Fijian Village

BARI
A pencil sketch from life by the author

Fijian Village

BY

BUELL QUAIN

WITH AN INTRODUCTION BY

RUTH BENEDICT

THE UNIVERSITY OF CHICAGO PRESS

CHICAGO · ILLINOIS

Publication of this book was made possible by generous support of the Viking Fund

THE UNIVERSITY OF CHICAGO PRESS, CHICAGO 37
Cambridge University Press, London, N.W. 1, England
W. J. Gage & Co., Limited, Toronto 2B, Canada

FOREWORD

THE study upon which this book is based was carried out during more than ten months' residence on Vanua Levu, Fiji Islands, in 1935 and 1936. Except for a preliminary survey of Bua Province and a four weeks' excursion through the villages of eastern Vanua Levu to learn something of the distribution of dialects and of variations in kinship classification, all time and effort were expended among the natives of the region of Nakoroka. I am indebted to Columbia University for the appropriation which made the study possible. For my training in ethnology I am deeply grateful to Professors Franz Boas and Ruth Benedict and to Alexander Lesser and Gene Weltfish.

For permission to pursue ethnological investigation among the natives of Fiji I am indebted to His Excellency Sir A. G. Murchison Fletcher, K.C.M.G., C.B.E., Governor of Fiji and High Commissioner for the Western Pacific; to the Honorable C. J. J. T. Barton, O.B.E., Colonial Secretary, and to his department in the Colonial Administration; to the Honorable H. C. Monckton, Acting-Secretary for Native Affairs and to his department; to Dr. Walter Foskett, District Commissioner of Cakaudrove and Bua Provinces; to Captain E. A. Meredith, Officer-in-Charge of Bua; and to Ratu George B. Toganivalu, Roko Tui Bua. I am particularly grateful to Captain Meredith and to Ratu George Toganivalu for the personal favors and friendship which they extended to me. To Mr. L. M. Anderson and his family at Delanisau I wish to express my thanks for the kindness with which they received me; during my sojourn at Nakoroka, Mr. and Mrs. Anderson were my nearest English-speaking neighbors, and I resorted frequently to the stimulating conversation of their home. I am also indebted to Mr. Anderson for many photographic negatives; some of his pictures appear in this book. To the natives of Vanua Levu, and particularly of Nakoroka, I am grateful for sustained friendship and for co-operation and interest in ethnological problems. To protect their privacy, I have changed the names of all persons and places associated with Nakoroka. I am also grateful to Ratu Dali, master of the Lekutu District School, and to young Emosi of Tavea. And for many cups of tea I am indebted to Mr. Mayok, the representative of the firm of Jang-Hing-Loong at Lekutu.

Of those European residents upon whose hospitality I depended during my excursions on Vanua Levu, I wish to thank Mr. and Mrs. Price and Miss Price of Savusavu, Captain Robby of Wainunu, Mr. Charles Hill of Silivakatini, and Mr. Alfred Edwards of Bua.

Of those who have offered helpful criticism of the study, Mr. George T. Barker of the Suva Museum was first to comment constructively. I am appreciative, too, of his kindness in permitting me the use of his private library. I am grateful to Professor Ruth Benedict for reading and editing the manuscript during its construction. I also wish to thank Mr. J. J. Lyons, who read and annotated large portions of it. For her generosity in sharing the results of her own ethnological investigation in Nasaucoko, Viti Levu, I am indebted to Dr. Dorothy Spencer; Dr. Spencer also read and annotated a large portion of the manuscript. For helpful criticism I wish to thank my parents, Dr. E. P. Quain and Dr. Fannie Dunn Quain; I am particularly grateful to Dr. Fannie Dunn Quain for accomplishing many necessary tasks without which the manuscript would never have reached completion —among them the arrangement of the Glossary. For the experimental printing and enlarging of many photographic negatives I wish to thank Mr. F. H. Neff. I am grateful to Mrs. A. I. Wolf for helpful criticism.

BUELL QUAIN

RIO DE JANEIRO, BRAZIL
March 1938

TABLE OF CONTENTS

INTRODUCTION

OUR neighbors in the Pacific have become increasingly interesting and important to Americans during these years since war
involved us with their island homes. Broad surveys of this area can
tell us much about them, but in many ways intimate and intensive accounts of small regions can tell us more. For, beyond all facts of economic geography and of colonial administration, we need to know
what kind of people they are. We need to know something about their
ways of conducting their lives, about their view of existence.

Fijian Village is such an account. When Buell Quain went out to
these islands on an anthropological field trip in 1935, they were still
remote from American interest. Even when in 1938 he sent back from
Brazil the last of the manuscript of this present volume, Vanua Levu
was still a region of strictly anthropological interest. He did not live to
see the outbreak of the second World War; in August, 1939, came word
of his tragic death in Brazil.

He had written that he was planning an introduction to this volume
which would give a sketch of Fijian culture to assist the reader in following the concrete descriptions of life in the village of Nakoroka. I
have carried out his plan of writing such an introductory sketch, but
all who knew him and recognized his talents will wish, with me, that
he might have lived to write it as he would so well have done.

The village of Nakoroka lies in an area of Fiji in which native ways
of life strongly persist. It has, however, had a complex history of acculturation. It experienced its first European influence not at first-
hand from white men but through the natives of the Polynesian
island of Tonga, who, stimulated by the promise of wealth from trade
with Europeans and equipped with European firearms, effected in the
first half of the nineteenth century a military, religious, and cultural
conquest of this area of Fiji. Even at the beginning of the nineteenth
century Tongan influence was not new in Fiji; Polynesian ideas of a
chiefly caste, taboos associated with their persons, and organization of
life under chiefly rule had, from Fiji's first contact with Tongans in
earlier years, been backed by prestige which those whom W. H. R.
Rivers calls the "kava people" have so often been able to exercise over
other aboriginal inhabitants of the islands of the Pacific. But before

about 1820 Tongan penetration was generally peaceful. The fifty years after that time the Fijians characterize as the "days of the wars." This period was not merely a military conquest of Fiji by Tongan chiefs; the whole region of Fiji was torn by warfare between small local kingdoms, and to Fijians today this warfare was not between Tongans and Fijians but between native villages. The Tongans not only effected military conquest; they spread a new religion—the religion of Wesleyanism, which had already been accepted by the Tongan chiefs. Cultural changes, like the organization of life under chiefs instead of through reciprocal obligations of family heads, as in earlier days, must also have been rapid, but we do not know how much earlier this change had begun. What we do know is that today in Nakoroka there are two parallel systems of mythology,[1] one which concerns animal ancestors and has no word of migration and conquest, and another which is an epic of warriors who reduced the known world to vassalage and whose kingdom "will stand victorious above bowed heads until the world tips over."[2] Equally, there are two systems of life, one which now persists almost as a supernumerary activity and consists in economic exchange between householders and lineage heads; and the other, now dominant, which insures the fertility of the land and the favor of the gods through ceremonies and exchanges initiated by the chiefs. To the Fijians there is no demarcation; the two cultures are inextricably mingled.

The present village of Nakoroka is a consolidation of the five villages of the kingdom of Inland Forest. These villages—Votua, Tovua, Nadroro, Rokowaqa, and Buleya—after their depletion in the "days of the wars," united about the middle of the last century, and the village therefore represents one of the native kingdoms into which Fiji was earlier divided. Each of these original villages had its own land and a chief who held the whale tooth, which was the symbol of his title. Each village had members of the chiefly caste, which is separated from all commoners by etiquette and privilege and manner of life; each had among its commoners four officiating groups which, following traditional usage, Mr. Quain calls "castes," though they were neither ranked nor rigidly hereditary. The members of the priestly "caste" received communication from the gods and other spirits and were generally the doctors; the "messengers of the village green" called out announcements to the village and spoke for the king or

1. Buell Quain, *The Flight of the Chiefs* (New York: J. J. Augustin, 1942).
2. *Ibid.*, p. 184.

chiefs or ceremonial leaders; members of the *bota* had special duties in caring for the bodies of the king and the chiefs; members of the "contents of the household" were proficient in the preparation of certain foods and performed certain household duties on ceremonial occasions. These castes of commoners still function today in Nakoroka, and a man is not merely a priest but a priest of Votua; he is not merely a "messenger of the village green" but a "messenger of the village green" of Nadroro. One entertains certain guests from other villages not merely as a member of the village of Nakoroka but as a member of Tovua or Rokowaqa. It is still a serious matter that the chiefly caste of Tovua has died out and that the sacred whale tooth is in the keeping of a commoner. In addition, not only each of the original villages but each caste within each village is identified with specific garden lands.

The king of Inland Forest, in the earliest days now remembered, was drawn from the chiefly caste of the village of Votua. He was the holder of the great whale tooth, "King Forest." In the "days of the wars" his kingdom had sufficient cohesion to make alliances with some kingdoms and to become involved in war with others. Making alliances after warfare was called "burying the blood" and was a ceremony initiated by the victorious kingdom, which solemnly sanctioned friendly relations with the vanquished. Strong bonds united all those who belonged to Inland Forest—bonds which depended upon their owning and using contiguous garden lands, their ties to the same chief and to the same gods, and the reward of renewed fertility that came from their individual initiative in building up the prestige of their kingdom. This identification with his kingdom, however, was not a man's sole loyalty. Kinship ties bound every man to relatives scattered far and wide in other kingdoms. The kingdom was not an endogamous unit. Marriages were contracted both within and without it and are so contracted today. The "heaviest" of all kinship obligations in Fiji is that to closely related male cross-cousins, especially to such of these as have married one's sister—and they are commonly of other kingdoms. Even in warfare men related by this particular tie carried to each other advance notice that their village was about to attack the others. In peace they are bound to each other today by economic obligations and by "heavy" responsibilities of formal respect. Social organization by kingdom and by kinship often supplemented and reinforced each other in Fiji, it is true; but they often conflicted.

Though these two schemes of social organization negate and cross-cut each other in so many ways, the people of Nakoroka are able to reconcile them by grounding them both in a fundamental view of life which no conversion to the Wesleyan church has succeeded in displacing. The land, the natives believe, belongs to local ancestor gods, and the fruits of it are the expression of these gods' satisfaction with their conduct of life. The aim of the community is so to conduct itself that the gods may be pleased and the gardens may flourish. In successful competitive gift exchange with all and sundry the fertility of Inland Forest is assured. These competitive feasts and gift exchanges are called "emptying the land," and this assures prosperity— not poverty, as we might more logically expect. Under native conditions, however, where any man's work will indeed replenish supplies, they speak quite truthfully in phrasing the matter of replenishment as merely a matter of providing strong motivation for renewed labor.

Fijian feasts and gift exchanges are of two kinds, one operating through the chiefs and one through kinship. The chiefly gift exchange with other kingdoms still functions, though Nakorokans lament its lessened glory. In the lives of people now living, distribution of goods even within the village was channeled through the chief. The bulk of the harvest was presented to him by all members of the kingdom, and he in turn redistributed it in ceremonial gift exchanges. Gift exchanges dependent on kinship also function today and occur in their most lavish form on the occasion of marriages "after the manner of the land," i.e., marriages following two families' formal betrothal compact in which virginity of the bride is part of the bargain. Prestige and self-respect rise and fall in Fiji, whether individual or village, with the role which one is able to play in such gift exchanges. And each "emptying of the land" sets in motion again the cycle that leads to increased prosperity.

The chief (king) has other functions besides those revolving around the gift exchange. In times of emergency it is the part of the chief to organize the community for action and to rouse men from the sleep which fear and discouragement seem to induce among them. Assisted by his council of elders, it is his duty, though some of these functions have been taken over by the native representative of the British government, to direct the many co-operative activities of his people, like clearing garden ground, planting, harvesting, and housebuilding. He is responsible for lavishly hospitable entertainment of guests. At all times it is his responsibility to see that quarrels are settled before they break out into violence, to advise in legal disputes, and to hear cases argued. He is the interpreter and channel of the will of the gods and derives his authority from them. He does not, however, speak with the gods directly, a role which is performed by the priestly caste.

Commoners address a chief with special respect-constructions of language, kneel before they enter his house at night, bow their heads in his presence, sit below him in any house, and eat only after he has tasted food. Chiefs walk with arms swinging, though commoners used to walk with hands clasped before the body, which was itself bent forward with lowered head; today commoners, too, may walk "like a chief." The person of chiefs is sacred, as is also anything that has been in contact with their bodies. Their children are absolved from work and training and indulged to the hilt.

The chief (king) who is to hold a pre-eminent whale tooth as sign of his office is selected from among the chiefly caste. This caste is hereditary in the mother's line. However, since for the chiefs endogamous marriage within their own caste is the form of marriage most highly approved, persons of this caste may be chiefly on both sides. They are then referred to as the "crown of the coconut"; if they marry a commoner, it is called "scattering the blood" and is lamented. A chief can be criticized on the grounds of not having had a chiefly father and of not having married a chiefly wife. A chief's eligibility to hold a kingly whale tooth may also be questioned on the basis of his hereditary title to land in that kingdom. Because of his pre-eminent functioning in relation to the fertility of the gardens, this is of extreme concern to the Nakorokans. Their own chief, Bulisivo, falls short in this, though he is "crown of the coconut"; his hereditary lands lie elsewhere. It is difficult for any incumbent to meet all the different requirements that are regarded as necessary "in the manner of the land."

Nakorokans who are not members of the chiefly caste are divided into two great exogamous moiety divisions, and these two moieties are present in the whole area of Fiji the natives know; moieties structuralize their relationships to all villages with which they have contact. Only the chiefly caste stands above the moiety division. Moieties are matrilineal, and one's moiety membership is the only Fijian status which is fixed at birth and not subject to choice or manipulation. All persons of one's own moiety and generation are, irrespective of blood ties, regarded as siblings.

The young people stage many dances and trips for courtships, and, in all these, two sides are lined up by inalienable moiety affiliation. In adult life, too, moiety membership structuralizes marriage, obligations, and gift exchanges for all commoners. A man who, like Nabadua in Nakoroka, claiming to be a chief, ignores moiety throws all village relationships into confusion.

Except for moiety, all Nakorokan relationships allow great leeway of individual choice. Even kingship is by no means automatic. The king must be chosen, and into this choice enter all kinds of balancing of genealogy, land ties, and ancestor gods. For commoners as for chiefs, a man's land affiliations are of very great importance for his whole life, but he may choose his mother's, his father's, or perhaps an affiliation which one of his parents forwent in their youth. All these possibilities are open to him. He is supposed to spend some years of indecision before he decides to which land he belongs. The land is the property of the ancestor gods, but his choice of an ancestor god may well be a separate choice for any man; he is fortunate if some sign or portent tells him which ancestor to choose. If he becomes ill from eating the flesh of some animal, he has received such a sign—he has discovered a taboo laid upon him and now recognizes his ancestor. In any event, he must, among a number of possibilities, discover his ancestor by personal choice or by trial and error. A commoner chooses his "caste" also in Nakoroka. A man decides on the basis of his gifts or of his desires whether he will take up the caste of the priest, the "messenger of the village green," the "contents of the household," or the *bota*. Among all the possibilities open to him, he must indicate his own preference.

Within the formal kinship framework, too, choice is rampant. A man selects among his kin a sister who stands to him as his great intimate; he chooses even a brother or a cross-cousin to be his "special" relative. From ancestor gods and caste to brotherly and sisterly obligations, the formal structure is a thing apart from the specific individuals who will fill the roles in the formal structure. The individuals choose their roles.

Nakoroka thus presents a cultural picture in which quite rigid formalization of differential behavior coexists with great lack of rigidity in the ascription of an individual to his role. The brother-sister relation is strictly defined as involving mutual help in love affairs. There is no trace of a brother-sister taboo, and with his sister a man relaxes; she is his go-between and confidante in love affairs. But he may select his "special" sister among a great number of possible women. The strongest cross-cousin ties, too, are set up by such choice—not by genealogy. The strongest uncle-nephew ties are similarly between a

young man and his mother's "special" brother or between an older
man and his "special" sister's children.

Since kingship, land, and kinship ties are the bases upon which
community activity is organized, Nakorokan life is unintelligible in
terms of biological genealogies or of rigid matrilineal inheritance such
as often occurs in societies with matrilineal moieties. It is clear, moreover, that in this area of Fiji the extreme lack of rigidity in personnel
in no way militates against continued strict definition of role in the
formal structure. Fijians are as extreme in one as in the other. Differentiation of role in Nakoroka provides minute prescriptions for behavior of "owner of the village"—one who has taken up his land rights
there—to nonowners; for the behavior of castes, both chiefly and of
the commoners; for contacts of chiefly caste and commoners; and for
behavior of all different categories of kin.

Kin behavior is most heavily differentiated within one's own generation. The formality of cross-cousins is strongly separated from the
informality of siblings, and the differentiation is extended in kind if
not in degree to all coevals in one's own moiety and in an opposite
moiety. This informality among siblings and within moiety is carried
very far in Nakoroka and has unusual connotations, as, for example,
in the complete lack of brother-sister taboo. A man watches also over
his sister's virginity before her marriage. This is phrased as his desire
to give a good woman at marriage to his prospective brother-in-law
(opposite moiety), and it is important as a means of insuring a satis-
factory relationship in this "heavy" affinal (cross-cousin) bond which
persists throughout life.

Informality between brothers takes a different form. Their relation
is one of extreme freedom. Brothers by known kinship ties take food
and goods from each other without asking, and this is specialized in
the case of own younger brothers, who have extreme claims on an
elder brother. Even moiety "brothers" co-operate throughout life in
providing for feasts and gift exchanges, and tit-for-tat accounting is
not invoked.

This very free and informal relation to brothers and sisters even in
extended categories has in Nakoroka another side to the coin. Brothers, and especially own brothers, as Quain reports in chapter viii,
"may give way almost freely to wrath or jealousy. To explain a folk
song in which a warrior, exasperated with two companions, bashes
their heads together, people say knowingly that they must have been
brothers." Sisters, too, can be freely critical of a brother's marriage

and can openly refuse co-operation. If they do so, his marriage is practically untenable, for many of them are married within his village, and, when he has brought his wife there, they can obstruct their brother's every move. He is helpless if they do not make suitable displays at his wedding, furnish his house, and care for his household during his wife's recurrent childbirth periods of taboo. His sisters can be drastic in withholding these services. Open wrath and free helpfulness are the obverse of each other in Nakoroka.

With cross-cousins (which include affinals) the story is quite different. Anger and criticism are taboo or are released only in a traditional and uneasy joking relationship. Cross-cousin punctilio is, as Nakorokans say, "heavy," and their mutual obligations generally override all loyalties which conflict with this kin tie, as, for instance, when cross-cousins in the "days of the wars" invited their own kingdom's defeat by informing enemy kingdoms of attacks upon them. Similarly in those days a man always spared his cross-cousins in warfare; "fathers" and "brothers" were not spared. Cross-cousins must "support" each other's interests but always with punctilio. No cross-cousin request for assistance can be refused, but *he must ask*. To Nakorokans this separates the relations of siblings and cross-cousins into two contrasting categories. With cross-cousins one is formal, and this formality includes both the taboo on anger and the compulsion to grant a cross-cousin's request for material goods.

Nakorokan life is co-operative and marked by what many other cultures would name extreme generosity. Not only through hospitality and gifts "in the manner of the land" but also through constant work-parties, where men pool their labors in others' gardens or on others' houses, every man's plan of life and enhanced status pivots on assistance and the support he contributes to others and which they freely render back to him.

Nevertheless, men's personal relationships in Nakoroka are uneasy. As Quain points out, Nakorokan men are obsessed by anxiety about their relative status, and advancement in status must be achieved; such advancement does not depend on automatic progression into an older age group or on automatically stepping into any honored position whatsoever. But Nakoroka has no objective standard for stating achievement. "Rank depends on subjective judgment and random proof." One's version of one's own rank differs constantly from others' versions, and men are baffled and touchy.

In addition, the most opposite virtues are invoked in determining status. The "strong man" acts aggressively and sweeps all before—and to be a "strong man" is to be chiefly. Contrariwise, the "good man" is fabulously generous; he is sweet-tempered and forbearing—and to be a "good man" is to be chiefly. Thrift or extravagance, acquisitiveness or generosity—each is used to praise or to disparage.

This contradiction in ethos has a historical background, the same which underlies the dual set of origin legends: the ethos of aboriginal Fiji and the quite different ethos of Tongan invaders. It works itself out in the character structure of contemporary men in Nakoroka by building within them strong status anxiety and a burning sense of shame which, they say, can cease only with death.

Nakorokan men are presented with two incompatible sets of goals, ideals, and behavior patterns. Their culture assures them of no green light ahead whether they are ruthless or whether they are co-operative. It gives them no objective standard by which to measure achievement. In spite of their common commitment to the village and its concerns, in spite of their far-flung kin reponsibilities and the personal advantages they derive from kin generosity, Nakorokan men walk warily among their fellows, and the most passive among them consolidate their positions most satisfactorily. The more active are obsessed by anxiety about their status and court defeat.

RUTH BENEDICT

COLUMBIA UNIVERSITY
NEW YORK City
November 1947

CHAPTER I

VANUA LEVU, AN ISLAND OF FIJI

EARLY in August, 1935, I arrived at Savusavu Bay on the windward coast of Vanua Levu. It was easy to see that the people of the coastal villages were no longer bound by their old customary restraints. Young men were seeking eagerly for the money wages of British enterprises—particularly the gold-mining company, a recent enterprise of Australian politicians, who, after Great Britain had fallen from the gold standard, found Fijian gold a profitable business. The warnings of the old were no longer heeded because the time was new. Only the younger generation could learn to appreciate the thousand petty vices money could buy and with proper delight anticipate a journey to Suva, that hilarious fleshpot of the Pacific, which is the source of songs built on new harmonies, tales of happy drunken brawls, and vices too delicate for all but the seasoned epicure. Opportunity was there, a whole new vista, open for him who chose to learn these new delights. One girl had been at Suva and came back dancing the Charleston. A new life, not well understood but withal cheerful, had supplanted the old.

At least a third of the coast villages boasted Chinese trading stores, which, with their knives, axes, rice, sugar, bright calico, and paste jewelry to be exchanged in the absence of money for native copra, dried kava root, kauri resin, or conch shell, had greatly disrupted native industry. The old as well as the young had neglected their gardens to tickle their palates with new foods and their vanities with printed calico.

The Chinese had come in large numbers only during the last decade. But for at least a century the Lauan descendants of Tonga had visited these coasts, bringing new songs and jokes and strolling through the villages. More than fifty years ago, Solomon Islanders were imported as plantation laborers. There are still a couple of small Solomon Island settlements on Vanua Levu. Indians also were brought from Punjab and other regions of India, both Hindu and Mohammedan, to work on sugar plantations. Though some have returned to India, many have found land in the more gently sloping regions on the leeward coast of

Vanua Levu, where they plant rice, grow goats and cows for milking, and found large families. European planters have never deserted the coast; they have shown special partiality for Savusavu Bay, where half-a-dozen plantations dot the jagged shore for fifty miles. To a high degree, each group maintains its cultural identity, but Fijians of today are far more sophisticated than their ancestors of a century past; even the most thoughtless among them has developed a taste for comparative ethnology which is rare among European nations. The Fijian feeds his curiosity with comparisons of the speech, etiquette, personality, and customs of birth and burial which he observes among these alien squatters on his soil. The Solomon Islander has a peculiar halting speech, teeth blackened by betel nut, and a body which the Fijian's fancy deems a caricature of himself. The Chinese deal sharply in exchanges, eat strange foods, and lead puzzling solitary lives without women of their own race. The Indians, who have flourished on Fijian soil so that they now number 85,002 to the Fijian's 97,651[1] and whose expansion may someday create an actual land shortage to the Fijian, symbolize the ridiculous, unclean, and sly. Sometimes they are hated. But still Fijians find them good gambling companions; their festivals, with choice dairy foods, are an amusing interlude in Fijian affairs; their poultry coops supply fowls to be borrowed furtively at feast time. Interbreeding between Fijian and Indian is rare.[2] With childish lack of control, Europeans usually abandon themselves to the emotions of the moment, love their personal belongings with a strange passion, lack cleanliness in some respects and are squeamish in others, and, worst of all, disregard the rules of social etiquette and decorum. Despite these faults, the steamboats, houses, and tools of the European bespeak an admirable cunning, and it is said that chiefs among them are really great people. This admiration has led to more careful observation of Europeans so that they can be separated into classes: the German can be distinguished from Englishman or Frenchman by the unpleasant sound of his speech; whenever I passed through a strange community, the native noticed my queer manners and always wanted to confirm his suspicion that I was American and not British.

I left the villages of the coast on August 16 and climbed the rain-soaked jungle slopes which rise behind Savusavu to three thousand

1. Population figures are taken from Commander W. Burrows, *A Report on the Fiji Census, 1936* (Suva, 1936).

2. I heard of only one such half-caste—a woman whom Fijians considered comely except for hair which was sadly "weak," like an Indian's.

feet and descended into inner Macuata Province, to the legendary
kingdom of Flight-of-the-Strong (see Map I). I followed the Dreketi
River to its mouth, but the scattered villages seemed small. Bari, my
guide and porter, had been provided by the district commissioner at
Savusavu. Though, according to local standards, he spoke English,
it was his knowledge of white man's needs and his ingenious use of
gestures which made communication possible. Secretly afraid of the
reputedly bloodthirsty natives of Macuata Province, he persuaded me
that the inland population of eastern Vanua Levu was too sparse for
ethnology. In high colors he pictured inland Bua, to the west, as just
the place for work. So we went to Bua Province, to the villages of Sarowaqa, Nakoroka, Lekutu, Nacula, Nalauvia, Great River, Bua, Driti,
Narowai, and Duleniwai. That I eventually settled in Nakoroka depended as much upon Bari's persuasion as my own decision; he carefully indicated its virtues, its well-kept paths, its large population of
a hundred persons,[3] and its relative isolation from outside influences—
all of which were substantiated by further experience. But the real
motive for his enthusiasm was his distant relationship with Nakoroka's
chiefly family, whom he had never visited but had always wanted to
know.

On a strip of land as narrow as Vanua Levu, a European map-
maker would hardly classify the villages as inland and coastal. The
island is a hundred and twenty miles long, and its greatest width is not
more than thirty miles. Mountains range from two thousand to thirty-
five hundred feet in altitude and, extending longitudinally in a chain,
divide it, according to native concept, into a "living" and a "dead"[4]
seacoast. But to the Fijian the division into interior and coastal is crucial. The population of the interior compares insignificantly with the
far greater concentration on the coast. Influences pass back and forth
and have always done so. But the coastal villages communicate with
one another more easily along their less precipitant paths or by boat
through lagoons. News eventually reaches the interior; but it must
follow the few cross-island paths which slip and bog in the mud by
turns, leap cascades and unbridged canyons, and vanish in the tangled
forests of mountain slopes. Many of the villages in the interior communicate with one another only by way of the coast because there

3. The number who slept at Nakoroka the night of the 1936 census was sixty-three, but
Nakoroka elders claimed one hundred. Though some of these hundred are expatriate from
the village, it is still one of the largest inland villages on Vanua Levu.

4. Windward and leeward.

MAP I

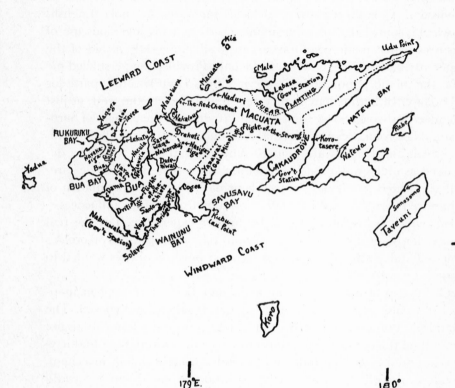

VANUA LEVU

_.._.. Provincial boundaries

PROVINCES

●← Modern villages

✿← Legendary kingdoms

Villages at Dama, Bua, Lekutu, Sarowaqa, Dreketi, and Yanawai are named for the rivers upon which they are situated.

Villages at Bua, Dama, Dreketi, Natewa, Solevu, Vuya, and Somosomo (on Taveuni) still occupy sites of the nineteenth-century kingdoms of these names.

Except for Nagadoa on the Dama River, a village near Solevu, and another near the Cakaudrove border, all modern villages of inland Bua are represented. But many villages of Macuata, Cakaudrove, and coastal Bua have been omitted. Names of inland Bua villages have been changed, and the map of this region has been slightly altered, with the hope of concealing Nakoroka's precise identity.

are few inland paths.[5] A tradition of long standing recognizes clear distinction between the rude inland peoples and their more polished maritime neighbors. About 1847 an old chief in the Natewa Bay region of eastern Vanua Levu advised John Jackson[6] to go into the interior and show himself to the bush people, the *lialia* (insane or feeble-minded), who were "so extremely ignorant . . . . that, for all he could do to persuade them that there was such a thing as a white man, they would not believe it. . . . . There were tens of thousands of people that had never seen the sea, nor had their forefathers."[7] There is a dance song still in use which ridicules[8] a mountaineer's surprise at the contrast of the periodicity of tide with the constant flow of fresh-water streams. The baffled mountaineer sings:

> It is a very different thing at The-Place-of-Singing;[9]
> The waters murmur there and then the morning breaks.
> It is a very different thing here with you;
> There is murmuring, and then nothing.

Like all inland villages, Nakoroka links itself in commercial partnership with a village of the coast. Its trade partner is Tavea, a minute island off the north coast of Bua Province. Nakoroka exchanges yams, taro, bananas, and kava root for turtles, fish, and other products of the sea which Tavean maritime skills procure. This kind of relationship exists throughout Bua Province; the classification which it implies agrees with the old belief that the coast was settled by maritime immigrants who spoke a dialect different from the aborigines. Along the leeward coast of Bua and the western half of Macuata the peoples of the coast speak *t* and indicate *k* with a glottal stop, while the inland

5. The quickest and easiest way to travel from Nalauvia to Driti, for instance, is by way of Lekutu, Bua, and Dama (see Map I).

6. John Jackson, whose adventurous autobiography occurs as Appendix A in John Erskine's *Journal of a Cruise among the Islands of the Western Pacific*, was cast away in Samoa in the early 1840's and eventually found his way to Fiji. For several years he served as "chief's white man" in the greater kingdoms of Fiji. Though his vocabulary is unduly sensational, his accounts of actual participation in Fijian life at this early date are unique in Fijian literature.

7. John Elphinstone Erskine, *Journal of a Cruise among the Islands of the Western Pacific* (London, 1853), p. 431. The old chief's exaggeration of Vanua Levu's inland peoples was probably fashioned to impress Jackson with Fiji's magnitude.

8. "In Fiji the readiest and most emphatic form of expressing one's supreme contempt for another and of disparaging his skill and prowess is to apply the term *Kai-vanua*. So in Samoa the pithiest epithet for an ill-mannered, contemptible person is *Uta-fanua*." Both these native terms mean "people of the land, or interior" (W. T. Pritchard, *Polynesian Reminiscences* [London, 1866], p. 418).

9. His home in the mountains.

peoples speak a fricative palatal for *k* and indicate *t* with a glottal
stop.[10] Except for eastern Macuata, where the land narrows and there
are no inland villages, the distribution of present dialects agrees with
the old tradition.

Early in September, after a three-week survey of Bua Province, I
established permanent residence at Nakoroka. It seemed to be isolated
from the disruptive influences of the coast. There were no Chinese
stores, Indian settlements, or plantations within the immediate vicin-
ity. There was no native religious teacher in residence, and this led me
to assume falsely that there never had been; accidental contacts with
devout Wesleyans in Sarowaqa and Bari had prejudiced me strongly
in Nakoroka's favor.

Thirteen thatched sleeping-houses with their adjoining huts for
cooking marked a rectangle about the Wesleyan church, which shone
in its red paint from the center of the village green.[11] Groves of coconuts palisaded the village margin and emphasized the distinction which
small native children learn to make between *village* and "*bush.*" On
the northwest the screen of coconut palms became a corridor for the
avenue which led to the river Votua a hundred yards away. In contrast with the feeble rivers of Nalauvia and Duleniwai, which fail with
a month of drought, the Votua is a steady stream of cold, clear water.
It is only during the quickly passing floods that the women must put
pots beneath thatched eaves (or the much more efficient iron eaves of
the church) to catch rain water and avoid the red mud which roils the
river at these times. Down the river at Sarowaqa brackish tides pollute
the water and plaster the shores with muck.

Two or three miles to leeward of the ridge that divides the drainage
of Vanua Levu, Nakoroka lies cupped in a shallow valley at an altitude of perhaps a thousand feet.[12] Behind the village the land rise-
rapidly into rugged peaks covered with tangled forests. But toward the
sea to the northeast the slope is gentler, and heavy growth is confined
to the glens; here round knolls, wooded with groves of sparse ironwood
(*nokonoko*) or with an aromatic fern (*qato*), step almost gradually to
the sea. The ridge behind Nakoroka claims over three hundred inches
of annual rainfall out of the trade winds which prevail from the southeast to make the Wainunu region on the windward slope one of the
wettest in Fiji. But the leeward slope, on which Nakoroka lies, is con-

10. See the Appendix for a description of Fijian phonetics.
11. A diagram of Nakoroka is given in Map IV, p. 83.
12. This figure is my own guess.

A CORNER OF NAKOROKA

A FIJIAN BARGAINS FOR TOBACCO WITH A WANDERING INDIAN

Hoping to disparage its quality and lower the price, the Fijian examines it before agreeing to buy. The old man in the center and the boy on the right are Indians.

siderably drier.[13] Nakoroka seems wholesomely arid in contrast with the hothouse atmosphere of the windward coast. The seeming dryness, despite the rainfall, which viewed from American standards is very great, is due perhaps to the nature of the soil. The areas in which forest vegetation has not deposited a heavy layer of loam are composed of red clay from which rain water runs in torrents; the next sun parches the surface quickly, and the process of constant evaporation which humidifies the luxuriant windward slope is held partially in check. But, despite the lighter rainfall of the leeward region, wooded slopes persist along the water courses even near sea-level and provide ample loam for gardens of yams, kava, and especially taro. Though the coast villages of eastern Vanua Levu speak contemptuously of Bua and particularly of interior Bua as a "land of taro," the men of Nakoroka counter by saying that the eastern peoples must subsist on breadfruit and manioc because their land will not produce taro. To the east, where the island narrows and the streams cascade abruptly to the sea, there are few well-watered inland valleys, and the villages have clustered close to the shore, where taro grows poorly. Nakoroka is proud of the productivity of its soil.

Further acquaintance with Nakoroka disclosed that it was not free from outside influences. Seven or eight miles to the northwest on the Lekutu coast, and at Sarowaqa, eight miles to the north, there are traders who represent the firm of Jang-Hing-Loong of Canton. Every week or two someone from Nakoroka makes the slippery journey to the coast, usually to Lekutu, with a basketful of native produce to exchange for a few pounds of salt and sugar or for money to meet the colonial tax or a mission assessment. On feast days store supplies are always called upon: flour, rice, tinned butter from New Zealand, and jam. There is a settlement of Indians about six miles from Nakoroka on the way to Sarowaqa who have been in residence for more than fifteen years. Once or twice a month an Indian with eggs for sale passes through the village on his way to the gold mine on the windward coast. Once an Indian hawker came to Nakoroka with bright calico for sale, furtively because he had no license; he had to confine his circuit to the remoter villages. Three men of Nakoroka had worked in Indian rice plantations for short intervals. He who had worked longest

13. For a few days during the January dry spell of 1936 there was dust in the paths of Nakoroka, but 1936 was an unusually dry year. Mr. L. M. Anderson, who lives perhaps eight or nine miles from Nakoroka, near Lekutu on the leeward coast, reported 74 inches of rain for 1936 in contrast with the usual 120.

received the use of a cow as wage; his newly born twins needed more
milk than their mother could supply. Once, at the time of an Indian
festival, a group of Nakoroka young people returning from a funeral
feast at Sarowaqa stayed overnight at the Indian village on this path
and joined in the festivities. On Christmas Day, 1935, two Indians
played cards with a group of young Nakoroka men who had returned
from the gold mines for the holidays. But there is very little cultural
exchange between them. The boy who claimed to know more about
Indians than anyone else in the village knew but a few phrases of
their language: "Now I am going" and "Where are you going?" Most
Indians speak broken Fijian. Though Fijians like Indian food, they
have not bothered to learn how to prepare it. Apparently the only
Indian custom which has been borrowed outright is a kind of pelvis-
twisting dance; during funeral wakes, when dancing is most hilarious,
old Fijian women dance this gracelessly as the height of buffoonery.
With the Solomon Islanders, Nakoroka today has no contact.

British influence has been far more important. Mr. Anderson grows
copra just beyond Lekutu. He and Mrs. Anderson have lived there for
thirty years, planted extensive groves of coconuts, and reared a family
now in its second generation. Despite his long residence on the Lekutu
coast, he has never traveled inland to Nakoroka; like others of British
tradition, he prefers to travel by boat. But he has known all of Nakoroka's adult men; wages for work in his copra groves have been a convenient means for meeting the colonial tax. The only other white
residents in this part of Vanua Levu for whom the natives have worked
are in the Dreketi region twenty miles away as the crow flies, two
days' travel as a man walks in Fiji. About ten years ago three Nakoroka
men worked at a now defunct sawmill there. There is also a planter
at Dreketi for whom one or two men have worked for short periods.
The sugar mill at Lautoka, the seat of colonial government in Macuata
Province, is at least eighty miles away, more than a week's journey. To
the native it is as remote from Nakoroka as Fiji is to the American.
One expatriate young man had worked there, but his influence at
Nakoroka was slight.

Following the shore counterclockwise around the Bua coast, there
are no other Europeans in permanent residence until Nabouwalu is
reached on the southernmost tip of Vanua Levu.[14]

It has always been the policy of the colonial administration to

14. Mr. Alfred Edwards resides periodically at Bua to represent a British commercial
house.

shelter the native from outside influences, to preserve the native community, and to allow Fijian culture its own direction of development. Until recently this policy has in practice permitted the Wesleyan mission society to be the high judge and mentor of Fijian culture. The missionaries have regarded the native as possessed of many admirable qualities. They have channeled the Fijian desire for conspicuous waste into periodical assessments which have helped to finance the expansion of Wesleyan influence through Melanesia and even Australia. But the influences exerted by planter, colonial administrator, and even the missionary have been gradual and subtly interwoven with the internal structure of the community. They have not destroyed the aboriginal structure of society.

The gold mines, whose development has been prodigious during the last five years, have attacked Fijian culture on an entirely new front. Australian capital which finances them owes little allegiance to the local colonial administration, and it has no "native policy." In contrast with plantation work, which is sporadic, the mines offer an illusion of full-time employment. The old-fashioned planter arranged with the chief of a village to send his entire community to work the copra when the season was right. But the mines can hire and fire arbitrarily because their profits permit a higher wage than Fijian labor traditions require, and in consequence there is almost always labor surplus. In fact, however, these wages are just high enough to annoy the planter; they attract his labor to the mine. A communication from an old settler in Fiji expresses the planter's point of view:

Our Fijians are all heading for disaster. This mining business will ruin perhaps one of the finest of native races. . . . . The native women are all becoming dirty prostitutes. Venereal disease has broken out and is being carried broadcast over the country. . . . . There is prospect of trouble arising within a year if not earlier. There are nearly 1,000 natives today working [in the Viti Levu mines]. . . . . This reputed paternal Government of Fiji goes along with its eyes closed. . . . . In my opinion it was from a point of view of the natives a bad day when gold was found in Fiji.

When natives need money, they go to the mines in hope of being hired. Some young men who have found favor with the mine employers and gain permanent subsistence from their wages are divorced completely from their home communities. Others, and this includes nearly every other able-bodied man on Vanua Levu, seek employment at the mine only when there is need for money to pay government taxes or missionary assessments. Their gardens at home provide all necessary subsistence, so they can afford to await the chance of being hired. Men become accustomed to mingle with strangers from great distances, strangers who speak unfamiliar dialects but whose stories always hold some special news of the outside world. Among these men who share a common lot and destiny in the mining communities customs are exchanged. And, as these bands of would-be laborers wander through the land, some villages have already learned to qualify the lavish hospitality with which they have been accustomed to receive strangers. These are new problems for the villages to face.

Nakoroka has been affected. Two of its young men have been lost to the mine at Yanawai.[15] Wild hogs ravage their weed-choked gardens. Three other young men divided their interest between the village and the mine. Two older men went there for the first time in May, 1936. Sometimes the girls go in troops to mix kava for the workmen at a shilling a bowl.

The death of the old era is in sight even in this inland village. But still today the community is productive in its own right. If the mine were suddenly to be removed, life could still continue on the old basis. As yet no gold prospectors have come to Nakoroka. These men confine their searching to coastal regions. Since no native fully realizes that the industry will expand as long as gold mines continue to produce, most are happily unaware of their doom. When old Nabadua calls himself a "man in the bush," the only English phrase that he knows, he is making a proud distinction between the decadent villages of the coast and the people of his own community who still know how to follow the precepts of their ancestors. Even among the young men there are conservatives who plan their lives according to the old forms.

Sophisticated curiosity about other cultures is of long standing throughout the villages of Vanua Levu and may serve to preserve the integrity of their own cultures. It is a tolerant attitude which expects each group to work out its own way of life and each individual his own adjustment within his group. Before 1850 Jackson begged a chief in Macuata to forsake cannibalistic practices. The chief answered that "the priests always told him that bloodshed and war, and everything connected with them, were acceptable to their gods." Jackson told him that Fijian gods were false and that they were enemies of the true God. But the chief said, "Different countries, different fashions, and, in like manner, different gods."[16] The people of Nakoroka speak

15. In Cakaudrove Province. At the time of my arrival this was the only mine on Vanua Levu. During my residence, work had begun on a second, and there were rumors of a third; both of these were farther from Nakoroka than the one at Yanawai.

16. Erskine, *op. cit.*, p. 428.

this same phrase today. Not only does it excuse differences in dialect, ceremonies, and kinship obligations of neighboring villages, but, so long as it is possible to continue the old forms of production and of social control, it enables Fijians to observe the Chinese, Indians, and British without calling into question their own standards. Though Nakoroka's gardens are not so productive as they once were, there is still an abundance,[17] so that they are in no way dependent upon the Chinese for food. In contrast, Lekutu on the coast must devote much of its effort to producing commodities which can be exchanged with the Chinese for rice; the neglected gardens produce abundance no longer.

Except for the few wandering Indians, persons of alien race have rarely visited Nakoroka. Three or four years ago a government surveyor was in residence there for a few months. I met one old planter who claimed to have gone through the region twenty years before. The Edwards brothers, who grew up at Bua village twenty-five miles west of Nakoroka, know every mile of Bua Province; but with an adaptability enviable to ethnologists they know Fijian etiquette and a dozen dialects so well that natives themselves can pick no flaws, and they can pass through villages unobserved. Mr. Alfred Edwards spent a night with me at Nakoroka, the only white man I saw there in ten months' residence. To a large degree acculturation in Nakoroka has been chosen voluntarily and carried to the interior by the village natives themselves.

17. For a discussion of natural resources of Bua in the middle nineteenth century see Thomas Williams, *Fiji and the Fijians*, ed. George S. Rowe (London, 1858), I, 60–65. See also the section on "Food," in chap. v, below.

CHAPTER II

THE CONQUEST OF FIJI[1]

IT WAS expected that Tasman would effect a landing on all newly discovered territories, and that he would seek an interview with the natives. The landing party was to go on shore armed; but only for their own protection. They were to treat the natives in a kindly manner, and extract from them all information possible about their country, 'especially trying to find out what commodities their country yields' and, adds the naïvely crafty Council of Batavia, ... 'likewise inquiring after gold and silver, whether the latter is held by them in high esteem; making them believe you are by no means eager for precious metals, so as to leave them ignorant of the value of the same; and if they should offer you gold and silver in exchange for your articles, you will pretend to hold the same in slight regard, showing them copper, pewter or lead, and giving them an impression as if the minerals last mentioned were by us set greater value on.' "[2]

Tasman's journey through the Fijian group in 1643[3] resulted in no promise of gold and no knowledge of the natives. But the spirit which motivated the Council of Batavia has persisted. Two centuries later whaling vessels were plying a less spectacular but profitable trade with the South Pacific Islands, "giving a blue bead about the size of a marble for a hog weighing three or four cwt., or a piece of iron hoop six inches long for 500 yams."[4] Bligh's second journey through Fiji in 1792 was more effective than Tasman's had been; trade relations were established with the island of Moce in the southern part of the Lau Archipelago. Though he brought back no tokens of wealth, his charts opened paths in this reef-strewn sea for the ships that followed.[5]

1. This chapter is based on old accounts by Europeans.
2. George Cockburn Henderson, *The Discoverers of the Fiji Islands* (London, 1933), pp. 40–41.
3. For this and other journeys of discovery see Map II.
4. W. T. Pritchard, *Polynesian Reminiscences* (London, 1866), p. 199. Yams rarely weighed less than five pounds and sometimes over fifty; hence the iron hoop purchased several tons of yams.
5. Henderson, *op. cit.*, pp. 152, 153, and 165.

MAP II

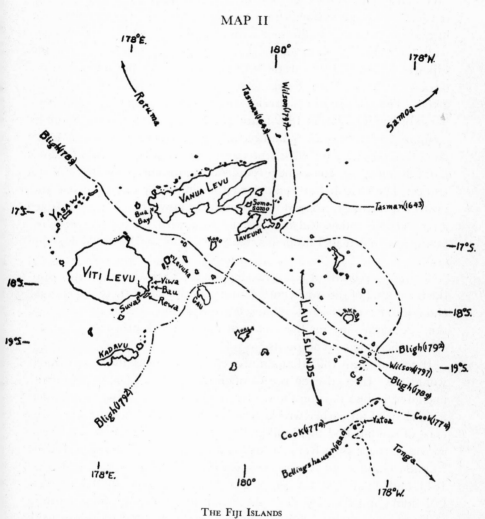

THE FIJI ISLANDS

Routes of discoverers have been sketched from maps in George Cockburn Henderson's *The Discoverers*
f the Fiji Islands (London, 1933).

The islanders soon learned to marvel at white men's commercial zeal. As early as the 1770's Captain Cook tells that the Tongan natives ridiculed his seamen's eagerness to barter, "offering sticks and stones in exchange and one waggish boy even presented a piece of excrement in derision to everyone he met with."[6] After a decade of intercourse with the sandalwood traders, in the early nineteenth century the Fijians had learned that trade with Europeans was not a competitive display of wealth but a debasing scramble to receive more than was given. The harassed missionaries who put up for repairs at an island north of Vanua Levu in 1809 found the Fijians sharp in their dealings compared with the less commercially experienced Tahitians; for a good fishhook they would sell no more than a few coconuts.[7] Today a more humanistic conscience requires a humanistic slogan for its tactics: The British have eulogized the simplicity of native life and protected it from European lust for wealth; now, though these natives have become thoughtful in their dealings with Europeans, they remain unschooled in Europeans' scales of value and still take lead for gold.

There are records of but nine ships that passed through Fiji before the beginning of the nineteenth century. Only one of these stayed long enough to have any lengthy intercourse with the natives: the tender of the "Pandora" lay for five weeks at one of the Lau islands, but the ship's officers left no accounts.[8]

It was not until 1801 that a native commodity was discovered which would have pleased even the Council of Batavia. The "El Plumier" anchored in Bua Bay, on the western end of Vanua Levu, and shipped a survivor of an earlier wreck, who secretly carried news of the existence of sandalwood to Manila.[9] By 1805 or 1806 the news had been spread abroad; ships from Australia, New England, the Dutch Indies, Manila, Guam, and Russia flocked to Bua Bay for cargoes which by 1814 had exhausted the supply.[10] This commerce shifted to New Caledonia and the New Hebrides.[11] But during this decade quantities of European hatchets, knives, mirrors, fishhooks, and red cloth were poured into the villages of the west coast of Vanua Levu, and the coast

6. John E. Erskine, *Journal of a Cruise among the Islands of the Western Pacific* (London, 1853), p. 159.

7. William Lockerby, *The Journal of William Lockerby*, ed. Sir Everard in Thurn ("Publications of the Hakluyt Society: Second Series," No. LII [London, 1925]), p. 144.

8. *Ibid.*, p. xxxi, contains the best summary of discovery, early contacts, and the sandalwood trade.

9. *Ibid.*, pp. xxxix and xli.   10. *Ibid.*, p. ci.   11. Erskine, *op. cit.*, pp. 15 and 18.

was well explored from Bua Bay to Dreketi on the border of Macuata Province.[12] The exhaustion of sandalwood did not discourage commercial visits to Fiji. From the northern coast of Vanua Levu *bêche-de-mer* for the Chinese market offered ample profits[13] until the supply began to fail in 1850. Then even the supplementary trade in tortoise shell, coconut oil, and lumber ceased to attract foreign ships and passed into the hands of the then intrenched missionaries.[14]

Contact with these traders shook the entire political equilibrium of Fiji. To gain a cargo of the precious sandalwood, traders would lend their military aid to any petty chief who agreed to supply them. During his residence at Bua in 1808 and 1809, Lockerby acted as mediator to make political bargains between the captains of trading vessels and native chiefs.[15] In 1813 Captain Robson agreed to assist the chiefs of the Wailea region to quell revolt among their subjects in return for a cargo of sandalwood.

The expedition set out for the island of Nanpacab [Nabekavu in the Dreketi River (see Map I)] situated about six miles up the river of the same name. It consisted of three armed boats carrying twenty musketeers, with a two-pound cannon mounted in one of the boats, and forty-six large native canoes, carrying near a thousand armed Fijians, while three thousand more marched overland to the scene of action. The Nanpacab river was entered . . . . and for fifteen miles up its course the native folk were driven away, their crops destroyed, and their homes burnt. . . . .[16]

But the Wailea people were slow to fulfil their part of the bargain, and Captain Robson grumbled. The rift became more acute until, with the assistance of native ships of war from Bua, Wailea was destroyed.[17] Terrorized by these new techniques of war which the more fortunate chiefs had cornered, entire villages fled far into the interior.[18] Favor of Europeans became a new criterion for political power.

12. Lockerby, *op. cit.*, pp. 59 and 69.

13. Charles Wilkes, *United States Exploring Expedition—1840*, III (Philadelphia, 1849), 222.

14. Thomas Williams, *Fiji and the Fijians*, ed. George S. Rowe (London, 1858), I, 95; Erskine, *op. cit.*, p. 269; Pritchard, *op. cit.*, p. 340.

15. "As it was a great point for us to pacify them [regions] on the North shore [of Bua Bay] that we might procure our cargo of wood, I offered them presents, which however would not satisfy them. I therefore agreed with the King of Myemboo (Bua), the King of Myendam [Dama], and some other chiefs, to destroy or drive them from the island" (Lockerby, *op. cit.*, p. 53).

16. *Ibid.*, p. xciii.   17. *Ibid.*, p. xciv.

18. The people whom Lockerby helped to destroy fled to inner Macuata (*ibid.*, p. 69). This destruction of Nabekavu may explain a peculiar dispersion of the descendants of Nadroro, a land group at Nakoroka. Nabekavu was related to Nadroro; today the people of the villages of Nakalou and Nasigasiga in Macuata claim inexplicable descent from Nadroro.

The name of the chief of Bua particularly resounded in the islands. To native eyes his wealth was great, including, in addition to the usual trade articles, some sheep and a wooden house. Either through desire to participate in this new wealth or to collect fiefs which the Buan chief in his new-found power chose not to pay, Bua became the object of the massed attacks of other ambitious chiefs. A premium was placed on European fighting methods so that beachcombers found an easy berth as mechanics for the king's muskets.[19]

It seems likely that many ships touched Fiji during this period and left no record. Castaway and expatriate seamen in the very first years of the nineteenth century existed in numbers out of proportion to the few ships that have left records. In 1808 the berths of deserters from sandalwood ships were easily filled by survivors of shipwrecks in the Bua region.[20]

Bau, off the east coast of Viti Levu, received an even larger share of beachcombers. Charles Savage, whose military prowess struck terror into the enemies of Bau, seems to have been using his musket with effect at the beginning of the sandalwood era.[21]

After the power and prestige of Bua Kingdom had collapsed with the end of the sandalwood trade in 1814, Bau's early advantage in possessing the services of Europeans who could teach the arts of musketry gained a political supremacy which was unchallenged until her old enemies had also learned the new techniques and until the arrival of the even more Europeanized Tongans toward the middle of the century. Bau learned to value her Europeans; the simple Jackson was received warmly there about 1848 because "Europeans are privileged in consideration of the wars they took part in, at the time Charles Savage and his party subdued all the islands that are now tributary to Bau. Before that time all the islands were independent of each other; but, by means of the fire-arms of the Europeans, Bau extended her dominions, and was feared even more than she is now."[22]

At this time Bau was well equipped with military supplies. The chief asked Jackson to cast a thousand balls for his muskets:

19. *Ibid.*, pp. lxxi, 25, 27, 198.
20. *Ibid.*, pp. xl and 83.
21. The exact time of Savage's arrival is unknown. Records state positively that he arrived almost every year between 1800 and 1808 (Henderson, *op. cit.*, p. 160; Sir Basil Thomson, *The Fijians: A Study of the Decay of Custom* [London, 1908], p. 28; Amasa Delano, *Narratives of Voyages and Travels* (Boston: E. J. House, 1817), pp. 460–65; Lockerby, *op. cit.*, p. 95, n. 1).
22. Erskine, *op. cit.*, p. 457 (Jackson's account).

I agreed, and went to his house, where I was surprised to see upwards of twenty chests of various sorts, and with a good many China trunks, forty or fifty pigs of lead, and upwards of two hundred kegs of powder. I asked where he got all these from. He said he considered himself very badly off, and wished some bêche-de-mer vessels would soon come, so that he could make up his standing quantity of powder, which, he said, was six hundred kegs, with pigs of lead in proportion. He also said that he had five thousand muskets, but that he had distributed them all but a few amongst his people. He then gave me a bunch of keys, and told me to unlock the chests, and I would find everything requisite for running the bullets.[23]

But amiable relations with Europeans were of short duration. As early as 1812 the sandalwood traders had incurred so much resentment against themselves that some of the natives had resolved to have no more dealings with them.[24] Punitive expeditions against those tribes who had killed a white man, in one of the sandalwood wars or other justifiable circumstances, caused a vicious cycle of increasing ill-feeling between natives and whites. European ships of war came expressly to display the power of their arms and to deal summary justice to those villages that were rumored hostile.[25] Eventually native anger was whipped to a heat which Europeans feared and respected. It became customary for traders to trick a chief of high rank into boarding their vessel and then to hold him hostage during the period of their negotiations[26] to avoid close encounters with native ships of war. The early hostility thus engendered may have served to maintain vitality in the cultures of many regions of Fiji; in spite of long contacts with Europeans, settlements have remained localized.

New political ambitions and this new kind of warfare took their toll from the population. In 1850 a chief of Viwa near Bau lamented the evil times: "All of the old people, and especially his own father, used to tell him, that these bloody wars, and this eating of one another upon the present enlarged scale, sprang up in their days, and did not obtain to such an extent in the generation before them."[27] Epidemics introduced by European ships as early as 1803 continued to sweep through the islands—measles, dysentery, and other unidentifiable diseases.[28] Close contact with expatriate whites had emphasized the decadence in some of the native capitals. Wilkes described a chief of

23. *Ibid.*, p. 455. Even after discounting for Fijian braggadocio, it is evident that European munitions had long been in use. For the rise of Bau see Williams, *op. cit.*, pp. 3–4; Lockerby, *op. cit.*, pp. lxxi–lxxii; Thomson, *op. cit.*, p. 23.

24. Lockerby, *op. cit.*, p. xci.

25. Erskine, *op. cit.*, p. 3.   26. Wilkes, *op. cit.*, pp. 127, 138, 221.

27. Erskine, *op. cit.*, p. 272, quoted from Lawry's *Friendly and Feejee Islands*, p. 95.

28. Thomson places the earliest epidemic in 1791 (*op. cit.*, pp. 25–26).

Rewa most flatteringly in 1840, commenting also upon his use of "table, chair, table-cloth, knives, forks, plates."[29] Within the next ten years, however, the eagerness of this chief to adopt foreign customs had cast disruptive influences in his villages. He catered to foreigners and levied oppressive revenues on his people to maintain a cosmopolitan household.

> He had ordered about seven or eight towns to supply four Tahitian natives with bananas, sugar-cane, and ti-root, and for their trouble he supplied them [the Tahitians] with wives, provisions, tortoise shell, etc. These Tahitians distill from the above about three or four gallons a day and . . . . then he and his companions (mostly English and American) drink it. . . . .[30]

Despite the demoralizing effects of acculturation, Bau profited for a time through her contacts with Europeans. Except for periodic contests for power with the neighboring Rewa, her superior munitions and able leadership initiated a process which might have led toward the unification of Fiji. But before this was fairly under way, the imperialistic advance of Tonga, which was motivated by another kind of contact with Europeans, interfered to divert the political growth of Bau.

Since long before the dawn of the historic era, there has been intercourse among Samoa, Tonga, and Fiji. Though this intercourse was sporadic and probably infrequent, the people of each group knew something of the diversity of custom in the others. A Samoan chief of the early nineteenth century traced his genealogy to Tonga and eventually through a maternal connection to Fiji.[31] There were also family traditions in the leeward islands of Fiji which traced connection with Rotuma, which is some three hundred miles northwest of Fiji and which in turn considers its progenitors to have been descended from Samoans.[32] Aside from the accidental contacts of lost navigators and fishermen,[33] these three island groups plied a trade among themselves and knew the special products of each region. Tongans made

29. *Op. cit.*, p. 122.

30. Erskine, *op. cit.*, p. 461 (Jackson's account). This chief also had a Spaniard from Manila as his steward (*ibid.*, p. 273).

31. Pritchard, *op. cit.*, p. 379.

32. *Ibid.* Captain Wilkes said: "There are in Macuata a greater number of light-colored Feejee men than are elsewhere to be met with. They are generally half caste, and this mixture has arisen from their intercourse with the Rotuma Islanders, of whom they are very fond" (*op. cit.*, p. 230).

33. In 1860 old men in Macuata Province remembered traditions of the arrival of Samoans who had drifted away from home while on fishing excursions (Pritchard, *op. cit.*, p. 379).

"On the island of Uea, one of the Loyalty group (near New Caledonia), more than 1100

trading journeys to Fiji in the early eighteenth century and probably earlier for the large timber which was lacking in their islands and for the bright red plumage of the Fijian paroquet.[34] An ancient Tongan legend places high value on fine Samoan mats trimmed with these same paroquet feathers.[35] Sometimes the Tongans, acting as middle-men between Samoa and Fiji, traded fine mats from Samoa for articles of Fijian manufacture.[36] The Tongans admired Fijian cleverness in contriving efficient practical devices; in addition to fine craftsman-ship in building canoes, the mosquito curtains[37] of Fiji and the soups and puddings were worthy of envy. But the influence of Tonga upon Fiji has been most profound within the historic era. Fijian admiration of Tongan chiefly etiquette is still waxing. Old men in interior Vanua Levu can still remember when sitting with legs crossed "in the manner of Tonga" was unknown, and it is only in very recent years that this practice has ceased to be a chiefly prerogative and has been assumed by those of low rank. Tongan types of house construction have found universal popularity only in the last ten or fifteen years. If impressions of early observers can be credited, the aboriginal Fijian attitude toward property was less Polynesian in flavor than it is today.[38] In this respect Fiji tended to resemble the more business-like peoples of eastern Melanesia.[39]

European intercourse with Tonga occurred earlier and with more effect than commentators have indicated, and this contact stimulated Tongan trade with Fiji. Shouten's description of the Tongans about 1616 suggests that they were already acquainted with European com-

---

miles west-ward from Tonga, there are now (about 1860) living a group of Tongans who were blown away from their homes in a large double canoe" (ibid., p. 404).

"In the district of Rewa and the contiguous island of Kadavu . . . . there is at the pres-ent day a tribe . . . . which maintains a distinct social and political status from Fiji, and which traces its origin from a fleet of war-canoes that was blown away from Tongatabu . . . . many generations since. Those who survived the perils of the storm and the wreck took to themselves Fijian wives, and taught their offspring the language, the customs, the traditions, and the worship of the gods of the land they had involuntarily left" (ibid., p. 380).

34. Williams, op. cit., p. 94.

35. Sir Basil Thomson, The Diversions of a Prime Minister (London, 1894), p. 298.

36. Williams, op. cit., p. 94.

37. Ibid., p. 138.

38. The missionaries who were forced to lay over on the north coast of Vanua Levu for a few weeks in 1809 may have observed validly that the Fijians were sharper tradesmen than the Tahitians (Lockerby, op. cit., p. 144). As late as 1860 Pritchard remarks upon the commercial aptness of the Fijians in contrast with Samoans and Tongans (op. cit., p. 414).

39. See A. Bernard Deacon's discussion of wealth in Malekula, a Vanishing People of the New Hebrides (London, 1934), p. 17.

modities: "They were very thievish and exceedingly desirous of iron, trying to draw the bolts out of the ship."[40] At the time of Cook's first contact with Tonga, Tongan admiration for Fiji was waxing. Since Tongans had been trading European axes and knives for Fijian canoe timber and paroquet feathers throughout the eighteenth century, this growing interest probably sprang from increased trade. European metal had provided wealth with which to purchase goods from Fiji. The first iron in Fiji probably came from Tonga long before Cook's initial voyage.[41] Wilson, who passed through Fiji in 1797, found that the Fijians "no doubt, would have been willing to trade with us had we found safe anchorage for the ship; for with these people the Friendly Islanders [Tongans] carry on a trade with the articles they got from us."[42] At the beginning of the sandalwood era Lockerby found no difficulty in remodeling a European boat because the king of Bua had "plenty of tools of all sorts."[43] He had received at least some of these through trade with Tongans, who at all times seem to have been more amply supplied with European goods.

The increase in Tongan commercial enterprise which followed upon their contact with European traders culminated in widespread trading expeditions in the early part of the nineteenth century. Natives of Eromanga in the New Hebrides were to be found in Tonga as early as 1830, brought there by Tongan trading canoes.[44] Superior munitions gave the Tongan traders a profitable advantage in their relations with more backward islanders. On one occasion a group of Tongan warriors, subsidized by Europeans, stormed an Eromangan village, "which, having no muskets, was defeated, with a loss of twenty-six killed, none of the intruders being injured." When the survivors took refuge in a cave, the Tongans pursued them. "After firing into the cave, which seemed to have no effect, the besiegers, pulling down some of the native houses, piled the materials in a heap at its mouth, and, setting fire to it, suffocated them all."[45]

There was also another newly introduced motive for the wandering of Tongan populations: European castaways had introduced new military techniques and accompanying political ambitions. This was true

40. Thomson, *Diversions of a Prime Minister*, p. 399 (extract from *Journal of Shouten's Voyage, 1615–1617*).

41. Williams, *op. cit.*, p. 94.

42. Henderson, *op. cit.*, p. 207.

43. *Op. cit.*, p. 26. Today there is no chief in the interior of Bua Province whose possessions could be thus characterized.

44. Erskine, *op. cit.*, p. 143.   45. *Ibid.*, p. 144.

also in Fiji, but such castaways came later to Fiji and in smaller numbers. At the times of Tasman's and Cook's first contacts, the Tongans seemed unaccustomed to the use of arms.[46] But they soon learned a new hostility toward strangers. Several European ships were seized between 1800 and 1804 as a result of the agitation of European deserters,[47] and there was already a need in these islands for European men and arms to prosecute their native wars. By Mariner's time (1806), a political reshuffling had begun which did not cease until Tonga was unified forty years later under the Wesleyan convert, King George Tubou. It seems strange that Sir Basil Thomson should blame association with Fijians for the change in Tongan political temper.[48] It is true that intercourse with Fiji had increased tremendously during these years, so that a Tongan chief considered it part of his education to travel to Fiji. But the introduction of European goods and munitions served to make conquest practicable in Tonga, as it did in Fiji a few years later. During this period of unrest, Tongan chiefs, newly risen to power, liked to send jealous contenders for chiefly authority to Fiji on pretext of a canoe-building expedition. Newly defeated Tongan chiefs, whose kinsmen had already traveled to Fiji and perhaps intermarried, sought the islands of the Lau Archipelago as refuge from the vengeance of their political opponents in Tonga. Travel stimulated desire for more travel until, in Mariner's time, the Tongans looked upon Fijian civilization as a thing to be emulated. Young men found something in Fijian bearing which suggested "a fierce, warlike and manly spirit."[49] It became common practice for Tongan armies to engage in Fijian wars.

The inflation of the market for whale teeth followed as an important result of increased trade with Tonga. Though whales had been plentiful about Fijian reefs, the natives had devised no means for capturing them. Dependence upon chance catches stranded by an ebbing tide limited the supply of whale teeth to such a degree that the high value in which they are still held is understandable. In the old days the gift of a whale tooth could bind the recipient to participate as an ally in war or to grant almost any request. The political rise of Somosomo (see Map I) on the island of Taveuni, which at one time extended its

46. Thomson, *Diversions of a Prime Minister*, p. 320.

47. Lockerby, *op. cit.*, p. lxiii.

48. *Diversions of a Prime Minister*, p. 318.

49. William Mariner, *Accounts of the Natives of the Tongan Islands* (3d ed.; Edinburgh, 1827), I, 204.

influence well into the eastern part of Vanua Levu, was made easier by the quantities of whale teeth which Tongan canoe-builders brought as payment for timber and labor. About 1850, when the Somosomo people were carrying their tribute to Bau, "the old chief then walked up to the Bau people with a bundle of whale's teeth, ... of from eighty to a hundred pounds weight and apparently as much as he could carry with both hands, and delivered them."[50]

European traders knew the value of whale teeth in exchange and used them in both Fiji and Tonga, but they seem to have favored Tonga with a greater supply. Jackson has described a method of classifying teeth according to color and "used to consider the difference between the white and the red teeth as the same as between our shilling and sovereigns, estimating the number of white whale's teeth through the Feejees to be twenty times as many as the red ones, the red teeth, which have become red by frequent handling and oiling for a number of years, they always told me were brought to the Feejees by the Tongans, by whom they were first introduced."[51] Thus, through trade relations with Tonga, certain kingdoms gained an adventitious source of wealth which could be used to political advantage. These were the kingdoms upon which the power of Bau and later of the Tongan conquerors depended.

In 1797 the ship "Duff," which had deposited missionaries at Tahiti, touched at Tonga, but no mission was established. It was not until 1826 that a mission was permanently founded there, with the aid of two natives from Tahiti.[52] Forty years after the arrival of the "Duff," Christianity "had spread throughout the three groups of the Friendly Islands [Tonga], and reached as far as Keppel's and Niuafoou Islands, Wallis's Island, and three hundred miles northward to the Navigator's Group [Samoa]. This extension of Christian influence was chiefly owing to the enterprising zeal of the new converts who, longing to give others what had so greatly blessed themselves, went forth, and preached everywhere, the Lord working with them."[53]

The political turmoil through which Tonga was then struggling

50. Erskine, *op. cit.*, p. 297. During the sandalwood trade many whale teeth were introduced into Bua as well by European traders. "The vessels from Port Jackson usually carried the teeth of the whale or sea elephant; but some vessels from India carried elephant's teeth, which they cut into pieces, and made into the shape of the other teeth. These, being very large, were considered of greatest value, and procured vast quantities of sandalwood" (Lockerby, *op. cit.*, pp. 174–75).

51. Erskine, *op. cit.*, p. 439.   52. *Ibid.*, p. 12.

53. James Calvert, *Fiji and the Fijians*, ed. George S. Rowe, II (London, 1858), 3.

turned to the advantage of the missionaries when George Tubou, an energetic though somewhat questionable heir to the kingship, espoused their cause and with his party won over a large majority of the population. The opposing minority, which the Wesleyans termed heathen despite its many Roman Catholics, fought valiantly and in 1840 defeated the Wesleyan party, even though the Wesleyan missionaries and an English ship of war had given their support.[54] By 1845 King George and the Wesleyans, with their superior munitions, had again gained ascendancy and had become virtual rulers of all Tonga.

But the missionizing of Fiji presented more difficult problems. The acceptance of Wesleyanism frequently entailed the acceptance of Tongan political supremacy as well. There were already large Tongan colonies in Fiji, and the Tongans, though received politely in some regions, had already begun to incur hatred because their entertainment brought famine to the regions which they visited. Though they went forth and preached everywhere, they attempted at the same time to imbue their converts with a reverence for Tonga and its King George which was hotly resented in some quarters.[55] In 1835 a group of missionaries left Tonga for Fiji and reached Lakemba in Lau. "King George of Tonga had, from the beginning, manifested his great interest in the undertaking, and now sent an influential person with a present to Tui Nayau, King of Lakemba."[56] Despite the retinue of Tongan teachers by whom they were accompanied, their efforts met with mediocre success. The missionaries were able to make headway only in those regions where descendants of Tonga dominated the population. Tahitian teachers fared better and by 1840 had succeeded in converting the few inhabitants of Vatoa in southernmost Lau.[57]

By 1840 contact with Tongans had already brought an awareness of Christianity to the people of Bua Bay. Bua was torn by civil war. "It was said that the chief had even made the people break up their canoes for the purpose of constructing palisades to fortify the village, and thus at the same time to prevent his people from deserting to the enemy."[58] The Bua chief, noting the political advantages attached to the profession of Wesleyanism and influenced by his family connections with the kingdom of Viwa[59] which had already submitted to

54. Thomson, *Diversions of a Prime Minister*, p. 195.

55. Pritchard, *op. cit.*, p. 294. " 'England, France and America are great countries, but Tonga is greater' " (*ibid.*, p. 296).

56. Calvert, *op. cit.*, p. 7.

57. Lockerby, *op. cit.*, p. xvi. Vatoa is indicated on Map II.

58. Wilkes, *op. cit.*, p. 214.　　　　59. Near Bau. See Map II.

Tongan Christianity, brought two native teachers to Bua, so that by 1845 there were three hundred converts.[60] Politics in Bua was in flux. Powers passed from Christian to heathen several times until the accession of Ra Masima in 1848.[61] This family of Buan chiefs were half-Tongan in blood, and, judging from the constant civil war, their power in the district was held in question. Hence it was necessary to engage the favor of the Tongans with their armed forces, the missionaries with their militant pacifism, and, better still, the British ships of war who brought the protection due British subjects. This definitely pro-Tongan policy matured slowly, and the chief of Bua delayed public profession of Wesleyanism until 1855.[62]

Throughout Williams' residence in Bua, from 1847 until 1853, war raged between the anti-Wesleyan nationalists (including Roman Catholics) and the Tongan Wesleyans. But toward the end of the fifties Wesleyanism was so well intrenched in Bua that Ra Masima, with an escort of well-armed Tongan generals and their troops,[63] waged war in Macuata and demanded the allegiance of the Yasawas in the far west of Fiji. Since the chief of Bua owed allegiance to King George of Tonga, and through his Tongan mother's hereditary obligations felt himself a vassal, the Tongans tried to increase the glory of their own kingdom by building an empire for the chief of Bua.

During the first half of the nineteenth century Tongan penetration of Fiji had proceeded without leadership and without definite policy. But, with King George's regime thoroughly established in Tonga, the time was ripe for organizing the Tongan colonies in Fiji into some kind of political solidarity. That King George had long been interested in Fijian expansion is evidenced by his co-operation at the time of the first Wesleyan expedition to Fiji in 1835. Maafu, the son of George's predecessor, recently converted to Wesleyanism and a likely competitor for power if hostility should ever again break out with the anti-Wesleyan party of Tongatabu, was therefore dispatched to Fiji; King George's mind was set at rest, and the Tongans in Fiji, many of whom, like Maafu, were political exiles, had an able leader. Tongan canoes had been built almost exclusively in Fiji since the close of the eighteenth century; Maafu easily assumed the subterfuge of seeming to be

60. Calvert, *op. cit.*, p. 360; Erskine, *op. cit.*, p. 226.
61. Calvert, *op. cit.*, p. 367. This may not have been the famous Ra Masima to whom the conversion of all Bua is attributed, but no other accession to power is mentioned between this instance and a definite reference of the Wesleyan Ra Masima in 1857 (*ibid.*, p. 404).
62. *Ibid.*, p. 394.   63. Pritchard, *op. cit.*, p. 307 *et passim*.

engaged in canoe-building. By 1853 he had organized Tongan forces throughout the Lau Archipelago and fought his way to political supremacy.[64]

Maafu's nominally Fijian allies were always more numerous than his Tongan followers. But the chiefs of these Fijian groups, like the chief of Bua, were frequently bound to Tonga by kinship ties which made their allegiance more Tongan than Fijian. The Tongans in his retinue "were the most reckless of his countrymen, ... young men who had fled from Tonga to escape the rigour of King George's laws and administration, and if defeated in Fiji would therefore have no retreat."[65] New allies and newly conquered warriors were always placed in the front ranks of the attacking army to guard against their changing heart. "They were pushed onward to the attack, as a shelter to the Tongans in the rear. If they hesitated, the Tongans fired on them."[66]

By 1860 Maafu had challenged the supremacy of Bau in her own territory, had advertised Wesleyanism throughout Vanua Levu, and, but for European intervention, might have conquered all Fiji. With Ra Masima as high chief in Bua and faithful vassal to Tonga, Maafu's supremacy in Bua was secure. Macuata presented more difficulties, but, by allying himself with the weaker of his adversaries against the stronger, he succeeded in splitting opposing forces into remnants which he could easily vanquish. In this he had the aid of the king of Bau, who, though fearing the rise of the Tongans, was also jealous of the power of Macuata; he sold his most powerful ally in Vanua Levu to Maafu in order to break the power of the last champion of Fijian nationalism in Macuata.

In the early 1860's those who opposed the Tongans had unified their forces on Vanua Levu. To fill their ranks and gain a European support which entailed no allegiance to Tonga, the principal chiefs had professed Catholicism. But the British Protestants far outnumbered the French Catholics; Wesleyan missionaries could mobilize more arms, more ships of war, and more sympathy to subdue the important coastal kingdoms of Macuata.

In the meantime Europeans had established permanent communities in the region of Bau and Rewa on Viti Levu and Levuka on Ovalau. In 1857 the Europeans helped to reinstate a chiefly family at Bau whose temporary loss of power had thrown white men into five

64. Erskine, *op. cit.*, pp. 132; Thomson, *Diversions of a Prime Minister*, pp. 360–61.
65. Pritchard, *op. cit.*, p. 290.   66. *Ibid.*, p. 291.

years of political disfavor in this once powerful kingdom. At the time of Pritchard's arrival in 1857 a few permanent colonists were attempting to raise sheep; tradesmen were carrying on profitable business in the regions open to them. Pritchard himself encouraged the planting of cotton. The growing colony of Europeans looked to the king of Bau to protect their settlements; he in turn learned to depend upon them for military supplies and, in an emergency, for military support. So it was that in 1858, when he was threatened from within by revolt and from without by the rising power of Maafu the Tongan, he agreed to cede two hundred thousand acres of land and general sovereignty over the whole of Fiji to Great Britain in return for the payment of debts he had incurred in ordering the manufacture of two European ships of war. Levuka, which contained the largest number of permanent white colonists, had long been in vassalage to Bau; hence the trading vessels that anchored there came to think of Bau and its king, Cakobau, as politically supreme in all Fiji. Thus this deed of cession received far more serious consideration than the extent of Bau's actual political domain warranted.[67] It did serve, however, to bind the destinies of British colonists with the fortunes of Bau. In 1862, aghast at the atrocities of the Tongan wars and the poverty which followed in their wake, Pritchard saw no other alternative than to support the warriors of Bau as police force for all Fiji. He traveled to Tonga to interview King George with the hope of checking Tongan advances; he made the king understand that friendship with Britain was at stake.[68] Joining the Catholic priests in an attempt to bring peace at any price, the British consul[69] persuaded the last Macuatan nationalist leader to retire to his village as a private citizen so that the Tongans had no adversary in the field. Maafu placed his governors over eastern Vanua Levu and rewarded the chief of Bua for his faithful support by allowing him to keep his kingdom.[70] During the next ten years, in a desperate attempt to maintain order, the army of Bau was officered and drilled by, and its ranks replenished with, Europeans.[71]

But the results of this half-century of war were not so easily erased.

67. Pritchard mentions "various chiefs in different parts" of Fiji who acknowledged and ratified this agreement, but we are not told what parts of Fiji they represented (*op. cit.*, pp. 215, 216).

68. *Ibid.*, p. 290.

69. Pritchard had inaugurated this office in Fiji in 1857 at Levuka on the island of Ovalau.

70. This period of Fijian history has been recorded by Pritchard in his *Polynesian Reminiscences*.

71. Thomson, *The Fijians*, p. 101.

One of the first catastrophes that followed upon the unequal distribution of European munitions, and the consequent imperialistic expansion of the more fortunate kingdoms, was the oppression and impoverishment of the conquered territories. Chiefly authority established by force of arms recognized no obligation to make the new regions flourish. When the castaway Jackson traveled with a brother of the king of Bau to one of the tributary islands, the canoes from Bau were blown by such a favorable wind that the islanders had no time to prepare a proper feast for their royal guests.

In their haste and desire to please, they took the victuals up before they were properly cooked, and brought them in the most humble way. The lazy courtiers and tasters informed Revalita [the Bauan chief] that the victuals were quite raw, and observed . . . . that it was an old offense of that place in particular. The chief flew into a passion, thinking that his dignity was slighted, and ordered the inhabitants to assemble before him. They did so, and it happened to be on a beach that was completely covered with pumice-stone. They crawled on their hands and knees, waiting with resignation the result of the anger of the chief. At last he . . . . began to abuse them at a tremendous rate, and said he did not know how to punish them, as it was of no use to kill them, because they would be glad to get off so easy. One of the courtiers observed that it would be easier for them to make a hearty meal of the pumice-stones, than for a chief such as Revalita to eat the pork undone. . . . . So he commanded them to begin . . . . which they immediately obeyed and dispatched such quantities of pumice-stone, that you could in a little while observe the quantity of the stone diminishing, although the beach was thirty or forty yards long.[72]

The entertainment of Tongan guests was another task which rested heavily on the less powerful communities. It was Bau's policy to receive the Tongans hospitably, but "the minor chiefs and people . . . . have different feelings, and call them impudent and greedy fellows, saying that they breed famine wherever they go."[73] The exorbitant tribute which the Tongans levied upon their conquered territories in Fiji injured the business of European traders in Fiji to such degree that they complained frequently to Pritchard. After a Tongan visit to Yasawa the trade "was totally ruined for a time; fully six months elapsed before the traders obtained either oil or pigs from the natives."[74] How the Tongans utilized the produce which they plundered is not certain. But at least some of the gains helped to advance the cause of Wesleyanism. As early as 1856 the missionaries were happy to report that their business was at least on a profitable basis and that the villages who had Tongan "teachers" were subscribing liberally to

72. Erskine, *op. cit.*, p. 456.
73. Wilkes, *op. cit.*, p. 144.
74. Pritchard, *op. cit.*, p. 310; see also *ibid.*, pp. 292–93 *et passim*.

their support.[75] There are lurid tales of the tactics which these armed
"teachers" used to extort produce from Fijian communities in the
name of the king of Tonga and the "Tongan" religion.[76]

Aside from the abuse which arose through the imperialistic expansion of Tonga and its vassal kingdoms in Fiji, constant warfare deci-
mated the population and disrupted industry. Estimates of the
population of Fiji as a whole for the early nineteenth century are too
inaccurate and contradictory to be considered seriously. About 1850
Williams estimated the population of Vanua Levu at 31,000[77] and the
decrease due to war to be 1,500 or 2,000 a year.[78] Even before the
great religious war was well under way the peoples of the Bua region
were poor in the ordinary products of the islands. The women no
longer beat cloth, and the men did not plait sennit. "Not knowing how
soon their houses might be in flames over their heads, they became
very careless in their manner of building, and quite slovenly in the
internal management of their homes."[79]

By 1870 peace had been largely restored, and all except the inland
tribes were nominally Christian. The king of Bau with his army,
officered by white men, was soon assisted in his maintenance of order
by the appointment of a British governor.[80] It is not clear how the
deed of cession, of which the king of Bau was principal author, was
ratified by chiefs throughout Fiji over whom Bau had no control. But
European fighting tactics were victorious, and, except for an occasional

75. Calvert, op. cit., pp. 398 and 400.

76. Pritchard, op. cit., pp. 304, 305, 306, 307. A statement by Chief Tongitongi from
Yasawa describes the arrival of the king of Bua and a Tongan teacher to his region in
1861: "The Tui [king] Bua, and the Tongan Wesleyan Teacher, Maika, were sitting
together waiting for us; and there were very many Tongans around them, and all armed.
. . . . [A Tongan said], 'You are a bad man, Tongitongi; how is it you do not follow
Maika the Teacher, and Tui Bua. . . . . You must throw away the Roman Catholic
religion, and you must follow the religion of Maika, the Teacher. . . . .' Tui Bua spoke,
and said, 'This is the day of the Tongans. The Consul and the white men have no power.
The Tongans have power. We want to make Yasawa good and religious.' A Tongan
warrior said, 'I am going to Maafu. He will send Wainigolo [a dreaded Tongan general]
down, and the land will be made bad for you, and flog you all again if you do not give your
land to Tonga, and all follow the true lotu [religion].' . . . . [Then the Tongans] went into
our houses and took away everything. They took our house-mats, tapas [bark cloth], sulu
[clothing], pigs, yams, taro, fowl, [etc.]." This community signed a paper vowing their
Wesleyan and Tongan allegiance.

77. Op. cit., p. 4.

78. Ibid., p. 53. The latter figure may refer to Fiji as a whole. Williams estimated the
whole population of Fiji to be about 150,000 (ibid., p. 162). But his criteria for estimation
were false in some instances (ibid., pp. 203–4).

79. Ibid., p. 364.   80. Thomson, The Fijians, pp. 54–55.

revolt in the interior, the sovereignty of Britain was unquestioned.[81] A period of peaceful colonial development was under way. Britons from New Zealand were attracted by the prospect of settling on Fiji's fertile land. The natives themselves were frequently anxious to bring a white man into their community as a source of money wages with which to buy iron tools or cloth of foreign make.[82] Between 1861 and 1869 the European population increased from 166 to 1,800.[83] According to *A Report on the Fiji Census*, by Commander W. Burrows, R.N. (Rtd.), there were 4,028 European residents in the colony in 1936. The British administration undertook the tedious task of setting up the kind of local political forms and system of land tenure which they learned at Bau and Levuka. Even today this process of remodeling communities to fit the Bauan scheme proceeds with difficulty.

81. The last denial of British authority occurred in Vanua Levu about 1895 in Flight-of-the-Strong [Seyaqaqa] territory in inner Macuata.

82. Pritchard, *op. cit.*, p. 250.

83. Thomson, *The Fijians*, p. 54. These figures refer only to the European colony at Levuka.

CHAPTER III

HISTORY AND LEGEND
AT NAKOROKA

THERE are no marked seasons at Nakoroka. During July and August it is cold at night, and the stiffened joints of sleepers must be tried cautiously in the morning until quickened circulation has warmed them; sometimes a fine cold rain blows instead of the steaming downpours of the December solstice. It is said that there is a cold time and a warm time. But the days are always warm, and the landscape is always green. Plants, more sensitive to the changing arc of the sun than the people are, indicate seasons for changing village activities. But changes in the rhythm of work are neither abrupt nor strict. So the years pass, not as carefully marked time units, but as part of a steady flow which heaps itself behind the present moment in an undifferentiated past. People live, are happy and ashamed, and, when they can no longer feel these two things, they look forward to death in a future which approaches as simply as the past has been laid away. They have no clocks.

In this timeless world, history consists of but few landmarks through which past events can gain perspective. The age of heroes merges with the old days of the wars; thence, through a series of vaguely defined periods, the old time becomes the new. In the heroic age the noble ancestors of all Bua Province lived at Flight-of-the-Chiefs and with their marvelous strength and craft in war conquered the known world and dragged their victims to the altar of their god, leveling the forests in their passage. Then there were the old days which barely elude the memory of the old men, when people dwelt in the same lands which they inhabit today. But they lived in close communion with their ancestors so that the land was fruitful beyond all measure. Then the days of war came, and men dared not sleep peacefully at night unless their spears lay near at hand. Fires were extinguished at dusk. He who coughed or sneezed had first to dig a hole in the earth to muffle his face and the sound which might betray the village to a lurking enemy. Women and children crouched uncertainly in their houses ready to

30

flee to the forest for refuge. The old men now living remember this time. Then the church came with its Tongan proselytes, and for a while the Wesleyan God received the first-fruits of the land, alienated the favor of the ancestors, and undermined the power of the chiefs. Then the British government came; this was the time of today's adult men. The five villages which were the survivors of the once great kingdom of Inland Forest were gathered together, and by order of the government they built the village in which they now live under the guidance of the chiefly heir to the kingship of Inland Forest. This was indeed a new time; it was about thirty years ago.

Long ago a canoe came to Bua Bay, bringing chiefs who sought new homes.[1] They chose a place near the headwaters of the Dama River, which thenceforth has been called Flight-of-the-Chiefs. They built a town and an empire whose glories are the subject of songs and tales still told. They conquered armies of fierce supernatural beings and under the wise guidance of their ancestors sailed into distant seas to levy tribute. Two noble women, angered with the people of Flight-of-the-Chiefs, fled to the mountains of Macuata, and their descendants peopled the region called Flight-of-the-Strong (see Map III). The old men think that they must have intermarried with an aboriginal people, though legend gives no clue. As the population grew at Flight-of-the-Chiefs, segments of the kingdom broke away and migrated to new regions in Bua Province, to Kubulau, Wainunu, Dama, Bua, Navakasiga, and Inland Forest.[2] The empire at Flight of-the-Chiefs decayed, and the jungle grew over the stone foundations of its houses. The wild forest cock flies up in the branches of the forest that has grown in the old village green. But the site of the old town is still a shrine for those who wish to honor the greatest of all their ancestors with an offering of roast pig or coconut-cream pudding.

From Viti Levu the wanderers sailed down the windward coast of Vanua Levu, depositing colonies whose descendants founded the various kingdoms of this region. If Flight-of-the-Chiefs was so founded, the two cycles of legend can be made to coincide.

Descendants of the village of Inland Forest peopled the region about

1. Stemming from European academic beliefs of the nineteenth century, a belief in direct migration from Africa to Viti Levu has spread through even the most remote villages. Fijians feel warm kinsip for Americans as well because the Fijian rendering of the names of the two continents, Africa and America, is confusingly similar.

2. The original village site of the chiefs of Inland Forest is in the mountains above Nalauvia. Thence they migrated into the lands which their descendants still inhabit. See Map I.

MAP III

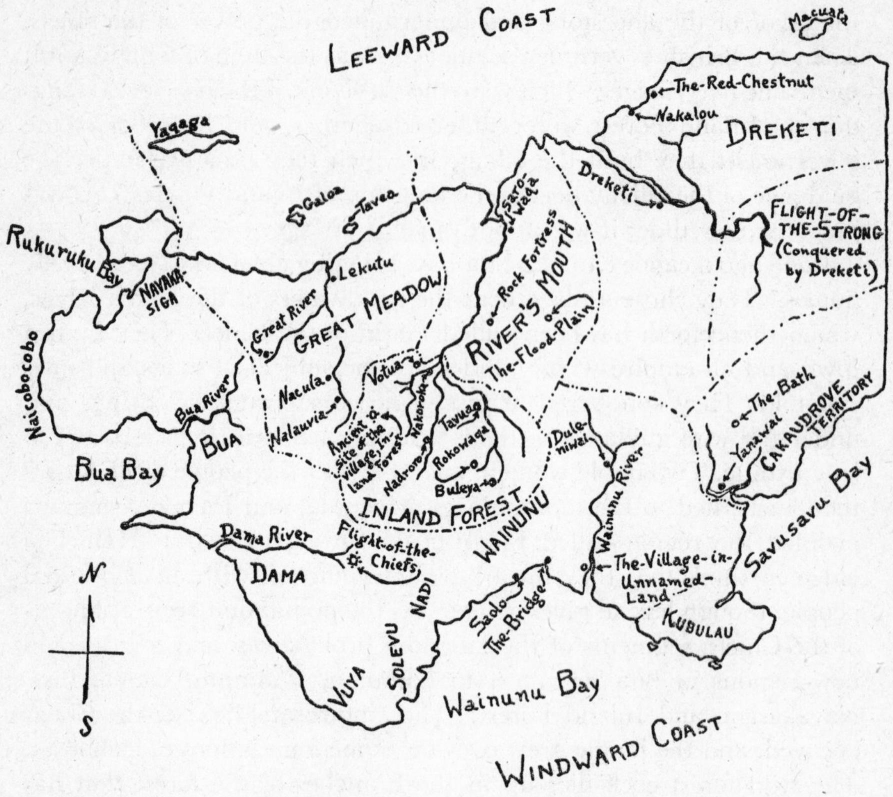

LEEWARD COAST

Yagaga

Macuaq

←The-Red-Chestnut
Nakalou

DREKETI

Rukuruku Bay

E.Galoa

Tavea

Dreketi→

FLIGHT-OF-
THE-STRONG
(Conquered
by Dreketi)

Naicobocobo

NAVAKA
SIGA

Lekutu

GREAT MEADOW

Great River

Rock Fortress

RIVER'S MOUTH

Savu
Savu

Bua River

Nacula

Votua

The-Flood-Plain

←The-Bath

Bua Bay

BUA

Nalauvia

Ancient
site of the
village, In-
land Forest

Naidromu

Tavuga

Nakoroka

Rokowaqa

Buleya

Yanawai

CAKAUDROVE
TERRITORY

Dulemuri

INLAND FOREST

WAINUNU

Dama River

Flight-of-the-
Chiefs

DAMA

SOLEVU
NADI

VUYA

Saolo
The-Bridge

Wainunu River

The-Village-in-
Unnamed-
Land

KUBULAU

Savusavu Bay

N

S

Wainunu Bay

WINDWARD COAST

SOME KINGDOMS OF WESTERN VANUA LEVU

o← Old village sites. Location of The-Bath is questionable.

●← Modern villages. There have probably been villages at Saolo, The-Bridge, and Great River for at least a century.

_.._.. Approximate extent of some of the kingdoms before organization under British adminis-tration. Because allegiances shifted frequently during the nineteenth-century wars, any attempt to reconstruct boundaries is doomed to inaccuracy; the concept of strict bound-ary lines does not exist at Nakoroka. Navakasiga, Vuya, Solevu, and Nadi were usually in vassalage to one of their greater neighbors. Except for Wainunu, which has been connected with Inland Forest by an ancient cross-island path, rugged mountains pre-vented intercourse between Inland Forest and the kingdoms of the windward coast. Military expansion was usually confined to coastal neighbors.

Nakoroka. In early times a large segment of Inland Forest seceded and migrated to River's Mouth (*Draka-ni-Wai*), which includes the present village of Sarowaqa, and increased in numbers until it had become six villages, some of them across the border in Macuata Province. The remaining segment of Inland Forest was driven eastward and built the five scattered mountain villages: Votua, Nadroro, Tavua, Rokowaqa, and Buleya. Each of these villages had its own chiefly family and its own system of rank in relation to that chiefly family, but the high chief of Votua carried the title to the kingship of all Inland Forest. The names of these five villages persist; though the chiefly families of all but Votua have died out, they still maintain separate land. In those village groups which no longer possess chiefly families of their own, chiefly duties have passed into the hands of influential commoners.

The chiefs of Inland Forest claim a sanctity greater than all the other chiefs of Bua Province. Their land is the land of "power." They claim that even the great chiefs of Macuata derive their ability to renew the fertility of the soil from ancestors who once lived in the land of Inland Forest. This claim is of little importance to the Macuata chiefs themselves, however, since their major concern is in tracing descent from the chiefly families of maritime Macuata who knew the haughtier traditions of Lau and Tonga. But it is through these claims to the sacredness of their chiefs that Inland Forest peoples maintain their self-respect; their glory as warriors is not great. Sometime before the advent of the British, the inland kingdom to the west, Great Meadow, which includes most of the inhabitants of modern Nalauvia and Nacula, conquered all of northern Bua Province including the small islands off the coast.[3] Inland Forest began to pay them a tribute which has always been begrudged because Great Meadow chiefs could boast fewer miracles, and their genealogical claim to descent from noble ancestors is questionable. It was not until Ra Masima, of Bua Kingdom on the sandalwood coast, the first Christian chief, had received the support of the British-trained troops of Bau that Great Meadow was defeated and converted into a district of Bua Province. Today, under the colonial administration, Great Meadow and Inland Forest belong to the same district, but their land is still separated by a distinction into "upper piece," which includes Inland Forest and its brother-kingdom, River's Mouth, and "lower piece," which is Great Meadow. Lekutu village, on the coast, also belongs to this district and comprises people of both Great Meadow and Inland Forest; but the main-

3. Yaqaga, Galoa, and Tavea.

tenance of its fertility depends largely upon the impostor chiefs of Great Meadow whose authority has risen by the "strong arm"[4] of war and not through rightful inheritance. Inland Forest people look with pity upon the failing garden crops of Lekutu and say knowingly that there is famine where there are no chiefs.

In the last century there has been some mixing of population and cession of land. A small group at Nacula, which is otherwise entirely of Great Meadow affiliation, claims descent from Inland Forest chiefs resident now at Nakoroka. This coastal region was disturbed by the sandalwood trade.[5] In 1840 a group of fishermen caste of Bau had settled at Tavea just off the coast from Lekutu.[6] When the power of Bua collapsed after the sandalwood trade had subsided, the king of Bua's relationship with the village of Lekutu was friendly enough so that he could take refuge there.[7] These cross-influences have confused the population so that it is difficult for them to formulate consistent accounts of descent from any localized group of ancestors.

But Nakoroka has no such difficulty; with few exceptions the residents have always been descendants of Inland Forest. Its component villages have not always been in political accord. They have made political alliances with foreign regions and sometimes fought among themselves. A century ago a segment of Nadroro moved to Nasigasiga, which is just across the border in Macuata Province. There are Tavua people living in Duleniwai on the windward slope of Bua Province toward Wainunu Bay. The last full-blooded descendant of Buleya has lived in Lekutu for perhaps ten years. Despite the various special affiliations of each of these five villages, they are bound irrevocably together in common dependence upon the chiefly tradition of Inland Forest to maintain the fertility of their soil.

4. *Liga qaqa* ("strong arm") is a specific term for this kind of authority.

5. In Lockerby's time Tavea was ruled by the nephew of the chief of Bau. Tavea was sacked several times during the sandalwood trade, sometimes with the aid of Europeans, once by Bau (William Lockerby, *The Journal of William Lockerby*, ed. Sir Everard in Thurn ["Publications of the Haklyut Society: Second Series," No. LII (London, 1925)], pp. 43–44).

6. According to Charles Wilkes (*United States Exploring Expedition—1840*, III [Philadelphia, 1849], 222), fishermen from the Bau region bought Tavea from the king of Bua for three hundred whale's teeth. "It is not long since they settled on it, having been driven from their former habitation by war parties of the Ambau people, and taken refuge there." This probably refers to the revolt and civil war at Bau when European aid assisted in the reinstatement of Cakobau's father, Tanoa, after his five years' exile at Somosomo. I have referred to this political trouble at Bau, above, p. 25.

7. "The town of . . . . Lekutu on Vanua Levu has been the residence of the Tui King MBua, since he was driven or expelled from Mbua Bay" (*ibid.*, p. 222).

The crags in the mountains behind Nakoroka bear traces of old house foundations and the stone fortifications of ancient villages. Some of these are former village sites of Votua, Tavua, Nadroro, Rokowaqa, and Buleya. But the history of many of them has been lost, and they are called "villages of spirits."[9] Some were obviously built to serve as fortresses with no thought for convenience of water supply or garden land.[10] A single steep approach may rise abruptly to a mountain peak six or eight hundred feet above the surrounding territory. At suitable intervals piled stone, uncut and not cemented, is heaped between large boulders to form ramparts; the path is effectively blocked so that but one man can pass at a time. Forest debris has accumulated so that the stonework is today rarely more than four or five feet in height; excavation might reveal that it was formerly more extensive. Such ramparts could conceal an army of defenders who chose to ambush an approaching enemy. Though the fortresses were impregnable to hostile attacks, they could not withstand sieges of long duration. Rain water and a few coconut trees, despite the elevation, could have prevented death from thirst, but food storage would have required arduous preparation. Usually there was a secret pathway by which the populace could escape when the siege became unbearable.[11] In ancient times the approaches to these strongholds were kept clean of forest growth so that the defenders ran no risk of a surprise attack. But even in peacetime the task of carrying food up the rugged slope must have twisted the backs of the workers.

Others of the old village sites were less difficult to attain. Palisades and moats protected them.[12] It seems probable that these, like the

8. This section and those of this chapter which follow it are based on native accounts at Nakoroka.

9. "Spirit" is a vaguely defined class of being which includes such divergent categories as forest spirits, errant souls, and forgotten ancestors.

10. Mr. George T. Barker of the Suva Museum is of the opinion that such fortresses were used only as temporary refuges.

11. One such fortress (Rock Fortress [see Map III]) could be reached only after two hours of rapid climbing from the nearest stream of water.

12. Lockerby (*op. cit.*, pp. 27–29) has described the building of a palisaded fortress at Bua in 1808: "The ground he [king of Bua] chose for the fort, was a dry spot of rising ground in the middle of a swamp, about twelve hundred yards in circumference. Round the dry parts logs of wood were placed at equal distances, about ten feet long and one foot thick, which had been collected by four hundred natives in the surrounding woods, where they cut and from thence carried them on their shoulders. Holes were then dug in the ground into which these posts were placed, and afterwards filling earth about them, that became quite solid. About these posts, two heights of small trees, were lashed length-ways with

mountain fortresses, were used only in times of danger. The close living which they imposed made them undesirable as permanent homes. The king of Bua built a fortress of this type only when the wealth which he had accumulated through the sandalwood trade attracted the notice and the hostility of his neighbors. The moats of the long-deserted village of Inland Forest can still be seen.

In the coastal regions there was a third type of village which served well as a military stronghold. This was built upon piles in a broad lagoon so that an approaching enemy could be seen far away in every direction. A village of old River's Mouth Kingdom was of this type, and the piles of its dwellings can still be seen on the coast near the present site of Sarowaqa.[13]

The old men of today remember the time of the wars, the time of perpetual danger, as the only authentic period in their history before the arrival of the Wesleyan church and British authority. Though this period may well have been of but a century's duration, they conceive

---

vines, the first three, the other six feet from the ground; to these two heights of trees they fasten in an upright position, bamboos, about forty feet long, which are placed close to each other all around the fort; the ends of them being buried in a considerable depth in the soil, and mould thrown against them. They form a complete and strong rampart. The fort has four gates, eight feet wide, at each of which they place perpendicularly four coconut trees, about sixty feet high; on the top of these platforms are erected sufficiently large to contain fifty men, and surrounded by a breast-work so strong and close as secures entirely those upon it, who by their slings and arrows have a great advantage over the besiegers. As an addition to the strength of the fort they place the plantain tree, which is of a spongy substance, inside the bamboos that surround it, which completely shelters them from the arrows, etc. of the assailants. When attacked in the day time they leave the gates open, but at night they are secured by logs of wood laid across them. This is the manner the fort is constructed, the outer works of which are equally calculated for defence. It is encompassed by a ditch full of water sixty yards wide, except for in front of the gates, to which narrow pathways run through it six feet wide. In the middle of these pathways they have a gate-way with a flanking barricade, so contrived that a number of men may conceal themselves behind it, and through which they have got holes for shooting their arrows, while they remain quite safe from the attacks of the enemy outside. At the outer extremity of the pathway there is also a barricade similar to that in the middle. This when forced is abandoned, and a stand is made in the inner one, and should this be carried, they retreat into the fort. The ditch, or the different divisions of it, is so planned as to keep it full, and not to allow it to overflow, the water being conducted underground by hollow bamboos. Such a fort as the above was completed in less than a month.

"The women were no less busy in preparing for war, than the men. They were employed in grating or rubbing down the plantain, the sweet potato and the breadfruit into a kind of jelly. This they wrapped up in leaves of the plantain, and deposited it inside of the fort in small holes covered with stones. The bodies of their enemies and this jelly or paste are all they have to live upon in time of war, the provisions outside being generally destroyed by the besieging party."

13. This is the village that delayed the army of Bua (see p. 38).

of it as extending far into the past and have forgotten that the old men of the middle nineteenth century remembered an even older time when each kingdom was content to remain within its own political boundaries and live at peace with its neighbors.[14] The fortresses have come to characterize the past. To the generation of today life in the "villages of war" has become a symbol of old Fiji, of the culture that existed before the arrival of the seeming pacifist church and white man.

During these hazardous times it is said that the villagers never left the security of their fortresses without arms. Men frequently did women's tasks of gathering firewood and carrying the food home from the gardens. Because only women knew how to use the nets for fresh-water fishing, men with their far less efficient technique of fish-spearing could not supply the village; an armed guard had to accompany the women's fishing excursions. Despite the highly charged dread and wonder with which the people of Nakoroka look back upon the days of their fathers, there are few actual battles within memory. Whenever conversation turns to the wars, everyone remembers the most recent of the battles of this region and discusses the military craft of the protagonists. But even after ten months' questioning, only seven tales of the wars were remembered. One of these does not concern the Inland Forest region.[15]

I

It is said that Ratu[16] Sameli lived four generations before the time of the present king of Inland Forest. With the help of all the villages of Inland Forest and River's Mouth, he built a great house in his village at Votua. It was so tall that it could be seen from Rukuruku Bay.[17] Maki-ni-valu[18] could see this house from his village at Lekutu and envied Ratu Sameli; there were no such houses at Lekutu. He called the chiefs together from all Great Meadow and prepared to make war on Inland Forest.

14. John E. Erskine, *Journal of a Cruise among the Islands of the Western Pacific* (London, 1853), p. 457.

15. Many of the villages and kingdoms named in the tales may be found on Map III.

16. "Sir" is perhaps the closest English equivalent for the Polynesian title *Ratu*.

17. This bay indents the west coast of Bua Province, twenty miles as the crow flies from Nakoroka. But mountains intervene so that none but an unnaturally tall house could have been seen from the bay. The house was a *vale* ("house") *leke* which is built with the long wall posts bent inward at their tops and bound to the ridgepole; roofs and walls are not distinct. This type of house prevailed in Vanua Levu before Tongan architecture became popular. In order to be bent, a procedure which is not used in the Tonga-like houses of today, the wall posts were much taller than those required by the present technique.

18. Whose name means "Skilled in Battle" and whose descendants of the third and fourth generation live today at Lekutu. At this time he held title of king for Great Meadow.

Ratu Sameli was forewarned of his danger and fled to the forest with his infant son. Thenceforth his house was called The-Greeting-without-Response.[19] It stood empty.

Maki-ni-valu was informed of the flight of Ratu Sameli. He sent whale teeth to the chief of Nadroro, to Sir Empties-the-Land at Wainunu,[20] to the chief at The-Flood-Plain,[21] asking these chiefs not to receive Ratu Sameli. These strong villages were the most likely places for Sameli to seek refuge. At each of these villages Sameli asked if he might deposit his basket of belongings. But the villages were already "crowded full with the whale teeth of Maki-ni-valu"; the acceptance of the whale teeth had pledged the chiefs to refuse Sameli.

Finally, he wandered to Rock Fortress.[22] Here the whale teeth of Maki-ni-valu had been refused, and Sameli found refuge.

Then Maki-ni-valu sent a whale tooth to the father of Ra Masima at Bua, requesting his aid in the destruction of Inland Forest and River's Mouth.[23] But one River's Mouth village, which was built on boxwood piles in a wide lagoon beyond the river's mouth, delayed the army of Bua and proved impregnable. In the meantime the forces of River's Mouth assembled and destroyed the army of Bua; only one warrior escaped to bear the news to Maki-ni-valu at Lekutu.[24]

Then Maki-ni-valu traveled with his army to all the villages of Inland Forest inquiring for Ratu Sameli. Maki-ni-valu's person was peculiarly sacred, in truly Polynesian tradition rather than that of inland Vanua Levu. He was always carried in a litter so that his feet never touched the ground. At length he reached Rock Fortress, and its strong men replied that Sameli was there indeed.

Aside from a single tortuous and well-fortified path, ascent into Rock Fortress could be gained only by climbing a tall coconut tree, which grew at the base of the highest cliff. Its summit was lashed within the ramparts. Fifty of Maki-ni-valu's men began to climb this tree. Just as they neared its top, the lashings which bowed it were cut; it sprung straight and catapulted the warriors far into the valley below.[25] When Maki-ni-valu saw the disaster, he ordered the rest of his army to ascend the fortified path, while he watched the battle from his litter. The path was so narrow that two men could not ascend abreast. Fifty more were killed before they had reached the ram-

19. *Na-Kara-Wale* ("The-Greeting-Only"). Upon approaching a chiefly house, one must first give conventional greeting; men say, "Duo! Duo!" and at night, "It is night!" The greeting of women is longer, and variation with locality is greater. If no member of the household answers, "Come in," and offers hospitality to him who greets, the house is disgraced.

20. The kingdom of Wainunu lay directly across the mountains from Inland Forest on the windward coast at Wainunu Bay.

21. Six or eight miles east of the present site of Nakoroka.

22. A village of River's Mouth, about four miles east of Nakoroka.

23. Some of the people of River's Mouth fled to the island of Tavea.

24. For this military service Maki-ni-valu ceded the village of Wailevu and its land to the king of Bua. There are many villages on Vanua Levu of this name, which means "great river." This particular Great River is located about ten miles inland from Bua Bay (Map III). Since Williams, the missionary, has recorded visiting it ninety years ago under the auspices of the king of Bua, the cession probably had taken place before his time.

25. This fortress is so difficult to attain that only two or three men now living have ever seen its site.

parts. Then the strong men of Rock Fortress said: "Now it is raining but gently; the sun is almost shining." And they charged down upon the remnant of Maki-ni-valu's retinue.

The porters of his litter fled down the mountainside, but Maki-ni-valu continued to fan himself, unconcerned. He called them back, but they did not heed him. Two warriors of Rock Fortress charged upon him, but he said: "You two are worthy only to be cooked as food for me." Daunted, they retreated, and Maki-ni-valu continued to fan himself. Then a visiting warrior from a distant Macuata town charged. When Maki-ni-valu taunted, this warrior answered: "You are blind. You cannot see your adversary." He struck Maki-ni-valu with an ax and killed him.

The few survivors fled back to Lekutu and the islands off the coast, Tavea and Galoa. In all, three hundred were killed, baked, and distributed[26] as food gifts throughout the countryside: to Tavua of Inland Forest, which was related to Rock Fortress by recent blood ties, and to distant Macuata towns. The grandfather of Monasa, Tavua's present priest, received one of these gifts and presented it to his chief.

Though the military prowess of Maki-ni-valu completely broke the military prestige of Inland Forest, the people of Inland Forest have never acquiesced complacently. Their chiefs view the "strong arm" of Maki-ni-valu and the chiefs of Great Meadow with contempt; presentation of the feast of first-fruits to Great Meadow has always been regarded as a sham of true ceremony. But the kings of Inland Forest have never built even a semblance of centralized authority in their kingdom. The allegiance of the various villages to the king has always depended upon supernatural sanctions: the king and his priests are the interlocutors with the ancestors; they alone can make an offering of first-fruits which will effectively maintain the fertility of Inland Forest land. Though bound in this religious rite, the villages act independently in other relationships. Tavua has long felt strong allegiance for Rock Fortress, which was a village of River's Mouth Kingdom; River's Mouth people, who now live at Sarowaqa, always stay at Tavua houses when they visit Nakoroka. There has been much intermarriage. Nadroro is closely bound with The-Flood-Plain, where many years ago a group of Nadroro prople migrated. Some families of Nadroro are also closely bound with Great Meadow. Votua has special affiliations with Great Meadow and also with the chiefly family of River's Mouth. There was never any military solidarity in the kingdom of Inland Forest. Though the strong arm of Great Meadow held military authority over all Inland Forest, which vaguely included River's Mouth, this authority by no means created military loyalty throughout Inland Forest. The subdivisions of Inland Forest separately honored Great Meadow's claimed right to receive first-fruits

26. Including the chief, Maki-ni-valu, despite his high rank.

only when Great Meadow chiefs could support their immediate claim
with an armed force.

II

During the time of Ratu Sameli's great grandson, Ratu Seru, who was father of
Bulisivo, the present chief of Votua and king of Inland Forest, a chief of Great Meadow came to a feast of first-fruits at Votua. These two chiefs were kinsmen though not
of the same land. Lacking one whale tooth to make equitable distribution of gifts in return for the first-fruits of Inland Forest's five village groups, Ratu Seru had asked this
Great Meadow kinsman to assist him. Instead of bringing one whale tooth, the Great
Meadow chief, whose name was Korokoro-i-vula, brought ten. To maintain prestige
in spite of Korokoro-i-vula's display of wealth, Ratu Seru might have given his entire
feast in return. But instead he chose to act in a "strong manner."

For a long time Ratu Seru had coveted an anciently famous ax which Korokoro-i-
vula possessed; the fame and antiquity of weapons enhance their supernatural power
to kill in battle. Korokoro-i-vula knew of Ratu Seru's desire for his ax, and, when he
arrived at the hill which overlooks the old site of Votua, he saw that several hundred
men of Inland Forest were assembled there, and he was afraid. He stopped there on
the hill. But Ratu Seru saw him and sent a messenger to escort him into the village.
Korokoro-i-vula was afraid and refused; if Ratu Seru should request his ax, Inland
Forest forces were too strong that day at Votua to risk refusing. He gave the whale
teeth to the messenger. Without receiving his share of the first-fruits, he returned to
his home at Lekutu on the coast. Still fearing, Korokoro-i-vula prepared to go to Bua,
ostensibly to "sing for bark cloth."[27] He gathered three hundred men of Galoa to accompany him.

When Ratu Seru heard that Korokoro-i-vula was preparing to travel to Bua, obviously for protection, he stuffed a roast pig with ten whale teeth and sent it westward
to the inland villages of Great Meadow, requesting them to kill Korokoro-i-vula and
procure the ax. The pig was sent first to Nacula[28] because Korokoro-i-vula had kinsmen there; it traveled on to Great River,[29] which possessed a "strong man"[30] and bore
an old grievance against Korokoro-i-vula: The-Hunchback, a chief of Great River,
had begged a pig from a fellow Great Meadow chief at Lekutu. This Lekutu chief had
granted The-Hunchback's request and had presented him with the pig. But Korokoro-
i-vula had rudely ordered the return of the pig and banished the generous chief from
Lekutu. The inland villages of Great Meadow, especially Great River,[31] were insulted

27. It was customary for the young men to descend upon a neighboring village and
parade upon the village green until anything they desired was satisfied. Frequently this
technique was used to obtain bark cloth, for which a special song accompanied their prom-
enades. If their request was not granted, violence might occur; but hosts usually treated
these marauders politely and retaliated with a reciprocal visit at a later time.

28. A Great Meadow village to the west of Nakoroka.

29. See n. 24 above.

30. "Strong man" is the term applied to famous warriors, who frequently were not of
chiefly caste.

31. Though formerly presented to Bua by Maki-ni-valu (see n. 24 above), Great River
maintained its traditional alliances with inland Great Meadow.

and angered against their high chief at Lekutu. They sent a pig stuffed with whale teeth to Rokowaqa[32] in the hinterland of Inland Forest, with the request that the Rokowaqa people ambush Korokoro-i-vula. Hence Korokoro-i-vula, aware of his unpopularity throughout the interior, had had reason to fear the men of Inland Forest who were assembled at Votua's feast of first-fruits; many Rokowaqa men were there.

The path from Bua to Lekutu passes near the garden land of Great River. The strong man of Great River worked his garden daily, awaiting Korokoro-i-vula's return from Bua. His spear, tipped with a sting-ray spine, was hidden in a hedge near by. One day the strong man saw Korokoro-i-vula's party approaching. He shouted, "Greetings, Korokoro-i-vula!" and hurled his spear with such force that its sting-ray tip and half its length stuck out from the front of Korokoro-i-vula's chest. Then Great River's warriors sprang from the surrounding forest. One of Korokoro-i-vula's retinue cried: "This is war!" and fled into the forest. He and two others survived. Many were struck down, and the rest driven off a cliff.

Revolt against the tyranny of the Great Meadow chief did not remove the dominance of Great Meadow military authority. It was merely a temporary flurry of co-operation between the villages of Inland Forest and inner Great Meadow against a common enemy, an alliance against an intruder[33] who had somehow come to hold the title of king for Great Meadow. Each village chief felt bound in allegiance to the other villages of his kingdom only when opposed by a common outside enemy. If this enemy were a neighbor, cross-ties of marriage or kin would split military loyalty within the kingdom, and traitors would inform against their own villages. In the perpetration of Korokoro-i-vula's murder, inland villages of two different kingdoms had united in common hatred against the more sophisticated chiefly authority of the coast. In retaliation, Korokoro-i-vula had looked to the alien kingdom of Bua for protection against the kingdom over which his own title gave him authority.

There are multiple examples of the instability of extended feudal structure in Fiji. Except for the relation between chiefs and their immediate subjects in their own villages, there have been no lasting obligations. Despite the wide extension of some titles to kingship, the supernatural sanctions which support a chief's status are usually of local nature only and place strict limits upon the chief's effective authority. The vacillating policies of powerful vassals in the empires of Bau and of Maafu, the Tongan imperialist, and the constant military

32. Far in the mountains behind the present site of Nakoroka (see Map III).

33. Korokoro-i-vula, who had close ties with Bua; his traditional background was not exclusively of Great Meadow.

intrigues during the great wars of the nineteenth century, grew out of this widespread lack of centralized authority in Fijian politics.[34]

"Strong men" flourished in the days of the wars. Any man, regardless of the caste into which he was born, could gain fame and respect through military valor. The more outrageously daring his act, the more surely it proved that the ancestral spirits had chosen him as military protector of his village. He violated all usual social restraints because his privilege was special. He took women without ceremony. When he beat himself on the chest and said, "I am a man,"[35] he embodied all that is "strong" in Fijian personality. Lisala Namosa was the greatest of these warriors in recent Nakoroka tradition. When he was an infant, his parents had bathed him in a pool at the forest shrine of the greatest ancestor of their village Nadroro. Tales III and IV which follow, recount the exploits of Namosa translated from a text which Vatili of Nadroro dictated.

III

At Nabekavu[36] there are four chiefs and Ra Namosa. One day they travel to The-Young-Man.[37] They go. But Ra Namosa stays at Nabekavu; he does not go. Straightway they climb to the village. Yes, but the village stands empty, the Dreketi people[38] are gone planting. Straightway they climb to the village and set fire to the houses there. Now the smoke of the timbers of the burning village arises, and the people of Dreketi come quickly climbing to the village. Yes, and those others, they flee. Now the chief of Dreketi[39] sees them fleeing. And now he tells the people of Dreketi to go smite them. Now they of Nabekavu are surrounded.

Now the sound of the guns is heard at Nabekavu. And Ra Namosa speaks: "I hear a certain thing. It is surely the sound of guns." Now he questions the people of Nabekavu: "Where have your chiefs gone?"

And they of Nabekavu answer: "Those? They are absent."

Now Ra Namosa speaks: "Perhaps they are fighting there with the Dreketi people. I keep hearing the sound of guns."

He hastens outside and takes up his gun and thrusts his outrigger canoe into the water. He embarks for the farther bank. And the name of his gun is Sea-Water-Is-Forbidden. He hastens to the place where they are fighting. And they of Nabekavu

34. Source material on nineteenth-century politics in Fiji can be found in W. T. Pritchard's *Polynesian Reminiscences* (London, 1866), pp. 329–42; supplement with Erskine's *Journal of a Cruise among the Islands of the Western Pacific*, pp. 425 and 437. For the rise of Maafu in Fiji see above, pp. 24–26.

35. There is no gender in Polynesian languages; in usual speech men are referred to as "persons." Hence, by contrast, the noun "man" has a special connotation of masculinity.

36. Nabekavu means The-Palisade-of-Mist, a village of River's Mouth Kingdom on an island near the mouth of the Dreketi River which Nadroro people frequently visited.

37. *A-Gone-Tagane*, a village of Dreketi Kingdom in Macuata.

38. I.e., the people of The-Young-Man.

39. This is Ratu Inoke, whose exploits of later time are recounted below, pp. 49–53.

are circling about inside [the lines of the massed enemy]. There is no direction in which they can escape, for there are hordes of men from Dreketi. And now Ra Namosa goes there.

And the chief of Dreketi speaks: "*Isa!*[40] That Namo is coming. We of Dreketi shall be struck down today."

Shouldering his gun, Namosa walks about. And he shouts to the people of Dreketi: "Be of good mind, all of you; go back, you chiefs of Dreketi! When I am at Nabekavu, there is not a single male in the Dreketi region. I know that of all men I stand unchallenged. I have with me Sea-Water-Is-Forbidden. Be of good mind, all of you. Return to your villages."

Now the chief of Dreketi speaks: "Very well. Go home, all of you." And now those of Nabekavu go home.

Because there is not a single "strong" one at Dreketi who is equal to Ra Namosa, this thing comes about. When Namosa is at Nabekavu, there is not a single person from Dreketi who goes fishing in the sea; when Namosa returns inland to Nadroro, then they go fishing. When he is at Nabekavu, not one of those Dreketi people go fishing, because of this: The name of his gun is Sea-Water-Is-Forbidden. And the reason for this name: When he is staying at Nabekavu, the people of Dreketi do not go fishing in the sea; if he comes back to Nadroro, then they go fishing.

IV

One day those of The-Flood-Plain[41] came to report at Sivoa.[42] They tell about a certain village which they have been besieging and which is too strong for them. Now Ra Namosa[43] asks: "What is the name of this village?"

Now they of The-Flood-Plain answer: "It is Nakega."

Now Ra Namosa says: "Very well. You return. I shall go to the chief at Great River. I shall go and tell him about it."

It is morning, and the people of The-Flood-Plain go away. It is morning, and they go. And Ra Namosa hastens to report at Great River.

Now that chief of Great River (Isacodro) answers: "Very well. Instruct one to go and tell them to prepare food for us at The-Flood-Plain. We shall travel there on the second night."[44]

And Ra Namosa returns to Sivoa and instructs a messenger to go to The-Flood-Plain to report there that they are starting on the second night.

In the morning the men of Nadroro, of both Sivoa and Great River, prepare. They sleep. It is morning again, and they go. They arrive there at The-Flood-Plain, and a

40. An exclamation of dismay or surprise.

41. See Map III. The-Flood-Plain was very friendly with Nadroro.

42. Sivoa and Great River (see Map VI, facing p. 106) lying along either bank of the river Nadroro, comprise the village unit of Nadroro. Each division has its chiefly family and alternates with the other in performing religious rites to renew the soil's fertility. Of all the village groups that comprise Nakoroka today, Nadroro is unique in this respect. At least ten miles separate this Great River from the Great River which is mentioned in n. 24 above.

43. Of Sivoa division of Nadroro.

44. In common speech nights and not days denote the passage of time. Hence "the second night" means "day after tomorrow."

feast is presented straightway. They finish eating, and kava is prepared.[45] Now the kava bowl is empty, and the chief of Nadroro (Isacodro) speaks: "In the morning we go with all you people of The-Flood-Plain to storm Nakega."

Kava-drinking finished, they sleep. In the morning they go forth. And quickly they arrive at the foot of the crag of the village Nakega. Yes, and the thing that makes the village impregnable is that there is but one path to it. Yes, and all sides of the village are edged by sheer cliffs.

Now Ra Namosa speaks: "Entirely alone, let me lead. Yes, and all of you follow."

They have ascended to the village. A palisade is there, and not a single place lies open. Now Ra Namosa says: "Let me climb alone into the village."

Now the chief (Isacodro) answers: "No. Let us uproot a timber of the palisade."

Now forthwith a timber is uprooted. Now they fire into the village. When the first guns sound, then the chief of Nakega (Sir The-Red-Sandalwood) comes. Now he speaks: "From what land does this fighting come?"

And Ra Namosa answers: "Do you question? Do you not know? We fight as rightful owners of this land."

Now Ra Namosa fires. The-Red-Sandalwood is struck in the thigh. The thigh is shattered, and he sits down. Now there is a second shot, and a warrior of Nadroro says: "With all this shooting we are like women."[46]

Straightway he lays aside his gun. Now he leaps to the top of the palisade and jumps down within and smites Sir The-Red-Sandalwood and cries: "To Nadroro in the daylight."[47]

His battle cry is not yet finished, and the people of Nakega have slipped away,[48] have fled because their chief is struck down. And that Nadroro warrior uproots the palisade. Now it lies wide open, and the men of Nadroro and The-Flood-Plain rush in. And they set fire to the village. And they go home straightway. They shoulder Sir The-Red-Sandalwood. And they take him quickly to The-Flood-Plain. There at The-Flood-Plain they shout the victory song. Now it is destroyed, the village which stood impregnable before the men of The-Flood-Plain.

In the morning ovens are prepared for the men of Nadroro, and the people of The-Flood-Plain present a feast. It is morning, and the people of Nadroro go home, return again to their villages at Sivoa and Great River. Now those of The-Flood-Plain are at rest, because the village which warred constantly with them is destroyed. If they had not consulted Nadroro, it would have been impossible to destroy Nakega.

Today in Nakoroka it is difficult for strong men to find expression for their energies. Though the tradition is still flourishing, aggressive behavior is likely to keep one embroiled with the British authorities,

45. Proper treatment of a guest requires the presentation of a feast and the drinking of kava afterward. Kava must be served on all formal occasions.

46. Fighting with muskets required no strength, no bravery, and so was effeminate. Strong men liked to insult their opponents by throwing away their weapons and attacking with bare hands.

47. Upon striking an enemy, it was customary to shout the name of one's own land, perhaps as a promise that this victim would be cooked for the village ancestors. The shout has a generic name, *vaka cau cau*.

48. Literally, "[they] have withdrawn from a horizontally inserted position."

who are intent upon maintaining the political and social status quo.
It is the strong men who chafe most under the restraints of British authority.

In the tale which follows, the kingdoms seem to function in proper
order as organized political systems. The king of Bua, with English and
Tongan police power, had established a semblance of stability throughout Bua Province except for the Wainunu regions.

V

One time the chief at Wainunu, Sir Empties-the-Land,[49] is sick. His sickness: The
father of Ratu Monasa, Ratu Luke, has worked the leaf of a tree[50] against him. Now
Sir Empties-the-Land dies because the sickness is strong against him. It is in that time
when the church is not yet flourishing. They have submitted but lightly to the church,
and likewise to the government of Britain. And now it is noised about to Bua, to Ra
Masima.[51] Now Ra Masima says to go to Wainunu and hold an inquiry because of it.
And now it is noised abroad to Wainunu that a certain Chief of the Law[52] is coming;
they mention his name. Now Ratu Luke says: "You people of Wainunu, go and await
this Chief of the Law at The-Sand. He comes tomorrow."

And in the morning the men of Wainunu hasten there to the beach. They are waiting there, and it is high noon. Now the Chief of the Law comes. Now they shoot. Now
this Chief flees back to Bua.

Now this Chief of the Law goes and informs at Bua. Now Ra Masima says: "Wainunu is always fighting."

They remain at Bua.

And now at Wainunu they decide to build a palisade about one of their fortresses.
And now they begin to palisade The-Village-in-Unnamed-Land.[53] Now it is heard
at Bua that the people of Wainunu are raising a palisade, that they are expecting war.
Now Ra Masima says: "Very well. Inform Ratu Meli[54] at Lekutu. Then let it be the
task of Ratu Meli to inform River's Mouth. Let Ratu Tevita of River's Mouth[55] inform Ratu Inoke[56] of Dreketi that the people of Wainunu are raising a palisade."

The speaking is finished. Now a certain one hastens to Lekutu and informs Ratu

49. The time of this tale is two generations later than Tale I, in which another Sir
Empties-the-Land is mentioned. The perpetuation of names in family lines is still frequent
practice at Nakoroka.

50. The formulas of witchcraft are known as "tree leaves" (dra-ni-kacu).

51. See chap. ii, n. 61. This half-Tongan chief of Bua Kingdom, Ra Masima ("Sir
Salt") brought Christianity to all Bua Province. With the aid of the British-drilled troops
of Bau, he became nominal chief of all territory now included in Bua Province.

52. "Chief of the Law" (Turaga ni Lawa) is the title which applies today to the officer-
in-charge of a province. Today such officers are British.

53. Na-Koro-Tiki, not far from the modern village of Saolo. Today it is almost deserted
(see Map III).

54. Grandson of Maki-ni-valu (see Tale I).

55. Ratu Tevita appears also in Tale VI. The flight of Sameli from Votua (pp. 37–39)
occurred during the time of Tevita's father.

56. Ratu Inoke is mentioned in the narrative of Tale VI.

Meli: "The people of Wainunu are raising a palisade. And it has been said to inform River's Mouth also. Let it be the task of Ratu Tevita of River's Mouth to relay the report to Ratu Inoke at Dreketi."

Yes, and Ra Masima goes to Levuka,[57] goes there to inform the government at Levuka that the people of Wainunu are raising a palisade. Straightway he embarks in his ship and anchors at Levuka and informs the governor. Now it is the decision of the governor that his contribution shall be two hundred "soldiers of Fiji":[58] "Yes, and you return again to your kingdom at Bua and prepare for the fighting at Wainunu."

Now Ra Masima comes back, arrives at Bua and instructs a certain one to go to Lekutu and tell them to prepare the materials of war, and tell them also to send someone to River's Mouth and likewise to Dreketi. Yes, and the day for assembling there at Wainunu is not specified. And so it is the decision of Ratu Tevita of River's Mouth to send someone to Votua, to Ratu Seru,[59] to say: "We of River's Mouth and those of Dreketi will sleep here at Votua tomorrow."

And a messenger hastens from River's Mouth to Votua and informs Ratu Seru. Now Ratu Seru says: "Very well. Now go back again. Go tell Ratu Tevita that I agree."

And in the evening the messenger goes back again. He goes to River's Mouth. When it is night, those from Dreketi arrive there. They sleep at River's Mouth. Those of River's Mouth prepare a feast during the night. In the morning they present the feast, heap it before those of Dreketi. When they have heard each other's formal speeches, the feast is divided. They are eating. Now Ratu Tevita comes and suspends a whale tooth before them and says: "This is my presentation, this whale tooth. Now we prepare to go to Inland Forest [i.e., Votua], to sleep there tonight. We are about to battle at Wainunu."

His speaking is finished, and the men of River's Mouth and those of Dreketi prepare straightway. And they hasten to Votua. They arrive here at Votua, and the feast is presented. When they have exchanged formal speeches with the chiefs of River's Mouth, they make presentation to Dreketi. When these have finished exchanging formal speeches, the feast is returned to the men of River's Mouth.[60] Now Ratu Tevita orders that the feast be apportioned. When the apportioning is complete, they eat. And they sleep.

It is the same night at Lewelewe.[61] Now the priest of Wainunu speaks: "A certain animal will come in the morning.[62] Very well. Go and wait in the path at the River Nameless."[63]

57. Then the capital of the British colony, on the island of Ovalau.

58. Warriors of Bau and Levuka served as police force for the British authority. This episode probably occurred about 1870.

59. See n. 85 below.

60. This is somewhat puzzling procedure. It depends upon the complex political relations of Dreketi and River's Mouth. Vatili, who dictated the text of this tale, says that the feast could not be presented directly to Dreketi because Dreketi was "in the back of" River's Mouth at this time; "in back of" probably means "under temporary obligation to." Vatili himself is confused on this point.

61. A village on the windward slope, in the forest above Wainunu.

62. The priest delivers his oracle in obscure manner. He refers to the approaching army of Inland Forest, River's Mouth, and Dreketi.

63. In the rugged mountains near the height of the land on the path which leads from the Wainunu coast to Nakoroka.

And it is morning, and they hasten to lie in wait at the River Nameless.

During the night the people of Inland Forest bake food in the ovens. In the morning they present a feast. The presentation finished, Ratu Tevita orders that it be apportioned. When they have finished eating, they prepare to go. Now Ratu Seru decides upon the method of their going: "Now let two men go ahead as scouts." And he appoints Paola and Care to go ahead.

They are going on through the forest. Yes, and those from Wainunu are waiting in the path. They are awaiting the men of Inland Forest. Yes, and the place in which they are waiting is a small place. It is not possible for many men to pass there. There are sheer cliffs on both sides of the path. Yes, and a small stream lies before. Yes, and those from Wainunu are on its farther bank.

It is not long, and those two, Paola and Care, descend to the stream. They climb up the other side. Care is in the lead. Yes, and Vatili-the-Great[64] is standing in a certain lemon tree. Now he shoots forth at Care. Now Care is shot in the side, here. Now he is pierced through to the other side, here. And Care slumps down and he cries: "I am dead!"

Now he pushes off his head-wrapping and ties it about his ribs. Now he speaks: "You are males, you men of Wainunu.[65] I am wounded. But if I were not wounded, not one of you would remain."

Frightened, the men of Wainunu take flight.

The men of Votua and River's Mouth approach. And Care is sitting there. Paola is standing by. Now Paola shouts: "Care is killed. The men of Wainunu are in flight."

And the chiefs say to fashion a litter. Straightway a litter is made, and Care is lifted upon it. And some carry him back to Votua. And some go on to war at Wainunu.

Now they arrive at Wainunu, at The-Village-in-Unnamed-Land. And those from Bua are fighting there, and those from Solevu,[66] and those two hundred soldiers of the governor at Levuka. They are firing at the village. In the morning they go right to the edge of the village. Straightway the soldiers of the governor scale the palisade. And, inside, two men are struck down: one, a boy from Nairai; one from Village. And they are baked in the camp of the soldiers.

In the night the chief of Wainunu orders his people to take flight, because there is no food and the water is used up. The women and their children are in need. There is no food for them to eat. It is night, and they hurry away. In the morning the soldiers begin to fire at the village. And the firing is not returned. And straightway they know that the village is empty. And Ra Masima commands that they go burn the village: "When the village is burned, that is enough. Dismiss and go home."

And the soldiers are dismissed. And the men of Inland Forest and those from River's Mouth and those also from Dreketi come home again. And the men of Solevu go home. And the men of Bua go home with Ra Masima. And the soldiers embark again for Levuka.

And the people of Wainunu take flight, and they go to The-Bath.[67]

One year passes, and Ra Masima decides that those people who are staying at The-Bath shall be brought forth. Ra Masima prepares himself and hastens to Levuka, goes

64. A Wainunu warrior.

65. Care is questioning the sex of his adversaries, a high insult.

66. Solevu, on the windward coast southwest of Wainunu was given to Bua Kingdom by the Tongan conquerors in return for military services.

67. East of Wainunu beyond the authority of the Bua Chief.

to tell the governor that the people of Wainunu are arriving in bondage. Now it is the order of the governor that they be brought in bondage to Bua. And now the soldiers embark, returning with Ra Masima. And they hasten to Bua.

They anchor at Bua, and their food is prepared. In the morning, when they have finished eating, they travel by land and sleep at Solevu. And they ask those at Solevu to come along to The-Bath, and also those at Nadi.[68] And they hasten forth, and they sleep at The-Forest-Banana. And they hurry on to Yanawai[69] in the morning. And they sleep at The-Bath. And during the night they tie up those from Wainunu.

And as they are brought forth from The-Bath it is morning. And they sleep at Wainunu. In the morning they climb inland and sleep at Driti.[70] And straightway they arrive at Bua and stay there in bondage.

Five years pass, and now the church is strong in the land. Now it is the Roko's[71] decision that the people of Wainunu return again to their land. And it remains so to this day. The affair at The-Village-in-Unnamed-Land has been an end to war. To this day there has been no other war. Now the church extends throughout the land.[72]

Such reshuffling of population was extensive during the wars of the nineteenth century. Those whose parents migrated because of the wars have adjusted with difficulty to the community of their adoption. Vatili's mother, the oldest woman in Nakoroka, was born at Wainunu and fled to The-Bath from the soldiers of Ra Masima. Her village of birth had a special land relationship[73] with the people of Nacula in Great Meadow Kingdom. Eventually she traveled there and married a man of Inland Forest affiliations. Thenceforth her time was divided between her husband's household at Nacula and that of a distant classificatory brother at Nakoroka. Vatili was born at Nakoroka. The individuals descended from such expatriates still live in great insecurity; if their rights in the land of the village in which they reside can be traced back but a few generations, they are held suspect, their prosperity is resented, and they are reminded of their foreign affiliations whenever they attempt to express an opinion. Vatili's status at Nakoroka is like this.

With the fall of the fortress at Wainunu, British and Christian authority was nominally established throughout Bua Province. Remembering the efficient police power with which the British enforced their

68. A kingdom on Wainunu Bay just east of Solevu.
69. The site of the first gold mine on Vanua Levu, in western Cakaudrove.
70. Near the ancient site of Flight-of-the-Chiefs at the headwaters of the Dama River.
71. Title of highest native official in a province. See below, p. 63.
72. Vatili's mother, the oldest resident at Nakoroka, was of this group who were taken to Bua in bondage. Vatili's statement that this ended war in Fiji is not true; rather, it ended organized opposition to British authority in Bua Province.
73. The two villages were "land together."

decrees, the most remote villages had been affected to a degree which allowed their forces to be united against a common enemy. But within the kingdoms themselves vacillations of allegiance continued.

The story of the sack of Nabetenidiyo may be of later date than the conquest of Wainunu, but its scope was local so that the police force at Bua was not involved. This is the most recent and thoroughly understood of all war stories. When the old men gather together in the evenings to talk of the days of the wars, this is always the episode which is analyzed.

VI [74]

One day Ratu Tevita of River's Mouth[75] comes, comes to Ratu Jone, the chief at Nabetenidiyo,[76] comes here to beg a pig from him. And he does not comply with the request of Ratu Tevita, who returns then to River's Mouth. Then Ratu Tevita goes to procure a whale tooth. Straightway he goes to Dreketi to Ratu Inoke, the chief at Dreketi. And he has also taken some earth from River's Mouth. Then he arrives at Dreketi and goes straightway to the house of this chief. Then he suspends the whale tooth[77] before this chief and speaks forth: "I suspend this whale tooth before you, Ratu Inoke. Today I have come to you. I have been to Ratu Jone at Nabetenidiyo. I went there to beg one of his pigs because of a certain need of mine. And he did not give me consent. Thence I returned to River's Mouth. Because of this thing I have come straightway to you today. Because of this thing I suspend a whale tooth before you, so that you will go raze this Nabetenidiyo. If this be possible, then the land at River's Mouth shall be your sustenance.[78] For this purpose, the earth here before you. If it be possible to raze Nabetenidiyo, the land at River's Mouth shall be your sustenance forever."[79]

His speaking is finished. And Ratu Inoke accepts, clapping.[80] Now Ratu Inoke

74. This tale is translated from a text dictated by Vatili of Nadroro.

75. This River's Mouth is the kingdom of that name.

76. This village was built in Tavua land and inhabited by Tavua people at the time when Wesleyanism had newly arrived and wars were nominally at an end. Hence Nabetenidiyo was not fortified. It was situated on a point of land bounded on the east by the river Tavua and on the west by the river Votua, about a mile and a half from the present site of Nakoroka. Five of Nakoroka's present inhabitants were born there. The coconuts planted along its margin near the watercourses are still luxuriant and productive (see Map VI, facing p. 106). Today Nabetenidiyo is said to lie in Nadroro land.

77. This is the proper procedure in making a request of a chief.

78. The class of pronouns which specifies food is used in this sentence. Land, as the source of all food, is frequently classified in this manner. As Ratu Tevita spoke this phrase, he suspended the parcel of earth which he had brought with him from River's Mouth.

79. Such ceremonial occasions require that the speaker drone in a sort of rhythmic chant. He salutes his host by clapping his hands, with fingers of one hand held perpendicular to those of the other, and the palms cupped to achieve deep resonance.

80. This clapping is also prescribed in the ceremony. It inaugurates the speech of acceptance. Chiefs rarely engage in ceremonial speeches themselves; usually their "messenger" (*Matanivanua*, "Face-of-the-Land") performs ceremonial tasks. Perhaps the urgent

speaks: "It is well. Return again to River's Mouth. Then I shall decide when to start. Just go and wait."

After some time has passed, Ratu Inoke orders all the people of Dreketi to gather in his house. The people of Dreketi assemble. Now Ratu Inoke speaks: "Tevita of River's Mouth has come here and brought a gift of earth from River's Mouth. Here it is, before all you chiefs of Dreketi. One day he went to Nabetenidiyo, went to get a pig from Ratu Jone. Ratu Jone did not give it to him, and he returned again to River's Mouth. Then he thought of coming here to us, the chiefs of Dreketi. For which, this whale's tooth. He wished that Nabetenidiyo be razed. If this be possible, the land at River's Mouth shall be our sustenance. Because of which, this bit of earth is an accompanying gift. Here it is."

Now the chiefs of Dreketi[81] discuss for a while.[82] Now Ratu Inoke speaks: "We go to destroy the village at Nabetenidiyo on the second night."

When their discussion is finished, they go separately to their villages to prepare the materials of war: the bark cloth, the black paint, the fringed girdle,[83] the spear, the war club, the gun.[84] When their preparation is complete, they return separately to the village of Ratu Inoke; they assemble in his village at Men-of-the-Forest. There is one named Ratu The-Sun-Is-High, a chief of Tavua. It is hardly night in the land when he hastens back to Nabetenidiyo, and there he informs Ratu Jone. And he speaks: "They of Dreketi are coming here in the morning, coming to raze this village because you refused to give a pig to Ratu Tevita of River's Mouth."

Now Ratu Jone speaks: "Let the chiefs of Nabetenidiyo assemble here."

They assemble at his house. And now he speaks: "You have gathered here, you chiefs of the land, that I may tell you a thing. The-Sun-Is-High has come here today. He [the Tavua chief] came to say that they of Dreketi are coming here in the morning. They are coming to destroy this village because of the pig which I refused Ratu Tevita of River's Mouth. Ratu Tevita has journeyed there to Dreketi, presented a whale tooth to Ratu Inoke. And they are planning to come here in the morning. I have informed you: Decide upon a plan so that all may understand. Then go and inform at Votua and Nadroro."

They discuss, and they reach understanding. Now a messenger hastens to Ratu Seru at Votua[85] to tell the plans of the Dreketi people, that they are coming to destroy Nabetenidiyo.

---

nature of the occasion caused Ratu Tevita to travel alone, but more probably it is a stylistic omission for the sake of brevity.

81. Dreketi is, here, the kingdom with its several villages and not the village Dreketi which is the capital of that kingdom.

82. All issues are thus formally discussed before a final decision is reached. Nabetenidiyo and all other place names refer to tracts of land and not to village, house, kingdom, or river. Hence it is the "village at Nabetenidiyo" and not the "village of Nabetenidiyo."

83. These are the regalia for ceremonial occasions and war. When a troop of warriors are so dressed, their ancestors will take pride in assisting them. These are the "clothes of chiefs."

84. Or *bow*. When muskets were introduced in Fiji, the Fijians classified them as "weapons with mechanically lengthened range" and called them *dakai*, which had previously meant only "bow and arrow."

85. Ratu Seru was father of the present high chief at Inland Forest and Nakoroka (see Chart I, p. 87).

Now Ratu Seru speaks: "Let someone go straightway to Nadroro, go and inform the chief, Isa-Momo, at Nadroro that the people of Dreketi come to destroy Nabetenidiyo. When the informing is finished, let them hasten here to me at Votua so that we may go together to Nabetenidiyo and hold discussion there."

The messenger of Votua hastens to Nadroro, hastens to tell the words of Ratu Seru to that chief of Nadroro. The people of Nadroro are gathered together. They assemble straightway. The chief at Nadroro tells the words of the chief at Votua about the coming of the chiefs of Dreketi to destroy Nabetenidiyo. And also he says: "I have finished speaking. Prepare quickly for your journey to Votua so that you may go in company to Nabetenidiyo."

The young men of Nadroro prepare quickly. They prepare the materials of war: the bark cloth, the fringed girdle, the black paint, the club, the gun, the spear. They hasten to Votua. The young men of Votua have prepared also.

Now Ratu Seru speaks: "We go hence to Nabetenidiyo. We go to discuss a certain thing, to decide where we shall await the people from Dreketi."

They hasten to Nabetenidiyo to hold discussion there. A feast is prepared there for the young men of Votua and Nadroro. Arrived at Nabetenidiyo, they hold discussion. And they decide to hasten to Sarowaqa, when the feast has been apportioned and eating is finished, to sleep there and await the men of Dreketi.[86]

One day had passed, and it is morning again, and they remain there at Sarowaqa. Yes, and the day is bright with sun; indeed, there is no rain. As they wait, the river at Sarowaqa becomes red with mud.[87] Now they say: "A mysterious flood.[88] Perhaps there is rain at the land's head[89] that causes this appearance of a flood."

They do not know the true reason for it: The men of Dreketi have not followed the path that comes to Sarowaqa, but they have climbed inland. It is their fording of the river that riles the water. They have ascended to the mountains and then traveled inland along the stream. As they wade, the river becomes red with mud. There has been no rain at all.

They hasten to Nabou.[90] And at Nabou, this chief of Dreketi speaks: "Let us not be carrying our weapons. Let us carry some firewood and some leaf containers for food so that, when the women of Nabetenidiyo see us, they will not suspect; for the sake of the battle, let them think that we are just wandering about."

Now some of them shoulder firewood and some find leaves for food containers. Now they hasten to Nabetenidiyo. They reach the bank of the river Tavua, and those women [of Nabetenidiyo] see them and think: "These men, they must come from Sarowaqa. They carry firewood and parcels of food."

And they do not know that these men are the men of Dreketi. And these men arrive at the village. Now they leap forth suddenly. Now they fire their guns, now burn the houses. And now they of Nabetenidiyo know this is war. The women, the children, are struck down.

86. Tavua, of which Nabetenidiyo was a descendant, felt closely allied with Sarowaqa, of River's Mouth.

87. Rain and accompanying floods are the only climatic cause of turbid water.

88. The word translated as "mysterious" usually means "stolen" or "accomplished in a stealthy manner."

89. The mountains of the interior.

90. The site of a deserted village in the mountains beyond Nabetenidiyo.

Now they [the Dreketi army] hasten along the path toward River's Mouth. They hasten to The-Women's-Altar. But they go to the seashore, straightway to Nukuseva, and they swim the river Sarowaqa at its mouth. They cross The-Old-Yam-Patches and hasten along the coast. They arrive at Place-of-Stagnant-Pools, at The-Painted-Rock. And quickly they have returned to their village.[91]

After more than how many years, Ratu Seru travels in procession to Dreketi, with his people.[92] The time of the wars had passed. Now they are going to a gift exchange (*solevu*) at Dreketi, because of a certain need of Ratu Inoke. After the people of Inland Forest have exchanged gifts at Dreketi and returned home, those from Dreketi followed them, come to exchange gifts at Votua.[93]

Now Ratu Inoke suspended a whale tooth there and says: "I suspend a whale tooth before you, Ratu Seru, because you granted my invitation and traveled hence to Dreketi. I tell you another thing also, about the land of River's Mouth. I give it to you; let it be your sustenance forever, because of your people whom I destroyed at Nabetenidiyo; let it bury the blood of your people. Let the land of River's Mouth be your sustenance forever, indeed until the end of the world comes."

And so it has remained until this day.

Bulisivo,[94] the son of Ratu Seru and heir to the kingship of Inland Forest, was very young when his father, Ratu Seru, journeyed to Dreketi and thence with Ratu Inoke to Labasa, which is perhaps sixty miles up the leeward coast from Dreketi. Inoke had been formally visited by the chief of Labasa, but his wealth was not great enough to repay this visit. Hence he called upon Ratu Seru, who was a distant kinsman, to assist him. Bulisivo remembers the time when all the peoples of Inland Forest domain pooled their property resources so that Ratu Seru could grant the wish of Inoke. In payment of this debt Inoke, who had no other resources, gave Seru the right to first-fruits of the land at River's Mouth. Bulisivo must be seventy; hence the feast episode must have happened before 1870. The sack of Nabetenidiyo could not have occurred more than ten years earlier: two young men of Nabetenidiyo escaped death because they were at Galoa, off the

91. From this list of place names, any native of the region would know that the men of Dreketi had detoured to the seacoast to avoid approaching the village at Sarowaqa, where they knew the men of Nabetenidiyo with their allies were prepared for an attack.

92. Ratu Seru was king of all Inland Forest villages, which included Nabetenidiyo, Nadroro, Votua, and others.

93. These chiefly visits with the accompanying feast and formal exchange of gifts were the principal means of intervillage trade. A chief's prestige depended upon his returning such a visit.

94. Present chief of Nakoroko. His real name is Ratu Meli, but the awkwardness of using the title, "Sir," or *Ratu*, which must always precede the name of chief, has popularized nicknames. *Bulisivo* means "Buli (chief official) who has been sacked." It is an honorary nickname. About thirty years ago, Bulisivo was recognized by the colonial administration as high official in his district until he was charged with appropriating the government taxes which he considered his rightful tribute.

coast of Lekutu, receiving instructions from a newly arrived Tongan religious teacher; in the 1850's Christianity was making but feeble inroads into Bua Province.

When the old men tell this tale, they are baffled by the stupidity of decision which centered the defensive forces at Sarowaqa. Bulisivo blames Ratu The Sun-Is-High; if he had learned what trail the men of Dreketi intended to follow, there would have been no massacre. Bulisivo says that if he had then been chief, Ratu The-Sun-Is-High would have been killed for his stupidity; this seeming stupidity may have been merely a subterfuge for a secret alliance with the chief of Dreketi.

After leaving Nabetenidiyo, the Dreketi army destroyed Votua, but, though it lay near the line of their march, Nadroro was not destroyed: the old men of Nadroro had prostrated themselves in the path and begged that Nadroro be spared.[95] This rite of humiliation could theoretically have been employed at Nabetenidiyo and at Votua. But there were no old men at these villages, only women; and women cannot be expected to act intelligently in an emergency. Furthermore, Nadroro was bound to Dreketi by the bonds of marriage, and in-laws must love each other. Because of affinal bonds, the Dreketi men granted Nadroro a respect which even blood relationship does not require.

To establish peaceful relations between two warring regions, a gift exchange served "to bury the blood"; when Ratu Inoke of Dreketi gave River's Mouth to Ratu Seru, he was observing this ceremony of pacification. Especially when warring villages are related by blood, which was almost always so, there were special funereal rites of exchange through which the bereaved group must be compensated with gifts. About eighty years ago in the Nacula region there was another occasion for "burying the blood."

VII

One day they of the windward coast decided to come to the Nacula region to a village named Tall Rock with which they are related by blood ties. When they come, the village is empty. Yes, their men have gone to Dry Village, gone to make a presentation to the chief of Great Meadow, Maki-ni-valu. Only the women remain in the village.

And they of the windward coast come. And straightway the women of Tall Rock open the gates of the palisade. Yes, these women think that it is their men returning from Dry Village. And straightway they of the windward coast enter the village. Now

95. This rite of prostration is termed *sau rabo*. A man of messenger caste blocks the path with crossed spears and lies before them with his head in the mud. When the enemy approaches, he may offer them gifts or tribute.

the women know that it is war, a horrible thing because women and children are struck down. Now they are piled together there. Yes, some only escape by leaping down [from the palisade], and they hasten to tell their men at Dry Village. When these return, the fighting has ceased, and those from the windward coast have gone home again.

Now much time passes, and now they come from the windward coast to bury the blood at Nacula. Now they give a piece of land called The-Bridge[96] to bury the blood. And to this day whenever there is a time of need at Nacula they go to The-Bridge because there are coconuts there. All because it was a war between relatives.

In native interpretations of these accounts, war is described as necessary to gratify the vanity of chiefs and ancestors. Ancestors maintained the fertility of the soil and the health of the populace, but in return they expected periodic gifts of human sacrifices. The more frequent the gift presentations, the closer was the rapport between ancestors and community. Victory honored the ancestors and at the same time gained their support for future wars. The jealous pride of a chief usually provided the immediate motive for war and determined what village should be attacked. Though informants insist that, in Bua Province, murdering expeditions were never a part of funeral ceremonies of prominent citizens, as they were in Macuata, yet even the death of a small child at the hands of a strange village was an insult worthy of military vengeance. Wars to collect tribute and wars of vengeance, no matter how frivolous the chiefly whim which precipitated them, were all justified in terms of their religious necessity and concerned the community as a whole: fertility raised everyone's standard of living, and the honor of a chief was reflected among all his retinue. The village, the chief, and the village ancestors were all bound together in this co-operative attempt to maintain prestige.

Like villages within kingdoms, households within villages honored relationships with outside groups above loyalty to the village. Marriage ties produced the most powerful of extra-village bonds. On the eve of preparation for an attack, someone who had affinal relations in the village to be attacked always felt impelled to warn them; warriors usually found their prey fled to the forest, and the village deserted except for a cripple or old person too feeble to take flight. But these victims, ineffective though they were in daily life, were quite acceptable as human sacrifices and gave ample excuse for the victory song when the conquering army returned home. Thus, before Tongans, Wesleyans, and Catholics had mobilized native military forces into

96. A village is situated in this land (see Map III).

opposing camps with annihilation of opponents as goal, there was slight occasion for great slaughter in Fijian wars.

Jackson, the castaway on eastern Vanua Levu before the middle of the nineteenth century, has left the only accounts of warfare which was carried on without the aid of European fighting methods.[97] A chief of far eastern Vanua Levu, Bonavidogo, led an attack against the people of Male:[98]

The inhabitants of Male live on the very top of a mountain, in shape like a sugar-loaf, with only one path up it. At the top they can easily guard the path, and defy ten times as many as themselves by rolling large stones upon them as they advance upwards. Aware of the safety of their natural defense, they sometimes sally forth and commit great depredations on the main land, taking off women as prisoners, and killing the men for food.[99] As soon as we were close enough to distinguish the natives on the mountains we saw that they were "bole" [challenging] by their antics and beckoning to us with their hands; and when we got on shore, and could hear what they said, we made out their speech of defiance to be, that they were extremely tired of waiting for us, especially as they had anticipated our visit for so long, but, as we had at last made our appearance, they were quite ready to begin at once. . . . . [They said that they had plenty of ammunition.] . . . . They said they saw that we had all the Feejees and Tongans with us, but they hoped that we would not have the presumption to attack until we had collected the whole world, Bulatangani [Britain], Franse [France], and Meriki [America], [which they thought composed the whole], to assist us. Each party continued for some time this kind of banter to each other, till three of the Male people ventured half-way down the path, where they stood and dared any or all to come up. As they were shaking their "masi" [or waist-belts] behind them, in the most deriding manner, all our party that had muskets fired and killed the three (one being completely riddled through and through), and then rushed up and caught the bodies as they rolled down the path. A number of our people were wounded, and as some of them, or perhaps all, went rather for amusement than for revenge, here the affair ended.[100]

The following describes an act of vengeance on the part of Bonavidogo against a village called Tuneloa, on Natewa Bay.

They had their faces blackened and new waist-belts on, their fine head-dresses that resembled gauze of different colors flowing behind them, and most of them with a kind of knee-buckles, as I used to call them, being composed of a quantity of small roots lashed very tightly round each leg under the knees. The use of them, they told

97. Even at this time motives for the wars in which Jackson participated were affected by the existence of European wealth and the imperialistic policy of the already acculturated Bau. But, in contrast with other early records of warfare, no armed body of Europeans under European command directed the procedure of these battles.

98. See Map I. Male lies off the north coast of Macuata.

99. All early travelers in Fiji were so shocked by cannibalistic practices that they were ready to believe natives' tales of their own ferocity and the ferocity of their enemies.

100. Erskine, op. cit., p. 425 (Jackson's account).

me, was to brace in the muscles of the legs, and they said they felt themselves stayed and firmer with these than without them. A great many had "sausauwais" on their middles. They looked extremely savage, their faces being blackened completely over, and the white of their eyes and their beautiful white teeth showing as they moved their enormous moustaches, also blackened, as well as their whiskers and beard, which hung down their breasts. Their numbers, and gigantic as well as athletic figures, had a most imposing and formidable appearance. They ran up to the front door of the king's house . . . . one by one, with their arms in their hands imitating the way they would use them on their enemies, each declaring his abilities or willingness to defend him, the great chief, by different quaint sayings, which sometimes caused great merriment and laughter. This business occupied four or five hours, and as soon as it was done they proceeded toward the tributary town, intending to lie in ambush until the Tuneloa people should arrive and begin to commit their usual depredations. They lay down in the scrub, but most of the young men preferred lying on the hard, shingly beach in rows, just above the high water mark. They said it was to inure themselves to hardship, and it tended greatly to harden their bodies. That night the mosquitoes were wonderfully numerous, so much so that I was unable to take any rest. The natives said they durst not kindle a fire for fear of being discovered, as they did not know whether the enemy was lurking about or not. I told them I did not want any fire to prevent the mosquitoes from stinging, as I should not dare go to sleep under such circumstances because at no time, that I had observed, was there a single watch kept, not even in the most imminent danger. . . . . In the morning the people fancied, or really did hear, a cracking of sticks; they were all immediately on the alert, and soon after they discovered the enemy at their work dispersed about. One of our people fired a shot without being ordered, and without effect. The enemy immediately drew up into one body and returned the compliment by firing a whole volley into us at once, and then took to their heels and ran off, I thought for good, but no such luck, for as soon as they saw that our people were not following them, they returned and fired a second volley into us, which our people as quickly returned, doing some execution on both sides. A pretty sharp fire was then kept up a few minutes, and the people that had no muskets were chasing and retreating on both sides, menacing one another with death. At last Bonavidogo, not liking this kind of undecisive work, asked the men if they would follow him. They said they would; he then watched the time when the enemy slacked their fire and not many had had time to reload, and rushed forward followed by his men with tomahawk in hand. At this the enemy turned around as though they were going away for good, and ran their hardest, occasionally looking around, and as soon as our party relaxed their speed the enemy turned to meet them. Our party then turned and ran off in their turn, allowing the enemy to be almost at their heels and then turned suddenly around, making a still stand; they were in momentary collision, but our people, being more prepared with their tomahawks, directed their blows well, and dealt with great destruction. Each party, or rather the majority of each, retreated from the other, while others were seizing the dead and wounded indiscriminately, each party trying to save his own dead and wounded from the ignominious end of being eaten, and, on the other hand, to secure the dead and wounded of their enemies, for the sake of eating them and dishonouring their memories. The conflict had not entirely subsided, but two or three detached parties were still disputing the victory. I observed Bonavidogo disputing it with a very powerful and determined antagonist, and was getting the better of him, when one of the enemy's party ran up to his friend's assistance with his tomahawk lifted to despatch Bonavidogo; I leveled my musket . . . . ; the ball entered the middle of his forehead and he fell dead. Bonavidogo told me afterwards that he saw it all, which inspired him with fresh courage, and, making the last and almost desperate effort, he warded off the blow of his antagonist's tomahawk, and then drove his own into his neck, almost severing the head from the body. Here ended the whole, our people threatening the Tuneloa people with further retaliation as they retreated, and saying in a short time they would go to Tuneloa and destroy it all together, and take their chief and make a cook of him afterwards and eat him; advising them to make haste home and repeat what had been told them, and prepare themselves for an assault on their "kolo" (fortification).

The Tuneloa people answered that we might come as soon as we thought proper, and might depend on a warmer reception than we had received today. They went home, but our people stayed to prepare food and cook some of the dead bodies.[101]

Muskets were already in use at this time, and it is probable that the bloodshed which these battles describe was far greater than that which depended only upon Fijian weapons. Despite the relative bloodlessness of their wars, the Fijians of today look with envy upon the customs of European war, which they imagine to be carried on by wireless; the few Fijians who were enlisted in the British army during the first World War spent their time far behind the lines on the coast of France, and their stories of the war are not realistic. The chiefs of Nakoroka admire European "chiefs of war" who, it is thought, send their commoners out to risk all danger, while they themselves live comfortably far from the site of battle and direct the progress of events. As a gesture of friendship toward visiting white men, Fijians frequently express verbal gratitude to the British for bringing a more humanistic concept of warfare.

In fact, the pacification of Fiji toward the end of the nineteenth century was a boon to the native population. Religious war was ended, and the political status quo was maintained firmly by an efficient and well-meaning British justice. War had ravaged especially the population of Bua Province. Though there are no written accounts from which an opinion may be drawn,[102] all of the old men of Nakoroka remember a time when their land was thickly populated. Of course, it is impossible to know how far their memory is colored by a childhood view of the world which saw adults and their activities in heroic proportions.

In supporting the chiefly lines in power at the time of Britain's first

101. *Ibid.*, pp. 444–46.

102. The population estimates of the old writers are contradictory and are not to be trusted.

ascendance in Fiji, British authority succeeded in removing to a degree the motives for civil strife within villages. Rival chiefs could no longer battle for power. Poisoning unpopular chiefs by witchcraft was condemned in British courts and punished in British jails. But this crystallizing of the political structure into incontestable stability brought a new evil. There was no longer any mechanism by which the community could assert itself toward reorganization of the relations of authority: chiefs who felt firmly intrenched could become lax in their concern for the community's welfare without fear that a rival would popularize himself with the commoners and usurp authority. The result, in Nakoroka at least, has been that the kingship of Inland Forest has fallen into listless hands which are effective only in religious functions and in passive disapproval of violence. Executive functions have been taken over to a large degree by commoners who have adventitiously gained popularity with the colonial administration and in return received official recognition of their will to power. Frequently personal political ambitions motivate such leaders rather than interest in the community's prosperity.

ARRIVAL OF CHURCH AND GOVERNMENT[103]

When the Tongan bearers of Wesleyanism first came to Inland Forest, Ratu Seru, who was chief in his great house at Votua, was absent in a secret forest retreat holding communion with his ancestors. Only the snakes, which his chiefly power permitted him to tame and control, guarded his home. The awful bearing of the pet snakes startled the Tongans; they knew that Seru must indeed be a great chief. But Seru's heathen ardor did not long discourage them. When they came a second time, all Inland Forest gave allegiance to the new religion and to the half-Tongan Ra Masima, chief of Bua Kingdom. This was the time of the church, and a new era at Inland Forest. Tongan teachers came to the coastal villages to teach the people to desist from cannibalism, patricide,[104] violent funeral practices, and, most important of all, to wear cotton skirts (in which it is rumored the missionaries had invested large sums) and to avoid all manner of productive work on the Sabbath. Any negligence in observing these rules was considered an insult against the person of the chief of Bua and was

---

103. In this section I have depended upon native sources entirely. References to the purposes of colonial administration are presented as the natives see them. Because most of my informants were illiterate, inaccuracy of detail in colonial regulations should be excused.

104. For which practice there is no remembered evidence at Nakoroka.

punished accordingly; climbing rocky paths on bared knees was a favorite penitential device.

But after a few decades the organization of missions expanded and grew independent of the chiefly authority upon which it was based. Schools were established in several outlying provinces,[105] and effective Christian propaganda reached the most remote villages. The missions began to draw subordinate teachers from their native localities. Eventually a Wesleyan hierarchy developed which, though independent of British authority, in natives eyes has an official British sanction of its own: power of the British state depends upon the Wesleyan God. Native officials and missionaries may co-operate to sustain their authority over the communities which have been allotted to them. Of Nakoroka's thirty adult[106] males, six have status within the church which permits them to tell Bible stories from the pulpit in ringing cadences two or three times on Sunday and once on Wednesday. Two others are recognized as apprentices and have authority to maintain order during church services; one of these, Raitova, who is meek and retiring on other occasions, wears deep furrows in his forehead and raps the knuckles of whispering children with more assiduity than he can ever muster in his private household. Monasa once belonged to the fold, but he fell from grace; many years ago he was officially charged with witchcraft,[107] and, though his friends knew that his offense is common to almost every native of the region, publicity which his case aroused required that the community seem shocked and that Monasa lose his status. He used to spend long hours perusing a bundle of loose leaves from a once-bound volume of the Fijian Bible; he could not read, but it pleased him to trace the lines of print with his index finger in a trance of intense concentration. Losing status in the church ranks high in local psychology. Every native knows that his name will be struck from the records of the nearest Wesleyan teacher, then of the mission office in Suva, and, finally, of the great missionary who lives at Sydney; his disgrace will be broadcast throughout the world. Only two of the men who hold status in the church are of chief-

105. One man of Nakoroka, who is about thirty-five years of age, has attended the mission school of Bua Province, located at Nabouwalu, near the southernmost tip of Bua Province at least fifty miles by path from Nakoroka. Until about ten years ago this was the only means open to natives of inland Bua for European education. Unfortunately, instruction was based largely upon Bible stories translated into the missionary's version of the language of Bau.

106. Past puberty.

107. Monasa had tried to use a magical formula to heal an invalid.

ly rank, and neither of these has claims to chiefly title in the community. Bulisivo, king of Inland Forest, remains aloof in quiet amusement at the antics of the devout, although he knows that there is advancement in the church for political upstarts and that his prestige grows yearly more pale in the "light"[108] of the church.

It is the desire of the church to maintain a trained teacher in each community. No Nakoroka boy has ever been fortunate enough to attain this status. More than ten years ago a Lekutu man, who had been educated at a mission school, lived at Nakoroka as a "guard" of Wesleyanism. He went mad and used to wander through the forest without aim or purpose, until the Nakoroka people resolved to send him to the government hospital at Suva to avoid the constant obligation of searching for him. In February, 1936, another teacher arrived at Nakoroka to inaugurate a modern campaign against overindulgence in kava and Sunday card-playing; he receives two pounds from the collection box every three months, and the community supplies him with food and plans to build him gardens for private use. Over each group of eight or ten towns a mission teacher of long standing supervises Wesleyan activities. He receives five pounds every three months for his services and considerable maintenance work in his gardens and houses. A man of this status is resident at Lekutu. Once during my stay at Nakoroka he traveled through the inland villages to warn the people against an imaginary measles epidemic and to inaugurate triweekly prayer meetings to maintain the continued health of the district. The head man of mission administration on Vanua Levu resides at Nabouwalu, and he lives "just like the white missionary at Suva" who is head of all Wesleyanism in Fiji. The salaries of these men are paid by periodic assessments in the regions in which they govern Wesleyan policy. To check misappropriation of funds, a treasurer appointed from the community holds a fund surplus from which the teacher's salary can be drawn in lean months.

The Wesleyan system of organization works so efficiently that special assessments for purposes as various as sending a teacher to enlighten the peoples of Australia[109] or buying paint for some church are always fulfilled. Though punishment for delinquency in payment of colonial taxes has harassed many communities since the copra market collapsed as the Fijian symptom of the world-wide depression, per-

108. Wesleyan usage in Fiji.

109. It is boasted that four Fijians are proselytizing in the hinterlands of Australia. The people of inland Vanua Levu are proud that their contributions have made this possible.

sonal honor depends upon giving liberally to the church. The collection box is never empty.[110]

There is advancement in the church. Though Wesleyanism demands chiefly courtesies for those high in the hierarchy and permits them the chiefly right to indenture labor without pay to satisfy their personal wants, it recognizes no caste of birth. The pleasure of speaking from a dais raised high above hereditary peers is easily available to every energetic young commoner of talkative temperament; for those who are ambitious there is the limited chance of promotion to one of the privileged positions within the church. Thus Wesleyanism has gained an impetus throughout Fiji that both colonial tax collectors and Catholics envy. But, except in so far as it has usurped some of the religious functions of the hereditary chiefs, the church is a social institution and provides slight opportunity for religious experience. Ascendance of the church has outlawed the priest and driven the temples of ancestors from the village; but those who would have communion with the supernatural still offer sacrifices to their ancestors at a secluded waterfall, monolith, or ancient grave. Though it was the chiefs who first espoused Wesleyanism for political reasons, commoners rapidly discovered the social feats which they could perform by serving this new cause.

When British authority had come to Nakoroka and an armed police force had put an end to strife for civil power in Bua Province, a "village chief" was set up in each village to supervise the observance of British decrees. His office is of uncertain tenure, depending upon his popularity and efficiency. The community builds his gardens for him —unwillingly because it is he who reports their misdemeanors to higher officials. He must assemble the village elders every week to discuss the performance of tasks which have been assigned by higher officials. He blows the conch shell to call men to work upon projects of public significance, such as housebuilding, cleaning paths, or even gardening. Those who do not respect his authority may be fined or jailed if he chooses to report them as negligent. A man for this office is chosen from the community in which he is to hold authority. Usually he is a commoner. Many of Nakoroka's adult men have held this office. Those who have not have been too shy to accept the responsibility and publicity which the position entails. It is generally difficult to keep the office filled; men do not like to tattle to a higher authority. There are

110. See Sir Basil Thomson, *The Diversions of a Prime Minister* (London, 1894), pp. 187–90.

few commoners who can execute the tasks of the office without constantly threatening fine and arrest. Chiefs at Nakoroka will not accept the office because the highest official of the district is a commoner.

The old kingdoms of Inland Forest, Great Meadow, and River's Mouth have been united into one district, that of Lekutu. There are nine districts in Bua Province. The head official of each is called "Buli." Linguistic significance of this title cannot be traced in Nakoroka. The term denotes a kind of highly valued mollusk shell used to decorate the doorways and rafters of chief's houses and the sennit "tails" of kava bowls. But, aside from its reference to the head official of a district, it has no sociological meaning. About thirty years ago, Bulisivo, king of Inland Forest and resident today of Nakoroka, held this office for Lekutu District. He received taxes from the villages as his chiefly right, and the land flourished because the ancestors were pleased. But Bulisivo has never been a strong executive. He considered it beneath his dignity to threaten his men with jail in Suva when they were lax in clearing the paths or their village greens.[111] He did not press the people to hasten with their housebuilding so that each family might have a house of its own. The British have considered the issue of housing of vital importance to native sanitation. But the Fijians rarely agreed; the old ways of living in crowded houses gave fewer roofs to be mended against the rain, and less time had to be consumed in this unpleasant task. Finally, Bulisivo was crafty in his handling of tax money,[112] and the British disapproved and removed him.

The office of Buli has come upon evil days in Lekutu District.[113] Hereditary chiefs whose power has wide scope are few, and the office has fallen repeatedly to those commoners who through contact with white men seem to have learned something of Britain's colonial policy. These men, whose hereditary status gives them no executive right, have had to use British police power, fines, and jails to enforce their authority. And since no chiefly tradition is associated with the office, they have had to depend upon British courts to support their demands for chiefly courtesies and privileges. Their demands have been granted, and it is customary to address the Buli with plural pronouns regardless of his birth; but the displeased ancestors have caused bush pigs to multiply and destroy the crops.

111. He himself says that the paths were never cleaner than when he was in power.
112. See n. 94 above.
113. A new official was appointed to this office after my departure in 1936. The discharged official had served since 1931.

The Buli is assisted by a clerk who knows how to read and write the missionary version of the language of Bau in which all government decrees are written.

The Roko governs the province. There are three on Vanua Levu, one in each of the three provinces of Bua, Macuata, and Cakaudrove (Savusavu). Like the term *buli*, *roko* has no place in old Nakoroka sociology. As a verb it means "to bow down respectfully," but at Nakoroka it was not a title until after the arrival of the British. The Roko of Bua Province lives in European quarters at Nabouwalu with a small staff of clerks. He speaks excellent English. Though he holds title to hereditary chiefship in the old kingdom of Bua, his hereditary status has today little meaning among the people of the eastern and northern parts of the province. Two or three times a year he travels to the official towns of each district. Sometimes he is accompanied by the officer-in-charge of Bua, who is the only British official in Bua Province; sometimes by the British district commissioner from Cakaudrove, who serves also as medical officer for the provinces of Bua and Cakaudrove. On these occasions courts are held to hear the Buli's complaints and charges against members of the villages under his jurisdiction. Fines and sentences are levied. The Roko, who works under the supervision of the British officials, is directly responsible for the solution of all problems concerned with the administration of Fijian population in his province. The British officials, who suffer the added responsibility of supervising the Indians, the Chinese traders, and the European planters, find their major concern to be the amicable solution of Indian troubles about land rent and taxes. The Roko is concerned with levying fines and charges against Fijians whom the district Buli has reported as delinquent in taxes or truant from statute labor.

Almost every month the Buli must call the "village chiefs" of his district to meet and discuss the program of work, an industrial routine which has developed under British influence. A calendar has been imposed upon the hitherto unscheduled process of time so that the months have English names, and many natives know the number of the year. It has now become government decree that houses be built in January and that ground be cleared for planting coconuts. February is for housebuilding and clearing the private paths about the village. March is for housebuilding and clearing those paths which are recognized by the government as official paths. April is for cleaning yam plots and preparing to plant. May and June are used to collect money for taxes, either by working for a European or by trading native produce with the Chinese. The tax must be paid in June; every adult and able-bodied male who has fewer than five children pays a general tax of thirteen shillings, special taxes of three shillings to support the government schools, and five shillings to support the Department of Lands and Survey. Old men, boys, and women are exempt. July and August are for planting: yams, manioc, sweet potatoes, kawai, etc.[114] Planting should be finished in September and housebuilding resumed. October and November are for housebuilding. December is a month of vacation, but, if housebuilding has been slow, the Roko may ask that work be continued.

Housebuilding is the greatest chore for both official and citizen. It has become customary in Lekutu District for all the men to assemble to build collectively where building is required. Because Nakoroka manpower is superior to that of many of the other villages of the district and their houses are in relatively good condition, it is necessary for a large percentage of the male population to work in other villages. During my stay at Nakoroka the men spent more than three months away from their homes and gardens; those who stayed home because of family obligations or garden work, without first consulting the Buli, were arraigned and fined. Nearly every man has been fined several times; all are anxious. Fines are paid today with money earned at the gold mines; the man in distress borrows from a relative who has recently been working for white man's wages.

That the component villages of the district feel no political unity but are drawn involuntarily into co-operative housebuilding enterprises is one reason for the dissatisfaction which makes the work desultory and inefficient. There is frequent friction, occasionally an outbreak of open hostility, between groups of varying traditional and political affiliation. On one occasion at Lekutu the men of Great Meadow accused those of Inland Forest of laziness, which is a serious insult: the men of Inland Forest had been unable to lift a house timber into the crotches of the wall posts which the men of Great Meadow had failed to sink to proper depth in the house foundation. In response to the jibe, the Inland Forest men threw their heavy timber to the ground and refused to work until the Great Meadow men dug deeper postholes. The Buli sided with Inland Forest and harangued the Great Meadow men until these, too, were insulted and refused to work. Before housebuilding could be resumed Inland

---

114. Taro is planted, too, at this time; new ponds are prepared for it. But it is planted at odd times throughout the year as well.

Forest had to present an elaborate feast to Great Meadow with apologies to wash away the Buli's insult.[115] In all, a week passed with no work.

According to old tradition, it is right for vassal villages to build the houses of their chiefs and to perform other labor which they require. In return a chief should feast them for their work. But the Buli of Lekutu holds no such hereditary right, nor does he feel obliged to feast the workers. Since the gardens of the interior are more productive than those on the coast, and those of Nakoroka particularly luxuriant, the women made almost weekly journeys to the site of work with burdens of food for their men. This task is accepted willingly, because Nakoroka likes to display its wealth, but it saps the strength of the community and diverts energies away from maintaining the home soil.

The natives realize the strain which housebuilding regulations place upon them. Housebuilding has become a symbol of oppression. The work languishes from one year to the next and is never completed on schedule. Carelessly constructed houses require more effort to repair. As time passes, the task increases in magnitude so that it has come to extend far beyond the limits set for it in the official calendar.

Next to housebuilding, payment of the head tax is the most unpleasant obligation which the British administration has brought to Nakoroka, and delinquency in payment has long troubled colonial officials. In 1935 freedom to search for tax money was extended from two months to three, in hope that payment would be more easily fulfilled. But the new policy brought more delinquency than ever. In officialdom old proverbs were cited as freshly proved. "Offer a finger, and they take the hand"; "Spare the rod and spoil the child." But to the people of Nakoroka that extra month was a busy time. One of their young chiefs was married, and the entire village prepared sweet puddings to celebrate the occasion. The island village of Tavea, with whom Nakoroka has a special trade relationship, completed a great turtle net, and the people of Nakoroka had to prepare and present a large quantity of food to them to make their net productive. Then toward the end of the month the Buli at Lekutu ordered them to prepare elaborate gifts of food and whale teeth to make a presentation to the chiefs of Macuata in return for a visit that had occurred the year be-

115. Though the Buli's strongest hereditary affiliations were with Great Meadow, in supporting Inland Forest against Great Meadow he had assumed the role of defender of Inland Forest; hence it was Inland Forest who had to apologize.

fore; in so doing, the Buli was attempting to fulfil the role of a truly hereditary chief. During the remaining period for earning tax money the men of the entire province scrambled for the few available wage jobs; few were prepared to pay their taxes to the Buli at the appointed time. So "freedom" was limited again to May and June. In May, 1936, nearly all the able-bodied men of the northern half of Bua Province passed through Nakoroka on their way to the gold mine. But the mine was already crowded with laborers from other parts who likewise were seeking tax money. The men stayed in the congested villages [in the mine area until food was exhausted and then came home discouraged; several had contracted "Indian boils," which were rampant [in the congested area. At one time fifty of these travelers were housed at Nakoroka.

Young Namo's fifth child was born a few months before I arrived at Nakoroka, and Namo looked forward to exemption from tax payment. But shortly before taxes fell due, his seven-year-old son died. Disgruntled, Namo went to the mine to earn tax money for one more year.

Better education facilities, sanitation, and improved medical service are viewed as pledges of British good faith, as ritual in the tedious process of learning to benefit by the white man's superior craft. It is the special duties and assessments imposed by the Buli at his own discretion that rankle most. Thirty years ago when Bulisivo, king of Inland Forest, was Buli, the British recommended that one day a week be set aside for work of public benefit. The Buli's judgment was supposed to determine whether freedom from local wants warranted the assembling of the entire district for large work projects. Under no circumstances were gardens to be neglected. A village which closely neighbored the Buli's town might sometimes be engaged to clean the Buli's village green, but this task was not intended to be an obligation for the district as a whole.[116] But the decline in hereditary chief's authority which followed upon the rise of commoners in the officialdom of church and government, and the relegation of hereditary chiefs to the religious sphere, has thrown more and more executive responsibility and initiative upon the shoulders of the Roko, Buli, and "village chiefs." Those in power have long forgotten the day-a-week limit for public work. With greater obligation, the officials have acquired greater privilege and prestige until today they can command personal services and impose tasks at their own discretion. The trimming of the village green at Lekutu requires an assembly of the entire country-

116. This discussion from Bulisivo of Nakoroka.

side. The building of a sailing ship of European design, which is largely a personal luxury for the Buli and of utterly no use to the people of the interior, required assessments from the entire district and labor without recompense. The women of Nakoroka must carry seed yam and taro stalks for eight miles to plant the Buli's gardens. When the Buli has been flattered by the visit of a true chief from another province, the people of the district must augment this prestige by contributing liberally toward a return feast. But the people do not give their private allegiance to these chiefs whose only power depends upon British law. Their false prestige is satirized: the honorary title "Crown of the Coconut Palm," which suggests permanence and dignity and belongs only to those chiefs whose rights have descended through both parental lines, in paraphrase to apply to officials, becomes "Crown of the Mammy Apple"; the mammy apple, or papaya, grows to a height of twenty-five feet in six months and then quickly rots and shrivels.

Official requirements for housebuilding and sanitation have lowered the morale of the citizens. All kinds of petty excuses are used to avoid labor on houses. Sometimes there is pride in a slovenly house; it may be counted a symbol of childish revolt against an irrevocable authority. And while work for the Buli becomes more time-consuming, the Chinese trader begins to vie with the gardens as the principal source of food; yearly the exasperated people find their gardens less productive and trade with the Chinese more a necessity.

Today there are eight government schools in Bua Province. Government supervision of education is of recent date; for half a century it was left largely to the missionaries, who confined their teaching to Bible stories with a smattering of arithmetic, geography, and history of Pacific exploration. The British regime has attempted to give a basis for learning in classical English tradition. For six or eight years four "classes" have been available to every child in Bua Province.[117] Truancy is punished by the British courts. Teachers are Fijians who have been trained at higher missionary or government schools. Parents have rapidly learned to send their children away to Lekutu when they reach seven or eight years of age. Unfortunately, these children finish the four classes at school before they are old enough to test their new knowledge and enjoy their newly awakened desire for participation in the "foreign" life at the gold mine. British law protects them from

117. The oldest Nakoroka person to have studied at the Lekutu school was about twenty years of age in 1936.

child labor until they are eighteen or thereabouts. But if the child is not lucky enough to be able to pay tuition for one of the higher schools in Savu or Lau, which, though only a couple of pounds a year, is high according to Fijian standards, he must spend an awkward period at home readjusting to village life or in the mining community learning the card games and jokes which will make him socially successful there when he is old enough to become a laborer.

British administration has tried to meet educational needs. A few professions are open to the young man if he can afford to pay tuition. He can learn to be a missionary, teacher, artisan, government clerk, or medical practitioner. Girls can learn to be nurses. All these callings, however, require that their followers travel far from their home communities to study, and, when the student has completed his study, the scarcity of openings creates a new problem. Government service supplies a limited number of jobs. The inland villages offer no field for plying a trade. Hence there is a tendency to drift toward Suva or some lesser European center as a potential domestic. Though the colonial attitude has always been kindly paternalistic, it is unfortunate that education has not been tempered to realistic needs. Motivated by a fatherly desire to protect the Fijian from the evils of our civilization, all but highest education is accomplished in the language of Bau; I did not see more than half-a-dozen Fijians on Vanua Levu with a working knowledge of English, and most of these had been imported from more sophisticated regions to perform official duties. The sheltered Fijians have been deprived of all knowledge of the structure and purpose of European civilization; to them European history is a tea party of kings and queens. Adjustment to the new conditions which have grown out of contact with European industry is the greatest problem in Fijian life; to date the educational policy has hindered rather than helped.

The present growing Fijian population probably owes its existence to efficient quarantine, sanitation, and health propaganda. Groups of Fijians are trained every year at a large modern hospital in Suva and sent to stations in the provinces as medical officers. Medical stations range from a thatched house and small dispensary to large frame buildings with facilities for major surgery. The four or five in Bua Province are located in the Buli towns and are inspected once or twice a year by the district commissioner (in charge of Bua and Cakaudrove) who, for economy's sake, is physician as well as administrator. The leeward half of Bua Province is served by the medical station at Lekutu, which is the least pretentious kind of Fijian hospital; the native medical officer of Lekutu, who was born in the island of Kadavu, speaks English and French. This medical officer establishes quarantine in times of epidemic and inspects the water supplies of the villages of his region several times a year. He tries to enforce the sanitary law which states that all domestic pigs must be denied the freedom of the houses of the village and confined within pigsties. He spreads valuable propaganda about aseptic first aid, infant feeding, and maternity care. He is also on call for emergency illnesses throughout the region. At his medical station he can diagnose and perform minor operations and, with limited facilities, offer hospital care. He is assisted by a "nurse," who has had some kind of training under European medical men, and by those with severe cases of ringworm who are required by law to remain inpatients at the medical station.

In inland regions, however, there is much to be desired in relations between medical administration and populace. The village women who are appointed to supervise the health of children and give first aid to the injured[118] follow the letter rather than the spirit of the law in many instances. Though they are effective in sending the children to bathe every morning and in administering iodine and salicylic acid to spots of ringworm, these regulations are observed as a magic ritual to appease the colonial administration and avoid the supernatural curse of disease and do not rise to an understanding attempt to decrease the ringworm. Bandage for first aid is considered clean if it is white, regardless of its previous history.

Likewise the observance of other sanitary laws is done in fear of punishment and without understanding. When an official is seen to approach the village, there is a tremendous scuffle and din while the children scurry in and out of the houses and through the coconut groves to catch pigs and carry them squealing to their pens. Sometimes a pig is overlooked, and then there is a fine. Diseased people are usually afraid to apply for medical service for fear they will be detained against their will at the medical station. Living at the medical station is a hardship because it means that relatives must carry food down ten miles of slippery path to Lekutu; there are no facilities for feeding patients. The people of the village have tacitly agreed that such fugitives from the medical officer can be given secret shelter. Native medical remedies are used constantly, and a strong sense of guilt

118. The two in Nakoroka received gardens for their services.

and mistrust has developed toward the medical officer, whose job it is to ferret out these practices and outlaw them; an invalid who has tried native remedies will fear official medical service lest his sin be discovered.

There are other difficulties which can arise from the native medical officer's own problems of social adjustment. His education is the best that is offered. His long residence and contact with Europeans has taught him a standard of living that is considered superior to that of the village. His official status gives him power and prestige, and it is customary to grant him chiefly courtesies. His own social ties have long been broken, and he finds himself living as a stranger in a strange land. It is tempting for him to try to compensate for his unhappy social plight by capitalizing his power and prestige and preening his personal ambition. He may eventually conclude that maintaining his household as a model is better pedagogy than either precept or medical practice. It is unwholesome to get wet and hence incumbent upon him to avoid visiting the sick on rainy days. Though nauseous to the Fijian palate, milk is a valuable addition to the diet; therefore, he must be a model dairyman and spend the late afternoon riding through the groves in search of his milk cows.[119] His status is such that it is difficult for him to serve those of all castes equally.

Compared with other colonies of the Pacific, however, Fijian health administration has been and is exemplary. The official organization of medical service makes possible effective campaigns against such diseases as yaws and hookworm. The knowledge of well-trained Europeans is at hand to serve those of the native population who are fortunate enough to come into contact with them. Money has been spent. But there is still great work to be done.

ACCULTURATION

Before 1800 a desire for metal tools and other European goods had already sprung forth in Fiji, so that the early traders found a ready market for their trade goods and a warm welcome in the villages of the chiefs. Old technology languished, and products of European industry became necessities. Soon native value ranked muskets above all other articles of exchange; kingdoms which had been lucky in the European trade developed ambitions of conquest. But Wesleyan imperialism, manned by the Tongans and financed by the missionaries' adroit con-

---

119. Efficient care of domestic animals is alien to Fijian culture and, consequently, is a most difficult chore for those who set themselves the task of learning how.

version of conspicuous waste into a productive mission business, came to disrupt all semblance of home-grown political amenities. Political interchange of civilities in Fiji degenerated to a chaos of civil war so that the ascendance of Great Britain was hailed as salvation. Wesleyan hatred of the devil-worshiping priests colored the entire British attitude; without realizing the intimate interdependence of priest and chief, British law condemned forever the former and by so doing weakened the entire native political structure.[120] Too late, Britain tried to reinstate the executive powers of the local chiefs; but the falsely royal "chiefs" of church and colonial administration were well established, and the old authority continued to crumble. Since the commoners seem always to have leaned heavily upon their chiefs for initiative and enterprise in maintaining economic and social standards, they must depend now in part upon the foreign authority whose power they respect but whose attempts to maintain the public welfare lack the certainty of fulfilment with which ancestors supported the authority of the old hereditary chiefs; the completeness of the relationship between chief and commoner has been broken; executive functions have been usurped by a growing foreign power which has not succeeded in keeping alive the old-fashioned vivid interest in living. But some aspects of Fijian culture have flourished vigorously under British authority. Reshuffling of populations during the wars, and the easier communication which resulted when wars were outlawed, has stimulated broader knowledge of cultural variations; native literature, the dance, and the innuendoes of everyday conversation have attained high polish and show no languor even today. Church and state have mixed with community life and assumed vigorous forms distinctly Fijian. Christmas and Easter are feast days; enthusiastic preparation for these has replaced the now rare feasts which once entertained visiting chiefs. Mother's Day is an occasion for children to honor their parents with elaborate displays of food which parents must reciprocate on another Sunday to avoid shame. The monthly meeting of the Buli with his "village chiefs" of the district, which occurs by turn in all the villages of the district, retains some of the pomp and all the ceremony of former times.

On March 29, 1936, Vatili, who is "village chief" at Nakoroka, blew the conch shell to call the elders to his house. Naicadra mumbled a

120. Sir Basil Thomson discusses this at length in *The Fijians: A Study of the Decay of Custom* (London, 1894).

prayer in ministerial cadences. He mentioned Vilomena, who had been buried the week before, because a special stalk of kava had been brought as her feast of the "fifth night."[121] Bulisivo, who sat in the place of honor as king of Inland Forest, spoke quietly to inaugurate the meeting. While Matua prepared the kava and served it with effortless ceremony, to which the group responded by clapping at ritually timed intervals, Vatili led discussion. Many men had been delinquent in the housebuilding activities of the past month. He spoke to each man individually, and some responded with vigorous denunciation of all truancy, but most of all his words were meant for Nabadua, who sat meekly between his two eldest sons and pondered his guilt. Vosalevu, whom Nabadua hated, spoke with fire; it was every man's duty to remember the name of his village and cast no clouds upon its reputation. Only Vosalevu dared to make a direct charge. Monasa, usually reticent, chattered volubly because his conscience was clear; he had gained official freedom from statute labor a month before. Matua, whose importance was eclipsed by the presence of Monasa, his elder brother, dozed between the rounds of kava.

Conversation turned to the evening's important topic: The Buli and the high church officials of Lekutu District would arrive on the following Friday. People from the entire district would assemble at Nakoroka for the occasion; only the elders would participate in discussion, but many others would come too, because everyone knew that Nakoroka feasts were bountiful. It was necessary to decide what houses could be allotted to the guests and how the work of preparing food could be apportioned equitably among the Nakoroka people. It is customary to divide the work of preparation among the five old village groups whose descendants compose Nakoroka: Votua, Nadroro, Tavua, Rokowaqa, and Buleya. But Buleya is defunct, and the few survivors of impoverished Rokowaqa can trace descent from Votua as well. So Votua, Nadroro, and Tavua were charged each with the preparation of ovens which would contain specified numbers of yams, taro, and pigs; each group also planned the gathering of food and kava from the gardens to present to the guests upon their arrival. The feast of the month before had been held at Nalauvia of Great Meadow which was an ancient rival of Nakoroka; and the men of Nakoroka remembered carefully how many pigs, yams, and taro had been consumed on that occasion so that their own feast could be prepared just enough more lavishly to "win" the competition without overtaxing the food resources.

121. See below, pp. 366–67.

On Thursday, April 2, six young men went hunting for wild cattle. They killed three bush pigs instead. All the women fished with nets in the rivers. The older men brought firewood for ovens. Garden food had been gathered during the week, and in the evening both men and women flattened strips of cane and plaited supporting stays about the large yams to keep them from breaking in the ovens. When all preparations were complete, eight men heated stones for the ovens and drank kava at Nabadua's house until just before sunrise, then laid the food so that it would be freshly cooked yet not overdone when the guests arrived.

On Friday the men who had drunk kava the preceding night at Nabadua's house made three ovens: one was called the women's oven and contained fish and yams; another contained pigs, yams, and taro—this was the men's contribution; Votua, as chiefly group, prepared a third oven to welcome the guests. When the sun was halfway to its zenith, the ovens were opened. Leaders of Tavua, Nadroro, and Votua managed the work of their special groups, but the younger men worked as tasks were assigned to them. The food which the women had gathered was prepared in Tavua's oven. Nadroro cooked the men's contribution. Before noon the Buli and his retinue and the mission official from Lekutu arrived and were ushered to the house of Naicadra, which was the largest in the village except for the chiefly house; the latter was useless for the democratic feasts of these days because of its fettering taboos. In all, there were sixty or seventy guests.

There was great bustle among the women of Nakoroka. Hastily they freshened themselves after the work of food preparation, donned the calico which was reserved for Sundays and state occasions, oiled their arms and faces with scented coconut ointment, and assembled behind Nabadua's house to drape plates of food from the Tavua oven with streamers of freshly plaited coconut leaves. They marched in stately procession to the house of Vatili, where kettles of fish, prawns, and vegetables were boiling. Hot kettles garnished with leaves and hung on carrying-poles were too heavy for the women; four young men were enlisted. Now the food-bearers, with their platters steaming and trailing leaves, swept an arc across the village green and marched in review before the lesser guests who were gathered around the doorway of Naicadra's crowded house. Votua's chieftainesses, too haughty to join this pageantry, met the procession with their food gifts at the mango tree beyond Naicadra's house. The procession passed the lower door. As Kelera, Nabadua's wife, took the food gift from each woman and passed it inside the house, each pivoted neatly and stepped aside to make way for the next. Wakesa, whose breasts were just beginning to swell, took part in this, her first appearance in formal ceremony. Nabadua and Vatili waited inside the house to make presentation speeches, and Peni, who is strong and dextrous, was there to serve the food. When the officials and elders had been served, the less illustrious guests replaced them at the eating-mats, until all were satisfied. The people of Nakoroka ate only the scraps of food which the guests had left. Nabadua's sons were busy making last hasty trips to their gardens for more kava and food.

Toward the middle of the afternoon the official meeting assembled at Inland Forest,[122] the house of Nakoroka's chiefly family. The Buli, the high mission official, and visiting elders sat on new mats which had been spread for them in the upper part of the house—a place which on other occasions is taboo to all except very high chiefs. There were six old men who sat in chiefly places, but only two had hereditary titles to chiefship. The others were venerable because of their age; the Buli and missionary assumed chiefly places because of their status in state and church. Thirty guests sat in the lower region of the house. While the missionary opened the meeting with prayer, each rested an elbow on the matted floor and supported the bridge of his nose with thumb and index finger.

Almost every person in the district is included in a vague category of extended kin. Since those who have not seen a dead kinsman's face before his burial must offer a propitiatory gift before entering his village,[123] it was necessary for the Buli to collect money from the leaders of the district; within the year two of Nakoroka's people had died. Two pounds, three shillings, and three pence were set aside for this purpose. Then the meeting proper began. Vatili, who was "village chief" for Nakoroka, entered as Nakoroka's only representative. Conversation which concerned Nakoroka centered upon the questions of whether Ratu Luke, a young Nakoroka chief, was justified in neglecting his pregnant wife, and whether old Raitova should retain the chiefly title of the ancient Rokowaqa village. The Buli called on the "village chief" of each village in the district to speak; and, when each had spoken, the others applauded and said, "It is well." Though there may be no real business to discuss, the Buli conscientiously fulfils his official function by meeting the "village chiefs" each month.

122. This house name is a variant of the name "Inland Forest."
123. See below, pp. 369–70.

Nabadua entered bearing a great stalk of kava which he presented
to the visiting elders, on behalf of Nakoroka. Ratu Kitioni of Lekutu,
who had been sitting with the chiefs, slid quietly down into the rank
of commoners; his strong Wesleyanism and weak digestion prohibited
his enjoying the quiet intoxication that kava brings. Young Nakoroka
men entered to mix kava in Nakoroka's largest bowl. As they poured
water into the bowl, guests clapped out lusty songs which he who
mixes must follow in the rhythm of his movements; the clapping with
cupped palms resounded pleasantly through the village. Ratu Luke
came to sit before the bowl with Vatili as a presiding chief while the
kava was served to the visitors. Peni came to serve the cup, which was
a coconut shell: he squatted on his strong haunches while the kava
strainer was squeezed until its fine trickle half-filled the cup; then he
rose gracefully with his elbows pointing outward and the cup before
him, crossed diagonally[124] before the bowl to the rhythm of a chant,
and, kneeling, served the Buli. There was a sudden flurry of confusion;
Peni had forgotten that the church comes before the state. The Buli
refused the cup and indicated the missionary. But Peni was not embarrassed; he likes to carry the kava, which temporarily absolves him
from all taboo. Peni rose again gracefully, refilled the cup[125] and knelt
before the missionary, who drank as the assembled guests clapped out
the song that always accompanies the first cup of kava and the drinking of the highest chief. Then a commoner drank as "messenger"[126] for
the missionary. Then the Buli drank to the song which indicates the
second highest chief. A hereditary chief from Tavua followed the
Buli's "messenger." When all visiting elders in the upper part of the
house had drunk, Vatili and Ratu Luke took their turn; Vatili's status
as "village chief" permitted him to drink on this occasion as a true
chief at Nakoroka. The cup went the round of "chiefs" again before
the kava bowl was twisted on its base as a signal that the more formal
part of the ceremony was complete and that now commoners could
drink in their turn. Though a brief ceremony of clapping and conventional phrases continued to accompany the serving of each man, tense
formality was ended, and conversation turned away from serious
topics. One of the old men, who had occupied a chiefly place in the
house and functioned as a chief in the kava ceremony, shook himself

124. In Macuata Province it is taboo to cross in front of the bowl.

125. A cup, once offered, cannot be drunk by another.

126. One who functions as *Matanivanua*, talking chief or messenger, must drink after
each chief.

from the doze into which formal discussion had thrown him and began to speak gaily of a feast he had attended thirty years before: a gust of wind had blown out the coconut oil lamps, and in the dark he and his brothers had each grabbed a woman of the host's household.

In the evening the men of Nakoroka presented their food from the Nadroro oven. They heaped it before the chief house where the visiting elders were still drinking kava. There were half-a-dozen large coconut-leaf baskets of yams and taro,[127] and for "garnish" there were three pigs which had been speared in the bush the day before and roasted whole. Four large stalks of kava, enough to intoxicate an entire village, were piled near the food; the guests would slice this so that it could be seasoned in the sun and take it home with them. Nabadua, as "messenger," made the presentation speech; four other Nakoroka men squatted with him to act as chiefs in the presentation ceremony.

In the evening the mission official from Lekutu led the church service. Like the houses, the church has an upper and lower end. At the upper end there is a raised platform on which elders and chiefs sit and the speaker stands behind his pulpit. On this night the lower region was so crowded that no aisle could be left between the men on the left and the women on the right; men who came late had to sit on the women's side. After a ritual of hymns and prayers the mission official from Lekutu led the service: he and the Buli had received special knowledge of a measles epidemic which threatened the entire countryside.[128] A stir of uneasy fear swept the listeners. They remembered the influenza, the most recent foreign epidemic. Whole villages had been sick and unable to feed themselves; many had died. But the missionary comforted them. If they obeyed the laws of church and state with clean consciences, they had nothing to fear. The state would protect its people with quarantines when the time came, and the church would plead for supernatural aid to drive out the pestilence if the people remembered well to pay their church fees. Prayer meetings were to be held three evenings a week to please the Christian god in this emergency. The Buli graciously gave precedence to the missionary because "the government had come to Fiji only after the church was well established." Elders from each village were called upon to express opinions. But Bulisivo, high chief of Nakoroka, who had worked in his gardens all day, did not deign to come to church. When turn came for

127. The *sova* basket frequently contains more than a bushel.

128. The native medical official at Lekutu had not been informed of this danger. It may have been a true rumor; but it is also possible that it was deliberate fabrication on the part of the Buli and missionary.

Nakoroka's opinion, there was hesitation: Vatili, "village chief," was sitting below with the commoners so that he had no voice. But Nabadua as titular head of Nakoroka's Tavua people, sat with the elders, although he held no status in the church. He rose to the occasion and spoke politely, and, when he had finished, the listeners whispered, "It is well," as though no flaw had arisen in the ceremony.

Church dismissed, and the guests retired to the houses which had been allotted to them. The girls of Nakoroka danced to entertain the Buli; but there was no hilarity because these guests were not young. The elders of Nakoroka met at the house of Bulisivo to discuss the preparation of a feast in return for the unexpected money which the Buli had collected to remove the "death taboo."[129] Bush pigs can be used to feast the government and the church, but only domestic pigs can pay an ancient ceremonial obligation. The sole large male pig in the village was being held in reserve for the funeral feast of the aged Kaiyava—who was still alive a year later. Nabadua, as titular head of the group to which Kaiyava belongs, sent a messenger to persuade Kaiyava that another pig could be fattened before he should require it. With self-righteous generosity Kaiyava assented, and the young men scoured the village kitchens for firewood with which to heat an oven during the night. Six young men and three elders drank kava at Nabadua's house until long after the guests had gone to sleep; the pig was inclosed in the oven at just the proper time. A few hours after the sun had risen, the hot pig freshly cooked was presented to the guests, who ate and prepared to depart. Bulisivo kept the money which he had received to remove the "death taboo"; Kaiyava has always expected that he would receive a few pence for his portion, and he murmurs secretly.

At about ten o'clock on the morning of April 4, 1936, the Buli assembled with his retinue at the "face of the path" to Lekutu at the southwest corner of Nakoroka's village green. The Nakoroka people had heaped taro on either side, with stalks tied together in bunches for carrying—in all, perhaps four hundred pounds of taro. There were also baskets of yams and fresh kava stalks. Nabadua made the speech of presentation. The visiting young men shouldered the food gifts on carrying-poles and turned down the broad path toward the river. Many of them shook hands with their Nakoroka friends because it would be many months before they met again.[130] The taro swung on its

129. See below, pp. 369–70.
130. Short parting never warrants shaking hands.

long stalks as they walked. The Buli and the mission official took their
leave slowly; the path was steep and slippery for their corpulence of
many years' official service; they were pleased in mind with the chiefly reception which they had received and pleasantly filled with the
morning's pig and rich Nakoroka taro. The people of Nalauvia were
shamed because their feast of the month before had been less lavish,
but they went in good spirit. Bulisivo said that the Sarowaqa people
would try to outdo Nakoroka when it came their turn to feast the Buli
in May; but they would fail, because poverty in food was already forc-
ing them to draw upon their Nakoroka kinsmen for taro. The Sarowaqa people tallied Nakoroka's food gifts with discouragement as they
went home. A young Nakoroka chief who had worked at the mines
said, "These visits of the Buli are to no purpose; they are just a lot of
trouble and waste." But the elders of Nakoroka remembered the old
days when the garbage from their feasts choked the river Votua, and
the people at Sarowaqa village would see food refuse floating out to
sea and say, "They must be feasting at Nakoroka."

The effects of a peaceful era with its easier communication have
been twofold. Aside from its stimulating aspects, disruption proceeds
as well. The young people are being coaxed from the villages. Each
year the more progressive among them look to European industrial
centers for their future. Of the young people, only the dullards remain
stubbornly attached to the old standards. British authority realizes this
problem and is searching for a remedy, but none has yet been discovered. Tremendous natural resources in Fiji have permitted a wide
margin for economic adjustment in the past. It is only in recent years
that the gold mines have introduced economic forces which are lower-
ing the productivity of the inland villages to subsistence level. Though
colonially enforced public work has harassed the native, it does not
expatriate him from his village; it does not effectively dilute his allegiance to his village, household, or the soil of his gardens.

There is a long clause in the colonial law which was paternalistically
formulated to stimulate private initiative among individual Fijians.[131]
According to this law, a Fijian who pays a special tax of ten shillings
to the colonial administration every year receives an indulgence and is
freed from the obligation to work for the public good under the supervision of the Buli and "village chief." In 1908, as proof of the efficacy
of the colony's system of administration, Thomson pointed to the fact

131. Thomson, *The Fijians.*

that practically no Fijians had taken advantage of this law. But this is no longer true. Many coastal towns in Bua Province are flanked by the scattered holdings of individual Fijian planters. To maintain an individual plantation on a profit basis, the Fijian entrepreneur must deliberately break all contact with his village and outrage all traditions of kinship obligations which require that produce be dumped back into the common pot of the extended kin group and that he who produces has only the common share and the glory of giving. The Fijian who courageously sets out to live this new life and succeeds in gaining the recompense of even the simplest European comforts is rare. Usually after a few years the once enterprising native returns disheartened to his village and tries to pick up the threads of community life. His status in the village has, of course, been permanently injured; he feels a new discontent, and, more frequently than the others, he says, "It is all right if I die quickly."

In April, 1936, Tomasi Raturaga[132] returned to Nakoroka from the Labasa sugar mills where he had been working seasonally for several years. He asked his brothers and a distant father to build him a house in the bush about four miles from Nakoroka, while he went to the gold mines and earned enough money to pay the special indulgence tax. He planned to become rich raising kava in the hills behind Nakoroka. I suggested that, rather than break away from the village, he use the money which he would earn at the mines to free the other able-bodied men in Nakoroka as well, so that the village as a whole could attempt collectively to raise its production standard without disrupting its family organization.[133] I suggested that attempting to benefit by the law would be a more effective means of satisfying wants than grumbling about colonial injustice. The suggestion was considered seriously. Six months after leaving Nakoroka, I received word that five Nakoroka men had applied collectively for exemption from public work. They took fifty shillings to the Buli, who sent them down the long fifty miles to the government station at Nabouwalu, to the Roko, for final verification. They were happy on this journey, which they imagined was

132. Tomasi died late in May, 1937, "and we of Nakoroka are sad because he was just a young man."

133. From conversation with D. G. Ball of the Education Department at Wellington, New Zealand: "It has been found necessary to re-establish the Maori according to their old community organization. Individuals who had broken away from the village lost incentive to work. By maintaining community structure, one village has learned to operate a modern scientific dairy (including milking machines) which competes effectively with European dairies."

the last task that the Buli would assign them. But the Roko refused to accept their money and sent them home without their freedom; if so many men from the interior were exempt from government supervision, there would be no way to control their activity. The avidity with which the natives flock to the wage jobs at the gold mines is justification, perhaps, for the Roko's attitude. Mines are not wholesome. They are a real problem to the administration.

Most of the primitive people of the world who have clashed with Western European civilization have found the adjustment to our tremendous emphasis on wealth and technology the most serious of their problems. Few can survive. Few can learn mechanisms of our production system before their own resources have been destroyed and they have become paupers on the hands of their respective colonial administrations. In directing this adjustment, there are two alternative policies: (1) Shelter the primitive community from all outside contact. Permit them only the certain benefits of our civilization, of which I can name but one—our knowledge of sanitation and disease. (2) Teach them to participate in what we regard as basic in our world—business. Teach them to exploit their natural resources as white men would do it. Teach them to produce with machines.

The first alternative is probably impossible for the future, even if it has seemed possible in the past. The second alternative meets obstacles in the path of its fulfilment; disillusioned primitives listen without interest to talk of machines. We must then sell them the desire for our machines; our method of producing for a profit must be advertised to them. To avoid destroying the primitive's incentive to live, our modes of production must be adjusted to his kind of family structure and social life. A hundred thousand Fijians, yet naïve, must learn to participate in the intricate economics of our world.

So long as the colonial government protects Nakoroka from real economic need, its people will retain the attitudes derived from centuries of economic plenty. Though there has yet been no real subsidizing of native communities, the natives are very much aware of those times in the past when the government has given them rations to help them through the periods of food shortage which followed hurricanes.[134] No successful attempt has been launched to stimulate inde-

---

134. Mr. L. M. Anderson of Delanisau cites an instance of this sort in recent years and suggests that the natives look forward to other opportunities to get something for nothing. Of course, as employer of native labor, he sees their problems from a white man's viewpoint. But it is highly probable that even a single instance of government help, after one of the rare acts of God which result in food shortage in Fiji, would have far-reaching psychological effect.

pendent attitudes in the native without removing him completely from his own village background.

So long as the native can fall back on his status as ward of the colonial government and be assured of a subsistence level of necessary goods, he has no real motive for wanting to compete economically with Europeans; hence he has no economic root in European culture. Money and what it can buy are luxuries. He imagines that his subsistence level is secure for the future. Present-day contacts with Europeans, though they may predispose the introduction of new necessities which cannot be had without the expenditure of some effort in European industry, tend to coax the native away from his own cultural background. Native medical practitioners, habitués of mining centers, and even individualistically minded planters who have paid for their exemption from community duty have lost touch with their own people. Though they may be economically aware of European culture, the emptiness left by alienation from their own culture has been left unfilled except for useless odds and ends of Europeanism.

CHAPTER IV

HOUSEHOLDS OF NAKOROKA

O F THE hundred persons whom Nakoroka claims as citizens, some sixty spend their greatest energies in village work and inhabit its twelve sleeping-houses (see Map IV). Of this group, twenty-one are small children. Houses are rectangular. At the lower end there is always a door. In one side wall, and sometimes in both, there is also a door which divides the upper from the lower end of the house. Food may enter the lower door, but the upper door is reserved for chiefs, honored guests, and owners of the house; food cannot cross this threshold.[1]

A large bed, sometimes eight feet in width, framed of timbers and mattressed with ferns and covered with mats, almost fills the upper end of the house. On the bed or under it near the upper wall there is always at least one large box or basket which contains the personal belongings of the owners of the house; the upper region is forbidden to all but the owners.[2] Bici has a sea chest with a key in which he has stowed books, papers, and pencils from his school days at Nabouwalu. Bulisivo has a large wooden packing case from some Chinese trading store in which his bark cloth, extra *sulu*'s, and shirts for Sunday are stored. Whale teeth are hidden here if the household possesses any. It is said that Bulisivo's box is fairly overflowing with hidden wealth. Less durable luxuries, such as soap and tobacco and sometimes even sugar and tea, are also cached there from the hungry gaze of kinsmen. Though in theory husband and wife share each other's property, a man usually speaks of the largest box in the household as his own and excludes his wife. Bici especially considers it a favor to give space in his sea chest to the belongings of his wife. He shares more willingly with his son and father. Ancestral weapons and ceremonial clothing may be contained in the box, or they may be wrapped carefully in bark cloth

1. However, in the houses of men of such low status as Bici, Raitova, Isacodro, and Orisi there is little distinction in function of the doors.
2. All those who plant land in Inland Forest Kingdom and who are habitual residents of a Nakoroka house are known as "owners" (*taukei*) of that house.

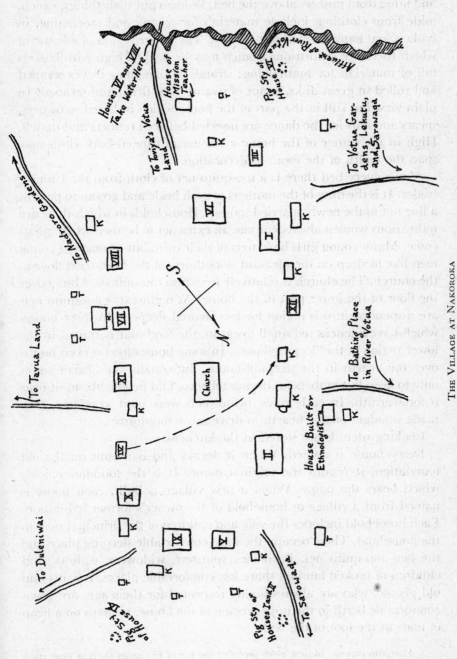

THE VILLAGE AT NAKOROKA

House numbers correspond with the list on p. 85. *K* indicates kitchen; *T*, latrine

and hung from timbers above the bed. Women put their things, which, aside from clothing, include materials for sewing and crocheting, in baskets and hang them above the bed. The upper region of a house in which there are industrious women may be heaped high with baskets full of materials for matmaking; strands of pandanus leaves scraped and rolled in great disks, heaps of swamp reed dried and scraped. In plain view but still in the part of the house which is sacred to owners, spears and fans for the dance are inserted between timbers and thatch. High in the center of the house a banner of fringed bark cloth may span the width of the room as decoration.

Above every bed there is a mosquito net of cloth from the Chinese trader. It is the duty of the mothers of both bride and groom to present a fine net to the newly married spouses. Households in which there are industrious women always contain an extra net to be used when guests come. Many young girls have nets of their own, but unmarried young men like to sleep on the pleasant smoothness of the hardwood floor in the church. The church is relatively free from mosquitoes. Mats cover the floor of the lower part of the house. At night extra mosquito nets are suspended in this region for less favored sleepers. In those houses which have kitchens too small to eat in, the food mat is spread in the lower region of the sleeping-house. In some houses food is even boiled over the hearth in the sleeping-house. But usually the hearth serves only to keep live embers for drying tobacco. Old people like to sit near it for warmth. In early days, before nets were used so widely, they made smudges on the hearth to drive away mosquitoes.[3]

Cooking utensils are stored in the kitchens.

Every house is named. When it decays and is rebuilt on the old foundation, it retains the original name. It is the foundation itself which bears the name. When a new village is built, each house is named from a village or household of the owner's former habitation. Each household includes the wife and children of the principal man in the household. These occupy the most comfortable sleeping place and the best mosquito net. Bachelors, spinsters, widowers, widows, and children of broken families share less comfortable places. Parents and old people, who are always highly respected for their age, are given comfortable berth in the upper region of the house, perhaps on a heap of mats at the foot of the bed.

3. Mosquito curtains of bark cloth preceded the net of European cloth in some parts of Fiji. But in inland Bua in the old days men say that smoke offered the only relief.

All the heads of households are married men or widowers with children.[4] If a man has a large family of his own, the title-holder of his land group may suggest in the council of elders that a house be given over to his use. Thus Namo, who before his eldest son died had five children, heads a Tavua household, although in ceremonial functions he is still a "young man." The elders discuss housing problems and solve them according to the best interests of the village as a whole. Adding a new house to the village is a rare event and worthy of serious discussion. Since the population does not expand rapidly, it is convenient for the newly married to join the household of the groom's father. When kinsmen come to town and claim rights in the land, it is the council which decides where they shall be housed; usually some kinsman who is the head of a household has already volunteered to take them in.

"Head of the household" is not a title, but each house is known for its most active male member. These are the men who gather to discuss problems of village politics. Such councils vary in formality from casual kava-drinking to "discussion in the manner of the land" in the presence of the king of Inland Forest. But attendance is not strictly limited to heads of households. Because of his age and the respect which people felt for his judgment, the voice of Akuila bore more weight than that of Bici or Namo. Bici and Namo have houses; Akuila has none. The housing of guests at the time of great ceremonies, the apportioning of feast food, and, with less strictness, the sharing of property obligations at times of feasts and exchanges are organized according to household membership; at such times household groups are known by the names of their houses.

To avoid introducing twelve new proper names, I shall refer to Nakoroka houses by the names of their principal occupants:

Households of Votua:
 I. Bulisivo
 II. Big Di Litiya
 III. Toviya
 IV. Isacodro
 V. Raitova (a Rokowaqa house but usually considered a part of Votua)

Households of Nadroro:
 VI. Naicadra
 VII. Vatili
 VIII. Orisi
Households of Tavua:
 IX. Nabadua
 X. Monasa
 XI. Namo
 XII. Bici

4. The chiefly household of Big Di Litiya was atypical. Lest her husband, the outsider Vosalevu, assume the role of "head" in this house, the house was always spoken of as belonging to Di Litiya's son, Ratu Seru.

HOUSE I

The roof of Bulisivo's house is low, though the area of its floor space is equal to that of all but two other houses. To shelter so great a man it is poorly constructed and in a sorry state of dilapidation. The floor is raised but slightly above the level of the village green. Alone among the sleeping-houses its walls are plaited of bamboo strips, but this is no worthy distinction. Cane has been in fashion for several years, and the material of this house marks it as outmoded. The many women of Bulisivo's household have kept the floor well spread with newer mats than one finds in other houses. There are only three kitchens in the village which are larger than Bulisivo's, but his kitchen requires repair. It serves well enough, however, as an eating-house. During many evenings he drinks kava there with the women of his household. Ratu Luke serves it when there are no commoners to do this task.

Bulisivo may be seventy-five years old. His skin is light in color like his sisters and his daughters. His muscles are well formed, though less developed than those of most men. Despite the slow dignity with which he walks, his gait lacks grace. He has a scrotal hernia.

He rarely enters other houses in the village except the large chiefly house of Big Di Litiya and the large house of Naicadra, where men gather for serious discussions. Though Big Di Litiya tries to hide her luxuries from him and his snooping wife, yet she shares more tobacco, sugar, and tea with Bulisivo's household than with any other. Almost all the members of these two households—Bulisivo's and Di Litiya's—belong to the chiefly caste and hence are free to beg from each other. Except for Ratu Luke, who is also of chiefly blood, the only persons outside his own household with whom Bulisivo recognizes kinship are those of Di Litiya's noble household.

As holder of the kingly title for all Inland Forest Kingdom, Bulisivo has rights to the first-fruits of all Nakoroka land. But influential men in Tavua and Nadroro, particularly Vatili and Nabadua, have often questioned his right. It is in the rich garden lands of Votua that his titular claims are strongest (see Map V). Those who plant in Votua land do not fail to give him gifts of food when their gardens ripen. Two dry gardens are considered his personal property. One of these, which is the largest and most productive of any in the village, lies half a mile or more beyond Isacodro's garden at Cold Water. The entire village planted it, and even Nabadua is proud of its luxuriance. It contains excellent taro, sweet potatoes, and manioc. Papaya trees cast their lean shade among the taro stalks. Coconut palms fringe its upper mar-

MAP V

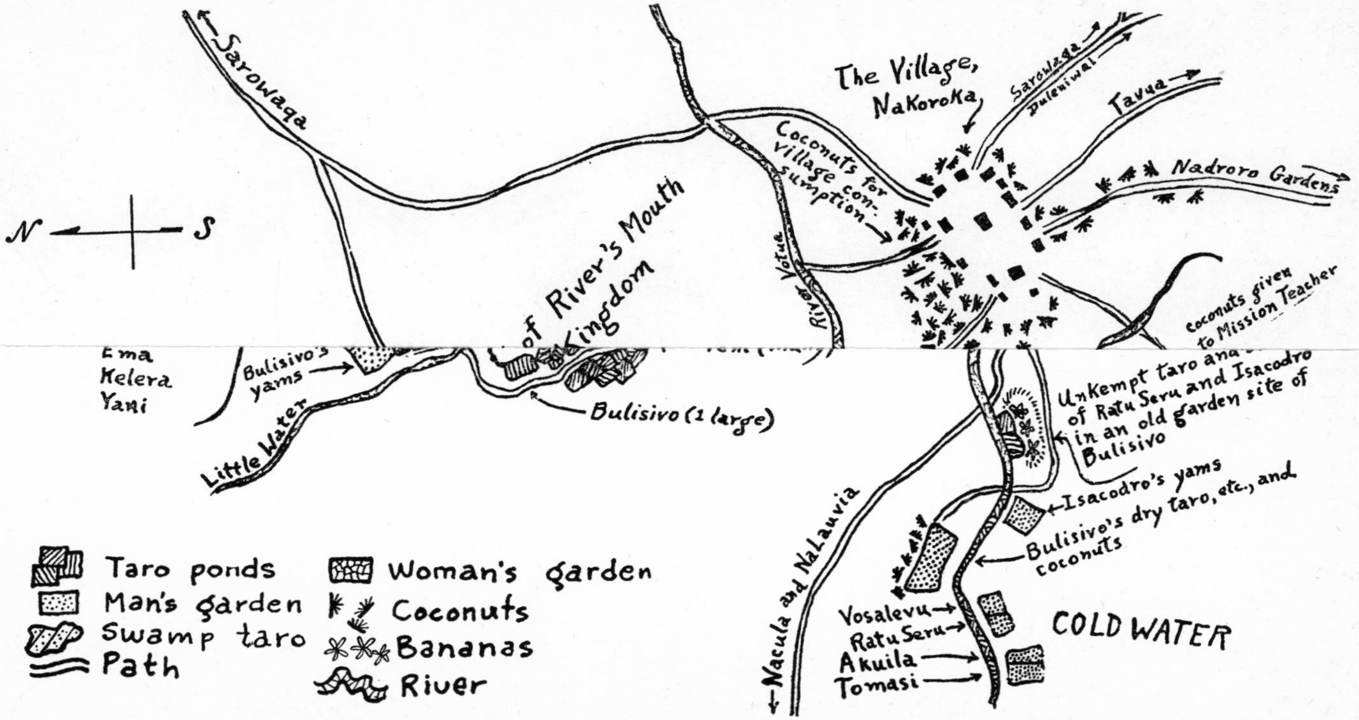

CHART OF VOTUA GARDENS

CHART I

House I

F(U) —— F(U) Noblewoman —— M(U) Ratu Seru —— M(C) BULISIVO (Votua)
+M(C) Chief   of River's Mouth   His claim upon Votua   +F(U) Noble-
at Votua   +M(C) Chief at   land depended upon   woman of wind-
              Dama   his mother's super-   ward coast who
                                 natural impregnation   had distant claims
                                 by Votua ancestors   on Votua
                                 +F(C) Noblewoman
                                 of Saolo on wind-
                                 ward coast

M(C) Chief at Wai-
nunu (Ratu Luke's
father [see
House III])

Children of BULISIVO:

M(U) Ratu Meli (*see* House II)
F(U) —— F(U) Little Di Litiya (Votua)
+M(C) Chief at Dama   +M(C) Noble kins-
F(U) Di Sereima (Votua)   man of Bulisivo's
                          from windward
                          coast

M(U) Ratu Keleme-di (Votua)
F(U) Di Vara (Votua) —— M(U) Ratu Tevita (Votua)
+M(C) Chief at Navakasiga
F(U) +M(C) Chief at Navakasiga —— M(C) Tomasi (Votua) Son of Viniyana's first marriage

F(C) Vini-yana (Toviya's division of Votua) (widow of M[U] title-holder of a land division at Nacula)
M(C) Akuila (*see* House III)
F(C) Di Kabu (*see* House II)
F(C) Big Di Litiya (*see* House II)

The name of him to whom the house is said to belong is printed in capital letters. His parents appear in the column to the left; his children, in the column to the right.

C and U indicate moiety membership.

M indicates male; F, female. *M* or *F* indicates males or females *living* in 1936.

Siblings are listed in order of age and are connected by vertical line. If this vertical line is broken, it indicates a socially important classificatory sibling relationship.

In compiling these genealogies, I attempted to ascertain true biological relationships. But at Nakoroka it is the sociological relationship rather than the biological which is remembered. I have probably included many classificatory sibling relationships of past generations as though they were biological. Native informants invariably exhibited great faith in my method of diagramming; whenever the diagrams showed confusion in the moiety affiliations of past generations, informants revised their opinions until the charts were consistent with the moiety principle.

Hereditary land affiliations appear with each name. But because each individual recognizes several potential affiliations, the charts are neither final nor indisputable. Of those living today at Nakoroka, the land affiliations appear which were considered strong in 1935 and 1936.

gin. But Bulisivo's yams and kava grow in a smaller garden which lies near the source of a northern tributary of the river Votua called Little Water. Though small, it produces abundantly. Aside from yams and kava, it contains dry taro. Men of the village co-operated in its planting. There are coconut trees near its lower margin and a dozen banana trees about it. Toward the village along Little Water there is a large taro pond of Bulisivo's; water drains from it into a large cluster of small ponds of the men of Votua and Nadroro. Perhaps three hundred yards below these ponds there are four large new ponds which Bulisivo built with his own hands. High in the swampy land called Nairoro, which lies less than half a mile from the village, Bulisivo has another large taro pond which his sisters have kept well planted. The large grove of coconuts (four to five hundred trees) which lies below the many taro ponds in Nairoro also belongs to him. Higher on the river Votua bordering the taro ponds of Ratu Seru and Vosalevu, there are some two hundred banana trees of Bulisivo's and some scattered coconuts.

Bulisivo eats finer foods than anyone in the village, except perhaps his own grandchildren. Sweet puddings are spread more often on the food mat of his household. He drinks tea at least once a week and during some periods almost every day. He has a file to sharpen his knife. He has several kerosene lanterns, and his house usually contains a can of kerosene to burn in them. But his personal belongings are not conspicuously fine. He alone, however, has a fathom of wool serge which he wears as a *sulu*. Others content themselves with printed cotton. He also has a battered felt hat and an umbrella; though Nabadua and Naicadra also have these luxuries, they are marks of distinction.[5] Except for Big Di Litiya's kitchen, that of Bulisivo contains a larger supply of cooking and eating utensils from the Chinese trader than any other household in the village: iron pots, buckets, plates, cups, knives, forks, and spoons.

Viniyana, who is a commoner and Bulisivo's wife, theoretically shares his bed and mosquito net in the upper part of his house. She is perhaps in her late forties, recently past the menopause, lithe and vigorous. She chatters boisterously, but the women of other households do not enjoy her company. Her clothing is of costlier quality

5. I did not take complete inventory of each household. I do not know with accuracy what Bulisivo had stored away in his various boxes. But I have mentioned these easily apparent possessions so that they may be compared roughly with the possessions of other households.

than that of other women who are commoners. Though she has all the
utensils of Bulisivo's household to make her work easier, she possesses
no wealth in her own right. Among the gardens of six other Votua
women near Bulisivo's yam garden at Little Water, she has a small
garden of manioc, tomatoes, kava, and sweet potatoes. No coconuts
are spoken of as belonging to her. When she approaches the house of
Big Di Litiya, she is always careful to observe the proper respect greeting. Her closest ties of kinship are with her true brother Akuila and
her son Tomasi, whose father, a native of Nacula, died long before
Viniyana married Bulisivo.

Viniyana's son Tomasi, now deceased, was a little older than Bulisivo's blind son. Through his father he claimed title to a land division
of Nacula. But for at least ten years he had considered Nakoroka his
residence. As Akuila's sister's son he had claim on Akuila's Votua
land. He showed marked interest in Akuila's shamanistic powers.
Across the valley from Bulisivo's large taro garden at Cold Water,
Tomasi and Akuila planted yam gardens close together. They assisted
each other in the planting. In Nairoro swamp land Tomasi had five
taro ponds. Above these, near Bulisivo's four new ponds, he had a scattered grove of coconuts, perhaps two hundred trees. Across Cold Water
among the great expanse of Votua coconuts, he had two more luxuriant groves. But Tomasi spent but little time at Nakoroka. He did not
dance with the other young men because one of his legs had been badly crippled in infancy, and it never grew to its full size. He used to
work for long periods at the sugar mills in distant Labasa and at the
mine. With his wages he bought long trousers so that only the limp of
his infirmity was apparent. But he did not squander his wealth. He
did not join in the gay life of other workmen. Women never found him
interesting.

Until his death in 1937, Tomasi planned to become wealthy on his
land at Nakoroka. Bulisivo used to commend his judgment. He slept
in Bulisivo's kitchen or in the church with other men who were unattached. He was guilty of the shameful practice of peeking at women
while they bathed.

All Bulisivo's children were born from an earlier marriage with a
noblewoman. The eldest of his daughters married a chief of the Dama
region. His youngest daughter married a chief of Savusavu. Both live
in the land of their husbands. But his two middle daughters still live
with their father at Nakoroka. The elder of these, who is Little Di
Litiya, is about thirty-five years of age. Her face is overplump and has

begun to sag, but she is still deemed beautiful. Like all other noble-women of Votua, it is said that she is tattooed about the vulva. Though unmarried, a daughter, Di Sereima, was born to her about 1931. Until 1936 poverty prevented the chiefly father of this child from publicly asserting his paternity. He is a young kinsman of Bulisivo's from the windward coast. Though he has now validated his paternity, he has not yet ventured to establish a household of his own. Little Di Litiya continues to reside like a spinster in her father's household. Her un-married husband lives on in his own distant village. Di Sereima spends most of her time in the house of Big Di Litiya, whom she mistakenly calls "mother." Little Di Litiya spent her childhood and youth at Saolo during Bulisivo's long sojourn there. Hence no coconuts or ba-nanas at Nakoroka are spoken of as hers. She has a small garden of manioc and sweet potatoes next to that of Viniyana, Bulisivo's wife.

The younger of these two middle daughters, Di Vara, also grew to maturity on the windward coast. She is perhaps thirty-two years old. Her right eye appears duller than the left and looks steadily in one di-rection from under a drooping lid. Like all Bulisivo's family, her skin is "red" and not "black." About 1925 she married a chief of Navakasiga on the westernmost extension of the leeward coast. But her marriage was unsuccessful. She returned to her father's household early in 1935. Later in the same year her son, who was then about ten years old, came to join her there. Like her older sister, no coconut trees are spo-ken of as hers. She has no land in her own right and has not yet planted a garden. However, in 1935 the men of the village planted a taro pond for her in payment for her services as "nurse." But as Bulisivo's daugh-ter she is, of course, free to take food from all gardens of the Votua nobility.

Her son Ratu Kelemedi, like all noble children, has been well fed and towers above common children who are his age-mates. But he is awkward. When he plays tag with the other children, they must pre-tend that he is difficult to catch. When the children leap with shouts from the fifteen-foot bank that overhangs the bathing place in the river Votua, he, too, shouts feebly and makes false starts to leap and then retreats. More modest than the other children because his noble soul is more mature, he always shields his genitals with one hand, so that the other children must sometimes give him support as he stum-bles among the slippery rocks of the riverbank. He has no gardens.

Bulisivo's daughters and Di Vara's awkward son spread their private sleeping-mats on the floor below Bulisivo's bed and hang mosquito nets, with which Bulisivo's house is well equipped, to make their sleep comfortable. But Bulisivo's blind son, who is his youngest child, sleeps alone in the kitchen. Every day he bestirs his childlike limbs and, with a stick to tap as guide, waddles to the shallow ford in the river Votua to bathe; nevertheless, his lack of cleanliness is a problem for the household. Then he returns to sit in the kitchen and whine for tobacco and, with loose-jointed gestures which caricature his father, scratch his head where the lice are biting. His features, too, resemble Bulisivo's, but his mouth hangs more loosely even when he eats. He has no gardens, but he sings in church and sometimes at dances. His speech is not coherent, because he has nothing to say. According to government records, he was born in 1914. It is said that he masturbates. His lack of circumcision is not worthy of conversation.

HOUSE II

Big Di Litiya's house is the largest in the village. The timbers of its frame are greatest, its roof is most lofty, and its foundation lifts it high above the village green. It was built for Bulisivo before his departure for the long sojourn on the windward coast. Di Litiya lived there during his absence while she held the kingly title for Inland Forest. But it is rumored that he will again take residence there and that she will move her goods into his dilapidated house. Since her marriage to Vosalevu, the commoners in the village have resented her use of this fine house; they speak of it as belonging to her son Ratu Seru rather than to her and her foreign husband.

Though the house lacks the fine decoration of the chiefly houses of Macuata, it is well constructed. Industrious Di Litiya and her sister Di Kabu keep its spacious floor littered with materials for matmaking. Many mats, designed bark cloth, and materials for the dance are stored in its upper region. The largest kava bowl in the village leans on edge against the wall near the lower door. In the middle of the floor there is a large sewing machine which does not work. As in Bulisivo's house, commoners feel shy of laughing freely when they are inside. Though Di Litiya likes gaiety, the people of the village feel reserved when they have crossed the threshold of her house; despite her persuasion, they do not stay late.

Uniquely in the village, this house is adjoined by a special house for eating. This eating-house is as well constructed as Bici's sleeping-house. It is well supplied with utensils for eating and cooking. Sometimes Di Litiya and Vosalevu sit there alone after dark and drink tea.

Cooking is done in a poorly built shelter which leans against one end of the eating-house. The latrine of this house is newly built and spacious.

Big Di Litiya passed the menopause some ten years ago. Though her hair is grizzled and her face is lined, and on her upper lip there are many black hairs, she is still lithe and fresh with health. Burdened heavily with copra or kava, she can travel swiftly along the slippery path to the Chinese trader on the Lekutu coast. Many women among the commoners enjoy her boisterous company. She matches her wits with men over the kava bowl in Nabadua's house. Her laughter is the

CHART II

HOUSE II

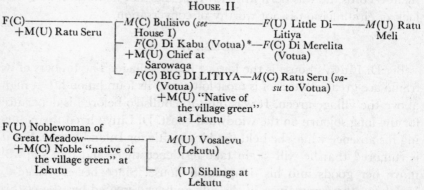

```
F(C)————————————┌—M(C) Bulisivo (see————————F(U) Little Di————M(U) Ratu
  +M(U) Ratu Seru  │   House I)                  Litiya         Meli
                   │   F(C) Di Kabu (Votua)*—F(C) Di Merelita
                   │   +M(U) Chief at            (Votua)
                   │    Sarowaqa
                   └— F(C) BIG DI LITIYA—M(C) Ratu Seru (va-
                        (Votua)               su to Votua)
                        +M(U) "Native of
                         the village green"
                         at Lekutu
F(U) Noblewoman of
  Great Meadow——————┌— M(U) Vosalevu
  +M(C) Noble "native of │   (Lekutu)
   the village green" at │
   Lekutu           └— (U) Siblings at
                         Lekutu
```

* Di Kabu is sometimes said to head the chiefly caste of Rokowaqa land, to which Votua chiefs are bound by distant genealogical tie. Though Raitova (House V) holds the title to chiefly authority in Rokowaqa, he is considered part of Votua and owes special allegiance to Di Kabu.

one noise which habitually disturbs the silence of the village; others usually speak in well-modulated voices. Unlike her brother, she visits freely about the village. Of those houses which are not of Votua, she is seen most frequently at the kava bowl of Nabadua or with Naicadra's wife. Sometimes she stops in at Bici's house because it lies on the path between her house and that of Bulisivo. Before she had returned the kingly title to her brother, the people of Votua sometimes gathered to feast in her kitchen. But she and her husband are known for their private consumption of luxuries.

No gardens are known as hers, but sometimes the gardens of Bulisivo and the women of his household are spoken of collectively as belonging to the Votua chiefs. She works vigorously to keep the taro ponds of her brother, husband, and sons well planted. She assists Bulisivo's wife and his daughter in the planting of their gardens. She takes food freely from these sources. A grove of coconuts in the division of

Votua to which Toviya holds the title (Nakabalemai) is known as hers. Except for the woolen sweaters which the noblewomen of Votua persuaded my houseboy to buy for them from a Chinese trader on the windward coast and which they wear in church on Sundays, these women wear no clothing which marks them as chieftainesses.[6]

Vosalevu, the husband of Big Di Litiya, is more than forty years of age. His chiefship comes through his mother only, who in turn was only half a chief because her father was a commoner. Yet, because of his noble marriage and his aggressive bearing, all commoners address him with the plural pronoun. He is gaunt and leathery. His teeth are prominent and well preserved, which is unusual at Nakoroka. Though his muscular development seems slighter than that of most men, they all fear him for his reputation as one who knows how to box. Uniquely he has a habit of wearing his *sulu* high, just below the armpits, like a woman. Perhaps this is because his chest is narrower than most men, or it may be from modesty, since he is a man of the church. He has four large taro ponds which lie in Votua land among Bulisivo's bananas and coconuts, near the point where Little Water joins the river Votua. Near the gardens of Tomasi and Akuila at Cold Water, Vosalevu and Big Di Litiya's son Ratu Seru have helped each other in the planting of yam gardens. Though he does not like menial tasks, Vosalevu is vigorous; though he is intelligent, he turns his mental energy to action rather than to speculation. With Di Litiya he shares the bed in the honored place in Di Litiya's household.

But Di Litiya's bed is long and easily accommodates two large mosquito nets. Sometimes Di Kabu and her daughter share the second net. Sometimes during their sojourns at Nakoroka, Little Ratu Meli or Ratu Seru have this place, and Di Kabu sleeps on the floor or moves temporarily to her brother's house. Like her sister Big Di Litiya, Di Kabu is tall and lean, but her manner is mild like that of Bulisivo. She is older than Big Di Litiya and at least five years younger than Bulisivo. Since she is Vosalevu's "small wife" and cannot speak in his company, she spends much of her time with the women of Bulisivo's house-

6. When Bari came to Nakoroka in my employ, he brought word from Bulisivo's youngest daughter, whose husband is a distant kinsman of Bari's at Savusavu. Di Litiya accepted him as her special guest. She showered him with gifts of food. He ate without restraint in all Votua households. When he departed, they requested that he send them woolen sweaters which a Chinese trader was displaying on the windward coast and which were coveted by all who saw them. Bulisivo was angered that his sisters and his daughters should be so outspoken in their request; it would have been far more fitting for noblewomen to accept with pleasure whatever gift Bari chose to give them.

hold. Because she married a chief of Sarowaqa and lived there with him until his death, she has never planted extensively in Nakoroka land. She has a small garden of manioc, kava, and sweet potatoes near the yam garden of Bulisivo. She helps to weed Bulisivo's gardens and plant his taro ponds.

Ratu Seru, who was born about 1910, spends most of his time on the windward coast. However, during two or three months of every year he lives at Nakoroka. He is rather tall. His muscles are less well developed than those of other men. Yet he is described as a man of great strength; it would be impolitic to disparage the prowess of so great a nobleman. He is aggressive and overbearing; the entire village takes pride in his reputation as an executive. Big Di Litiya, his mother, holds his mosquito net in reserve for him in her house, but frequently he prefers to sleep about the village. He is no gardener. Four of his taro ponds lie near Vosalevu's among Bulisivo's bananas and coconuts. Three have been well planted and cared for by the noblewomen of Votua, but the young people who came as guests to Nakoroka early in January, 1936, built the fourth. He has planted a small patch of taro in the wet soil at the edge of Cold Water, downstream from Isacodro's garden. Few coconuts or bananas are spoken of as his. Yet his status as Bulisivo's sister's son is high; he is *vasu* to Nakoroka land and lives in greater personal luxury than anyone else—even Bulisivo himself. In theory all garden lands at Nakoroka are his to lay waste if he chooses. Actually he forages among the gardens of Votua noblemen only.

Di Merelita, the only daughter of Di Kabu, is perhaps a little older than Ratu Seru. She is an industrious girl. In the evenings she stays at home and plaits mats. With Naicadra's daughter and Ivamere, she is known as a woman who will make a good wife. Though, because she is chiefly, people say that she is beautiful, her nose is far too large and her complexion blotchy. Her skin is darker than that of the rest of Bulisivo's kinsmen. But her figure is of the right plumpness. No coconuts or bananas are said to belong to her, but she has a yam garden next to Bulisivo's at Little Water. Under Vosalevu's direction, Isacodro and Raitova cleared this land and planted it. Big Di Litiya carried some of the seed yams. Di Merelita has made a mosquito net for herself. Sometimes she visits for long periods in Sarowaqa, where her father's kinsmen live.

Little Ratu Meli, who is Bulisivo's namesake and grandson through Bulisivo's eldest daughter, was born about 1920. Though healthy and well fed, he seems weak and awkward compared with commoners of his age. Like Di Merelita, his skin is dark. As a small child he lived in the Dama region with his father and mother. But his father's household is crowded with many small children. Now that he is old enough to travel, he prefers to live with Big Di Litiya as her *vuona*, "beloved grandson." Like Ratu Seru, he is *vasu* to Nakoroka, but his youth and milder temperament prevent his exploiting this hereditary privilege. Ratu Seru treats him like a small boy, and he accepts such treatment. Little Ratu Meli has no gardens and no coconuts or bananas. He leads a carefree life teasing the older girls and tormenting small children. He has attended the mission school at Nabouwalu, and in March, 1936, his powerful kinsmen paid his fee at a higher school in Suva, and he went there.

Di Sereima sleeps with Big Di Litiya and Vosalevu. Sometimes her mother, who is Little Di Litiya, or some woman of Bulisivo's household cares for her, but most of the time she is a member of Big Di Litiya's house. She is large for her age and very pretty despite her tiresome self-consciousness. The entire village remembers her with choice foods. Only Bici admitted that he favors his own child more. Vosalevu has made two small taro ponds for her next to Bulisivo's large one at Nairoro. She has no coconuts or bananas. People speak of her as "the little noblewoman."

HOUSE III

Toviya's house needs repair. It is no larger than Bulisivo's kitchen. Though it is said that many whale teeth are stored in Toviya's private box, no one has ever seen them. The ancestral weapons which are the "houses" of Toviya's ancestral spirits are also cached safely in his box. But the goods of this household are meager. The few women of the household have been busy for months with the chores consequent upon the confinement of Ratu Luke's wife and have had no chance to make new mats for the floor. Frequently the house is crowded, but most of the inhabitants are equally at home in households at Sarowaqa and divide their time. No kitchen adjoins. Cooking is done in the kitchen of Naicadra's house, which is near by.

According to government records, Toviya is older than Bulisivo. Though he is not strong, he looks as if he were at least ten years younger. His muscles are soft and spare, but he moves with grace. He is not a good man and is not kind to his kinsmen. Yet it is known that his ancestral spirits make constant demands upon him, and he is forgiven in part for his meanness. His clothing is poor, but he is rarely without to-

CHART III
House III

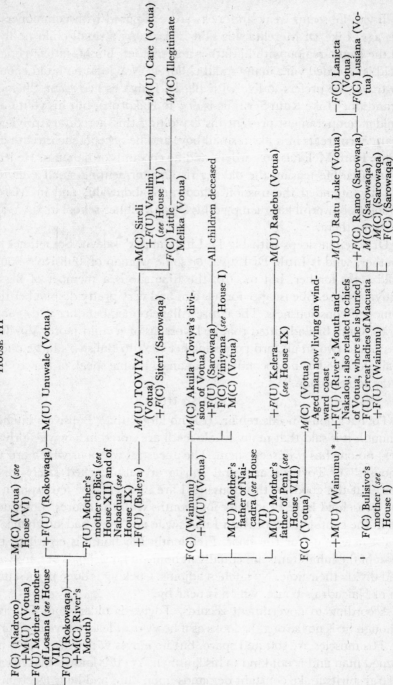

* Either this Wainunu chief belonged to moiety C and married within his moiety or his relationship with Bulisivo's mother was "sibling-cousin" and not "sibling in moiety."

bacco. All respect his intelligence, and no one questions his knowledge of past events. His position as title-holder for the division of Votua land called Nakabalemai gains serious voice for him among the men, yet all happily anticipate the time when Akuila will inherit this title. Toviya likes to work alone. More rarely even than other old men does he participate in casual gatherings in the evenings. In the past he was friendly with Bici's uncircumcised father; but Bici's father's mind has shrunken with his age, and Toviya no longer seeks his company. Sometimes he drinks kava with Bici.

The land called Nakabalemai lies to the south of Cold Water, which is a tributary of the river Votua. It contains no gardens, but coconut groves grow luxuriantly there. One small grove is known as Toviya's, but upon Naicadra's advice he divided the rest among the people of Votua after the death of his son Sireli. Across Cold Water in the land called Slice-of-the-Moon, he has made taro ponds for many years. Today only one of these is clean and well planted; several others still contain a few stalks of taro. He built a large taro pond at Nairoro in March, 1936. He also has garden land in Naicadra's division of Nadroro. In the land called Bau[7] the old banana trees which are scattered on the slope below Peni's yam garden are Toviya's. Perhaps two miles farther along the path there are three luxuriant and extensive banana groves which are his. Among the bananas he has planted a few stalks of kava.

During the latter part of 1935 and most of 1936, Ratu Luke's wife slept in the place of honor in Toviya's house. When Toviya is in the village, he frequently shares the large mosquito net in Naicadra's household; he calls Naicadra "cross-cousin."

For several years Siteri, who is Toviya's wife, has lived with her brothers in Sarowaqa. She is more at home there than at Nakoroka. She is known as an "old woman," bui. For perhaps ten years, ever since she fell among the rocks at the river Votua, her right arm has been almost useless for heavy work. During her brief sojourns at Nakoroka, she assists with the cooking and tries to plait mats. No food resources at Nakoroka are considered hers.

Toviya's daughter Little Melika, who is perhaps thirty years old, also spends most of her time in Sarowaqa. A son was born to her in 1934, a sickly child with a large head. She is a bad woman. She has not yet married. With Bici, who is her cross-cousin, she jests grossly. She has no food resources at Nakoroka.

7. See Map VI, facing p. 106.

Vaulini, who is the widow of Toviya's son, sometimes sleeps with her six-year-old son Care in Toviya's household. But she usually considers herself a part of the household of Isacodro, who is her father. When Toviya dies, Akuila will hold his title in trust for Care until Care's maturity, but Care will probably be an old man before he attains adequate maturity. The title will doubtless pass through the hands of many trustees. Toviya considers him his true grandson (*vuona*), but they spend little time together. When Sireli died, Naicadra adopted Care; Care prefers Naicadra's larger household. He receives the affectionate attention of adults in all three houses. Already he can whisper scandal to amuse his admiring adult audience. He is too young to have gardens of his own.

Akuila and his wife are also owners in Toviya's household. They are almost fifty years old. Like Toviya, they spend much time in Sarowaqa. During their brief periods of residence at Nakoroka they sometimes sleep in the house of Bulisivo, sometimes in Bulisivo's kitchen. Akuila has an extensive grove of coconuts in the land to which he will someday inherit the title. Across Cold Water from Bulisivo's taro gardens, Akuila and Tomasi have planted yams in adjacent gardens. Near Ratu Seru's taro ponds, Akuila has built five ponds among a grove of coconuts which are his. At Nairoro he has two more ponds. No food resources at Nakoroka belong to his wife. Like Toviya, Akuila knows how to conceal his tobacco so that he always seems to have a small supply. His clothing is poor.

During the pregnancy and confinement of Ratu Luke's wife Ramo, Ratu Luke acted as head of Toviya's household. All other inhabitants withdrew so that he and his wife could live comfortably during this trying period. In 1936 he was less than thirty years old. His skin is much darker than the chiefs of Bulisivo's immediate family. Despite the birth injury which has hindered the full growth of one of his legs, he is muscularly more powerful than any other man in the village. With Peni he is the most skilled of Nakoroka's huntsmen. Bulisivo is his closest kinsman in the village. Ratu Luke calls him "father," but there is little affection between them. Though his birth binds him irrevocably with the chiefly caste, his status at Nakoroka is insecure. He likes to dance and joke among the young men, but he is shy and ashamed in the presence of strangers or his elders. His yam garden is at the distant end of the planted area in Nadroro land. There are also banana trees and dry taro there, but wild pigs have destroyed the taro and injured the yams. He has a grove of coconuts in Toviya's section

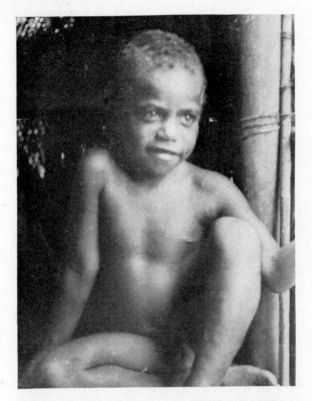

"SOMEDAY HE WILL OWN A CHIEFLY TITLE"

AN OLD CHIEF
Beside him is a drum with drumsticks

of Votua. One taro pond at Nairoro is his, but it was exhausted early in 1936. Above Nairoro his wife's father built five new ponds for him which began to produce late in 1936. These ponds are among a few coconut trees which are also Ratu Luke's. Though his household is not managed in chiefly fashion, he takes great pride in his personal appearance and in that of his wife and children. He always dresses in white cloth and keeps his skin well oiled. As a native of Sarowaqa, his wife Ramo has no claims upon the land at Nakoroka.

When Sakariya, the troublemaker, who is the last survivor of Buleya land, comes to Nakoroka, he too shares Toviya's house because Toviya likewise has claims upon Buleya land. But since 1931(?) Sakariya's visits to Nakoroka have been rare and brief. He now considers himself a resident of Lekutu. A small grove of coconuts in Toviya's Votua land still belongs to him. He also has a grove of bananas in Naicadra's division of Nadroro.

HOUSE IV

When Isacodro came to Nakoroka with his family about 1930, he was given the house in which the aged Unuwale and the widower Samu with his two children were living.[8] But the house fell into disrepair, and the village, busied with other tasks, failed to assist Isacodro in rebuilding it. He moved his family into the kitchen and dismantled the sleeping-house of its walls. The kitchen is small and poorly built, but it served as sleeping-house for many months. When a house was finally built for Isacodro, it was placed on the opposite side of the village green from where his kitchen is. Now, rather than carry cooked food across the village, it is convenient for the family to take meals in the kitchen despite its small size. The new sleeping-house is neatly built, but it is too small. It is barely twelve feet in length and six feet in width. No stone foundation raises it above the village green. Isacodro's daughters are not industrious, but there are many of them for so small a house, and they have made more mosquito nets than can be conveniently hung. Isacodro's wife possesses a small sewing machine which is run by a handcrank, but no other tools of outstanding value grace this house. Isacodro's ornaments for the dance, the family clothing, and perhaps some ancestral weapons are stowed away in the upper region. Because Ema, who is Isacodro's wife, and Nabadua are "small brother" and "small sister," there is a strong bond between the people of Isacodro's household and Nabadua's.

8. See below, p. 105.

CHART IV

HOUSE IV

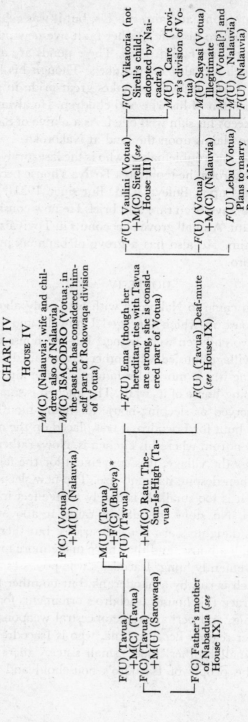

M(C) (Nalauvia; wife and children also of Nalauvia)

M(C) ISACODRO (Votua; in the past he has considered himself part of Rokowaqa division of Votua)

F(C) (Votua)
+M(U) (Nalauvia)

—F(U) Vikatoria (not Sireli's child; adopted by Naicadra)

M(U) Care (Toviya's division of Votua)

—F(U) Vaulini (Votua)
+M(C) Sireli (see House III)

M(U) Sayasi (Votua) Illegitimate

M(U) (Votua[?] and Nalauvia

M(U) Nalauvia

F(U) (Nalauvia)

—F(U) (Votua)
+M(C) (Nalauvia)

F(U) Lebu (Votua) Plans to marry Peni of House VIII

+F(U) Ema (though her hereditary ties with Tavua are strong, she is considered part of Votua)

M(U) (Tavua)
+F(C) (Buleya)*
F(U) (Tavua)

+M(C) Ratu The-Sun-Is-High (Tavua)

F(U) (Tavua) Deaf-mute (see House IX)

F(U) (Tavua)
+M(C) (Tavua)

F(C) (Tavua)
+M(U) (Sarowaqa)

F(C) Father's mother of Nabadua (see House IX)

*Their descendants live at Duleniwai.

Nabadua's children sometimes eat in Isacodro's kitchen. Isacodro's daughter's frequently sleep at Nabadua's house.[9]

Isacodro's only prestige is gained through his quiet personality and his skill as a workman. He rarely speaks among men. He seems to be resigned to his low status. On the few occasions when he speaks, his voice bursts forth in erratic fragments. But he takes great pride in his motor skills. Among the older men he is the most sturdy. Though he is perhaps fifty years of age, he looks much younger. The native medical practitioner has warned him that his heart is enlarged from overwork. Like his entire family, he is light in color; his skin is darker, however, than that of Bulisivo's family. He is a successful gardener. Aside from his luxuriant yam garden at Cold Water, he has a large garden downstream from the taro ponds at Nairoro. This second garden contains dry taro, kava, two banana trees, tomatoes, and many supplementary foods which his wife has planted. It is one of the few fenced gardens at Nakoroka. He has one taro pond among the large cluster at Nairoro. Above Ratu Luke's five new taro ponds, Isacodro has five new ponds among a small grove of banana trees. Across the river from Toviya's section of Votua land a large grove of coconuts belongs to him. In Toviya's land itself he has forty more coconut trees. Near his yam garden at Cold Water some taro carelessly planted among a few banana trees belongs to him.

Though her oldest child is already thirty years old, Isacodro's wife Ema is still pretty. Her face is weathered, but her body is firm and full. She moves gracefully and carries her burdens with almost as much vigor as Big Di Litiya. Though both her parents were of Tavua land, she has considered herself a member of Votua since her marriage with Isacodro. Her garden is with that of the Votua women, above Bulisivo's yams at Little Water. She is true sister to the microcephalic mute who lives in Nabadua's house. Sometimes she plaits mats with Melika, who is her "small sister" and Naicadra's wife.

Vaulini and her son Care are usually a part of Isacodro's household. The girl Vikatoria, who was born to Vaulini shortly after her marriage to Sireli, has been adopted by Naicadra. But, like Care, whom Naicadra has also adopted, she spends much of her time in Isacodro's household. In 1935 and 1936 she was at the district school at Lekutu. At that time she was perhaps nine years old. Vaulini is known as a foolish woman of easy virtue. She has no food resources of her own.

9. Because of Nabadua's marriages within moiety, the young people of these two households are all of the same moiety and call one another "brother" and "sister."

Isacodro's second daughter is a year or two younger than Vaulini, who in 1935 was perhaps twenty-eight. Though this daughter is married to a young man of Nalauvia, she comes frequently to visit Isacodro and stays for long periods. She has four small children whom she brings with her, and she shares the task of caring for them with her mother and her sisters. Her oldest child, Sayasi, who is eight or nine and was born before her marriage, lives permanently with Isacodro and his wife. Sayasi is now in the district school at Lekutu. Isacodro's youngest daughter, Lebu, planned to marry Peni in June, 1936. None of Isacodro's daughters have food resources of their own. They are all known as foolish women who like to visit about. Isacodro's house is so small that there is good reason for their sleeping wherever they can find comfort. Often they visit kinsmen in Lekutu or Nalauvia for long periods. Particularly Lebu and Vaulini make young men pay heavily for their favors; with prim superiority to the other girls in the village, Lebu says that she only smokes tobacco that has been tinned in Australia.

HOUSE V

Raitova's house lies between that of Big Di Litiya and Nabadua. It is built on an old foundation, which is faced with stone and rises high above the village green. The timbers of its frame are old but sturdy and of good thickness, and the ceiling is lofty. Though the floor space is not quite so large, it is a better house than the one in which Bulisivo lives. Since mosquito nets are not plentiful, the women and the children of the household sleep comfortably inside the nets, while the men make shift wherever they can find space. The child Karalai usually occupies the bed in the upper part of the house. The food mat is usually spread near the lower door because there is no eating-house. Not being constructed on a proper house frame, the kitchen does little more than break the wind.

Raitova is younger than Isacodro, though he looks older. His abundant hair is gray, and a gray beard hides his chin. He is well muscled, but he moves with languor. His slowness is a village joke. For many years he has suffered with the fever of filariasis, and in recent years his left forearm has become swollen with this disease. When Raitova first came to Nakoroka, Naicadra recognized a cross-cousin bond of kinship and took him into his division of Nadroro. But Raitova's father was of Rokowaqa, and this is the land upon which his claims to ownership are strongest. Though he holds the chiefly title for Rokowaqa, he functions ceremonially as a lowly member of Votua. His personal be-

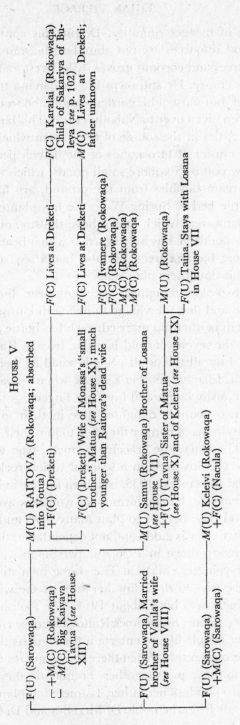

CHART V

HOUSE V

F(U) (Sarowaqa) —— M(U) RAITOVA (Rokowaqa; absorbed into Votua)

+M(C) (Rokowaqa)
M(C) Big Kaiyava (Tavua) (see House XII)

+F(C) (Dreketi)

F(C) (Dreketi) Wife of Monasa's "small brother" Matua (see House X); much younger than Raitova's dead wife

F(C) Karalai (Rokowaqa) Child of Sakariya of Buleya (see p. 102)
M(C) Lives at Dreketi; father unknown

F(C) Lives at Dreketi

F(C) Lives at Dreketi

F(C) Ivamere (Rokowaqa)
F(C) (Rokowaqa)
M(C) (Rokowaqa)
M(C) (Rokowaqa)

M(U) (Rokowaqa)
F(U) Taina. Stays with Losana in House VII

M(U) Samu (Rokowaqa) Brother of Losana (see House VII)
F(U) (Tavua) Sister of Matua (see House X) and of Kelera (see House IX)

F(U) (Sarowaqa) Married brother of Vaula's wife (see House VIII)

M(U) Keleivi (Rokowaqa)
+F(C) (Nacula)

F(U) (Sarowaqa)
+M(C) (Sarowaqa)

longings are of meager quantity. Despite his control of Rokowaqa lands, his food resources are not abundant because, except for a few old banana trees and coconut groves, wild forest and wild pigs, Rokowaqa land is empty. He still owns fifteen banana trees in Naicadra's Nadroro land, but most of his gardens adjoin the section of Votua land which has been given over to Nabadua's use. This land, which is called Spring Water, lies at the source of the stream which waters Nairoro. In the great cluster of taro ponds of the Tavua people, Raitova has built two new ponds. Six more small ponds, which are near the place where the stream bubbles from the ground, are filled with ripened taro. Along the bed of Spring Water he has planted kava and taro, The few banana trees which grow above the stream are his. Near his six small taro ponds he has a dry garden which bears yams, kava, dry taro, and more banana trees. He also has a few stalks of pandanus from which his daughters plait mats.

Raitova's two older daughters have both been discontented in their father's house and fled the village to live with kinsmen in the Dreketi region. Though neither has married, each has borne a child. The child of the eldest, the seven-year-old Karalai, lives in Raitova's household and is favored by all the adults. She is small for her years, but she is lithe and swift. Like her mother's sisters, when embarrassed, she turns her head with a shy laugh and bites her fingers.

Raitova's two younger daughters live in their father's household. But sometimes in fits of temper they flee to join their sisters in the Dreketi region. The elder, the graceful Ivamere, who wore virgin's coiffure until she was involved in a scandal which rocked the village in November and December, 1935, is known for her industry and virtue. For several years she has performed all woman's work for her household and found time besides to plait many mats and plant foodstuffs. But the younger sister is giddy and not dependable; though her virgin's curls were already shorn in 1936, she persists in wasting her time in play with the younger children. The young men still regard her as a child; Ivamere tries to discipline her so that she will someday learn to work. Ivamere was born about 1914. The foolish sister is perhaps three years her junior. Sometimes Raitova's house is spoken of as Ivamere's. Young people like to entertain their guests there because Ivamere is a generous hostess. When there are no guests, the young women gather there to make mats together. Frequently they stay all night.

Near the taro ponds of her father, Ivamere has planted a small patch of manioc. Aside from the noble Di Merelita and Di Sereima, who did not plant their own gardens, Ivamere is the only unmarried girl to have shown such industry. Naicadra's daughter Meremanini also has a garden, but the men of Nadroro helped her plant; her household chores are fewer than Ivamere's.

Raitova's elder son of fifteen years, whose voice has barely changed, is already known as lazy like his father. When the other boys of the village built small taro ponds for themselves at Nairoro, he was not among them. Raitova's younger son, who is eight or nine, lives at the district school at Lekutu.

Keleivi is Raitova's "small brother." Though he looks much older than Namo, it is said that he is younger—not yet thirty. Late in 1935 he married a woman of Nacula. It was not until several months later that he brought her to Nakoroka. He is tall and sturdily built but, like Raitova, is slow. Though the food from his gardens helped to feed Raitova's household, Keleivi slept in the church with other unattached men until he was married; but, when he brought his wife to Nakoroka, he shared with her the bed and the best mosquito net in Raitova's house. Both Keleivi's parents were of Sarowaqa, but he came to Nakoroka with Raitova to become a member of Naicadra's Nadroro group. Then through Raitova he was permitted claims in Rokowaqa land and has finally been absorbed by Votua. Among the taro ponds of the Tavua people at Spring Water, Keleivi has built two new ponds. Near Raitova's six ponds, Keleivi has two old ponds which are overgrown with weeds. In Naicadra's Nadroro land he has three patches of taro which are planted in swampland (*lau-levu*) and poorly cared for. A little farther from the village he has a few banana and papaya trees and a small patch of dry taro and corn. In distant Rokowaqa land he has a few coconuts and bananas. Keleivi is famous in the village for his deep sleep; he lies all night in whatever position he has dozed off and cannot be roused.

Samu, who is a widower and the brother of Vatili's wife Losana, also has claims on Rokowaqa land and on Raitova's household; he is Raitova's "small brother." He is about thirty-five years old. When his mother died, he and the aged Unuwale gave their house to the king of Inland Forest and disbanded their household. Unuwale went to Nabadua's house, and Samu joined Raitova. Samu's son, who is about fourteen years old, usually stays with his father as a member of Raitova's house; but Samu's daughter, who was born about 1931, lives with Vatili's wife. Both Samu and his son visit frequently in Vatili's house. Samu has planted a yam garden next to Vatili's in Vilomena's

division of Nadroro. Near a banana grove of Vatili's, Samu has planted a small patch of manioc; he is the only man in the village to own a
garden devoted exclusively to this food. Through his father, Samu has
bonds with the Votua people; he has two groves of coconuts of about
forty trees each in Toviya's Votua land; along Little Water he has
built eight or ten new ponds. Though still young in appearance, he is
rapidly growing fat. He learns the routine of dances with greater ease
than anyone else in the village.

With four other boys, Samu's fourteen-year-old son has built a
small taro pond just above Nairoro in Votua land.

HOUSE VI

Naicadra's house is almost as large as that of Big Di Litiya, but its
foundation is not so high. Built as a meeting-house in which the men
of the village could discuss co-operative enterprises without suffering
the embarrassment and restraint which descends upon them in the
houses of chiefs, it is also convenient as a place to house official guests
who are not of chiefly caste. It is an honor for Naicadra to preside over
a house of such importance to the village. The house is well furnished,
and in its upper regions there are many baskets and boxes. To accommodate guests, it is well supplied with mosquito nets. Naicadra and his
family prefer to reserve the bed for guests, while they themselves sleep
in a single long mosquito net which they hang lengthwise in the house.
But the kitchen is inconveniently situated and badly in need of repair.
The invalid Waseroma occupies most of it, so that cooking for guests
must frequently be performed in the open.

Many years ago Naicadra's father, who was of chiefly caste, gave
the title for all Nadroro land to Vilomena's chiefly father. Though she
was considering a return of the title to Naicadra, Vilomena was still
holding it at the time of her death. But Naicadra is in permanent possession of the title to the half of Nadroro Valley which rises from the
far bank of Nadroro River. He fulfils his office well, and men like to
plant in his land under his direction, although, of all garden land, it is
most distant from the village. Naicadra's own gardens are productive.
Along the path to his land one comes first to two of his taro ponds and
a patch of taro planted in swampy ground next to Keleivi's. Farther
along, past the gardens of other Nadroro people, Naicadra has three
small patches of kava and a large tract of swamp planted with taro.
Near by there are a few bananas, mingled with those of Keleivi's,
which Naicadra calls his (see Map VI).

MAP VI

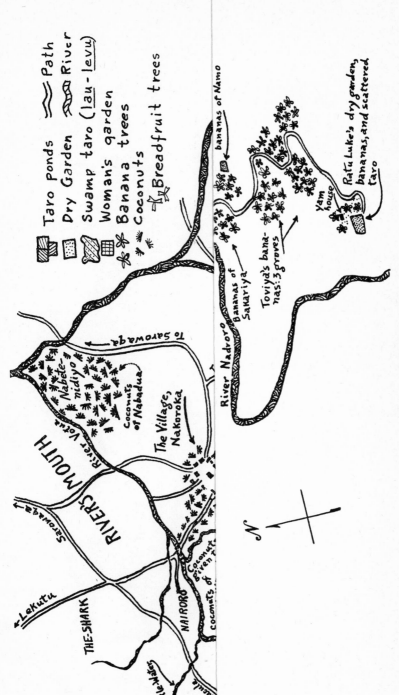

Taro ponds — Path
Dry Garden ≈ River
Swamp taro (lau-levu)
Woman's garden
Banana trees
Coconuts
Breadfruit trees

To Sarowaqa →
← Lekutu
THE SHARK
Little Waters →
RIVER'S MOUTH
River Votua
← Sarowaqa
Nabete-nidiyo
Coconuts of Nabadua
NAIRORO
The Village, Nakoroka
Coconuts of seven ...
Coconuts of ...

N

River Nadroro
Bananas of Sakariya
Toviyo's bananas: 3 groves
bananas of Namo
yam house
Ratu Luke's dry garden, bananas, and scattered taro

Chart of Nadroro Gardens

CHART VI
House VI

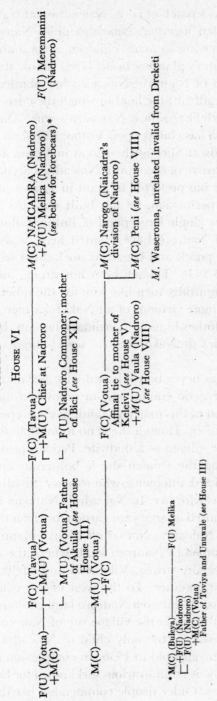

F(U) (Votua) —— F(C) (Tavua) —— F(C) (Tavua) —— M(C) NAICADRA (Nadroro) —— F(U) Meremanini
+M(C)   ⌐+M(U) (Votua)   ⌐+M(U) (Votua) Chief at Nadroro   +F(U) Melika (Nadroro)   (Nadroro)
                              │   (see below for forebears) *

             └ M(U) (Votua) Father └ F(U) (Votua) Nadroro Commoner; mother
               of Akuila (see House   of Bici (see House XII)
               House III)

M(C) —— M(U) (Votua)   F(C) (Votua)   M(C) Narogo (Naicadra's   M(C) Peni (see House VIII)
     +F(C)   Affinal tie to mother of   division of Nadroro)
                       Keleivi (see House V)
                       +M(U) Vaula (Nadroro)
                       (see House VIII)

                                                  M. Waseroma, unrelated invalid from Dreketi

*M(C) (Buleya) —— F(U) Melika
 ⌐+F(U) (Nadroro)
 └+F(U) (Nadroro)
  +M(C) (Votua)
  Father of Toviya and Unuwale (see House III)

Above Keleivi's patch of corn, Naicadra and Namo have planted a large yam garden together. Naicadra pities Namo for being son to Nabadua and having so many children at such an early age; he has encouraged Namo's planting in his land. Across the river Nadroro in Vilomena's half of Nadroro, Naicadra has planted a small grove of oranges and breadfruit; the land in which these trees grow is spoken of as that of Big Melika, who is Naicadra's wife. Through his mother's father, Naicadra has claims upon Votua. The land which adjoins Toviya's taro ponds at Slice-of-the-Moon in Votua and contains Isacodro's extensive grove of coconuts is Naicadra's according to this claim. But in Votua he has preferred to plant in a more convenient location; with Bulisivo's permission, he has built ten taro ponds along Little Water below the single large pond of Bulisivo. But they are not well kept. Others of Nadroro have planted here as well. At Nairoro he built four large ponds and began to stock them with taro during the early months of 1936. Though he is not strong, and though his conversation is unamusing, men like him for the quietness of his disposition. He is the most virtuous of all Nakoroka men. He is almost fifty years old. He clothes himself in ordinary fashion, but he has the only pair of spectacles at Nakoroka; he wears them when he speaks in church.

Big Melika has never been pleased with her marriage to Naicadra. She was an energetic young woman renowned for her beauty. Her parents approved of this marriage, and, like a proper daughter, she respected their wishes. Though she is no more than forty, she is already renowned in the village as a midwife. People speak of her as a "wise woman." Among the women she is boisterous and well liked. She pitied the disfigured Vilomena, who was her "small sister," and planted many gardens with her. In Naicadra's Natovoli land their kinsmen from Nacula planted a large yam garden for them near the three small kava patches of Naicadra. Not far off Melika planted a small patch of manioc. In Vilomena's Nadroro land, where the claims of Melika's mother are especially strong, Vilomena and Melika planted another patch of manioc together. To the west of the village, Melika has a grove of coconuts; in this area Nadroro land extends all the way to the river Votua and includes the village site of Nakoroka.

Meremanini, who is the only child of Naicadra and Melika, was perhaps nineteen years old in 1936. In complexion darker than either of her parents, she is an industrious girl known for her wisdom in dealing with property. Older people commended her thoughtful planting of tobacco and her restraint in consuming the ripened product; she took a quantity of it to the windward coast, where the climate is too wet for tobacco, and sold it there for a fine price. Meremanini does not visit about in foreign villages like the daughters of Isacodro. She stays home in the evenings and plaits mats. Her virtue depends in part upon her figure, which is much too fat. And Peni, who is her "small father," takes pleasure in her fine reputation and insists that she keep it so. She has a garden next to Peni's in Naicadra's division of Nadroro land. Its products are more diverse than any other woman's garden. It contains yams, but she did not plant these herself; Peni assists her in her gardening. The bananas and papaya which grow in her garden are hers, but she has no groves of coconut.

Narogo, brother of Peni and son of Vaula, is also part of Naicadra's household. Perhaps thirty-three years old, he is Naicadra's younger "small brother." He sleeps with the young men in the church or in some kitchen where they have been singing or drinking kava, but his few extra *sulu*'s and his tobacco, on the rare occasions when he has any, are stored in Naicadra's house. Narogo will never marry because he is so lazy. Though a few years ago Peni insisted that he allow the native medical practitioner to circumcise him, Narogo is still known as uncircumcised, and the women laugh behind his back. He takes no interest in dancing and has never courted girls. For food he depends upon Naicadra's household. He wears the cast-off clothing of his younger brother Peni. In Vilomena's Nadroro land he has a small dry garden of taro, which Peni keeps clean, and a poorly maintained yam garden. He built three very small taro ponds at Nairoro, but many months passed, and he neglected to plant taro in them. In Toviya's Votua land he shares with Peni the ownership of a grove of forty coconuts.

Though there are few people who are permanent members in Naicadra's household, his house frequently contains a guest. When the young mission teacher came to the village, he lived with Naicadra until a house of his own could be prepared for him; for several months he continued to eat in Naicadra's kitchen. Naicadra and Melika distribute their food generously among less fortunate neighbors. He has adopted Vaulini's two children, Care and Vikatoria, and the fatherless daughter of Namo's wife; these children, when they grow older, will plant gardens in his land and spend more time in his household.

The invalid Waseroma, who came to Nakoroka many years ago with a group of wandering young men, took up residence in Naicadra's kitchen and has never departed. He has no kinsmen at Nakoroka. Paralyzed, because yaws has made lesions in his spinal cord, he has lain helpless ever since his arrival. Naicadra would hardly claim him as a member of the household, but Melika and Meremanini give him food. On rare occasion Naicadra has given him a fresh *sulu*. When the odor of his filth becomes too oppressive, Melika or Meremanini douse him with a bucket of water.

HOUSE VII

Vatili's house is nearly as large as Raitova's, but its foundation is not so fine. It is well supplied with mats and utensils. Though Vatili's resources are not great, his family is always adequately clothed. His new kitchen, which was built while he, as "village chief," was foreman among the housebuilders, is larger than Isacodro's sleeping-house and quite as well constructed. If Vilomena had not died, she would have been permanently situated in the kitchen with her two children. While his own house was awaiting repairs, he moved his family into the kitchen and lived comfortably there. He and his wife Losana share the bed in the upper part of the house and the largest mosquito net. At the foot of the raised platform, which is their bed, he has prepared a place for his mother to sleep—several new mats spread upon a heavy mattress of fern.

According to government records, Vatili was born in 1900. He still looks young, but his long terms as "village chief" have softened his muscles. During 1935 and 1936 he grew fat. Until his quarrel with Losana in May, 1936, his strongest kin bond outside his own household was with Samu, his cross-cousin (brother-in-law). Though he called Vilomena "sister," she was actually the daughter of his maternal grandmother's sister. It is through his mother's brother, recently dead, that he gains his claims in Nadroro land. But these are not strong. His father was of Great Meadow Kingdom. His mother's ties with Nadroro are maternal only; her father was also of a foreign kingdom. In the distant region of Vilomena's division of Nadroro he has planted a yam garden next to Samu's, but his tasks as "village chief" consume his time so that he cannot weed it properly. A little closer to the village he has eight or ten taro ponds which a cross-cousin from Nacula built during a sojourn at Vatili's house. He also has a small grove of coconuts and a hundred luxuriant banana trees.

Vatili's wife Losana has sound claims in Rokowaqa land in Raitova's household. She has some old coconut and banana trees in distant Rokowaqa, but since her marriage she has spent her efforts in Vatili's gardens. Sometimes, too, she assists her brother Samu. No food

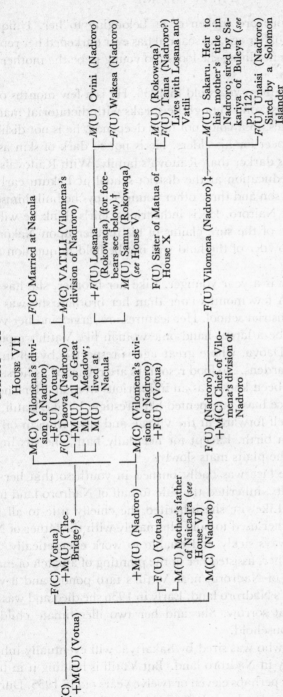

CHART VII
HOUSE VII

F(C) (Votua)
+M(U) (Votua)

F(C) (Votua)
+M(U) (The-Bridge)*

M(C) (Vilomena's division of Nadroro)
+F(U) (Votua)

F(C) Daova (Nadroro)
+M(U) All of Great Meadow;
M(U) lived at Nacula
M(U)

F(C) Married at Nacula

M(C) VATILI (Vilomena's division of Nadroro)

+F(U) Losana (Rokowaqa) (for foro-bears see below)†
M(U) Samu Rokowaqa) (see House V)

F(U) Sister of Matua of House X

M(U) Ovini (Nadroro)

F(U) Wakesa (Nadroro)

M(U) (Rokowaqa)
F(U) Taina (Nadroro?)
Lives with Losana and Vatili

M(C) (Vilomena's division of Nadroro)
+F(U) (Votua)

+M(U) (Nadroro)

L M(U) Mother's father of Naicadra (see House VI)
M(C) (Nadroro)

F(U) Vilomena (Nadroro)
+M(C) Chief of Vilomena's division of Nadroro

F(U) (Nadroro)

M(U) Sakaru. Heir to his mother's title in Nadroro; sired by Sakariya of Buleya (see p. 112)
F(U) Unaisi (Nadroro) Sired by a Solomon Islander

F(U) Vilomena (Nadroro)‡

F(C) (Votua)
+M(C)
F(U) Mother's mother of Unu-wale (see House III)

F(U) (Rokowaqa)
+M(C)
F(U) Mother's mother of (see House III)

F(C) (Votua)
+M(U) (Nakalou)

F(U) (Rokowaqa)

+M(C) (Votua)
F(C)
+M(U) (Nakalou)

F(U) Losana (Rokowaqa)

+M(C) (Votua)

+M(U) (Nakalou) (When Samu fled from Nakoroka, these "parents" in Nakalou accepted him as one of their family. They belong to a group which traces descent from Nadroro. When they come to Nakoroka, they feel at home in Vatili's house.)

* The-Bridge belongs to Wainunu Kingdom. This man was one of those who fled to The-Bath after the last act of defiance of the power of Bua and Great Britain. See pp. 45–48 and 54.

† F(U) Losana (Rokowaqa)

‡ Although Vilomena was of opposite moiety, Vatili chose to call her "sister."

resources in Nadroro are spoken of as belonging to her. Uniquely among the women of her age, no scandal has ever darkened her reputation. Though she is not lithe, she looks too young to be the mother of a fifteen-year-old son.

Vatili's son was fifteen years old in 1935. He is a few months older than Raitova's oldest son. Though he speaks with dictatorial manner among his age-mates, in a voice not fully deepened, he is not disliked. He has proper respect for his elders. He is not so dark of skin as his father, but yet he is darker than Raitova's family. With Raitova's son he completed his education at the district school at Lekutu early in 1936. With Samu's son and three other younger boys he built himself a small taro pond at Nairoro. He is industrious. Girls think he will be handsome. Because of the sure claims of his mother upon Nakoroka land, his status as owner of the land will not be held in question as is that of his father.

Vatili's daughter is a year younger. Like her brother, she has just reached puberty. A few months later than her brother, she was discharged from the district school. Her features are large, and her voice is hoarse. She will be a large, handsome woman like Vatili's mother.

Vatili's mother Daova, whose great age is respected by all in the village, plants no gardens. No food resources are regarded as hers. But in the past she has been known as an industrious woman. Her knowledge and intelligence have augmented her prestige. Unlike Vatili, she did not thrust herself forward in the village and risk criticism on the score of her foreign birth. Except for her daily bath, she sits in the house; sometimes she plaits mats slowly.

Vilomena, whose face was badly burned in youth so that her appearance excited pity, inherited the title to half of Nadroro land from her chiefly father. Likewise she inherited the chiefly title to all Nadroro which her father used to hold alternately with the father of Naicadra. She was always sickly and unable to work energetically. But Melika, who pitied her, assisted her in the planting of a patch of manioc in her own half of Nadroro, near Vatili's taro ponds, and a yam garden in Naicadra's Nadroro land. Early in 1936 she died and was not mourned with great sorrow. She and her two illegitimate children crowded Vatili's household.

Her son Sakaru, who was sired by Sakariya, will eventually inherit her title to authority in Nadroro land. But Vatili is holding it in trust for him. Sakaru was perhaps eleven or twelve years old in 1935. During 1936 he grew tremendously and showed signs of puberty late in the year. But he is sickly like his mother. People say that he will die of the same disease. Men say that he talks too freely and fear that he may grow up to be a troublemaker like his father. His "soul is mature" for his age. He planted a small taro pond next to that of Vatili's son. He still attends the district school, but until his mother's death he came to Nakoroka on frequent visits.

Vilomena's daughter Unaisi is perhaps nine years old. Unaisi's head was shaped poorly in infancy, and people laugh about her ugliness. Her mind is not well developed, and, though her unbridled chattering amuses other children, she is often the butt of their jokes. People say that her father was a wandering Solomon Islander. No food resources are spoken of as hers.

Samu used to bring food to Vatili's house before Vatili quarreled with Losana. Samu's daughter is truly part of the household. She calls Vatili "father" and demands that he hold her in his arms every night until she falls asleep. She sleeps in the same mosquito net with Vatili and Losana.

Vaula and Peni eat frequently at Vatili's house, but they are more properly a part of Orisi's household, which is next door. Peni dislikes Vatili and resents the suggestion that they are of the same household.

HOUSE VIII

Orisi's house is slightly smaller than Vatili's and in bad repair. The foundation is lower, but his wife has carefully landscaped the door-ways with shrubs. Before a kitchen was built for them in 1936, they cooked on the hearth in the sleeping-house or in Vatili's kitchen. Orisi and Vaula, who share Orisi's house, are of Vilomena's Nadroro group. The lot of Orisi's wife has been difficult because she has no sisters at Nakoroka and Orisi's sisters have not accepted her whole-heartedly. Though she is not lazy, her house is inadequately supplied with mats. Her three small children are not well clothed. Utensils and tools in the house are poor. Orisi's is the poorest of Nakoroka's families. But, instead of attacking the problem of his poverty by planting in his own lands and gaining respect in the village, he prefers to live among the Indians and work for a wage. During long periods Orisi takes his family to live among the Indians and work in their rice fields. From the Indians he has learned something about the care of domestic animals. In payment for his work, the Indians gave him a horse to ride and a yearling heifer.

Men who are not of Nadroro say that Orisi is a fool. He is extremely

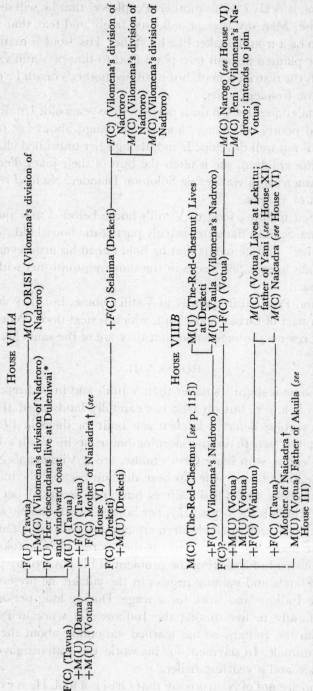

CHART VIII

House VIIIA

M(U) ORISI (Vilomena's division of Nadroro)

F(U) (Tavua)
+M(C) (Vilomena's division of Nadroro)
F(U) Her descendants live at Duleniwai* and windward coast
M(U) (Tavua)
+F(C) (Tavua)
F(C) Mother of Naicadra† (see House VI)
F(C) (Dreketi)
+M(U) (Dreketi)

+F(C) Selaima (Dreketi)

F(C) (Vilomena's division of Nadroro)
M(C) (Vilomena's division of Nadroro)
M(C) (Vilomena's division of Nadroro)

M(C) Narogo (see House VI)
M(C) Peni (Vilomena's Nadroro; intends to join Votua)

F(C) (Tavua)
+M(U) (Dama)
+M(U) (Votua)

House VIIIB

M(U) (The-Red-Chestnut) Lives at Dreketi
M(U) Vaula (Vilomena's Nadroro)
+F(C) (Votua)

M(C) (Votua) Lives at Lekutu; father of Yani (see House XI)
M(C) Naicadra (see House VI)

M(C) (The-Red-Chestnut [see p. 115])
+F(U) (Vilomena's Nadroro)
F(C)?
+M(U) (Votua)
M(U) (Votua)
+F(C) (Wainunu)

+F(C) (Tavua)
Mother of Naicadra†
M(U) (Votua) Father of Akuila (see House III)

* These descendants at Duleniwai attended the marriage feast of Vaulini and Sireli. Many of them stayed in the house of Orisi, but they were related more directly to Monasa and Nabadua.

† Mother of Naicadra appears twice in this chart.

A SMALL HOUSEHOLD IN SUNDAY CLOTHES

timid, but he is given to committing rash acts; once he crossed Buli-sivo. Though he is spoken of as head of his household, he has no voice among the village men. Short of stature but strongly built, he is per-haps thirty years old. In the most distant part of Vilomena's land he has planted his yam garden. Nearer the village, in the region of the gardens of Peni and Vaula, he has many banana trees. This central portion of Vilomena's Nadroro land is spoken of as his, and the un-claimed trees which grow in it are his. Near Peni's garden there are four breadfruit trees. In a small banana grove he has some dry taro which is overgrown with weeds. According to government records, the land upon which the village itself is built belongs to Orisi and Vaula, and thus Orisi considers the coconuts which grow about the village to be his own private property. But it has long been customary for each family to use the trees which grow nearest; hence Orisi's claim is un-heeded. The coconuts which grow along the path to Nadroro gardens are spoken of as his. Though his ties with Votua are very remote, he has built six or eight taro ponds at Little Water in Bulisivo's land.

In the central region of Vilomena's Nadroro, in the land which is spoken of as her husband's, Orisi's wife Selaima has planted a patch of sweet potatoes. A little nearer the village among her husband's ba-nanas and ill-kept taro she has planted some pandanus for mats. But no land, coconuts, or bananas are spoken of as hers. She is a for-eigner.

Of their three children, the oldest is perhaps six. All are badly in-fected with yaws. Lacking the co-operation of the women of the village, the children are poorly cared for. Like their mother, their heads were poorly shaped in infancy, and they will all grow up to be ugly. During Selaima's confinement, Melika, who is Naicadra's wife and lives in the big house next door, assisted as midwife and for several months prepared meals.

When Orisi lives in the village, Vaula and Peni share his household and eat at his food mat. When he is away, they join Vilomena in Vatili's house. Neither of them has mosquito nets. But Vaula, who is about fifty years old, is a man of the old school who needs no modern comforts, and Peni likes to sleep about the village. Vaula's mother was a woman of Vilomena's division of Nadroro. She married a man of the village called The-Red-Chestnut in Macuata and lived there until her death. Vaula did not come to Nakoroka to reside until his marriage. He has lived quietly and worked leisurely, at a pace far beyond his years. Men say that he is good, because he has never tried to assert his

voice among them. Though he is not a man of the church, he is friendly
with Bici and Naicadra. He is the hairiest man in the village. In the
central region of Vilomena's Nadroro, he has a luxuriant grove of
seventy-five banana trees among which he has planted kava, manioc,
dry taro, and tomatoes. With the help of Peni, whose own garden lies
near by, he has kept this region well weeded. Near the yam gardens of
Narogo and Orisi, in the most distant region of Vilomena's land, he
also has a yam garden. But Peni has not assisted him here, and his
yams are choked with weeds. Some of the coconuts along the path near
the village are spoken of as his. He also plants in Naicadra's division of
Nadroro. His dead wife was bound to Naicadra by devious biological
ties; they called each other "sibling" (see Chart VI). In swampy land
he has planted two careless patches of taro among some scattered
banana trees which are spoken of as his. But Vaula's wife was more
closely bound with Votua; among the taro ponds at Little Water
Vaula has built four. At Nairoro he has also built two new ones, but
these are not yet planted.

Peni, unlike his father or lazy elder brother, is an energetic workman. Born about 1910, he is strong and very dark of skin. He planned
to marry Lebu in 1936 and establish a household of his own. He has
many gardens. In the central part of Vilomena's Nadroro land he has
a small dry garden of taro next to Narogo's. Below Vaula's garden in
the same region he has a grove of fifty bananas and another well-kept
dry garden of taro; joining the taro garden there are six taro ponds,
and below these, where the land is swampy, he has planted more taro.
In Naicadra's Nadroro land, next to the garden of Naicadra's daughter, he has a large garden of yams and divers dry-garden products;
Vaula, who had formerly used this land, persuaded Peni to plant it.
Near by Peni has planted some kava among a few banana trees which
are also his. Through his mother he has claims also in Votua land. In
Toviya's section of Votua he shares a grove of forty coconut trees with
Narogo. Among the taro ponds in Bulisivo's land at Little Water he has
built more than ten ponds which he keeps well stocked with growing
taro. Peni is proud of his gardens and will extend his planting as he
grows older. Except for Ratu Luke, he is the most skilled of huntsmen.
But he is timid and dares not raise his voice.

HOUSE IX

Nabadua's house is as large as Bulisivo's. It is smaller than Naicadra's, but it was built for Nabadua's use and not as a public house for

village meetings. Though the tools and utensils which it contains are old and broken and its atmosphere is shabby, still Nabadua takes great pride in it. Nabadua and Kelera sleep comfortably on the large bed behind which the family clothing is stored. In the lower part of the house Nabadua's many children sleep. His oldest daughter, however, usually sleeps in the house of her brother Namo. A large kitchen was newly built for Nabadua in 1935. It is not so large as Vatili's, but it serves amply as an eating-house; several persons can sleep comfortably in it.

Nabadua has always been energetic, but his extravagance has exhausted his large resources. In 1935 and 1936 he was so harassed with deaths and sickness in his family that he had little time for planting. He is about fifty years old. He inherited his title to chiefship in Tavua land through his father and chooses to remember no other caste affiliation but those with his father's chiefly caste. His mother was of Nadroro through her father and of Rokowaqa through her mother. Since the garden lands of Tavua are far from the present village site, it has been convenient for the people of Tavua to plant in Votua land. The chiefs of Votua have given over the fertile slope at Spring Water for the exclusive use of the Tavua people (see Map V). Nabadua controls the planting of this area, and the land is spoken of as his. Four of the many taro ponds there are his. They are very large and located in the best region near the top of the slope; but they were completely emptied of their products early in 1936. Near the source of Spring Water, in the region of Raitova's bananas, Nabadua has inserted a few taro stalks among the rocks of the stream bed (*vatui*). In the land called Nairoro, he has one large pond, but this is not yet fully stocked with taro. He is well supplied with coconuts and bananas. There are luxuriant groves of nuts at the site of the old Tavua village, Nabetenidiyo, which lies in the point of land made by the joining of the rivers Votua and Tavua. In more distant regions of Tavua land there are additional groves of coconuts and bananas which are his.

Nabadua's third and present wife, Kelera, was born soon after 1900. A swollen thyroid gland makes her neck bulge, and she is languid. Nevertheless, despite her many children, she has found time to plant a garden of manioc and various garnishes among the gardens of the Votua women. Kelera's hereditary claims are exclusively in Tavua, but she was formerly the wife of Akuila's brother, now dead, who was of Votua. Her garden is next to that of Viniyana, who is Bulisivo's wife and Akuila's sister; they are cross-cousins (sisters-in-law). In the land

CHART IX

House IX

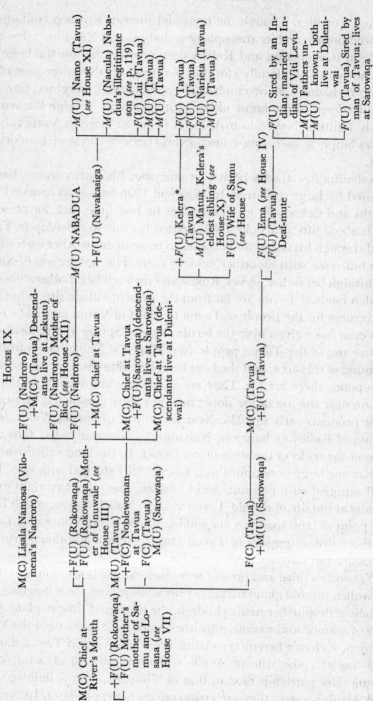

* Kelera was at the time of her marriage to Nabadua the widow of Akuila's brother (see House III). Their child was the girl Radebu (U) (Voiua), now dead.

of Monasa, who is Kelera's "small brother," she has planted some pandanus for mats. But Kelera is not skilled at plaiting.

Kelera's daughter by the earlier marriage was Radebu, who died at the age of twenty-one in 1937. Among the young women she was notorious for her sexual vigor. Unlike her mother, who is tall and spare, she was sturdily built and heavy. Her complexion was darker than that of Nabadua's family. Through her father, Radebu had claims in Toviya's Votua land, but only five coconut trees were spoken of as hers. She was given to wandering and rarely assisted her mother with the chores of Nabadua's household. Sometimes she lived with Monasa and his wife, to whom she was related through her mother.

Of the four children who have issued from Nabadua's marriage with Kelera, the oldest is a girl who had almost reached puberty in 1936. Though she has not completed her term at the district school, Nabadua kept her at home for several months to assist Kelera and was fined before the provincial court for her truancy. A younger girl lives at the district school. Narieta, who was perhaps eight years old in 1936, still stayed at home and accompanied Nabadua on his excursions to the forest for wild pigs and yams. The youngest is an infant son.

The children of Nabadua's former marriage with Namo's mother are all residents of Nakoroka. Four are still living. Namo, who is the eldest, has a household of his own and plants gardens in Nabadua's land. Lui, who was born about 1912, frequently lives with Namo's household. She has no food resources in her own name. The third oldest child is a son who was born about 1916; in 1935 and 1936 he spent long periods at the mines to assist his father and elder brother with their taxes and fines. He has planted no gardens. Nabadua's youngest son by this marriage is perhaps fourteen years old; he is an age-mate of the eldest son of Raitova and the son of Vatili, but he as yet shows no signs of puberty. With four other boys he has planted a small taro pond for himself at Nairoro. Between the births of Namo and Lui, a Nacula woman bore a son of Nabadua's; this young man lives at Nacula and claims rights only in his mother's land.

Nabadua's microcephalic "small sister" also shares a lowly place in his household. Though she brings firewood and assists Kelera in the making of mats, she is incapable of filling a social role. Since birth she has been deaf and dumb. She has borne several children who were sired by men of the village of Duleniwai. These children plant in Du-

leniwai land; but, when they come to Nakoroka, they stop at Nabadua's house.

Bici's father likes to sleep in Nabadua's kitchen because it is more
comfortable than Bici's dilapidated house. It is his father's strong bond
with Tavua land which prevents Bici from deserting Nabadua and
joining Naicadra.

HOUSE X

Monasa's house neighbors Nabadua's. It is small but firmly constructed. In 1935 Monasa moved his possessions into the kitchen and
allowed Kelera to live in his sleeping-house.[10] Soon afterward he built
a house near his gardens in the land of his wife which lies beyond Nabadua's jurisdiction. Thenceforth Nabadua used Monasa's house to
accommodate guests. Nabadua's children and members of Isacodro's
crowded household frequently sleep in it.

Monasa is lean and lightly built and is one of the few Fijians whose
faces are clean of hair. He does not have to shave. Though he is at
least as old as Nabadua, his hair is not grizzled, and most of his teeth
still remain in their sockets. He is not sociable and rarely participates
in co-operative enterprises. Though the utensils of his house are poor,
his gardens are by far the most luxuriant in the village, and he is constantly engaged in their cultivation. He has claims upon Nabadua's
Tavua land; he is Nabadua's "small brother." Among the Tavua taro
ponds at Spring Water he has three taro ponds which are still producing. In 1934 he abandoned a large number of ponds in that region, and
they may still be seen, now choked with weeds. He prefers to plant in
his wife's land, which belongs to River's Mouth Kingdom and begins
just across a small valley from Spring Water. This region is called The-
Shark, and it is here that Monasa has built his new house. He has
planted a large dry garden of taro near by. Down the valley slope his
extensive banana groves begin and grow luxuriantly throughout the
land which he cultivates. With his "small brother" Matua, who is a
widower and spends most of his time at the gold mine,[11] Monasa has
built twenty or more taro ponds and stocked them well. On the banks
between the ponds he has planted kava. In the swampy land below the
ponds he has planted more taro and a small garden of kava. Toward
Sarowaqa he has developed another region for extensive taro cultivation. It is said that these gardens are even more luxuriant that those at

10. For Kelera's separation from Nabadua see below, pp. 374–77.
11. He is the true brother of Nabadua's wife, Kelera.

The-Shark. Near the village of Sarowaqa itself, he has devoted much labor to gardens which are spoken of as his wife's.[12]

Monasa's wife is also an energetic gardener. Aside from the assistance which she gives Monasa, she has planted a large garden of manioc, kava, and papaya trees among Monasa's bananas. Though the women do not regard her as good company, they admire her industry. She is not pretty. She works hard at plaiting mats. Her habit of interrupting Monasa and finishing his sentences for him is a joke in the village.

CHART X

House X

```
┌─F(U) (Nadroro) Affinal bond with
│    father's mother of Vilomena (see House VII)
└─F(U) (Nadroro)──    F(U) (Sarowaqa)—M(U) MONASA
   +M(C) (Saro-    ┌─ +M(C) (Tavua)      (Tavua)
     waqa)         │                      ┌ +F(C) (Sarowaqa)—┌─M(C) (Tavua
                   │  F(C) (Sarowaqa)—└    F(C) (The-Red-    ├─F(C)   and
                   │                        Chestnut) *      └─M(C)   Saro-
                   │  +M(U) (Saro-                                    waqa)
                   │    waqa)
                   │
                   └    M(C) (Tavua)    ┌─  M(U) (Tavua)
                        +F(U) (Ta-      │   +F(C) (Dre-
                          vua)          │     keti)────────M(U) (Tavua)
                                        │     Sister of Rai-
                                        │     tova's wife
                                        │     (see House V)
                                        ├─  F(U) Kelera (Ta-
                                        │     vua) (see House
                                        │     IX)
                                        ├─  F(U) Wife of Samu
                                        │     (see House V)
                                        └─  M(U) (Tavua)
                                              Formerly betrothed
                                              to Ivamere of
                                              House V
```

* The village of Peni's father (see House VIII).

Monasa's eldest son,[13] who is perhaps eleven years old, is one of the boys who planted the five small taro ponds above Nairoro in Votua land. His other two children, a nine-year-old girl and a seven-year-old boy, attend the district school at Lekutu.

Monasa's "small brother" Matua, who is about thirty-five years old, lives in Monasa's household during his sojourns at Nakoroka. He sleeps in the church with the unattached young men. Below Monasa's

12. Monasa is the only man at Nakoroka who plants extensively in foreign villages. But this practice is not uncommon. Four taro ponds at Nairoro were planted by residents of Sarowaqa who have claims upon Votua land. Higher along the river Votua there is one more. In Nabadua's land at Spring Water there are at least thirty ponds and five banana trees which belong to Sarowaqa residents who have claims upon Tavua.

13. A much older son died several years ago.

gardens at The-Shark he has built a tremendous taro pond among a grove of sixty banana trees which are his. (Though there is no natural boundary between this area and Monasa's ponds at The-Shark, this land belongs to Votua.) He also has a yam garden next to Raitova's near the source of the stream which waters the ponds at The-Shark. Among the Tavua ponds at Spring Water he has a pond which is still producing and one which is exhausted. Matua's gardening depends on his association with Monasa; he himself does not choose to participate in life at Nakoroka. He has a ten-year-old son who attends the district school at Lekutu. He has separated from his wife, who is of a foreign village.

Matua's younger full brother, who is between twenty-five and thirty years of age, is also part of Monasa's household. But he has lived at the mine for several years. Though he comes home for the feasts of Christmas and New Year's, he does not plant gardens. He is clever at cards and gambles for a living among the workmen at the mine. For several years he was betrothed to Raitova's daughter Ivamere, but their agreement was dissolved in 1935.

HOUSE XI

Namo's house is larger than Vatili's and built on a loftier foundation, but it is poorly equipped. Namo is too young to head so large a household. He is still dependent on Nabadua, and, now that poverty has descended on Nabadua, Namo suffers. His kitchen is dilapidated. During 1935 and 1936, when the sickness of Namo's eldest son disrupted the management of the household, Namo's family usually ate with Nabadua in the large kitchen which adjoins Nabadua's house. Namo's mother and all the children she has borne to Nabadua deem themselves a part of Namo's household; however, they feel at home in Nabadua's house.

Namo is past thirty, but he looks much younger. Though his skin is "red" and not "black," he is the darkest of Nabadua's children save his sister Lui. His mother comes from Navakasiga on the westernmost extension of the leeward coast. Her dialect differs from that of Inland Forest Kingdom; she speaks *t* and elides *k*. Namo was the first of Inland Forest children to speak the strange dialect which is today current among Nakoroka young people; from his mother he learned to elide *k;* like his father, he elides *t*. All subsequent children copied his phonetics. Namo is proud to be the youngest head of a household. He is proud of his large family, which is a badge of his virility. Like his father, he is proud of his claim upon the title to chiefship in Tavua land. When Nabadua dies, he will inherit this title.

During 1935 and 1936 Namo had little time to care for his gardens. They all became choked with weeds. In his father's land at Spring Water he has two taro ponds which were still producing and four which were empty. The few banana trees which grow on the banks between the ponds are also his. In Nairoro land, where everyone plants because it is easily available from the village, Namo has two partly consumed ponds and a banana tree, four ponds which are freshly planted, and one newly built pond which in June, 1936, had not yet been stocked with taro. Since his marriage with Yani, whom Naicadra regards as a sister, Naicadra has encouraged Namo's planting in

CHART XI

House XI

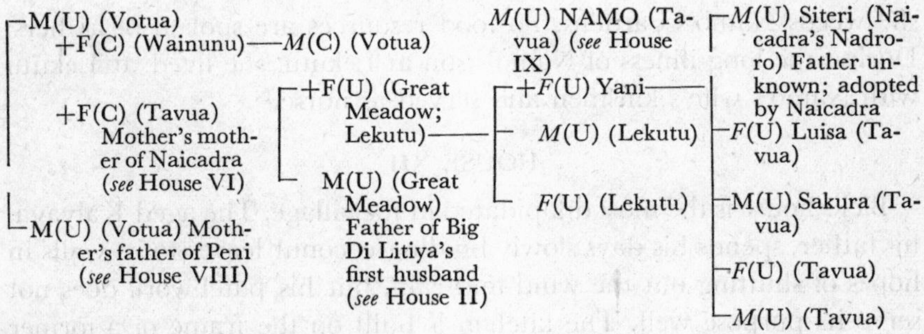

┌─M(U) (Votua)		M(U) NAMO (Ta-	┌─M(U) Siteri (Nai-
│ +F(C) (Wainunu)──M(C) (Votua)		vua) (see House	│ cadra's Nadro-
│		IX)	│ ro) Father un-
│	┌─+F(U) (Great	┌─+F(U) Yani──	│ known; adopted
│ +F(C) (Tavua)	│ Meadow;	│	│ by Naicadra
│ Mother's moth-	│ Lekutu)──	├─ M(U) (Lekutu)	├─F(U) Luisa (Ta-
│ er of Naicadra	│	│	│ vua)
│ (see House VI)	└─ M(U) (Great	│	│
│	Meadow)	└─ F(U) (Lekutu)	├─M(U) Sakura (Ta-
└─M(U) (Votua) Moth-	Father of Big		│ vua)
er's father of Peni	Di Litiya's		│
(see House VIII)	first husband		├─F(U) (Tavua)
	(see House II)		│
			└─M(U) (Tavua)

Nadroro land. Together, Namo and Naicadro planted a large yam garden there. Not far away a grove of Namo's banana trees lie scattered about a small garden of kava which is choked with weeds. Nearer the village Namo has another dry garden of yams and taro. Among the first cluster of gardens which one encounters on the path to Naicadra's garden land, there are two half-consumed taro ponds and some swampland planted with taro which are Namo's. All Namo's gardens are ill kept. He also shares the wealth of Tavua coconut groves with his father Nabadua.

By a distant and uncertain biologic tie, Namo's wife Yani is related to the maternal ancestors of Peni, who were of Votua. In Toviya's Votua land she has a grove of coconuts. With the women of Votua she has planted a garden of manioc and other supplementary foods. In Monasa's land called The-Shark she has planted some pandanus near those of Kelera. The languid Yani is becoming fat. Though she is no older than Namo, she looks staid and matronly.

Siteri, the oldest child whom Namo calls his, has been adopted by Naicadra. No one except Yani knows the name of her true father. But she usually eats with her half-brothers and half-sisters in Namo's household. She and Namo's next oldest daughter have attended the district school for several years. In 1935 they were perhaps ten and eleven years of age.

Namo's eldest son, who was about seven, died in 1936. His three-year-old daughter and his infant son still require the care of their mother and older sisters. Peni, who calls them "sister's children," showers attentions upon them.

Namo's mother is a lean woman who in appearance resembles Big Di Litiya. She is probably more than fifty years old and has quietly accepted her role as foreigner in the village. Unlike Di Litiya, she rarely laughs. Where Nabadua's land at Spring Water joins that of Monasa at The-Shark, she has planted two small patches of pandanus. Though she weeds Namo's gardens, no food resources are spoken of as hers. During the long illness of Namo's son at Lekutu, she lived at Lekutu with Namo's wife's kinsmen and served as nurse.[14]

HOUSE XII

Bici's house is the most dilapidated in the village. The aged Kaiyava, his father, spends his days slowly binding coconut leaves to its walls in hopes of shutting out the wind and rain, but his patchwork does not serve its purpose well. The kitchen is built on the frame of a former sleeping-house; it is well roofed but has but one wall. Not infrequently cooking is performed on the hearth in the sleeping-house. The bed, which Bici shares with his wife Ana and his small son, so crowds the little house that his aged father prefers to sleep in Nabadua's kitchen. With the possible exception of Orisi's house, Bici's is most poorly furnished. But Bici is proud of his few possessions. Besides the mosquito net which is hung above the bed, there is a net for Ana's mother, who sleeps uncomfortably on the damp floor.

Bici is proud of his few gardens. Because of his failing eyesight and his twisted limbs, he gains frequent indulgence from the "village chief" and need not work regularly at housebuilding; hence he has ample leisure to attend his gardens. Though he is but thirty-five years old, he works at an old man's pace. Through his father he has claims in the land

14. Namo's two full brothers and his sisters are discussed under Nabadua's household. They speak of themselves, however, as members of Namo's household.

MAN WITH HIS FAMILY

In his hand he holds his iron spear for hunting wild pigs

of Tavua and Rokowaqa, but his father feels strong loyalty toward Tavua only. Among the Tavua taro ponds of Nabadua's land at Spring Water, Bici has five which have been emptied of their products, two which are ripe and well stocked, and six small new ones which he was planting during the early months of 1936. His ponds are at the lower margin of the slope, which is the least favored of all locations. In land made swampy by the seepage from the ponds, he has planted three patches of swamp taro. There are also a few banana trees in this area which are his. One large pond at Nairoro is his. Through his Tavua claims, he planted in Monasa's land at The-Shark in 1934;

CHART XII

HOUSE XII

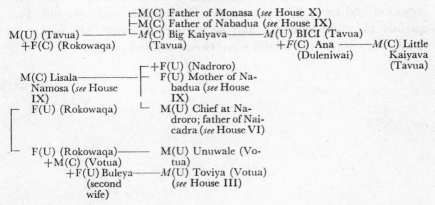

Monasa is his elder "small brother" in Tavua. But Bici prefers his maternal claims upon Naicadra of Nadroro, whom he calls "cross-cousin" and cherishes. He approves of Naicadra's interest in the church. It is in Naicadra's land that Bici has planted his garden of yams.

Though Bici's wife Ana accomplishes much of her husband's planting, she has planted a patch of manioc as well in Vilomena's half of Nadroro. Perhaps it is her sibling relationship with Peni which has gained her this privilege. She has no hereditary claims upon Vilomena's land. In Monasa's land at The-Shark she has planted some pandanus for mats. Though she is not lazy, her strength is not great. Planting and the chores of preparing food for Bici's small household exhaust her energy so that she plaits but few mats.

Ana's mother, though vigorous for her age, is slight and wizened. She and Bici are taboo to each other and observe strict silence in each other's company. She is skilled in women's dances and instructs the young, and her popularity among the women is greater than that of her daughter. Though she is capable of garden work, to carry water or firewood taxes her strength. In Nabadua's land at Spring Water she has planted a patch of manioc.

Bici's six-year-old son, Little Kaiyava, likes his father's company. Bici says jokingly that one of his own taro ponds at Spring Water belongs to his son. Little Kaiyava planted it himself and was very angry when Bici found it necessary to uproot some of the stalks and replant them. Like his mother, his eyes bulge and he suffers from nasal infections. Like his father, his belly is bloated and his legs are wobbly; he looks rachitic.

Bici's aged father, Big Kaiyava, the uncircumcised, suffers from indigestion and cannot sleep at night. He is feeble and very old. Frequently his mind wanders, and he mutters nonsense. He awaits his death. All his claims to land have been assumed by Bici.

CHAPTER V

LIVELIHOOD

FOOD

AT NAKOROKA food is chiefly a matter of starchy roots, and, though a good meal includes fish or meat, these are considered mere "garnish" for the starchy roots. Fruits serve principally to amuse the palates of children. Though many nutritious plants grow wild in the forests, it is considered impossible to subsist without the security of garden produce. In the gardens every household can grow an abundance worthy of pride. Though rank of birth and achieved status in the village can increase or decrease a man's rapport with his ancestors and so influence the fertility of his gardens, yet the most important factor in garden productivity is the vigor of the gardener's own zeal—a zeal which is in proportion to his ambition. Even women may advertise their industrious natures by displaying initiative in gardening enterprises, but their plans are more modest and their gardens far less extensive than those of the men.

Maintenance of the supply of staple foods is largely man's responsibility. Each man worthy of adult status is expected to have at least one yam garden and an ample supply of taro. Organization of garden work varies with the status of garden owner and the nature of the work; planting usually requires greater organization than garden maintenance. Some planting projects may include the entire village; on other occasions garden work may serve to divert a visiting kinsman who is bored with too much leisure. Most of all, the planting of large yam gardens requires carefully planned work organization.

Isacodro, of the Votua land division of Nakoroka, had discussed his garden at the meeting of village elders the night before. Everyone had known privately for a long time that this yam-planting would be a village project. It was a large garden at Cold Water,[1] a tributary of the river Votua, about three miles upstream from the village. For many years Isacodro had planted the land there. When Indians and Chinese plant repeatedly in one spot, they find it necessary to fertilize the soil;

1. See Map V, facing p. 86.

127

but the ancestors of Nakoroka could keep the land productive if it were allowed to lie fallow for a year or so after each crop had been harvested. This land had lain fallow for some time but not long enough to become overgrown with heavy timber. Isacodro was a conscientious gardener, and long ago he had removed all the creeping roots from which shoots might arise. One day during the past week he had cut away the mat of light vines, pulled out the small weeds, and spread all in a tangled mass to be burned when the sun had dried it.

Before sunrise, on September 30, 1935,[2] Peni and Namo prepared separately to hunt according to the plan of last night's meeting. Their troops of dogs barked about them anticipating the chase. Small children were excited too. Some clamored to go along. Especially Peni enjoyed the children's attention and gave them unnecessary orders. Namo went to the forests of Tavua, the land of his father's ancestors; Peni to Nadroro, the land of his mother; each stalked the streams in search of trampled foliage where a newly wakened boar had had his morning drink and the dogs could find the scent. Isacodro returned from his mature gardens laden with yams and taro and with his wife and daughters prepared cooking materials with which to feast those who would plant his new garden. When the sun was two hours high, Bici and Monasa were breakfasting at Nabadua's house.[3] The village bustled. Men sharpened their knives with files bought from the Chinese. Children scurried through all the houses searching for digging-forks which, even with rotted handles and broken tines, were superior to the old-fashioned digging-stick. Within an hour the village was moving along the path which followed the course of the river Votua. Women carried baskets of cooked food. Men carried their knives (machetes) and digging-forks. Isacodro was laden with heavy uncooked food, and his wife carried clusters of pots. Very small children, sitting in slings made from discarded calico, straddled mothers' backs. Four-year-olds rode the shoulders of their older kinsmen. But six-year-olds ran ahead to shake the dripping foliage which hung over the path and wet themselves in the cold, growth-producing[4] dew. Bici cursed his whining son, who had defecated awkwardly and soiled his buttocks, and with an extravagant lecture on the virtues of cleanliness doused

2. The people of Nakoroka are unaware of dates, but I have included them for the sake of precision.

3. Nabadua held the chiefly title for their land, which was Tavua, and was their elder classificatory brother.

4. This is a half-believed superstition. Adults jokingly preach it to children so that they themselves will get less wet.

BREAKING THE SOIL OF ISACODRO'S GARDEN

him gently in a shallow eddy of the river. Naicadra, whose tumorous shoulders bore no proper callouses for the carrying-pole, carried his adopted grandson on his back. There was no order in this procession: twelve men, seven women, and eleven small children (those between eight and puberty were at the district school at Lekutu) straggled along the path in small family groups or friendly couples. Toviya, the most venerable of the ancients to work on Isacodro's garden, arrived alone and last of all, just in time for the midday feast.

Nabadua was first to arrive. With his fingers he was raking the now parched weeds, which Isacodro had left strewn about, into heaps and firing them. When the others began to gather below the garden plot, he joined them to discuss procedures. The five digging-forks which the village possesses were distributed among the younger men. Nabadua, too, used a fork for a while until the plot of soil to be loosened was well demarcated. Then he gave it to plump bachelor Narogo and joined the older men who were breaking the already loosened lumps of soil with their hands and throwing woody debris and rocks toward the garden's base. Isacodro went off to gather the kind of firewood that makes a hot, quick fire, while his wife Ema laid out cooking utensils. The young women bound up their skirts, took fishing nets, and disappeared among the boulders of the river bed in search of a likely fishing place. Children played in the swift water; the occasion was gay because not often did so many playmates find themselves together in a strange part of the river, among boulders with unfamiliar shapes, and Nabadua shouted in vain for his young daughter to fetch his knife from the tree crotch where he had left it. Even the five-year-old darling of the chief's family lay unchaperoned on a sun-warmed boulder and dabbled her cautious toes in the water.

The plot of earth which Nabadua had marked out to be loosened was almost finished. Peni arrived with a small pig. Namo, less fortunate at the hunt, brought a heavy load of seed yams from the village. Work ceased. Nabadua called his daughter furiously, this time to bring a lighted tinder from the cook fire to dry his tobacco. The men smoked reclining and let their sweat dry in the hot sun. Suddenly they rose and completed turning the soil. The younger traveled back to the village for more seed yams, while the elders pulverized the lumps of earth with their fingers.

The young women had returned with their catch of fish and prawns. Isacodro and his wife had scraped the skin from yams and taro and set them to boil. The young women spread plantain leaves about and served the food. There were a few plates and knives which had come from the Chinese store. Nabadua chattered gaily during the meal; though it was frequently said that he "cackled like a bird but said nothing," he made everyone laugh. The women leisurely ate what the men had left. Orisi's two-year-old son slept with his thumb in his mouth.

Namo was first to begin carrying yams up the short slope to the gardens. His father Nabadua continued to entertain the older men, while Isacodro and the women gathered up the cooking utensils. The younger men dug holes in diamond pattern in the already broken soil, each hole two or three feet from the next. First planting holes and best seed yams were placed at the base of the garden slope where loosened soil was deepest. For years soil had been washed toward the base of this deforested plot so that its angle of ascent had lessened; it was decided that a deep ditch must band the garden halfway up its slope, to increase the angle of ascent and drain the almost swampy soil. Straightway the ditch was complete. Men held their forks with left hand near the tines and right hand near the top of the handle, in the manner in which they grasp digging-sticks, and plunged them deep into the soft earth. Rarely did they need to force the fork downward with a foot in European fashion to loosen an especially hard-packed area. Isacodro, who prides himself upon the violence and efficiency with which he can work, came to finish the planting. The thin soil of the upper slope was worthy only of halved and quartered seed yams of inferior quality. Isacodro's wife planted some sections of kava stalk in the soft soil at the garden's base. A large tree blotted the afternoon sun from a portion of the garden plot, so Naicadra felled it skilfully with his machete.

That night Isacodro served kava and food in the house of Monasa; his own house, which neighbored Monasa's, was too small. Ladies of the chiefly family, although they had been occupied with their own gardens during the day, came to Isacodro's feast. A year later when the yams had matured, Isacodro would present several basketfuls to Bulisivo, who held the title to kingship of Inland Forest, and these would be apportioned among the households of the ancient village groups: Votua, Tavua, Nadroro, and Rokowaqa.[5]

After Isacodro's feast the men assembled at the house of Nabadua, drank kava until long after midnight, and planned to finish the planting of Bulisivo's garden on the morrow. During the previous two months more than twenty plots had been planted with seed yams. Few,

5. Buleya was practically extinct at Nakoroka.

however, had received the extensive co-operation of Isacodro's enterprise. Small family groups, supplemented when necessary by a more
distant kinsman of the same ancient village descent group, worked together on garden plots as the individual owners required. But now the
season was late. Many houses were scheduled for building before December, and the quick completion of the gardens was a concern of the
entire village. Gardens of members of the chiefly family of Votua,
which included Bulisivo, king of Inland Forest, received more co-
operative effort; demands for assistance included Isacodro, the best
worker of Votua, although no traceable blood ties bound him to them,
the old Raitova of Rokowaqa whose chiefly ancestors were genealogi-
cally interlocked with those of Votua. Bulisivo's garden would be complete by the middle of the morning of October 1, but there was a more
serious problem to discuss: seed yams were exhausted, yet one large
plot lay cleared but unplanted in Nadroro land. The owners of this
garden—Melika, wife of Naicadra, who held a potential right to the
chiefly title in Nadroro, and Vilomena, who was Melika's sister-in-
Nadroro-land and then holder of chiefly title there—had followed
the path of kinship and called upon relatives in the neighboring village
of Nalauvia to bring yams and plant the garden. Preparation for the
Nalauvia guests had to be elaborate; they had to be feasted according
to old Nakoroka tradition.

When the feast which closed the work on Bulisivo's garden had been
served by the women of Votua, all the able-bodied men in Nakoroka
hastened to Melika's garden in Nadrora to prepare the soil for planting. Early next morning all the men brought food and kava from their
gardens against the arrival of the Nalauvia people. Nabadua, of
Tavua, and Isacodro, of Votua, worked also in their private gardens
for a time pulling weeds and cutting the growth which encroached
from the surrounding forest. But the men of Nadroro were busily anticipating their guests. That evening four men arrived from Nalauvia
bearing seed yams.

Next morning, which was October 3, ten more guests arrived and
went directly to Melika's garden.[6] Some of the older men of Nakoroka
who were not members of Nadroro continued work in their own gardens. Young men prepared ovens and brought firewood. The village
women went fishing. Naicadra and his wife Melika and two young
women of their household scraped yams and taro for the ovens. The
young men clubbed Naicadra's only domestic pig, because wild pig

6. In all, nine men of varying ages, two old women, a girl, and two small children.

is no honor to a guest who has come to perform a traditional service. When the ovens had been covered and food for the guests was cooking, the men dressed in their Sunday[7] attire and rested in the shade near Naicadra's house; two young men prepared kava, because it is proper, when guests have come to do garden work, for hosts to cook food at their leisure and to rest and converse over the kava bowl. No one of Nakoroka had accompanied their guest kinsmen to Melika's garden.

It was late in the afternoon when the planting was finished and the guest workers returned to the village. Vatili, who had just returned from a week's errand in his capacity as "village chief,"[8] made the presentation of kava to the guests. The Nakoroka girls danced for them until far into the night. Next morning, before the Nalauvia people started home, they received kava stalks and large bunches of uncooked taro and a few small baskets of cooked food to be eaten on the path.

Yams and kava are not the only dry-garden products.[9] Each may contain as well a varied assortment of manioc, sweet potatoes,[10] kawai and bulow,[11] bananas, eggplant, tomatoes, papaya (oleti), a few bushes which produce spinach-like leaves, or a few stalks of corn and dry taro.[12] Sometimes tobacco grows in a corner of the plot, but in the last ten years production of this commodity has passed largely into the hands of the Indians.

Yam gardens and dry gardens intended especially for taro are al-

7. Significance of Sunday and the organization of the Wesleyan church have been described in chap. iii, pp. 58–61.

8. In each village there is a "village chief" who represents the colonial administration. He is appointed by the Buli, who fills an analogous function for the district as a whole, and who is appointed by the Roko. The Roko is the highest native official in a province. Usually he is supervised by a British district commissioner ("district," in this titular usage, usually refers to a province, never to the subdivision of a province, which is ordinarily termed "district"; district commissioners may even hold authority over more than one province). For further discussion of organization of colonial administration see above, pp. 61–67. At Nakoroka, almost all middle-aged men have held the office of "village chief." But Vatili was generally considered to be especially well suited for it.

9. The Fijian term were, which is applied to these gardens, may also be used as a verb to denote "weeding a garden, village green, or path." Since dry gardens must be constantly weeded, the term distinguishes them in this respect from the other important type of garden, the taro pond (vuci), which is continuously flooded with eight or ten inches of water and hence produces no weed growth.

10. Kumala, which in the literature is the Maori word for yam, but which in Fiji is quite distinct from yam.

11. Starchy roots, smaller and sweeter than the yam.

12. Most kinds of taro may be grown in dry gardens, but, when so grown, the flavor and texture suffer.

ways built on a sloping hill for proper drainage and depth of soil. The other products are scattered through any available space. But gardens devoted exclusively to sweet potatoes, or particularly to manioc, are frequently built on level hilltops. Such gardens, usually planted by women, form an auxiliary but not essential food supply. A good woman who has passed the period when young children require most of her time finds leisure from plaiting mats and preparing food to plant large quantities of these foods.

All men of importance have yam gardens. Eighteen men had twenty-four well-kept dry gardens. Only five of these contained dry taro and kava to the exclusion of yams as principal crop. Fifteen women had dry gardens. Only three of these contained yams and the wide range of products which make them comparable to men's gardens. One contained a large supply of dry taro. Ten were small, built carelessly on level ground; nine were devoted chiefly to manioc; one was a garden of sweet potatoes. All were crowded at the margins with eggplant, peppers, or tomatoes. Samu was the only man who had planted manioc; he was a young widower who had no household of his own and no unattached women relatives to help in his yam gardens.

Though women frequently assist with their brother's and husband's planting, men do not often return this favor. In 1935 the men of Nakoroka assisted the women only with those three of their gardens which contained yams. Women's planting is gay and informal. Sisters, sisters-in-law, mothers and daughters and small sons, wander day after day through the bush in groups of threes and fours, always on an errand—to get firewood, to bag a netful of fish or a basketful of prawns or snails, or to bring food from their husband's gardens—but their route brings them past their own small plots, and they plant a basketful of seed supplies which they have prepared before leaving the village. Their tomatoes, tobacco, eggplant, and papaya have no traditional sanction as feast food but are of inestimable value in adding tastiness to an otherwise monotonously starchy diet. When the stately yam is planted even in women's gardens, the occasion must be formal; men must be engaged to perform the more laborious loosening of the soil, the more careful removing of the roots which tangle the topsoil. When men work together, each man works in whatever part of the garden strikes his fancy and, unless a program for work has been laid out carefully, casts debris thoughtlessly upon the area which his fellow-worker has cleaned. But, when women plant, there is no tension, no confusion, and no need for a program of work. Men laugh at women's gardens: they have no aura of traditional sanction; ancestors are but slightly concerned with the fertility of a patch of manioc.

The yam harvest[13] occurred in October and November with a gift of first yams from each garden presented to Bulisivo. Those whose gardens had been co-operatively tended by the entire village made formal presentation to Bulisivo, who then ordered general distribution throughout the village. But the harvest from each garden was presented and distributed separately; the collective harvest of all the village gardens and the elaborate feasts which accompanied its distribution have passed from use. Aged Daova[14] had vague recollection of yearly festivals celebrated after all yams had been harvested, a lull in the year's round of work which was filled with feasting and dancing. She did not associate this with the elaborate feasts of first-fruits, which all remember and which occurred earlier in the year. The feast which Daova remembered was in December and January, the months which are now gay because they are an extended Christmas and New Year's holiday. She remembered no precise religious significance, except that everyone was happy because the land was fertile.

The garden areas, which lie in clusters exclusively in Nadroro and Votua land, have been planted for many years, so that it is rarely necessary to clear large timber from proposed planting sites; in a day or two, one man can clear away such tangled brush as grows in a few years' time so that the soil is ready for turning. Isacodro had so prepared his garden on the river Votua. But sometimes a new family moves to town from a neighboring village and immediately needs a large block of new garden land. About 1930 Isacodro had come suddenly to Nakoroka from Nalauvia because his brother at Nalauvia had been using the aid of spirits to attract the beautiful Ema, Isacodro's wife. Ema had been a Nakoroka girl, and Isacodro could trace descent from ancient Votua; hence he and his family had claims on Nakoroka which were easy to utilize when relations with his brother became tense and violence threatened.

According to customary obligations toward affinal relatives, Ema's

13. The elaborate first-fruits feasts of early days were first condemned by missionaries because their connotation was considered un-Christian. The colonial administration encouraged their re-establishment in the late nineteenth century when it was realized how intimately chiefly authority depended upon them. But colonial decree probably had little effect upon the Nakoroka region. The decline in the importance of first-fruits ceremonies has a local history which ties closely with Bulisivo's personal history (see below, pp. 221–22).

14. Mother of Vatili, perhaps ninety.

classificatory brothers and fathers at Nakoroka prepared new land for Isacodro. The site on the river Votua, which Isacodro planted on September 30, 1935, was cleared of its great timber,[15] and lower along the course of the river several plots were cleared for taro-planting. The men of Nakoroka chuckle now when they remember how they piled the cut timber and brush in such tangles in the middle of the clearings that it took Isacodro, their cross-cousin, weeks to prepare the ground for actual planting.[16] But the clearing of land is not a usual problem. The jungle stays within bounds because men cut it gradually as it encroaches from year to year.

A man's prestige depends partly upon the cleanliness of his gardens. When he is free from other tasks, he goes to inspect them, binds supports to the heavy stalks of kava, chops out a large invading root, and pulls some weeds. But the work of a man in maintaining gardens is chiefly that of supervision. His sisters, and particularly his daughter-in-law and her sisters, do most of the actual cultivating. When they have been negligent, he will call them to task and send them on a special garden-cleaning expedition. They work in good spirit with their friends or with a few small children as helpers and chaperones[17] and probably return with a basketful of forest fruit or some bush-pineapple leaves for rolling cigarettes. But cultivating requires men's supervision. Peni would frequently return from several weeks' absence housebuilding in a neighboring village to find his gardens neglected and overgrown, although he had carefully instructed the energetic Meremanini, his classificatory sister, to remember to care for them; though she willingly performed many personal services for him, his immediate presence was required to activate her. Peni was not angry when he saw the condition of his gardens, but he would say sadly, "It is the custom of women."

Taro is grown in larger quantity than yams. But a feast of taro is less spectacular than a feast of yams, for yams are an honorable and chiefly food loved by the ancestors. The preparation of pond gardens for taro consumes more time than that for yams, but it is less spectacular and requires less concentrated effort. There is no special time for planting because warm rains of the summer months have no effect on the submerged taro roots. Stalks of taro which has been eaten are saved in a

15. Such timber, though large, is not first growth. Even in most dense jungle regions there are evidences of former habitation and agriculture; ancient irrigation canals for taro ponds are now choked with the roots of great trees.

16. This obligation to perform garden work is termed *tave*.

17. The chattering tongues of children are proof against love trysts in the forest.

cool place and replanted while still turgid; some man or woman in each household used to replant several times a week, whenever he went to his ponds for a fresh supply of food. The building of ponds is difficult and may engage the labor of the entire village. But since a day in January is as good for the purpose as one in September or May, there is no driving need for haste. Though women may assist in a day's co-operative work at building taro ponds, it is predominantly within men's scope. Of more than two hundred taro ponds, only three were spoken of as the property of women. Two very small ones belonged to the pampered five-year-old granddaughter of the king of Inland Forest; one large one was co-operatively built for Melika and Di Vara in return for their services as "nurses," when, for several years, they had held periodic inspection of the children and with the viscid iodine that the government distributes had dosed spots which looked like ringworm.

For six months during sunny days Bulisivo, king of Inland Forest, worked alone on his land, building four large taro ponds and a canal which ran for a hundred yards to the nearest stream. Behind his back younger men jeered at the flimsy wall of earth which he had built to force some of the water of the stream into the mouth of his canal; the first flood would wash it away, and then on instant notice the men of the village would have to rebuild it so that his taro ponds would not run dry. They laughed, too, at the slowness of his progress and at his self-righteous claim to industrious character. But their laughter was very private because they considered him chief of highest rank in Bua Province. But Bulisivo was old. As a chief he loved his land. Like many old men, who were no longer responsible to colonial administration for taxes or for statute labor, he liked the solitude of his gardens which permitted him to set his own pace. Old men like to work alone. Vaula, Toviya, and Naicadra frequently strengthened the walls of their taro ponds or planted at Nairoro, in Votua land less than a mile from the village; though they were within calling distance of one another or even in adjacent ponds, they exchanged few words, and these perhaps to borrow tobacco. They were friends, had grown up together on Nakoroka land, yet any one of them might leave off work and go back to the village without bothering to notify the others. Monasa, whose taro ponds were the most extensive of any in Nakoroka, spent weeks alone, often sleeping near his gardens to protect them from bush pigs.[18]

18. Though fences can afford a kind of protection against wild pigs, only two or three of Nakoroka's gardens were fenced. When other work is finished, 'no time remains for build-

It is customary for guests whose sojourns are lengthy[19] to build gardens for their host. Vatili's cross-cousin from Nalauvia built eight new ponds in Nadroro land. Though the agricultural work obligations between affinals are usually phrased as an obligation of child-in-law to father-in-law, Ratu Luke's father-in-law embanked and planted five taro ponds for Ratu Luke just beyond Nairoro.

But there is a definite pattern for co-operative work in taro production. He whose gardens are so built must serve a feast bearing a name distinct from that which follows co-operative yam-planting.[20] When the work is complete, the men chant and in great united shouts count the number of finished ponds so that the women and children who hear the rhythmic shouts resounding in the village will know and marvel at the quantity of work which the men have accomplished that day.[21] As in co-operative yam-planting, a program of work is decided upon before the day of work arrives. Co-operative taro enterprises supply food resources for newcomers and individuals to whom either the chief, "village chief," or Buli decide the community is indebted and also increase the village supply when elders and chief decide that it is failing. So ponds were built for the two women who had served as "nurses" and for the young mission teacher,[22] the native Tavean who took up residence at Nakoroka in February, 1936, and who, since he had no food resources, had to spend his mission wage at the Chinese store to bring tea and bread for the workers' feast which followed. Theoretically ponds should have been prepared for Vatili, "village chief," but that year other work pressed too heavily, and they were not built.

Work under Ratu Seru's direction was different from the usual co-operative enterprise. Ratu Seru, perhaps twenty-six years old, sister's son to Bulisivo and namesake of Bulisivo's father, spent most of his time wandering through the villages in the mining area on the windward coast. The white boss at the mines appreciated his executive

---

ing fences. Old men say that it is only in modern times, since the rapport between ancestors and chiefs has been disturbed by foreign administration, that pigs have increased to the extent of becoming a garden menace.

19. Which means that they are bound by kinship ties to their host.

20. *Kaurau* is the name for this taro feast.

21. This habit of marveling at booming sounds and counting them centers an unsolicited attention on blasting in the gold mines forty miles away. The entire village pauses to count the blasts; four in succession are worthy of exclamations; eight or nine warrant remembering a month later.

22. Organization of the church has been discussed in chap. iii.

ability and sometimes used him to gather young men when the supply of labor at the mines was slack. But Ratu Seru rarely worked. He preferred to idle where his chiefship was recognized, utilize his chiefly prerogatives, which through Bulisivo's mother were widespread in the region, and visit about, exhibiting his truly great skill at ukulele-playing and his rasping tenor singing voice before an audience who were hereditarily destined to appreciate. As oldest "nephew"[23] of Bulisivo his status in Nakoroka was unique. Women, pigs, and chickens of the entire countryside were at his disposal.

On January 10, 1936, Ratu Seru decided that he needed new taro ponds in Votua land. Like other expatriate young men, he had come home for the Christmas and New Year's festivities. He went directly to his taro land and saw the old ponds dry and weed-grown; back in the village among his friends he lamented his neglect. For nearly ten days Nakoroka had been crowded with young people. Six young men who traced their lineage along devious paths to Nakoroka had come for the famous holiday food. Four girls from Dreketi were visiting their distant sister Ivamere, who had been Nakoroka's most recent virgin. When Ratu Seru said that ponds should be built that day, there was no need for discussion. Ratu Seru had planned the program of work. His curt nasal commands left no question as to each man's task. The young women fished with nets. The young men plied the village digging-forks to embank the walls of the ponds. Schoolboys, free this month from the district school, made sweet puddings so that Ratu Seru could feast the workers when the ponds were complete. Workers could depend upon Ratu Seru's initiative in any enterprise that he undertook. They obeyed to avoid his snarling insult and to please the village ancestors, who approved his command. Unlike his mild uncle Bulisivo, Ratu Seru knew how to make slaves work; he had seen the commoners of the windward coast groveling before their chiefs.

On another day in January five prepubertal boys built a row of five small taro ponds just beyond the large area of intensive cultivation at Nairoro. The project was hatched co-operatively among them. As they worked, they chattered because they were too young to feel man's proper dignity. But each boy built and planted his own garden. Sakaru, who was sickly, said to his distant brother Ovini, whose sturdy voice was already changing: "Come, I beg you to help me a little so that my pond shall be finished this day."

Though most taro is planted in carefully irrigated ponds, the canals

---

23. This term also includes grandchild; in chiefly families it determines *vasu* rights.

of which may extend for more than a mile, there are other methods of planting. Nabadua had planted some in a manner called *vatui*:[24] stones in a shallow stream bed support bare taro stalks which send out feeding roots to grow loosely in the water. Such taro approaches the desired hyaline consistency even more closely than pond taro, but these gardens are too fragile for large-scale production. Canals which water the ponds of Tavua taro[25] are lined with stalks hastily planted in soil muddied by canal water. Ponds which have gone without care for a year or so become filled with debris and sediment so that they approximate the *lau-levu*,[26] which is the taro planted hastily in the swampy floors of ravines. Taro requires much more water than yams. Hence even that which is planted in dry gardens requires a cupping-out of soil about the planted stalk so that rain water will form a small puddle; the cupping-out should be as deep as the mature taro is expected to be long.

Except for dry-garden taro the maintenance of taro plantations is less exacting than that of yams. Sometimes a kind of watercress fills the ponds, but its growth is gradual. Floods wash away the canal walls at their intakes or fill them with debris, and quick repair work must be done lest the ponds run dry. On rare occasions a leak springs through a precarious point in the canal where it must flow parallel with a deep ravine; repair must be quick lest the entire embankment wash away. A few bamboo pipes or troughs which carry water across a gulley require frequent inspection. But the eyes of those who daily wander through the land are focused for such dangers, and supervision is not a chore. The maintenance as well as the building of ponds and canals is the work of men. Though the women fancy themselves too weak, they are capable in an emergency; when all the able-bodied men are absent building houses in a neighboring village and a flood damages the irrigation system, the women will try to persuade an old man to leave his house and mend the damage, but, if no men are available, the women will do their best, though "they do not know" the work.[27]

Of other foods, bananas form an important though lowly item. Usually boiled long before ripeness has brought flavor, they are almost tasteless and of nutty consistency. A meal of bananas would be offered to a guest only by the most poverty-stricken host; it has become

24. *Vatu* is the word for stone.
25. Located in Votua land.   26. For which there is no translation.
27. In recent years European influence has helped to discourage heavy work among women and to support their belief in their own weakness.

the simile for poverty. Yet most households serve them every day. Though banana trees are not an annual crop that must be harvested and replanted, they are usually found in groves along the paths in garden areas; Rokowaqa and Tavua land, the garden sites of which have long stood empty, still produce an important supply planted in former years. Individual trees and groves are spoken of as belonging to various men of the village. Land which is well plotted in gardens and surrounded by groves of banana, coconut, breadfruit, chestnut, and citrus fruit trees is called *wiligau;* it is a great compliment for a traveler to describe his host's land with this term.[28] Since banana groves need little care when once planted, even men who have few gardens control a quantity of bananas as food supply.

The only magic ritual which ever concerned planting, other than proper observance of the ceremonies of everyday life and consequent pleasing of the ancestors who insure fertility, occurred in ancient times with the planting of bananas, breadfruit,[29] or any easily destructible tree food. The old men searched their memories, but only Vaula could remember a magic chant; it was a rite to protect against the marauding attacks of parrots. As the shoots were placed in the ground, he who was planting tamped the earth over them with his right foot and sang:

> I have planted a shoot of banana[30]
> Fly hither, Parrot:
> Swoop down to the garden of So-and-So
> Fly hither, Flying Fox:
> Hang well exposed on these branches.
> *Ogei ogei ogei.*[31]

The parrot, which attacks fruit that is still hard and green, fears the flying fox, which eats fruit only after it has ripened. Hence the crop is safe if it is carried to the village before being fully ripe. Of course, a shaman may be specially consulted to insure safety of crops of all kinds; but such precautions are superfluous for those who have clear consciences.

A coconut is the symbol of permanence. It requires perhaps fifteen years to mature and bear fruit. Once bearing, it outspans a generation.

28. The only true *wiligau* are to be found on the wet windward coast. The gardens of Namo in Nadroro land lie in a region named "Great *Wiligau,*" but they are choked with brush and weeds and no longer warrant the title.

29. Breadfruit, though frequently slips of it are started, is scarce at Nakoroka. There are perhaps ten trees in all, these all in Nadroro land, planted by Naicadra and Vatili.

30. Or breadfruit.   31. The cry of the flying fox.

Groves planted in fortresses of the days of war still produce. Though cream squeezed from the grated coconut ranks high in Fijian cuisine, as everyday food it is not important. The juice of the green nut is cool and refreshing for a pause in a hot day's work. The transparent sweet jelly of the young nut excites the palates of small children and infants. Sweet crumbling roots of the young shoots which grow inside last year's fallen husks supply confection to the wanderer in the woods and names for young girls. But, except in combination dishes, coconuts never form part of Nakoroka's meals.[32] With the spread of knowledge of the copra trade in recent years the importance of coconuts as economic goods has increased. All the groves which extend along the river Votua and in old village sites are claimed as property under British law. Every adult man and woman has his share. Occasionally arguments arise which must be settled by litigation in the court of the Buli. Coconuts which grow about the present village site, however, are used by him whose house they adjoin. If a family changes its residence from one side of the village to another, which rarely happens, its supply of coconuts for use also changes.

Of other tree foods, chestnut, *dawa*,[33] Tahitian apple, mandarin, orange, lemon,[34] mango, guava,[35] and others—any or all may be planted, and ownership can be claimed as personal right. But except for the *dawa* and giant chestnut, which rank as food fit for feasts, their value is considered insignificant, and they belong to him whose land contains them or to whoever wants them. Chestnut, *dawa*, and mango are all delicacies, but their season is so short that they have never gained importance as staples.

Pineapple and sugar cane have been introduced. Though probably planted in many of the plots in which they now grow, they propagate themselves from year to year without attention. Like the green coconut, they are refreshments for hot days. A meal never includes them. These products are spoken of as belonging to him in whose land they grow, but whoever passes may eat. During December and January the path to Lekutu was rancid with trampled pineapple which had ripened too fast for consumption and had fallen rotting. Though the fibrous bush pineapple, which is an entirely different variety within the pandanus family, supplies leaves for rolling cigarettes, the coarse fibers

32. An old British resident in Fiji once told me that the coconut was the Fijian's meat—that they always ate with a coconut in one hand and a piece of yam or taro in the other.
33. Vaguely similar to the plum.
34. Probably introduced but now growing wild.
35. Introduced but now almost a pest.

of its flowers bind the teeth and cut the gums so that it is unpleasant
to eat.

The forest supplies abundant varieties of food. Chestnuts, guava,
oranges, and other introduced fruits are available to him who knows
where to look. But more than this the many varieties of yam which
grow wild can supplement failing gardens. With his eight-year-old
daughter, Narieta,[36] and a digging-stick, Nabadua would frequently
search for yams along the valley slopes in Tavua land; to be prepared
for a chance wild pig, he would take his spear, his machete, and his
dogs as well. The year had impoverished his gardens so that he was
disgraced and had to depend upon wild yams to feed his family. Even
young Narieta could tell by examining the leaves and tendrils of yam
vines whether the yam was mature enough for use. She also knew
many varieties by texture, color, and shape of leaf or vine. But Nabadua had to correct her frequently on this score because she made mistakes. Digging for yams was hard work. Sometimes Nabadua would
return late at night with no food to show for his efforts, and his family
had to eat bananas boiled green. Frequently he would dig for an hour
in the hard soil along the path of the vine to find that it disappeared
in the crevice of a boulder too large to dislodge. But sometimes he was
fortunate and returned burdened with a hundred and fifty pounds[37]
of yams bound to his digging-stick, which he had converted to a carrying-pole. Narieta, too, could carry burdens for long distances through
the forests. Yams stored in houses keep for several months.

Rarely has anyone tried to subsist entirely without gardens. It is the
consensus that it could be done only if there were plenty of bananas as
supplement. But he who can be characterized as a habitual searcher
for wild yams is disgracefully impoverished and symbolizes the antithesis of chiefliness. Once, visiting in a Macuata town, I bragged to my
host of having learned to hunt wild yams in company with Nakoroka's
chiefly family. My companions from Nakoroka were embarrassed and

36. Accurate determination of ages is impossible in a community which does not mark
the passage of the years. Everyone knows that he is younger than some of his fellows
and older than the rest, but attempts to rate age differences in terms of years are ludicrous.
Peni, who must have been between twenty-five and thirty, ardently defended his statement
that he was twelve until I indicated children in the village who I thought might be twelve;
then he recanted and decided that he was forty-four. Government records of births and
deaths have been kept upon occasion since 1921, but it is frequently difficult to equate
names in the records with those in use; a few flagrant errors incline the observer toward
suspicion of all of them. To please foreign guests, Fijians frequently say, "We are so stupid.
We don't know how old we are."

37. My estimates of weights and dimensions are rough.

surprised at my disloyalty, because now their ancient Macuatan rivals would know that there was no smooth rapport between chiefs and ancestors at Nakoroka. That the chiefs must live like "men of the forest" was evidence that the gardens had failed. It was true that the entire village of Nakoroka had suffered shortage during the month of November, 1935, and the people lamented: "Our yams are exhausted. Our taro is not yet mature. We have nothing but bananas; so we must hunt wild yams." But disgrace did not weigh heavily upon the shoulders of the women and children; they trooped off gaily to have picnics of roast yams in the forest. Sometimes an older man accompanied them. Sometimes a couple of big boys did the heavy work. On the whole, men preferred to search with solemnity, accompanied if at all by a youngster to perform errands, to climb a coconut tree and throw down nuts for a cool drink, to gather vines for tying yams to the carrying-pole, to retrace steps for a mislaid knife. Bulisivo, upon whose head responsibility for this shame rested, would giggle shyly and turn his head when wild yams were mentioned.

The many varieties of wild yams are all distinct from those which are cultivated. Appearance varies, but, in general, wild yams are lighter in color, coarser in texture, and larger in size. Wild yams sometimes grow to more than a fathom in length, but, though longer than those of the gardens, they never attain such thick diameters. Economically the important distinction lies in the fact that garden yams are a sure supply while wild yams are uncertain. The quantity of food which a garden contains can be roughly estimated, and the length of time required to dig a certain number in the soft garden soil is known; wild yams, which may be almost incased in the bedrock of the island, require greater effort because they permit no such prediction.

Compared with Melanesian regions, domestic pigs play but a small role in life at Nakoroka. Yet there are certain ceremonial and economic obligations which require domestic pigs instead of wild ones. To include a domestic pig in the funeral feast is a great honor for the corpse. To serve a bush pig to a group of guests who have performed a service in fulfilment of the obligations of kin or chiefship is the custom only of people impoverished in chiefly tradition. Yet there are few pigs at Nakoroka. Some households have none. A few consecutive feasts may exhaust the village supply; then begging from relatives in neighboring regions must replenish the stock. On April 4, 1936, the supply of domestic pigs at Nakaroka was temporarily exhausted.[38]

38. See the account of the entertainment of the Buli at Nakoroka, above, pp. 72–78.

There are indications that pig culture received more attention in earlier times. Curved boar tusks were highly valued as ornaments. Though chance malformation of jaws or accidents may prevent proper grinding and thus permit tusks to grow, I observed no such cases. The curved tusk is still valued, but the only ones now at Nakoroka were found at old village sites. A now forgotten dentistry may have produced them, but natives think that aged bush pigs sometimes grow long curved tusks. Remarks in published literature suggest far greater pig culture in other parts of Fiji than exists today.

Each household that has a pig has a pen made from upright stakes or piled stones;[39] though colonial regulations enforce this usage, pigs are usually at large in the village. The men and women of some households may throw their garbage into the pen consistently for a while, but it is usual, too, for small pigs to loiter in the shadows of the household and snatch taro from a platter on the spread eating-mat.

Early historical references, as well as inferences from comparative ethnological study, indicate that the pig was not introduced into Fiji by Europeans. Schouten's expedition to Tonga as early as 1616 noted the "wild black pigs" there and contrasted others of European varieties.[40] The ceremonio-economic role of pigs is well established and seems to have been so from earliest times. But the role of domestic pigs in maintaining the food supply is negligible, and the fact that, in contrast with Melanesian regions, few gardens are fenced as protection against domestic pigs gone wild suggests that the development of today's hordes of wild pigs is recent. Primarily domestic pigs are emblems of wealth far above subsistence level.

Only in part can hunting the wild pig be classified as work to supply food. Every mile of excursion along a forest path startles a pig, which grunts and crashes off through the brush. The gardens produce as much as they do only by good luck. They lie unprotected far from the village, some of them four or five miles by circuitous paths. As ancestors maintain the soil's productivity, so they also protect gardens from the ravages of pigs, but it is truly supernatural that only the misdemeanors of Nabadua and Ratu Luke should bring about the com-

39. In coastal villages piled stone pens serve for both sea turtles and pigs. Such pigs must wallow in salt water and drink the rain.

40. Sir Basil Thomson, *The Diversions of a Prime Minister* (London, 1894), p. 399. Very early immigrants from Tonga may have brought their domesticated pigs to Fiji, and either in Tonga or in Fiji they may have acquired their agouti-like color from disorderly breeding of several European varieties. At any rate, early traders dropped anchor at both Fiji and Tonga to replenish their supplies of pork.

plete destruction of their gardens. Though Monasa revered his ancestors in the old-fashioned manner, it was a practical consideration which led him to sleep near his luxuriant taro ponds when the moon was full. Likewise, acting upon an adage similar to "God helps those who help themselves," one man usually performs the office of hunting through the forest areas around garden lands several times a week. Colonial administration recognizes this depredation and authorizes group pig hunts. On March 11, 1936, all able-bodied Nakoroka men and dogs assembled with others from the district. The drive continued for ten days in garden lands throughout the area. But unfortunately work under the Buli's direction was so spiritless that few pigs were killed. Thus pig-hunting is to a large degree concerned with garden maintenance. Though a man kill several pigs during a fortunate day's hunt, he may bring only a couple of hindquarters to the village. He leaves the rest to rot.

But there are occasions when the catch of the hunt forms welcome food. When Isacodro feasted those who planted his yams, Peni brought a bush pig. Those who ate were all of Nakoroka; Isacodro's depleted prestige among them did not warrant the killing of a domestic pig. Sometimes a sudden desire to eat pig causes a group hunting excursion among the young men. Usually, however, such an excursion is for wild cattle. Cattle, which European vessels brought to Fiji from Tonga in the early nineteenth century, arrived in a culture that contained no dairying technique to sustain a tradition of domestication. They ran wild. In later years cows errant from dairy herds of planters joined the original deserters from Fijian villages. Early in the twentieth century a beef-producing enterprise was started by British commercialists in Taveuni and eastern Vanua Levu, but it was abandoned, and the herds ran wild through the tangled jungles. However, wild cattle are scarce and too timid to graze in the gardens. Though a man who chooses to travel at night may startle a grazing herd in a moonlit clearing far from human habitation, the hunter who concerns himself principally with beating a patrol about garden territory seldom encounters them. Dogs, who form a snarling ring about a pig so that the hunter has only to deal the death blow, are of little use in cattle-hunting. Cattle are fleet, and the hunter must outrace them and risk an angry charge. Hence only three of the young men of Nakoroka can boast of having killed wild cattle. Two boast authentically. The third is Ratu Seru, the chief's nephew, whose word no one dares question. But beef is a delicacy which ranks high above bush pork. At Nakoroka there is never enough domestic beef to make the flavor common and thus to minimize the value of wild beef. Sometimes young hunters, discouraged with only pigs to show for the day's catch, kill a docile yearling recently strayed from the herd of an Indian dairyman.

On January 11 Ratu Seru organized a hunt among the young men. Several of the guests who had come for the Christmas and New Year's feasts departed early in the morning. When the Dreketi girls had started home, Ratu Seru mobilized the young men in two groups which penetrated the forest in two directions. Entertainment had been costly. Ratu Seru had been lavish in his use of taro and yams. Frequently he had sent a fourteen-year-old to the Chinese store at Lekutu. The last chickens had been boiled the night before when Ratu Seru had feasted those who built his taro ponds. The young men were glutted with feast food and eagerly anticipated the exertion of the chase.

While Ratu Seru, who wanted beef, planned to circle through Votua land, Peni led two youngsters of fourteen years and ten dogs far into Tavua land. As they paused for a drink at a cold stream, Peni told them how he had once killed a wild cow in this same spot: He had just stooped for a drink when a startled cow raised her head from a clump of wild cane on the farther bank. With a stone Peni struck her above the eye, momentarily stunning her. But her calf must have been hidden near by, for, instead of taking flight, she charged into the stream. Peni made for the trees. But two boulders of the rugged ford caught his foot and he fell sprawling. Before he could gain the safety of the nearest tree, the cow was upon him, pinned him to the bank of the stream and tore his flank with a horn. (He indicated the great scar which the horn had made.) With his right hand he reached his spear and drew it from the tangled vines in which it lay. While the cow still bore heavily upon his chest, he thrust through her heart and killed her. The fourteen-year-olds interjected words of wonder and admiration. Later, in private discussion, they said, "Had it been any other, had it not been Peni, the cow would have been victor. Peni is indeed a man." Of course, they had heard the tale many times before, but their admiration was real.

Peni directed the two boys to gather firewood and stones for an oven at a certain spot where the forest was not so dense and the stream ran deep and to wait there until they heard the peculiar cry which dogs make as they encircle a pig. Peni himself spatted his hands to call the dogs to the chase and disappeared with them into the forest which walled the steep ravine. The boys found dry wood and twenty-five or thirty stones about the size of baseballs. Long before the dogs gave the signal of a catch, the boys had laid the wood in a hole dug for an oven and piled the stones on top. They were cross-cousins, so the larger ragged the smaller as they waited and ridiculed his ignorance of proper oven-building and his awkwardness with the knife in cutting wood. Repartee, though weak, was in good spirit. Then a cloud of mud was seen to rise in the deep clear river pool. The larger boy ordered the smaller to run to the nearest bamboo clump and bring a shaft split into many points at one end to serve as fish spear. It was an eel four feet in length that roiled the water. Both boys hurled many times but failed because the spear was at fault: the smaller boy had wrought it clumsily. At length one of them dived into the water, with some misgiving because an eel can bite, to search out the hole in which their quarry might have taken refuge.

Far up the mountain slope the snarling yap of the dogs sounded. The boys stood tense, listening to ascertain the precise direction. Then they dashed recklessly through the brush, leaping vine-hidden logs and boulders, slashing passages through the nets of tougher vines that hung from branches of the large timber. As they jumped sideways to avoid a ditch in their path, their machetes waved carelessly; but there was no danger of fall or injury because the ancestors allow only those who have a bad conscience to be hurt. They ran up the steep slope, finding hasty footing on the great roots where rain had washed away the soil. They paused for a moment when the vegetation gave way to solid growth of cane, which is the most difficult of barriers. As they lunged upward through it single file, they changed places frequently so that the erstwhile leader could follow in the path broken by his fellow and catch his breath.

Peni was standing in a clearing with his foot on the throat of a fat sow. A live young pig lay near by fettered with vines and bound to Peni's spear, which he had been using as a carrying-pole. He had not speared either of the pigs because the dogs[41] had performed well; Peni had merely grabbed the pig's hind legs and thrown it on its back. The boys found tying vines and a sapling shaft for a second carrying-pole.

At the oven Peni was displeased with the boys' preparation. There

41. The present dog of Fiji is a mongrel mixture of European and Indian varieties with a basic native stock which early accounts describe as small and yellow. A rough average of today's types might approximate an undernourished fox terrier.

were not enough stones. The firewood had partially rotted and could not be used lest during the roasting process it communicate its infirmity to the meat. Rearrangements complete, Peni gutted the pigs and singed them carelessly over the fire in which the stones were heating. When the oven was closed over, each found himself a comfortable stone, piled leaves upon it, and, except for the stings of large black ants, slept peacefully until midafternoon. When the pigs were cooked, they feasted and gave liberally to the hungry dogs. They wrapped the best of the remaining meat in leaves and carried it to the village. That evening Ratu Seru brought a yearling which had strayed from an Indian's dairy herd, and the young men feasted in his kitchen.

On some occasions when meat has been scarce, a large bush pig may be carefully singed, washed, and apportioned to all households; though such distribution reaches the same households as formal distributions of food, it lacks ceremony. To avoid carrying the extra weight of entrails, butchering usually occurs where the pig has fallen in the forest. On the evening of October 6, 1935, Vosalevu had killed a fat boar on his way home from Lekutu. Next morning he engaged Peni and Orisi to butcher it.[42] A troop of children followed because it lay close to the village. On the way firewood was gathered. Children helped. Vosalevu, who was of chiefly caste though of questionable status at Nakoroka, did not choose to dirty his hands. He watched while Peni first cut out the testes and threw them on the fire to broil under the children's supervision and then incised a long triangle through the abdominal wall including scrotum and umbilicus, which was thrown to the dogs. Through this hole he removed all entrails cleanly. But when the esophagus had been disentangled from lungs, heart, and liver, the latter were replaced. The testes, now broiled, were a delicacy for the children.[43] Peni and Orisi grasped the pig by four legs and turned it above the fire. The sizzling smoke from scorched hair and flesh mixed with Vosalevu's leisurely tobacco. At either end of a carrying-pole, Peni and Orisi shouldered the pig to the ford in the river Votua, from which a palm-lined avenue leads to the village. They washed it carefully, letting the river flow through it. In contrast with European technique, the slaughtered pig bleeds only through the wound which has killed him; there is no deliberate attempt to drain the freshly killed meat of its blood by slashing the jugular veins.[44]

42. *Solo* is the Fijian word for disemboweling and singeing.
43. The broiled testes have no magical significance.
44. The method of dressing a domestic pig is similar.

Hunting and butchering are masculine tasks. As the domestic pig has usurped the sacrificial and ceremonial function of cooked human captives of the days of the wars, so hunting the wild pig has gathered some of the reckless glamour of old military excursions. There is actually little danger in hunting pigs. But the rare occasions on which a wounded boar trees a hunter supply adventurous facts which can be exaggerated into valorous experience. In May, 1936, a boar charged a young hunter whose dogs were too few and tore away "the source of his manhood." He bled to death before a search party from his village could find him.[45]

Endurance necessary for the chase might prohibit the participation of most women. But one day Di Litiya, the sister of Bulisivo, haughty and lithe despite the fact that she was ten years past the menopause, persuaded Bulisivo's noisy wife to go with her as hunting assistants for the young chief, Ratu Luke. Di Litiya's chiefly status allows her to outrage the bounds in which femininity confines most women. Her hunting expedition was worthy of comment for several weeks. On rare occasions Nabadua might take his small daughter Narieta to run errands during a day's hunting.

Frequently the village contains chickens. But there is little regularity in care of them. Ratu Seru's feasts had consumed all the chickens of the chiefly family, which were the only domestic fowls at Nakoroka, and during the first half of 1936 the supply was not replenished. Had a need arisen, it could have been satisfied by begging from a relative in another village, stealing from the coops of the nearest Indian village, or outright buying. Eggs, though sometimes boiled to treat a sophisticated guest, do not especially please the Fijian palate. Hence, except for the pilfering of young Ratu Meli,[46] who cooked eggs secretly in my kitchen, all eggs were allowed to hatch at the discretion of the hen who laid them. Only the ravages of the mongoose limited multiplication of the stock. Sometimes hens wander in the bush with their broods because, though the falsetto call of *toa-toa-toa* which announces food for them may be of the same historic stream that prompts the Iowa farm wife, feeding is erratic and intermittent. As in the case of pigs, either man or woman may assume responsibility for feeding them.

The aboriginal land fauna of Fiji was poor. Earliest accounts mention the snakes that crowded the undergrowth, writhed in the forest

45. This occurred at Duleniwai, which is about fifteen miles by path from Nakoroka, across the height of land on the windward slope.

46. Grandson and namesake of Bulisivo, home from a Suva mission school.

branches, and hissed noisily at travelers. They were important as food and are still remembered as a delicacy. Early European settlers, recoiling at contact with the harmless but numerous snakes, brought the mongoose, who quickly emptied the islands of its hereditary enemies and began to consume the eggs of birds.[47] As a result, bird life at Nakoroka is conspicuously dull. Snakes can be found only on the small islands to which the mongoose has not come. Wild pigeons, numerous in the old days, supplied an appreciated delicacy. But they are now extinct. In the old days bird snares were set at favorite roosting places of pigeons. Prey was caught by its feet. Today the children snare the mongoose by its throat for fun, but it is not used as food.

Large tree lizards, which are still supposed to exist, ranked with the turtle as food fit for feasts. But these seem always to have been rare. The mongoose has probably completed their extinction as well as that of the once numerous parrot, valued for feathers and not as food.

Introduced rats abound in coastal regions. Frequently they gnaw the callouses from the feet of sleeping natives. But there was probably an aboriginal rat. Descendants of Rokowaqa identify their earliest ancestor with a rat; though it is taboo to them as food because of its place in their genealogy, it was never an important item in diet.

Of insect foods wild honey is known but rarely used. There is a kind of fat grub, pleated like an accordion until it has been allowed to drink its fill of sweetened coconut milk as preparation for eating. It is said that uncircumcised men should not eat it. Among the old men of today it is a rare delicacy. It is found in chance pieces of rotten firewood, but no one makes special search for it.

When a visiting chief is feasted, several pots of boiled fish almost always accompany the yams and taro. Though spearing fish is sport for boys, and some men have recently learned to fish with hook and line in imitation of British colonists, it is the women who are responsible for supplying fish in large quantity. Women know how to fish with nets; though there is no taboo upon men learning this technique, they do not because it is considered especially suited to feminine temperament. Many sizes and types of nets are adapted to group or individual fishing. Fishing to supply food for a feast is usually done co-operatively by all the younger women of the village, while fish for the family pot are supplied by the younger women of household or family.

The most desirable of fresh-water fish is the *kadroka*, which is similar

47. It has been suggested that the purpose of importing the mongoose was to rid the islands of rats as well.

"THEY WASHED THE PIG AT THE FORD IN THE RIVER VOTUA"

GRATING COCONUTS FOR SWEET PUDDING

to trout. Though rather rare, eels are valued highly, because they are "fat." But there are other fine foods which the streams supply. Snails and prawns, more than twice the size of our shrimp, are gathered singly as the women ply their nets. Sometimes a woman devotes a whole day to searching the rocky eddies in the streams for prawns. Obligation to keep her family well supplied with these fresh-water foods bears constantly upon her. Whenever she travels to or from her gardens, or through the forests for firewood, her eyes are focused for chance delicacies in the streams. When she must journey to another village, perhaps to visit a dying relative whose kinship cycle does not include others of her family, she may perform a magic rite to insure her household a supply of fresh-water foods. She knots a few wisps of grass and, as she draws them tight, spits into the knot; then she grinds the knotted grass into the mud of the path with her heel, calling the names of the foods which she wishes the men and children of her household to eat—eels, snails, etc. Then, lest evil spirits descend upon her, she dashes down the path until she has passed a fork in it; with a few twigs she builds a symbolic barrier behind her so that pursuing spirits, fooled by her device, will follow the other fork of the trail.

In villages of the coast, salt water provides greater variety of marine food—turtles, crabs, clams, and many kinds of fish. Women fish the reefs for crabs and small fish, but men supply turtles and shark in those regions where shark is not a favorite disguise for ancestors. Since turtles rank as chiefly food, men's role as fishermen surpasses that of inland regions. Turtles are caught with the largest of Fijian nets; each catch is heralded by a trumpet blare of the conch shell. In former times priests were frequently consulted to insure a good catch. The frequently recurring belief that misdemeanors of a man's family are reflected in his fisherman's luck is found also in Tavea, an island village off Lekutu. In general, sea foods are considered far superior to those of inland streams. Thoughts of a journey to the seacoast cause the mouths of mountaineers to water. On this basis trade relationships have been established between island villages and the sea people.

The possessive pronouns of most of the dialects of Fiji classify all things which may be taken into the mouth as either food or drink. According to this classification, pineapple, oranges, or stewed taro leaves are "drunk"; tobacco is "eaten." Of those things which are eaten, some are "food," others are "garnish." "Food" includes yams, taro, bananas cooked green, manioc, chestnuts, sweet potatoes, breadfruit, and, of European foods, rice, bread, and potatoes—all foods of starchy consistency. "Garnish" includes meat, fowl, fish, stewed taro leaves,[48] eggplant, and, of European foods, corn, jam, or butter (as garnish for bread), and, practically all vegetables of low starch content. "Food" satisfies hunger, while the various "garnishes" make "food" more tasty. Yet all meals and always all feasts should be accompanied by garnish (*ai laya* in the dialect of Nakoroka, in Bauan *ai coi*). "Accompaniment" is perhaps a better translation for this word. Only poor men eat food without garnish.

Aside from broiling, which is sometimes a hasty method of preparing food in the forest, boiling and baking are the two principal classes of cooking. In recent years frying has been copied from Europeans and Indians and gained considerable popularity, but fried food is always a luxury and has no place on the regular menu. Boiling is the method of every day. In early times it was done exclusively in earthenware pots procured by trade from Tavea off the Lekutu coast. Iron pots, however, have been in use for more than a century. The old earthenware vessel was oval in sagittal section with a small mouth which, during use, was partially closed with leaves and grass; the cooking principle was steam which rose from water in the base of the vessel. But the wide-mouthed iron pots have necessitated the use of much more water and a consequent deterioration in cuisine. When large quantities of food are prepared, for guests or at the time of a village feast, ovens are used for baking; baked food is considered superior to that which is boiled. Though ovens require lengthy preparation of both food and firewood, they accommodate a tremendous quantity at one baking, so that the work of preparing food for many people is actually made lighter by this method. Since occasions for baking rarely arise more frequently than eight or ten times a year, baked food retains its status as a delicacy. Though no sharp categories are drawn, preparing ovens is usually the work of men, while boiling is women's work; but men of common caste (and some chiefs) always pride themselves on their knowledge of the preparation of special boiled dishes.

Yams, taro, green bananas, or some other "food" is boiled in every household every day, in most cases twice a day. The chore of feeding the household regularly is woman's. "Garnish" is more likely to be passed from house to house, especially if it has been boiled in the cream squeezed from grated ripe coconut; the heat of the day turns such cream rancid if kept from one meal to the next. Pork or beef is usually

48. Some "garnish" may be either eaten or drunk.

boiled and reboiled. The broth is considered more delectable than the meat itself. Fish soup served in a coconut shell is also valuable "garnish." Taro leaves, prawns, and eggplant are usually boiled in coconut cream and flavored tastily with small peppers. Women know best how to flavor the pot. Extensive use of coconut, however, is self-indulgent and unwholesome; the people of Nakoroka attribute the fat, sleek appearance of the natives of Lau and Tonga to their constant use of coconut cream in cooking.[49]

The word for sweet pudding means literally "with coconut cream." The puddings may be prepared from baked or boiled taro or breadfruit prepared in various ways; the one constant is always coconut. The more hyaline varieties of taro, boiled and pounded to a rubbery mass and pinched into small balls, makes the simplest pudding. Over this the sweetened liquid squeezed from grated coconut is poured. The coconut has been seared with a hot stone to give it flavor. Half of the balled taro is rolled in the discarded coconut gratings and receives a special name; epicures argue its virtues over against the simpler kind. Another kind requires that the taro be beaten under water until it attains a glassy texture; then it is sliced and served in sweetened coconut cream. Baked puddings are more difficult to prepare and more highly valued. Some kinds are coated with a sweetened coconut preparation which looks like cold brown gravy, wrapped in banana leaves, and baked in an oven. The kind which requires most lengthy preparation, and in consequence is prepared least often, is made from taro which is grated raw, pressed into balls, tied in banana leaves, and baked for four or five days. During the baking process the ovens must be opened and the puddings turned several times. Once baked, this chiefly pudding may be served in a variety of sauces.

Both men and women know how to prepare puddings. Since puddings are almost always served to guests, along with feast foods, men frequently participate in their preparation.[50] Any person or group of persons may decide to prepare a quantity of pudding, particularly at

49. Upon these same physical criteria early travelers noted the contrast in appearance of Fijians and Tongans. The Polynesian is variously described as fat, fine-skinned, graciously proportioned, in contrast with the Fijian, who is lean, angular, rough, and graceless.

50. Dr. Dorothy Spencer has said that the men always prepared the pudding at the village of Nasaucoko on Viti Levu. She indicates the hard labor involved in the pounding process as requiring masculine strength. At Nakoroka women occasionally performed all the tasks of preparation, but their product was considered inferior. Usually, when women wanted to make pudding, they engaged the help of a male kinsman of low status.

the conclusion of any group activity. The baked varieties keep for several days in hottest weather; hence they are a choice gift for departing guests who have a long distance to travel.

In former times baked ti root was used as the sweetening principle. Its syrup was wrung from it in hot water. The same technique may be used to squeeze the sap from sugar cane. But today most regions depend upon sugar which is purchased from Chinese traders. A European missionary invented a coconut sauce sweetened with caramelized sugar which is widespread today. There is willingness to accept new recipes and to experiment.

Early in November, 1935, Bulisivo, who was returning from a long sojourn at his mother's village of Saolo on the windward coast, spent a night at Duleniwai. Nabadua, who was one of Bulisivo's escorts, and who had relatives at Duleniwai, was ashamed of that village's niggardly treatment of its chiefly guest. He decided to make pudding. Unfortunately, no sugar could be begged or borrowed; the village was poverty-stricken. But Nabadua found a small bag of salt. Nabadua is a man of old tradition. He remembers the days when chiefs dug yams in the forest to find them already baked and when chiefs who were caught in the rain and wanted to smoke tobacco could pick burning cinders from the flood. So Nabadua prepared the pudding and used the salt as though it were sugar. Bowing, he presented it to Bulisivo and watched his face anxiously as the chief took his first mouthful. There was no miracle, but Nabadua will try again sometime.

There are other dishes which may be prepared on occasions of group work or merely because someone is hungry for them. Manioc grated and boiled with grated bananas, which may be green or ripe, makes a kind of porridge which is served with sweetened coconut cream. Manioc pounded with grated coconut and allowed to ferment before baking produces a food of which Fijians consider bread to be the European counterpart; such "bread" keeps for many days. In most of the above preparations, breadfruit can substitute for taro or manioc.

On first experience Fijian cuisine seems singularly lacking in seasoning and variety. In inland regions salt is a luxury. In former times it was traded in from coastal regions, especially from certain areas on Viti Levu, but now it is purchased from the Chinese, though many days pass in which salt is lacking from the menu. The tastelessness of Nakoroka food, however, is apparent and not real. To a carefully schooled palate the multitude of varieties of yams and taro each has its distinct flavor. Each pudding has subtle differences of flavor which may create violent likes and dislikes.

Men as well as women pride themselves on their knowledge and skill in preparation of special dishes. Though women assume the task of daily preparation, yet men perform even these chores when there is a temporary shortage of women.

HOUSEBUILDING

Vatili had promised the Buli of Lekutu District that eleven houses and kitchens would be built or repaired at Nakoroka before December. On October 5, 1935, he blew the conch shell at sunrise to call the village men to work. According to a plan previously formulated, the older men went to the bush to gather tying vines and to cut cane for plaiting walls. Peni and Orisi, young and best fitted for heavy work, cut timbers to repair the frame of the old kitchen which stood behind the site of Vatili's dilapidated dwelling house. It was Vatili's plan to use the house that would be newly repaired for dwelling and to convert the former dwelling into a kitchen; though this arrangement would cause the kitchen to face upon the village green, which guests might say spoiled the appearance of the village, yet press of unfinished work required that a minimum of effort be expended upon the satisfaction of each man's needs. The men's shrill calls of exultation sounded like loon cries from the bush as they worked. Vatili dug a trench about the old house foundation for drainage.

By midmorning the men had returned to eat their morning meals separately in their houses. According to old traditions of housebuilding, Vatili should have prepared food for all the workers, but in these modern times, when the colonial administration requires that almost every family group have a house of its own and, with little regard for the immediate food resources of the houseowner, rules the time for housebuilding, ceremonial obligations for housebuilding within the village have fallen almost into disuse. The men loitered in their houses when they had eaten; Vatili had to blow the conch shell several times before they returned to this most unpleasant of chores.

In the afternoon some guests arrived from Nalauvia to speak at the church service next day, which was Sunday. Naicadra and Vaula, who had been bringing cane from the bush, left off working with the housebuilders and went to their gardens to bring food. The Nalauvia men would eat and sleep at the house of Naicadra because, in the absence of a trained missionary teacher, Naicadra's status in the church was highest in all Nakoroka; he had never sinned, and all spoke of him with affectionate pity as a good man. Nabadua pleaded an illness in the stomach from drinking too much kava the night before and went to his house to sleep. Monasa shivered and complained of a headache. Even slight disabilities made house work seem unbearably distasteful. But the younger men, who had not known work under the regime of hereditary chiefs, were more nearly inured to this modern routine of work; commoners among them did not resent Vatili's prestige as "village chief" and foreman of work procedure. Peni cut light timbers to size and passed them to Vatili and Orisi, who, perched high on the rafters, lashed a frame for the roof. Isacodro, though nearly as old as Nabadua, worked vigorously plaiting the cane walls; eight years earlier Isacodro had been disgraced and lost what little social status he possessed,[51] so that his only remaining resource for prestige lay in his physical energy and technical skill. Bici and Samu, who were clumsy at plaiting cane, tied it fast after Isacodro had placed it properly.

On the following Monday the walls were completed. The old men brought bundles of leaves for thatch, and, when they had deposited their bundles in piles near the new house, they sent seven-year-old Sayasi to search for a burning tinder to dry their tobacco. Samu and Vatili and Orisi and Bici worked in pairs to bind down the thatch. One of each pair stood outside on the rafters and, after having placed a bundle of thatch, made it fast by pressing it tightly with a light pole laid transversely. Then he passed a strip of freshly peeled bark of known tough variety about the pole and threaded it through the roof to his partner who sat on a scaffold inside the house. He on the outside sang; at the conclusion of each phrase in his song he struck the pole with a heavy timber as the man inside tugged the bark binding rhythmically and punctuated the song with sharp grunts, until the thatch was snugly fitted to the roof. The song has two functions: it enables the coupled workers to exert themselves at moments when they need to be most efficient and it magically prevents the roof from leaking. Monasa hurled bundles of thatch to the workers on the roof.

It was Wednesday morning before all sides of the roof were thatched and the ridgepole packed tight with grass and covered over. Vatili brought kava from his garden and invited all the men to drink in his new house that night, but the older men of the village did not come. Tradition has decreed that kava be drunk in new houses before occupancy; this is the last vestige of ceremony that is performed regularly

51. See the account of Vaulini's marriage, pp. 329–41 below.

in everyday housebuilding. But Vatili has never been well liked at Nakoroka. Nabadua excused himself because he had fallen and bruised a rib, Monasa felt sick, and Naicadra disapproved of kava-drinking. Vaula was the only elder present; he is of Nadroro, which is also Vatili's land, and frequently a member of Vatili's household. Bici was the only one not of Nadroro who came, but Bici always goes where there is kava to drink.

In former times hereditary chiefs authorized and controlled the work of housebuilding. Each caste group seems to have had its own large eating-house. Ceremonial exchanges occurred through the chief which, though reciprocal and ineffective in changing wealth distribution, pleased the ancestors and fertilized the soil. The chief in supervising such ceremonies performed a necessary service which he alone could perform. But today in Lekutu District natives who hold positions in the heirarchy of colonial officialdom have assumed the authoritative role without accepting its obligations. Bulisivo, hereditary king of Inland Forest, sits quietly in meetings which discuss the procedure of work. If a dispute should arise, he would be called upon to arbitrate. But it is Vatili, officially recognized "village chief," who relays the orders of the Buli at Lekutu and reports those who have been delinquent in their work. Though most men of Nakoroka over forty years of age have filled this role of "village chief," it has been a distasteful task to most of them because the chores which the Buli imposes are greater than the community will fulfil without threats of the colonial courts. Vatili's terms of office have been long; though he claims to dislike the task, it is whispered that he enjoys it secretly. Greatest difficulty in organizing work occurs in attempting to regulate the activities of young chiefs; young Ratu Seru, the nephew of Bulisivo, fled from Nakoroka whenever tasks sanctioned by the government were in order. Rather than bow to Vatili's authority in group work at Nakoroka, he preferred facing the Roko and the Buli and perhaps an English official in a session of the colonial court. The young chief Ratu Luke was less intractable, but he, too, was frequently delinquent. In contrast with Ratu Seru, Ratu Luke had no hereditary authority at Nakoroka, although his rank of birth was unquestionably royal; hence fulfilling an inconspicuous role in group work did not outrage him so violently as it did Ratu Seru.

The work of housebuilding is apportioned according to age and ability. The old men performed the light tasks of cutting thatch and cane. The middle-aged men, who are technically more skilful than young men and still sturdy, plait the cane walls and tie thatch. The young men carry the heavy timbers and serve as assistants to someone more skilled in lashing the house frame together. An age classification which has gained wide use because it has been incorporated in colonial tax regulations groups adults into old men (*qase*, who are exempt from taxes), married men (*uwabula*, who range from perhaps thirty to fifty years of age), and young men (*caurevo*). It is impossible to classify an individual with finality. Thirty-five-year-old Bici[52] was too feeble to perform any but old men's tasks, and yet he lacked the status of an elder. There are unmarried men of thirty-five, while young Namo, hardly thirty, had five children. In any particular situation the roles of the participants fall roughly into these classes, but in varying situations an individual may shift from one class to another. In the rebuilding of Vatili's house, which required more than three full days, seven men worked as old men, five as middle-aged men, and three as young men.

Individual skills or preferences may also determine one's role in group work. Fat bachelor Narogo was the oldest "young man" in the village. He was perhaps thirty-five. His clumsiness and inability to work except under immediate direction will keep him classed as a young man until old age enfeebles him. He fled the circumcision ceremony and has been deemed socially inadequate ever since. Isacodro, who is renowned throughout Bua Province for his speed in plaiting cane walls and his strength and accuracy in building house frames, is past the age when men begin to be allotted lighter tasks. But if his rapid plaiting should cease to press upon those who are tying, and if his impatient cries for more cane no longer send the old men scurrying to the bush for another load, work would languish. Vosalevu, though lithe and only forty-five, prefers the dignity of old men's tasks and the perspective which leisure gives him. He likes to comment upon the general policy of the work.

The last garden was planted on October 29. During the month a small sleeping-house had been built for Isacodro, and new walls and thatch had been raised on the large frame of Nabadua's old kitchen. From early in November until the middle of December the men of Nakoroka built houses at Lekutu and Tavea, off the Lekutu coast. The

52. I have previously spoken of the impossibility of accurate age determination. But with the aid of Mr. Anderson, who for thirty years has lived on the Lekutu coast, I was able to date a few landmarks in recent history; with this knowledge as premise the adult natives could arrive at estimates of their ages.

"WHILE THOSE WHO ARE SKILLED CRAFTSMEN PLAIT WALLS OF
CANE, THE YOUNGER MEN CUT TIMBERS FOR THE ROOF"

Pictures of housebuilding were taken shortly after my arrival, when natives were still
painfully conscious of the presence of an outsider; they wore their Sunday clothes for
everyday work.

"THE WALLS ARE ALMOST COMPLETE"

Some of the men have already gone to the brush for thatch

PLAITING THE WALLS OF A SMALL KITCHEN

PLAITING A HOUSE WALL

Because of the unusually clumsy construction of this house frame, a third row of knots must bind the cane to the eaves. Usually two rows of tying secure a wall.

renovation of Monasa's kitchen, completed December 17, was the last work on houses to occur before the long Christmas holidays. Nakoroka's quota was far from filled. For six weeks following January 21, 1936, houses were built at Lekutu and Sarowaqa. Toward the end of February, Vatili's dwelling house was renovated so that he could move again from his kitchen into his proper dwelling house. For three weeks in March building proceeded in Nalauvia and Nacula. On slack days some of the men found freedom to come home to Nakoroka to construct a kitchen for Orisi. Between April 6 and May 2, two large houses were built for the native medical practitioner[53] at his station near Lekutu. Then it was time to prepare the gardens for another planting and to seek for money to pay colonial taxes, which fell due toward the end of June. The wind and rain still blew through the houses of Bulisivo and Bici, and Raitova's house had no kitchen.

Sometimes, because of housebuilding in other villages, Nakoroka was almost emptied except for the very old. Someone of Bici's household always had to stay in the village to cook for Bici's aged father. Vatili's wife cared for his mother, the aged Daova. Naicadra, who was ailing, was detailed to hunt pigs and inspect the gardens, but his household also assumed the responsibility of caring for paralyzed Waseroma. Old Bulisivo and his blind son required that one of the many women of their household remain at home to prepare their food. But, more often, several men would find excuses for staying at home. Nabadua, Ratu Luke, and Bici sometimes had legally recognized reasons to stay in the village. Frequently they were delinquent without excuse.

During the holidays a spirit of gaiety sprang forth which lasted far into the next year's work. Vatili was able to feast the men of the village while they worked on his dwelling house. During the January and February sojourn at Lekutu the women did not resent the eight-mile journey along slippery paths with burdens of food for their men. The young people of all the villages of the district who were assembled at Lekutu entertained one another with dances during the long evenings. Even the middle-aged men danced until the cocks crew to herald the sun. The older people watched and clapped time; sometimes they even joined in the dancing. The Buli, glutted with holiday foods, demanded little precision of the workmen. When the time arrived for work at Tavea, the Nakoroka people pleasurably anticipated the feasts of fried dough and tea with which the Tavea people would re-

53. The official of the colonial department of medicine who supervised sanitation and health in Lekutu District. This office has been discussed above, pp. 68–70.

gale them. Tavea's island gardens were small, but their land was rich in coconuts; with copra they could afford to buy European delicacies from the Chinese traders.

Even during the gayest season, however, each village group which was assembled at Lekutu lived as a separate economic unit. There was no pretense of observing the ceremonial exchanges which in the old days would have occupied all the participating villages. Each village group lived in the houses of relatives in Lekutu, purchased food from the Chinese, and sent hurried expeditions to Nakoroka gardens for food. A few Nakoroka women always stayed with the men to prepare their meals; Isacodro's daughters took turns with his wife in attending the housebuilders or staying in Nakoroka with the small children of their households. Sometimes children were brought along and temporarily joined the households of their distant relatives at Lekutu. Men of different villages rarely worked together on the same house; each village group performed its separate tasks and vied with the other villages in its attempt to create a superior product. But the evenings contrasted with those during the November period of work at Lekutu: formal visits were exchanged between village groups, and men no longer gathered with their fellow-villagers to drink exclusive kava in their private kitchens. Sometimes the owner of the house which was being built would make a feast for the workmen.

Work at the medical station was of a different order. Though colonial authority required that needs of the native medical practitioner be satisfied by work levied on the community, this man was a native of Kadavu, and the people of the district owed him not even the spurious allegiance which they gave the Buli; the Buli at least was native to the district, and, though he was not of chiefly rank, his title to homage in the district was sustained by British rights of conquest, the right of *liga qaqa*, the "strong arm." The medical practitioner needed two houses, one for inpatients and another small one for his "nurse" assistant. Men of Navakasiga, ten miles west along the coast from Lekutu, built the nurse's house. The men of Nalauvia, and other descendants from the old kingdom of Great Meadow, divided the tasks of building the large house with the men of Nakoroka and Sarowaqa, descendants of Inland Forest; each of these groups brought its timbers, built the frame for its walls and its part of the roof, wrought the cane panels for its walls, and thatched its portion of the roof. Inland Forest and Great Meadow performed their separate tasks on the same house with rivalry, and it happened that serious argument broke out between them,[54] so that the Buli had to speak quietingly to them and demand that gifts be exchanged to expiate their anger; the holiday spirit of good will had worn thin through two months of labor. The medical practitioner presented feasts to the workers as each stage in the building of the house was completed. When the frames were complete, he made formal distribution of food "to insert the wall panels"; when the houses were complete, he feasted them again to "bathe the workers." During the month of work seven cows, which he purchased from surrounding Indian settlements, were slaughtered and baked. Because the medical practitioner had the new kind of prestige which evokes chiefly etiquette, he felt impelled to sustain this prestige among the housebuilders as though he were a true chief; but, because he had no hereditary retainers, the feasts had to be prepared by those whose severe infection with ringworm gave cause for their confinement at the medical station. Though the feasts were elaborate, and though the medical practitioner had met the obligations incumbent upon him who would be chief with far more lavish display than the Buli bothered to observe, still he was merely imitating the traditions of ceremonial exchange associated with housebuilding. Had the Buli chosen to recognize him as an alien chief desirous of fulfilling the "rules of the land" and reciprocated with presentations of feast food, mats, and whale teeth, the medical practitioner's display would have appeared poor and inadequate. The hospital community, which included all to whom he was chief, was lacking in size and supernatural sanction as a political entity so that it could not participate in ceremonial exchange like a village native to the region.

According to traditional theory, groups which have worked in the construction of a house enter into prolonged ceremonial relationships with the houseowner. Within the local community these ceremonies of exchange function as part of that interminable series which formalizes the relations between chief and community. As the chief makes his initial request for a new house, he should present whale teeth in large numbers[55] to be distributed among the participating groups.[56] Then as each village group brings its allotment of wall posts, it presents food gifts to the chief "to imbed the wall posts." When the frame is complete, the chief presents an elaborate feast to the workmen and accom-

---

54. See above, pp. 64–65.

55. During the nineteenth century the whale-tooth market was flooded, so that it is impossible to estimate the original value.

56. See Song VII in my *The Flight of the Chiefs* (New York, 1942), in which a request is made along the path of relationship for the building of a chiefly house.

panies his presentation with a distribution of whale teeth "to insert the cane panels." When the walls are complete, each village hangs clusters of whale teeth on the wall posts which it has inserted; these are "to place the thatch." The chief will distribute these whale teeth among all those who have contributed toward his presentations. As each village completes the thatch of its section of roof, shells of a large sea snail[57] are tied in as decoration for the ceiling. If one village group lacks these shells, other groups donate from their surplus so that the shells design the ceiling symmetrically. Whale teeth, however, are not passed freely about; when the village groups hang them on the wall posts, each wants the prestige of its own contribution, because the value of whale teeth is insuperable. When the thatch is complete, the houseowner presents a feast and gifts of mats and whale teeth to "bathe the workmen."

In entirety the series of exchanges should be almost reciprocal. The presentation by the workmen to the chief "to place the thatch" is the largest of all and outranks any return presentation by the chief during the building process. But the chief will have occasion at a later time to level the score. If the exchange has occurred within the community, the chief will return the surplus wealth at a fertility feast; if an outside community or kingdom is involved, the chief of the group who owns the newly built house will pay a formal visit to his creditors to present gifts. There is no payment for labor except that all concerned will enjoy the favors which the ancestors of the region will cast among those who have engaged in ceremonial exchanges. Hence, to receive supernatural benefits, a commoner must serve a chief; and a chief must initiate activities in which reciprocal exchange is well formalized.

Frequently members of one political group call upon a neighboring kingdom to perform a task for which their skill is renowned. Several years ago the Buli at Lekutu had engaged the men of Macuata through negotiations with their chiefs to build a tremendous house at Lekutu. Exchanges between two separate political groups are of more highly competitive nature: the Buli levied taxes upon all the people of Lekutu District so that his return gifts to the Macuata men might exceed what he had received. The periodic exchanges set up during the period of housebuilding continued long after the house was complete; in April, 1935, the Buli Lekutu carried an elaborate gift presentation, which he had levied upon a grudging populace, to the chiefs of Macuata. This will be reciprocated at some future date. A region's ancestors are

57. The *buli* shell, which is sometimes considered the insignia of a chiefly house.

pleased when their descendants engage in competitive displays of this sort to publicize the fertility which these ancestors have made possible. But the economic relations within Lekutu District have fallen upon evil days because of disruption in the relations between ruling chiefs and their subjects. The ancestors of Nakoroka have little interest in displays which are initiated by the Buli Lekutu, who is not their descendant; the Buli in his turn is not careful to redistribute among his subjects the gifts which he receives.

There has been constant change in architectural technique during the past century. The concept of the chief's house lashed with sennit of coconut fiber seems to have spread gradually from Tonga through Lau and arrived in Lekutu District within the last generation. It is this type of house which requires the most elaborate ceremonial observances during its construction. The most-admired houses of this type have been built recently in Macuata Province under the strictly centralized authority of Macuata's chiefly family, which has been strongly influenced by Tongan tradition. In the old days Lekutu District built *vale leke*, tall houses with thatched roofs extending to the ground and with no walls. In more recent times a rectangular house with wall panels of cane thatched on the outside has found wide popular use throughout Vanua Levu; chief's houses of the present day are elaborations of this type. Within the last decade a new type which has been borrowed directly from common house types of Tonga has become popular. The walls are plaited from cane in a single panel broken only by doors; no thatch is bound to the outside, and wind and light penetrate. Almost all houses built in Lekutu District in 1935 and 1936 were of this last type. Some even have rounded ends in true Tongan style.[58] Many variations on these last two house types occur in every village of Vanua Levu. Minor differences in patterns of plaiting probably depend upon the varying skills of individual workmen. At some period during the past, houses with walls plaited from split bamboo were fashionable. Bulisivo's dilapidated house is the only bamboo house at Nakoroka.

Any manufactured thing of unusual workmanship may be called "chiefly" in character, but respect for such chiefly quality is not buttressed by supernatural sanction. An influential commoner may build a house of chiefly proportions which will be described as a chiefly house. It is the presence of a hereditary chief which creates the respect

58. This house type is called *lotoa*. Natives speak of it as Tongan.

taboo. In the old days, when the powers and prestige of the chiefs were greater, there was doubtless less distinction between houses of chiefly workmanship and houses owned by chiefs. Today houses owned by chiefs, regardless of the nature of their construction, must still be held in respect.

According to old tradition, houses of chiefs should be thatched with a special kind of leafy shrub. The wood of the greenheart of India, *vesi*, is still reserved for the construction of chief's houses.[59] Before a greenheart tree is felled, kava must be mixed in the forest, and each workman must drink.[60] An accident will befall him who neglects to drink, but any man, regardless of his rank of birth, may cut the sacred tree after having drunk. To avoid carrying a heavy bowl to the forest, kava is mixed and served in a banana leaf. In the old days the felling of trees was accomplished with a stone wedge held in the left hand and a heavier stone used as a hammer.

A large timber may be brought to the village according to several methods, each of which has its special songs to co-ordinate group effort. When the branches have been removed and ropes attached for dragging, a crowd of both men and women assemble and take places along the ropes. Those in front sing: "Pull the rope to death in the rear." Those in back respond: "Pull the rope to death before." Then together they chorus a chant which ends in united jerks of the ropes to jar the timber from its settled position in the soft foliage and mud. With a cry they run, hauling upon the ropes, while a master of ceremonies chants in rhythm to their running. After short progress there is resting, and special songs fill the interval until the entire process is repeated. During the last interval of dragging, the workers dance violently, especially the women, and with a final shout drop the ropes. If possible, the timber will be rolled into a stream and floated at least part way toward its destination; for this there are also special work songs. If the timber is not too heavy, poles for carrying may be bound to it. The workers sing:

> Lift up the great wall post,
> Lift up the great wall post,
> To the village of the great sky.

As they carry the log, two men sit upon it; one chants so that the workers may respond in unison and work rhythmically; the other swings a

59. It is also used for making kava bowls.

60. Though the boxwood, *buabua*, is even more durable than *vesi* and is frequently used in chiefly houses, it may be cut without ceremony.

dance club and blows the conch shell. Old Kaiyava, father of Bici, says
that these principals in the ceremony must be of chiefly caste, but the
younger men do not corroborate him. When the timber lies in the village, the people gather about it with sticks and beat upon it in rhythm
to a song which ends with a victory shout:

> Gather, gather, people of Nakoroka,
> Gather at the greenheart log[61]
> And sing the victory song in great voice:
> *Suru kobelo-o-o, ho ho hi hi-i-i!*[62]

If the log is to be used as a wall post in a chief's house, it must be
peeled of its bark and sometimes shaped near its top into a symbol of a
human head and neck set upon a columnar trunk. To protect it from
the rain while skilled men finish it to proper smoothness, a shelter is
built. Women or children cannot go to this place. He who has been the
craftsman will tell those who accidentally trespass this taboo how to
expiate their negligence: whether to prepare kava or sweet pudding as
offering for the village ancestors. A bark-cloth signal is tied conspicuously near the log's shelter as a warning that the place is sacred. When
the timber has been inserted in its place in the house, the taboo automatically dissolves.

It is said that human victims of war must be buried beneath each
house post in Macuata. The people of Bua, however, consider human
sacrifice barbarous and disclaim its use, even in ancient times. It is
possible, however, that introduced Christian mores have brought re-
valuation of old practices so that the people of today like to cast responsibility for all sin upon their neighbors, in hope that their own
character will so be beatified.

Ceremonial observances still exist in modified form. The song for
carrying timber was used when the posts were brought for the large
house at the medical station, but no priests rode upon them to conduct
the chants. The song which accompanies the dragging of timbers has
not been used since the great house was built for the Buli at Lekutu
several years ago. This represents Lekutu District's greatest achievement in housebuilding. Macuata workmen were engaged to help with
its construction. Architecturally it is a poor reduplication of the more
carefully wrought chiefly houses of Naduri, Nakalou, Nasasa, and
Dreketi on the Macuata coast. It lacks the carefully designed tying

61. Or whatever kind of log has been felled.

62. *Hi-i-i* is a nasal whinny which begins on a shrill falsetto note and falls laughing to a
grunt in deep bass. It is the cry of exultation which punctuates group work of all kinds or
marks the completion of a task or a feat of strength.

with coconut fiber sennit, a skill known only to a few Macuata chiefs. Its wall posts are but carelessly finished. Yet it is Lekutu District's only attempt to co-operate in united effort to produce an architectural monument in the elaborate style of the islands to the east.[63] The new house at the medical station employed the new techniques of decorative tying with sennit, supplemented with hemp rope from the Chinese store, but its proportions were not monumental.

Though it does not occur exclusively in chiefly houses, one characteristic of all carefully built houses which commands respect is the raised earth platform on which the house rests. Though all houses are slightly raised for purposes of drainage, some houses rest on platforms faced with stone and more than four feet high. The margin between the edge of the platform and the outer wall of the house is sacred and taboo to all but the houseowner. According to legend,[64] the platforms of some chiefly houses could serve as temporary sanctuaries for warriors tired of battling. Doorways to houses with high foundations require an approach; these range from a simple log cut to give foothold, to earthen ramps paved with stone and set among artfully cultivated shrubs.

Most of the chores of housebuilding are concerned with repairing the more perishable thatch and walls in old house frames. Once the house frame has been constructed, the housebuilder needs to use but little architectural thinking. But, in constructing a new house, he must carefully determine size, shape, and type before work begins. Each young man who goes to the bush for timbers knows precisely how many timbers he must procure of each kind. All the timbers of the house frame are named and classified according to function, so that the young man, who knows the dimensions of the house in fathoms, can choose the timbers in the forest and cut them almost to size; hence the heavy work of carrying timbers to the village is minimized. In the meantime the older men have been preparing a shallow excavation about the proposed house foundation to secure good drainage. They throw the excavated dirt on top of the foundation to raise it. Holes for the wall posts are not sunk until the beams, the "sacred timbers," which will rest upon the wall posts and determine the dimensions of the

63. Great houses built at Bua village in the kingdom of Bua at the beginning of the Christian Era were strictly Tongan in pattern. The great house posts of an oval house of the half-Tongan Ra Masima are still in existence. But this style of building was never used in elaborate detail in the interior of Lekutu District.

64. See Song I in my *The Flight of the Chiefs*.

house, have been placed on the foundation as measures. Symmetry of contour is admired; but, since the dimensions of the house are usually adjusted to the size of the already cut timbers, exact symmetry is luck rather than design.

All houses built during 1935 and 1936 were of small proportions. Even the house frames at the medical station were small enough so that the timbers could be lifted into place without the aid of mechanical devices. But the large houses of chiefs may require considerable mechanical ingenuity. In 1894 Sir Basil Thomson assisted with the erection of a great house, probably on Viti Levu:

It once fell to my lot to build a native house which was to gratify the natural vanity of the mountaineers in Fiji by surpassing all other houses in size and magnificence. The main posts were enormous logs of *vesi* [greenheart of India], a timber heavier than oak, and each of them must have weighed more than ten tons. I had the holes dug to receive them, and lined them with two feet of stones to prevent the trees from driving farther into the earth than the measured depth. Then I borrowed some strong tackle-blocks and ropes, and summoned all the able-bodied men of the district to help in lifting them. I carefully explained the use of the tackle, and tried to get them into their places; but a council of the elders sat on the case, and flatly declined to use it. There was only one way, they said, of raising heavy weights, and that was the way of their fathers. What could one lone white man do against an army of pig-headed ancestor-worshipers? I gave in and watched them. They spent the first day in getting stout logs with forked tops. With these they built a solid platform sloping upwards to a height of 15 feet above the holes. Then they fastened strong vines to the end of the logs, and rolled them to the base of the inclined plane. Butt-end first, they dragged them inch by inch along the platform—100 men on either vine—until the logs lay at length horizontal, with their bodies projecting over the platform, above the hole. Then the council of elders sat on them, literally and metaphorically, and had them shifted an inch or two to the side. When they were satisfied, two men with axes hacked at the logs that formed the end of the platform. One by one these snapped until, as the supports were cut away, the great butt-end overbalanced, and the huge log began to tip up. Its head rose to an angle of 45 degrees, and then with a crash and a deep thud it shot down into the hole, and then men swarmed up and fastened vines to its summit by which it was easily hauled into position. I must say, in parenthesis, that I was unlucky enough to intervene at this juncture with my block-and-tackle. I made it fast to a cross-beam lashed to two trees, but no sooner had my twenty men begun to strain upon the rope than the beam snapped like a watch-spring, and swept the council of elders into the hole; so that, until this accident is forgotten, the primitive method of raising weights is likely to prevail in that district. I asked the old men what they did with heavier weights still, and they immediately answered, "We make the platform of earth, and dig it away to make the log tip up."[65]

Like symmetry, rigidity in the house frame is attained, as it were, accidentally. If it were not for the firm imbedding of wall posts, the

65. *Op. cit.*, pp. 380–82.

frame would collapse like a bottomless shoe box, because no diagonal braces are used. The nature of the roof requires triangles which produce rigidity, but the mechanical principle involved is unknown. Hence all shelves, beds, benches for drying copra, and modern imitations of European tables must be built upon legs which are firmly sunken into the earth, or they will collapse. The only observed attempt to build a movable table met with ludicrous failure. Doors made from cane bound to parallel cross-braces quickly degenerate into sagging parallelograms.

Strangely, too, builders overlook the principle of allowing gravity to support heavy timbers upon firm bases and thus to minimize stress. The frequently heavy beams which support the gables of the roof are allowed to rest in the frail vine bindings by which they are fastened to the horizontal beams that rest upon the wall posts. While the house is under construction, the frame is frequently supported by scaffolding until the support of thatch and cane-plaited walls adds sufficient firmness. Resting the weight of the roof on top of the horizontal beams, instead of hanging it under them, would produce a more efficient structure with less strain upon construction materials. Nevertheless, Fijian houses never need repair because of failing firmness of house frames. The thatch of roof and walls decays long before the house frame shows signs of weakness. When the roof is rethatched, the beams of the frame can always be retied.

The plaiting of the walls and the laying of thatch, and particularly the rapid tying of these, are accomplished according to set rule. The individual artisan shows little inventiveness. Isacodro, most renowned of artisans, never adjusted his method to the particular curve of the wall; in bending and tying the cane to edge doorways, he invariably bent three stalks in a bunch regardless of their variation in size. In supervising my progress at the same task, he insisted that I undo my work because I had deemed a fat stalk the equivalent of two; in spite of the fact that my adjustment made a tighter fit, it was the "wrong way" and had to be redone. Such dogmatism in technique makes for high speed in work at the expense of perfection in the finished product. Skill in work consists in learning to perform routine motions quickly. The result is in native terms "good enough" and, in fact, both sturdy and handsome; but on close inspection most houses show gross imperfections due to compliance with the dogmatic rules.

Considerations of the rank which the house symbolizes color the aesthetic judgment of its beauty. Fine wood, coconut fiber tying, shell decorations—all speak of chiefliness and are held in high regard. Workmanship, if noticeably bad, becomes an important criterion; but, if it meets the demand of utility, it rarely gains further notice. There is one purely decorative structure which all houses must have to look complete; thin shafts of the black porous wood of the sago palm must protrude from the thatch at either end of the ridgepole.[66] Europeans have frequently speculated as to its esoteric significance; no one has ever discovered its "meaning." Once when I asked Bulisivo whether it was, perhaps, the dwelling place of ancestral spirits, he silenced my questioning. He laughed and, pointing to the village church, which bore a small upright cross at either end of its ridgepole, he said: "If there were no crosses on the church, it would not be a church." Young Namo once said that if he saw a house without these projections, he would go to the bush, find some shafts of sago palm, and insert them; it is unpleasant to see a house which lacks them.

OTHER INDUSTRIES

Aside from the timbers, cane, thatch, and many kinds of vines and fibers for tying, the land supplies an abundance of other resources which are useful for industry. The unwooded hilltops, the land which is called "sunny" in contrast with the dark forests, are covered with the wild fern, *qato*, which grows waist high and higher. The young women gather it in huge bundles, spread it on the village green to dry crisp in the sun, then lay it cleverly with stems hidden to make a heavy carpet on the floor of a new house. Its fragrance resembles the evergreen of temperate climates. Its softness reduces the wear on the mats which are spread upon it. In hot rainy months it molds with the dampness that pervades everything and must be renewed.[67] Fern mattresses of two hands' thickness soften the table-like beds made from rows of unfinished saplings; after several months red ants and colonies of centipedes infest them and necessitate renovation.

Bamboo water containers grow ready-made. The swamps provide a reed which makes a soft pliable mat for sleeping. The Kauri pine exudes resin which burns slowly and with a brilliant flare that serves well as a torch or, in a broken coconut shell, as a lamp to use indoors at night. A poisonous tuber bleaches cloth. Medicinal roots and leaves abound, some of real potency as cathartics. Dyes for bark cloth, the

66. This structure is called the *balabala*.

67. Women must take advantage of every sunny day to dry all household textiles and check the growth of the ever present mold.

many-colored coiffures which Fijian fashion decrees, and face and body paint are extracted from the red turmeric root or a black brew of chestnut leaves. Fragrant leaves and flowers decorate the dancer's costume. But pandanus from which washable mats are made must be cultivated. Five Nakoroka women had each planted a few stalks of pandanus in shady places.

Coconut palms are not indispensable, although they have many uses. The leaves make baskets both temporary and permanent, fans of multiple use, thatch for kitchens which is more fireproof than that used on sleeping-houses, and mats for rough wear. When dry, leaves serve as quick-burning torches and as kindling to make the smouldering ashes of last night's fire blaze. The petioles, carved sharp, make temporary spoons for eating the soft unripe jelly inside the coconut. The fiber of the husk makes sennit. The stem upon which the nut cluster hangs sweeps rough debris into the hearth. The trunk bridges streams and chasms. Oil squeezed from the ripened nut or allowed to seep into a wooden oil dish in the heat of the sun can be mixed with wild scents to produce a salve which is valued as an article of trade and which makes the bodies of visitors glisten in the evening.[68] It beautifies and at the same time protects against mosquitoes. The industrious Di Litiya used to busy herself at casual evening gatherings with a piece of sandal-wood which she grated to fine powder for scenting her salve.

Mat production is Nakoroka's industrial specialty. The swamp reed which makes the most pliable kind grows abundantly near the path to Lekutu. The supply of pandanus is small at present; though rougher than mats of swamp reed, those of pandanus are more durable.[69] Mat-making, women's special industry, consumes much of their time. The wife of Monasa frequently worked at plaiting until far after midnight; sometimes she began again before sunrise because she needed a large supply to carpet the new house which Monasa was building near his garden lands.[70] Once five young women each made mats to take to the mines on the windward coast in hope of lucrative sale. Whenever there was occasion for gift presentations to guests, and at the ceremonial presentations of birth, marriage, and death, mats were a usual com-

68. In 1850, according to Thomas Williams (*Fiji and the Fijians*, ed. George S. Rowe [London, 1858], I, 119), use of this salve was newly introduced on Vanua Levu from Lau and Tonga.

69. There is a third material, a woody fiber for making the most durable of house mats. But its incidence is rare.

70. Monasa was planning to sever his connection with the village and produce for a surplus as an individualist (see above, pp. 78–79).

SUN-CURING *QATO*

The young women have spread fresh *qato* to be cured in the sun before they place it on the floor of a new house.

MAKING THE PALM-LEAF MAT

POTTERY OF THE ISLAND TAVEA

DRYING HAIR NEWLY BLACKENED WITH A BREW OF
CHESTNUT LEAVES

modity of exchange. The large floor mats of the houses depreciate constantly and must be repaired or replaced and the old ones relegated to kitchen use. Though most of this work is done individually, on several occasions during the year the press of work required co-operative effort. On December 14, 1935, Melika, Naicadra's wife, engaged the help of the village women to prepare a large floor mat of pandanus for Naicadra's large house. Five women worked all day until about ten in the evening, when Melika served kava to celebrate the completed mat.[71] Vatili has said that one woman working undisturbed can plait a sleeping mat, which is six to eight feet long and four to six feet across, in four days.

Preparation of materials for mats requires considerable work. On every sunny morning the village green is littered with pandanus leaves spread to dry and bleach. Then, when groups gather casually in various households to visit in the evening, industrious women bring armfuls of leaves to be split in proper widths. Superfluous fiber must be scraped away with a shell or a piece of broken glass. Especially sleeping-mats are patterned with interwoven strands of pandanus dyed black; the dying process requires chestnut leaves and twigs. Swamp reed, too, must be carefully dried, bleached, and scraped before it can be plaited. On April 20, 1936, these reeds were in proper state to be harvested. The women and children spent several days in the swamp cutting reeds and laying them in bundles near the path where the men, returning from housebuilding at the Lekutu medical station, would find them and bring them home. Preparation of materials was extensive during April because the women planned to make many mats during May and June, while their husbands were at the mines searching for money with which to meet the colonial tax.

Mat-designing is the only decorative art in which the women participate. According to legend, the idea of patterning mats came to Bua from the Yasawa Archipelago west of Viti Levu. But patterns are free to all who will copy. All women invent designs. Long ago parrot feathers were used to design mats, but the early introduction of wool yarn has completely replaced this art. The artistic productions most admired today are embroidered borders made with gawdy yarns purchased from the Chinese. Embroidering is crude; triangles and circles a foot in diameter are stitched on in stitches six inches long. The ladies of Nakoroka's royal house spent their rare leisure planning designs to be appliquéd with yarn. My services in drawing circles with a string

71. She had been working on it for several days without assistance.

and a pencil were much in demand; natural objects never supply exact circular contour which can be traced. Woolen fringe also mars the simplicity of mats otherwise unblemished.

Women's industry determines the number of mats which a household contains. A man is wise if he marries a woman skilled in mat-making.

The small mat made from two coconut leaves with interlocked midribs has no value as an exchange article but serves many useful purposes. It carpets the house floor near the lower door, where muddy feet would spoil a more delicate fabric. Frequently it is a kitchen mat. It may curtain the doorway to shut out rain and pigs. Though in a similar manner men plait the coconut leaf as thatch for cookhouses, the trick of interlocking the midrib is woman's special knowledge. It takes only an hour to make a mat of this kind.[72]

Coconut leaves also make fine baskets. Women like to make two kinds of round basket, with capacity for about a bushel, in which to keep rolls of prepared strands for mat-plaiting. In the old days the women made large baskets of coconut with lids which were used for personal belongings of both men and women; but in the early nineteenth century whaling vessels brought sea chests which could be locked. More recently traders have brought boxes which serve well for storage, and the technique for making the basket with lid has gradually been forgotten. They can also make a pliable bag of coconut leaf. Some women also plait small baskets of pandanus in which they keep their tools, tobacco, playing cards, and perhaps perfume.

Both men and women make the temporary baskets of coconut leaf (*ketekete*) which are used for carrying food from the gardens, for presenting feasts, and, when once used, for disposing of garbage and refuse; in the last instance the basket is discarded with its contents. The "true *ketekete*" is shaped like an envelope without a flap. During construction the midrib serves as a base for plaiting, but when complete it is split to form the lips of the basket. The plaiting of the "*ketekete* of Tonga" begins similarly, but the ends of the leaves are braided and tied to form a handle instead of being incorporated into the walls of the basket. Nabadua could make either of these baskets in about three minutes. Di Litiya's work was more firmly plaited; she spent perhaps five minutes on a basket. Small yams or taro are sometimes woven into "*ketekete* of Tonga" to be baked; the basket incases

72. These mats were called *cabakau* and, perhaps by an accidental twist of the tongue, *cakobau*. The first name, however, is correct.

the food, and the midrib is not split until the food is ready to be eaten. The *sova* basket is made from a length of coconut leaf halved along its midrib. The midrib, which has served as a base for plaiting, is bound into a hoop to form the rim of the basket. The trailing ends of the leaflets are tied haphazardly at the bottom. Size varies, but some *sova* can hold a couple of bushels. When a great feast is to be served, both men and women busy themselves with the preparation of these temporary baskets. They are rarely made in long anticipation. A man going on a journey may sit down at the edge of the village to make a *ketekete* for his awkwardly packed belongings or his "food for the path," as an after-thought just before starting.

Crafts of Fiji are highly localized. All regions make mats, but Nakoroka specializes in matmaking at the expense of all else and depends upon trade to maintain a balanced supply of industrial products. Before the influence of European trades had become widespread, tools, pottery, salt, bark cloth, wooden bowls, drums, oil dishes, and headrests were almost all imported into Nakoroka from other Fijian communities. The lavish exchanges of gifts which accompanied intercommunity marriages, formal visits between chiefs, trade partnerships between individuals, and formal trade games[73] between villages of coast and interior permitted lively diffusion of products throughout the islands. All but the most crudely carved wooden utensils came from Lau. Great kava bowls of the sacred greenheart wood, decorated kava cups of coconut shell, carved walking-sticks, and drums were imported into Nakoroka largely through their special trade relation with the small island village Tavea off the Lekutu coast. Whenever the people of Tavea weave a turtle net, the people of Nakoroka still must feast them to make the net productive. The maritime Taveans have always maintained lively trade relations with the islands to the east, which they can utilize upon the request of a Nakoroka chief. Though in recent years wood-carving techniques have spread among the chiefs of interior Vanua Levu, their output is not great, and Lau must still supply kava bowls and other wooden articles of which the Chinese trading store carries no stock.[74] Itinerant craftsmen from Lau find employment carving drums in the coastal regions of Vanua Levu. Drums are too heavy to be readily shipped about. Bulisivo has carved the village

73. The game *Ago* and its modern counterpart are described below, pp. 347–50.

74. When I wanted to purchase a kava bowl, Bulisivo sent a request to Tavea which was fulfilled in a few weeks.

drum[75] at Nakoroka; in his plentiful leisure he also carves walking-sticks of sandalwood or ironwood. But he alone at Nakoroka knows these arts. His mother's brother, a sophisticated chief of the windward coast, taught him. The other men at Nakoroka who consider themselves skilled woodworkers know only the crude technique for hollowing large timbers to make rough mortars for chopping kava. Wooden headrests are widely used. But those native to Nakoroka are simply cylinders of bamboo; the only two which show skilful craftsmanship were imported.

Weapons were made at Nakoroka in the old days, but the art has long been forgotten. Metal axes, brought by whaling vessels, rapidly replaced clubs of native manufacture. Today these axes, like all ancestral weapons, have become sacred receptacles of supernatural power. Some of Nakoroka's ancient spears tipped with the spines of the sting ray may be of local manufacture. But clubs and spears with carved decorations were probably made in Lau. Within historic memory chiefs have battled for the possession of famous weapons; cross-cousins or in-laws might exchange them as gifts over wide distances.

Pottery was essential for cooking. Greatest variety in pottery forms are found on Viti Levu, where pottery is still in everyday use.[76] Nakoroka today has less than half-a-dozen articles of Fijian pottery. These were all made on the island of Tavea, where old women still know the art; much of Tavea's population is descendant from Bau, whence they may have brought their knowledge of pottery-making. Tavean style, however, is distinct from that of other regions. Three forms predominate: a large oval pot with a wide mouth for boiling food (*kuro*), a spheroidal form with small mouth for heating water, and a wide-mouthed pot into which he who wished to dye his hair could insert his head. Today Nakoroka buys its cooking utensils at Lekutu from the Chinese. Iron kettles belong to every household.

The bark-cloth industry has become almost extinct at Nakoroka. Women there never produced it on a large scale and never designed it. Of the several kinds of bark cloth, they knew how to make only the simplest. Bici says that he remembers when the older women could smoke their bark cloth to produce a brick-red finish. The process, however, is no longer known. Nakoroka bark cloth is suitable only for gee-

75. Each village has a large drum to beat on special occasions so that neighboring villages will know that the day is festive.

76. Dr. Dorothy Spencer, who worked in Colo West, Viti Levu, during the same period in which I resided at Nakoroka, reports that metal cooking pots of European make are more rare in that part of Viti Levu, and pottery utensils still extensively used.

Top, finger bowl; *left to right*, throwing-club; a dart for the ancient game called "hurling the chicken head"; axes brought to Fiji by nineteenth-century whalers but now honored as ancestral weapons; *lower left*, a head rest of wood.

Top, a wooden bowl (*dreli*) for bathing infants or for making coconut oil; *center left*, wooden finger bowl (*dari kacu*); *center right*, clay bowl (*dari soasomu*) used for drying hair; *front*, drum for the dance.

IMPORTED ARTICLES OF WOOD AND POTTERY

Left, a wooden platter and pestle for making taro pudding; *right*, mortar for chopping kava; the pestle is of European iron.

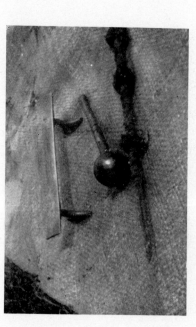

Top to bottom, ancient head rest; throwing-club; spear tipped with sting-ray spine.

WOODEN ARTICLES MANUFACTURED AT NAKOROKA

BASKETS OF PALM LEAF ON A PANDANUS MAT

On the left, the true *ketekete;* on the right, a fine basket (*kato drika*); in the foreground, a *noke*.

BASKET- AND MATMAKING ARTICLES

Left to right: Rolls of pandanus leaf prepared for matmaking; a temporary basket of palm leaf and a basket of pandanus; two fine baskets of coconut leaf (*idre*); a *noke*, a *kato drika* containing pandanus which has been split into fine strands for mats.

THREE BASKETS ON TWO MATS OF PANDANUS

Left, a temporary basket of palm leaf (*ketekete* of Tonga); *center*, a decorated basket of pandanus (*kato voivoi*); *right*, a basket of unknown origin, probably Indian.

FANS AND A ROUGH MAT OF PALM LEAF

strings and secular use. Striking designs in black and red which both men and women must wear to dance on ceremonial occasions come principally from Lau and Taveuni. The chiefs of coastal Vanua Levu are supplied amply with bark cloth to decorate their walls, but it is rarely of local manufacture. Even the white variety used as a shroud at Nakoroka can no longer be prepared locally. Bici begged a large piece for his own shroud from a relative at Lekutu. Designing may be relatively recent in Fiji. The centers of highest development are those which have experienced most Tongan influence. In the literature of Bua Province luxuriance of the mulberry trees of Tonga, from which bark cloth is made, characterize Tonga in contrast with Fiji.

Salt was also important as a trade article until the expansion of Chinese traders made it easily available to all Vanua Levu. Though all villages of the coast have learned how to extract it from sea water, the best salt has always come from Viti Levu. The old men remember visits of Viti Levu chiefs in Bua Province at which mats from Nakoroka were exchanged for bricks of dark-colored salt; a sleeping-mat was considered equivalent to a brick about a yard long. Nabadua claims to know how to make salt; but perhaps to distinguish himsel he is merely boasting of unfounded accomplishments. He says that a hole is dug in a mangrove swamp where tide water evaporating in the mud precipitates salt and raises its concentration. When water accumulates in the hole, it is boiled dry in a pot, and the process repeated until the pot is full of muddy salt.

In recent years a new stimulus for trade has arisen. Every Fijian has financial obligations toward church and state. European knives, iron bars for making pig spears, axes, cooking utensils, soap, and kerosene are no longer luxuries. Hence, aside from the wealth of his land, he must have money or some commodity that can be reckoned in terms of European values. The European copra market fulfils this need. On November 1, 1935, all Nakoroka men cut coconut meat from the shell and carried it to the Chinese at Lekutu to obtain money for a school tax, three shillings per family. On December 14 the young men cut copra and built a rack for drying it; though undried coconut is heavier, it brings a lower price. The people of Nakoroka needed money for their Christmas feasts: sugar and flour, which are the ingredients of a modern delicacy, and fat to fry them in, can be bought from the Chinese. Every month or so there is collective demand in the village for money; the need is discussed by the elders, who determine the time for cutting nuts. Besides these co-operative enterprises individuals who are not free to work at the mines find it convenient to cut a basketful when they need a fathom of calico for a new shirt. Though kava brings a higher price than copra, consumption in Nakoroka itself is too great to permit great export.

On December 26, 1935, the Christmas feast had exhausted the food stores in the village. Almost all the ripe coconuts had already been sold to the Chinese to buy sugar, tea, and flour for the Christmas feast. But the season was still festive. Guests remained and expected food in harmony with the season. So the women of Votua, the group which contained the chief of all Inland Forest, took the initiative in organizing a women's expedition to search in the forest for resin of the Kauri pine which the Chinese value highly. The women knew where every tree grew; in past years the trunks had been tapped so that the resin would flow more freely. Because the trees were scattered and in the remote bush, they asked Isacodro to accompany them and build a temporary shelter somewhere near the trees; two or three days would be required to complete the work. On such excursions it is always advisable to include some man who can prepare kava and offer libations to forest spirits, particularly to the spirits of the Kauri pine.[77] Isacodro, who was well schooled in ritual for dealing with the supernatural, knew how to make the expedition auspicious. After several days in remote Tavua land they returned with a couple of small basketfuls, which sixteen-year-old Ratu Meli, grandson of Bulisivo, sold to the Chinese, purchasing in return jam and milk canned in New Zealand.

The small supply of pine resin (*makadre*) prevents its becoming an important economic asset. The trees which supply it are ancient and must choose their own sites for growing. Each large tree supplies a limited quantity. But on occasions when there is quick demand for money, pine resin may serve as a convenient resource.

Turmeric root also has value in foreign markets. The Indian immigrants buy it from Fijians to flavor their curry. In forest regions it grows wild and invades garden plots. But worth-while returns require great quantities. Grated turmeric has value as dye. On November 12, 1935, the women of Nakoroka grated turmeric at the house of Vatili under the direction of his wife Losana. The Buli Lekutu had levied

---

77. Forest spirits are difficult to place in the hierarchy of Nakoroka ancestors. Though the ancestors are omniscient and rule both the land and its forests, the world is peopled as well with several orders of beings who were never human and whose attitude toward humanity is capricious and indeterminable.

this work upon them as a special assessment to pay for administrative work in the district. The grated root would be sold for a good price in Suva. The women worked gaily, and at midday the younger ones among them prepared a feast of taro, taro leaves, and pudding for the workers. In the afternoon eight-year-old Sayasi was sent scurrying up a coconut tree to pick green nuts for the women to drink. They worked noisily and were interrupted frequently by Di Litiya's wrestling with her cross-cousin, Iliseveca, who had just arrived from a sojourn on the windward coast; they both wanted to smoke the same piece of tobacco leaf. Melika danced the hip-swinging dance of the Indians and kept them laughing. They worked for two days preparing the turmeric. Each evening they drank kava at Losana's house. All but the old men were building houses at Lekutu; on the second night these old men joined the women's kava-drinking and sat somberly in the shadows while the women in two groups entertained each other noisily with dancing. The noble women had co-operated but little in the work of this group project.

Sometimes braiding sennit occupies the men who are old or disabled. During the month of April the house at the medical station, which was finely built in chiefly fashion, required large quantities of sennit for tying. At the Buli's discretion varying levies were placed upon each village. Old Kaiyava and Vaula worked more consistently than anyone else at this task and discussed the days of the wars. Sometimes Nabadua, excused from a day's housebuilding to bring garden food to his wife, whose nursing child prevented her from properly managing her household, would spend an evening making sennit. He would twist strands of fiber of the coconut husk by rolling them on his thigh and then braid them onto the seventy-fathom roll which the older men had made. Isacodro, who had pierced his foot with a bamboo stalk, and young Tomasi, whose leg was infected with "Indian boils," worked with the old men for a week or more. But after pounding the coconut husk into its constituent fiber, rolling it into strands and braiding, it was aged Kaiyava who stayed up all night to boil the newly manufactured product. Nabadua and Vaula ridiculed Kaiyava's braiding: "The work of one uncircumcised." It was true that Kaiyava had fled the circumcision ceremony and had borne the shame all his life; for this reason he could not be skilled in man's techniques. But such criticism of his work was never spoken while he was within earshot; the word "uncircumcised" had never been uttered in his presence.

Nakoroka houses are not tied with sennit. Forest vines bind the timbers of even the chiefs' houses. The small quantity which Nakoroka produces for its own use serves as handles for baskets or as binding for bundles of personal belongings in traveling. It is probable that the production of this commodity has developed only since the introduction of Tongan architectural style for chiefly houses.

SEXUAL DIVISION OF LABOR

As in gardening and hunting, there is sexual division of labor in industrial activities. Housebuilding falls entirely within men's scope. Though it is said that women can build houses in emergency, no such occasion has ever arisen. The work of carrying timbers is considered too strenuous for them. Except for minor work of restoring thatch or broken doorways, tasks of housebuilding and maintenance are predominantly co-operative. Like gardening activities, co-operative work of all kinds among men must be carefully planned in advance. The experience of working in groups has special emotional connotation for men which it lacks for women. When the men were preparing to return to work on houses at Lekutu after a week end at Nakoroka, they painted black designs on their faces and began the journey with wild shouts which only men know how to make, like their ancestors who had cried the same shouts and blackened their faces in the same way to go to battle. Each man was jealously proud of his own skill and feared lest this group test of his ability should disclose his inadequacies. Work itself always proceeded with utmost dignity. Each man performed the task which he had been allotted as fast as he could but, except when procedure required a chant, in silence.

Work within the community was less charged with self-consciousness. But, though men of the village all knew each other's failings and abilities, each fulfilled his task with decorous regard for his social status. It was especially on occasions of district-wide co-operation that the men took special pains to appear spectacularly fierce as they entered upon the scene of work with a great shout. Men carve all the crude wooden tools, weapons, or utensils which Nakoroka makes. This work is usually performed during solitary leisure.

Women's industrial activities, of which matmaking is the most important at Nakoroka, are almost always performed in groups. As in gardening activities, co-operation is rarely formalized among them. They work together from preference. Women who intend to spend a morning plaiting mats gather in groups so that they can chat, accuse

each other of outlandish sexual ventures, and strike each other in pretended anger when colloquial repartee has been exhausted. At night
co-operative work on mats is economically efficient because several
women can work by the light of a single lamp and save kerosene. No
man at Nakoroka knew how to finish the borders of mats. But in strong
contrast with common North American Indian sex attitudes, women's
skills were considered almost unattainable by men; the one man of
Lekutu District who could make mats was admired for his special en-
dowment which made women's work available to him. Those rare
occasions upon which women's work is formally co-operative, and has
been planned in discussion before the actual procedure begins, are
hilariously gay and contrast sharply with the somber formality of men's
groups. When the women grated turmeric, the days were festive and
the nights noisy with celebration.

Special tasks in housebuilding are assigned according to age and
ability. The categories of activity are not strictly observed. He who is
temporarily disabled does old men's work. A chief or able executive
may choose to work as an elder. A vigorous old man performs tasks
which are considered fit only for the strength of youth. But there are
tendencies for this division of labor to be observed in practice as well
as theory. Aged Kaiyava used to work in solitude at the leisurely repairing of his dilapidated house; he tied coconut leaves to those walls
through which the wind whistled most easily. No young man had time
for this task. It is the very old men who are responsible for the preparation of coconut fiber sennit, though the younger men occasionally assist them. Among women age is less determinative. Aged women cannot do garden work, but even Vatili's mother, the oldest person in
Nakoroka, slowly plaited mats. Sixteen-year-old girls can make mats,
though their skill is noticeably inferior to that of their mothers and older sisters. Young girls frequently assist older women and perhaps weave
portions of their mats. Elderly women preserve their youthful boister-
ousness; in contrast, men grow more reserved as they mature.

In former times, it is said, high rank prohibited participating in such
menial tasks as gathering firewood or carrying water. The tasks of
everyday food preparation were fit only for slaves and women. Capturing a chief and converting him into a cook was more severe revenge
than killing and serving him as a feast to the ancestors. Bulisivo, who
observes old tradition to a high degree, is helpless in the absence of his
women attendants. Though he is old, his age is not entirely responsible
for his helplessness; rather it is that he has been sheltered all his life

from everyday routine chores. But Vosalevu, who is also of chiefly rank, carries water for his wife Di Litiya; he uses his privilege as chief to outrage custom. Carving of drums, finishing of wall posts, and other tasks which require leisure and aim at an artistic product are theoretically skills only of chiefs. But Monasa and a few other old men claim to know the rudiments of this work. Bulisivo carves the best handles for European knife blades. The beams of the chiefly houses of Macuata Province are decorated with complicated interweaving of red and black sennit; all this is the work of one chief who has learned the art in the Lau Islands to the east. Di Litiya and her sister Di Kabu apply colored wool to their pandanus mats with a skill that all the women envy. But their economic position as women of the chiefly caste, which permits them to accumulate more materials for working than common women, determines their skill rather than a feminine parallel to the special artistic talents of chiefly males.

CHAPTER VI

CASTES[1] AND CHIEFSHIP

THE people of Nakoroka trace their descent from five ancestral villages—Votua, Nadroro, Tavua, Rokowaqa, and Buleya—which comprised the ancient kingdom[2] of Inland Forest. They represent most of the survivors of this domain; each individual still regards himself as a member of one of the ancient villages of it. He who holds the kingly title for Inland Forest resides here; and, except in so far as the role of the modern village as a unit in the colonial organization of Lekutu District confuses the modern scene, the village of Nakoroka is the ancient Inland Forest Kingdom. Now, stimulated by colonial parlance, Nakoroka is the usual appellation of the natives, but use of the ancient names still lends formality to an occasion. Affectionate conservatism associates them with the days before European infiltration began to disrupt the relations between chiefs and ancestors, and these earlier names and concepts of this golden age still dominate Nakoroka's political organization.

There are no general native terms for groups in the political framework; each is known by the place name of the land upon which its village is built. Nativity in this land grants membership in the political group to each person and to his children—membership which may or may not be taken advantage of at the option of the individual.

This system of land-naming forms hierarchies the structure of which parallels that of more typical Polynesian political systems. The land called Inland Forest includes half of Lekutu District. Within its limits the lands of Votua, Nadroro, Tavua, Rokowaqa, and Buleya trace their boundaries; each of these territorial units includes a river and the sloping sides of the valley to the summit of the ridge which bounds the

1. Despite the usually more rigid meaning of "caste," a meaning which does not apply in Fiji, I have used it as a convenient word to indicate groups of persons whose heredity predestines them for specific tasks in chiefly households and ceremonies. Except in the chiefly caste, there is no preference for caste endogamy.

2. "Kingdom" refers consistently to the large land divisions which include several ancestral villages. Inland Forest and Great Meadow are of this category. For legendary history and for history within memory and organization under British authority see above, pp. 31–34 and 62.

river drainage. Each of these lands is composed of many subdivisions of varying extension, ranging from large forest tracts to the earth platforms upon which houses are built. Land names are static to a high degree except that the place name of the land on which a village is built may gradually be applied to the entire land division. Inland Forest once referred only to the chief's village in the large territory of another name, but, as the fame of the chiefly family grew, the name of their village came to mean the entire kingdom. When a village is moved also, it may still be known by the name of its earlier, now distant, lands. During the past century the ancient villages of Votua, Nadroro, Tavua, Rokowaqa, and Buleya have all been moved, but the old names have been retained.

Rules governing kinship determine individuals' rights in specific land divisions. A man is *vasu*[3] to the land of his mother and *cadra*[4] to the land of his father. In Nakoroka it is said that *vasu* ties ought to be the stronger, but every individual must discover for himself which of these possible blood ties is stronger in his case. His decision frequently requires long trial and error until he eventually discovers what his true blood ties are. Since each parent also had *vasu* and *cadra* rights, these, too, must be considered by the individual who is uncertain as to his status.

Ratu Luke's parents were both of chiefly caste, but they came from different lands. Now about thirty years old, he had not decided until he had reached his twenties which of his various land ties was stronger. He had lived in his mother's village, Nakalou in Macuata, where a colony of *émigrés* from the Nabekavu division of Nadroro had settled. Here *vasu* rights exalted his chiefly status so that all his desires were laws. But he did not feel that he belonged to that land. For several years he lived with his aged father in the land to which his father's father belonged, at Wainunu on the windward coast. Here the British tried to persuade him to assume the office of Buli for Wainunu District, which was a great honor for a young man. But he felt discontent

---

3. The term *vasu*, much discussed in the literature, is interpreted at Nakoroka to mean specifically this right to belong to the land of the mother. Etymologically it seems to be a contraction of *vaka sucu*, "being born."

4. *Cadra* appears to mean "their name." Though children are frequently named from the father's family, they may also be named from the mother's family; proper procedure is to alternate after naming the first child for one of the father's parents. But genealogies show that no strict observance of this rule has been followed. According to some theories, it is also proper for children whose parents are not of chiefly caste to be divided alternately according to birth between father's and mother's land groups and castes; this propriety, likewise, has been observed only in exceptional cases.

inside and returned finally to the land at Nakoroka, where he was born and where a great platform faced with stone marks the site of his mother's grave. Ratu Luke's father's mother had belonged to Votua; his father had resided at Votua until after the birth of Ratu Luke and the death of his wife, when he returned to the land of his father at Wainunu.

Choice of land affiliations is open also to commoners. Peni was *vasu* to a division of Votua land. His mother had been a "*bota* who wipes away feces"[5] at Votua. While he was still in his teens, a classificatory father[6] came from his father's father's land at the distant village of The-Red-Chestnut on the Macuata coast with whale teeth as gifts for Peni's land group at Votua; the classificatory father had come to adopt Peni into a land group at The-Red-Chestnut. Peni resided there for about two months, but he felt that he did not belong. One day he fled back to Nakoroka. Through a maternal tie Peni's father was then a member of Nadroro's priestly land group. Peni, who is now about twenty-eight years old, was taken into this group and has remained there ever since. But, when his father dies, he plans to return to the group into which he feels himself born, the "*bota* who wipes away feces" at Votua.

It is said that in former times the *vasu* (maternal) tie was much stronger than it is today. In many regions British colonial policy has exerted considerable pressure toward creating a uniform system of patrilineal inheritance. But at Nakoroka, except for Vatili and Nabadua, everyone insists that the maternal tie is still the stronger determinant of rights in the land. Of all Nakoroka men, Vatili's rights in Nakoroka land are most questionable. His position in society depends largely upon governmental decree; hence it is natural that he should support British edicts. Nabadua has claims on higher status through his father than through his mother; he prefers to consider maternal ties of but secondary importance. Of Nakoroka's older men, only three belong to Nakoroka land through both parents: Nabadua's father was chief at Tavua through both parents, while his mother was bound to Rokowaqa and Nadroro through hers; Naicadra[7] is of Tavua and Votua through his mother and of Nadroro and Votua through his

---

5. See below, p. 188.   6. In this case a father's father's brother's son.

7. *Naicadra* is a contraction of *na yaca dra*, which means "their name," a polite mode of reference to a chief's name. His real name is Ratu Lala-a-vanua, the title being included in the name. But, because he is a commoner, it is disrespectful to the chiefly name to address him with it; hence he is called "Their Name." Every village contains someone who is known thus.

father; Toviya is of Votua and Nadroro through his father and of Buleya through his mother. Only these three men speak what is called the true Nakoroka dialect. Others have polluted their speech with intermarriage and travel. Even Bulisivo, though of chiefly caste and possessor of the title of kingly authority over all these ancestral villages, lacks status as a village owner when compared with any one of them. Only these three are bound unquestionably to the soil of Nakoroka territory. But even among them there is no objective method of determining which of Nakoroka's ancestral villages and which of the caste divisions within these villages draw them with strongest blood ties. They must depend upon their own intuitions.

Each ancestral village and each division within these villages has its first ancestor who is sacred to his descendants. Though all of Nakoroka's people are traditionally descended from the kingdom of Flight-of-the-Chiefs, there are no genealogies which connect the sacred village ancestors and the legendary kingdom. The two traditions are distinct. In contrast with the chiefs who migrated from Flight-of-the-Chiefs to found the villages of Inland Forest Kingdom, the sacred ancestors of each village are identified with animals; Votua's great vagina is associated with a female dog. Siri, the ancestor of Nadroro, was a man with a tremendous penis, but sometimes he is identified with a snake; the ancestor of Rokowaqa was a rat. In contrast with the Flight-of-the-Chiefs legend, the sacred ancestors are first owners of the local land divisions where they had always dwelt.

Food taboos are theoretically associated with these animal ancestors, but the inheritance of taboo observance does not coincide with ancestral village affiliation. All present members of Nadroro feel tremendous repulsion for snakes, and many would be stricken with yaws if they ate snake; but Peni, who says that his father told him that this taboo is no longer effective, inherited a taboo against chicken through his father's mother's land in Nadroro. Among those who have close ties with several ancestral villages, genealogies show that the father's *vasu* (maternal) tie was frequently chosen as the determinant of food taboo. As in the case of determining by trial and error the strongest ties with the land groups, the individual must frequently suffer from a breach of taboo before he discovers which he must observe. After the illness has appeared, possible breaches will be reviewed in hopes of finding a clue; if a gift presentation to an ancestor removes the disease, the line of inheritance of the taboo is established pragmatically.

In Nakoroka, legends of marriages of these first village ancestors establish the *tauvu*[8] relationship between these villages. Rokowaqa is *tauvu* with the island of Gau because its rat ancestor married there and bore children. *Tauvu* relationship consists of satirizing formal ceremonies. Individual *tauvu* relationships require practical joking.

Each village traditionally contained within it all the castes into which Nakoroka is divided; in theory each individual is hereditarily specialized, and a complete community should contain members of each caste living in correspondingly divided territories within the village lands. There are five castes at Nakoroka, but a great gulf is fixed between the chiefly caste (*turaga*) and the other four, which are filled by commoners. Commoners must show abject reverence for all those who have been born chiefs. Men of common castes, those who are "just men and not chiefs," receive a dilute form of this reverence only when they have reached old age, and then only if they are old in a wise manner and not foolish with age.

In inland Bua the chiefly caste must be chiefly not only by inheritance but specifically by inheritance through the mother; if they are to exercise their chiefly function according to tradition, they must have clear rights not only in a land division but in the land division of the village in which they are then living. The chiefly caste procreate only through the maternal line. Though male chiefs may bequeath a chiefly title to their sons along with chiefly authority in their land division, and though sons of such chiefs have more respected status in society than other commoners, yet the greatest of all gulfs in everyday behavior exists between chiefs hereditary through the mother and the rest of the population. No matter how strongly one feels himself a chief, public opinion prohibits his assuming a chiefly role and ridicules any expression of desire to do so. Nabadua feels inside himself that he is a chief. His father, of Tavua's chiefly caste, bequeathed to him the chiefly title for Tavua land. Though he drinks kava before any other member of Tavua,[9] directs all Tavua's internal affairs, and speaks for the entire group at meetings of the elders, he is not granted the respect etiquette or the privileges of a true chief. He chafes constantly under the insult which he imagines the community is dealing him and in reprisal makes himself ridiculous by attempting to seize chiefly prerogatives; he has married two of his classificatory sisters, an incestuous

8. "Ancestor together." Arthur M. Hocart and others have discussed this at length for other regions of Fiji. See discussion of *tauvu* below, pp. 247, 288–90.

9. Except for an older classificatory brother who lives with a small group of descendants of Tavua at Duleniwai on the windward slope.

breach which is permitted only to chiefs; he explains secretly to visitors, who smile when he has finished, that he alone is responsible for Nakoroka's prosperity; beyond the hearing of the other men of Tavua, he pretends that they are the abject slaves of his every wish. Nabadua is Nakoroka's most acute social problem.

Bulisivo, Vosalevu, Ratu Luke, and Vatili are all highly ranked by the government. The first three are all of true chiefly caste, conscious of their status and defensive of it. In contrast with Nabadua, these men suffer because of the questionable nature of their status as village owners; their land claims are strongest in alien villages. Nevertheless, except for Ratu Luke, they all play authoritative social roles.

Besides the chiefly caste, there are at Nakoroka six "castes" which are filled by commoners. They differ fundamentally from the chiefly caste, and I use the term only because it is common usage in the literature. In these commoner castes there is no preference for caste endogamy, and they are not formally ranked in order. These castes are: priest (*bete*);[10] "natives of the village green" (*kai rara*); "contents of the household" (*lewe ni vale*); and three kinds of *bota* (untranslatable).[11]

10. For a discussion of priests see below, chap. vii.

11. Chiefs, priests, some group which acted as messengers and spokesmen for the chief (cf. the "talking chiefs" of Polynesia), and another group which performed duties in the chiefly household seem to have occurred generally in Vanua Levu. The term used in Bau for the messenger caste is *Matanivanua*, "Face-of-the-Land." *Mata* means "eye," "face," "front," and, in one form, "first"; by extension, "forerunner or herald." When used with the possessive of "the day," it means "sun." *Matanivanua* can be used without reference to caste to mean anyone who serves as messenger, who drinks after a chief in the kava ceremony, or who plays a specific role in ceremonies of formal presentation (cf. A. H. Hocart, "Heralds and Envoys in Fiji," *Journal of the Royal Anthropological Institute*, XLIII [1913], 109–13). In Macuata, castes which perform these ceremonies receive various names, but all are considered kinds of "messengers." In eastern Macuata and in some villages of Natewa Bay in Cakaudrove Province there are legends of an original family (sometimes fused with Degei, the snake-god of Viti Levu against whom the missionaries waged their battles until he became popular throughout Fiji). The order of birth of brothers within this family determined the caste of their descendants for all time. In neatly formalized fashion an old man of the village of Korotasere on Natewa Bay attributed caste origin to seven such brothers whose status according to order of birth ranked in the following order: chief (*turaga*), assistant chief (*sau turaga*), warrior of the distant borders (*bati balavu*, "distant edge"), guardsman (*bati leka*, "near edge"), priest (*bete*), domestic servant (*lewe ni vale*, "contents of the household"), and fisherman (*kai weli*). Each of these established a household or village of his own and procreated his caste; descendants drank kava in the order of the birth of their ancestors. Each caste contained a head man, loosely called "chief" but not of chiefly caste. Coast villages of Macuata omit several of these castes but add others, such as mourners (*nasi ni tagitagi*, "bark cloth for weeping"), who functioned at the funerals of chiefs, and "pillows of the dead" (*lokuloku ni mate*), who served as slaves to be buried with a chief's corpse.

Many of these castes have never functioned in the communities which claim to have

"Natives of the village green" function as messengers of the chiefs; they carry private messages and announce publicly in booming voices from the center of the village green.[12] When food is distributed to various households at times of great feasts, it is a member of this caste who calls the names of the recipient groups.

"Contents of the household" are skilled in preparing food and performing all manner of household tasks; when I hired Peni, who was a *bota*, to cook for me, Bulisivo expressed great regret that I had not asked his advice. Bulisivo would have recommended Samu, a young man of the "contents of the household" group; though Samu had had little experience as cook, yet his hereditary predestiny would produce perfection in cooking which Peni could never achieve.

The "true *bota*," *bota dina*,[13] cared for the chief's body from the hips up. Cutting the chief's hair in a carefully guarded and secluded house was his most important function.[14] Today, though the sacredness of the

contained them. Traditions, without practice, have been borrowed freely, particularly from Bau, whose prestige skyrocketed when Europeans accepted its chief as king of all Fiji and whose political structure the British used as a model for the colonial organization. The Land Commission, to stabilize land inheritance, classified all Fijians into "clans" (*mataqali*) and defined descent in these groups as patrilineal. *Mataqali*, however, properly means "kind" and may refer to any classification; the term has this meaning in interior Viti Levu also (see Dorothy Spencer, p. 6). Applied to humans, it may mean rank, caste, temperament, or sex, as well as affiliation with descent groups. Government records, however, which record the answers of all Fijians as to their *mataqali*, consider the answers they have received to be indications of descent-group affiliations. Etymologically, *mataqali* seems to mean "façade of subordinate community" (*qali*, "soil"; *mata*, "veneer of population"). In folk tales *qali* consistently refers to subsidiary political groups of varying extension. In the kingdoms of Inland Forest and of Great Meadow the compound term had no reference to political structure at the time when the colonial administration introduced—or reintroduced—it.

With this in mind, it is perhaps not surprising that in eastern Vanua Levu, which has been most influenced by the colonial administration, castes are today held even by the natives to have been coextensive with villages. In the Dreketi region of Macuata, for instance, villages are said by present-day informants to have consisted of single castes. It is, of course, possible, but it is hard to reconcile with the nature of Fijian castes. Unfortunately for the adequate investigation of the problem, Macuata chiefs, schooled in the tradition of Lau and Tonga, have reorganized their entire province in the last century; old men in the interior barely remember the old political structure. Old government records might offer a clue.

12. In modern Nakoroka the "village chief" appoints some commoner who almost every evening announces the procedure of men's work for the morrow. He calls from either end of the village green so that all may hear if they choose to pause from their work or entertainment.

13. Or "he who grasps the upper part" (*tara i cake*).

14. Though the *bota* caste occurs in other parts of Vanua Levu, the secluded barbershop, taboo to all but chiefs and *bota*, which was the only place in which chief's hair

chief's head still creates difficulties in hair-cutting, *bota* do not consistently perform the task. Though chiefs are theoretically prohibited from hair-cutting, the wickedness of modern times permits Ratu Luke, who holds chiefly rank but no effective status, to cut the hair of the six-year-old chieftainess Di Sereima; the fact that Ratu Luke's mother has a distant classificatory brother of *bota* caste justifies this breach in part. Laying out the upper part of a chief's corpse was also the duty of the true *bota*.

"*Bota* by theft," *bota butako*, tended to the needs of the chief's body only in the absence of a true *bota*. Isacodro has affiliations with this caste. He could cut hair in an emergency, but afterward he would have to prepare a feast, distribute it in the village, and make public confession.

"*Bota* who wipes away feces," *bota cara da*,[15] cares for the lower part of the bodies of chiefly children until they are three or four years old. If a "*bota* who wipes away feces" should cut the hair of a chief, the *bota* would be stricken with a disease similar to smallpox. Bulisivo's wife, who cuts his hair, is of this caste; but the fact that she has sexual relations with him removes the danger of the disease.

Caste and land divisions were created when the first ancestors settled the land; perhaps even these ancestors searched for land to which they felt they belonged and settled according to land divisions which they assumed mystically to be already delimited. According to theory, new land divisions or new castes have never since been created.

Despite individual mobility within the caste structure, in theory castes themselves and the special tasks which they entailed were once fixed strictly in accordance with divisions of the land. Territorial divisions have perpetuated themselves without regard for their constituent membership. Though individual affiliation with ancestral villages is subject to individual adjustment, the villages themselves remain unalterable subunits of larger land divisions. Though personnel of the divisions fluctuates, and though one individual can perform functions without conflict in two castes at the same time, the functions of each caste and land division remain distinct. Toviya, through his father's father, has inherited the title for political authority among the "*bota* who wipe away feces" at Votua. Through his mother's people he has

---

could be cut, was exclusively an institution of the kingdom of Inland Forest. Despite the fact that its purpose was to conceal the hair and nails of the chief, all knowledge of the widespread Oceanic witchcraft which utilizes this refuse is disclaimed for all time at Nakoroka.

15. Or "he who grasps the lower part" (*tara i ra*).

rights in the priestly land group at Buleya; through this channel he has gained some special accoutrements for shamanistic practice and in former times, before the religion of Wesleyans outlawed the formal religion of Fiji, would have functioned politically as a priest at Buleya. A valid tie with chiefly caste theoretically prohibits participation as a member of any other caste; but even this rule is subject to qualification.[16] Ceremonial exchanges are organized carefully on a basis of land divisions; but, when there are not enough persons of the proper land group to perform the ceremonial function, someone else can readily substitute.

Though individuals are free within limits to select their own affiliations among the castes of commoners, opinions of their parents are usually paramount in formulating the final decision. If a child shows special temperamental proclivities toward a contemplative life, parents are quick to observe and prophesy his destiny as a priest. Some near-relative who is skilled in priestly knowledge will begin to coax the child's interest; as the relationship between pupil and mentor develops, people will say that a true blood tie is asserting itself. More frequently the child of commoners grows up with little regard for his caste affiliation. When the occasion arises, he will be prepared to function ceremonially as *bota*, "native of the village green," or "contents of the household." Among commoners, only priests or heirs to a title of political authority require exceptional training. Choice of commoner-caste affiliations are much less troublesome than choice of affiliation with the land of an ancestral village.[17]

Precise statement of the structural principles underlying the organization of ancient Inland Forest Kingdom is bound to err grossly. But there is belief that they were more systematic than they are at present. An established tradition states that each of its ancestral villages contained households specific as to caste. Each of these households had its elder who represented it in town meetings, but only members of the chiefly household were chiefs. It is said that, within each of the five ancestral villages, a title for political authority over each caste group descended along the tortuous path of blood ties. Someone, preferably of the chiefly caste, who had inherited a whale tooth from his predecessor as emblem of office held executive power over the entire vil-

16. Vosalevu, though of chiefly caste at Nakoroka, could function as a "native of the village green" at Lekutu, where his father had been a member of a land group of Great Meadow Kingdom (see Ratu Luke's functioning as *bota*, above, p. 188).

17. It will be remembered that each of these contains all castes.

lage.[18] Likewise, someone with some blood tie with the priestly caste served as "priest" and, with the "chief," had specific functions in first-fruits ceremonies. There was also the "native of the village green" who served as special herald for him who held the chiefly whale tooth. It is probable that he who held the chiefly whale tooth also held title to the executive office of the land of the chiefly caste; he who held the office of priest for the entire ancestral village, however, did not necessarily hold the title for headmanship in the land of the priestly caste. Each caste group contained a holder of this title who, together with title-holders of other caste groups, composed the council of village elders. Those who held office as priest and "native of the village green" functioned primarily at times of ceremonial exchanges or when the village as a unit was fulfilling a ceremonial role within the structure of the entire kingdom. Each village was a complete social unit.

The kingdom of Inland Forest as a whole was organized in similar fashion. The chiefly land group at Votua controlled the descent of the whale tooth, named "King Forest," from the name of the kingdom, Inland Forest; it contained within itself the right of kingly authority[19] over the five constituent villages. To maintain proper rapport with the ancestors who controlled the region's fertility, the kingly office had to be held by a hereditary member of the chiefly caste. If a true chief fills the kingly office, this fact compensates in part for the religious breach of allowing a commoner to hold the chiefly whale tooth in one of the constituent village groups. Bulisivo is a true chief. His parent and his parents' parents were all of chiefly caste. But the king should also have unassailable rights of ownership in the chiefly land group of his kingdom, and Bulisivo's rights within Votua's chiefly land division are not unquestioned. His father's mother had married an outsider; though he was a chief, he was from Dama,[20] and the marriage "scattered the blood" contrary to the wishes of Votua's ancestors. As a result, she was sterile in her marriage until she returned to Votua to be treated by Votua's priest with a medicinal ash. Though Ratu Seru, Bulisivo's father, was thus conceived parthenogenetically under a cloud of ancestral disapproval, the land flourished under his regime. Bulisivo, his only male heir, was born in his mother's village at Saolo on the windward coast. Ratu Seru's marriage to the Saolo chieftainess

18. The name for this office, *turaga*, is the same as that for the chiefly caste, but it is clearly recognized as an office distinct from the caste.

19. The office of king is *tui*, distinct from the word for chief, *turaga*.

20. South of the village of Bua on the coast (see Map I, p. 4).

had been stormy and of short duration. Bulisivo lived on at Saolo and still considers the *vasu* (maternal) tie his true blood affiliation. But the whale tooth "King Forest" could not be left unpossessed and uncared for. The elders of Votua sent gifts to Bulisivo and requested that he reside in their land to make it fertile.

Today Bulisivo and his sisters, whom he brought with him from Saolo, and their children comprise Votua's chiefly family. Though Bulisivo holds the title of the chiefly land at Votua as well as that for king of Inland Forest, all the other members of Votua, who all consider their prime affiliation to be with the land of "*bota* who wipes away feces," feel that he is but a guest among them. This chiefly group is today composed of Bulisivo; his two daughters, who are Little Di Litiya[21] and Di Vara, and their two children; Bulisivo's blind son of twenty-one years; Bulisivo's grandson and namesake, Ratu Meli, by the oldest daughter of Bulisivo, who married a chief of Dama; and Bulisivo's two sisters, of whom the elder, Di Kabu, has a marriageable daughter, and the younger, Big Di Litiya,[22] is the mother of the young chief Ratu Seru, namesake of Bulisivo's father. In recent years Big Di Litiya married Vosalevu against the wishes of the entire community, so that his position in Votua is even more tenuous than that of the others.

The difficulties within the chiefly caste that are raised by the necessity of squaring hereditary caste with rights as "owner of the land" are duplicated in the same manner for commoners. Toviya, whose genealogy is completely separate from that of Bulisivo, received from his father's classificatory brother the chiefly whale tooth of his land division of Votua. Toviya's group includes Ratu Luke, who is himself of chiefly caste and connected with Toviya only by most devious ties of blood, and Akuila, and their families, and Bulisivo's wife, who is of Votua's "*bota* who wipes away feces." Isacodro, though already "*bota* by theft" at Votua, has considered himself as part of a Rokowaqa group; but he, like young Peni of Nadroro, plans to join Toviya.

Nadroro land is typical in that it is divided into two large territories, Great River and Sivoa, which lie on either slope of the valley of the river Nadroro, and each of which has held its own title to chiefly authority and had its own internal caste organization. At one time these two divisions were separate villages, but today they have become a single political division of Inland Forest Kingdom. A whale tooth

21. *Lailai*, "little," because she is the namesake of Bulisivo's vigorous sister.
22. *Levu*, "big" (see n. 21).

which signifies chiefly authority descends within each, but the chiefly title for Nadroro as a whole is held alternately by a rightful heir in either group. Vilomena, of Sivoa, who died in March, 1936, held the title until her death. Then Vatili, who with his mother and children have questionable rights as "contents of the household," now holds the titular whale tooth in trust for Sakaru, Vilomena's illegitimate son of twelve years. Vilomena's father was of full chiefly caste at Sivoa. He had received the Nadroro title many years before when the land failed to produce. Naicadra's father, who was of full chiefly caste at Great River, and who had been holding the title for many years, passed political authority to that chief at Sivoa, hoping to please the ancestors and renew fertility. The advisability of returning to Naicadra the title of Great River has been discussed heatedly in recent years. Naicadra and his daughter are the only living members of Nakoroka's population who have strong ties with the Great River division of Nadroro. The others belong to the priestly group of Vilomena's Sivoa: Orisi and his family; Vaula and his two sons, Peni and Narogo, who are at the same time bound to Votua through their mother; and Melika, Naicadra's wife, who is Sivoa's "native of the village green." Atypically, also, Nadroro claims to have maintained its own fertility in the old days without the aid of Inland Forest kingship. As proof of its right to act independently, Naicadra may point to the time when Ratu Inoke with his army from Dreketi destroyed all Inland Forest except Nadroro; Nadroro, of its own initiative, had bowed down before the conqueror.[23]

Tavua, says Nabadua proudly, will soon be the largest ancestral village group at Nakoroka. Nabadua holds title to chiefly authority there which, when he dies, will pass to the eldest of his four sons, who already, at barely thirty years of age, has three daughters and a son of his own. Nabadua refuses to admit any hereditary bonds except those with his father, who was of chiefly caste at Tavua. Despite the impossibility of inheriting claims upon the chiefly caste through the father, Nabadua insists that he and all his sons are of strong chiefly blood. Bici and his father, old Kaiyava, belong to the "native of the village green" land of Tavua. Monasa heads the priestly caste group at Tavua not because of an inherited right but because he is the oldest member of the group; furthermore, his two classificatory brothers who share his claims are partially drawn into Bici's group by maternal ties. Peculiarly the priestly caste at Tavua includes the functions of *bota;* this is

23. See above, p. 53.

an easy fusion, says Bici, because "when the work of *bota* is ended, it is the priest who personally serves the chief"; when the priest's services are ended at the chief's death, it is the *bota* who lays out the corpse.

Raitova holds the title at Rokowaqa because he is the only adult male who has close ties with Rokowaqa land. Keleivi, his much younger classificatory brother, also belongs, though both maternal and paternal ties bind him to the village of Sarowaqa (see Chart V); Keleivi has ties to Rokowaqa only through Raitova. When Isacodro came to Nakoroka about 1930, Raitova presented a whale tooth to Isacodro's land group at Nalauvia to bring him into Rokowaqa and increase its depleted manpower. Though Isacodro and his family have since been part of Rokowaqa, with no hereditary ties to support their membership, they have never slackened their older affiliation with Votua. Recently the Buli has intervened and confused Rokowaqa's membership. He directed Vosalevu, a chief whose ties with Nakoroka are questionable, to supervise the garden and housework of Raitova, Keleivi, and Isacodro, perhaps to function as titular head of Roko-waqa. After eight months of Vosalevu's supervision, Isacodro chose to reassert his claims on Votua and permanently separate himself from Rokowaqa. In effect, Rokowaqa functions ceremonially as a subsidiary group of Votua; sometimes Bulisivo's two sisters, who live in the great house next to that of Raitova, participate with it.

Buleya land lies far in the mountains beyond Rokowaqa. Descendants of its early population have gradually affiliated themselves with other groups at Nakoroka so that it can no longer function as a political entity. Sakariya, the last member of Buleya, fled to Lekutu in disgrace about ten years ago. Buleya once possessed the family from among whom king of Inland Forest chose his special "native of the village green"; Sakariya can still fill this role for Bulisivo.

The influence of colonial authority has created a trend toward patriliny. People say that the *cadra* tie has grown strong under British influence. Hence, except for chiefs, most children of today are considered part of their father's group regardless of their mother's affiliation. When a child displays unpleasant traits of temperament, it is customary to cite the similarity to his father's personality and to quote a phrase from the Wesleyan Fijian Bible: "The child of a king is just a king" ("Luve ni tui e na tui ga").

Under the regime of government appointees, the Buli and the "village chief,"[24] it is possible that a new system of patrilineally descending

24. For discussion of the organization of colonial officials see above, chap. iii.

political functions may develop. As Sakariya of Buleya belonged to a family which had become specially marked as producers of "natives of the village green" for the king of Inland Forest, so Orisi's descendants might be marked as those to whom the task of announcing for the "village chief" was hereditarily suitable. Though five of Nakoroka's adult men have been "village chief," they dislike the task; only Vatili has been willing to incur social disapproval by serving long terms. Hence, though tradition credits the present caste structure with immemorially long duration, yet it is possible that each political reshuffling has arranged land groups into new caste relations. Likewise, the ascendance of a particular chiefly family with their special set of ancestors might change the emphasis in inheritance from matrilineal to patrilineal, or the reverse, in accord with their own special traditions.

In effect, except in the case of chiefs, the groups which function ceremonially as land units have lost caste connotation. Though all males know the caste to which they are bound by hereditary ties, yet this fact does not influence their choice of group affiliations; Peni prefers Votua, where he is a *bota*, to the more dignified caste of priest at Nadroro; he does not like Vatili of Nadroro. Most women and children, if not of chiefly caste, are unaware of their caste affiliations.

Secular leadership in a group may be determined by ownership status within a group rather than by political title. Though Toviya holds the title for chiefship among the "*bota* who wipe away feces" at Votua, his priestly inclinations suggest that his Buleya heredity is active within him; Peni considers Akuila, who as second in seniority will control the chiefly title of the group when Toviya dies, as the actual leader of the group.[25] Akuila's mother was of Wainunu on the windward coast, but Akuila feels bound by his paternal tie alone.

CHIEFSHIP

Of Nakoroka's hundred men, women, and children, twelve are of chiefly caste. Commoners address them with a plural vocative, cower in their presence, and always sit below them in the houses. At the eating-mat all wait until he of chiefly caste has tasted his food, then they clap with cupped palms before beginning to eat. These twelve chiefs have "backs of Samoa." It is impolite to pass behind the back of anyone, particularly if he is old and in consequence deserves respect, be-

---

25. Akuila will merely be holding the title in trust for Toviya's grandson, the six-year-old Care. But for all purposes Akuila will act as though he were Toviya's true heir.

cause the back is where one's soul perches, and a chief's back is especially sacred. In former times only chiefs could sit "in the manner of
Tonga" with legs crossed, tailor fashion; commoners squatted on their
heels or sat with one leg flexed to the fore and the other to the side. In
former times only chiefs could walk in the manner of Tonga, with arms
swinging; the arms of commoners, when not laden with burdens, were
clasped before the body, which was bent forward as they walked about
the village with bowed heads. Today commoners may sit like chiefs,
but on a journey it is still a mark of chiefship to be without burdens so
that one's arms may swing freely. Upon first seeing a chief in the morning, or approaching his house, a commoner must greet him with a conventional call: men say, "Duo, duo!"; women have a more complex
phrase which varies with locality in its plaintiveness. When a commoner approaches a chief's house at night, he must say, "It is night," and
wait for an invitation to enter. He must kneel before entering and, if
he is of lowest rank, sit on the dirty mats near the door. The persons
of chiefs are sacred: whenever a commoner must pass them a plate of
food or even a tinder to light their tobacco, he must clap afterward to
remove the danger of being infected with the chief's sacredness. Commoners object to Bulisivo's careless waste of tobacco; he is always losing large leaves of it which he has been carrying behind his ear; but,
no matter how great the need, tobacco which Bulisivo has dropped
cannot be touched; commoners must avoid contact with it, almost with
disgust. Commoners can never speak chief's names without first speaking the proper title; *Ra* or *Ratu* for male chiefs; *Di* or *Adi* for noblewomen chiefs. Any breach of these observances displeases the ancestors, who bring disease or accident upon the offender.

Bulisivo, king of Inland Forest, is of chiefly caste through both parents, who were likewise chiefs through both parents. Such a chief, born
from a marriage within the chiefly caste, is called "crown of the coconut palm" to distinguish him from those whose chiefliness comes
through the mother only.[26] Of all Nakoroka's chiefs, Bulisivo receives
most careful observance of respect etiquette. His seniority within the
chiefly caste rather than his political status as king of Inland Forest determines this precedence. His two sisters, Di Kabu and Big Di Litiya,
are likewise "crowns of the coconut palm." But they wilfully defied
their elders and married commoners and "scattered the chiefly blood,"
so that their children are not "crowns of the coconut." Di Kabu's hus-

26. In contrast with inheritance in Bua Province, chiefliness in many regions of Macuata can be inherited through either or both parents.

band was the son of a chief, hence her daughter Big[27] Di Merelita is carelessly called "crown of the coconut" but not with justice.[28] Big Di Litiya married as her first husband a "native of the village green" at Lekutu village and bore Ratu Seru, namesake of her father. Although he is not a "crown of the coconut," young Ratu Seru alone is free from infection with Bulisivo's personal sacredness. This is because he is Bulisivo's sister's son, his *vasu*. He alone can eat as an equal with Bulisivo. Usually, however, he prefers to identify himself with the young men, whom he treats as his personal slaves. At evening entertainments which include large numbers of men and women of all castes, he frequently prefers to sit near the lower door with the young men and drink kava after the chiefs and elders have finished. Nevertheless, his mother, the lady Big Di Litiya and his stepfather, Vosalevu, who is Di Litiya's second husband and chiefly through his Great Meadow mother, serve meals at his convenience and clap when they pass him food as though he were far above them in rank.

Big Di Litiya held the whale tooth "King Forest" during the many years when Bulisivo was sojourning in his mother's land on the windward coast. During this period she ranked first at all meetings and kava ceremonies at which she was fulfilling her role as king of Inland Forest. She drank kava before the village elders and sat in the most honored place. But at casual gatherings, though she was always served kava before any of the commoners, she would frequently sit near the lower door in her role as a woman. Even during her regency as king of Inland Forest she served her son Ratu Seru with greatest respect.

Di Kabu, though older than Di Litiya, has a mild disposition like her brother Bulisivo. She has never held political office. At casual gatherings about the kava bowl she receives precedence over Di Litiya, but she avoids formal ceremonies. Her daughter Big Di Merelita is likewise sister's child to Bulisivo; since she is a woman, her field of influence is far less than Ratu Seru's. Within the household, tasks of preparing daily meals naturally fall to her, while Ratu Seru is free to organize hunting expeditions among the young men.

Di Litiya's second husband, Vosalevu, is chiefly through his mother, a lady of Great Meadow Kingdom; but he has no direct chiefly tie with Nakoroka, and his claim to chiefly respect is resented. People always remember that his father was no more than a "native of the vil-

27. "Big" to distinguish her from Bulisivo's granddaughter, five-year-old Little Di Merelita Sereima.

28. Because her father's mother was not chiefly.

lage green" at Lekutu. His rank is anomalous: though he usually takes precedence over even elderly commoners, among chiefs his status is low. But he receives full support from Bulisivo and Di Litiya. In contrast with Bulisivo's mildness, Vosalevu's blustering bearing and his willingness to fill executive roles make him useful as a spokesman and lieutenant for Bulisivo. Especially during the regency of his wife Di Litiya his political influence was highly resented, but his reputation as one who knows how to box in the British fashion requires that resentment be confined to secret confidences between friends. Though commoners address him with a plural vocative, no title is ever used with his name; though he sits high in the house in relation to commoners, without great risk a commoner might smoke tobacco which had fallen from behind his ear.

Three of Bulisivo's children by a lady of the windward coast reside at Nakoroka: Little Di Litiya, perhaps thirty-five years old, namesake of Bulisivo's sister, is the mother of five-year-old Little Di Merelita, who, though her father, a chief from the windward coast and a classificatory cross-cousin of her mother, has never chosen to verify his paternity with gifts to validate marriage and birth, is given all respect due a "crown of the coconut." Di Vara, Bulisivo's third daughter, fled from her husband, who was a Great Meadow chief, and for several years has lived in Bulisivo's household at Nakoroka with her noble son of ten years, Ratu Kelemedi. Bulisivo's oldest and youngest daughters have married chiefs in distant regions. Sixteen-year-old son of the eldest, Ratu Meli, namesake of Bulisivo,[29] has made his home with Big Di Litiya for several years, and, though his mother and father reside at distant Dama, he considers his true heritage to lie in Nakoroka land. Ratu Meli's father is of the family of the old chiefs of the now defunct Bua Kingdom.

Bulisivo's daughters are usually preoccupied with the menial tasks of cooking and matmaking in his household. But when they choose to join a casual gathering, they receive all the honors due chiefly women. Usually they like to sit in lowly places near the doors, but they drink kava before any of the old men among the commoners. No one dares to stand in their presence. Though Bulisivo's second wife, Viniyana, of "*bota* who wipes away feces" caste, works constantly with the chiefly women of his household and joins them with her noisy laughter, she carefully performs all the duties of respect toward them.

29. "Bulisivo" is a nickname. Commoners need not use a title in addressing him with this name.

Bulisivo's only son, Ratu Tevita, who was born blind about twenty-one years ago and who leaves the house only to bathe once a day, or to join a feast or group of singing young people in the evening, receives all etiquette due his rank of birth. His person is sacred to all commoners. When Bulisivo and Ratu Seru are away, the chieftainesses patronizingly serve him first at the eating-mat or in the kava ring. But his blindness and consequent undeveloped personality will always preclude his filling a political role.

Everyone grants that thirty-year-old Ratu Luke is a true "crown of the coconut palm." But he has little status at Nakoroka. He grew up in his mother's village in Macuata, where he was *vasu*, and later made his home with his chiefly father at Wainunu on the windward coast. His position in Nadroro, though he was born there, is compromised because his land affiliations are elsewhere. Whenever he participates in kava-drinking, he is served as a chief if he chooses to sit with chiefs. Frequently he performs the rather menial task of preparing and serving kava in Bulisivo's household in the evening. Though his father is Bulisivo's cross-cousin, Bulisivo gives him but slight recognition as a member of the chiefly family; early in 1935 Ratu Luke married a pretty commoner of Sarowaqa, in spite of Di Kabu's plans for his marriage with her still maidenly daughter Di Merelita. Bulisivo's two sisters and their children and Vosalevu live at the large house called "Inland Forest" and are considered chiefly above all others at Nakoroka; Bulisivo with his children, grandchildren, and common wife lives in the house called "Na-Vusodrumate," which is dilapidated but respectworthy because of its noble inhabitants; but Ratu Luke lives precariously as an adjunct to the commoner Toviya's household.

Within the chiefly group, precedence of the individual in eating and kava-drinking depends upon degree of chiefliness in the hereditary background, age, sex, and special kinship status. Political or ceremonial role at any time may temporarily override this distinction. All but Ratu Seru would suffer from contact with Bulisivo's back or head. All address Bulisivo with a plural vocative and use plural pronouns in referring to him. All move away from the upper part of the house when he approaches to give him the cleanest space on the mats. But in informal contacts all but Bulisivo address one another with the familiar vocative, *Lale*, which is used among commoners. Great discrepancy in age sometimes results in more formal observance: young Ratu Meli addresses Ratu Luke with the respectful vocative. But kinship ties frequently qualify attitudes which would result if rank alone were considered; child chiefs address many of the elder chiefs with kin terms.

The children of commoners learn to use respectful language to chiefs of all ages as they learn to speak. Bici shames his six-year-old son when he neglects to use respectful language to his chiefly playmate, the five-year-old Little Di Merelita. Likewise children who talk in the presence of chiefs are ridiculed and berated with the strongest of Fijian invectives. Soon they learn to flee when Bulisivo approaches. Child chiefs rapidly learn that they are distinct from ordinary human beings. They learn to expect other children to give up tidbits of food to them. Though most children receive constant attention from the adults of their households, chiefly children receive even more. Five-year-old Di Merelita almost always rides on the back of an adult chief or chieftainess: her age-mates have long since been held responsible for their own locomotion. Other children her age know how to swim with ease and security, but she rarely ventures to the water without an adult as special chaperone. Sometimes she has tantrums when adults fail to pay attention to the funny faces she can make. Her negligence in performing the small errands which, as in the case of other children, are assigned as an essential part of her training creates amusement for her elders in which she participates.

As a result of this adult supervision, the muscular co-ordination of chiefly children seems to fall rapidly behind that of their commoner age-mates. Better nourished, they grow to full stature more rapidly, but their physical skills do not grow with corresponding rapidity. Ten-year-old Ratu Kelemedi, grandson of Bulisivo, played tag in the water with the other children. Though he was a head taller than any child of his age, he was treated with constant care lest an accidental collision should send him sprawling on the rugged riverbank. He liked games and participated in their excitement, but he was easy prey, and the other children were obliged to tolerate his awkwardness so that he would not be "it" too often.

Bulisivo, Ratu Seru, and Ratu Meli habitually sleep until the sun is high in the sky, while their age-mates have long since been working at daily chores. But no one criticizes; they are chiefs, and hence their behavior cannot be adjusted to the rules which govern ordinary mortals. A chief who seriously considered criticism which stemmed from commoners would lose face as chief. Hence, when Ratu Seru outraged the village sense of propriety by sleeping night after night in her kitchen with Lebu, Isacodro's red-skinned daughter, people tittered but admired the courage with which he openly defied the restraints of modesty that inhibit most people. He is indeed a chief.

But this sacredness of chiefs has degenerated far below old standards. They say that in former times one who had accidentally touched an object which had been infected with old-fashioned chiefliness would cut off a finger to propitiate the chief's offended dignity. Now begging forgiveness is usually sufficient; but, if an angered ancestor sends misfortune as punishment, then the offender knows that he must make more elaborate amends. The land at Nakoroka is especially endowed with sacred power. The old men claim that even chiefs at Macuata trace their chiefly power[30] to Nakoroka. Chiefly families of the windward coast are even more closely related. Before the advent of the Wesleyans and the British, which was followed by widespread negligence in "remembering" ancestors and chiefly tradition, all chiefs were miracle-workers. Bulisivo's father could put a lighted cigarette in a safe place for the night; in the morning it would still be burning, and the tobacco would not yet be consumed, When he dug wild yams in the bush, one could hear the steam hissing out through the holes his digging-stick made; when he unearthed the yams, they would be already cooked. Ratu Luke's grandfather was once caught away from the village in a cloudburst. As he took shelter under a tree, he felt a desire to smoke tobacco. The rain had soaked the forest so that there was no dry wood in which fire could be plowed.[31] But no sooner had he expressed the wish to his companion than a burning tinder came floating in the flooded path. A generation past, chiefs could uproot great trees with their bare hands.

Though all members of the chiefly caste have special supernatural endowments which associate them with the spirit ancestors of the village, he who holds the sacred whale tooth plays a ceremonial role which expresses the function of the entire chiefly caste as intermediaries between the village population and the world of ancestors. All chiefs are necessary to the community's well-being. Observing chiefly etiquette, honoring all whose mothers are chiefs, is in itself a religious ritual which helps to make the land prosper. The ancestors like to see life in the village moving along traditional paths. But he who holds the

30. The term *mana*, impersonal supernatural power, is understood at Nakoroka and occurs in ceremonial chants. But the equivalent in the local dialect is *sau*.

31. Though matches are widely used today, even adolescent boys still know how to make and use fire-plows. They also know which of the forest woods fire most easily.

sacred whale tooth is the executive who initiates the great ceremonies that please the ancestors. Although any direct communication with the supernatural—such as certain extreme emergencies of the people might dictate—is regarded as unsuitable for any chief, and a priest was employed for the purpose, yet the king is nevertheless regarded as closely associated with the ancestor gods. It is he who best knows how to advise in legal disputes so that the ancestors will be proud of the conduct of their descendants and anxious to cast favors among them. It is he who is responsible for the reception of guests according to traditions of lavish hospitality, so that the name of the village will travel far and people in foreign lands will speak of the great power of Nakoroka's ancestors; the ancestors will know and be pleased that honor has been brought to their names. His primary responsibility is to maintain rapport with the ancestors by conducting the affairs of the kingdom in such conformity with tradition as will please them and with such distinction as will flatter them.

In relation with other kingdoms, this involved, in the old days, playing for his kingdom a respect-worthy part in the competitive gift exchanges, which actually functioned as the means of distribution of goods, and providing the ancestors with occasional sacrificial delicacies in the form of baked human bodies, which provided the main rationalization for military aggression. Within the realm also, goods were distributed through his hands, since the bulk of crops were presented to him, and he in turn redistributed them through the mechanism of ceremonial gift exchanges. He, assisted by the council of elders, further functioned in directing in detail the many co-operative enterprises of the people, such as housebuilding and the heavier agricultural tasks like clearing ground and harvesting and planting, which required the collective labor of the community. In large measure the titular chief carries out these responsibilities at the present time.

According to the structural principles of society, he who holds the chiefly whale tooth for each ancestral village group should be of chiefly caste. His ceremonial role presupposes it. But except for the title of king of Inland Forest, the chiefly whale tooth of all groups at Nakoroka has fallen into the hands of commoners because there were no chiefly heirs. In Tavua and Nadroro the descent into commoner caste has occurred within the last generation. Nabadua received the Tavua whale tooth from his father, who was of chiefly caste; the fathers of both Vilomena and Naicadra, holders of chiefly title in Nadroro's two subgroups, were chiefs. Bulisivo, who now holds "King Forest," the whale tooth which embodies the sacred power of all Inland Forest ancestors and gives the owner the kingly title for all Inland Forest, will have difficulty choosing an heir for his office from among the chiefly caste. His two sisters, one of whom has already held the title, are old and will outlive him by only a few years. Of these two, the younger, aggressive and able Big Di Litiya, has married the alien Vosalevu, and his influence in Nakoroka's family has already caused almost open resentment. A younger heir would be preferable; of his and Big Di Litiya's two daughters who reside at Nakoroka, neither shows promise as a leader. Besides, a male title-holder is always sought; even the energetic Big Di Litiya was unable to maintain proper rapport with the ancestors, and the land failed under her regency. Bulisivo's only son, Ratu Tevita, who has been blind since birth, is utterly undeveloped in the simplest social requirements; his only active participation in village life occurs at group sings, when he carries the higher voice with great assurance. Ratu Seru, son of Big Di Litiya, prefers to spend most of his time on the windward coast, where his chiefly claims in the land are secure through his maternal grandmother. He neglects his gardens at Nakoroka; he does not "remember the land." He displays wealth with extravagance but has no thought for his own or for the community's resources; hence he is frequently destitute. Ratu Luke, though his blood ties with Bulisivo are more remote, is a possible heir whose heredity is impeccable. Ratu Luke has not Ratu Seru's failings. He likes to live at Nakoroka; his eyes blur when he speaks of his love for Nakoroka's land. But he did not avail himself of his land rights in this village until he was fully grown. Besides, Bulisivo points out all Ratu Luke's faults to rationalize a personal disapproval of him: Ratu Luke has continually embroiled himself in responsibilities which he has been unable to fulfil, both of ceremonial nature and with the colonial administration; rather than experience temporary loss of face, he has changed his residence from Macuata to the windward coast and now to Nakoroka. Though Ratu Luke feels at home in Nakoroka, he has fulfilled no obligations there as a member of the chiefly caste. And, worst of all, in Bulisivo's private estimation, he has failed to remember that the land needs chiefs of unimpeachable heredity; he spurned Bulisivo's noble niece, Big Di Merelita, for the prettier commoner of Sarowaqa, by whom he has sired twins.[32] Now Ratu Luke is unable to fulfil

32. Though Bulisivo himself married the commoner Viniyana against the wishes of the entire community, he had already produced four chieftainesses and a blind chief by a lady of the windward coast who had distant connections with Nakoroka. Because of their mother, Ratu Luke's twins are commoners.

the gift obligations of marriage and paternity, which need not be costly, because his marriage was informal and with a family of commoners. Through his wilful conduct he is dispossessed of all the economic support which he would normally receive from Bulisivo's family, who are his nearest kin. So Bulisivo is in a quandary, and the village is losing faith in its chiefs.

The ideals upon which the populace pattern their criticism of chiefs—and particularly their titled chiefs—are fraught with contradictions, so that even the most conscientious chief has cause for private guilt and public self-justification. A good chief disapproves of violence and discourages it among his subjects. He disregards personal slights and never raises his voice above a mild, polite, conversational tone. Such restraint befits a chief; in itself it pleases the ancestors and encourages "a good soul" among all the people who, as ordinary mortals, are incapable of learning such thorough self-control. But a male chief must also be a "man."[33] He must have courage to overlook the chattering of commoners and follow his own counsel. If he satisfies his own desires blatantly and overrides all social regulations, people will say that he is "bad," but they will also say that he is "indeed a chief." Ratu Seru, who uses a "strong arm" on his women and whose lack of modesty shocks the village, is indeed a chief; people will speak in voices hushed with awe and admiration of a certain chief of Rokowaqa, long dead, who used to wait near the children's bathing place so that he could choose a particularly fat child to bake for his supper.[34] Such statements of the outrageous appetites of the ancient chiefs should be discounted to a high degree. Several early commentators have recorded the contrast between the sweet-tempered Tongan and the Fijian's equation of shocking conduct with manliness; the informant who gave me this tale was enjoying the shock himself and proving to me that his forebears were virile men who ate their own children. The ancestors, too, are proud of producing chiefs who are men so that their names will resound through the countryside; but the chief's masculinity is, first of all, a problem of his own social adjustment within the village and only secondarily a concern of the ancestors.

For many years Bulisivo has realized that he commands no admiration for his physical prowess or commanding presence. His conversa-

33. Fijian language completely lacks gender distinctions; hence, whenever the word "male" is used, it bears special force.

34. A great premium is placed on all foods which contain fat. In describing foods, "fat" is almost a synonym of "delectable." Of fat, starch, and protein in diet, fat seems least abundant.

tion receives little attention at casual gatherings; though he may find a temporary companion who will listen to his well-modulated voice as it drones below the vigorous yarns of other men, he resigns himself with a light laugh when he sees that his companion, out of concentrated politeness, has fallen asleep. Instead of pressing his views upon his subjects, he prefers to take refuge in holy isolation. He has become shy of interrupting even a young commoner to verify a fact for one of his few stock stories. People say that his conversation is like a woman's. Yet Bulisivo is ideally mild. In the last ten years there have been less than half-a-dozen near-outbreaks of violence; only one of these occurred while Bulisivo was resident at Nakoroka.[35] This is because Bulisivo is a "good" chief and hates anger. In contrast with Bulisivo, Nabadua has sought to assert his ungrounded claim to true chiefship through outrageous behavior. Neither has struck the precarious mean.

A chief should be lavishly generous on all occasions. Even if his own larder be lean of food, which does occur in fact though it is logically impossible if he has maintained friendly accord with the fertility-producing ancestors, abundance of food throughout the village must be his first concern. His obligation as intermediary between ancestors and community should be placed above his personal comfort. Yet he should maintain a house in fresh repair and a surplus of food with which to entertain guests so that all who pass will know the power of Nakoroka's ancestors. He should live in comfort, so that outsiders will know that his person is of high value. By realistically admitting that times were bad and attempting to maintain a plausible compromise, Bulisivo tried to avoid the dilemma. People grumble when his kitchen serves sweet puddings to the chiefly household. But when they think of his ramshackle house, they accuse him of lacking the spirit of a chief; they remember that the community as a whole had to take the initiative in building the great house called "Inland Forest," of which Ratu Seru, Bulisivo's nephew, is nominal head. Now it can be said that Nakoroka has a house suitable for the residence of chiefs.

Nabadua, in his attempt to emulate chiefly tradition, has involved himself in a paradox. He, too, blames the times for his poverty, but, unlike Bulisivo, he has emptied his gardens and impoverished his relatives in a frantic attempt to impress visitors. He compensates for the shoddy appearance of his house by stressing the virtues of the woods of

35. Though Bulisivo was a resident of Saolo on the windward coast through most of this ten-year period, men at Nakoroka generally attribute their peaceful temperaments to Bulisivo's influence. The few outbreaks of violence occurred because of his absence.

which it is constructed.[36] He points to the two other Tavua households, those of Bici and Monasa, and explains that his responsibilities as chief of Tavua have diverted his attention from the deplorable condition of his many houses. (People say that Nabadua cackles like a bird.)

A major criticism whispered against Bulisivo stems from his questionable blood ties with Nakoroka land. When today's lack of prosperity is compared with the abundance of former times, Bulisivo always receives his share of blame. He, like young Ratu Seru, has neglected his charge; he has wandered to foreign parts and has not "remembered the land." After a personal slight, which to Nabadua seems miniscule in retrospect, Bulisivo deserted Nakoroka for a sojourn of many years in the village of his mother at Saolo on the windward coast. A titled chief with the true spirit of chiefly blood leaves the boundaries of the land which is his charge only on formal visits to other villages; on these rare occasions he conducts gift presentations, the lavish wealth displays through which, best of all, ancestors receive honor in foreign kingdoms. Bulisivo's conduct has betrayed that he loves neither the land at Nakoroka nor communion with the ancestral spirits who reside there.

When poverty and famine have proved the unworthiness of the chief who holds the kingly whale tooth, or when some violent provocation has caused him to resign his title, there are mechanisms for choosing a successor. Discord among commoners may be the signal which motivates the chief's resignation. There need be no personal ignominy attached to his retirement. When poverty has descended, the title-holder will sorrowfully beg other chiefs to accept the whale tooth, in hopes that by trial and error some choice will eventually meet with ancestral approval. *Masi ca* is the condition of the land when it requires a change of chiefs. *Masi* is the common word for bark cloth and in this context seems to refer to the bark-cloth covering in which the title-bearing whale tooth is wrapped; *ca* means "bad." Choosing a new chief should produce a condition of *masi re*. *Re* means "good"; hence, as the whale tooth is wrapped in more suitable bark cloth, so the land will be more prosperous. When the fathers of Vilomena and Naicadra, chiefs of the Sivoa and the Great River divisions of Nadroro land, exchanged Nadroro's whale tooth, they hoped to produce a condition of *masi re*.[37]

36. The house is not built of chiefly wood, but nevertheless its wood is very sturdy.

37. Those regions which are called "land together" can exchange chiefs. Aside from those lands which are actually adjacent, like Sivoa and Great River, the phrase exists to

Toviya of Votua has said that, when a successor was to be chosen in the old days, the entire village repaired to the garden land and made a tremendous feast. The priest especially was stuffed with food. As names of prospective title-holders were called out, the priest, in whose bowels the feast did not yet lie comfortably, jumped repeatedly over a prone log. The name which was called as the priest broke wind marked him who would succeed to office. A spun coconut could also divine the proper chief to hold the whale tooth. But in recent times the choice of chiefs has been so limited that such devices are superfluous; the relative suitability of the few available candidates can almost always be determined by reviewing genealogies and personal history. Even when a divining technique has suggested a successor, the choice is not clinched until practice has provided its correctness.

When one has been chosen to rule the land or rather to reciprocate the services of the ancestors with the pleasing observance of traditional ceremonies and the maintenance of proper conduct within the territorial limits, he weeps sorrowfully because he mistrusts his ability to fulfil the responsibilities which are being thrust upon him. Ratu Luke, who is oppressed with unfulfilled private economic obligations, has said that the drain upon the chief's private wealth which accompanies the holding of a title and his responsibility as entrepreneur in intervillage exchanges of gifts give true cause for weeping and doubting one's capacity; beginning a career as a title-holder is a serious undertaking. Furthermore, it is a crucial test of one's chiefliness; if the ancestors fail to respond with a renewal of prosperity, question of the hereditary validity of one's caste and of the righteousness of one's past conduct gains glaring publicity. From his observations about 1850, Thomas Williams has described the choosing of a successor to titled position:

On Vanua Levu the election of a successor has the appearance of being done by surprise. The leading men have assembled and consulted awhile, one of their number advances to the person chosen, and makes him their *Mata* by binding a blade of the red Ti-tree leaf round his arm between the shoulder and elbow. It is the fashion for the man thus bandaged to weep and protest against his election, asserting his incompetency, and pleading low birth, poverty, indolence, ignorance of official phraseology, etc.; all which objections are, of course, met by others declaring their choice to be good.[38]

---

denote relationship of long standing, the cause of which has been forgotten. Nadroro has such a relation with the village of Narowai, which lies beyond the kingdom of Great Meadow near the kingdom of Bua; of reasons for this particular relation only the name "land together," persists.

38. *Fiji and the Fijians*, ed. George S. Rowe, I (London, 1858), 28.

This description may apply to the choice of successor to an office other than that of chief. Use of the title *Mata* and the candidate's complaint of ignorance of official phraseology suggest that the office to be filled was that of "messenger," *Matanivanua*. However, the reticent attitude of the elected might apply to a chiefly successor at Nakoroka. Since false modesty is a sign of good breeding, such reticence, both in this description and at Nakoroka, may have been ritual rather than genuine.

Some say that commoners can be influential in determining who shall be chosen as chief. Some commoners even say that the choice of whether to use respect language toward one who claims to be of chiefly rank is theirs to make. Yet, despite the general criticism of Bulisivo's caching of tobacco, sugar, and other luxuries for his private use, no one dares to neglect meticulous use of chiefly etiquette toward him; if people are reminded of the inconsistency in their theory and practice, they always remember quickly that Bulisivo is a chief who has rarely forgotten to be "good."

It is said that communities who possess more than one possible chief of any particular age group frequently suffer from rivalries for the status of title-bearer. The kingdom of Wainunu on the windward coast has always possessed three or four vigorous claimants; discord among them has annoyed the ancestors, and the land has failed in consequence. In the old days poisoning by witchcraft offered a convenient means for disposing of rivals; but the danger of detection, particularly by British authorities, who are severe in such cases, and the danger from the power of the poison itself, which may strike back upon the practitioner or his children, has saved chiefs from sorcery in recent years. The noble chief Empties-the-Land was poisoned at Wainunu during the last generation, but three ardent rivals still claim the Wainunu title. At Nakoroka there is a supernatural safeguard against such misfortune: neither the chiefs nor the chiefly women at Nakoroka can bear more than a single son. If two sons are born to the same chiefly family, misfortune befalls one of them. Ratu Luke's mother died when he was born, so he has no brothers. Big Di Litiya bore Ratu Seru but has since been childless despite her second marriage with the chiefly Vosalevu.[39] Bulisivo's Ratu Tevita was born blind because he is too

39. Her marriage to Vosalevu, however, is still considered "scattering the blood" of Nakoroka's chiefs. His only chiefly tie is through his mother, whose father was a commoner. Furthermore, his chiefliness is that of the kingdom of Great Meadow, the ancestors of which are despised despite the respect which military success has brought them.

near the age level of the slightly older Ratu Seru; had he been vigorous, the two might have contended for the kingship. Such contention would consist of whispering campaigns, secret alliances, and a striving for popularity within the village.[40]

The whale tooth "King Forest" did not come to Bulisivo until sometime after Ratu Seru's death. Ratu Seru's cross-cousin held it for a year or two, but he soon realized that its sacred power was far stronger than his own chiefly blood. He prepared gift offerings and journeyed to Saolo, where Bulisivo was residing and begged him to accept "King Forest" with the obligations it entailed. After difficult persuasion Bulisivo accepted it and moved his family to Nakoroka. By 1912, however, open dissent had arisen in the village centering about Nabadua's insubordinate attitude. The Saolo people had been begging constantly for Bulisivo's return to them because their land was failing. Besides, Bulisivo's wife had died giving birth to the blind Ratu Tevita, and Bulisivo, unable or unwilling to find a nurse among the women of Nakoroka, remembered a friendly British planter on the windward coast who could lend him a milk cow to feed the ailing son. The elders at Nakoroka rubbed ashes upon their heads and, presenting whale teeth and gifts of food, begged him to remain with them and protect their land.[41] Though Bulisivo wept as he saw them, he was adamant in purpose and departed for his mother's land. He left "King Forest" in the custody of his sister Big Di Litiya. Not until February, 1936, was the whale tooth again returned into Bulisivo's hands.

In October, 1935, Bulisivo had sent word that his long sojourn at Saolo, his mother's village, was at an end and that his personal belongings were packed and ready to be carried to Nakoroka, where henceforth he would make his home. Immediately the village was in a turmoil of preparations. Viniyana, his wife, and Ratu Luke left for Saolo to help him with preparations, and ceremonies began at Nakoroka.

During the day of October 14, 1935, Big Di Litiya and Vosalevu

40. As a check against rivalry within the immediate family, it is thought that a *masi re* condition could not be produced by passing the whale tooth to a true brother of the erstwhile title-holder. The change of chiefs is more effective when the chiefs have contrasting hereditary backgrounds. The best possible choice is a chief of a family line of the region which is "land together," and consequently "ancestor together," with the home community. Cases of actual exchange, however, are so rare that informants must speculate as to the proper procedure; their theory is drawn from the few existing cases, of which Nadroro is the most striking.

41. This ceremony of humiliation is called *ai soro*.

prepared an oven with the aid of Akuila, Isacodro, and Samu. In the evening Nabadua, Naicadra, Vatili, and Raitova gathered in Di Litiya's kitchen as representatives of the four ancestral villages which had no true chiefs. Each brought whale teeth from his household and arranged himself on the mat behind Nabadua opposite Big Di Litiya and her Votua group. Nabadua, fulfilling the ceremonial role of *matanivanua*, "spokesman,"[42] held the whale teeth in a cluster dangling on the rope handles which bound both ends of each tooth. He laid them gently on the mat, eight in all, between his own knees and those of Akuila, who was *matanivanua* for the receiving group. When he had clapped twice with cupped palms, he spoke in the respectful language of ceremony and with an index finger twisted a lock of hair against his forehead nervously:

"My presentation. Whale teeth for the chiefs of Inland Forest to bring Bulisivo back from Saolo where he has been staying, together with his box of personal things which has remained there at Saolo for many years. Be of good soul, do not be angry. It is a small thing that we give, but there are many needs among the people. Some of us have done evil and because of it we suffer need. Do not be angry, you chiefs of Inland Forest. My presentation of whale teeth is finished. *Soso ratu.*"

Naicadra, Vatili, and Raitova joined Nabadua in a deep voice to chant: "Iye-e-e."

As spokesman for Big Di Litiya, Akuila touched the whale teeth gently, clapped, and said: "I accept the whale teeth. Let us be united that our land may prosper. *Mana!*"

And those sitting with Akuila chanted: "It is true! *E! O! Duwasa-a-a.*"

Akuila continued, "*Madua, madua, madua,*" and his companions joined him in a tremendous "*Madua, madua, madua!*" Then Big Di Litiya, Vosalevu, Akuila, and Samu began to clap out of time and say, "It is good. It is good."[43]

Akuila turned to Di Litiya and said: "Di Litiya, the whale teeth lie inside the house. I have accepted the presentation. It is ample. I name the chiefs. This is the naming. May I be correct."[44]

Di Litiya clapped and said: "It is well."

42. Translated otherwise in other contexts.
43. The conventional phrase of thanks.
44. The text for this speech is garbled; our translation is probably inaccurate.

Akuila addressed Vosalevu and Samu in turn and said: "The whale teeth." Each clapped and responded: "It is well."[45]

Di Litiya had joined but sparingly in the chanting, because "women do not know these things." Isacodro had piled food fresh from the oven behind Akuila, who now turned, placed it before Nabadua, and began to present. The tables were turned. Akuila took the role that Nabadua had played a few minutes before. But instead of opening with "My presentation," he said: "My acceptance of the whale teeth," which was the name of the feast he was presenting.

The feast included a pig and a large number of yams and taro. When Nabadua had accepted it, Bici came to help cut it into shares for the households which had contributed whale teeth. He called the names of the households loudly, and, if no one responded, someone of the group which had gathered at Di Litiya's kitchen delivered a share of the food. Though all there had already eaten a boiled meal earlier in the evening, they gathered again to taste the freshly baked food. All households, except those of Big Di Litiya, Bulisivo (then absent), and Isacodro, who were the "owners of the feast," received a portion. Though, of the nine other houses, each had not contributed a whale tooth, each shared in the responsibility for the contribution according to its affiliation with other households descendant from the same ancestral village. Vatili represented the Sivoa division of Nadroro, which included the household of Orisi as well as his own. Nabadua's whale teeth were the collective gift of the households of Monasa, Bici, and Nabadua's oldest son, Namo, as well as his own.[46]

45. Though I did not observe its beginning, this ceremony is constructed from recordings of text for similar ones which were observed in entirety. Though the content of the speeches varies somewhat with the nature of the particular presentation, the general outline is constant for all occasions of formal presentation. The untranslated words have lost specific meaning at Nakoroka. *Mana*, which occurs in the acceptance speech, is probably the widespread term for sacred power. *Mudu*, in combination in the same speech, means "shame" and "respect." When the occasion concerns high chiefs, those who participate in the ceremonies sit with bowed heads and speak with taut throats; only at appointed places in the ritual do their united voices rise in mournful crescendo. The ceremony is holy. (Dorothy Spencer has said that the effect of ceremonies is very different in Cola, West Viti Levu.)

Though local variations in phonetics and vocabulary remodel the ceremonial words in each village, a native of any part of Vanua Levu would recognize the presentation ceremony of any other part; if he tried to participate, however, he would embarrass himself by erring in the pronunciation of a word or chorusing with the spokesman at the wrong time.

Such a ceremonial presentation requires about five minutes.

46. The status of Toviya's household in this exchange was not recorded. It might have been that of "owner" of either feast or whale teeth.

At a formal meeting that night, kava, which Vosalevu had brought from Bulisivo's garden land, centered the attention of the elders. Nakoroka was in turmoil deciding who should go and who should stay at home; men half-intending to depart changed their minds and planned to continue housebuilding on the morrow. Vatili had informed the Buli at Lekutu and had gained permission to free five men from their tasks of housebuilding; but the men whom the Buli had designated were old or infirm, and Nabadua, who knew best of all how to make glib ceremonial speeches, was not of the chosen number. But there was no consternation among the women; the chieftainesses plaited mats at the house of Big Di Litiya until far into the night. They did not care who went or who stayed at home; arriving at a decision concerned the men alone. Big Di Litiya, as sister to Bulisivo and then holder of "King Forest," would certainly undertake the expedition regardless of what men accompanied her. A few hours before sunup the men reached a decision and went to sleep.

On the morning of October 15 the time for departure had already passed. Nabadua, who the night before had decided to go, complained of pain in his side where he had barked his ribs against a boulder the week before. The way was long and slippery. If Vatili used his authority as "village chief" to forbid the truancy of Isacodro from the housebuilding project where he was badly needed, Nabadua might have to shoulder part of Bulisivo's belongings on the way home. Vatili threw up his hands, saying that he himself would go on the morrow if the men did not act quickly. Privately Vosalevu said that Vatili was not relaying the Buli's words correctly and that all men had permission to go. Ratu Kitioni, a chiefly relative of Bulisivo, who had arrived from Lekutu the night before, waited impatiently at the mouth of the path to the windward coast with his suitcase and umbrella. Nabadua dictated a letter to young Ratu Meli, who had attended school in Suva and could write the missionary dialect; it was to be delivered to Nabadua's older classificatory brother at Duleniwai on the way to Saolo. Nabadua still considered himself too ill for the journey.

Suddenly Vosalevu and Big Di Litiya joined Ratu Kitioni at the edge of the village with their small parcel of personal belongings. Isacodro hastened to the gardens to cut a stalk of kava to present to their host wherever they should spend the night. Nabadua took up the empty baking-powder tin in which he kept his personal leaves of tobacco and a few matches, bound a heavy strip of calico about his sore ribs, and with a great shout said, "Let us be off!" (Now there was no need for the letter which he had dictated.) Naicadra and Raitova dropped their work as housebuilders and joined the departing group. Half the village assembled to wave goodbye and exclaim upon the length of the path to Saola. It was midday.

Frequently they rested on the way. A young man from Nalauvia, on his way to the mines, carried Kitioni's small suitcase so that, relieved of his burdens, he could "walk with his arms swinging." But Kitioni proceeded but slowly. By late afternoon the procession had only reached Duleniwai, hardly ten miles away. At the last river crossing all bathed the mud from their bodies; some donned fresh calico skirts (sulu's). With a table knife which he had purchased from a Chinese trader at Lekutu and filed to sharpness for the purpose, Nabadua shaved without soap. Big Di Litiya caught a shrimp and boiled it on the riverbank. The laggards arrived: young girls who came to help with food preparation at Saolo; Ratu Kitioni; Isacodro, with a tremendous stalk of kava on his shoulder. They entered the village in procession. The first native of Duleniwai whom they met ushered them to the house of Nabadua's elder brother.

The kava which Isacodro had brought was formally presented to the people of Duleniwai and to Nabadua's brother, who, though not of chiefly blood, held the highest title in this region. Later the Nakoroka people formally displayed the whale teeth. In return Nabadua's brother presented one tooth which, added to the others, was placed safely away to be presented at Saolo; thus Duleniwai was included in the venture of bringing Bulisivo home. Through his mother, Bulisivo's chiefly blood was recognized at Duleniwai; many of the people there could trace their descent from Tavua of Nakoroka's territory.

Next morning the Duleniwai people presented a stalk of kava to Nakoroka. It arrived unexpectedly while the Nakoroka girls were seated in the lower part of Nabadua's brother's house. Big Di Litiya barely had time to call a warning to them so that they could scramble out of the house; as women, they could not attend a chiefly presentation of kava. Di Litiya only, whose capacity as title-holder at Nakoroka necessitated her presence, was free from the danger which threatened the other women. Even Bulisivo's thirty-year-old daughter, Di Vara, was not immune; she scurried off with the other girls.

When the sun was well risen, the straggling procession continued on its way to Saolo. Vosalevu, Big Di Litiya, and Di Vara walked most rapidly. They walked on through Cogea and Daria,[47] where all who

47. See Map I, p. 4.

met them fell prostrate before Di Litiya and brushed their noses against her graciously extended hand. This was the land of her mother, and her people knew her as their *vasu*. Here the path was less rugged. Once descended to the coast region, it looped about round knolls always in sight of the sea. But the windward coast is wet, and the rare intervals of sun never dry the paths. The traveler must extend his toes and dig them into the mud for footing. Sometimes the path spreads itself on a broad strand of beach, but more often it is lost in the muck of a mangrove swamp. Heavy forest growth descends nearer to the sea, and the soil which produces it also makes gardens flourish. The people, distributed more densely than in the Nakoroka region, build their gardens closer to the villages and line them with groves of orange trees and bananas, which grow luxuriantly.[48] At The-Bridge (Nakawakawa) a young girl ran to meet Di Vara, who was her old friend; for a while they sat on a fallen log with arms entwined and expressed their mutual sadness at the long separation. When the sun had passed behind the great ridge which rises abruptly from the windward coast, Di Litiya and Vosalevu halted to wait for the others so that they could enter Saolo as a single group. They washed the mud from their limbs in the muddy water of a coral lagoon, but there were no fresh streams to wash the sweat from their bodies; tide flows high into the mouths of rivers and scoops out deep caverns in which sharks like to bask.[49] Di Litiya found a clump of "bush pineapple"[50] and gathered an armful of dry leaves, to split, scrape, and roll into packages while they waited. She had brought fifty leaves of tobacco as a gift for Bulisivo. The tobacco on the windward coast grows feeble and lean and has no flavor. A few rolls of pineapple leaves prepared for making cigarettes would add polish to her gift.

At Saolo a young chief met the procession on the margin of the village and ushered them quietly to a house specially emptied of its owners for the convenience of the guests. When they had freshened themselves from their drenching of rain and sweat, kava, which Isacodro had carried all day from Duleniwai, where it had been presented to the Nakoroka people, was presented to the houseowner and to the

48. This garden land is classified as *wiligau*.
49. In home territory sharks are harmless to him who is without sin. Ancestors frequently assume shark form. But in foreign waters one has no rapport with the ancestors of the land. If they had chosen to smear their bodies with the sticky, brackish water, Di Litiya and Di Vara could have bathed with safety because they were related to the land. But Vosalevu and the others were strangers, and the risk would have been great.
50. Of distinctly different variety from the wild-growing edible pineapple.

chiefs at Saolo. Nabadua spoke at length in his presentation. He told that the party had traveled for two days, that the path was long, that the land from which they came was poor, and that the gift was unworthy of his hosts. He begged them not to take insult at his presumption in making such unsuitable offering. When he had finished, the men of Saolo expressed their admiration for Nakoroka's kava, and Saolo presented kava to Nakoroka for use during their sojourn there. Perhaps as a gesture of politeness Vosalevu played the role of *matanivanua* in the acceptance speech; Vosalevu's claims to chiefly blood through his mother were valid, while Nabadua's through his father were not, and it may have honored the hosts for a chief to speak humbly as *matanivanua*. During the presentation which preceded Vosalevu's acceptance, Nabadua, who now sat in the shadow, interrupted the Saolo speaker with quietly spoken chants of "It is well; it is well."[51] As Vosalevu spoke, he scratched his thigh and shoulder vigorously. When he verbally apportioned the kava among the Nakoroka men, Nabadua pulled strands of hair over his forehead, Naicadra scratched his chest, Raitova sawed a finger between his toes. Ceremonial clapping was subdued. All spoke in whispers. Raitova and Isacodro, of lowest rank and hence most sparingly adjusted to the sanctity of the occasion, moved their lips without sound and gently touched palms together with only the gesture of clapping.[52]

When Bulisivo had had ample time to prepare himself for the meeting, he joined the Nakoroka people in the house which had been allotted them. He entered through the upper door, and a great silence fell among them. In one voice they murmured, "Iye-e-e."[53] Formally Nabadua presented the cluster of whale teeth for Bulisivo's inspection. A commoner of Saolo acted as his *matanivanua* in the acceptance speech. That night Vosalevu and the Nakoroka men presented the whale teeth formally to the chiefs of Saolo. The ceremony occurred in another house, and Bulisivo did not bother to attend. Before removing the

51. Such behavior, though acceptable and polite, is unusual. Perhaps Nabadua resented losing the limelight.

52. The striking similarity of individual attitudes during these ceremonial occasions and church services suggests a strong psychic identification which informants substantiate. The bowed head, the lowered voice, the abject appreciation of the speech of the pastor or the presenting *matanivanua* with quiet interruptions of "It is well"—all express the "shame" which is felt in the presence of supernatural powers and of chiefs.

53. "Duo, duo," the more frequent phrase at Nakoroka has come from Macuata. The clapping with cupped palms is also of recent introduction from Macuata. Throughout Bua Province, snapping the floor mat with the fingernail formerly took the ceremonial place of clapping.

whale teeth from the mat where they lay, the Saolo chiefs presented a large stalk of kava as an "acceptance of the whale teeth."[54] Later, word came from Saolo's title-holding chief that two ovens of feast food, including two domestic pigs, would be prepared for the Nakoroka people and that they were expected to remain as guests at Saolo for five nights.[55]

Days at Saolo were a long round of idleness. The Nakoroka girls, to whom a kitchen had been allotted, served two meals a day of the feast food which the men of Saolo had baked. In the middle of the morning one of the Nakoroka girls would come to announce that the mat was spread for eating, and again in the late afternoon. Bulisivo always filled the place of honor at the head of the mat. When the women had filled his plate with food cooked in the Saolo ovens and with a fresh fish which they themselves had netted on the reef earlier in the day, those who occupied the places along the sides of the long mat, ranging from women and commoners to chiefs, passed his plate to him and clapped as they released it from their hands. All waited until his lips touched the food, then clapped in unison. There was no loitering about the mat when one's plate was empty; as soon as a place was vacated, it was filled by someone of lower rank.[56] The chiefs, however, ate more slowly. When the men had finished, and the girls at the foot of the mat had sponged clean their plates, women filled the eating-places. Big Di Litiya held the place of honor among the women. Even Bulisivo's daughter Di Vara and his wife Viniyana clapped as they passed her plate.

Among the Nakoroka men, intervals between meals were filled with dozing, kava-drinking, and lazy conversation. The Saolo people went about their usual tasks during the day and left the Nakoroka people to their own devices in their guest house. But the hosts were not remiss in supplying an abundance of food and drink. Ceremonies of

54. Dire misfortune follows handling whale teeth before a return gift of other whale teeth, kava, or mats has validated the acceptance.

55. On the occasion of any visit guests are informed as to how long they are expected to stay. Departing before the time which the host has appointed is as much a breach of etiquette as overreaching one's stay.

56. The order in which the men sat was Bulisivo, Ratu Luke and Ratu Kitioni on Bulisivo's right and left, beyond them Vosalevu and Naicadra or Nabadua, and lastly Raitova and Isacodro. When Bulisivo's *matanivanua* of Saolo joined the group, he sat above Naicadra but below those of chiefly rank. On rare occasions a chief who was traveling on the windward coast and was related by immediate blood ties to Bulisivo took a place at the Nakoroka mat among the chiefs.

presentation and acceptance of food and kava[57] filled more than an hour of each day. During his participation in ceremonies, Nabadua always twisted his forelock, Vosalevu scratched his thigh and shoulder, and Raitova scraped the crevices between his toes.

But at night the unaccustomed quiet of the day's procession had produced no desire to sleep. Kava-drinking was resumed with vigor. A few men of Saolo would pay visits to the guest house and, in the voice used to make guests feel gay, cry, "Let's have conversation, conversation from the people of Nakoroka." Vosalevu, shaking away his drowsiness, would draw closer to the kava bowl and in histrionic tenor and artfully rounded cadences describe a hunting adventure: a wounded boar had treed him until night had fallen in the forest; a companion, likewise in refuge from the boar, was so precariously situated that he could not urinate despite the long passing of the hours. Sometimes his own laughter, timed to bring best effect upon his audience, made him inarticulate. Then a Saolo man, with mannerisms tuned to his literary style, would tell of a dangerous escape. Sometimes they told humorously obscene stories of the ancestors of the land, sometimes of the days of the wars or of the supernatural. More often they made anecdotes about government officials or missionaries, or a Saolo "man of schooling" tested his knowledge of Bible stories and the discoverers of Fiji against the dull but learned wit of Ratu Kitioni. Each raconteur had mannerisms of his own. Frequently his timed laughter brought no response from the listeners, but he continued as he had privately planned to do, outwardly unabashed. If the story were too lengthy or if the audience were bored with the heaviness of its humor, another spokesman might draw all attention with a different yarn, but he who was bereft of his audience would continue speaking until he was sure that his story had failed; then his voice would fade gradually into silence.

Not all conversation was stylized in this manner. Sometimes a serious issue of general importance almost swept away self-consciousness. All were concerned with the rise of the Indian population in their territory. All had opinions about the relative worth and danger of the gold mines to the future of Fiji. Ratu Luke, Nabadua, and two Saolo men heatedly condemned the Buli of the district in which Saolo is located; each contributed to the long list of the Buli's sins.

Sometimes late at night the girls of Saolo entertained the kava-

57. Identical with the presentation of whale teeth which has been recorded in detail (above, pp. 208–10).

sodden men of Nakoroka with dancing. But there were no young men of Nakoroka who could reciprocate the dancing. The girls danced for these venerable guests out of politeness and not with the vigorous grace which they call into play when they wish to attract the admiration of gay younger visitors. Nakoroka people always "lost": it had been many years since Nabadua and Vosalevu had danced before an unfamiliar audience, and they were ashamed to expose the stiffness of their joints, lest they appear foolish. Ratu Luke, who alone of the guests was still young enough to participate in dances of the young people, had gone to visit his aged father in a forest retreat several miles away; so the girls would rise in disgust, after a few attempts to persuade these old men to "return a dance." On the third night of the visit, long past midnight, three Saolo boys came to dance. Big Di Litiya, who frequently drank and conversed with the men,[58] rose to the occasion and routed the Nakoroka girls from their beds to smear scented coconut salve on their sleepy faces and tie garlands of leaves about their arms and throats. But these were not the prettiest of Nakoroka's girls; their dance was sluggish, and the Saolo boys commented rudely and left the house. Again Nakoroka had "lost."[59]

There was no need for the Nakoroka men to sleep at night. No responsibilities oppressed them. Vosalevu said: "We sleep at home, at Nakoroka. While we are guests, we rest and enjoy ourselves." But the days of the Nakoroka girls were filled with chores which they performed under Big Di Litiya's direction. Salt-water fish was a rare delicacy to these mountaineer palates, and the girls procured it fresh from the sea every day. One day they gathered conch shell on the reef to trade for sugar and tea at the Chinese store three miles down the coast, so that the chiefs could drink. The girls' entertainment consisted of quick card games played with interruptions between their chores. One morning Meremanini, Naicadra's daughter, drew playing cards from beneath her, where she had placed them as she fell asleep the night before, and wakened Di Vara to have a quick game of rummy before Di Litiya should call them to begin the preparation of the morning meal; they played without changing the postures in which they had slept all night. But the game was barely under way when Big Di Litiya's voice boomed from outside: the sun was high. The women used the house that Bulisivo had been allotted during his long sojourn there;

58. People said that her conversation was like a man's.
59. Fijians have borrowed the English word "lose" and pronounce it *lu-si*, whispering the second syllable. It refers specifically to "being outdone in a reciprocal relationship."

to the Nakoroka people this was the "women's house" in contrast with the house in which the men conversed, drank, and performed ceremonies of presentation and acceptance.

Bulisivo never joined the evening entertainments in the "men's house." Sometimes he sat quietly in the kitchen, dozing and whittling leisurely on a new handle for his steel machete. He was proud of his skill as a wood-carver. He went to sleep early with the women in their house, but sometimes late at night he woke his wife Viniyana to ask her to stir up the fire and find his tobacco so that he could smoke. There were a hundred little personal chores that he could invent to disturb the women; his voice was always plaintive when he called upon them. Men say that his conversation is like a woman's; he always tells the same stories, always with the same pointlessness, and he can chatter idly about nothing. He consoles himself with a belief in the farsightedness of his views; other men think only of this day's pleasures.

Naicadra, Isacodro, and Raitova tired of the idleness and of the formality which thrust them constantly into the shadows as commoners. Idleness, they said, is a talent of chiefs. On the fourth day they worked with distant Saolo relatives at garden-planting.

On the morning of the sixth day of the visit the men, sodden with kava and too much feasting, blearily roused themselves before the middle of the morning to prepare their departure. Nabadua, whose kava consumption had been prodigious, rubbed his swollen eyes and drained the kava bowl of its dregs from the night before. The Saolo men presented kava and sweet puddings as food for the path. Baskets (*ketekete dina*) were hastily wrought from coconut leaves which Isacodro had freshly cut. Big Di Litiya and Nabadua did the plaiting. Though Nabadua's fingers were shaking with jitters from too much kava, he plaited more rapidly than Di Litiya. When Bulisivo's wife and his daughter had completed his final packing, the Nakoroka people moved toward the "mouth" of the path which led home. The titled chief of Saolo, with a few retainers and one to function as *matanivanua* in the ceremony of presentation, made a final gift to Bulisivo of four whale teeth and half-a-dozen mats. The village gathered to shake hands with their departing guests and sniff the hands of their two *vasu*, Bulisivo and Big Di Litiya. Many traveled far along the path to postpone separation.

At The-Bridge the elders gathered to present more kava to Bulisivo. While the travelers rested and fanned away the heat of the hot sun, Raitova and Isacodro prepared the kava for drinking and served it to

Bulisivo and the chiefs of The-Bridge with whom he was chatting, Vosalevu acting as presiding host of the kava bowl. Ceremony of the kava-serving required meticulous correctness so that the people of The-Bridge would say that the men of Nakoroka knew how to behave in the presence of their chiefs.

Constant delays along the path, and Bulisivo's leisurely progress, a result of both his age and his chiefliness, retarded the tempo of the march so that nightfall halted the procession at Cogea. Though Duleniwai was not far distant, the path thenceforward led away from the sea and up the steep slope of the mountains. Bulisivo preferred to remain at Cogea even though Nabadua and Naicadra were obviously chafing at the delay; they worried about the condition of their gardens and wanted to feel at home again in their own land. Bulisivo's heavily laden packing box (obtained from some trader) swung on a pole between the shoulders of Isacodro and Raitova; to halve the rigors of the ascent into two days' travel, these two had carried their burden on to Duleniwai.

Every member of the party except Bulisivo helped carry the overflow of his goods that could not be packed away in the chest. Vosalevu, who had been shouldering a tremendous basket of goods, traded loads with Big Di Litiya, who was clumsily bearing a roll of mats upon her shoulder. Though the basket was much heavier than the mats, the exchange relieved both: carrying upon the shoulder is a masculine technique; Big Di Litiya could bind sennit ropes about the basket and carry it comfortably like a knapsack, which is woman's way, while it had been balanced with difficulty upon Vosalevu's shoulder. Vosalevu was sensitive about his status as chief, and, had he carried a burden like a woman, people might have commented upon it.

Cogea had but few ties with Nakoroka; hence the party did not loiter in the morning. They reached Duleniwai by high afternoon. But Bulisivo preferred to rest there until the following day. The last stretch to Nakoroka was steepest and roughest of all. But food at Duleniwai was scarce. The people there, in spite of their great respect for Bulisivo's chiefship, could prepare but a meager oven. Nabadua, especially, was chagrined at the poverty of his Duleniwai kinsmen. Isacodro, whose affinal ties with Duleniwai produced joking attitudes toward him among the men, helped with the preparation of this oven while the other travelers rested. That night when kava was served to Bulisivo, Isacodro tugged for the kava strainer with one of his brothers-in-law; each wanted to prepare the beverage and ridiculed the other's technique. Late at night Duleniwai girls barely past puberty entertained Bulisivo with dancing, but all others went to sleep. All but Bulisivo had exhausted their supply of tobacco, and Duleniwai had none to offer; when there is no tobacco to smoke as "garnish" for kava, all gaiety vanishes. At Duleniwai the last of the Saolo men, who had been accompanying the Nakoroka party, turned back home; it was he who had served as Bulisivo's *matanivanua* when the Nakoroka party first greeted their chief at Saolo.

Next morning all prepared to depart in good time. But as an afterthought Bulisivo decided to drink kava and detailed Isacodro to prepare it. As Bulisivo called to his wife and daughter to bring mats to spread in the village green so that he could recline comfortably in the open air, Isacodro fetched a kava bowl, water, and the kava mortar. Bulisivo's whining calls to his women gained no response, and he had to spread the mats himself. Nabadua muttered: "This is the trouble with traveling in procession with chiefs. You never know when they will demand delay even though night is falling." Quickly he and Naicadra found the sweet puddings which had been received at Saolo and munched noisily, full in Bulisivo's vision. When Isacodro was ready to serve, and Bulisivo called plaintively for the Nakoroka men to join him in the kava circle, Nabadua and Naicadra indicated their half-eaten puddings; it is generally believed that mixing food with kava, particularly sweet food, causes stomach disorder. But Raitova, who had not created an excuse, had to drink. Though Bulisivo did not press Nabadua and Naicadra to drink, they were obliged to join in the ceremony with clapping and conventional phrases until the bowl stood empty.

With late departure the party straggled into Nakoroka after dark. It was October 23. No feast greeted the returned chief because Vatili had constantly driven the young men in their work on Nakoroka houses. All but Vatili were weighted with this shame of neglecting to honor their chief. But Bulisivo's immediate family—his blind son, his daughter Little Di Litiya, sixteen-year-old Ratu Meli, and old Di Kabu and her daughter—greeted him warmly. That night he opened his chest and his bundles of goods and gave gifts to all these members of his family: a few spoons and knives, but principally new calico skirts to his grandchildren.

Though Bulisivo had been escorted back to Nakoroka in the manner of a chief, a month passed before the men of Nakoroka were prepared to celebrate his return. During the lull in housebuilding activities, Ratu Luke seized the initiative and organized food-gathering in all the ancestral village groups. Men, young and old, were enlisted. More than a hundred large taro and two domestic pigs for garnish filled two ovens. Bulisivo received them in formal ceremony and late at night ordered that Big Di Litiya's pig be butchered and baked as a return feast to the people of Nakoroka. The men drank kava heavily that night, but Bulisivo remained in his house and smoked tobacco in solitude.

All formal behavior in relation to chiefs stimulates fertility in the land, but there are also special ceremonial exchanges specifically for this purpose. If ever an unusual fish is caught or a pig with an unusual growth of tusks, the fisherwoman or hunter presents it to Bulisivo, who returns a gift of acceptance. Ana, the wife of Bici, caught a tremendous eel on January 16; if she had not presented it to him, she would never have caught another eel. If Bulisivo had not presented her with a return gift, on this occasion a man's shirt, she would never have presented to him again. If either had neglected his share of the obligation, this relationship, which alone could keep a large population of eels in Nakoroka waters, would have been broken. Ana would no longer have found eels, and Bulisivo would no longer have deserved the position of chief. Likewise an unusually formed papaya, orange, or mango should be presented to Bulisivo, or whatever chief holds the "King Lekutu" whale tooth. Then fertility of these food products will increase.

Formerly a presentation of first-fruits of the chestnut was carefully observed, but Bulisivo and Big Di Litiya have never responded vigorously to such presentations. Formerly the ripening of yams gave occasion for the most spectacular of all ceremonies of first-fruits.[60] Now they have become simple exchanges between individuals and require no elaborate preparation. Among the descendants of the "*bota* who wipes away feces" group of the ancient village of Votua a commoner should present his yams first to Ratu Luke, who alone among them is chief by blood. Ratu Luke would give a mat and perhaps some boiled food in return. Then Ratu Luke, together with the commoner, should present the yams to Toviya, who formerly held the whale tooth for this division of Votua. Toviya in turn would present a small return feast and a mat; but the commoner, who had already received gift food from Ratu Luke, would insist that this return gift be Ratu Luke's exclusively. Then all three should present the yams to Bulisivo together with a

60. See above, pp. 40–41 (the first-fruits of Ratu Seru).

whale tooth.[61] Bulisivo should return gifts to Toviya, including a whale tooth. When the first yams of all groups had so accumulated with Bulisivo, a grand division would occur. In former times this was the occasion for the great feast at which relatives from other villages came to participate with the ancestral village groups to which they were tied by blood. The more whale teeth and mats which a chief could distribute at these times, the greater loomed his prestige. Today, however, the title-bearing whale teeth of all subsidiary units of the kingdom of Inland Forest have fallen into the hands of Bulisivo, and men bearing titles to chiefly authority, commoners like Nabadua and Toviya, no longer have the right to accept first-fruits. Today each man presents individually to Bulisivo. After a small return gift, Bulisivo distributes each man's yams among the households of the village. He no longer delays the distribution until yams have accumulated from all village gardens.

Both Toviya and Monasa, who have liens on ancient priestly land groups, claim that a separate presentation to the priest formerly preceded that to the chief. These yams were for the priest's personal use, and in return for them he gave a small gift of mats and perhaps some boiled food. He to whom the presentation is made can never refuse to accept. Toviya says that, no matter how small one's supply of new yams, such presentation will invariably produce an abundance for the following year. He who neglects will suffer famine.

Periodically he who held the titled whale tooth "emptied the land anew." It has been many years since Bulisivo sent messengers to the title-holders of each ancestral village group with a whale tooth as gift and the request that preparations begin for this great feast to promote fertility. Sometimes several years passed before preparations for return feasts were complete. It was usual for each village group to respond separately; months or years might interpose between the various responses of Tavua, Nadroro, and Votua.[62] Strict taboo was laid upon many gardens, pigs were encouraged to reproduce and fatten in their pens, and the people avoided extravagance in daily cooking and even treated guests with meager fare. The taboo which the title-holder in conference with the elders laid upon his land took precedence over all needs that might arise; it was sanctioned not only by the sacred power which lay within the whale tooth of the ancestral village land but also

61. Probably not the tooth which bore the group's administrative title.
62. Rokowaqa has long been considered as incorporated in Votua for most ceremonial purposes.

by that of the "King Lekutu" whale tooth, which embodied the power of Nakoroka's greatest ancestors.

By responding separately to Bulisivo's request, each ancestral village group could include the food resources of relatives who would otherwise function as members of other groups. Thus Bici, though he considered Tavua his closest land affiliation through his father, would assist Nadroro in preparation of their feast, because, through his mother, he observed a kin tie with Naicadra. He is also bound by kinship to Toviya's group in Votua. People came from distant villages, and all brought food gifts for their host kinsman at Nakoroka. Bici said that Bulisivo would instruct each ancestral village group as to how many hundreds of taro and yams to prepare, how many pigs, and how many whale teeth. The titled chief of each ancestral village met with his elders, and together they decided how much each could expect from kinsmen in other villages. Invitations were issued to villages near by; kinsmen in distant villages would hear of the preparations and come without invitation, bringing a gift of whale teeth for their Nakoroka host. So it was that new mats were spread for twenty fathoms on the village green to receive the last feast which Tavua presented to Bulisivo.

It is always a titled chief who, with a new mat spread on his shoulder, carries pigs to present to Bulisivo's "contents of the household." One pig at a time is presented, cleaned, and butchered. He who carries it tries to cast it violently to the ground; but Bulisivo's "contents of the household"[63] would catch its legs to prevent this and so preserve their reputation. The association between carrying a pig and holding the titled whale tooth is so strong that, though the whale tooth of Toviya's land has long since mysteriously disappeared, Toviya still holds the title, because everyone remembers that long ago he carried the pig when his land made a feast to Bulisivo. A chief too feeble for this task would pass it to his heir; likewise he would pass on his title of chief and the whale tooth which authorized it.

Bulisivo's "contents of the household" would feast all guests who had come from other villages for the occasion. Such guests are classified according to the households of their hosts. Feasts must be apportioned among them so that none who have brought gifts are neglected. It is this apportioning of feasts which wearies every host. Those who come with no gifts receive no portions of their own; nevertheless, there is abundance for them to eat because a host's prestige is reckoned in the quantity of his garbage.

63. Raitova and Samu would fulfil this function today.

.After such feasts food abounded for several years. It was Bulisivo's obligation to observe the condition of the land and inaugurate
such renewals of its fertility. The whale teeth which embodied the
chiefly authority of each ancestral village fell into Bulisivo's hands at
these times, not to be returned until the period of abundance had
passed and Bulisivo deemed it necessary to begin preparations for another great feast. During the intervals in which the title-holders of
each ancestral village held in their possession their own whale teeth,
first-fruits were presented to them, but, during the period of abundance which followed, Bulisivo received first-fruits directly from the
whole population. Discussion of the whereabouts of the whale teeth
of ancestral villages requires great delicacy. It is certain that Tavua's
tooth has remained in Bulisivo's possession ever since the last renewal
of Tavua land, which occurred more than twenty years ago; for many
years Nabadua, as Tavua's title-holder, has borne this grudge against
the chiefly family of Votua, not always secretly. Nadroro's whale
tooth is still in the possession of Nadroro's heirs to the title;[64] hence
Naicadra, who has been the most venerable member of Nadroro since
Vilomena's death,[65] feels that Nadroro is almost independent of Bulisivo's jurisdiction. Toviya, erstwhile title-holder for the "*bota* who
wipes away feces" at Votua, has long been silent about his whale
tooth; there are those who say that he has lost it; some even suggest
that he sold it to Chinese traders, and the men of the group have begun
to look to Akuila, the next oldest, as their leader. It is said that the
whale teeth of both Rokowaqa and Buleya are hidden away in the
bottom of Buliviso's great box of private belongings. So for many years
the land at Nakoroka has failed steadily.[66]

In recent years villages of Bua Province have feasted one another
without the sanction of their chiefs. Early in September, 1935, the
good Wesleyans of Nakoroka went to the village of Bua to celebrate
the century anniversary of the arrival of missionaries in Fiji.[67] They
carried gifts to the people of Bua which will someday be lavishly reciprocated. But in the time of Bulisivo's father Ratu Seru only chiefs

---

64. See above, pp. 191–92.

65. Vilomena's death is described below, p. 367.

66. Because of the great length of time which has elapsed since this feast was performed,
descriptions of it are mingled fact and theory. The term by which this feast is more widely
known is *solevu ni vanua. Solevu* may be a contraction of *sosou levu,* "great arrival," *ni vanua*
is "of the land"; or it may be derived from *sole levu,* "great giving."

67. The first missionaries arrived at the island of Lakemba in 1835.

initiated such intervillage feasts. When Bulisivo was but a young man, Ratu Inoke of Dreketi came to Votua to feast Ratu Seru and "wipe away the blood" of the sack of Nabetenidiyo.[68] The Dreketi people had spent the night in the region of Sarowaqa, but there was not enough food there to satisfy them. At Nabetenidiyo they paused, and that village[69] presented them with several ovens as "food for the path." At Votua, Ratu Seru had long been planning for their arrival. He had begged the aid of his kinsman chief at Nadroro, the father of Naicadra. And the Nadroro people brought great quantities of uncooked yams, which were placed in a temporary shelter and held in reserve. The slaughter of pigs at Votua and the baking of yams and taro were such that, when the feast food was piled together, it loomed high like a great hill.[70] Every two men at Votua had prepared at least one oven; every oven contained at least one pig. (In those days the population was much greater than it is today.) The night was advanced before the feast was apportioned among the people of Dreketi. Though the guests were famished, they could consume but a fraction of the feast. The river at Votua was so dammed with food refuse that the boulders at the ford could not be seen. At Sarowaqa,[71] near the mouth of the river Votua, people saw the floating carcasses of pigs and the great yams half-eaten and said: "It is the people of Nakoroka who are holding feast today." One ill-bred Macuatan, who had but little taste for taro, asked for some *kawai*, a sweet starchy root used more extensively in Macuata than in Bua. Ratu Seru ordered two large baskets to be cooked and heaped before him. Ratu Inoke saw and said: "Are you hungry that you ask for food? Have you eaten your entire share of feast food?" The man looked at the heap of uneaten taro near by and was ashamed, because a well-fed guest does not ask for food. It was on this occasion that Ratu Inoke returned the land of River's Mouth to the kings of Inland Forest.[72]

Though Bulisivo speaks affectionately of the days when chiefs of Macuata came laden with gifts for him, he has made no effort in many years to reciprocate such attentions. Some thirty years ago the people

68. See above, pp. 52–53.
69. Tavua descendants lived there.
70. To give me some conception of the amount of food, Bulisivo indicated a hill several hundred feet high.
71. Perhaps eight miles as the crow flies from Nakoroka, but much farther along the river's course.
72. See above, p. 52.

of Dreketi came with their chiefs, bringing several large sacks filled
with whale teeth. Bulisivo has never returned their visit. Hence today's chiefs in Macuata carefully avoid visiting Nakoroka.[73] Several
years ago the Roko of Macuata engaged the services of Nakoroka's
young men to build houses in a distant part of Macuata. He escorted
them home in his sailing boat as far as Sarowaqa but refused to come
to Nakoroka; he preferred not to embarrass Bulisivo, whose long-
standing neglect to return a visit to Macuata could mean only that
Nakoroka's chiefly family was impoverished. With graciousness which
carried a deep insult, he sailed the men up the Sarowaqa River as far
as the draft of his vessel would permit but did not deign to disembark
into land ruled by the now declassed "King Forest."[74]

During the time of Maki-ni-valu[75] the kingdom of Great Meadow
conquered Inland Forest. But Great Meadow chiefs have never dared
to take the whale tooth "King Forest" from the possession of the
Nakoroka chiefs. The inland region holds all chiefly sacredness; coastal
peoples, less firmly rooted in the soil, dare not question the rights of the
chiefs of the interior. Though Great Meadow included the inland regions of Nacula and Nalauvia, its chiefly family was of the coast. Its
present title-holder is a resident of Lekutu whose father, a true chief
of Flight-of-the-Strong in inland Macuata, married a commoner of
Great Meadow and settled with her there. Since Maki-ni-valu left no
male heirs, his whale tooth passed through devious lanes of succession
to its present holder. Ratu Kitioni, who is a descendant of one of
Maki-ni-valu's daughters and also tied with Inland Forest through his
relationship with Bulisivo, has formed a plan by which the whale
tooth of Great Meadow will again be held by a true chief. Ratu
Kitioni's son has married the daughter of the present title-holder;
hence, when the whale tooth falls to her, Ratu Kitioni's son will be
its virtual possessor, and the lands of Great Meadow will flourish again.
Perhaps then the people of Inland Forest will grant rights of first-
fruits to Great Meadow's title-holder. Though the conquered chiefs
of Inland Forest should have granted this courtesy long ago, they have
never deigned to humble themselves before chiefs of questionable
blood. No one blames Bulisivo for neglecting to present first-fruits to

73. In contrast with the chiefs in Bua Province, the Macuata chiefly family has held
official positions under the British colonial regime. Hence recent years have brought no decline in their chiefly authority.
74. The "King Forest" whale tooth carries with it the kingly title of Inland Forest.
75. See above, pp. 38–39.

the title-holder of Great Meadow; then the land at Nakoroka would
fail even more rapidly.

The village, however, resents his lack of interest in fulfilling his role
as chief in reciprocal trade relations. Neither Bulisivo nor Di Litiya
has ever responded properly to gifts of first-fruits. The failure of Nakoroka land is attributed to their lack of initiative in "emptying the land
anew." With shame the people whisper of Bulisivo's lack of pride in
never returning the visit of the Macuata chief. Nabadua says that both
Bulisivo and Big Di Litiya have "insides of commoners"; as proof he
points to the disappearance of the title-bearing whale teeth of Tavua
and of Toviya's division of Votua. Nabadua remembers also that the
whale teeth presented to Bulisivo by the chiefs of Saolo, in October,
1935, were never distributed among Nakoroka's households. Though
Nacula, the inland division of the kingdom of Great Meadow, is
favored with no such chiefs as Bulisivo's family, yet their yams flourish
in abundance in contrast with Nakoroka's rather limited supply. This
is because all chiefly ceremonies are observed at Nacula. Though
chiefly titles have long since fallen to commoners, the title-bearing
whale tooth of each division of Nacula land can still enlist ancestral
favor.

As the power of chiefs has declined, British influence in local administration has increased. Its deliberate concern was to check war. In
theory it left local authority in the hands of local chiefs and supported
the heir to chiefship regardless of his qualifications. Such strict succession to the title limits the expression of talent for leadership to him who
is hereditarily ordained, and instances are rare in which the luck of
succession has coincided with great personal gifts. In the old days it
was ceremonially possible to shift the title-bearing whale tooth among
chiefs until one was found who bore the title well. But today it is more
difficult to utilize such devious blood ties as that miraculous birth
which bound Bulisivo's father to Votua. Offensive chiefs in former
times could also be poisoned by witchcraft. If black magic proved ineffective, alliance with a neighboring village could free the people from
a tyrant's yoke. But with the arrival of the British all such devices for
reshuffling authority within the community were outlawed. The Land
Commission has tried to stabilize nativity, and hence the choice of
candidates for chiefship is still further limited. Bulisivo and his family
have always been unable or unwilling to initiate and sustain economi-

cally beneficial activities in their village, yet their unshakable position as Nakoroka's chiefs has resulted in progressively more authority falling to him who has sanction of government officialdom, the "village chief." But the village is confused because these "village chiefs"[76] usually have no hereditary rights to authority, and much wasteful effort is cross-purposed. Commoners still expect chiefs to lead them.

76. Titles of native officials in government service have been discussed above, pp. 61–63.

CHAPTER VII

PRIESTS[1] AND PRACTITIONERS

SOME commoners find blood ties with the priestly caste to be strong within them. These are marked as' deserving respect. Though priests play formal roles at times of chiefly ceremonies and though they use formal ritual to control weather and the fortunes of war, their talents are principally directed toward developing personal rapport with ancestral spirits. Such rapport can validate their role in ceremony. Though they play a true priestly role as interpreters of traditional methods of rapport with the supernatural, their application of these methods requires high capacity for shamanistic communion with spiritual informants. To the ancestors each moment in the history of the village is unique, and it is the priests who must discover what ceremony is most fitting to the needs of the moment. Men so talented, even though they may bear titles to chiefly authority in the land castes other than priestly, are singled out as eccentrics to be humored with awe. Toviya, most clearly marked as a hereditary priest at Nakoroka, rarely participated at casual evening gatherings; when he did so, a hush fell among the others. Of commoners, he was first to receive the kava cup even when an older man was present. He felt secure in his eccentricity because no one doubted its social necessity.

Everyone makes clear distinction between affiliation with a priestly caste and the ability to deal with spirits. Caste affiliation means specific role in ceremonies of fertility or in predicting the fortunes of war. One whose blood ties with a priestly caste are weak cannot perform these tasks, but any commoner can deal with spirits if he is temperamentally fit. Such shamanistic talents are deemed substantiation of strong priestly blood only when associated with priestly heredity.

The ceremonial function of priests is almost extinct at Nakoroka. Temples for ancestors were once common in Vanua Levu villages. Long ago missionary doctrine forbade the presentation of the priest's portion of first-fruits at temples. They became shrines of Satan. Com-

1. I have translated *bete* as "priest" because, though Fijian seers hardly fit the ethnological definition of this term, the translation is sanctioned by use in the old accounts of Fiji.

munities soon realized that pleasing the whims of missionaries would gain European support in the nineteenth-century wars, and ancestors were relegated to forest, rocks, and waterfalls.[2] Presentation of first-fruits to the chief alone pleased the ancestors well enough. Yet, before the people learned to depend upon Wesleyan prayer meetings for control of climatic emergencies, priests conducted community-wide rituals in times of drought, flood, or hurricane; it was they who advised wholesale repentance. In 1850 Williams described such a ceremony near the present site of Bua village:

> When the Tiliva [village of old Bua Kingdom] people found their land parched with drought, notwithstanding the presentation of the ordinary offerings, they repaired in company to the bush, to dig up the *yaka*, which is a creeper with edible roots from two to three feet long, taking care not to detach the long vines springing from them. On returning, each man wound these round his neck, leaving the roots to hang beneath his chin, while the rest of the vines dragged after him on the ground. To this was added a large stone carried on the back of the neck. Thus equipped, the whole company performed a pilgrimage to the *bure*[3] on their hands and knees, making a noise as though they were crying. At the end of this painful journey they found the priest waiting to receive them, and to him one of their number stated their distress and begged him to accept their prayer and offering. "The *yaka* is for you to eat; the stones are for strengthening the base of your temple. Let our *soro*[4] be accepted, and procure us rain." Some who took part in this humiliating scene gave me the particulars.[5]

In Nakoroka it was the chief who realized his own inadequacy in times of drought and sought the priest to determine what measure to use to appease the angered ancestors. It seems that the priest, independently of chiefs, could influence ancestors to wreak vengeance upon the community to settle scores for a personal slight; in such cases a chief might recommend a ceremony of humiliation before the priest, to persuade him to use his private influence with the ancestors once more in the community's behalf. In less severe weather emergencies the chief would present the priest with a stalk of kava and the request that he intercede with the ancestors for rain. When hurricane threatened, the chief presented bark cloth as well as kava, and the priest made presentation at the shrine of the ancestors with the bark cloth wrapped around his head. If gardens were poor, the chief in extremity might request that every man in the village plant a yam in a garden

---

2. Forests, rocks, and waterfalls undoubtedly have always been shrines of supernatural beings. I do not mean to suggest a post-European invention in religious practice.

3. Literally, "a small house"; in this instance, an ancestral shrine.

4. Ceremony of humiliation.

5. Thomas Williams, *Fiji and the Fijians*, ed. George S. Rowe, I (London, 1858), 232

specially prepared for the priest; then the priest would exert his influence with the ancestors. He might also be persuaded to provide ancestral protection against wild pigs in private gardens. Though observance of chiefly ceremonies themselves pleased the ancestors, there was no standard by which complete observance could be measured; possible flaws in the ceremonies were multiple, and the ritual prescriptions too vaguely defined to fulfil with certainty. Hence there was real necessity for specialists in supernatural matters whose talents of close rapport could determine in what way relations between chief and commoner were at fault in the eyes of the supernaturals.

The old men of today place those who divined the fortunes of war in a separate class. Monasa has vague claims to membership in an ancient group of war priests. He describes their role in warfare:

Priests were always consulted before the attack. The chief said: "Who is game to attack Sarowaqa?" If men of Nadroro responded, the chief presented whale teeth to them and a great stalk of kava so that they could spend the night in drinking and "making themselves brave." In the meantime the women prepared prawns, whose shell is red, and red yams as a private feast for the war priest. After the priest had retired to commune with the ancestors, he returned to advise about the auspiciousness of the time for attack and to predict the minimal number of victims each warrior would kill. When the battle was over, the ears of victims were cut off and presented to the priest, who ate them raw. Then, while the corpses of the enemy were presented to the chief, who relayed some of them to the ancestors of the land, the priests joined the warriors in the victory song.

Nabadua compares the priests to European "war chiefs" because, too precious to risk their own lives, they never left their villages in times of danger. As the generals of Europe use wireless, the ancient priests far behind the lines conducted battle with their supernatural powers.

Williams and others have stressed the role of the priest as a popular mouthpiece to check the authority of chiefs. But in Nakoroka those who knew how to commune with ancestors supplemented the chief's authority in social control.

Perhaps the outlawing of formal priestly rites has been instrumental in diffusing shamanistic talents through the entire male population. More probably, however, occult practices and special relations with the supernatural have always existed independently of the priestly caste. Only chiefs feel that the shamanistic temperament is not congenial to them. In former times the priestly caste functioned as the special shamans of the chief and filled a role which the chief's own specialized nature made impossible for him. Their status was extraordinary, and they were treated with some of the gestures of respect which are otherwise reserved only for blooded chiefs. At Nakoroka today the greatest shamans have blood ties with a priestly caste, but, except for chiefs, almost every man has some private communion with the supernatural. There are many kinds of relationships with spirits which descend to chosen heirs completely independent of priesthood.

Articles of ceremonial dress and spears and clubs for both war and dance become sacred when they are older than a generation. Articles which date from the days of the wars have repeatedly accumulated the respect which the younger generation feels for the older until they have achieved the highest sacredness: wrapped carefully in bark cloth, they are never displayed except to him who would join in ancestral communion; offerings of kava and tobacco are placed lovingly within the wrappings, because it is said metaphorically that ancestors use such wrappings as "houses." In the old days sacred weapons generated military power; newly wrought weapons, laid next to them overnight, absorbed enough of their sacredness to effect great slaughter in battle. No one carried ancestral weapons to battle: none dared risk the loss of these bonds with ancestral spirits. Men on their deathbeds will their sacred objects to whatever descendant has seemed most congenial;[6] these heirs have already shared in the ceremony of communion and learned the ritual and the special endowments of their ancestral "friend." Bulisivo's father's "things" were buried in his grave because he had never achieved any spiritual companionship with Bulisivo. Yet Bulisivo sometimes goes to his father's grave for ancestral advice. In ancestral presence, however, he need not assume the extremely respectful attitude which is required of commoners, because his chiefly blood causes opinions of his own creation to accord automatically with ancestral will; a true chief's status is almost that of ancestor. It is probable that all Nakoroka men treasure some sacred object in secret, but everyone knows that Akuila and Vaula possess their fathers' war clubs and that Toviya holds the weapons and the ceremonial paraphernalia of his mother's brother.

People regard Toviya above all others as priest. When questions arise as to ancient ceremonial procedure or even as to history, Toviya's opinion is infallible because it comes directly from his ancestral in-

6. As in the inheritance of rights in land, such congeniality is proof of blood tie.

MAN OF PRIESTLY HEREDITY, WITH
ANCESTRAL WEAPONS

formants. Through his maternal ties with a caste of weather priests, Toviya alone of all Nakoroka's men can be possessed by a true ancestral spirit. On January 22, 1936, I explained that my energy in investigating Nakoroka sociology was flagging and that I required supernatural aid; my collected genealogies were inaccurate, and I wanted a supernatural check. Toviya motioned me to silence and beckoned that I follow him to the margin of the village where, in the dark, we could whisper in secrecy. Confronting me there, he asked whether I "knew him." His voice rattled with the sudden tremors of his body. My response did not satisfy him as to my authentic interest in his priestship. Secretly he sought out Peni, who had been managing my household, and Bici, whom the village generally considered my closest friend. Peni, who was young and of low status, respected Toviya as belonging to his parental generation; furthermore, Toviya bore the chiefly title of the land group in Votua with which Peni planned soon to affiliate himself. Toviya could trust him. Bici, though in his middle thirties, had always flattered Toviya with personal interest in his talents and sometimes assisted at interviews with ancestors. Bici's father and Toviya had cherished each other as cross-cousins; hence Bici viewed Toviya with added respect, and Toviya knew that Bici would keep his secret. Many years ago someone had tattled to the British of Toviya's occult practices, and he had been ordered to bring his sacred objects into colonial court and display them before the vulgar eyes of all the strangers assembled there. He feared a repetition of this insult to his ancestors—a repetition which would surely mean sickness for himself. Finally, he decided that I could be trusted; but, first, I had to promise that whatever Toviya's ancestors asked of me I would grant "with a strong spirit." Toviya drove a hard bargain: before our agreement was sealed, he asked that I pay his daughter's debt with the Chinese trader at Lekutu as a gesture of mutual friendship. Then, quickly, Peni prepared kava so that we could drink together. To absolve himself from the danger of contact with the supernatural, Toviya drank two cupfuls in quick succession without the usual ceremony between, and gradually his agitation subsided.

Upon my first request for supernatural aid I expected only to gain the assistance of one of the inferior classes of spirits who abound in the forest and are distinct from ancestors, an *uwawa* or a *veli* who dances in moonlit forest glades. But, as we continued to meet secretly about Bici's kava bowl, Toviya discovered that it would be possible for me to establish communion with a true ancestral spirit. There was an ancestor who wanted to be my "friend." Each time we met, we presented Toviya's ancestor[7] with a few yards of red calico, which is especially pleasing to spirits, some kava, tobacco, or a few shillings.

Sometimes we boiled taro for sweet puddings secretly at night and beat it into glassy consistency beneath the water of the river lest the others of the village should hear and suspect; before dawn we would meet with Toviya and serve him kava while he presented the puddings in quaking voice to his ancestor. Ancestors are chiefs, and, in addressing them, Toviya always used plural pronouns and the most archaic language.

When the hollow thump of the kava pounder resounds in the village, all pause to wonder who is drinking; hence Bici found it difficult to pound our kava secretly. Since he frequently pounded that which was served at Nabadua's house in the evenings, he was sometimes able to prepare two portions at a time without exciting suspicion. Then, carefully concealing one portion in the folds of his calico *sulu*, he would drink with those at Nabadua's house until they had retired for the night.

When several months had passed, I began to suspect that Toviya was growing fat on my offerings and had no intention of producing my ancestor. Sensing my suspicion, he sent Bici to explain to me that a final presentation of a fathom of calico and a few shillings to "bind" the gift would bring lasting rapport with the spirit. An hour before dawn, Bici and I nervously awaited Toviya's arrival at my house. Suddenly he appeared at the doorway and whispered rapidly to Bici. When Bici asked me if I was prepared to receive my ancestral spirit adviser, I fumbled sleepily for words, and Toviya, shocked at my indecision, fled. Next day when Bici described the episode to Peni, he spoke of the dazzling light which, he said, issued from some object which Toviya kept concealed behind his back.[8] Until darkness began to fade, Toviya raced madly about the village in silence; then he returned to my house to drink kava in hopes of avoiding the dangerous consequences of annoying an ancestral spirit. But the noisy yawns of

7. The plurality or singularity of Toviya's source of supernatural information is questionable. Though he could address it by name, he used a name far distant in his genealogy. Yet it included the spirit of the man who had taught Toviya his occult practices. It was a composite of many forebears and yet seemed to be a single entity. Toviya was skilled as well in the arts of the Children-of-Water cult, which has been flourishing on Vanua Levu for at least eighty years (Williams, *op. cit.*, pp. 237–39). When he addressed his "Ancestor," he included as well the spiritual informants whom he had gained through participation in this cult.

8. Bici has cataracts which make him nearly blind.

Big Di Litiya in her house near by gave warning that she was about to begin her daily chores. Toviya leaped behind my mosquito curtain lest she discover us drinking kava at such an unusual hour; knowing Toviya, she would suspect that we had been dealing with spirits.

Toviya's troubles had just begun. Next evening, after drinking a great quantity of kava at a casual evening gathering, he found himself unable to urinate. Frightened but anxious to use the privileges which are granted the acutely sick at Nakoroka and also to exploit my responsibility for his sickness, he requested me to prepare a meal for him of the European delicacies, rice and tea with sugar. Peni was sure that it was my attitude which had brought the sickness; Bici, however, thought that the spirit might have been angered because our last presentation of pudding was boiled instead of baked. On the third day Toviya felt hungry for the bush pig which was being served in his household; he ate a large meal of it. He attributed the gradual restoration of his normal functions to this satisfying of the desire for pig which his ancestors had expressed through him. My plans to possess a spirit were temporarily dismissed. I believed that Toviya had never intended more than a program of mild extortion. Priests, not so strictly bound by the obligations which among chiefs preclude accumulation of property, are expected to become prosperous through the favor of their special ancestors. Now well stocked with delicacies from the Chinese store, Toviya could use his illness as an excuse for dissolving our relationship; his ancestors were angry that he had permitted a skeptical foreigner to invade their privacy. If he ignored this first warning, he might expect the spirits to smite his daughter or his grandson, as they had killed his son four years before. I spoke with Peni about my suspicions of Toviya's integrity, and he agreed that Toviya was "difficult"; Akuila, who was himself a seer of sorts and already suspected my relationship with Toviya, whispered to Peni that he knew of a spirit who would willingly grant me its aid.

But Bici's faith in Toviya remained unshaken, and he continued to instruct me in the etiquette which must be used toward an ancestral helper. Before drinking kava, I must pretend to find a bit of grass or an insect in my cup, pick out a pinch of the liquid and flick it away, concentrating my thoughts for a moment upon my spirit helper. Before going on a journey, I must never forget to leave an offering of tobacco or kava in the spirit's "house." In an emergency six pence or a shilling might be substituted. In America, where kava is not available, a few drops of whiskey would serve as well. Bici assured me that once possessor of a spirit I would "know" exactly what to do without being told. I saw little of Toviya until I was preparing to leave Nakoroka for the last time. I had already said goodbye to those who had assembled at the mouth of the Lekutu path. Those who intended to accompany me to the coast were already straggling along the path beyond the ford of the river Votua. Bici drew me unexpectedly aside and informed me that Toviya was in hiding at a certain lemon grove beyond the village and that I must loiter behind the procession on the Lekutu path and travel secretly to meet him. I found him there weeping. He presented me with an ancient throwing-club bound in bark-cloth wrappings, the "house" of his ancestor. A sacred ax remained in his possession, but the club shared in sacredness, and parting with it not only decreased his power but endangered his life; if I should be remiss in my respect for it, if I should neglect to give it offerings of tobacco and whiskey, the angered ancestor would surely return to Nakoroka to wreak vengeance upon him who had so carelessly shared sacred favors with a foreigner.

Aside from the general abilities of Toviya's ancestors, some of them have special talent for singing songs to him which he can teach to other men. These songs, a distinct literary type, were the poetic accounts of the adventures of the heroes at ancient Flight-of-the-Chiefs to which Toviya's ancestors had been eyewitnesses. From other ancestral spirits Toviya had power to teach and compose spear dances and their accompanying songs. Only the older generation associate these artistic forms with sentimental memories of the past and give them traditional value, but the young men regard them as awful manifestations of the supernatural, so that Toviya's prestige is heightened in all strata of the community.

Though his talent in no way compares with Toviya's, Monasa, too, is known as one who deals in the occult. From childhood he has been marked as the kind of human to whom the solitude of the forest is especially congenial. He used to flee to the forest when strangers visited the village. As a youth he lived with a group of descendants of war priests at Tavua, but aside from this affiliation people noticed his pleasure in solitude as a portent that someday he would have dealings with spirits. For days he would wander alone in uncultivated regions, eating the forest foods and sleeping in hastily erected shelters. The people realized that there was danger to him in this trait of temperament. They remembered a man on the windward coast who from such beginnings had changed into a forest spirit. The people of his own household decided to take special pains to socialize him. They brought him back to the village and showered him with attention, stroking his body, feeding him good foods. Before he had reached adolescence, he was "cured." But Monasa still likes to wander alone in the forests or sit quietly in his kitchen contemplating a few torn leaves from some Wesleyan teacher's Bible. In 1936 he built a house near his taro gardens and moved his wife and children away from the village.

Many years ago he was involved in a scandal on the windward coast and expelled from participation in church activities. Officials of both government and church discovered that, with some men of the Duleniwai region, he had been sacrificing to spirits. Ever since, he has led an even more private life. No one knows what sacred objects he possesses nor with what spirit he deals. but everyone surmises that he is a holy man.

Though Akuila's father was of Votua's "*bota* who wipe away feces," his shamanistic abilities included composing and teaching the same kind of songs and dances that Toviya knows. During the time of Bulisivo's father at Votua the teacher of songs and dances died and left no heir. Bulisivo's father, then holder of the whale tooth "King Forest" had always encouraged intercourse with all manner of spirits as a part of his task of maintaining the fertility of the land. Hence, he personally requested Akuila's father, who was already dealing with lesser spirits, to use the sacred objects of the deceased teacher of dances to establish a rapport with the spirits and instruct the people of Votua in singing and dancing; these arts are pleasing to the ancestors. Akuila has inherited these materials and the techniques of rapport, but a wilful marriage prevented his receiving his father's full support as mentor. While his father was dying, he requested that the sacred materials be buried in the grave of Ratu Seru, Bulisivo's father, not to be removed until the holder of "King Forest" should decide that a great need had arisen in the village. Akuila has had little opportunity to ply his knowledge, because Bulisivo rarely patronizes the arts. But in 1936, perhaps with the hope of interrupting the great ravages of wild pigs in Nakoroka gardens, Bulisivo instructed Akuila to open the grave of Ratu Seru and bring forth the sacred materials. Though the sacredness of these materials cannot rival those of Toviya in priestliness, they reflect the glory of "King Forest" and have grown in sacredness during their contact with the grave of the great Ratu Seru.

From his father, Akuila also learned to cure several sicknesses and to deal with many kinds of lesser spirits, the *veli* and *uwawa* who teach the modern sitting dance, bring luck at cards, and assist a thief who wishes to steal from the Indians or a Chinese store.[9] He has also dealt extensively with the Children-of-Water. These are useful in all manner of trickery; they rank just below true ancestors and are sometimes addressed as such. But his father's displeasure at his marriage has bereft him of heirs. Though five children were born to his wife, all died soon after birth. His sister's son, Tomasi Raturaga, who had already learned Akuila's skill in the treatment of "Indian boils" and had received several stalks of kava for his services in bestowing the favor of spirits upon young men who wanted luck at the cards with which they gambled at the gold mines, would doubtless have been his heir. Tomasi's congenitally shriveled limb prevented his achieving prestige as a hunter or conqueror of women's favors; young men sometimes teased him about his pretensions to shamanistic knowledge. But his spirits had already begun to bring him respect, and this would increase as his practice continued. But Tomasi died in May, 1937. Akuila has no other heir in view.

Naicadra has but the vaguest ties with a priestly caste, and no one would suspect him of serving a spirit, because he is a dignitary of the church. But he has a special penchant for communing with the souls of the recently dead. Even though other elders have prepared themselves with kava to receive such souls, it is Naicadra whose tongue they will use in speaking. On the fourth night after burial[10] a lantern placed on the grave attracts the soul, whose reflection may be seen in a mirror held near by. After Vilomena's death[11] the young people of the village, including the missionary teacher from Votua, watched mirror fragments which had been purchased from the Chinese trader. At length, eyes straining upon the rain-splashed mirrors, someone claimed to see a second light above the grave, and Keleivi went to extinguish the lantern and carry it to Namo's house.[12] There, aged Kaiyava and Vaula had drunk themselves into kava stupors in hopes that Vilomena would speak with their tongues. All lights in the house had been extinguished, and half the village crowded there expectantly in the dark. Soon all

9. There is no known case of such theft. Perhaps this is mere braggadocio.

10. The third night will less probably bring results because the soul has not had time "to become strong."

11. March, 1936.

12. No one but Keleivi would dare to venture close.

were discouraged with waiting and returned to the usual pursuits of
the evening. Hours later Melika, Naicadra's wife, shrieked, and all
knew that Vilomena's soul had possessed Naicadra. That night no one
dared to verify this belief, but next morning people who had conversed
with Melika whispered that it was true.

Likewise upon the death of Sakiusa, the grandson of Nabadua, it
was Naicadra whom Sakiusa's soul chose to enter and explain the
cause of his death: Nabadua had spoken too freely in the village, had
presumed to be a chief, and the ancestors had found their revenge in
smiting his grandson. When Sireli, the son of Toviya, died, his soul
told Naicadra that the ancestors disapproved of Toviya's management
of the land of the "bota who wipe away feces" at Votua. Toviya received the chiefly title for this land upon the death of uncircumcised
Unuwale, who had decreed that rights in this Votua land be shared
with Votua's "children in Nadroro,"[13] but Toviya had neglected to
share the land. And so it was, said Naicadra, that Toviya's son had
been taken by the ancestors. But Toviya disagrees. No one, he says,
can hold intelligible conversations with the souls of the recent dead;
one can discern only outlines blurred as by a deep fog; and Naicadra
is not even of priestly blood. It is too bad, says Toviya, that there is
no certainty in our intercourse with the recent dead; they can do no
more than inspire us with a suggestion and a guess. In the case of the
death of Nabadua's grandson, Toviya admits the accuracy of Naicadra's diagnosis; "but everyone in the village knows how Nabadua
has been behaving through all of these years."

Naicadra is also subject to portentous dreams. Before Sakiusa,
Nabadua's grandson, had become seriously ill, Naicadra saw an ap-
parition in his sleep. A child, hazy and difficult to identify, yet surely
familiar to him, came whimpering; only the penis shone distinctly so
that Naicadra knew that it was a boy child. Next morning people wondered whether Sakiusa's soul could have been wandering during the
night. It was not until Sakiusa died and illness threatened two of his
sisters that Naicadra could explain the true meaning of his dream:

Naicadra had adopted Sakiusa's oldest half-sister into his household
and land group. But Namo, who is Sakiusa's father and Nabadua's
son, had never presented Naicadra with a feast of domestic pig. Namo
had been fattening a pig for this purpose but, since Tavua land was
impoverished, he had no yams, and a feast without yams is meaning-

13. Almost all Nadroro people, to whom Naicadra belongs, have maternal ties with
Votua. It is to these that Unuwale referred.

less. Before he could find food to accompany the pig, a new and pressing need had arisen. His wife's brother, whom he called "cross-cousin" (*tavale*),[14] the most "heavy and difficult" of all relationships, was marrying at Lekutu and needed a pig for his wedding feast. In desperation, Namo gave the pig which he had been saving for Naicadra. The ancestors, already angered at Nabadua's lack of respect for tradition, had been driven to this disciplinary measure by Namo's neglect. Sakiusa's soul had spoken to Naicadra, hoping that some action would be taken in its behalf.

Naicadra grew strong in self-confidence and expanded upon the moral of his dream: Namo, he said, was evil in the eyes of the ancestors. Not only had he neglected his obligation to Naicadra but he had failed to carry gifts of kava to the various "medical" men who had been consulted about Sakiusa's illness and who had prepared "waters" to heal him. Hastily, because his two daughters were already failing, Namo shouldered a stalk of kava to the house of the wise man of the island village of Tavea who had offered suggestions for Sakiusa's treatment. Also Namo prepared sweet puddings for Naicadra. But Naicadra shook his head: ancestors are not likely to cast favors upon those who delay in the fulfilment of their obligations until ancestral wrath is manifest in sickness. But Namo's daughters did not die.

The village loves Naicadra. He is a good man. He has never broken the rules of the church. He never drinks kava to excess. He has never worked on Sunday. For years his household had fed an invalid to whom he is bound by no kinship ties. He is always adopting other people's children. His fat daughter is industrious and almost chaste. He is a quiet man and, except in church, never speaks his mind publicly. Since childhood he has been sickly. As a young man he was continent. In contrast with most other men he does not "deal with spirits"; all his sacrifices to gain supernatural aid have been offered to the Wesleyan god; he has no other "friend" in the spirit world. The word "priest" bears associations which are antithetical to his particular shamanistic talents.

Isacodro is not of shamanistic temperament, but upon occasion, like all men of the old school, he has learned to prepare "waters" for several diseases which include leprosy, dysentery, and conjunctivitis. These he has obtained through long-continued gift relationships with men to

14. *Tavale* also means "brother-in-law."

whom shamanistic experience is more congenial. Meticulously he gives gifts of tobacco to the sacred bundles which contain the power of his "waters."[15] He is especially skilled in massage. He prescribes "waters" for stiff joints. He knows considerable supernatural lore and can interpret supernatural manifestations with accuracy. When Bari[16] was troubled with nightly apparitions of a malignant being, Isacodro first diagnosed it as the dead soul of one of Bari's kinsmen; but, when Bari continued to complain, Isacodro realized that Bari had been chopping firewood upon the site of the house foundation of a woman who had been dead for many generations. After Bari changed his place for chopping wood, his troubles disappeared. Isacodro received perhaps half-a-dozen leaves of tobacco for his services.

An ancient ancestor of Isacodro's land is a *vi'eki*,[17] an anthropoid being with a tremendous belly who can consume gardens full of food; this accounts for Isacodro's skill as a garden worker, for his ravenous appetite, and for his ability to eat raw meat which would disgust anyone else. Perhaps Isacodro's skill as healer is also associated with his peculiar ancestry. Nabadua says that all those who cure disease must offer sacrifices at the graves of their ancestors. It is said that Isacodro knows a spirit who, in exchange for a gift, can inspire any woman with desire for the donor. Formerly he participated energetically in the cult of the Children-of-Water.

Vaula is a hereditary priest at Nadroro, but his functions as such are largely undeveloped. Like Isacodro, he understands supernatural phenomena; but, rather than a special talent, his understanding is the wisdom which comes with age. He is well acquainted in the Dreketi region, where techniques for dealing with lesser spirits are highly efficient. He has observed and participated in these rites but is incapable of initiating them himself. He receives mild inspirations of intuitive knowledge, however; some years ago he "felt" that it would not displease his ancestors if his two sons should thenceforth desist from observance of their hereditary food taboo, chicken.

Aside from siring a large family, Raitova's influence in the commu-

15. Such bundles were not observed. Since "waters" are illegal under British law, descriptions of their secret use must be held suspect. All whom Isacodro treated, however, gave small gifts to him which he presumably relayed to some supernatural being with whom he had indirect relationship.

16. The young man whom I had brought from the Savusavu region as porter and assistant.

17. Perhaps *viteki*.

nity is slight. Likewise, though he knows a few "waters," he rarely attempts to practice supernatural arts. People say that he is not one to talk much. He has no ties with priestly blood.

Nabadua and Vatili are abnormally ignorant of all supernatural arts. Vatili has a cross-cousin at Nacula whose supernatural powers enable him to compose and teach the modern sitting dance and to prepare "waters" for several diseases. Once Vatili tried to learn to use one of the "waters" to help a sick acquaintance on the windward coast. Though he cured the sick man, spirits began to "eat" away one of his own legs; he knew immediately that medical practices were impossible for him. Quickly he returned the medicine to his cross-cousin. Nabadua, however, is proud of his ignorance, which he attributes to the chiefly blood he has received through his father and which he feels strong within him. He says that chiefs have their own tasks and responsibilities; knowing the spirit world is the work of priests.

In careless speech Akuila, Toviya, and Monasa are all called "priests." Dealing with spirits may be termed priestly activity; but, when a caste distinction is intended, "priest" applies most aptly to Vaula and excludes Akuila. Despite the complete antithesis which exists in the temperament of priests and chiefs, Bulisivo's father was known as one who dealt with spirits. For weeks he would retire to the forest to commune with ancestors; but it is said that these retreats were in company with his retainers. It is probable that the chief himself was merely a spectator and that he received shamanistic communications only through the medium of priests or shaman. To expect Bulisivo to know about occult practices is mildly insulting. Though Naicadra's status in the church prohibits classing him as priest, yet his mediumistic talents are considered priestly.

Women at Nakoroka have no direct contact with the supernatural. "They are unable to understand these things." In the Dreketi region an old woman who has a young lover will be said to deal with spirits. But at Nakoroka this concept has meaning only as a joke. Bici's old mother-in-law knows many ancient dances. In preparation for church celebrations, for which women practice standing dances in chorus to imitate ancient festivals, she acts as dance master; but she works without supernatural aid and has no power to compose. Though in most villages it is a man who teaches women's dances, there is no such man at Nakoroka; hence the village is not very proud of the dancing of its women. But there is a great field of knowledge in which women exclusively can gain fame for wisdom: the practice of obstetrics and gynecology, the molding of infants' heads while the bones are still soft into beautifully receding shapes, and tattooing thighs and vaginal lips of pubertal girls.

These skills require no special caste affiliation. Melika, who is a *bota*, and Big Di Litiya, a chieftainess, consider each other the wisest women in the village. Though all women have assisted on occasions when wise women ply their arts, there are few in these times who are stronghearted enough to preside at a confinement. The difficulty with which wise women find pupils thus precludes any semblance of a hereditary pattern. Women are jealous of the skill of one another's pupils and ridicule their clumsiness.

Most fame accrues to those women skilled in treatment of the menopause, of which there are none at Nakoroka. Any stopping of the menstrual flow suggests disease; the cervix must be artificially opened. Thus many witless abortions are produced among young girls. Older women must frequently consult a wise woman to determine whether their menopause is a result of pregnancy, the normal progress of events, or fatal disease.

CHAPTER VIII

KINSHIP

A S INDIVIDUAL choice is effective in forming the affiliations of caste and land, so it is a determinant in the kin framework of the village. He who is growing into a place in village life may choose persons with whom to build strong bonds of kinship. To rationalize his final choices, he may refer to theoretical rules; but even in theory it is the well-established relationships of the past, rather than connection through the biologic family, which determine the present. Kinship does not stem from genealogies; in contrast with more truly Polynesian regions, Nakoroka preoccupies itself but slightly with remembrance of family trees. Charting the terms which each individual calls every other individual makes clear the manner in which kinship is reckoned. It is irrelevant that A is B's father's father's mother's brother's daughter's son's son's wife; they call each other cross-cousin because they are of opposite moiety and of the same generation, or, in other words, the parents of each have had brother-sister relationships with those of the other.

Status in village life, claims on village wealth, rights in the land, obligations to contribute gifts for ceremonial exchanges—all these stem from a man's place in the kin framework of the village. In this framework moiety division is a fundamental category. Moiety descent is transmitted through the mother and is fixed and unalterable from birth. Before a child has learned the rights and obligations of kinship, he has classed his playmates according to their moiety affiliations. Though some boys and girls reach puberty without knowing to which moiety they belong, they always know which of their companions is of their own moiety and have assumed a teasing attitude toward those of the opposite moiety.

The names of Nakoroka's two moieties, *turaga* and *caurevo*, occur throughout Vanua Levu to indicate dual classification of the populace. But the basis for this classification varies with locality. Throughout Macuata and Bua provinces the terms may be used to classify as to rank. Those who habitually sit in the upper part of the house during formal kava ceremonies are called *turaga*, "chief," as distinct from

244

caurevo, "young men" or "commoners," who flank the kava bowl and perform the duties of preparation and serving. But throughout the inland regions of Bua Province which have been controlled by the ancient kingdoms of Inland Forest and Great Meadow the terms also classify the population into two matrilineal exogamous groups. Men of Nakoroka deny philological connection between the two meanings of these terms; yet confusion sometimes arises as to which is intended.

Upon close questioning, someone usually suggests that *turaga*, meaning "chief," should be spoken with a *t* despite phonetic habit at Nakoroka which requires the substitution of a glottal stop for all *t*'s. Except in recently borrowed words the elision of *t* is consistent; this phonetic tendency is so strong that the *t*'s which persist in recently borrowed words are sometimes voiced and preceded by nasalization, which identifies them with Nakoroka's *d:* Vatili says *wai dui* for *wai tui,* "kingly water" or "ocean," widely used to mean "salt water for cooking." There are those who say that the moiety name *"uraga (turaga)"* has no paronym in dialects which speak *t*. There are also many who say that the moiety name is *uraga,* phonetically quite distinct from the word for chief. These same men contend that the name of the other moiety is *caravou,* not *caurevo*. But confusion persists.

The Flight-of-the-Strong region of inner Macuata, which least of all Macuata regions has been affected by the political regimentation under Macuata's present chiefly family, has moieties which are similar in name and function to those of Nakoroka. Like that of Nakoroka, also, the dialect of this region elides *t*. But on the coast, from Naduri eastward, and throughout the Udu Peninsula, which extends beyond Labasa, *yavusa turaga* and *yavusa caurevo* refer exclusively to rank classification.[1] This region speaks *t* and elides *k*. Though the same kinship terms are used in both regions, the persons whom the terms specify vary with absence or presence of moiety, while the behavior associated with the terms remains constant; thus "brother-in-law," which implies joking affection among the men throughout Bua and Macuata, includes cross-cousins in regions which have moieties and excludes them in eastern Macuata and the adjacent territory where moieties are absent.

The general term *yavusa* or *yavosa*[2] designates "moiety." But it also

1. My hurried excursion through this region could, of course, produce only superficial observations. But evidence points to the complete absence of moiety concept in this region as well as along the north coast of Natewa Bay, in Cakaudrove Province from Korotasere eastward.

2. At Nakoroka *yavosa* is usually applied to moiety, *yavusa* to "descent group."

means "kingdom" or "descent group." Colonial administrators use
yavusa to mean "tribe," inclusive of several *mataqali*.[3] Since in Nakoroka
dialect, size and structure of *yavusa* is not specified, it is more accurate
to translate this term there as "descent group." If Bulisivo, who is of
highest rank in Inland Forest Kingdom, is asked to what *yavusa* he belongs, he says, first of all, "Inland Forest." If asked whether he belongs to *yavusa turaga* or *yavusa caurevo*, he might consider the question
ridiculous or insulting; everyone knows that he is of chiefly rank. Only
with greatest difficulty could an investigator discover that his moiety
affiliation is with *yavusa caurevo*. Though individuals are always conscious, from early childhood, of whether others belong to own or opposite moieties, moiety names must be recalled to mind with deliberate
effort.

Throughout the Nakoroka area there is a strong tendency to describe own moiety as composed of siblings in contrast with opposite
moiety, which is loosely identified with cross-cousin. Moiety thus becomes a dual grouping of society in single generations, and it is within
own generation that moiety actually functions. Only in own generation does the kinship system correspond with moiety structure. Only in
own generation do the interobligations of brother and sister groups
involve moieties in reciprocal exchange.

Moiety classification cross-cuts descent groups and caste, villages,
and kingdoms and includes persons of formerly hostile regions. The
moiety division, however, which primarily concerns the individual is
that which lies within the limits of his own village. As he matures, he
will learn to extend his concept to include persons of foreign villages or
even foreign kingdoms to which marriage, traceable genealogy, or traditional relationship associate him. But these always remain mere re-
flections of the moiety ties in his own village. Among his own moiety in
his own village he is at ease and on familiar terms; members will assist
him in garden work or in special building. Garden produce and personal property, such as clothing, bark cloth, whale teeth, money, and
tools, pass easily among them. He can speak angrily within his moiety
without great breach of etiquette or fear of embarrassment. His own
moiety, which depends upon descent through women, is "of his own
blood." Though his cross-cousins, who compose the opposite moiety,
may have grown up in his own household, he views them as especially
privileged outsiders whom he must patronize and cherish. Relation-

3. See above, chap. vi, n. 11.

ship with members of the opposite moiety is tense with obligatory affection.

With the following terms Nakoroka classifies all people of the village and many persons in distant villages. The definitions given here do not include extensions. A possessive pronoun almost always occurs as suffix;[4] the terms appear here with the possessive third person singular:

Taci-na:	Sibling of either sex
Tuaka-na:	Older sibling of either sex but usually restricted to older brother, woman speaking[5]
Gane-na:	Sibling of opposite sex
Tavale-na:	Cross-cousin; sibling-in-law
Dauve-na:	Female cross-cousin or sister-in-law, woman speaking
Tama-na:	Father
Tina-na:	Mother; father's sister
Luve-na:	Child; man speaking, any brother's child; woman speaking, any brother's or sister's child
Tubu-na:	Mother's brother and grandparent
Vuo-na:	Grandchild and, man speaking, sister's child
Wati-na:	Spouse
Vugo-na:	Specifically parent-in-law or child-in-law but loosely applied to any affinal relationship
Lailai:	"Small," as a qualifier of these, distinguishes "classificatory" from "real" in native terms. A traceable biologic tie or tradition of established kinship warrants classifying as "real." "Small" brothers are those of same moiety who have grown up in same village. Extremely distant relationships may be qualified with *levu*, "big," which refers to the scope of extension.
Tauvu:	Vatili insists upon including *tauvu*, "common ancestor," as a kind of kinship. Though individuals may be *tauvu* to each other, the term refers primarily to the relation of the groups in which the *tauvu* individuals are members. Within the relationship group, *tauvu* may coexist with any one of the above twelve terms. As a rule, any of the above terms takes precedence over it.
Vasu:	Nor is *vasu* a kinship term. Though theoretically dependent upon a kin bond, it is a claim of an individual upon his mother's land. It coexists with the kin term, *vuo-na* and, in broader extension, with all the terms which apply to kinsmen in mother's land.

4. When the possessive pronoun occurs as a suffix, it denotes inseparability.

5. Admission of youth in relation to another lowers one's status in relation to him. Hence it is understandable that a woman usually recognizes the status difference between herself and an older brother and calls him *tuaka-qu*, whereas men usually use *taci-qu* to elder brother and *gana-qu* to elder sister, neither of these latter terms having reference to age. The status of women is categorically lower than that of men.

BROTHERS

Brothers call their relationship *tau-taci*.[6] They may be children of the same parents, of two sisters or two brothers, or of any two sets of parents in which one of each calls the other *taci-qu*. Frequently there is great discrepancy in age. Theoretically anyone of the same moiety and generation may be included, but, since age is a poor criterion of generation, individuals whose acquaintance is of short standing and who do not know what relationship term their parents applied to each other qualify their brotherhood by calling themselves "brothers in moiety." Such extensions of the kinship category are not accompanied by the privileges and obligations of the brotherhood. Young men of the same moiety who have grown up together in the same village, when pressed to distinguish such relationships from those of close genealogical ties, refer to one another as "small brother."

When young Tomasi Raturaga planned to pay the special tax which would free him from statute labor under colonial law, he expected his "small brother" Peni to build him a house in the forest while he himself went to the mines to work for the tax money. Peni was not surprised when this task was thrust upon him; he expected his brothers to make such requests. Tomasi and Peni had long been companions of the same moiety in the same village. Both had claims on Votua land through their mothers. Tomasi belonged to Akuila's division of Votua. Though Peni was of Nadroro, he planned to join Akuila's group.

If Peni passed the garden of his biologic brother, fat Narogo, he would doubtless remove weeds which he saw choking his brother's food plants. In this instance, Peni's conduct was motivated by the fact that they both shared in Nadroro land rather than by the biologic tie; Peni's mother had died in his childhood, and Naicadra had virtually adopted Narogo so that the lazy father would not be burdened too heavily with paternal responsibilities in a motherless family. Likewise Peni felt free to ask Narogo to run errands to the gardens for food when he himself was too busy to go. They called each other "brother."

If Peni had objected when Narogo walked off with the pair of shorts which he bought from the Chinese trader with the first money he had earned in my employ, people would have said that he was evil inside, that he had the soul of one fit to be baked and eaten. But Peni bought many bright scarfs of silk, bottles of perfume, and pairs of blue, white,

---

6. *Tau*, reciprocal; *taci*, sibling. In address, *taci-qu*, "my brother." In reference, *taci-na*, "his brother," etc. *Taci* is a general term for siblings of either sex. But the special cross-sex term, *gane*, is usual in cross-sex usage. Hence *taci* usually refers to someone of the same sex.

or khaki shorts with the wages which I paid him. When Narogo regularly possessed himself of Peni's finery, those who were not envious so sympathized with Peni that some weeks later, when Ratu Seru, a "small brother," asked Peni to buy him some long trousers from a wandering Indian hawker, Peni could pretend falsely to be penniless without fear of social censure; people said instead that he had become "cunning" (*qase*)[7] and almost admired him.

But Narogo was Peni's older brother. As such he should have had superior economic resources; Peni should have been using his younger-brother privilege to depend upon Narogo. But, like his father before him, Narogo was lazy. He had a small, ill-kept yam garden and very few taro ponds; Peni's garden products were abundant. Of the young men, Peni was the most vigorous and skilled as a housebuilder, most fortunate at the hunt, and fleetest of foot and strongest of wind to carry a message or bring hurried advice from a healer of diseases in another village. He was burdened constantly with the demands of others upon his time and energy, yet he had planted many flourishing taro ponds and conscientiously saw to the weeding of his three dry gardens. When Peni said that Narogo was his older brother, *tuaka-na*, people tittered. It was disgraceful that under these circumstances Narogo should possess himself of Peni's new clothes. Narogo's obedience to Peni, who frequently ordered him to run errands to the gardens, signalized forfeiture of his right as older brother. Narogo accepted his lowered status with humility.

Bici begrudged Nabadua the respect due "older brother" and called him merely *taci-qu*, "brother." Monasa, Bici, and Nabadua were all brothers in Tavua land as well as in the *turaga* moiety. Though they knew that the blood lines of their genealogies interlocked somewhere in the remote past, there was no traceable biologic connection. Though Nabadua's seniority in years was unquestioned, resentment of his status as older brother was acute; he was always trying to impress everyone with the importance of his position as chiefly title-holder for Tavua and with his "older brothership" among his brothers. Bici countered, utilizing the rights to private property which he possessed under British law; Monasa moved from the village. But Nabadua pretended not to notice. Outwardly undaunted, he continued to offer hospitality with a lavish hand and expected Bici to prepare his kava. When Nabadua's gardens failed, his obsession with status did not desert him;

7. *Qase* also means "old"; in this context it refers to the wisdom which comes with experience.

rather than allow himself to depend upon the resources of his younger brothers and thus lose status as older brother, he preferred to remove taro from their gardens and plead innocence about its disappearance. Bici, with his "soul of a commoner," spoke secretly in anger because Nabadua refused to emulate Narogo's relationship with Peni.

To use a brother's property for convenience need require no adjustment of status and no subterfuge. When Peni traveled at night from Lekutu to Nakoroka to obtain food for the men who were building houses, he sometimes took taro from Tomasi's ponds which were nearer Lekutu than his own. At some future time he would casually tell Tomasi what he had done. There was no necessary embarrassment.

When the young men make excursions to neighboring villages bearing gifts for their girl cross-cousins, brothers and "small brothers" like to go in company because only brothers can dance pleasurably together. The same girls are available to them, and, though a boy feels no shame at dancing before a sister, he will not exert himself to dance attractively unless he feels that there is some distant hope of exciting the girls who are his audience. Hence groups of three or four brothers make the best dance teams. Likewise when girls visit Nakoroka, it is a group of brothers who entertain them.

Though brothers rarely exchange sexual confidences, the companionship of such excursions is of long standing. Old Vaula likes to tell his friends of his visit to Nacula many years ago in company with Nabadua, his "small brother"; each found a girl cross-cousin who seemed willing, and they were able to find furtive privacy in a house empty except for a sleeping child. Considering Vaula of low rank and hence less deserving of comfort, Nabadua possessed himself of the bed.[8] But the bed creaked on its timbers so that, whenever Nabadua moved, the child roused and raised a clamor. When Nabadua would subside from his sprawling attempt to frighten it with ill-directed kicks and bad language, the child would doze soon because it was sleepy. But it always wakened easily. Vaula lay near the lowly hearth, undisturbed. (Vaula does not tell this in Nabadua's hearing.)

Among the young men of today, Ratu Seru[9] and Peni sometimes included Ratu Luke in their excursions. But Ratu Luke married early in 1935 and can no longer accompany them. Though Ratu Luke is their cross-cousin and four or five years older than either of them, he

8. Framed of timbers and softened with ferns, the bed always occupies the most honorable position at the "upper" end of the house.

9. Son of Big Di Litiya, *vasu* to Nakoroka.

dances well, and they enjoy the prestige of his company. The only other brother with whom they might have danced was Tomasi, whose leg had been so crippled from birth that he had never participated fully in the gay courtship which preoccupied the other young men.

Peni never admitted that Lebu was in all probability pregnant. He planned to marry her as soon as he returned to Nakoroka after accompanying me to an American-bound steamer at Suva. For several months Lebu had been Ratu Seru's mistress; now, to avoid litigation in colonial courts, it suited Ratu Seru's convenience that Peni should marry her and pretend paternity. In this way Ratu Seru's child would be legitimate under the new law, and his freedom to wander and play the ukelele would not be hindered. In official eyes Ratu Seru was already conspicuous for his truancy from statute labor. Theoretically chief and *vasu* to Nakoroka, he held life-and-death authority over all Nakoroka subjects; but it was the established brother relationship which, though Ratu Seru was perhaps the younger of the two, permitted him to expect Peni to stand by him in this extremity. Peni did not begrudge Ratu Seru his pleasure with Lebu.

More than a year before, Peni and Lebu had informed their relatives of their intention to marry. But each suspected the other of flagrant breaches of fidelity: his reputation for philandering had already broken a formal betrothal with Nabadua's daughter, which had been sanctioned by the presentation of a whale tooth; Lebu, on her part, was beautiful and liked to visit about in other villages. One moonlight night Ratu Seru and Ratu Luke invited Peni to accompany them to Sarowaqa to dance for the girls there. Peni acquiesced gladly; many girls of the opposite moiety lived there. But Lebu intercepted him as he was leaving the village. Quickly she grabbed the clean calico print which he had been intending to don fresh as he approached Sarowaqa and hid it in her house. Left thus in his ragged shorts, he was sorrowfully deciding to stay home when Ratu Seru volunteered a new pair of long trousers, brought from the windward coast as an emblem of rare sophistication. Triumphant, Peni again set forth across the village green, but Lebu spied him and raised such a tumult that Ratu Luke, perceiving the seriousness of her intent, advised Peni to deliver the long trousers also into her keeping. Thus Peni stood alone and watched Ratu Seru and Ratu Luke cross the river at Deep Pool and grow small in the moonlight as they climbed the hill toward Sarowaqa.

But it was not until the entire village had heard about Peni's tryst with her wily sister (biologic) Vaulini, in Bulisivo's latrine, that Lebu annulled the betrothal "once and for all."

Some months later Ratu Seru, home for the Christmas holidays, proved his strong soul and his chiefly disregard for social opinion by sleeping with her in her kitchen every night. Though in local belief promiscuous cohabitation never causes pregnancy, Ratu Seru's constant attention caused people to make prophecies about her. When he returned to the gold mine in March, she followed to mix kava and serve it for pay to the laborers in their leisure time. In April she returned to Nakoroka, and one night she made a secret tryst with Peni inside a mosquito net at Nabadua's house. Peni waited until he saw Nabadua leave the house to urinate, then darted agilely through the lower door. Inside her mosquito net they lay in silence until Nabadua had returned, and they were sure that he slept. Next morning Peni said that she had asked him a "certain thing"; coyly he refused to specify her request, but he assured me that no one knew but me. Thenceforth until our departure for Suva, she avoided the village and divided her time between Lekutu and the gold mine. Peni went to the mine and spoke with Ratu Seru. When he returned, his decision was fixed, but sometimes in private he spoke longingly of his other loves. Once I witlessly remarked that Lebu looked fat; Peni was immediately defensive and angry. Thus Ratu Seru's worries about illegal paternity were dissolved as Peni casually fulfilled the plans of his chief and brother.

More than with any other group in the community a man is free to express his true opinion among brothers. Even with violence he may enforce discipline among them when he deems it necessary. Thus Peni claims to have beaten his now deceased "small brother" Sireli, son of Toviya; in Peni's estimation Sireli was mismanaging his marital affairs. Toward a brother one may give way almost freely to wrath or jealousy. To explain a folk song in which a warrior, exasperated with two companions, bashes their heads together, people say knowingly that they must have been brothers.

Especially among chiefs a brother relationship may be a source of serious discord.[10] Vatili attributes the division of the tribes of Fiji and their emigrations from Kauvadra, Viti Levu's mountain home of pri-

10. Danger of rivalry for the title-bearing whale tooth among chiefs is discussed above, pp. 207–8. This danger was far more serious when the chiefs were brothers.

SISTERS

mordial man,[11] to disagreements between chiefs who were brothers. "Brothers are constantly competing among themselves," he says. He goes so far as to interpret all war as a result of brotherly discord. "Why should we fight strangers, of whom, necessarily, we can know no evil? Of those whom we know thoroughly enough to hate, it is only against brothers that we may act. Other relationships are burdened with respect or most difficult affection." Thus freedom to hate, together with sensitivity about status, centered tension among chiefly brothers.

SISTERS

Like brothers, sisters perform their chores co-operatively and share property among themselves. The same boys are available to them; they dance together and pay wooing visits to their male cross-cousins in other villages. Like brothers, too, they are free to disapprove of one another, and because, according to the men, women at Nakoroka are congenitally unable to understand dignity and the need for restraint, their disapproval is voiced openly. But among women there is less consciousness of kin distinction, perhaps their "congenital" lack of understanding, which permits them to vent their wrath even upon female cross-cousins,[12] precludes growth among them of the deep personal antagonisms nurtured by the men.

The lady Di Kabu says that it looks bad for sisters to wrangle among themselves. With malice aforethought she points to the unseemly demeanor of the lovely commoner Ivamere, who sometimes whips the legs of her already grown sister. Bari, the boy whom I brought from the Savusavu region, pretended to want Ivamere in marriage; his pretense was successful enough to excite the jealousy of the royal Di Kabu, whose daughter Big Di Merelita, now abandoned by the faithless Ratu Luke, industriously plaited mats in the evenings as a virtuous woman should who wants to make a good marriage. Since Bari, who comes of good family, might have saved Di Merelita from spinsterhood, Ivamere incurred the spiteful wrath of the entire chiefly house. Perhaps her treatment of her younger sister was not really unseemly. Though discord of any sort is recognized as dangerous to society, and therefore bad, Ivamere's bearing was as restrained as could be expected of a woman. The measures with which she disciplined her wilful younger sister were carefully calculated and half in jest.

11. The popularizing of the Kauvadra legends probably resulted from the Wesleyan's campaign against Degei, who, Satan to them, is remembered as Kauvadra's chief god.

12. See the case of Ivamere and Radebu, below, p. 265.

Lebu and her true sister Vaulini, both daughters of Isacodro, and Lui, who was Peni's erstwhile betrothed among Nabadua's daughters, were all three rivals for Peni's favor. As classificatory sisters, they were free to accuse one another almost openly. Lui broke her marriage agreement with Peni because she feared that, once married, "he would remember a certain woman, and then evil times would come." Everyone knew that she meant the widow Vaulini, whose virtue was notoriously easy. But as Vaulini neared thirty and showed no sign of losing her beauty or her hold over Peni, Lebu and Lui gradually spent their anger. Vaulini, they said, was just like an animal. They learned to accept life in an unmarried state until their elders began to worry for fear they would never marry. Peni was happy, and his favors passed from one to the other. Only when public scandal threatened did the most recently jilted girl visit friends for a few days in a neighboring village. When Lebu broke her first betrothal, she knew that the entire village was laughing at his most recent infidelity; when Bulisivo found Vaulini breathless in his latrine and in an unlucky shaft of moonlight saw Peni rushing headlong down the palm-lined avenue toward the river Votua, he called with his aged voice, "Why do you run so fast in the dark? You shall surely gash a foot against a hidden stone," and laughed loudly so that the women came pouring from his house to understand the joke; with head hanging, Vaulini emerged from the small thatched house that screened the latrine, and the women of Bulisivo's household tried to smother their laughter until they were again indoors. Before such public ridicule Lebu had to act: she denounced Peni among her friends and traveled to Nalauvia and Nacula for a prolonged visit with her relatives there. Peni turned again to lithe, small Lui because the village was watching Vaulini. But Nabadua's failing food resources required that Lui marry. Since Nabadua smarted more than Lui from Peni's first infidelity, and resented this lack of respect to a daughter of his, who to him was a chieftainess, it was well that Lui accepted the proposal of a young man from Nalauvia who had been coming to dance before her for several years. Thus Lebu was left with but one rival in the field—a rival whom scandal temporarily held in leash. Because of her recent affair with Ratu Seru, people were beginning to remark upon how like her sister Vaulini she was; it was important that she marry to maintain status, and Peni was a good worker with many gardens.

But rivalry and anger among women are of little importance to the functioning of society. When sisters spat, men shrug their shoulders. A woman can initiate no serious change in social arrangements. Not so among brothers. With awe people remember Isacodro's anger when he left Nalauvia with his household to take up residence at Nakoroka.[13] For months they had watched in suspense as Ema, more than twenty years the wife of Isacodro, traveled the path from Nalauvia to distant Dreketi for trysts with Isacodro's brother. The path crossed a clearing visible from Nakoroka. At night people saw her silhouette against the sky or her lantern blinking in the rain. She traveled alone and sometimes, forgetting all caution, passed in broad daylight. People could not blame her, for no woman would behave so were it not for the supernatural tricks that her lover was using. Isacodro knew and was powerless to reason with her. At length, when Isacodro's brother returned to Nalauvia, the entire community waited in suspense. These were two brothers of the same father and mother. Both of low caste, their status in the community was almost equal. They were free to hate each other. If Isacodro had not folded his belongings in haste and departed for Nakoroka with his family, violence would surely have occurred. But departure was a drastic step; communities will humble themselves before one who feels injured rather than lose a valuable male member. Isacodro is a famous builder of houses, and his gardens always flourish.

Among women of chiefly rank sisterly anger is serious enough to be avoided. Like men, they treat one another with restraint and politeness. Big Di Litiya gives a place in her household to her older sister. They work together at gardening and matmaking. While Big Di Litiya was holding the whale tooth "King Forest," which gave her kingly power in Inland Forest Kingdom, she would insist graciously that Di Kabu's superior age be honored with precedence in the casual kava-drinking at which both chanced to participate. It is whispered that they do not like each other; in the past they have been jealous. At casual gatherings today Big Di Litiya more frequently drinks kava and converses among the men, while Di Kabu prefers the company of the women of Bulisivo's household.

In sharp contrast with the brother-sister taboo which occurs in the *t*-speaking region of eastern Vanua Levu[14]—the region which recognizes no moiety division—brothers and sisters at Nakoroka live easily with each other. Sisters feel no embarrassment in washing a brother's

13. See above, p. 134.   14. See the Appendix and Map VII below.

dirty clothes, a task which is strictly forbidden in regions where strong taboos exist. But the degree to which brothers feel free to use obscenity in their sister's presence, and the degree to which they require chastity among their sisters, varies with individuals.

Namo, Nabadua's oldest son, was most lax, and Peni considered him foolish and undignified for his laxity. Not only would he speak bawdily before his true sister Lui but to a friend he privately recommended his sister's lovemaking.

Bari, the boy from Savusavu, charmed Namo with his tales of the decadent life in coastal villages. At Nakoroka Bari was unhampered by the restraints of kinship which limited the choice of most boys to half the girls in the village, but likewise he lacked the strong security in emergency which a kin group can give to one who through sexual misdemeanors is temporarily unpopular. When he chose the virgin Ivamere for his mistress and witlessly forgot the babbling tongue of her sister's seven-year-old child, anger smoldered among her brothers until Bari felt impelled to request a few elders to present gifts formally to her father and speak for her hand in his behalf. Namo sympathized with Bari and his trials. Bari had ready cash and had spoken often in detail about his wealthy relatives at Savusavu and his luxuriant gardens there. Namo was influenced by these things, and besides he was capable of quick genuine affections which caused the community to consider him unstable like his father. He romanticized Bari's love for Ivamere and remembered his own dramatic marriage against odds. Once he said wistfully: "How sad it is that Bari has not found one of my sisters attractive. Lebu and Vaulini[15] can be persuaded easily, and Lui is very clever. I, as oldest of their brothers, would not object."

Peni would have been shocked and dismayed had anyone discussed with him the lovemaking of his sisters in moiety, Big Di Merelita or Ivamere; these two were known widely for their industry and in sharp contrast with the sisters of Namo, who were of the opposite moiety, they rarely wandered about the village at night. When they planned excursions to the gold mine or even to neighboring villages, Peni would advise them not to go, and frequently they listened to him. It pleased him to think that, because of him, his sisters were good women, the sort of women he would like to marry. But even outsiders were willing to admit that he played a strong role in maintaining his sisters' virtue. Sometimes Ivamere, who managed the women's work in the household of her father, the widowed Raitova, watched sadly as her gay

15. Remote classificatory sisters.

cross-cousins, the sisters of Namo, prepared themselves for an excursion; she would complain that her lot was like that of an old woman. When her virgin curls were shorn,[16] Peni let it be known that he would no longer call her sister. A brother has material interest in his sister's virtue; the great ceremonial exchanges of betrothal and marriage occur most elaborately when the girl is a virgin.

Perhaps Big Di Merelita listened to Peni because she knew that he had the ear of her noble brother Ratu Seru. Perhaps Peni's deliberately secret boasts that he would beat any man whom he knew to be stealing his sister's favors deterred those who otherwise would have wooed falsely. There is a tradition that outsiders who tamper with unwilling girls may be "turkey-tramped," stamped upon by all the village's adult men. Actually such violence has never occurred at Nakoroka. In a gathering of men even Peni's braggadocio deserts him. Though Ivamere was not averse to Bari's advances, it was this tradition which made him fearful when he heard about her brother's anger.[17] In contrast with Peni, Namo has a "strong soul" and can speak out in a crowd, but his big talk is even less likely to be substantiated in action than that of Peni.

A young man rarely uses another man to act as a go-between in a love affair. This task falls to sisters. Exceptionally, Peni used a fifteen-year-old distant brother for this purpose. But Peni looked upon him as a child in his service and not as a younger brother; they were fond of each other. Usually Peni spoke to Selaima, wife of Orisi, or to Yani, wife of Namo, who as his older classificatory sisters would bear gifts to a girl cross-cousin and arrange a trysting place. Frequently girls took the initiative and spoke with the desired young man's sister. The foolish Semi, who sometimes fled to distant kinsmen at Nakoroka to evade the clutches of some native medical practitioner who hoped to confine him in a sulphur bath and cure his stinking body of its ringworm, was butt of many sly jokes because he had once asked Namo, his classificatory brother, to speak to a girl in his behalf. Thus in contrast with young men, girls know the love affairs of their brothers in detail; since

16. See below, p. 281.

17. The "turkey-tramping" of outsiders does not contradict Vatili's emphasis upon the limitation of violence to the brother group (see below, pp. 296–97). In former times a man never entered territory in which he had no kin. The tendency to remain within the circle of one's ancestors' influence is still strong among men of the interior. But in recent years government projects have brought strangers temporarily into every community. Men of acculturated regions have dared though with trepidation to visit foreign villages for no motive other than curiosity. Turkey-tramping functions where kinship does not apply.

258 FIJIAN VILLAGE

most of the young men who are not their brothers are potential lovers, they know the love arrangements of the entire village. Peni says that he would beat any man whom he knew to have slept with one of his sisters; his boast is safe because he will never know. It is only the women who know these things and can discuss them among themselves. Though men may be curious, they can only suspect.

Nakoroka lacks all concept of the sister's right to curse which is widespread in Oceania; Nakoroka sisters cannot bring sterility upon their brothers or their brothers' descendants. Such supernatural power is reserved for fathers and the men of older generations of one's moiety. The only magic function which belongs exclusively to sisters is but theoretical and probably has never occurred at Nakoroka; when a woman suspected of infidelity is suffering difficult delivery, a sister of the man who might be father drinks a broth brewed from her brother's loincloth. If delivery proceeds more smoothly thenceforth, the suspected brother's guilt is proved.

But there are good practical reasons why a brother needs his sister's good will when he plans to marry and establish a household. Peni's "sister" Yani had acted as go-between in the serious matter of his marriage. When Lebu had decided to renew her betrothal with Peni, she first discussed the matter with Yani and came to an agreement. It was Yani who arranged their secret tryst in the mosquito net at Nabadua's house. Yani's approval was essential, because, if she refused to accept her brother's wife, "who would help them when Lebu was ready to bear children?" Who would assist with household tasks during the taboo period of early infancy when mothers cannot leave their houses? Peni's other sisters were young and might marry outside the village.

Sometimes Peni sadly remembered the "dry vagina" in the Udu region of Cakaudrove, which had the delectable texture of "an onion's skin." On our January excursion to learn the distribution of phonetic systems, he had made the acquaintance of this girl; she had served us with food in a distant Cakaudrove village. But the distance was far too great for Yani to make her acquaintance. Peni had considered marrying her and bringing her home with him. He was sure that she would charm his sister Yani. But, on second thought, he realized that the expense of a return trip, in case Yani should disapprove, was prohibitive.

Yani, already an experienced matron with five children of her own, was Peni's "special" sister, whose children he would always cherish above all others. Except for Selaima, wife of the lowly Orisi, she was the oldest of all whom Peni called "sister." Since Peni had no true mother and few from whom he could expect maternal indulgence, it was doubly important for him to respect Yani's opinion: she would supply many of the mats and household goods which he would need to establish a household of his own. In contrast with his attitude toward younger sisters, Peni's respect for Yani and Selaima made the thought of disciplining them seem absurd.

As in all things, Orisi had been a fool in marriage. Without consulting Vilomena of Nadroro,[18] senior sister in his land group, he had married Selaima informally at Dreketi and brought her home to Nakoroka. Vilomena lived in Vatili's house, which lies next to Orisi's. It was she who controlled ancestral favor for the land which Orisi planted. But she refused to accept Selaima as wife of her brother. After Orisi's children were born, she refused to recognize them as kin and drove them angrily from her kitchen when they came looking hungrily for a tidbit from the food mat. Selaima was unhappy. At length Orisi gained an ally in his distant sister Melika, who was Naicadra's wife, and together they asked Bulisivo to hear Selaima's grievance. Late on the night of November 17, 1935, the elders assembled at Naicadra's house, and kava was served formally to Bulisivo. Orisi charged Vatili, who as Vilomena's brother of the same household acted as her spokesman, with the evil nature of his sister. He said that she behaved like a commoner of lowest blood. Selaima wept without restraint and said: "I know that my face is ugly. In the morning I shall return to my village and send back a wife for Orisi who shall be pleasing in the sight of Vilomena and whose children she shall love and deem worthy to mingle with her own and share their food."

People had always pitied Vilomena despite her high birth. Long ago her face had been hideously burned so that strands of skin bound her chin to her neck and tore her mouth awry. Her breath was unwholesome. Her children had both been conceived "in the path," the elder a boy by the philandering Sakariya, the younger a babbling half-wit girl by a wandering Solomon Islander. But older people remembered her as a young girl, and a legend had grown that she had once been beautiful as Lebu.

Vilomena denied the charges against her, but when her brother Vatili was moved to substantiate them, she wept. Then Bulisivo addressed them: "This my word is right in the traditions of the law of the government of Britain, of chiefs, and of the land. Henceforth let there

18. See above, p. 113.

be an end to hatred. Let us live happily together. Let Vilomena love
Selaima. And let their children divide food, one with the others, as is
proper among true cross-cousins. This is my word; I have finished."
Thenceforth Vilomena loved Selaima and her children. Melika and
Vilomena resumed their sisterly garden work together. In March,
1936, Vilomena died; though she had held high political status in
Nadroro land, her funeral caused little sorrow. The dancing of the
mourners was but mildly hilarious.

Because it is easier for women than for men to establish themselves
among affinal kinsmen in a foreign village, or because men like to live
among those with thom they have grown up and women are powerless to move them, it is considered better for bride and groom of different village affiliations to establish themselves in the household of the
groom rather than that of the bride.[19] Hence a woman who chooses to
marry an outsider need not worry about her spouse's adjustment with
her kinsmen. In the village of her husband there will be no need that
he have everyday contact with her kinsmen. Peni says that he would
drive away any suitor of his sisters whom he considered lazy or ugly.
He would refuse to co-operate in making a marriage feast or donating
whale teeth to the dowry. But if one of his sisters should choose to
marry and live outside the village, she would hold Peni's opinion lightly. In the competitive giving at marriage a woman is supposed to be
"weak"; she can "lose" with good grace. Her only great problem lies
in her adjustment to her husband's sisters in her new home.

Above all others a young man's sister, particularly the one whom he
has selected as his "special" sister, may serve as confidante in all things.
It was only a sister whom a sorcerer could trust to free him from the
danger of his own evil power. People of Nakoroka deny all knowledge
of the technique which poisons an enemy by tamping a bit of his spittle
or food refuse into a length of bamboo together with a leaf medicine
brewed to prescription. When a victim had died of such poison and the
nature of his quick decay had roused suspicion of murder by witchcraft,[20] his grave was dug in such a way that the shaft descended
crookedly; then the murderer could not thrust a spear through the
soft earth of the grave's mouth to pierce the corpse and disperse his

19. Matrilocal marriages do occur. But the man who can build status for himself in his
wife's village is rare.

20. The jaws of those who have been murdered by witchcraft rot quickly and drop from
the corpse.

medicine's evil power which was regenerating within the corpse and preparing to strike back upon him. Brothers and sisters of the deceased watched his grave for at least four nights to guard against suspicious-looking prowlers.[21] Though Bici denies the existence of such practice at Nakoroka, in another breath he explains how a sorcerer can evade this danger by enlisting his sister as ally. For at least a night after death the corpse lies in a house, wrapped loosely so that all relatives may gaze upon its face for the last time and mourn. As mourners enter, it is polite for them to cry out shrilly and rush with passion to the side of the corpse. A sister, forewarned of her brother's guilt as murderer, could easily pierce the corpse with a needle as she crouched over it to wail her last respect. A sorcerer would dare to trust no other; if his wife should discover his guilt, she would inform her kinsmen straightway.

A sister feels that she owns her brother's property and, even after both have married, feels at home in his household. Peni never admits resentment when his sisters take the new calico which he has bought from the Chinese. In contrast with his attitude toward his elder brother Narogo, he is glad to see his sisters well provided for. In return he feels free to ask them to perform the numerous services for which men must depend upon women. At least until his marriage such dependence is essential. They make mats when he must provide a gift for a wedding or funeral. They sew and wash his clothes and, when he is prosperous, make him a mosquito curtain of muslin, though they may decide to take it for themselves when it is complete. When Melika needed seed yams, and the Nakoroka supply was exhausted,[22] she called upon her classificatory brothers in Nalauvia to supply her. Good men are ashamed to take personal belongings from their sisters; such an act, indeed, would contradict the male's status as provider. Yet, despite cold weather, Bici feared to allow his wife to wear a heavy wool shirt I had given him; he said Narogo or some other classificatory brother would take it from her. But Bici, who had little status in the community outside the church, was not ashamed to impute to others the white man's hunger for personal property which he feels himself; pitied and impoverished, he takes the disgrace of seeming mean before his kin as but a small price to pay for the personal belongings which he desires with true European possessiveness.

21. At the end of this time the evil medicine would have grown so strong that piercing the corpse would avail the murderer nothing. The soul of the deceased grows strong within the corpse and departs on the fourth night.

22. See above, pp. 131–32.

CROSS-COUSIN

The term *tavelena* applies to all whose parents have had brother-sister relations. In extension it includes all relatives of opposite moiety of own generation; also, just as "brothers" refers loosely to all members of one's own moiety, so "cross-cousins" loosely includes all members of the opposite moiety.[23] A cross-cousin of any degree of closeness may be addressed with respect language as a mark of affection;[24] or a man may assume a humble position in the kava ceremony to honor his cross-cousin. Actually the most poignant cross-cousin relationships are those which have been carefully taught to the children of two affectionate cross-cousins of the same sex. Thus the son of Toviya on his deathbed had asked Bici to teach their two-year-old sons to cherish each other in the manner of cross-cousins. Though at the age of six the two small boys had little affection for each other, Bici was far from despairing: Care, the grandson of Toviya, who had been adopted by the kindly Naicadra upon his father's death, with his playful and athletic hazing and his petulance nurtured in a houseful of adults, annoyed Bici's malnourished son, Little Kaiyava, whose "mature soul" was his father's pride; the pedantic Bici was sure that his son would learn to disregard Care's blustering manner and take pleasure in sharing food with him. Jokingly, Bici would threaten to beat his son for disregarding Care's cross-cousinhood; but he had faith that his son's intelligence would soon perceive the social import of his relation with Care. Bici's father, the aged Kaiyava, and Toviya had cherished each other as cross-cousins and passed the relationship on to their sons; now it was in its third generation.

Those, too, who have married a man's "special" sister are particularly "heavy and difficult" cross-cousins to him. No matter how greatly Peni disapproved of Namo, the husband of Peni's sister Yani, he would never speak evil of him. When Namo requested, through Yani, that Peni travel to the distant Nakalou to obtain the advice of a medical practitioner,[25] Peni acquiesced willingly regardless of other tasks. When he heard others say that Selaima's husband Orisi was a fool, he was always hurt.

Vatili had no vigorous brothers to make him repent when he ordered his wife Losana from his house. Never in her eighteen years of

---

23. In work obligations (see above, pp. 135 and 137).

24. Plural pronouns used in addressing chiefs refer to great numbers. Respect pronouns to a cross-cousin are dual or trial in number.

25. See the discussion of Sakiusa's illness and death, below, pp. 370–71.

marriage had she been unfaithful to him. No one had ever spoken evil of her. Uniquely among Nakoroka women she had worn virgin's coiffure without challenge until her curls were shorn ritually at the end of her wedding ceremony.[26] But once in June, 1936, during Vatili's absence she smoked up his tobacco. He ordered her to return to the household of her brother. The entire village buzzed with hatred against Vatili: "tobacco is but a small thing." His cross-cousins, who were Losana's brothers, avoided him; but not one of them dared show anything but good humor toward him. Though Samu, who is Losana's true brother, felt deep sympathy, he did not dare even secretly to express his opinion of Vatili. He could say only that the whole affair was unfortunate. He gave up eating at Vatili's house, and he glowered when his name was mentioned. But to suggest by his behavior that he bore private malice against his sister's husband would cast unpleasant shadows on his status as a socialized adult.

Mild joking characterizes cross-cousinhood and occurs between all members of opposite moieties who have no other relationship which proscribes it. Thus when Ratu Vuki came from Sarowaqa, he would bluster into Raitova's house and with cross-cousin humor remark upon the poverty of the food. He borrowed Bici's knife and file and never returned them; Bici smiled slyly and made plans to get even. These men have no traceable relationship with Ratu Vuki; but they expect him to act like a cross-cousin because he is of the opposite moiety, and they have always classed him as such. Samu's and Raitova's younger brother once embarrassed their cross-cousin Tomasi by poking at his penis. Though Bici says that such behavior is common and proper for cross-cousins, it is actually rare and considered indecorous among men. Only women cross-cousins can tussle playfully and insult each other sexually; women know no better. Particularly old women can be entertaining as they clown among themselves, but men pretend to ignore their humor. The relations of men with their female cross-cousins[27] provide the only occasions upon which men relax from dignity without danger of social reproof. Even in such relationships it is only Bici, with Little Melika, daughter of Toviya, who dares to be joyfully obscene. Most men confine themselves to interrupting

26. Formally promised in marriage at puberty, she had had little opportunity to experiment with sex before marriage. Such a youthful marriage is unusual.

27. At Nakoroka a man's female cross-cousin is the keeper of his ceremonial bark cloth, *solesole ni masi*. It is also her duty to prepare him for the dance: rub his body with ointment and prepare leaf garlands.

games of cards which their female cross-cousins are playing or tangling the strands of their unfinished mats.

Work obligations between cross-cousins provoke the same delight in practical joking. When Isacodro's cross-cousins cleaned land for him upon his arrival at Nakoroka, they left it piled high with rubbish. In contrast, when Melika's classificatory brothers came to plan her yam garden,[28] they worked with dignity in the manner of "blood relatives."

Property relations between male cross-cousins are reciprocal. A request for property, no matter how great, is always granted. Of possible requests for favors, that of cross-cousins is the heaviest.[29] In distinction from the property relations between brothers, a cross-cousin must always ask, and this in a formally abject tone. He is not of the same blood. Granting his wish is a special dispensation to a privileged outsider. No one would use the garden products of a cross-cousin without first making a formal request. Requests for property among cousins result in far-flung trade of valued objects. Thus Isacodro's large kava bowl was taken to Sarowaqa by a chief there who is his wife's classificatory brother. Vosalevu brought a great kava bowl to the house of his wife Big Di Litiya from the windward coast; he had begged it from the aged Ratu Sailiya, who was Ratu Luke's father and Big Di Litiya's distant brother.

Though reciprocal in theory, the property of male cross-cousins within the same village tends to flow toward sisters' husbands. A woman feels at home and shares control of property in the household of both her brother and her husband. But the consumption of goods for which she feels economically responsible occurs principally among her children in the household of her husband. Property relations between moieties is balanced, because every man has a sister. In theory every man's wife is the sister of his sister's husband; but, since only a few women are selected for the specially intense sister relationships which entail complete sharing of property control, it is usual that a man's wife is merely the sister-in-moiety of his sister's husband.

Female cross-cousins have a special name for their relationship to distinguish themselves from male or cross-sex cross-cousins (*tau-dauve-na*).[30] They are less formally restrained than men. They can possess

28. See above, pp. 131–32, 135.

29. Among the people of Nakoroka, traditional obligations, sorrow, and burdens of great weight may all be described as "heavy."

30. For the significance of *tau* see n. 6 above. Bici distinguishes between *tau-dauvena*, which he says are sisters-in-law, and *tau-yavena*, which he says means cross-cousins through

themselves of each other's clothing without making formal requests. Their relations are easier, less tense, with deliberate good humor. Melika and Big Di Litiya, cross-cousins, friends and confederates in midwifery, preferred each other's co-operation in work to that of any of their sisters. Frequently they visited about the village together. Since women cross-cousins have served as go-betweens in each other's love affairs, their jesting is more accurately pointed than that of their brothers; sometimes lewd accusations, shouted across the village,[31] make even the men chuckle. But as women are less capable of restraint in all things, so they are less able to direct controlled affection toward their female cross-cousins.

Several years ago young Radebu[32] and her cross-cousin, the then virginal Ivamere, were hurling playful insults at each other. But Ivamere, whose virgin's coiffure was a matter of village pride, resented the charge that she was falsely pretending to be a virgin. Incensed, she demanded an inspection of all the young girls of the village. On an appointed day the village women repaired to the shallows in the river Votua and squatted in the water while an older woman inspected them and announced the report. But Radebu had fled to the bush. It was late evening when she returned.

In the days of the wars cross-cousin affection was put to serious test. When an attack was to be made upon a neighboring village, it was the duty of a man who had a cross-cousin in that village to carry him warning. On some pretext the forewarned cousin would busy himself with some work in the forest until the danger had passed, then return to his village and feign surprise at the destruction that had occurred during his absence. Frequently such cousins were ''weak in spirit'' and warned the entire village so that the conquering army found none but the aged and sick to slaughter; these, however, could serve as justification for the victory song and as food offerings to the ancestors. Even in the heat of battle a warrior spared his cross-cousins. No other relative went free; a man felt at liberty to kill a father, brother, or even a *tubu-na*.[33]

A cross-cousin can best call the soul of a dead man to return to the

---

tradition or descent. However, the distinction is questionable. Affect is identical in both classes.

31. Unless he were making a formal announcement, a man would never shout.

32. Radebu died in July, 1937.

33. Grandparent or mother's brother.

village.[34] Instead of placing a lantern on the grave on the fourth night after burial, as is done today, an earlier practice required that a coconut leaf be imbedded in the soft earth so that only its tip protruded. When the soul had time to grow strong in the grave, it was the task of the cross-cousin to tug lightly upon the coconut leaf, calling the while for the soul to return to its beloved friend, its cross-cousin. Soon the leaf would quiver as signal that the soul had heard and was prepared to follow. The cross-cousin drew the leaf from the grave and dragged it slowly behind him to the village, crooning to the soul lest it be frightened and take flight. Today it is Keleivi who must bring all souls from their graves. Only he is unafraid.

Those of the same sex who are cross-cousins through descent from classificatory brother and sister are not distinguished in treatment or attitude from those who have become cross-cousins through marriage. In theory cross-cousins become in-laws, and only cross-cousins can become in-laws. Actually, however, since the extended moiety involves many who are strangers to one another, such widely extended terms connote a large range of varying affection and respect. So those among whom acquaintance has developed only through marriage between villages are bound by tenuous ties of cross-cousinship; respectful and affectionate etiquette, rather than provocative banter, predominates in their relationship. But the supervising interest which men assume in their sisters' potential husbands lessens the danger of creating uncongenial cross-cousin relationships through marriage. Peni would drive away those potential cross-cousins whom he considered "lazy or ugly." Should his sister disregard his opinion, he would refuse to recognize her spouse as cross-cousin, unless open discord should make it necessary for the chief to demand that a loving relationship be established. Disciplining a sister's sex life is in part motivated by the desire to give a good woman to one's cross-cousin. If women are faithful and industrious, and if brothers can keep them so, no chance for affinal discord will arise; cross-cousins can maintain their cherishing relationship with ease. Though discord between women cross-cousins may disrupt life within the household,[35] men feel secure in their power to control conflict and avoid violence; it is fear of violence between men which looms large as a danger to society. Thus intervillage cross-cousin-

34. For a description of the return of the soul on the fourth night see below, pp. 265–66.

35. See the case of Vilomena and Selaima, above, pp. 259–60.

hood served in the old days as a safety device against war and today produces amicable bonds for trade.[36]

Cross-cousinhood between man and woman is less frequent after marriage, because a taboo relationship between a man and his wife's sisters and a woman and her husband's brothers replaces it. The term "small spouse," designates such taboo relationship.[37] One cannot speak the name of his "small spouse" or address her in any way; words which suggest the name must be avoided. "Small spouses" cannot remain alone together, because, as Bici explained, "if you put a cat and a rat in a house together and leave them alone, what do you think will happen?" A kava cup may not even pass between them. Despite such relationships in every household, family life runs smoothly because even a small child may serve as mediator between those who are taboo. When Vosalevu makes kava in his household for private drinking, he asks five-year-old Di Sereima to pass the cup to "that person," by which he refers to his "small wife" (his wife's sister Di Kabu) who shares the same house.

The change from cross-cousin bantering to "small spouse" taboo need not wait for formal betrothal or marriage. When Lebu and Ratu Seru shocked the village with their almost public love affair, Peni decided to consider Lebu his "small spouse" and feel shame in her company. He refused to speak her name. In daytime, at least, he observed strict taboo. Others said that this was his private custom, that tradition required no taboo until after formal betrothal. Peni liked to consider himself a champion of propriety.

Before Lui had accepted the proposal of the young man from Nalauvia, Peni used to go stealthily to her mosquito net at night. Sometimes she would come to his bed and tug his leg to wake him. Then she decided to marry. Her betrothed was, of course, of Peni's moiety and therefore Peni's "small brother." But Peni preferred not to consider this new complication in his affairs. When the village slept, he sought Lui in her mosquito net as usual. She said: "Aren't you ashamed to

---

36. All Nakoroka residents have blood ties in other divisions of Inland Forest Kingdom, and at least half have strong claims upon other regions as well. Among women who come to Nakoroka to reside in their spouses' households, claims of the villages of their birth usually predominate in their kinship obligations. Thus, of the cross-cousinhoods whose strength depends upon marriage, those between men, rather than women, more frequently serve as intercommunity bonds. Women tend to be coresident with their affinal cross-cousins (i.e., those created by their own marriages, the brothers and sisters of their husbands). In-law relationships created by women's siblings' marriages are of very minor importance in inland Bua unless strengthened by coresidence.

37. *Wati-na*, "his spouse," plus *lailai*, "small."

seek your 'small wife'?'' Crestfallen, he returned to his bed. For several days he pondered his guilt. The wife of a "small brother" should be held in even more strict taboo than that of one with whom the brother relationship is well established. Thenceforth Peni held Lui as "small spouse."

Among men and women relatively of the same age, only cross-cousinhood of strong traditional standing, like that between Bici and Toviya's daughter Little Melika, can override the "small spouse" taboo and persist in spite of it. Those cross-cousins of opposite sex who are children of true blood brother and sister, and in consequence ashamed to look upon each other sexually, usually deem their blood tie an excuse for overlooking the taboo which would otherwise come with marriage. Such cross-cousins distinguish their relationship with the descriptive term "brother-sister cross-cousin."

The only biologic first cross-cousins at Nakoroka who were of close enough age to regard each other sexually were Vatili's daughter Wakesa and the son of his wife's blood brother, Samu. These children were barely reaching puberty, not old enough to appreciate the significance of cross-cousinhood. As they grow older, their relationship will contain many elements of brother-sister relationship. It is probable that Peni's children will consider those of Yani, who is Peni's especially chosen "sister," as cross-cousins toward whom they never need establish a taboo relationship, that is, as "brother-sister cross-cousin."

A "small spouse" relationship, once established, is difficult to dissolve. If the marriage upon which it depends gives issue, the taboo persists in spite of the death of either one of the partners to the marriage. So long as there is a child who classifies the husband and his "small wives," or the wife and her "small husbands," as father and mother, shame will persist. If all such children die so that there is no living person whose kin status depends upon the marriage, the taboo can be dissolved; usually the older member of the taboo relationship takes the initiative in its dissolution. In such a case a man who has courage may grasp the arm of a "small wife" even older than he is himself if she seems too shy to make the first advance. But most men reflect the shyness of their erstwhile "small spouses" and maintain the taboo. Cases in which these taboo relationships are dissolved, or in which death has created an opportunity for dissolution, are rare; I know of no actual case.

Before his marriage a man maintains cross-cousin relations with the sisters of his brothers' wives. The "small spouse" taboo is limited to the true wives of a man's brothers and of his "small brothers" and to his own wife's sisters and her "small sisters." Hence an individual's extension of the term to include all those of same generation and opposite sex and moiety cannot occur until his or her own marriage. But moiety-wide extension is largely theoretical. Whenever possible, the inconveniences of the taboo are avoided; on some pretext it is circumvented and never established. Monasa, who is Bici's older brother in Tavua, prefers to consider Bici's wife as "small daughter," a relationship which he can establish only along a tortuous path through the genealogies. The community considers Monasa justified in his excuse for avoiding this taboo. On the other hand, when Raitova's "small brother" married, Raitova neglected to observe a taboo toward his wife; people point to this neglect as another symptom of Raitova's foolishness.

If Peni were not so much younger than Big Melika, the wife of his older "brother" Naicadra, she would be taboo to him. She is more than ten years his senior. Such wide discrepancy in age permits her to look upon him as a child.

Peni and Vaulini have been taboo to each other for many years. Vaulini's husband had a well-established brother relationship with Peni. Peni classed Vaulini's son as "child." When Vaulini's name is mentioned, Peni always pretends embarrassment. Only with greatest difficulty can he be persuaded to speak her name confidentially. Yet, for several years tales of their secret trysts by night have buzzed through the village. When Peni has money, Vaulini always wears new calico from the Chinese store and smokes tobacco tinned in Australia. Peni admits his guilt, but he feels little shame. He says it is because everyone knows that Vaulini is a foolish woman without restraint or dignity. But in the daytime she is "his taboo."

If "small wives" are unmarried, they are supposed to make themselves useful in the households of their "small husbands." They are needed particularly at times when their married sister is confined. Together with the sisters of their "small husband," who are their cross-cousins, they perform the chores of nursing and kitchen management. If there are "small husbands" in the household of a married woman, she must prepare their food with special care; though she observes strict taboo toward them at all times, she must be solicitous for their wants.

"Small spouse" taboo receives unusually high development in the

Nakoroka area. In eastern Macuata, where there is strong brother-sister taboo, sibling-in-law is a joking relative[38] similar to cross-cousin at Nakoroka.[39] Along the Wainunu and Savusavu coasts it is a man's "small wife" who cares for his ceremonial bark cloth and prepares him for the dance; she receives the special term, *solesole ni masi*,[40] which at Nakoroka applies only to a man's female cross-cousin. Bici and Vatili say that, except in the village of Daria in Wainunu Kingdom, which is like Nakoroka, people of the windward coast apply "small spouse" only to the immediate sisters of one's wife; it is only in inland western Macuata and the leeward half of Bua Province that the term receives wide extension to very distant siblings.

The term for true spouse, *wati-na*, is never used in address except as part of mourning etiquette. When a mourner approaches a corpse, it is customary for him to use a kin term as he wails his first polite greeting. Uniquely, "spouse" is avoided even in reference on all other occasions. Within the village, everyone knows all marriages; personal names are adequate identification. This avoidance which insures that one shall not speak of any man or woman as spouse of another appears to be an aspect of modesty. In case of necessity a young man might indicate his intended betrothed as his intended wife, but even then he would not address her as such. Use of "spouse" even in reference is insulting. In vulgar banter Ivamere once playfully insulted Vaulini, saying that Samu was Vaulini's "spouse."

There is the greatest variation in attitudes between husbands and wives. Companionable relationships are not the rule, but they do occur. Big Di Litiya and her husband Vosalevu usually visit about together when both are in the village. As chiefs, however, they are not typical of the whole community. Big Di Litiya says that their attitudes are like those of white people whom she has heard about. Others say that she follows Vosalevu wherever he goes to make sure that no other woman excites his fancy. She is fully ten years his senior. But when they are alone in their house, they laugh together so that the village resounds. Nabadua, whose younger wife is at least twenty years his junior, calls her "friend" during the intervals in which he is not avoid-

38. For examples of the kind of "joking" which occurs widely on Vanua Levu, see above, p. 263.

39. Affect and term are constant in both regions. *Tau-tavelena* seems to suggest joking wherever it occurs. But the term includes a different group of persons in each region. In eastern Macuata both parallel and cross-cousins are called "sibling"; *tavelena* is used exclusively for "sibling-in-law" and functions only after marriage.

40. See above, n. 27.

ing her in a jealous rage.[41] His voice is usually quavering with the emotion of a recent reconciliation. Bulisivo's wife Viniyana is constantly busy with the chores of his large household and serves him as nurse in his old age. The wives of Bici, Vatili, and Naicadra, during the time which they can spare from their household chores, mingle indiscriminately with groups of spinsters and widows, of whom there are many at Nakoroka. They rarely go visiting with their husbands.

According to Bici, a wife's prime function is as supervisor of women's work in the household. Bici expects his wife to obey him, to search the forest for some special food to please him even though she may be ill; if she does not obey him, whom then will she serve? No household can be whole without a wife. Yet her social adjustment in the village must depend to a large degree upon herself and upon the women friends she chooses in the village. Most husbands are ashamed to betray any public hint of affection for their wives. They prefer to spend their leisure with men. Sisters and cross-cousins are better company than wives.

Despite Peni's vivid interest in sex, he insists that sexual charms are no criterion in choosing a wife; her industry in the household, her skill in plaiting mats, can far outshine her beauty of face or figure. Yet for his own marriage he accepted the attractive Lebu, whose skills as housewife are mediocre; her habit of wandering to other villages for long visits is notorious. Though his decision to marry was not his own choice, the prospect pleased him. For feminine companionship Peni has depended heavily upon his "special" sister Yani and plans to continue doing so.

The choice of a spouse is limited by moiety, age, and kinship. Marriage within moiety is called "marriage of siblings"; it is always highly improper. Chiefs can marry their sisters-in-moiety, but their right to such marriage is the chiefly privilege to disregard the restraints which bind common people; courage to commit an impropriety is a badge of

41. Nabadua had never allowed British or missionary law to ratify his marriage. He was proud of the money he had paid to the authorities as fines for living with a woman "in the manner of a devil." The mother of his four older children lived sometimes in his household, but she preferred the house of his eldest son. Kelera, mother of his four younger children, of whom, in 1936, the youngest was still an infant, looked attractively younger than forty. She shared his house most of the time. Nabadua also had a son at Nacula by a woman with whom he had lived *en ménage* before he joined Kelera. Nabadua's large family as well as his polygamy were unique at Nakoroka. Polygamy has been a prerogative of chiefs and strong men. Though illegitimacy is frequent, sharing a house with more than one wife at a time is very rare even among chiefs. The British and the missionaries have disapproved effectively.

chiefliness. Among young people discrepancy in age can prevent sexual intercourse. A boy who has sexual contact with an old woman, or a girl who allows herself to be seduced by an old man, risks contracting the dread wasting disease. Though this danger does not exist among the older age groups, even with difference of chronological age, it is effective throughout the period when most marriages are made.[42] Generation in kinship coincides but roughly with age groupings, and marriage occurs within the generation as determined by kinship. Since everyone is related to everyone else along several genealogical paths, it is conceivable that a man could marry a woman who, according to one genealogical path, is his daughter. Such a marriage is not specifically taboo, provided that the persons concerned are cross-cousins by some other genealogical path and have never observed father-daughter behavior toward each other. Despite separate moiety affiliation, persons known to be biologic first cousins cannot marry.

In considering potential spouses, a young man must class the girls in his generation of the opposite moiety, all of whom he vaguely terms cross-cousins, in four categories: (1) those who are his first cousins and whom he may describe as sister-cousins; (2) those whom he has come to regard as special joking cross-cousins;[43] (3) the remaining girls of his generation and opposite moiety toward whom he observes no "small spouse" taboo; and (4) "small spouses." He must choose a wife from Groups 2 or 3. Of Group 2, he can marry anyone who is not also a first cousin (and who, therefore, belongs to Group 1). Before his marriage a man observes "small spouse" taboo only with the true wives and fiancées of his brothers and "small brothers."[44] Hence there are usually a few girls in his own village and in neighboring villages whom he may class as Group 3. But sometimes the number of possible spouses is seriously limited. When Peni decided to marry Lebu, she was the only girl in the village who did not fall into a forbidden category; and even she had almost become a "small spouse" during her affair with Ratu Seru. A girl of Group 2 is preferred as wife; one of the man's parents and one of her parents were either strongly affective but nonbiologic brother and sister, like-sexed brother-sister cross-cous-

42. There is no specified age for marriage, but most first marriages have occurred at Nakoroka between the eighteenth and thirtieth years.

43. Some of the girls with whom he jokes may be biologic first cousins toward whom he feels but slight brotherly modesty. If pressed to *describe* these first-cousin joking relationships, he would probably call them sister-cousins and include them in Group 1.

44. Moiety-wide extension of "small spouse" taboo does not occur until after an individual's own marriage.

ins, or like-sexed joking cross-cousins of traditional standing. In the
Korotasere region of Natewa Bay the term "face of marriage," *mata
ni wati*, indicates a group from which a preferred wife is selected;
though this term is not institutionalized at Nakoroka, it can be used
descriptively to specify a man's relation with a woman of Group 2.
Nakoroka parents approve of a Group 2 marriage because it will
"keep the blood from scattering."[45] Among commoners, the most elaborate preparation of marriage gifts and lavish displays of wealth can
accompany only a Group 2 betrothal and marriage.[46]

In theory chiefs can marry women of Group 1. Chiefs need not feel
the shame which prohibits commoners from marrying into this group.
Better than any extra-moiety marriage, a marriage with a woman of
this group can "bind the blood together." Despite ancestral approval,
however, no such marriage is known. Long ago Big Di Litiya, Bulisivo's sister, was betrothed to a first cousin who was a chief in the
Sarowaqa region. But he did not have courage enough to fulfil the betrothal in marriage.

Chiefs theoretically have the right to marry within the moiety. Bulisivo married his "sister" Viniyana six years ago. But rather than presume to use his chiefly prerogative, he prefers to plead utter ignorance
of moiety structure. Like others of chiefly caste at Nakoroka, he refuses
to classify the population outside his immediate family into these categories; but, in contrast with other chiefs, he will not even consider
commoners as *tubu-na*, which in the mouths of other chiefs means "distant relatives of unknown class." He refuses to admit any blood connection with them. Hence to him Viniyana is not a sister. No kin relationship has ever been established between them, and the genealogies
show no biologic tie, but she is of his moiety; in the eyes of the community she is his sister despite her commoner caste. Even Bulisivo's
biologic sister, the royal Di Litiya, recognizes moiety distinction and,
behind her brother's back, accuses him of incest. People are pleased
that there has been no issue from this marriage.[47] They are pleased
that their disapproval has been substantiated by ancestral wrath;

45. Though usually there is no traceable biologic tie between a young man and a girl
of Group 2, yet the strongly affective relationship between their parents is considered a
manifestation of blood bonds. The closest biologic (in European sense) relationship which
can exist between potential partners to a proper marriage is that of children of first cousins.
To be proper, such marriage must, of course, be of persons of opposite moiety.

46. Women classify men in similar fashion.

47. His first marriage, however, which was not within the moiety, gave him five children.

sterility is the usual penalty with which ancestors afflict commoners who marry within the moiety.

Bulisivo's ignorance of moiety and kinship structure may be a symptom of the rare blood which makes him so high a chief. Or perhaps through his maternal ties with the Wainunu coast, he preserves a chiefly custom of islands farther to the east which is foreign to Nakoroka. Regardless of cause, his plea of ignorance is the most passive way to greet the village-wide disapproval.[48]

Though Bulisivo's is the only known marriage within the moiety which can be remembered among Nakoroka's chiefs, it is said that chiefs and strong men of the old days were not afraid to test ancestral wrath. In keeping with this tradition, all Nabadua's children have been born to him by women of his own moiety. Like Bulisivo, Nabadua refuses to abide by moiety regulations. The fact that he is of the *turaga* moiety supports his inward belief that he is a chief. By marrying many wives within the moiety, he has hoped to prove his chiefly nature, both to himself and to the community. But the ancestors have allowed pigs to ravage his gardens. Disease has taken many of his own children and one of his grandchildren. Nevertheless, his family is by far the largest at Nakoroka. When people see him suffering in the throes of one of his frequent troubles, they remember that he has married his sisters and think him a fool. Though Nabadua's wives are of his own moiety, they have no closer relationship to him.

Nabadua's oldest son, Namo, has been well schooled by his father's temperament. Though his bonds with chiefly caste are even more distant than those of his father, he cherishes the tradition of strong men and chiefs in his family. About ten years ago he married Yani. She was living at Lekutu in her father's house. The parents of five suitors had already offered betrothal gifts of whale teeth; as sign of his approval, her father had kept the whale teeth of one of her suitors. But Namo eloped with her to Nakoroka, leaving a whale tooth in her place as wedding gift. Immediately her father and grandfather came to Nakoroka to return Namo's gift and escorted Yani back to Lekutu. For one night and two days Namo did nothing. Then on the second night he traveled the path to Lekutu in the dark. He found the village sleeping. Stealthily he listened at the walls of the houses. In a certain kitchen he heard women's voices. With his ear close to an aperture between the

48. That Viniyana has never been well liked influences the village attitude toward this marriage. Not only is she a commoner, but her hoydenish personality is displeasing. People fear that the sins of their chief will strike back and cause suffering throughout the kingdom.

plaited canes of the wall he recognized the voice of one of Yani's "small sisters." He spoke quietly to her and requested that Yani be brought to a certain place. He waited. Then great was their hand-clasping when Yani came. Together they traveled back to Nakoroka in the dark. At first Yani's people were angry, but now their anger has subsided. Namo did not give them the whale-tooth wedding gift again; he chuckles now when he remembers that he got both Yani and the whale tooth. Yani belongs to his moiety; she is his sister.

Though Namo and Yani have already had four children as proof that they have been spared the ancestral curse of sterility, they have suffered in other ways. Shortly after their marriage Namo found that Yani was already pregnant by a previous lover. Later, while he re-mained lithe and young, the charm of her languid torpor softened quickly to fatness. Today there is little friendship between them. Fre-quently their children are sick. While Namo combs the countryside to find new medicines, the pigs destroy his crops, and official tax-col-lectors gather grievances against him.

Samu, too, married within his moiety. His wife died giving birth to her second child. But in contrast with the incest of Namo, Nabadua, and Bulisivo, the community felt no resentment. Samu is of low caste, "contents of the household." He is not one to speak much and will never assume a responsible place in the community. People believe that he was truly confused about moiety classification. It is not his fault that pigs ravage the village gardens.

These four cases of marriage within the moiety are all that the com-munity remembers. Moiety relations in the marriages which occur in the genealogies are not remembered clearly. It is always assumed that there were no breaches of moiety regulation; in fact moiety structure is used as a clue to work out genealogies. Twenty-eight marriages of persons resident in Nakoroka observed moiety regulation.[49] The fact that the marriages of Nabadua and Namo have proved most fertile will create a preponderance of their moiety in the next generation. Because Nabadua has persuaded his sons that moiety does not exist in his fam-ily, Namo's younger brother is also expected to marry within the

---

49. This number includes marriages of which one spouse is now dead. Three women and Bulisivo each have been widowed and remarried; these four persons have been num-bered twice. Counting cases of marriage within the moiety according to the same principle, Nabadua's case must be counted three times. Hence, in a total of thirty-four marriages, there are six cases of marriage within the moiety. Temporary matches which produced il-legitimate children have not been included. Accurate data on such cases are hard to get; of two illegitimate matches in which the same man is father, one was within the moiety.

moiety. Unless the next generation chooses most of its spouses from outside the village, preponderance of a single moiety will offer further excuse for ignoring the moiety principle.[50] If memory of informants can be credited (and because genealogies can be reconstructed only by using the moiety principle to rebuild past relationships, this memory is questionable), marriage within moiety is a recent trend. It is possible that regulation against marriage of biologic first cousins, which predominates in eastern Macuata, will persist at Nakoroka after the concept of moiety has become obsolete. No one is ever known to have married a biologic first cousin even when such marriage has not conflicted with moiety structure.[51] Yet except for Samu,[52] who is said simply to have made a mistake, it is easy to understand these cases of marriage within moiety in terms of individual histories alone. Bulisivo chose to use a well-known chiefly indulgence and marry to please his whim. His lack of aggressive temperament prompted him to shield himself behind ignorance of the rule, which was especially easy because of the irregular manner in which chiefs classify kin. The particular circumstances in Nabadua's background made him a constant social problem. An intramoiety marriage substantiated his fantasy of chiefly blood. Nabadua's own explicit teaching led Namo to follow in his footsteps.

When marriage within moiety occurs, kinship attitudes must be adjusted within the village. The adjustment need not be difficult. When Namo married Yani, he brought her from a neighboring village. The entire village looked upon her as Namo's wife and built the relationship with her which suited this role in village activities. Though Yani was of opposite moiety and Peni should have looked upon her as his cross-cousin, he was already enjoying well-established cross-cousinhood with Namo. Peni chose to consider her as a sister, and through the years his dependence upon her as a sister has grown. Now he distinguishes her as his "special" sister and cherishes her children as though she truly were his sister. She procures girls for him from her own moi-

50. The degree to which the village may be called exogamous depends upon the definition of the in-group. If blood tie with the land is used as a criterion for classing people as in-group, all but two or three marriages are endogamous. If household affiliation at the time of marriage is used as a criterion, nearly half are exogamous. However, few marriages cross beyond the limits of well-established kinship (see n. 36 above).

51. However, since biologic first cousins are far less numerous than sisters in moiety, there is far less chance for such marriages to occur.

52. Of all cases, fewest data have been collected around the case of Samu.

ety as though these girls were her cross-cousins. They call her "cross-cousin."[53]

When Yani's children grow up, Peni's role as mother's brother to children who are not of his own moiety may prove embarrassing. Vatili has already felt this embarrassment in relation to the children of Nabadua's first wife. Like Yani, Nabadua's first wife was not reared at Nakoroka. She was brought there as Nabadua's wife. Because he is Nabadua's cross-cousin, Vatili chose to call her "sister," although she is not of his moiety. But recently a boy of Nalauvia village who is Vatili's sister's son, according to proper moiety classification, asked Vatili to be his spokesman for the hand of Lui, Nabadua's oldest daughter by his first wife. Vatili was embarrassed because he was mother's brother to both partners to the marriage agreement. Fortunately, Nabadua was absent from the village and Vatili could present the betrothal gift to Namo. Vatili opened his speech of presentation with an apology;[54] he could never have apologized to Nabadua, whom he hates.

Nabadua's third wife has had more difficulty in adjusting to her irregular marriage. She has always lived at Nakoroka. She already had status in the community as one of Nabadua's sisters in moiety. People have not readjusted their kinship attitudes toward her. She must even treat Nabadua's sisters as though they were her own. But some adjustment has been made toward Radebu, her daughter by an earlier marriage. Several young men of the village, who, according to moiety affiliation, were her cross-cousins, decided to consider her as sister. Peni was of this group of young men; he speaks of her with pity because her moiety status is ambiguous. One of Nabadua's sons by another marriage has already made sexual advances toward her, and, despite the fact that she is his sister according to moiety structure, it is said that he will probably marry her. It may be as counteraction to this proposal of Nabadua's son, which they consider incestuous, that the young men of the other moiety have come to include Radebu in their brother-sister group. The young women have been less charitable; they persist in classifying Radebu according to her hereditary moiety affilia-

53. Though Peni and Yani were both nursed in infancy by the same woman, it is said that this temporary adoption was not effective in establishing their present brother-sister relationship. The woman who nursed them was a "small sister" of Peni's mother and a biologic sister of Yani's father. Adoption does not change kin affiliations. See discussion of adoption below.

54. Namo, who is Lui's full brother, also has grown up as Vatili's sister's son.

tion; they chide her with especially biting accusations of sexual impropriety.[55]

Like Radebu, Samu's moiety affiliation is ambiguous. His wife, now dead, grew up at Nakoroka, and her kin relationships were as well established as his own. The same young men who took Radebu into their brother-sister group have chosen to consider Samu as their brother despite his belonging to the opposite moiety; but, unfortunately, he has well established affinal relationships which prohibit full participation with this group of brothers. Embarrassment may arise when Samu's two children attain adult status.

Adjustment of kin relationships to Bulisivo's marriage within moiety has been easier. Chiefs are not expected to feel kin attitudes toward commoners. Bulisivo's sisters and other members of the royal family grudgingly recognize Viniyana's kin status as Bulisivo's wife. Though Viniyana's relations with commoners are confused, she is secure in the chief's household. Since this marriage has brought no issue, its present complications will die with this generation.

The gift exchanges which occur at times of marriage, betrothal, birth, and death are organized on a basis of kinship. In theory two groups of brothers and sisters participate competitively in an exchange occasioned by the marriage of individuals from both groups. Most informants deny that moiety functions at all in these exchanges. They consider that individual ties through a woman, either sister or wife, must activate these affinal obligations. They point out other considerations also; participation in exchanges is conditioned by village affiliations and by ties to land divisions within the village (Votua, Nadroro, Tavua, and Rokowaqa). In addition, leaders in these exchanges must be persons with secure status in the kinship structure, so that large numbers of persons will be involved.

The truths which informants are stressing in these statements is that affinal exchanges are not moiety-wide. Nevertheless, each exchanging group should be wholly composed of the same moiety. Marriage within moiety therefore creates complications. Bici described one of the possible gift exchanges which could follow upon his own funeral, the gift of "living *yabo*." Upon the death of any adult his spouse—or "small spouses"— may present the brothers of the deceased with such a gift. The brothers and sisters of the deceased must reciprocate. If Nabadua's younger sister-wife Kelera should choose to honor the funeral

---

55. It is said that every village holds a woman who sleeps with everyone. Radebu is said to be this woman at Nakoroka (see above, p. 265).

of Nabadua's "small brother" Bici with the gift of "living *yabo*," her status as Nabadua's wife and Bici's "small wife" would permit her to do so despite the fact that all three are of moiety U. Kelera would collect food and a whale tooth from her brothers in moiety U with whom she has genealogical ties: Monasa and Matua. Under no circumstances could Nabadua assist in the gathering of property for this gift. But, in consequence of her marriage within moiety, Bici's brothers[56] are all of her own moiety—moiety U—and hence Kelera could not present gifts to any one of them. But she could seek out someone in opposite moiety C with whom Bici has genealogical ties through his mother; Bici's kinsmen through his father are related too closely to Kelera herself. The choice would proably fall on Naicadra, whom Bici calls "cross-cousin" and whose relationship to Kelera is very distant. Naicadra would collect gifts among his brothers in moiety C and present return gifts to Kelera and her brothers.

Unfortunately, in the accumulation of her "living *yabo*," Kelera would have to ignore Nabadua completely because he is her husband; in presenting the gift to her affinals, she would have to ignore him because he is her "brother." But, as Bici's eldest brother, Nabadua should play the principal role in acceptance and reciprocation of the gifts. To include him, Bici's wife Ana would have to collect gifts from among her brothers in moiety C and present them to Nabadua, Monasa, and Matua, ignoring Kelera. Though Bici's father is of moiety C, aged fathers are usually included in the group which their sons and small sons compose; if he were residing in the house of Nabadua, as he does intermittently, he would receive Ana's "living *yabo*" with the brothers of moiety U, to whom he is "small father." If Bici's son, who is of moiety C, were old enough to be of any help, he would work with his mother and her brothers.

Thus when Kelera wants to participate in a simple exchange between affinals, the exchange relations are doubly complex because of her improper marriage. Instead of presenting to the deceased's brothers, she must seek out a relative of his mother's in the opposite moiety. Actually she would never dare contemplate honoring Bici with a "living *yabo*." She would be ashamed to display her irregular status so conspicuously. There are many other ways to honor a corpse. More usual exchanges are arranged on a basis of land divisions, in which Kelera's status is secure. No actual case in which the "living *yabo*" was

---

56. E.g., Bici's brother Monasa avoids "small spouse" relationship with Kelera.

given is known to have occurred at Nakoroka. Other kinds of funeral gifts have always been more popular.[57]

PARENTS AND CHILDREN

Tama-na, "father," includes all father's brothers, and these are all men of the first ascending generation of the opposite moiety. *Tina-na*, "mother," includes not only mother's sisters but father's sisters as well, hence all women of the first ascending generation. *Luve-na*, "child," is the reciprocal for both these terms; when a man speaks, it means "children of my[58] brothers," or "persons of the first descending generation of the opposite moiety"; when a woman speaks, it means "children of my brothers and sisters" or "the first descending generation."

In contrast with sibling terms, "father" and "mother" are habitually used in address.[59] In abbreviated form—'*a* or *ta* for father, *na* for mother—they are the earliest terms which a child learns to use. Small children are inclined to classify all familiar adults as *ta* and *na* until the age of four or five, when they learn to distinguish *bu* or *bu-qu*.[60] Besides the usual method of distinguishing "classificatory" from "real" relatives by adding the qualifying "small," real parents only are addressed with kin term alone. In the case of "small parents," the kin term is used as an honorary title preceding their personal names. Samu's five-year-old daughter calls Vatili "*Ta*-Tili."[61]

Attitude toward "parents" in the widest extension of its meaning is one of respect. Children listen to the words of parents and run errands for them endlessly. To call the name of a "parent" without first speaking the title *ta* or *na* is impolite. At eleven or twelve intelligent children begin to know who of the smaller children will submit to their discipline and call them "parent."

In contrast with the shame-engendered respect toward a "small spouse," ancestral pleasure sanctions filial respect. Respect attains its

57. Funeral exchanges are discussed in detail is chap. ix.

58. Possessive suffix for the first person in -*qu* instead of -*na*.

59. Terms for brother and sister are rarely if ever used in address. "Cross-cousin" (*tavale*) may be used, though it is not habitual; it occurs vocatively in the folk tales.

60. *Tubu-na*, "mother's brother, grandparent." It will be difficult for the daughter of Samu to learn to make this distinction. Samu married within his moiety. At five his daughter still classes all men of her father's generation as "father."

61. Small children pronounce the *t*, in contrast with adults. This phonetic innovation at Nakoroka arises from the influence of the older children who attend the district school at Lekutu, where *t* is spoken.

greatest intensity toward real father.[62] Bici married Ana against the wishes of her father. Four children were born to them, but Ana's ancestors were angered at her filial disrespect and killed her children. Then Bici and Ana prepared gifts, traveled to her father's village, and humbled themselves ritually before him. When in 1930 their next child was born, he lived.[63] Akuila never repented before his father's anger; though five children were born to his wife, all died, and today he is old and has no children.

In property obligations and disciplinary attitudes parent-child relationship is similar to that of older and younger sibling. A father disciplines his daughter's morals as a brother supervises his sister's. A true father may feel too fond of his daughters to exact strict discipline. In the absence of brothers, a "small father" may whip an erring girl to preserve the dignity of the household. When Ivamere, of whose virginity the village was proud, met Bari secretly in her mosquito net and made a scandal, it was her "small father" Samu, then resident in her household, who whipped her. Shamed, she ran away to her mother's relatives in the Dreketi region for several months. Ivamere's true father Raitova had a ridiculously soft heart. His undisciplined daughters were always leaving his household, and he and his brothers had to do their own kitchen chores.

Peni treated his "small daughter" Meremanini like a sister. Sometimes in hasty speech he classed her with his sisters. When he wanted a fresh fern mattress laid upon his bed, he asked her to perform the task for him. Sometimes she washed his clothes. It was she who cleaned the weeds from his yam garden. Her garden lies next to his in Nadroro land. Like his sisters, she possesses herself of his new calico from the Chinese store. She rarely visits about in neighboring villages with her sisters, because Peni approves of virtue and industry in a young girl.

As long as a father is still an active producer of garden food, his property obligations toward sons are like those of an older brother toward younger brothers. Until age has brought him the honored status of an old man, it is disgraceful for him to be dependent upon his children

62. As in the case of siblings, "real" means "of long traditional standing" and not necessarily "biologic."

63. It is also well known that Ana's milk is poisonous. When their only surviving child was born, they followed Bulisivo's advice and gave the infant to another woman to nurse. Yet the causes of events are multiple, and Ana's lack of health does not preclude the anger of the ancestors.

for food. But this attitude does not extend to casual taking of food; when it is convenient to take food from the garden of a parent or a child, the true owner need not be consulted. He can be told at some future time so that the disappearance of food will be accounted for.

In contrast with the sibling group, those of the first ascending or first descending generations who share a familiar attitude toward each other are not necessarily of the same moiety. Fathers are not of the same moiety as their children. Father's sisters, who are called "mother," are also of the opposite moiety. The moiety-wide extension of brother-sister terms is understandable because of the sexual taboo that goes with them; but such wide extension of parent and child terms is meaningless because these require no obligations and set no comparable limit upon behavior. Aside from the mild respect which, regardless of relationship, one offers seniors, "parent" has meaning only in application to those toward whom one's real parents have developed strong sibling attitudes. Peni had a "small father" in the village of Nakalou on the Macuata coast who had shared in the sexual adventures of Peni's real father at Nakoroka. On the rare occasions when Peni went to Nakalou, he felt secure in his claim of kinship with this "small father." Yet he did not extend his claim to include this man's "small brothers" at Nakalou.

"Small mothers" do not act as go-betweens in the sexual adventures of their sons, but in other respects they are like older sisters. When a young man or woman marries and establishes a household, mothers and older sisters make mats and help furnish the interior.

Love for real parents makes a local proverb of the biblical Fourth Commandment, which most Fijians know. Peni does not like to wander far from Nakoroka because he always remembers his aging father Vaula. Because of his unusually great affection for Vaula, Peni was most active of all the young people at Nakoroka on that day when children honor their parents with a feast.[64]

Though the feast was not scheduled until May 10, which was Sunday, on May 6 Peni had already planned the tasks of all the young

64. On the first Sunday in April parents made small feasts for their children. Isacodro made *madrai*. Big Melika made *madrai* and served it with coconut cream. Bulisivo's and Bici's households boiled chickens. The Nadroro group postponed their feast until the second Sunday. Vatili brought food from the Chinese store, and Naicadra killed a domestic pig. On this day children like to give return gifts to their parents—a mat or a shilling. A feast to honor parents is scheduled on an early Sunday in May. Both these feasts were introduced by the church. Though the latter is Mother's Day to British Wesleyans, it includes both parents at Nakoroka.

people of Nadroro. The feast would be served in Naicadra's house because it was the largest of Nadroro's three houses. Peni was worried for fear the burden of feast preparation would fall entirely upon his own shoulders. His older brother Narogo was notoriously lazy and could not be depended upon for any unsupervised task. Orisi, the only other adult male among so many Nadroro children, had taken his wife to Dreketi to prepare a feast for her parents. The children of Vatili were willing but too young. Meremanini, the daughter of Naicadra, was not lazy, but she was a woman, and women do not understand the preparation of large feasts. But Little Melika, daughter of Toviya, could persuade the Chinese trader to contribute flour and other European delicacies from his store; she had been his mistress.[65]

Despite the large number of wild pigs which had glutted the village appetite for pork during the past week, Peni planned to kill his only domestic pig as "garnish" for the feast. When I reminded Peni that wild pig was rotting in the kitchen of every household, he said: "When I was very small my mother died. If my father Vaula had not loved and cared for me, what would have become of me?" When I laughed because Peni is healthiest and strongest of Nakoroka's young men, he looked hurt and said: "Isn't a pig a small thing to give in return for all that Vaula has done for me?" To Narogo, Peni said: "Let my gardens be emptied of their taro."

The day before the feast Peni sent Vatili's son to bring food from Little Melika's Chinese trader, Narogo to bring food from the gardens. Peni prepared wood for the ovens, while Meremanini scraped yams and taro in preparation for their baking. The feast was ready at noon. Vatili, Naicadra, Vaula, and Toviya, and the very small children were served at the first sitting. Vatili's aged mother, Daova, was not strong enough to come; feast food for her was carried to where she lay in Vatili's house. First there was a large pot of pig boiled with onions.[66] Its broth, served separately in coconut shell cups, was heavy with beef tallow purchased from the Chinese. Roast pig, baked yams, and taro on platters and banana leaves lay steaming from the oven. Before the

65. Though Toviya and his daughter usually acted with the Votua group, they would consider themselves of Nadroro for this occasion. The birth of Ratu Luke's twins in December had crowded Toviya in his house, and he had moved into Naicadra's large house next door. Ratu Luke had no house of his own.

66. No onions are grown at Nakoroka. These were purchased from the Chinese trader. Peni, who had been in my employ for several months, spent tremendous sums on European delicacies for this feast. It is probable that no such display of European foods had ever before been seen at Nakoroka.

first course was complete, Peni brought a great pot of pork boiled in broth which was thickened with flour; then, third, a large pot of eels, prawns, and chicken boiled together; then, fourth, a small pot of boiled beef. When each person had eaten from each pot, Peni sliced three loaves of bread and apportioned it among those who were eating. There was tea with lots of sugar and a tin of milk.

The girls served food and cleared away the dishes. When the older men had eaten, Peni ate with the other children of Nadroro. Naicadra's wife ate too. Though she was a parent, her status as woman would not permit her to eat until the men had finished. Hardly had the food mats been cleared when Peni set cheerfully about preparing "pancakes"[67] so that the feast could be continued in the evening. Of the other intravillage divisions, only Votua[68] parents were feasted. Nabadua, whose gardens were empty, had taken his family to the house of an older "small brother" in a neighboring village. Bici was ill, so Tavua held no feast. But the feast which Ratu Luke and the girls of Votua prepared for the elders of Votua was niggardly in comparison with Peni's lavish display. When the people of Votua came afterward to drink tea and eat the jam-sweetened pancakes left over from the Nadroro feast, Peni was triumphant.

The affection of real children toward parents is fully reciprocated. Fathers especially spend their leisure playing with their infant children. Mothers have less leisure about the household. As children grow older, parents frequently take them as companions and errand boys on planting and hunting expeditions. In large households the attention of brothers and sisters dilutes that of parents. But in small households, like Bici's, a parent may be the child's constant companion and mentor.

Vaula rarely came to my household until Peni entered my employ. Then he used to come often and sit silently for long intervals while Peni puttered about the kitchen.

Vatili treats the daughter of Samu as though she were his own. She will not go to sleep unless she is lying in his arms. Since Samu has been widowed, she has become a part of Vatili's household. During Vatili's quarrel with his wife,[69] his cause for greatest sorrow was that now this

67. Pancakes are lumps of sweetened dough fried in large quantities of fat. The European word has been borrowed.

68. Raitova of Rokowaqa and his household collaborated with Votua.

69. See above, p. 263.

"small daughter" could no longer share his household; his wife, who was Samu's sister, took the child when they separated.

Though parent-child attitudes are charged with affection and respect, the restraint which characterizes the relations of cross-cousins is lacking. In time of war a man could kill his "small fathers" or his "small sons" as though they were brothers. In theory, a man is free to hate his "small father" or "small son."

Tubu-na refers specifically to mother's brother and grandparents. Its reciprocal is *vuo-na*, sister's child and grandchild. More frequently than in any other relationship this one is expressed in its reciprocal form as *tau-tubu-na* or *tau-vuo-na*. Between the two terms there is little distinction in meaning. Because of matrilineal descent these terms, when used by men toward ascending and descending generations, designate those of the speaker's own moiety (as opposed to "father" and "child," which, for man speaking, designate those of opposite moiety). Though the privileges of the sister's son of Tonga and Fiji are notorious, at Nakoroka there is theoretically no difference between the privileges of sister's child and grandchild. Yet the significance of *vuo-na*[70] is primarily "sister's descendants," and the terms can be used as synonyms for "those of one's own blood," "true heirs," or *kawa*, which specifies sisters' descendants in own moiety.

The *vuo-na* privilege is similar in many respects to that of *vasu*. Functionally these two relationships overlap. Those who have *vasu* privileges toward a man's property probably call him *tubu-na*. But these two terms are distinct. *Vasu* is right of ownership in the land of one's true mother. *Vuo-na* is a privileged relationship toward men of the first ascending generation of one's moiety and toward all persons of more remote, ascending generations. Conspicuous *vasu* rights appear only in the case of chiefs. Ratu Seru is *vasu* to Nakoroka land, but it is his position as *vuo-na* to Bulisivo, ruling chief at Nakoroka, which places all of Bulisivo's chiefly rights at his disposal. Women, pigs, garden products, and even Bulisivo's personal belongings are theoretically his if he wants them. He is Bulisivo's sister's son. Through Bulisivo,[71] in the female line, he has inherited *vasu* rights to land on the Wainunu coast, the land of Bulisivo's mother; there he is *vuo-na*, "grandchild,"

70. There may be etymological connection between *vuo-na* and the word for "fruit of the tree," *vuo-na*, and "bearing fruit," *vua*.

71. Through his own mother as well, Ratu Seru has inherited rights in Wainunu land. But Bulisivo's sex lifts his status as chief far above that of his sisters; hence Ratu Seru's claims on Wainunu are usually spoken of as derived from Bulisivo.

to the chiefly brothers of Bulisivo's mother. In theory his privileges are equivalent in both places, at Wainunu and at Nakoroka. The *vasu* right of Big Di Merelita, who is *vuo-na* to Bulisivo through another sister, is identical with that of Ratu Seru. But, because she is a woman, it is unlikely that she will ever behave in a strong manner. She receives great respect as a chieftainess. But *vasu* rights need not 'coincide with *vuo-na* relationship. Peni calls the children of Yani *vuo-na*, but they are *vasu* to the land of Yani's mother at Lekutu. They have weaker *vasu* claims upon the land of Yani's father in the Votua division of Nakoroka.[72] Peni also has *vasu* claim upon this division of Votua land, but he has not utilized it extensively. Though he intends soon to strengthen his status in Votua and dissolve his bonds with Nadroro, at present most of his resources are in Nadroro land, and he is spoken of as a member of Nadroro; only after Peni has developed his Votua resources, can Yani's children be described as having claims upon his land.[73]

Since Yani is Peni's "special" sister, his attitude toward her children is highly charged with affection. The three-year-old Veitiniya likes to ride upon his shoulders. During the day, whenever leisure permits him, he seeks her out to accompany him on a casual visit to the house of a friend. Whenever he receives bits of choice foods, he remembers her. Frequently she sits between his knees to eat his portion of sweet pudding. These attentions are due only in part to her *vuo-na* relationship with him. All small children enjoy attention and affection from adults. Bici's son also sits between his father's knees to receive instruction in appreciating delicate foods. An older sister or brother may choose a child for a special pet. But from the child's viewpoint the *vuo-na* relationship makes for ideal companionship because it prohibits all disciplinary measures. Peni cannot even scold the children of Yani.

The grandparents of five-year-old Di Sereima[74] have chosen her for a pet. She rides upon the shoulders of her great-aunts, to whom she is *vuo-na*, more frequently than upon those of her mother, who is busy

72. *Vasu* rights include all maternal claims. Hence Yani's children have claims on the land of mother's father as well as mother's mother. But *vasu* claim upon the land of mother's mother is the stronger, the more purely *vasu*.

73. Peni and Yani have built a strongly affective sibling relationship with each other. But this relationship is largely independent of common claims upon land or of biologic ties. Nevertheless, Yani's children are Peni's beloved and privileged *vuo-na*. The lack of coincidence between *vuo-na* and *vasu* in this instance may depend in part upon the atypical kin basis upon which Peni has built his sibling relationship with Yani (see above, pp. 258–59 and 276–77). Yet the fact that this lack of coincidence is in no way considered abnormal is proof of the independence of the concepts, *vasu* and *vuo-na*.

74. Granddaughter of Bulisivo.

with women's tasks in Bulisivo's household. Vosalevu also calls her *vuo-na* because he is of her grandparents' generation in the chiefly family. He likes to feed her and always laughs at her humor.

As sisters freely use their brothers' tobacco or new calico, *vuo-na* also have rights to posssess the personal property of their *tubu-na*. But shyness usually restrains them from abusing this privilege. It is an unusually strong man who will dare to possess himself of the valued article of a *tubu-na*. Several years ago Namo took a new umbrella from the house of his *tubu-na*, Toviya. People are still pleasurably shocked and admire Namo for his audacity. Ratu Seru squanders the chickens and the garden produce of the entire chiefly family, but he is a chief and likes to display his audacity. Once he took a valuable kerosene lantern which belonged to Bulisivo; Bulisivo still remembers the occasion, though it happened five years ago. In contrast with his claims upon younger siblings and children, a man never expects a *vuo-na* to clean his garden or to run errands. But, through wide sibling extensions in the moiety, a *vuo-na* may be included with siblings in co-operative preparation for large ceremonial enterprises.

Bici and Toviya are *tau-vuo-na*. But their attitude toward each other's property is reciprocal and mutually possessive. Toviya and Bici's father are joking cross-cousins of long standing, and Bici has now come to fill his father's place in this relationship with Toviya. Noisily they demand tobacco of each other and worry lest their entire supply be confiscated; furtively Bici draws a small piece from the empty baking-powder tin in which he caches his smoking materials and pretends that he possesses no more. Yet neither would dare to take from the other without asking; though they are of the same moiety, they resemble cross-cousins in this respect.

Though less "heavy," in Fijian terms, than cross-cousinhood, violence is prohibited between *tau-vuo-na*. Love is obligatory. In a legend there is one instance in which a *vuo-na* threatened his *tubu-na* with violence; but the chief who made this threat risked ancestral wrath with a courage to which no man at Nakoroka would lay claim.

There are those among commoners who claim familial or affinal relationships with members of the chiefly house, but such claims are rare. Rarer still is the admission of such relationship by the chiefs themselves. Though Bulisivo refuses to classify commoners with a relationship term, most chiefs group all commoners together as *tubu-na*. Vosalevu, however, whose status as chief is held in question at Nakoroka, is willing to classify all but the lowly family of Bici according to the same kinship rules that commoners use. Even the commoners who claim special and varied relationships to chiefs admit that, regardless of other possible relationship, all chiefs are *vuo-na* because of their chiefly blood. Some commoners apply *tubu-na* and *vuo-na* indiscriminately to chiefs; Namo says that you call an older chief *tubu-na*, a younger one *vuo-na*. But the older men say that *vuo-na* is the proper term for chiefs because it implies privileges. Yet *tubu-na* is frequently spoken in awed whispers to mean collectively "all ancestors"; in this use it implies the great love and respect which one feels for chiefs.

If *tubu-na* were extended to coincide with moiety structure, it should mean "all men of own moiety of the first ascending generation and all persons of either moiety of second ascending and all preceding generations"; in like manner *vuo-na* should mean "all persons of own moiety in first descending generation (man speaking) and all persons of either moiety of second descending and all subsequent generations (man or woman speaking.)" But in these wide extensions the terms lose their force. The *vuo-na* and *tubu-na* relationships which require respect and affection stem from established brother-sister or parent-child relationships. When the terms express the bond between chief and commoner, they need not agree with moiety division. Sometimes *tubu-na* can be used without reference to moiety to mean "distant relative of unknown category."

"TAUVU"

Like classifications of kin, *tauvu* ("ancestors together") relationship imposes certain traditional modes of behavior into which an individual is born. In theory those who are *tauvu* to each other are descendent from original ancestors who were true brother and sister. Many obscene folk stories explain the *tauvu* relationship between various villages of Vanua Levu. With miraculous sexual prowess some legendary ancestor woos an ancestress of another region; during sexual intercourse he transports her to the region of her descendants, while her brothers and her brothers' children remain at home. The rat ancestor of Rokowaqa, a land division at Nakoroka, married a woman of the island of Gau and joined her household there. The people of Rokowaqa, who are descendants of the sisters who remained at home, are *tauvu* to his descendants.

But, in contrast with the bonds of kinship, it is inherited claim to land that determines the regions to which one is *tauvu*. *Tauvu* concerns lands and their earth. Bonds between these lands affect all those who till the soil. The land of eastern Macuata is *tauvu* with that of Bua Province. When Peni and I traveled to the Udu region of Macuata, our dialect betrayed that we had come from inland Bua. We were greeted jovially with insults about the poverty of our soil and our constant diet of the taro for which Nakoroka is famous.

Nadroro is *tauvu* toward a division of the land of Bua Kingdom. Several years ago a group of the Nadroro people traveled to Bua on one of the formal visits which their *tauvu*-ship permits them. They cleaned the village paths with the careless inefficiency that characterizes work both for affinals and for those who are *tauvu*. When work on the paths was complete, they received guavas and mammy apples[75] as feast and a dog roast as garnish for it.

Once a group of *tauvu* people came to Nadroro to build yam gardens in accordance with the request of a Nadroro chief now dead.[76] As *unudoka* feast, which according to the rules of the land must be presented before the first digging-stick bruises the ground, Peni and his agemates presented their guests with hot stones and coconut meat from which the juice had been wrung. Such coconut is food only for pigs.

This same group of Nadroro's *tauvu* reside today at Nacula. It is said that long ago their ancestors resided at the village of the first chief of Inland Forest. For some unknown reason they left the parent-village and wandered to the Wainunu coast, to the village called Two-Coconuts. During the time of the wars they were taken in bondage to Bua Kingdom. When the Bua chief Ra Masima freed them from their bonds, they took up residence at Nacula not far from the most ancient village site in Inland Forest Kingdom, where they already had claims to the land. Vatili's mother is of this group.[77]

Through his affiliation with this group at Nacula, Vatili retains a *tauvu* attitude toward Peni. Only for the purpose of enjoying the *tauvu* relationship is Vatili a native of Nacula. He uses a *tauvu*'s right to squander Peni's property despite the fact that Peni is his *vuo-na*. He distributes Peni's tobacco freely among his friends or the guests in his household. During the period of Peni's employment in my household, Vatili often found uses for Peni's wages. Peni's private plans can never be effected if Vatili hears of them. Their kin relationship (*tau-vuo-na*) prohibits anger or violence. Peni cannot even express his displeasure.

75. Pawpaw or papaya.

76. The father of Vilomena, who died within the last decade.

77. See above, pp. 45–48, in which the captivity of the people of Two-Coconuts is recounted. The land claim which the people of Two-Coconuts had upon Nacula stemmed from a gift exchange which buried the blood of warfare between the two regions.

His inferior age and status[78] and his meek disposition preclude his following the one possible path of retaliation: his *tauvu* relationship toward Vatili is completely reciprocal in concept, and in theory Peni could joke boisterously about Vatili's house; but it is only on feast days, or days of rare happiness, that he feels equal to Vatili in all respects. He prefers to avoid Vatili's companionship whenever possible.

"VANUA-VATA"

Relationship between regions, *vanua-vata* ("land together"), highly resembles *tauvu*. It is the result of frequent intermarriage or descent from a brother and sister. But, distinct from *tauvu*, the brother and sister forebears from whom the relationship derives postdate legendary times. It is said that people who are "land together" are "true kinsmen." Joking, playful insults, and taking possession of personal luxuries characterize this relationship between individuals. Between groups it stimulates competition in ceremonial exchanges. Nakoroka and Nacula are "land together." When a group from one of these villages visits the other, the etiquette for entertaining guests is observed meticulously. Conversation is especially polished. Vatili jovially pretends high rank when he drinks kava with a man of Sarowaqa with whom he is "land together."

The joking attitude between individuals in these categories suggests that of cross-cousins. But affection between them is not so strictly prescribed. Violence is not articulately prohibited. The groups concerned are not organized according to moiety affiliation. In general, these land relationships include large numbers of persons outside the limits of well-established kin.

"VUGO"

Those of the opposite moiety who are related only along the path of marriage are grouped together as *vugo*. It includes those brothers- and sisters-in-law who are classed as "small spouses," and the entire *vugo* group are treated with taboo and respect similar to that necessary toward "small spouse." One is *vugo* also with one's parents-in-law, children-in-law, and the spouses of *tubu-na* and *vuo-na* in first ascending or descending generation. The reciprocal relationship is called *tau-vugo-na*. Those of same sex and opposite moiety observe respect and demonstrative affection like that between cross-cousins of the same sex. As in

---

78. Though both are of equally common birth, Vatili's frequent terms as "village chief" make him an important figure in councils of the village elders. He speaks well in the church. Despite his relative youth, he is considered the "elder" in his household, of which Peni has frequently been an unimportant member.

the case of "small spouse," it is usual to circumvent the taboo whenever possible; but only firmly established kin relationship can super-
sede the taboo between affinals of opposite sex and opposite moiety.
The establishment and removal of the taboo is identical with that of
"small spouse."

Parent-child or *tau-tubu-na* relationships always preclude the observance of taboo toward affinals of either sex in the same moiety. The
parents of Bici's wife may both be described as *vugo* to him. But his
father-in-law, like the fathers-in-law of all males who have not married
within the moiety, is of his own moiety. In consequence Bici calls him
tubu-na and treats him as such. It would be improper to define *tubu-na*
as "father-in-law." Rather, in all proper marriages within the circle of
extended kinship the father of the spouse of either man or woman is
already *tubu-na*.[79] The nearest exception to the rule which proscribes
taboo relationships within the moiety is that of Ratu Luke and his
father-in-law. The respect between them is too intense for pleasurable
companionship. Though they speak politely together and on occasion
meet at the halfway point along the Sarowaqa path to trade garden
products and sea food,[80] Ratu Luke does not care to participate in a
casual gathering of which his father-in-law is a member. No established kinship binds Ratu Luke's family with that of his wife; but in
similar circumstances Bici found a path of relationship by which he
could call his father-in-law *tubu-na*. Ratu Luke's abnormal attitude is
conditioned by two factors: first, he is of chiefly caste, which confuses
his respect attitudes toward commoners,[81] and, second, since he is reputed to neglect the needs of his newly confined wife, the relationship
with his father-in-law requires special politeness.

Bici's affinals lived in the village of Duleniwai until the death of his
father-in-law. Then Bici's mother-in-law came to live with him in his
household at Nakoroka. Though they have eaten at the same mat for
several years, they never speak to each other. She cannot even mention
the name of the bird for which Bici is named. They rarely visit the same
households in the evenings. If they both happen to be spectators at a

79. *Tubu-na* in wide extension exerts little influence on behavior. It is probable that
marriage strengthens such weak *tubu-na* relationships between a man and his children-in-
law.

80. An example of institutionalized trade partnerships between men of the interior and
those of the coast.

81. In theory, a chief with "strong" personality could choose to overlook all taboo relationships. In fact, though he observes them among chiefs, he is not likely to do so among
commoners. But the respect in which commoners always hold chiefs makes an affinal taboo
redundant.

dance to entertain guests, neither will participate in the evening's gaiety. Yet when she is untrammeled by taboo, she likes to accompany dancers with the boisterous clapping in which old women indulge. In their own household they use six-year-old Little Kaiyava to relay messages between them. Since it is forbidden for them to be alone together, Little Kaiyava often acts as chaperone on those days when Bici's painfully failing eyesight confines him to the house.

In the absence of Bici's wife and son, Bici could speak respectfully to his mother-in-law if an emergency arose. But he does not often use this privilege. Even this is denied to his "small brothers," Nabadua and Monasa. These two men are almost old enough to look upon her with sexual interest. Because they are Bici's distant brothers and live in separate households of their own, she has but little familial contact with them to serve as constant reminder of the taboo; hence the taboo, as it affects them, is stated in stricter terms.

A *vugo* taboo seldom is extended to affect distant relatives (more distant than spouses, "small brothers," "small fathers," etc.), and usually some other relationship can be traced which will preclude the taboo. When no such relationship can be traced, the taboo must be observed. If individuals who are potentially taboo to each other lack the personal sensitivity which will lead them to observe it, public opinion within the village will press the obligation upon them. Word of unobserved violation of *vugo* taboo will spread through the countryside as scandal, and the name of the village will suffer. His own village will call him a fool who neglects to respect his *vugo*.

In the households of Namo and Nabadua, where all marriages have occurred within the same moiety, there are no proper *vugo* relationships.

Whenever Bici visits the household of an affinal relative in Duleniwai village, he must work in the gardens there. In April, 1936, when Ratu Luke's father-in-law came with gifts to see Ratu Luke's infant twins, he built four taro ponds for Ratu Luke in Votua land. Ratu Luke has worked for his father-in-law in the gardens at Sarowaqa.[82] Any work for an affinal may be loosely called *tave*, but its specific meaning is work performed by a man for his wife's kinsmen, including those persons toward whom he observes the *vugo* taboo. In own generation it is a work obligation laid on sister's husband for the benefit

82. See also above, pp. 135 and 264, where other examples of work in the gardens of affinals are described. Work is performed with the deliberate carelessness which expresses a joking attitude.

of wife's brother.[83] But no one at Nakoroka considers it one-sided. The man who works for his wife's brother today will be worked for by the husbands of his classificatory sisters tomorrow; the fact that the same individual does not reciprocate is not important in their estimation.

Occasionally affinal work obligations may exist within the moiety and need not coincide with the observance of *vugo* taboo. Toviya is father-in-law of Vaulini, but he calls her *vuo-na* because he and Vaulini's mother invoked their brother-sister relationship when Vaulini's marriage was planned. Yet she and her sisters have weeded the gardens of Toviya at his request. They have also brought fish for his household. It is probable that Toviya's claim upon Vaulini depends upon her true *vugo* relationship with his wife. Like the relationship of women who are cross-cousins, *vugo* relationships between two women implies great affection; it is proper for them to exchange fine foods. Through his wife's claims upon Vaulini, Toviya can balance the privileges which he is obliged to grant her as his sister's child.

Bici says that both affinal work obligations and *vugo* taboo are expressed more intensely on the islands of Tavea and Galoa, which lie off the Lekutu coast. It is said that one cannot board a boat which bears a *vugo* relative even though the boat be crowded to capacity with kinsmen and strangers. Between betrothal and marriage it is customary there for a young man to slave in the household of his father-in-law. To retaliate, the young man's father may press labor claims upon the brothers of his daughter-in-law.

Adoption cannot change a child's moiety classification or his place in the framework of village kinship. It is recognized as a formal institution only in so far as it adds new members to the group who have rights in land. A man or woman who has few children may take a child into his household and rear it as his own. The child may become his heir. But it is the change in land rights which requires an exchange of a whale tooth and a feast between him who adopts and the true parents of the child. Naicadra has adopted, among others, Yani's eldest daughter, who is not Namo's child, as an heir to his land, but the child knows her true blood relatives and classifies them as such. Naicadra calls his adopted daughter "sister's child," the same term which he applies to Yani's other children. Though residence in Naicadra's household will influence her choice of persons with whom to develop warm personal

83. Note that property exchanges, on the contrary, between male in-laws of the same village benefit sisters' husbands (above, p. 264).

relations, her kinship status in the village as a whole will always be "child of Yani."

Di Sereima, whose father is now, five years after her birth, considering a formal admission of her paternity, is said to be adopted by her paternal grandfather's sister Big Di Litiya. Sereima's mother is usually busy in the household of Bulisivo, who is Sereima's grandfather. Big Di Litiya and her husband have assumed the task of supervising the child's play and feeding her fine foods. But this is not true adoption. If the child's mother should die, Big Di Litiya would assume the task of teaching as well and, with it, the mother's privilege of whipping. Sereima classifies Big Di Litiya improperly with the diminutive form of "mother" instead of *tubu-na;* she will correct her error when she grows older, even though Big Di Litiya should assume all parental responsibilities. No question of land affiliation is involved; all are owners of the same land.

The word "adopt," *susuga,* is not clearly definitive at Nakoroka. It means "care for a child." It need not imply a change in the child's property rights. The head of a household which contains orphans or illegitimate children may describe himself as having adopted them. Such adoption is a virtue.

Though illegitimacy is viewed as a constant danger, and the woman who allows herself to bear a child out of wedlock is called a fool, disapproval is not directed toward the child. The child himself need make no special adjustment to find kin of all categories in the village. He does not lack adult attention. The entire village pities him because he has no true father to head his household and increase his claims in the land; they shower special kindnesses upon him. But the child himself may feel secure in the house of a grandparent or a mother's sister's husband. Like the fatherless Di Sereima, he may be the idol of a houseful of adoring adults. Only if he tries to attain some status which is considered out of keeping with his maternal heredity will the village deride him with the charge of illegitimacy. But the exchanges between affinal groups which follow upon marriage are necessary to keep wealth in motion and to please the ancestors; illegitimacy is an evil because it shirks these affinal responsibilities.

There are two kinds of relationships which individuals may establish with those who are not closely bound to them by kinship: trade partnerships and friendships. An individual trade relation, *vei wa,* is usually established by a man of the interior with someone of a coastal village. They meet at a halfway point on the path; he of the interior brings garden products, while he of the coast brings sea food. They vie with each other in displaying their wealth. But the custom has become unpopular in the last few decades because the more sophisticated men of the coast have learned to suppress their pride and enjoy the products of inland gardens without giving gifts in return. Sometimes Ratu Luke meets his father-in-law on the Sarowaqa path to exchange gifts. Though they describe their relationship as *vei wa*, it is rather a continuation of the exchanges which accompanied Ratu Luke's marriage and the birth of his children. Today at Nakoroka no one is partner to a true *vei wa* relationship.

Friendships, however, are especially frequent between acquaintances who can find no tie to kinship upon which to base their relations. The most common word for friendship is a compound of two prefixes meaning "reciprocal." *vei-i-tau*. *Tau-drega*, which means "gummed together," and the English word "company" are also used. Bari of Nasavusavu was called "friend" by all the young men at Nakoroka upon his arrival there. They would come to ask him to bathe with them and accompany them on evening visits about the village. Bari was particularly fond of Samu because of Samu's quiet demeanor and his great size. But after Bari's love affair with Ivamere, which caused public scandal, all except Namo ceased to address him as "my friend." Samu, who is Ivamere's "small father," was especially angry and avoided Bari for several weeks. During this period Namo had taken his family to live with his wife's people at Lekutu so that his sick son Sakiusa might receive medical treatment from the native medical practitioner of Lekutu District. Though he was never absent from Nakoroka for more than a week at a time, he would send frequent notes to Bari in the missionary dialect regretting his long separation and expressing deep sorrow at Bari's unpopularity among the Nakoroka people. Bari saved these affectionate notes. On the rare occasions when they were together they whispered confidences and exchanged sympathies. But their mutual affection did not last. When Ratu Seru returned to spend the Christmas season at Nakoroka, Bari preferred to seek his favor and discard his less useful friendship with Namo. Ratu Seru was Ivamere's "small brother." Namo's feelings were hurt, but the death of his son Sakiusa soon preoccupied his sentiments; quickly Namo began to plan secret trysts with Ivamere. When Bari had proposed marriage to her, and when Samu saw that Ratu Seru was accepting Bari as "friend," Samu prepared kava one evening and sent a small boy with a special invitation for Bari to drink with him. Bari, in his new security as "friend" of Ratu Seru, enjoyed ignoring Samu's invitation.

Friends provide relief from the strain of gaiety and politeness which cross-cousins require. Friends are free also from the property obligations and status distinctions which may cause tension among brothers. Occasionally a cross-cousin, wife, or sweetheart may be called "friend" as an expression of affection. Women also have friendships among themselves.

SUMMARY

Kin classification within the village permits easy fluctuations to accommodate individual choice. Bonds of residence in the same household or membership in the same landowning group qualify existing relationships and intensify their expression. Such intense relationships qualify others which are derived through them. Though almost inarticulate in the culture, moiety structure is fundamental in the classification of kin; it must be waived in case of marriage within the moiety, and this necessity makes ensuing relationships difficult. Within the children's play groups consciousness of moiety appears symptomatically in behavior as first knowledge of kinship in his own generation, but until adolescence they can rarely classify adults of households other than their own. But only within the group activities of young people does classification according to strict moiety principle attain wide extension; potential sexual excitement adds interest to this factor of kinship. Among adults the formal exchanges which occur between large groups of classificatory brothers and sisters, and so coincide with moiety structure, sustain the classification established during premarital youth. Though an adult is constantly aware of the classification of those of his own generation within the village, he often finds difficulty in classifying those of other generations with whom he has not participated in household or landowning group or whose connection with him cannot be traced through well-established relationships within his own generation.

The fear of violence which is always present at Nakoroka takes specific form in prohibitions of violence associated with certain classes of kin. All those to whom one is related along the "path of marriage" must be treated with prescribed attitudes which articulately forbid anger: cross-cousins must be loved and their slightest request honored; all other affinals who are not bound also by a strong familial tie must be respected and avoided as *vugo*. Affinal affection and respect increase in inverse ratio to the strength of bonds by the "path of blood"; hence he who marries among strangers not related to him by blood must respect a larger number of persons as *vugo* and love his affinal cross-cousins with especially strict affection. Yet despite affinal restraints it is unwise to become betrothed to a virgin of a very distant region, because her parents cannot be trusted to keep her chaste; village honor might require war to avenge the cheated bridegroom. Thus between regions which are not already bound together by sharing fertility rites or by ceremonial exchange, the most likely cause for friction is reduced.

Alone among cross-moiety relationships the attitude toward father and father's sister[84] is intimate. The father may whip his child. But the child who answers with violence to such discipline risks ancestral anger.

Within the moiety brothers are free to feel anger. But the "small spouse" taboo precludes fraternal interference in marital arrangements; in theory, after marriage no cause for jealousy can arise within the brother group. Classificatory brothers within the village must observe the strongest "small spouse" taboo. It is almost impossible for a father to compete for his son's wife's affection. His relationship to her is that of mother's brother, *tubu-na*, which imposes a familial attitude in regard to sex.[85]

In both ancestral and public opinion careless observance of the restraints of kinship is less dangerous when it occurs among women than among men; men are not afraid of women's anger.

Within own generation and toward affinals it is shame which buttresses taboo and respect. Between generations it is danger of ancestral wrath that prevents questioning the authority of parent or *tubu-na* and outlaws violence. Filial respect is "a thing of the land"; affinal respect is "a thing of shame."

Though chiefs recognize *tubu-na* relationship with the commoners of their community, the chiefs' circle of kinship extends into distant regions; sibling relationships, affinal obligations, and claims to inheritance in remote lands expand their interests over great areas which are unknown to commoners. Bulisivo considered it ridiculous to imagine that he had any kinsmen at all among the commoners of Nakoroka. Though the *tubu-na–vuo-na* relationship between chief and commoner bears certain similarity to that between two commoners, rather than a bond of kinship it resembles a system of feudal obligation between lord and serf and exists independently of any concept of blood relationship between these two different categories of beings.

---

84. Note that she is called "mother."

85. Though Bici's wife came from a foreign village, her relationship with Bici's father was *tubu-na–vuo-na*.

CHAPTER IX

LIFE-CYCLE

CHILDHOOD[1]

ADULTS never withhold their affection because a child is ill-tempered. Choice foods are thrust upon him. His whims are pampered. All bow to his comfort and convenience. Mothers and aunts (*tina-na*), fathers (*tama-na*), and mother's brothers (*tubu-na*), grandparents (*tubu-na*), and older siblings (*taci-na*), regardless of their sex or age, envelop the small child in an atmosphere of loving attention of which he is center. After the child's birth the mother is freed

1. I am indebted to Marion Quain Kaiser of the Child Guidance Clinic of Spokane, Washington, for adapting some of the principles of American mental testing to the comprehension of Fijian children. Though limitations of time prevented systematic experimentation with mental tests, the procedure itself was valuable in establishing rapport with individual children and in gaining insight into the wide variation of personality among them.

I have not attempted to rate mental ability. But among twenty children tested, there was extreme variation in speed of performance. Some children answered with slow deliberation. Samu's twelve-year-old son responded with such slowness that testing was abandoned when the second hour had elapsed. Children of Nabadua and Namo were quick and accurate. The son of Monasa's "small brother" Matua answered quickly, but his statements were redundant and contradictory; adult spectators laughed at his stupidity while they sympathized with the slow deliberation of Samu's son.

It is worthy of note also that a four-year-old girl performed commissions comparable to an American test of the fifth year. All children performed commissions with ease. Though all were below the American standard in their ability to repeat a series of numbers, all excelled the American standard in their ability to repeat phrases of many syllables. Inferior handling of numbers is understandable because arithmetic plays little part at Nakoroka. Furthermore, the Fijian words for all digits contain two syllables. Superiority in ability to repeat phrases is also conditioned by linguistic habit: two consonants (except for nasalizations) never occur together; the language is peppered with vowels; thus it is probable that a given thought content requires more syllables for expression in Fijian than in English (in testing, each fully stressed vowel was counted as a syllable). Most children rated high in tests of comprehension, but they failed in their ability to define words: the concept of a definition, other than *use*, was almost impossible to convey even to twelve-year-olds. Ten- to twelve-year-olds, however, readily stated the conditions which gave rise to emotions when they were asked to define the terms for these emotions (anger, fear, affection, etc.).

I am also indebted to the co-operation of the young chief Ratu Dali, who was schoolmaster at the Lekutu District School, and who not only permitted me to use the buildings of his school but assisted personally in administering the tests.

from household tasks so that she can devote her time exclusively to the nursing infant. Even when he has grown to a sturdy infancy of nine months and bathes daily in the cold water of the river, his mother interrupts her evening conversation to nurse him for a while and quiet his crying. On Sundays she takes him to church, and, though others are absorbed in prayer and shame in the presence of supernatural powers, she nurses him calmly whenever he makes his discomfort known. When he is old enough to eat yams and taro and drink the juice of oranges[2] and coconuts, the child weans itself rather than being weaned.[3] He is perhaps one year old. As he grows older and learns to run about the village and play with other children, newer infants divert some of the kindly attention which he has enjoyed throughout the village. But when six-year-old Kaiyava tripped sprawling on the soft grass of the village green and bawled out of all proportion to his hurt, Vaulini and Isacodro, who were the closest spectators of the mishap, came to embrace him and comfort him; they are his classificatory mother and grandfather, but to Kaiyava they were just "adults of the village." Older people preserve their affection for the young. But, as the child grows to maturity, only the adults of his own household, particularly his parents, and perhaps a grandparent in another household, or one with whom his mother has built a strong brother-sister relationship, continue to humor his whims. Though Ratu Seru was a bad son who during his short sojourns in the village wasted the food products which his mother's labor had made to grow luxuriantly, his mother Big Di Litiya dropped her work and hastened across the island to serve him when she heard an ill-founded rumor that he lay sick at the gold mine.

But there are many things which children must be taught. If children fail to learn how to participate in society, parents must bear at least part of the blame. Whipping a child to enforce obedience is a last resort. Vatili said: "It is a bad thing to exact obedience by continual coaxing and threatening; in former times whipping was in higher repute, and as a result today's adult generation knows well how to

2. Infants being fed orange juice may be due to the child welfare propaganda of the medical department of the colonial administration.

3. One male informant said that peppers were tied about the nipples to discourage the child. But no observations substantiate the practice. Women with whom it was discussed considered it cruel. The affection in which infants are held cannot be exaggerated. Thomas Williams speaks of the frequency of infanticide in Bua Kingdom during his residence there. But the women of Nakoroka are sure that a woman would kill her own child only if she were utterly insane (lialia).

work." Bici blamed the undisciplined behavior of Raitova's children upon Raitova's ridiculous kindliness. Raitova could not bear to whip his children. As a result two of his daughters became pregnant in the path and fled the village. Scandal had clouded the name of his third daughter, the industrious Ivamere. His younger children wilfully refused to help him weed his gardens, pouted in the kitchens of other kinsmen in the village, and threatened to desert his household. Raitova was at fault because his soul was weak, and he could not whip them. But Bici's own son was not unlike Raitova's children; though Bici sometimes yelled until he choked to persuade his son to perform some small errand, yet he considered his son most tractable and had never found occasion to apply the whip. But if his son should show some fault, Bici declares he would not hesitate to correct him at all costs. Ivamere sometimes switched the legs of her younger sister in hopes of persuading her to join in household tasks. Once Ivamere switched the legs of Karalai, the happy six-year-old girl of Raitova's household, because she had peeked through the walls of the latrine when someone was inside.[4] The child cried noisily, but Ivamere considered her disciplinary measure justified to blot out such an evil trait of character. Once a woman visitor from distant Bua village struck her two-year-old son for spilling drinking water in the house of her host; but, when he cried, she clasped him warmly in her arms and rocked him for a quarter of an hour until he was comforted. Bici considered her discipline somewhat severe.

Animals, like children, are treated with the same great forbearance. Few men dare to inflict physical pain. When Raitova's pig, which he had fed and watched from infancy to a lush fatness in maturity, was killed for the feast at Christmas time, Raitova came sorrowfully to my household and stopped his ears lest he hear the death blow which some sturdier man would deal. Once Vosalevu asked me to lance a fistula that was afflicting the horse which the chiefly family used on rare occasions to bear copra to the Chinese trader at Lekutu. I chose Vosalevu and Peni as sturdy men to assist with the task. A troop of children, thirsty for the excitement of watching such cool cruelty, followed to the place in the forest where the horse was standing with neck and forelimbs so swollen that it dared not move. I instructed Vosalevu to hold a rope which we had tied about its neck. In the absence of a twitch, I instructed Peni to insert his fingers in the horse's nostrils and

4. Though peeking is reprehensible, eavesdropping is considered an inevitable human weakness, and no one attempts to control it.

twist the nose, and to twist with force just as I raised my knife. There was a moment of tense silence as I prepared to jab quickly and puncture the hide lightly in a likely spot. But Peni screamed and lost his hold. Vosalevu hid his face. The horse jumped, and I plunged the six-inch blade to its hilt in the horse's withers; blood and pus showered among the shouting spectators.[5]

Like children, dogs who help the men in the hunt are fed with kindness and never whipped. When they creep stealthily toward the food mat to snatch a morsel from under the unwary elbow of some eater, a cry is raised against them. Angry blows whiz through the air, but they are carefully measured to miss their mark. The dogs yelp, uninjured, and tripping over their drooping tails find sanctuary in a shadowed corner of the house to whine in privacy. Soon they dare creep forth again slowly with their bellies dragging on the floor. In company with older dogs and through the wordless encouragement of their masters, these spineless animals somehow learn to enjoy the hunt. They attack an angered pig with courage and respond to the huntsman's signals. They perform their special function well. Of course, there are some lazy dogs whose individual bents preclude their learning to be useful; these exist inconspicuously on the periphery of society and receive their share of food.[6]

The maturity of a child's soul can be measured by his capacity to feel shame (*madua*) and fear (*rere*). These two qualities are considered to be fundamental in human character. Children learn a simple kind of fear before shame has grown strong in them. When a child wakes at night to find himself alone in the house, he is afraid; he learns readily to fear solitude in the dark. He learns, too, that there is more security from this fear in his own house than in the open, more safety in the village than in the forest. To keep children at home after nightfall, adults like to encourage fear. If children play outside at night and there is no moon, some adult will surely remind them that souls of the recent dead are stalking through the darkness to snatch them off. Aside from souls of the dead, there are other horrors in the night which belong to no

5. Despite such tender hearts, no one bothered to observe my suggestion that the horse be watched and that water be fetched for it now and then from the near-by stream. For fear that I should decline to perform the surgical task, the fact that the horse had fallen in a bamboo thicket many years before and that the pectoral girdle of its skeleton was entwined with bamboo splinters, had been deliberately concealed from me. The horse recovered from its wound, but the cause of its illness was not removed.

6. Though dogs are malnourished, it is the parasites with which they are infested and the nature of their diet rather than lack of food which brings about their leanness. Their food is largely vegetable. Feeding, though impulsively generous, is irregular.

specific class of being. As maturity increases, fear of darkness becomes less strong. But even grown men shudder in disgust and terror when they meet the soul of a dead friend in the dark. This "blossoming of the body," however, the gooseflesh and the bristling hair which contacts with a dead soul produce, are not regarded as symptoms of fear. Rather they are proof of the presence of a dead soul and proof that one's own soul exists and can react as is proper for an adult soul.

There are two kinds of shame (*madua*): that which prompts concealment of the genitals and that which is fitting before chiefs and strangers or during formal ceremonies of the land when the air is made oppressive by ancestral presences. All mature commoners must by definition know shame in both its forms and understand the conduct which it imposes. As the child's "soul of water" gradually loses its clearness and becomes thick, he learns to hang his head before the noisy admonitions of his elders. He learns embarrassment and how to cower in silence.

At the age of three or four, a child has already become sensitive to the disgust which elders display toward the smell of urine and feces. When an angry parent tells him not to dirty the house, to hasten to the forest at the village margin, through shame he obeys, and the parents rejoice that his soul is maturing. When there are guests, adults shoo him away from contact with them, saying derisively that children do not know how to keep themselves clean, that they smell offensive. It is not until a child is ten or eleven that his shame of personal uncleanliness is considered to have reached an intensity equal to that of adults.[7]

If a child raises his voice when there are guests in the house, if he crawls to the upper part of the house when there are elders present, reaches above someone's head or walks behind his back, the angry shouts of adults will accuse him of not knowing his place (*via via levu*, "want want big"); they will ask him whether he knows no shame.[8] The parents of the ill-behaved child themselves feel shame; and if the child is too young to see virtue in humility, if shame does not secure obedience, parents may warn him that spirits, chiefs, or white men

7. Even small children never offended my nostrils. But Fijian standards of smell are culturally determined. They like the smell of cloth brought freshly from the Chinese store. They put their clothes in my musty suitcase to absorb its odor. They themselves smell like tincture of iodine.

8. There is a perceptible difference in the treatment of commoner children who are heirs to titles and those who are not. Care, who would someday hold Toviya's title, was expected to be more forward than Bici's Kaiyava.

will come and "tie him up." Bici's six-year-old Kaiyava had already learned to flee or crouch in silence upon Bulisivo's approach. He used plural pronouns in addressing the five-year-old noble Di Sereima. But when he included her in the first person pronoun, he used the dual form; he had not yet learned that the inclusive "we" should always be plural when applied to chiefs. Bici said that he would whip Kaiyava should he fail to know his place and show respect to those of chiefly caste; but the occasion had never risen because Kaiyava's soul was mature beyond his years and he knew shame. The foolish Unaisi, who at the age of eight or nine still spoke baby talk, had not yet learned to be ashamed.

There are many ways in which children must learn to play a social role. With patience Bici sat with his hands in the kava bowl about a heap of chopped kava root and waited while six-year-old Kaiyava clumsily dipped water from a bucket and poured it over his father's hands. The house was filled with adults who were waiting to drink the kava which Bici was mixing. But it was amusing to mark the awkwardness of Kaiyava, who was new at this task. His hand shook under his father's continuous stream of instructions, and he spilled the water on the floor. He poured too fast or too slow. And his father's noisy advice, his asides to the adult audience, his laughter, and his ridicule were confusing: "This is a stupid child. He cannot even pour water properly into the kava bowl." The occasion, which was a casual kava bout, allowed Bici to display his wit, a wit more pleasing to himself than to his audience.

Nabadua's daughter, the eight-year-old Narieta, also had a soul which was mature enough to know shame and humility. Once, during casual drinking of kava in Nabadua's kitchen, he instructed her in the etiquette of serving kava. Himself more excitable than Bici, his shouts of advice boomed in explosive fragments, and Narieta was confused and hung her head, refusing to proceed. The coconut shell shook in her hands. The kava spilled on the mat. Her father's shouts redoubled in velocity. He told her to stand and walk with the cup: those who carry kava are absolved from the rule of etiquette which forbids standing while others sit. She persisted in walking clumsily on her knees. And as she sobbed quietly with hanging head in the full gaze of the adults who were waiting to drink, more kava spilled on the mat. Then she was confused and failed to offer the cup to him of highest rank. The cup had to be filled anew before she could present it again. Hesitating for long intervals while Nabadua assured her that she was an idiot, she eventually attained her goal and presented the cup to the proper person. She knelt before him who was to drink, but instead of clapping and speaking the words of the ceremony, she was preoccupied in trying to suppress her sobs. As soon as she dared, she fled to a dark corner of the kitchen where her infant brother was lying, flung herself face down upon the mat, and with one arm drew her brother close so that she could feel the warmth of his body. Nabadua was not satisfied with the lesson, but he knew that there was ample time to school her many times again before she would be called upon to fulfil this task seriously in the presence of a guest from out of town.

There is persistent fear that a child may find the solitude of the forest too comfortable.[9] The fear and shame with which he is possessed when strangers come to the village may grow stronger than propriety requires, and he may flee in panic to the forest, which then to him seems safer than the village. When one shows such symptoms, he is coaxed with kindness to find comfort again among his kinsmen, his body is caressed, and he is urged to enjoy the companionship of other children and to participate more often on social occasions.

Skilled conversation and dancing are valued as social accomplishments, and training begins early. Small children wake frequently at night and watch dances. Sometimes an adult holds an infant in his arms and claps time with the infant's palms between his own. Sometimes when the young women of the village are entertaining guests, Narieta or some other small girl sits at the end of the line of dancers to accustom herself to the gaze of strangers and learn the necessary poise for dancing publicly.

I saw no boys learn dancing this way. Young men dance with more zest than women, but the occasions of their dancing are confined more strictly than that of the women to courting favors of visiting cross-cousins. It is usually girls who dance for elderly guests; though the presence of a child in the line of dancers mars the symmetry of the dance, the girls do not mind because such guests have seen the dance many times before and are already dozing. Young men practice their dances during the evenings when there are no guests; at these times boys may learn.

Exposure to public gaze strengthens the soul. In this way children learn the postures of the dance and with companions of their own age practice them among the sun-warmed boulders on the riverbank.

9. See the account of Monasa's childhood, above, pp. 236–37.

When there is a scarcity of entertainers, nine-year-olds can perform skilfully for guests.

Especially for men it is important to know how to speak in company. Adult men take pride in developing the conversational powers of their sons and nephews. Laboriously Bici explains the puns in current slang to his son so that the son may learn to speak with wit. He also tells stories so that the son may learn their content and build a store of anecdotes of his own.

An adult never performs a task which a child can do as well. Even if it is only to reach for a smoldering tinder to dry tobacco, the adult will ask the child to serve him; if the child is but two or three years old, the adult may repeat his instructions patiently and with kindliness until the child understands and obeys. But if the child's soul has begun to mature, his response may be negative. He may wilfully hesitate or disregard the instructions. Then the adult must shame him into obedience. The child is exhorted with threats and angry shouts, and in extremity an arm is raised as if to strike. It is well for children to learn to listen well to the words of adults and perform small tasks as bidden, lest they grow up to be lazy. They must learn to be ashamed of laziness. Six-year-olds can be trusted to run errands across the village. Ten-year-olds can carry messages alone down the long paths to neighboring villages.

Four-year-olds often accompany the women on their excursions to the bush for firewood or to the gardens. On such occasions there are innumerable petty tasks for children. Some adults and elder children take delight in persuading their juniors to satisfy their whims. But, in the process of serving their elders, children learn much that is useful. They learn the uses of forest products. They learn geography and the location of wild food plants. When a man hunts, he likes the company of a spry eight-year-old, preferably a boy, who can climb a tall coconut tree and get him a cool green nut to quench his thirst and help him carry a burden of wild yams or pork back to the village. Such children are efficient and self-reliant in the forest; there they can wander freely, and there is no cause for shame. When children have attained the age of ten or eleven, they perform a test which marks the completion of their "learning the forest." Girls and boys go together in search of wild yams, and they decide upon a spot in which the new-found yams will be roasted. Then separately each searches until he has found several yams of good size. Without help from anyone, each finds firewood and stones for a private oven. From the wood of the forest he fashions a fire-plow, kindles his firewood, and roasts his yams. Together they await the opening of the ovens; together they raise a sorrowful cry for those whose yams are not properly roasted.[10]

The weeding of dry gardens and the replanting of taro ponds are constant chores. In company with girls and adult women children readily learn these tasks. But it is well known that a child works better if he is unaccompanied by other children; in a group children are foolish. As a companion for a friendly chat, Bici, whose infirm legs prevent him from enjoying the hunt, frequently took his six-year-old Kaiyava to assist in taro-planting. Though Kaiyava wanted above all else to prove worthy of his father's companionship, he was not much real help in the work of planting. But Bici tolerated his clumsy efforts and, despite Kaiyava's chagrin, cheerfully replanted the areas which the son had botched. The son was a most appreciative audience for the father's wit.

Except among chiefly children, muscular co-ordination develops precociously. With the exception of Bici's six-year-old Kaiyava, all six-year-old children could swim swiftly and without fear. During the sunny days of the warmer months small children sport continuously in the water at the village bathing place. They play tag on the steep slippery bank and from towering boulders leap agilely into the swift river. They race in the water with burdens of mud balanced high on their heads. When not employed with chores, older children and adult women join them in their games.[11] Even at flood time, when the water rises ten feet above its normal height and roars between its banks, laughing six-year-olds sail downstream with the current. But Bici's Kaiyava was slow to learn. He feared the chilling water. Despite his crying, Bici used to douse him in the river. With his son on his back, Bici would swim and suddenly duck below the surface so that the son should learn to hold his breath. After several such lessons Kaiyava lost his fear and ventured to the river alone to try his skill. But he dared not join the other children. He bathed during the cooler times of day and played alone. He chose the shallow eddies near the bank and with mock courage leaped into them shouting exultant verses as he plunged.

Children learn to climb tall coconuts, to walk with sure tread on the slippery paths, and to proceed through the tangled forest growth with grace and quickness.

10. The name of these ovens is "the crying-forth together" (*vei tagi cake*).
11. Men bathe only for cleanliness and to cool themselves; swimming is a sport for children only.

CHILDREN OF INLAND FOREST

BOY WITH A CANE OF
CARVED SANDALWOOD

Lacking only the wristlets of fresh leaves, he is
dressed for the modern sitting dance.

Both boys and girls learn to carry burdens at an early age. When the women carry food to men who are building houses in foreign villages, they make special parcels so that children can share the work. Even five-year-old Di Sereima has borne a small basket all the way to Lekutu. Men habitually carry burdens on a carrying-pole, while women sling baskets between their shoulders. Though women also know how to use a carrying-pole, their shoulders never become calloused or padded with the particular muscular overgrowth which shields the clavicles of the men. But small girls and boys carry loads with little discrimination as to method.

The play group at Nakoroka is small and of fluctuating composition. Of the twenty-one children of so-called "native adults" of the village who were not yet old enough to attend the district school at Lekutu,[12] five were infants or toddlers too young to play unchaperoned. Three were children of Orisi, who, with his entire family, resided for long periods in Indian settlements. Two were the children of Isacodro's middle daughter, who lived for long intervals with her kinsmen in Nalauvia. One died after a long illness. Three began to attend school during my residence. Of the remaining seven, two were boys and five were girls. The eldest, Unaisi, the illegitimate and happy moronic daughter of Vilomena, was eight or nine years old. Nabadua's daughter Narieta, who spent many days wandering through the forest with her father, was more than a year younger. Karalai, the illegitimate daughter of Raitova's wilful eldest daughter, was a little younger and frequently accompanied the women of her household on their various excursions. The two boys, Bici's Kaiyava and the sturdy Care, son of the widowed Vaulini and the darling of three households, were both about six. The noble Di Sereima, whose activities were almost always chaperoned by an adult of chiefly caste, was more than a year younger. Samu's shy daughter Taina was so young that she still clung constantly to the adults of Vatili's household, where she lived; when she ventured forth in charge of an older child, even Karalai and Narieta recognized her youth and helped her over the rough boulders of the riverbank. There was little homogeneity in the group. Each child belonged to a separate household to which he could flee and gain the kind attention of adults. Though Kaiyava and Care were of the same age and sex, and though Kaiyava's father was always trying to

12. Six girls and eight boys were of school age, roughly from eight to puberty. Of these, the oldest girl and the two oldest boys showed definite signs of puberty.

stimulate a cherishing cross-cousin attitude between them, they could rarely endure each other's company except as part of a group of children; Care's strength contrasted with Kaiyava's wobbly legs and made Kaiyava sulk.

When these children ran naked through the village in the rain, played tag in the river, or built miniature irrigation dams and ditches for imaginary taro ponds on the riverbank, each was conscious of his place in the scale of relative seniority. Before eight-year-old Sayasi of Isacodro's household began to attend the district school, he blustered among the village children and directed their activities. But when an older child came home from school for a week end, Sayasi's authority dissolved, and he would squall as readily as the younger children. He listened to the words of older boys and obeyed their instructions in the same way that he expected younger children to honor his senior status. After Sayasi left the village, the foolish Unaisi sometimes tried to assert her authority; though she found the two small boys intractable, sometimes she would slap Karalai, who was her junior by perhaps two years, and accuse her of not knowing her place; Karalai never slapped back, but she paid little heed to Unaisi's discipline.

During the Christmas interval, when the school children were home in the village, some twelve-year-olds caught some eight-year-olds smoking tobacco. An older brother slapped a small boy so that he cried. Then the older brother dragged him to their house. In shocked tones Namo's eleven-year-old Luisa told the foolish Unaisa, who was also guilty of smoking, that "it looked bad." To shame the small children, Nabadua's almost pubertal daughter said: "These are indeed old people; see how they smoke."

Once the eleven-year-old Sakaru, home from school, forcibly possessed himself of a coconut shell with which six-year-old Care had been amusing himself. Care cried. Sakaru laughed at first until he saw that Care's cries were growing louder. Then he returned the shell. But Care cried for a long time afterward. Had Sakaru persisted, Care would have sought the company of adults, with whom he could feel secure. Though older children may enjoy tormenting a sturdy six-year-old, even very small children cherish an infant and treat him with kindness. Once Yani was bathing her two youngest children, her three-year-old daughter and her infant son; the daughter capered in the shallows of the cold river, but now and then she came to sprinkle cold water upon her brother and make him laugh. She sprinkled him gently and with slow deliberation; she took great pleasure in his enjoyment.

Children of chiefly caste grow much faster than commoners. Choice foods and a quiet chaperoned existence are congenial to a rapid attainment of full stature. The noble Di Sereima, who is perhaps two years younger, was taller than the graceful Karalai. Bulisivo's grandson, the ten-year-old Ratu Kelemedi, was as tall as boys who were already showing signs of puberty. Both chiefs and commoners say that early growth is a constant characteristic among chiefs. But these chiefly children seem ungainly and awkward in contrast with the well-knit commoners of the same height. With them the period of infancy is prolonged. Long after the age when common children have become self-reliant wanderers in the village and the near-by bush, chiefly children are still riding the backs of kindly adults. Once with other small children Di Sereima ran naked through the village in the rain; a few minutes later her mother scurried after her, annoyed that she had become wet. Sometimes Di Sereima played about the houses with Bici's Kaiyava, who preferred her company to that of other more boisterous children. But more often she spent her leisure in the house of Bulisivo or Big Di Litiya amusing an audience of adoring adults with the wry faces which she knew how to make. Lack of adult attention angered her; she would whine and say, "Look at me." Proudly Big Di Litiya says that the children of Nakoroka's chiefly families have always evoked this kind of attention from adults.

Chiefly children need not be taught to keep their place. Their souls need not know the fear of shame. They need not learn the tasks of formal ceremonies; they need not learn how to serve kava because it is they who will always be served. Once with quiet kindly laughter old Bulisivo explained to the five-year-old Di Sereima that her speech was imperfect and that he could not understand her conversation. But he continued to listen attentively. Once both he and Big Di Litiya tried to persuade her to perform an errand to a neighboring household. They spoke persistently but with a pleading tone and were half-amused when she eyed them from many angles and deliberately failed to comprehend. Her failure to learn obedience was no defect in her chiefly character because there would always be commoners to run errands. With more regularity than other children she sat between the knees of some friendly adult when she took her meals. She would finger all the food before she found a morsel to her liking.

Once I presented a group of children with some toys from an American five-and-ten-cent store. They had no conception of how to play with objects; they admired the bright colors for a time, but eventually they either concealed them in their houses as valuable possessions or broke them and cast them aside. At the time of the presentation Di Sereima was among the children with some noblewomen as chaperones. When a verdict had been reached as to which were the most beautiful of the toys, the noblewomen saw that these were all given over into the possession of Di Sereima, who alone was bored by the proceeding. All the children yielded up their toys with good grace, among them Bici's son, to whom I had presented a special gift. But Bici, who sat in the background, was privately angry and at a later time used some argument to persuade a woman of the chief's family to return his son's gift.

At an early age commoners learn that a chiefly child is a special kind of being to whom the ordinary regulations of seniority do not apply. He must always be cherished like an infant, regardless of his age.[13] None would dare to tease him. Once I gave an orange to six-year-old Kaiyava, who was loitering in my household with the noble Di Sereima. He said: "Have you no orange for the noblewoman?" He was embarrassed when I said, "No," until upon his own initiative he found another one for her. When Bulisivo's grandson, the awkward ten-year-old Ratu Kelemedi, swam with other children at the bathing place, they pretended great pleasure in his company and with helping hands encouraged him to scale the slippery riverbank.

More than the other children of commoner caste, Bici's weakling Kaiyava looks to adults for companionship. But, unlike chiefly children, it is he himself who chooses to be so chaperoned.

Kaiyava is the only child in Bici's house; his father and mother are the youngest of other occupants. When the older children are attending the district school, almost every child is an only child in some group of adults. But even when the older children are at home, Kaiyava has but little contact with them. Except perhaps for the noble Di Sereima, Kaiyava is more isolated from young people than any other child in the village. Older children are not attracted to him; they prefer Care's jollity.

On April 3, 1936, several of Isacodro's grandchildren were in the village. With the sturdy Care they played tag on the village green and finally went to bathe together in the river. Kaiyava preferred to play separately with the foolish Unaisi. On April 20 Kaiyava joined Care and the small girls in a hiding game of tag about the village houses.

13. This classing of chiefs with beloved infants is reflected in the usages of kinship nomenclature; it is customary for a commoner to apply the term for beloved "sister's child" or "grandchild" (*vuona*) to all chiefs. See above, chap. viii, "Kinship."

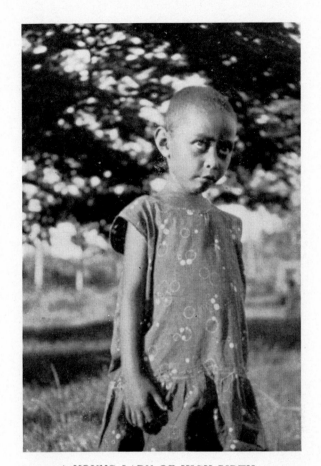

A YOUNG LADY OF HIGH BIRTH

Care was "it," and Kaiyava taunted him gaily. Then sturdy Care rushed upon Kaiyava, pushed him, and ran laughing to hide with the admiring girl children. Left alone on the village green, Kaiyava allowed his lower lip to droop and with his wobbling gait stalked slowly off to the adults of his own household. Later in the day, while the other children were bathing, he waited in company with his maternal grandmother on the path to the gardens so that he could greet his father's return.

On April 3 Kaiyava was licking a tin which had contained sugar. His mother ridiculed his greedy manners. Kaiyava merely opened wide his eyes, which bulge like his mother's, and let his tongue hang out. Bici exchanged glances with the mother, and they tried to repress their smiles. Kaiyava saw that he was amusing his parents, and with his tongue still hanging, began to roll his head from side to side.

But when Kaiyava sulks, Bici is proud because he interprets such display of anger as a symptom of a mature soul.[14] Almost alone among the adults of Nakoroka, Bici conceals his anger with poor grace; even on formal occasions his changes of temper are easily apparent. He is proud that the son is old beyond his years. He encourages Kaiyava's factual learning and hopes that some day the son will find a clerical career in the church or in the colonial administration. This is the easiest course by which a sickly child can gain prestige among good men; strong men at Nakoroka do not choose to be clerics. Thus, though Bici imagines Kaiyava's soul mature and fully conscious of shame, it is Kaiyava's weakness that has taught him to keep his place; in part the weakness has served as a substitute for shame, and Bici rarely finds it necessary to shame his son into observing social regulations. When the father hears the weeping of his son, he listens with concern and sometimes goes to find the cause of the unhappiness.

When boys of commoner caste reach the age of ten or eleven, their activities begin to separate them from the girls. In small groups they hunt pigs or at the bidding of some elder perform tasks concerned with the preparation of feast food. They know men's work in the gardens. For several years they have been errand boys for groups of men engaged in housebuilding. Now, under the instructions of older men, they are able to gather tying vines and thatch in the forest and shoulder them to the site of activity. But a boy likes to attach himself to

14. Ratu Seru bragged of having been dismissed from colonial service because he was always having trouble with women; though strong men apologize for their inability to control their passions, they are proud of the fault.

some young man, a "small father" or an elder brother, and serve him as his special "boy."[15] Thus Peni was well supplied with "boys" who enjoyed the stimulus of his leadership as wholeheartedly as he enjoyed issuing orders among them. The adolescent sons of Vatili and Raitova admired Peni's skill in hunting and his strength in work of all kinds. Alone among them, eleven-year-old Sakaru, who would someday control the chiefly title for Nadroro land, did not obey when Peni commanded. Sakaru already knew to which of the village children he was "small father" and chose to assert his status among them on this score. Before puberty most boys have classed their age-mates of both sexes according to moiety affiliation and have learned the different attitudes expected between siblings and cross-cousins.

An eleven-year-old girl can help effectively about the house. If she is industrious, she can carry water and firewood for her household. Already she has begun to carry three-year-old children about on her back and supervise their baths. Since early childhood she has accompanied young women on their fishing excursions and assisted in weeding gardens. Efficiently she helps to serve the family meals. Soon she will participate as one of the village women in serving food to guests. In contrast with boys of equal age, it is improper for young girls to visit about the village at night.

Segregation between the sexes is not strict. When the village pigs must be penned hurriedly for the visit of some colonial functionary, youngsters of both sexes race gleefully through the village after their squealing quarries. Twelve-year-old boys still like to play tag with the girls in the river. But girls at this age can no longer enjoy a senior status over younger boys. Boys will not listen to their attempts at authority. Even at six years of age the sturdy Care dared the ill-measured slaps of a meddling older girl and hurled his *sulu* at her angrily. Twelve-year-old boys like to tease their older sisters and excite a flow of exasperated comment. When the school children came home for the Christmas holidays, the eight-year-old Sayasi found refuge among the girls from the hazing of the older boys; squatting on the boulders of the riverbank, he used to practice dances with them. In the company of girls or women, boys can relax from the restraints with which consciousness of

15. The term *gone*, which I have translated as "boy" in this instance, really means "young." But it is used to designate all those whose status is servile. Thus Bulisivo spoke of thirty-five-year-old Samu as his "boy"; only a chief would describe a man of full adult status in this way. Toviya, however, who was too venerable to be even Bulisivo's "boy," was described as "one of Bulisivo's people." Regardless of age, those who serve in the kava ceremony are "young men" in contrast with the "chiefs" whom they serve.

status among other boys oppresses them. But if by chance some boy is left alone in the village with only girls and kava-drinking elders as companions, he longs for male company and grows disconsolate in boredom. For several days the adolescent son of Raitova was left in this unhappy condition; though I was a poor substitute for the glamorous Peni, the boy would come to my house and watch me work, regretting constantly that time hung heavy on his hands, that he had nothing to do. During the days he gardened with his old father, but in the evenings he soon tired of playing cards with the girls of his household. There were no young men whose banter with the older girls he could watch. Peni was not there to plot hunting projects for the future and use him as an orderly.

Before puberty, souls are quite mature, and children are already looked upon as distinct personalities whose desires and opinions deserve recognition. Each adult has his private standard of custom and ethics which all others respect, and it is natural that children whose souls are mature should be individually divergent, one from the other. With objective curiosity each personality is analyzed. If a child displays no traits which are deemed positively undesirable, his peculiarities are accepted calmly as his own invention and his special contribution to life in the village. Toviya believed strongly in the role of supernatural beings as determinants of personality. Left-handedness and deafness recur frequently in the same genealogy, and he was adamant in his support of the power of ancestors. But even he looked upon some of Peni's crotchets as individual invention. It is this easy tolerance of individuality which permits Fijians a sophisticated curiosity about other civilizations and which prompts them to say: "Different countries, different customs."

Though the prestige of parents may suffer from a child's faults, the child himself is held responsible for his misdemeanors and in extremity is expected to bear his own punishment or justify his behavior in a formal "hearing." Eleven-year-old Sakaru spoke in a formal gathering before the chiefs to refute a charge which Bici had brought against him;[16] Nabadua's twelve-year-old daughter tried to justify her truancy from the district school before high officials in a session of the provincial court.

Children are encouraged in economic enterprise. Peni very probably consulted his father Vaula before he contributed a gift to Vaulini's marriage exchange; at that time Peni had scarcely attained pu-

16. See below, pp. 413–15.

berty. Vaula undoubtedly encouraged him and was proud that his son showed promise of great initiative. Today when Peni intends to plant new garden land, he still depends upon Vaula's encouragement. When a child shows no initiative, parents are disappointed, but they exert no positive pressure upon him; they accept his laziness and look upon it as a symptom of his individual temperament. On the whole, adolescents of commoner caste take pleasure in obediently fulfilling parental hopes and accept their obligations to the village with well-developed sense of responsibility. Boys carry important messages. Girls in their teens, without the supervision of older women, hold conferences to decide how guests shall be fed and entertained on the morrow. Quietly encouraged by parents, both boys and girls of pubertal age plan their futures with practical intelligence. But the noble Little Ratu Meli, Bulisivo's fifteen-year-old grandson, used to loll in indolent boredom, beloved of all the village.

Among the boys puberty in itself is no great event. But in former times circumcision probably coincided with it. Big Di Litiya says that circumcision used to cause shame of nudity, an adolescent trait, until the modern practice of youthful circumcision broke the affective connection. Nabadua has said that newly circumcised young men were once expected to bring a victim of war as sacrifice for their ancestors; only then was the ordeal deemed complete. Others corroborate his statement that boys must have reached at least a sturdy fourteenth year before the operation was performed.[17]

Young men were circumcised in a group which became thenceforth "age-mates." Sometimes the rite was postponed until a chief's funeral; the great bloodshed would honor the death. Any skilled man might perform the cutting. The fathers of the newly circumcised presented them with a feast. Some man, whom thenceforth the boys affectionately called *tubu-tubu* or *tubu-na* (grandfather or mother's brother), served

17. This statement contradicts certain documentary evidence. Thomas Williams (*Fiji and the Fijians*, ed. George S. Rowe, I [London, 1858], 166) says: "Males are circumcized when from seven to twelve years old. The cutting instrument is a piece of split bamboo, and recovery is rapid. The operation is generally performed on a company of ten or twelve at a time, who for several days afterwards, live together in some public building, their food being taken to them by women." Cf. John E. Erskine, *Journal of a Cruise among the Islands of the Western Pacific* (London, 1853), p. 254. But William Lockerby, who, like Williams, spent most of his Fijian residence in Bua Kingdom, says: "At the age of sixteen the young men are circumcized. . . . . The youth of the district of the proper age assemble together in a house, their hands are tied to a beam above their heads—their feet barely touching the ground: in this position the operation is performed with a piece of bamboo" (*The Journal of William Lockerby*, ed. Sir Everard in Thorn ["Publications of the Hakluyt Society: Second Series," No. LII (London, 1925)], pp. 73 and 85).

them as nurse during their convalescence. While he served them, he dared not touch food or tobacco with his hands and had to supply his own needs clumsily with sticks as tongs. When a week or more had passed, the boys bathed ceremonially in the river. The *tubu-tubu* bathed also to wash away his contamination with genitals. Then the newly convalesced young men prepared a tremendous feast for themselves and their erstwhile nurses. No pig or chicken in the village was safe from their appetites. Thenceforth they were known as "young men" and slept together in a young men's house. Young women began to look upon them with favor.

Today's young men are circumcised separately at ten or twelve. They have no *tubu-tubu* to nurse their convalescence. Peni was circumcised at the ford in the river Tavua. One day he met Ratu Luke there, unexpectedly. Ratu Luke said: "It is time that you were circumcised. You are almost fully grown." And, before Peni had time to weigh the value of Ratu Luke's words, the operation had been performed with Ratu Luke's hunting knife. For a week Peni lay sick in the house, and the women of his household brought him food. Ratu Seru, whom Peni considers his age-mate, was circumcised somewhere on the windward coast.

In very recent years the native medical practitioner has circumcised without ceremony even the small boys who attend the district school. But it is still an ordeal for which they are primed from early childhood. Men grasp the penes of four-year-olds and threaten them playfully with knives. Small boys are taunted with foods which, according to tradition, only grown men can eat.[18] As eight-year-old boys they already know how to ridicule an awkwardly performed task as the work of one who has fled in fear from the circumcision knife. He who is circumcised imagines that he has braved an ordeal and feels proud that he can call himself a man.

First menstruation and the tattooing of the vulva which formerly accompanied it were viewed as the feminine parallel to circumcision. Though tattooing of the vulva adds to sexual attractiveness, its neglect is in no way comparable to the disgrace of the uncircumcised. It is not looked upon as an ordeal. In recent years, since through white contact girls have become ashamed to inform their parents of menstruation, parents make no feast to honor the occasion, and, except for

18. A fat grub which lives in rotten wood and a large land snail are theoretically disgusting to the uncircumcised.

the changes in their own physiology, girls pass imperceptibly through puberty. There is no fear of menstrual blood. Instructed in hygiene by an older woman, perhaps a sister, the girl goes about her usual chores without concern for her condition. She bathes more often in order to be clean. Perhaps from shyness she avoids crowded houses. Little anxiety attends first menstruation.[19] But it is a sign that growth has stopped; it means a girl is big enough to marry.[20] Lui is small because she began to menstruate too young. Meremanini's first menstruation was delayed; hence she is very large. It is said that in former times it came later than it does today.

But menstruation, which is called "sickness of the month," inaugurates a period of mild but constant worry. When it fails to appear, there is uncertainty as to the cause of failure: unless a woman has been cohabiting regularly with one man and therefore knows that she is pregnant, she believes that a disease which is peculiarly fatal to women has fallen upon her; she may travel long distances to some famous wise woman who will insert a twig in her cervix and draw forth the blood.[21]

SEX

Among infants, desire for tactile stimulation is readily gratified. Crying almost always brings maternal attention. Small children straddle the nude backs of adults. Though adults chide them mildly for their lack of independence, even six-year-olds who complain of fatigue may be so carried. Children who are eight or nine sometimes embrace the nude trunks of adults without embarrassment. Though modesty soon asserts itself as a symptom of a maturing soul and such obvious tactile stimulation of the genital areas becomes shameful, among men self-indulgent postures persist through life: at social gatherings they lie on their stomachs and swing their legs.

Knowledge of sexual differentiation occurs at an early age.[22] Chil-

19. Bici adds that women like to wear red cloth during the menstrual period because blood stains are less obvious.

20. However, girls usually do not marry for another ten years.

21. This is not considered abortion unless they believe that pregnancy has been previously established. Abortion is in disrepute, but the disease warrants pity. One girl, who was very active sexually, resorted frequently to this treatment. Though her prestige suffered because of her indiscreet promiscuity, the village sympathized with her in her diseased condition. This practice could account for a period of sterility which might seem to follow first menstruation at Nakoroka.

22. On one occasion I determined to ascertain the average age at which children become aware of their own sex. I began to question them methodically, but the question caused such hilarious embarrassment among the six-year-olds that I desisted. They all knew.

dren of both sexes swim together without shame until they have begun
to show signs of puberty. But there is a growing tendency in modern
times to urge even six-year-olds to conceal their genitals with a *sulu*
while they are in the village. Modesty is urged especially in the presence of strangers and chiefs. Yet no small child would seriously consider donning a garment on a rainy day. Though there is no gender in
the language, the words for male and female genitals fall constantly as
daringly shameful interjections from the lips of men, women, and children. The care with which adults and older children conceal their
genitals from elders and contemporaries, but less carefully from small
children of the same sex, stimulates a curiosity about the sexual classification of both humans and animals which is apparent among all
members of the village. I once traveled to an Indian village with a
fifty-year-old man of good standing at Nakoroka. Upon seeing a goat
which was very obviously a billy goat, he naïvely asked our Indian
host whether the animal was male or female. When a huntsman returns from the bush with word that he has killed a wild pig, he is frequently greeted with a question as to the pig's sex. Because of a boar's
greater ferocity, the killing of a boar is a greater achievement. But
in modern times the killing of pigs has become so commonplace that
it is only especially adventurous experiences with pigs that bring prestige. Yet the question about the pig's sex persists. When young people,
who understand the representative function of Western European
photography in a manner which their elders do not comprehend, saw
magazine portraits in my house, they invariably asked whether the
person represented was male or female.[23] Because small boys bear the
stigma of lack of circumcision, the chiding of adults and of older boys
who have already passed through this ordeal inspires them with consciousness of themselves as a class distinct from small girls; they are uncircumcised, unskilled, inefficient at all tasks. Once Bici's six-year-old
Kaiyava was proudly wearing the ragged trousers which some adult
had cast off. Bici said, "Sew up your trousers."

"This is my hole for urination," Kaiyava replied.

"You tear your pants to urinate," said Bici derisively.

"No," said Kaiyava, "a rat made this hole."

"Yes," Bici said humorously. "Rats are attracted to the stench of
the filth which has accumulated beneath your prepuce."

23. Once I witlessly displayed a photograph of a nude boy to a group of small children.
The pictured genitals fascinated them until Ratu Luke chanced to discover their preoc-
cupation. Angrily he thrust the picture in their faces and shamed them.

Also small children learn at an early age that there is social value in observing the sexual behavior of adults. Because of his favored point of vantage as son of the notorious Vaulini, the shameless conversation of six-year-old Care could enthral an audience of young adults; they used to hang upon his words, and he enjoyed this flattery. Once he told of how his slumber in his mother's arms had been disturbed by a certain man who came in the night and climbed upon his mother's back, as a child straddles the back of its parent; but the man was not content to stay there quietly but must jerk about in most unseemly fashion. It was Ivamere's little sister who publicized the scandal which drove Ivamere from the village; the child awoke at night and next day told the village of what she had seen. If a woman is habitually accompanied by small children and no scandal has yet touched her name, it is known with certainty that she is virtuous; small children are ruthlessly efficient chaperones.

The modesty which parents attempt to instil in their children becomes focused about the sexual and not the excretory function of the genitals. A certain adult man who had not been moved by mission teaching but was nevertheless of good standing in the community habitually squatted inside his *sulu* to urinate on the village green; once during the procedure he carried on a conversation with a group of women. The only shame attached to excretion is derived from its uncleanliness. But modesty is concerned with coitus. Modesty prompts absolute concealment of the genitals from those of the opposite sex only after sexual maturation has begun. Thirteen-year-old girls begin to wear the *sulu* when they play tag games in the river. They are modest in the presence of even very small boys. He who fails to learn modesty, even though his failure is apparent only in the careless manner in which he sits down without first ascertaining that his *sulu* is properly arranged to conceal his genitals, is considered a fool; his "soul is big." When adult men bathe together, each must employ one hand to shield his genitals from the gaze of others. If an alarm is raised that women are approaching, they rush hysterically to don their *sulu*'s. Missionary teaching has substantiated this belief in the virtue of modesty, and it has perhaps grown stronger in the last half-century. Parents urge their children to wear clothes in the village; in contrast with older women, young women have learned to hide their breasts from men, and all adults wear shirts when they go to church. But these innovations are observed as a mechanical ritual to evoke the favor of the Wesleyan God; they are not functions of the mature soul. Old accounts have often mentioned the modesty of Vanua Levu women.[24] On one occasion a boy whose voice had changed and who already showed signs of puberty sat naked on the riverbank while a troop of children and young women bathed about him. Adults disapproved his lack of shame. He had already been circumcised; hence his penis was of special interest to women. But Big Di Litiya explained his negligence, saying that in former times circumcision did not occur until the soul was mature and already knew shame; that clothes used to be donned to hide the glans, to which, more than to other parts of male genitals, modesty is sensitive. It is this developing modesty in young children which is used to deter sexual experimentation. Only one instance is known in which small children attempted to imitate coitus. The case was notorious in the village, and the principals were severely shamed. Eight-year-old Sayasi coaxed seven-year-old Narieta into a dense clump of cane near the bathing place. But they were discovered, and Sayasi fled to the forest because he feared that his mother would whip him.

Fear of a specific disease which is said to afflict those who cohabit too young with an older person is an effective check upon the seduction of adolescent boys or girls. The famous rape of a barely adolescent girl on the windward coast substantiates this fear.

Two old men were friends. One was healthy except for the cataracts which blinded both his eyes. But the other was afflicted with ringworm[25] over his whole body, his stomach was bloated, and his skull was abnormally small; he was known as a fool. Once, when the village was almost deserted, they attacked a girl whose breasts had just begun to swell. The fool held her while the blind man raped her; then it was the fool's turn. The ravaged girl felt ashamed and told no one of her experience.[26] But soon her vagina began to itch, and there was a

24. Of Bua Kingdom in the early nineteenth century, Lockerby said: "I . . . . went naked with only the belt made from the bark of a tree round my waist, that hung down before and behind like a sash. The islanders were also dressed this way. The dress of the women is somewhat similar to that of the men; only the belt or petticoat is made of grass about four inches broad, is tied into a knot before and hangs down to the ground. These dresses differ in quality according to the rank of the wearers; and in the manner the women walk and sit. They answer every purpose they are intended for" (op. cit., p. 23).

25. There was little ringworm at Nakoroka. But it is known that the disease produces an unpleasant odor. Badly diseased women sometimes have illegitimate children, but men are less fortunate.

26. It is the rule that a girl is ashamed to tell of a sexual experience. Though she likes to make fools of the men who court her favors, and keeps them standing in the rain all night at some appointed meeting-place while she herself is snugly laughing with the women in

copious discharge. She became very thin so that her arms were like stalks of cane. Then people recognized her disease. Her parents questioned her, and she told. When officials came to summon the culprits to the provincial court, the two old friends were plaiting sennit on the village green. The fool saw them coming and fell in a faint from fright. Together they were led from the village. Their kinsmen wept as they departed. During their trial the bond of friendship between them was nearly broken; as they sat handcuffed together, an argument sprang up as to who had broken the hymen. The fool said: "The vagina was lax when I mounted; you broke it." The blind man said: "You broke it." The officials who presided were uncertain and sent them both to prison in Suva. The blind man died there. After many years the fool returned to the village. He died in 1935. The ravaged girl recovered from her illness. She is now a fat matron with many children.[27]

This disease threatens prepubertal children with special dangers. But it augments the sexual timidity of boys until two or three years past puberty, or at least it serves as a rationalization for this timidity. It is impossible to know accurately the average age at which sexual activity begins. Statements of men are clouded with conflicting admirations for virtue and virility. Serious questioning of women was interpreted as obscene. Age itself is controversial. Yet one boy of fifteen[28] who had developed most signs of puberty before June, 1936, had no immediate intention of pursuing a sexual career. He still feared the disease, and this fear undermined his interest even in girls his own age. Aside from the disease there is fear of angering a young girl's brothers, who are particularly anxious that she shall pass through the pubertal period as a virgin. After first menstruation at least a year or two must pass before a girl has learned to deceive the members of her household.

Among the young men erotic dreams which produce ejaculation are shameful and colored with the fear and disgust which many men experience in close contact with supernatural beings.[29] Once Peni woke

---

some household, from shame she tries to conceal her serious sexual experiences and interests.

27. It is Bici who tells this story. The blind man was Bici's mother-in-law's younger brother. Though Bici honors his mother-in-law with observance of a strict avoidance taboo, he considers this tale a good joke on her. It amuses him that his mother-in-law should have wept when such a brother was led from the village.

28. Notice of his birth was entered in government records in 1920. Since the recording of births is sometimes delayed, he may have been older. This was the same boy who lacked modesty and bathed unclothed with the women.

29. Parallel information was not sought from young women.

angrily in the night and commanded a supernatural being to depart from his presence. A male *tuwawa*[30] had come to his bedside with the prepuce of its uncircumcised penis pulled back so that the glans was shamefully visible. It was about to perform manustrupation upon Peni; but, fortunately, Peni succeeded in frightening it away. Though he frequently dreams erotically about young women of the village, there is no shame associated with these dreams because they do not produce ejaculation; they result from contact with the souls of living women. Ejaculation is proof of visitation by a *tuwawa;* masturbation is the special task of these shameless creatures.[31] Once when the men of Nakoroka were traveling to a foreign village to build houses, the uncircumcised Narogo paused to rest near the grave of a once famed beauty. Though when he awoke he claimed to have slept with the soul of the famed beauty, everyone knew he was lying; the wetness of his clothing proved that he had been visited by a *tuwawa*.

Before puberty, marked differentiation appears between boys and girls in their satisfaction of desire for tactile stimulation. More conscious of their status in relation to contemporaries, ten-year-old boys have already begun to treat one another with the dignity and restraint which persists throughout their lives. Even in play they rarely find it necessary to touch one another. Once eleven-year-old Yavusai sat close to eight-year-old Sayasi and stroked his body affectionately; both were pleased. But their behavior was unusual. Everyone knows that Yavusai's soul lacks maturity. Despite the distance which each man keeps between himself and every other man, he is not embarrassed when, after a hard day's work, his sister massages his back with oil. Some of the games which are played at gay feast times require considerable physical contact, but such contact occurs between the sexes. Sometimes the women throw dirt upon a man to tease him and in a group descend upon him to throw him into the river. Highly pleased, he submits. Throughout life a woman feels free to embrace her friends and wrestle playfully with other women. Girls walk arm in arm. Occasionally two young women return from the bathing place in the same *sulu*. The wise woman who attends as midwife at childbirth or exam-

30. A spirit whose form is human but whose long hair hangs almost to the ground. The *tuwawa* does not warrant the respect which ancestors receive. It is of a lower order.

31. The Fijian equivalent for "masturbation" is one of the few words which can never be spoken without painful embarrassment in mixed company. Various words for coitus are likewise taboo. It is the shame attached to words for genitals which gives them their interjectory force; they are used constantly. Words for excrement evoke but little obvious emotional response, regardless of the company.

ines girls to ascertain their virginity never feels the same repugnance for contact with genitals that is exhibited by the *tubu-tubu* who nurses the wounds of newly circumcised boys. The hands of the *tubu-tubu* are defiled by his task so that it disgusts him to touch his food.

Boys learn the mechanics of sexual activity from discussions with young men whose sex lives have already begun. Though fathers and elder brothers take pride in all symptoms of aggressive sexual behavior which they see developing in a boy, they are ashamed to offer actual assistance; men do not procure. Nabadua, who champions "strong behavior," would be proud to learn that his twenty-year-old son had seduced a virgin in the face of village opposition. He would be ashamed if his son should be known to masturbate or to cohabit with an old woman. Yet he expects that son, independently of all assistance, to build his own reputation for virility. On rare occasions a young man may act as go-between for an older brother or a timid "friend," but this is usually the function of a sister. Girls learn from older sisters how to regulate their sex lives. But in contrast with men there is little prestige to be gained or lost through sexual adventures. Continence is mildly admired among unmarried young women, but no one expects a girl to remain a virgin. Women who are cross-cousins can trust each other with sexual confidences and procure each other's lovers.

Among men, and especially among those who covet the reputation of a "strong soul," inability to control their passions is a boast. It is also a fault which is used against them in the community and for which they must apologize. With great zest Namo and his younger brother, sons of Nabadua, describe their constant readiness for sexual adventures. With gusto thirty-year-old Namo distinguishes between youth and middle age, saying that youth—his own age is that of "youth"—is the time of perpetual eagerness for sexual satisfaction. Their mouths water as they think of coitus.[32] Yet even youths expect to resort to masturbation practices on occasion.[33]

Knowingly, Bici describes the postures for sexual intercourse: squatting face to face, which is called "boiling rice"; hanging from a beam with legs free, which is called "in the manner of the flying fox"; lying with heads to the wind so that the stench blows away, which is

---

32. Among men sexual intercourse can be described as "eating vagina." Sight of a beautiful woman is said to stimulate salivary flow.

33. In the myths an ancestor sees an old woman exposing herself and calls "his children to bring saplings and whip his penis to awaken it. They began to whip, and the penis awoke and began to travel like a snake." Mechanical means are employed to produce erection in life as well as in literature.

called "with the wind behind"; "mounting together," which is a leisurely method with conversation; "shouldering salt water," which requires that a woman flex one leg over the shoulder of a squatting partner; "husking coconuts"; and many others. But in practice sexual relations are never so colorful. Though plans for sexual adventures preoccupy young men, these plans are not often consummated. When the village is crowded with young visitors at feast times, young people slip away from the dancing in the evenings. But they always absent themselves on some pretext and never remain away so long that their claim to have gone to the bush to urinate seems ludicrous. If caught *in flagrante delicto*, even Ratu Seru would feel shame and beg that the event be kept secret. Only Nabadua and Ratu Seru have dared to take a mistress openly before marriage. Fear of discovery makes pre-marital coitus brief; the usual posture is standing. In foreign villages young men fear the anger of the brothers of their paramours.[34] Some young men admit that sexual prowess develops only after marriage. Yet all married men spend weeks away from their wives while they are housebuilding in other villages. Some men avoid their wives for weeks at a time, even though they are together in the same village.

Bici, who more than any other man was highly versed in the folk-lore of postures for coitus, was notoriously incapable sexually. Namo and Nabadua and even Ratu Seru needed reputations for virility to support their claims to high status. Peni, who with constant secret plotting, slept sporadically with three of the most desirable women in the village, was embarrassed whenever anyone suggested that his lik-ing to live constantly at home was sexually motivated. Peni found Bici's conversation disgusting and tiresome. Ratu Luke, whose lack of sexual restraint had embroiled him in scandals in three different ter-ritories, would leave the company when Bici began to speak of sex.

Before marriage women distribute sexual favors among men of their choice. No matter how ugly a woman is, she need not doubt her ability to attract some man if her approach is obvious. Even the hideously

34. Young men are more daring when women from other villages visit them. Visiting young women are rarely accompanied by their brothers. In January, 1936, when Nakoroka was gay with feasting and young women had come visiting from Nalauvia and Dreketi, young men who traced claims of ownership in Nakoroka land through distant channels came to join in the merriment and court the visiting girls. Aside from Ratu Seru's affair with Lebu, the only knowledge which the village gained of extramarital coitus was the case of a girl from Nalauvia who was notorious for her sexual vigor. Two young men of Nako-roka and three whose claims were questionable took her to the bush and cohabited with her quickly, each in turn. Such co-operation among men is bizarre. Nabadua was pleased that his second son was of their number and had thereby exhibited his strong soul.

scarred Vilomena bore two children. The microcephalic deaf-mute of Nabadua's household bore four children. Women think of men as waiting hungrily for an invitation. Women give their favors to men whose reputation for sexual skill rates high among women. Thus Peni had more opportunities for sexual satisfaction than his fear of detection allowed him to utilize. But women ignored men like young Tomasi, whose leg was shriveled and who was said to peek at women while they bathed. Naicadra and Bici likewise were ignored until their kinsmen assisted in arranging their marriages. But Naicadra is known for his virtue, and Bici, despite his interest in obscenity, sees virtue in continence. It is probable that men whom women ignore resort to despised masturbatory practices in solitude. Some adolescent boys masturbate. The blind son of Bulisivo is known to masturbate frequently. The fat bachelor Narogo masturbates. But no man admits that he himself stoops so low; the twenty-year-old second son of Nabadua claimed to know nothing of the practice; with contempt he described how some young men whose weak souls prevented them from seeking women would go to the forest and masturbate while they thought of the face of a desired woman.

Men classify the attractiveness of women. Abstractly they extol the virtues of the vagina which is deep and dry. But no women are known to be sexually incompetent. Frigidity is inconceivable. It is the woman who feels no shame whom both men and women consider abnormal. She who distributes her favors too easily and without regard for secrecy and who babbles afterward is undesirable both as a friend to women and as a mistress to men. Such a woman is said to possess a "big soul"; she has never learned the modesty which becomes an adult. The microcephalic deaf-mute of Nabadua's household had a "big soul"; she would gladly permit coitus on the path in broad daylight. The attractive Vaulini is also condemned for her laxity; sometimes she babbles too freely. Sometimes people say maliciously that she, too, has a big soul.

The uncircumcised are the only men whom women consider lacking in sexual appetite. Such men are classed sexually with children. They live comfortably on the edge of society and receive their share of food, but they participate mildly and on rare occasions.[35] But, un-

35. The tattooing of women may formerly have been associated with sexual prowess. A tattooed woman is proud to bathe with other women and display her patterned thighs. Yet the converse was never true; she who was not tattooed was not barred from sexual adventures. Big Di Litiya exaggerates the parallel between tattooing and circumcision; since she herself is tattooed, she likes to emphasize the importance of the women's puberty ceremony.

like children, theirs is the apotheosis of shame. They dare not bathe with other men. Aged Kaiyava used to go to the river secretly and, if he was interrupted in his bath, would cover himself hastily with bark cloth. Now that Narogo has been recently circumcised, he no longer bathes alone. But his shame persists, and he can look forward to no sexual future. He knows that he is a by-word for incompetence.[36] His voice will never command an audience. It is said that he tells the same stories over and over again.

It is interesting that, like sexually lax women, uncircumcised men are sometimes known to exhibit "big souls": two men of distant Macu-ata village, whose fame because of their uncircumcised condition has spread even to Bua Province, are said to discard their clothing upon occasion and stride through the village in complete nakedness. Narogo, too, has been accused of a "big soul"; his maturity is questionable.

Nakoroka is incredulous of the existence of any unusual sexual appetites among Fijians. Men describe sexually aberrant habits among Europeans, Chinese, and Indians, but the development of a strange appetite in someone of their own village is incomprehensible. The few cases of sexual perversion which have occurred within memory in other parts of Fiji are famous because of their novelty. All concern men. People at Nakoroka consider them funny stories. Three men in distant parts of Fiji are said to have experimented with bestiality; the colonial administration punished one man for necrophilia; a boy is known to have made an unsuccessful attempt at homosexual pederasty. Except for these five cases, no other instance of unusual sexual behavior is known to have occurred among Fijians.

Vatili of Nakoroka classifies pederasty, bestiality, and voyeurism in the same category. Men whom he describes as oppressed with shame, fear, impotence, or ugliness may sometimes resort to such practices because they do not dare to seek women. He says that the colonial administration deals severely with these offenders. Except for one young man who peeks at women, it is improbable that any man at Nakaroko has ever behaved abnormally. There is no conception of sexual inversion or homosexuality. No boy doubts that his sexual appetite is identical with that of every other young man in the village. When he has passed through the ordeal of circumcision, his sexual anxiety is focused upon his own courage to act.

Bici said that group masturbation occurs among the men of a king-

36. Clumsy performance of any kind may be termed "uncircumcised." Even a woman may be accused of behaving in an "uncircumcised manner."

dom on Natewa Bay. Their chief calls them to assemble, and, when he gives a signal, they race to see who can first produce ejaculation. The chief gives a prize to the winner. Though such behavior is deemed ridiculous, it is merely a strange and foolish kind of contest; it has no reference to the satisfaction of sexual appetite. The women of the same region also used to play a strange game. If a man who was foreign to their territory encountered a group of women, they would fall upon him and pin him to the ground. To produce an erection, one of them would tantalize him. Then they would drag him along the rocky ground. As soon as his erection disappeared, they would repeat the procedure. Though this game is unknown at Nakoroka, it bears certain similarities to the rough games with which Nakoroka women may tease men at feast times.[37]

No psychological disturbance attends menopause. There is anxiety until a woman can be certain that it is age which checks her menstrual flow; she worries for fear she is afflicted with the dread disease which may clog the cervix and prove fatal. But when she feels sure that she has become an old woman, she is relieved that her menstrual period is over. She does not sorrow because she is old. Big Di Litiya laughed at the suggestion that she feared old age and said: "As long as there is life in Fijians, they know shame and happiness. When I knew that I was old, I said, 'Now I am old.' "[38] Though there is a word for "old woman" which is frequently used in derision, menopause brings no change in status to a married woman. Growing impotence may cause anxiety to those men whose status depends upon virility; Nabadua shouted too loudly his claim to virility to be reconciled to old age, and others accept their status as "old men" more quietly. "Old man" also means "clever"; among men age is more venerable than among women.

ADULTHOOD

Even adult men and women depend heavily upon affectionate encouragement from parents in all their undertakings. Though individuals build their own lives, they continue to look anxiously for parental approval. As age advances, men return more closely into the seclusion of their own households. Though social participation may consume much of their time, gradually the definition of each man's role in coun-

37. Despite their capacity for these aggressive attacks upon men, women at Nakoroka are said to be passive during coitus.

38. The marriage of Big Di Litiya and Vosalevu is the most companionable in the village.

cils, ceremonies, and group work grows more clear in relation to other men's; each one tries to learn to play his part and confines his behavior within limits set by what he imagines to be his status. But he likes to spend his leisure among the women of his own household; there he can relax, secure in the place of greatest honor, while his women serve him kava and honor his commands. If a visitor from another household should join him, the atmosphere quickly grows tense with formal politeness unless the visitor's status is clearly defined as so low that it cannot rival that of his host. Thus in their leisure young men are accustomed to cluster about an older man, a father, or an older brother. Old men, whose parents are long dead, enjoy the solitude of their land, where they spend many hours affectionately tending their gardens and remembering their ancestors. But the importance of their social role need not decline as age advances. The influence of their voices may still be strong among men, and, as their contemporaries die, their status rises in the kava ceremony. Men need not grow foolish with age like Bici's father, the uncircumcised Kaiyava. Raitova, who is nearing fifty, is still encouraged to improve his social functioning. He was urged to act as sergeant-at-arms in church so that this exercise of authority might improve his discipline in his own household. Once when Vatili was preparing for a journey, he appointed Raitova to serve as "village chief" in his stead and call men to the work of housebuilding in the village. Vatili hoped that his new responsibility would cause Raitova to forget his slothful habits and spur him on to greater efforts.

Women, among whom status differences are treated lightly and without formality, attain their period of maximum participation in public affairs during the years before marriage when their dancing attracts the gaze of visitors and amuses chiefs. Thereafter, unless they are of noble blood and hold an important title, they play behind the scenes in the lives of brothers, sons, and husbands. As they grow old and wizened with age, their status falls even lower in the eyes of men. It is only their children who continue to honor them for their superior years. Finally they become "old women" who flock to the dances of young people and clap hands in time to the beat of the drums; this is a pastime which mature men disdain. When there is excuse to laugh, the old women raise a boisterous clamor and make fools of themselves buffooning without restraint. They have no dignity.[39]

39. The respect achieved by women wise in obstetrics and gynecology is limited to the women of the community; men take little notice of them. Vatili's mother is venerable because of her unusually great age; for many years she has been too old and feeble to participate in the gaiety of other old women. She has adult grandchildren.

Chiefs, who have not been taught to keep their place and who have never been shamed into performing duties, must learn to value the reputation of their kingdom and take pride in its renown in foreign regions. Their scope of interest is wider than that of commoners. They must learn, too, that their own prestige depends upon the commoners in their own kingdom. The ages of Nakoroka's chiefs range from five to seventy, and their functions at Nakoroka are various, so that the status of each is well defined in relation to the others. In theory commoners must continue to honor their whims and admire their weaknesses. With old age their venerability increases. Yet chiefs learn to feel responsible for the communities over which they hold title. In emergency mild Bulisivo can preserve his calm; in times of hurricane when houses must be bound with ropes lest they collapse, he can persuade common men to rouse themselves from the lethargy into which fear has thrown them;[40] when they hear his voice, they perform the work which must be done.

40. No woman has been known to feign sleep in an emergency. But women are foolish and rattle-brained.

CHAPTER X

CEREMONIES OF THE LIFE-CRISES

MARRIAGE

SOMETIME in the year 1925 Ema first spoke of the marriage of her daughter Vaulini. Ema was then living in Nalauvia as Isacodro's faithful wife; her infidelity[1] had not yet created the tension between Isacodro and his brother which forced Isacodro to take flight from Nalauvia and, with his family, to beg land of his Nakoroka kinsmen. Vaulini was very young, just past puberty. It was during a visit in Nakoroka that Ema said to Toviya: "You and I are brother and sister.[2] It will be a good thing for Vaulini to marry your son Sireli. Then our blood will be bound together again. Let it be a great marriage in the ancient manner of our land." Sireli was not yet twenty. Soon afterward Toviya took a whale tooth to Isacodro to seal the marriage bargain and assure his son a virgin wife. The name of this whale tooth is *gasau me cina;* it is a request to keep watch over her who will be bride.

Marriage "in the manner of the land" begins with betrothal and ends more than a year later when the mother of the bride presents a gift of mats called *sasavuta* to the groom's family, mats which were not complete at the time of the great wedding feast. Only virgins can be betrothed. Only the wedding of a virgin bride can please the ancestors and make the soil fertile. If the wedding involves an outside community, the ancestors feel even greater honor because the web of kinship of two communities will enmesh an even greater multitude of guests from distant regions, and tales of the land's fertility will resound in distant villages. But one is safe only in betrothing a woman of a

1. See above, p. 255.
2. No biologic tie is apparent between them in the genealogies. Ema had spent her childhood and youth at Nabetenidiyo, an old village in Tavua land (see above, pp. 51–53, for an account of the destruction of this village during the "days of the wars"). Toviya had lived in the now empty villages of Nadroro and Votua. Ema married Isacodro and took residence in Nalauvia before the five ancestral villages of Inland Forest Kingdom had been incorporated into the village of Nakoroka. But intercourse between these old villages was frequent enough for brother-sister relationship to grow between Toviya and Ema. They are, of course, of the same moiety.

near-by region because one cannot trust the men of foreign lands to respect the betrothal whale tooth. If the bride's village holds few toward whom the groom already feels strong affinal respect and affection, there is great fear lest violent dispute arise from broken troth. Thus cross-cousins in adjacent villages are the most likely choice for those who would marry "in the manner of the land."

The five ancestral villages of Nakoroka intermarried frequently among themselves, but each chose wives as well from the adjacent villages of foreign kingdoms. Thus affinal ties bind Tavua people to Sarowaqa on the northeast and Duleniwai on the southeast. Votua people have married with Lekutu on the northwest. Nadroro has intermarried with Nacula and Nalauvia. Through the experience of many ceremonial exchanges in the past, adjacent villages have learned to vie with one another on all occasions. When they entertain one another as guests, they are especially careful lest some flaw in etiquette give grounds for ridicule. If entertainment is not lavish, the guests will laugh among themselves when they have returned to their own villages. Since the building of the village at Nakoroka, Nalauvia[3] is the village toward which all the subdivisions at Nakoroka have come to concentrate their desire for competitive display. Nalauvia is the nearest of Nakoroka's neighbors. Exchange at the marriage of Sireli and Vaulini would indeed be vigorous. Though they who win are very proud, and their ancestors are highly pleased, the shame of losing warrants joking reprisals only; to be outgiven is but a mild insult. Tense bonds of affinal affection prevent real hostility.

After his betrothal Sireli felt ashamed when he met Vaulini's sisters, but he felt no shame toward Vaulini herself. Frequently he visited at her home in Nalauvia. He might have felt ashamed toward Ema, who would be his mother-in-law, but Ema said: "Do not be ashamed; you are my child." He continued to address Isacodro as "uncle" (tubu-na). Likewise Vaulini called Toviya "uncle." But toward her prospective mother-in-law Siteri, whose close kinsmen were of Sarowaqa village on the farther side of Nakoroka, she began to feel the affectionate respect in which one holds an affinal relative of the same sex.[4] Sireli's "brothers" in both Nakoroka and Nalauvia began to look upon Vaulini as "small spouse."

3. The villages of Nalauvia and Nacula lie close together on the same river. They form a single political unit, and the name of either village may refer to the people of both.

4. See discussion of tau-vugo-na in chap. viii. They are of the same sex but of opposite moiety.

When Vaulini visited Nakoroka, Ema usually accompanied her, and they slept in Toviya's house. When she came visiting with a group of girls, however, she had to seek out some "small mother" at Nakoroka as chaperone. Even when she visited about in her own village, her mother accompanied her. In contrast Sireli was not expected to be continent, and his behavior was not supervised. Yet, had his philandering become notorious, Vaulini could have demanded that her father return the betrothal whale tooth and break the marriage agreement.

Anticipating the marriage feasts, people of both villages began to fatten their pigs. They planted gardens with special care, some of which were marked to be held in reserve for the time when guests would come to see the gift exchanges. When many months had passed, Sireli prepared himself for the long journey to Nabouwalu, the seat of colonial authority in Bua Province, to obtain marriage permits.[5] Toviya made the oven which is called "food of the path for bringing forth the writs." Bici, Monasa, and Nabadua assisted in the preparation of this feast. They are all of Toviya's moiety. At the request of Naicadra's wife, who is Toviya's sister, Naicadra helped as well.[6]

Isacodro came from Nalauvia with his brothers and their families. When they had eaten the feast, they returned to their village, and Sireli went to Nabouwalu alone to obtain the marriage permit. A party of travelers could have accompanied him, but many local needs absorbed their attention. Vaulini could have accompanied him only as a member of a large group of men and women.

During the weeks that followed, Sireli and his parents sought among their relatives for pigs, whale teeth, and sulu's.[7] Thinking only to accumulate a large number, they piled up obligations along both the "path of marriage" and the "path of blood." Close relatives of both cate-

5. Theoretically the government issues a second permit three weeks after the first. But to accommodate those who come from long distances, both permits may be obtained at the same time and sent to the purchaser by mail three weeks later. The native who is highest mission officer of the district issues a third permit. Formerly these required the payment of 2s. 6d. to the government for Permits I and II and 5 shillings to the mission officer for Permit III. But since 1934 the price has been reduced to a shilling each. If more than three months elapse between the purchase of Permits I and II, Permit I is automatically void.

6. Monasa and Nabadua are Toviya's "brothers." Bici, however, calls Toviya "*tubu-na*" and classifies him with first ascending generation. But Bici is younger brother to Monasa and Nabadua; he is Nabadua's henchman and "native of the village green" in Tavua. Hence as a member of Toviya's moiety he was obligated to share the tasks of Toviya's other brothers in moiety. Naicadra could not refuse a request of Toviya, who is his cross-cousin.

7. The *sulu*, which is worn wrapped around the waist, is made from a couple of yards of printed cloth. Worn widely in Fiji, it has become the unit for measuring value in cloth.

gories were questioned and asked to contribute. Then three whale teeth were chosen for the gift called "the wedded see each other." To present this gift to Isacodro, Naicadra's household escorted the parents of the bridegroom to Nalauvia. Sireli remained at home, preparing for the feast and the gift exchange which would occur on the morrow. At Nalauvia, Isacodro had made no oven; he was obliged only to serve his guests with kava and an ample meal of boiled food. When they had eaten, the whale teeth were presented formally to Isacodro. Toviya asked whether Vaulini had been watched faithfully. Isacodro said: "Vaulini, is Sireli your true husband?" In a low voice she answered that he was.

Next day Toviya and his party journeyed to Lekutu, to the house of the native mission official. Vaulini and her parents and friends accompanied them. Sireli also came, from Nakoroka, with a group of young friends who brought food for a meal to celebrate this Wesleyan ceremony. Sireli brought five shillings as fee to make it right in the eyes of the church. All small children were left at home. When the food was spread upon the mat, Vaulini and Sireli approached from either side, each laden with twenty-five or thirty sulu's which their friends had wrapped about them. First, Sireli gave her two sulu's and two pinafores as his personal gift. Then, before the applause of their assembled friends and relatives, they exchanged sulu's one by one until Vaulini had no more to give. With a gesture of munificence Sireli presented her with his remaining few. There was great applause. It is proper that a man should be a little stronger in giving than a woman. They left Lekutu in time to reach Nakoroka by nightfall.

Several days earlier Bulisivo had called the elders to council so that Toviya could discuss the work of preparing the great feast which would greet the wedding party's return from Lekutu. They had decided who should go to Nalauvia and who among the young people should accompany Sireli to Lekutu. Though Peni was very young,[8] they permitted him to attend Sireli because upon his own initiative he had contributed a sulu to Sireli's gift. They assigned the work of preparing ovens, considered how many guests each household could accommodate, and decided which of the women would provide a fresh catch of fish and prawns. Toviya said that his fat pig should be roasted as garnish. The day before Sireli's departure for Lekutu the village bustled with preparation. Guests were already arriving and had to be fed and served with kava. From among the many sulu's which they

8. Perhaps fifteen; barely pubertal.

brought as gifts,[9] Sireli chose about thirty of the prettiest to present to Vaulini at Lekutu. During the day of the ceremony many who had contributed *sulu*'s to Vaulini arrived from Nalauvia.

When the party returned to Nakoroka from Lekutu, ovens were opened and the feast apportioned. Each of the guests received a share. Toviya's pig had been cut in many pieces to feed the hundred guests, but there was no pork left for the people of Nakoroka. When all had eaten, the remaining *sulu*'s were exchanged. Sireli gave Vaulini sixty or seventy before hers were exhausted. Thirty more remained with Sireli. Vaulini had lost; it was said she had "jumped into the water." The people of Nalauvia were shamed and requested that Sireli keep his surplus *sulu*'s. But generously Toviya said: "Give everything to the Nalauvia people." Despite the competitive nature of the exchange, woman has never been known to "win."

Isacodro and Toviya presided over the redistribution of *sulu*'s among their respective guests. Each who contributes a gift should receive one in return. That Vaulini received thirty more *sulu*'s than Sireli indicates that more guests came with gifts for Sireli. Hence Sireli was obliged to make the greater number of return gifts to his guests; and he had fewer *sulu*'s with which to fulfil his obligations. But the people of Nakoroka were glad to waive their claims so that guests who had come from other villages could receive as many *sulu*'s as they had brought. The local people went without, but the fame of their wealth resounded. Kinship ties had divided the allegiance of every Nakoroka household. Many men, like Toviya, Nabadua, and Bici, had given a *sulu* to each party of the exchange. When Isacodro prepared to supply these men with return gifts, Toviya said: "Do not. Let Nakoroka's share be distributed among the people of Nalauvia." When the distribution was complete, Vaulini had kept for herself only the two *sulu*'s and pinafores which Sireli had given her as his personal gift.

That night Isacodro's family slept in Toviya's house. Vaulini and Sireli could converse together in the presence of their parents. Even the young Peni began to feel shame in the presence of Vaulini and observed strict taboo toward her. Next day all guests went home.

No matter when the Wesleyan ceremony is performed, the "true marriage feast" always falls in April or May, the time when yam and taro gardens are yielding their fullest. Six months remained before

9. Those who brought more than one *sulu* were about as many as those who brought none. It is presumptuous to come empty-handed, but there were a few who admitted their poverty and presented a single *sulu* as gift from an entire family. To advertise the abundance of their goods, some men like to harbor such guests.

this last great feast would consummate the marriage of Sireli and Vaulini. Efforts of preparation were redoubled. Sireli and Toviya let the appointed day be known and rumor spread through the province. Very distant relatives began to prepare marriage gifts for the Nakoroka wedding; men gathered pigs and whale teeth; women plaited mats. At Nakoroka each household decided upon its obligations. Bici sent word by a chance traveler to a cross-cousin in Dreketi that he needed a whale tooth to contribute to Sireli's marriage property. Since by kinship he was also obligated toward Vaulini,[10] he begged another whale tooth from a "small father" of Nasigasiga village.[11] Bici's mother, since dead, and his wife plaited four sleeping-mats of swamp reed (*kuta-kuta*): two mats were gifts from his whole household to Sireli, the other mats were for Vaulini from Bici and his mother, since they two alone were bound to Vaulini by close ties of kin. Of Nakoroka households, Bici's was the poorest; little was expected from it. But his gift was ample and in good taste. As well as mats and whale teeth, Nabadua gave two pigs to Vaulini's mother and one to Toviya.

Nakoroka houses were too few to shelter the multitude of expected guests. During the last week before the great feast, Nakoroka men built hasty sheds (*bolabola*) of thatch for those who would find no other place of refuge from the rain. When the guests arrived, two days before the feast, the permanent houses were given over to their use; all natives of Nakoroka slept in sheds or kitchens. For those who came as guests of men who owned no houses of their own, special sheds were built. As guests of the chiefly family people came from distant Solevu, Dama, and Nabouwalu, because Bulisivo's daughter had married a chief of that region; from Saolo, the land of Bulisivo's mother on the Wainunu coast, a dozen chiefs came to Bulisivo, bringing their families; to the widow Di Kabu guests came from Sarowaqa, the village of her husband; they came to Big Di Litiya from Lekutu and the islands off Lekutu's coast. To Toviya's household fifteen guests came from Duleniwai; his wife's people came from Sarowaqa. To Ratu Luke, who shares Toviya's household, came his chiefly father from the Wainunu coast with his retainers. To Nabadua *émigrés* from Tavua came with their families from Duleniwai, thirteen in all; many more came from Sarowaqa. Twenty-five came to Monasa from Duleniwai, and the village there was almost empty. Namo's house was filled with

10. Vaulini's mother belongs to the group of classificatory brothers and sisters in Tavua land, in which Bici also is included.

11. Nasigasiga lies just across the border in Macuata Province. One section of this village was populated by emigrants from Nadroro division of Nakoroka.

his wife's relatives from Lekutu and those of his mother from Navakasiga. To Vilomena's father, who held the chiefly title for Nadroro land, guests came from Nasigasiga.

The kinsmen of Raitova's wife, now dead, who live in the Dreketi region, were too poor to come; but his house was filled with people from the windward coast and from the island Yaqaga, with which Raitova's land is "ancestor together." Samu had no house of his own; his guests from distant Nakalou, on the Macuata coast, and Dreketi were received in a temporary shed which Nakoroka men had helped him build. Few guests came to Orisi, for he had not yet married and had few kinsmen; but Duleniwai people who overflowed the houses of their proper hosts filled the house which Orisi shared with Peni's father.[12]

The great house of Naicadra and that of Vatili were held in reserve for their kinsmen from Nacula and Nalauvia. Guests came to Bici from Duleniwai and Lekutu; to his wife from Duleniwai, where she had grown up. Some guests had been specially requested to bring whale teeth. Others brought mats or *sulu*'s. Those whose hosts were obligated to both parties of the marriage exchange brought gifts for both bride and groom; Bici's guests contributed to the marriage property of both Sireli and Vaulini; those who came to his wife brought gifts for Sireli only. The head man of each Nakoroka household directed the work of his guests, sent them to the gardens for food, and ordered the preparation of ovens, so that all could be fed. Bici does not know how many guests there were in all; he says that there were at least two hundred. Fortunately the moon was bright; the young could dance on the village green. There was no rain, and the older people could sit outside to converse and smoke tobacco.

Next day the people of Nalauvia and Nacula arrived with the bridal party. They brought three pigs, baked whole in Nalauvia, and many basketfuls of cooked food. And they brought raw food and one pig, dressed but uncooked, for Isacodro's "oven of the father," which was made near Vatili's house. Ema's brothers at Nakoroka (Nabadua, Monasa, and Bici, of Tavua, and Toviya of Votua) built her "oven of the mother" near Nabadua's house. All Tavua gardens were drawn upon to fill this oven; two Tavua pigs were garnish. Toviya's house-

12. Peni's father Vaula was bound most closely with land of the distant village Navidamu in Macuata. He had utilized his wife's claim on Nakoroka land; his own local claims are not strong. Despite his long residence, he has never displayed much initiative in property exchanges at Nakoroka. Like his tenuous claims on the soil, his claims to kinship must be used sparingly.

hold made two great ovens: Toviya's "oven of the father" held ten pigs and many hundreds of yams and taro from the gardens of the men of his moiety (Nabadua, Monasa, and Bici); Siteri's "oven of the mother" held four pigs and food from the gardens of her brothers in Sarowaqa. Sireli helped his mother Siteri.

It was right that the ovens of Isacodro and Ema contained few pigs, since pigs are the task of the groom and not the bride. Above all, it is important that the bride's family and their guests be well fed by the ovens of the groom. The head of each household delegated his guests to work upon those ovens toward which he was obligated: some of Bici's guests helped in the preparation of Ema's oven; some helped Toviya. Bulisivo and the chiefs participated but slightly because Toviya alone was responsible for the smooth progression of the work. So long as obligations of kinship functioned smoothly, Toviya did not need to ask the chiefs for help. In emergency, however, Toviya could have asked Bulisivo to give executive support, because Toviya, like all people at Nakoroka, is "one of Bulisivo's men." The day before the feast Toviya's brothers and their guests baked sweet puddings according to an elaborate recipe.

Toviya chose two pigs, two basketfuls of food from his oven, and some sweet pudding as special food for the bride and groom; he concealed three whale teeth inside the pigs. The remaining contents of his oven, together with the food of Siteri's "oven of the mother," was presented formally to Isacodro, in the open, then heaped near Toviya's house, where Isacodro was staying. In return Isacodro presented Toviya with the food from his oven and that of Ema. Inside Toviya's house the mothers of the bride and groom arranged the two pigs and the baskets of food which had been specially set aside. Many years ago Siteri had fallen on the steep path at the bathing place and crippled her arm; her sisters, as "small mothers" of the groom, helped her with her tasks. They gathered the mats which the wedding guests had brought, all except those which were held in reserve for the next day's exchange, and, after selecting a large number to be spread upon the marriage bed, Siteri and Ema began to give competitively in the exchange called "counting of the mats." Ema would spread one mat upon the floor, then Siteri would spread one of hers on top until Ema had no more to give; Siteri was happy and Ema was ashamed. The mats made a big pile in the center of the house. Then above the marriage bed each mother hung a mosquito curtain which she had sewed from cloth of the Chinese trader.

The bride and groom were separately preparing their entrances into Toviya's house. Their friends wrapped them in *sulu*'s brought as wedding gifts, smeared their faces with sweet-smelling salve, and combed their hair. They carried clusters of whale teeth in each hand. In all, Vaulini brought ten. She was first to enter Toviya's house. People whispered among themselves about the number of whale teeth she had brought and pitied her because they knew Sireli's marriage property was far greater than hers, that again she would "jump into the water." The many *sulu*'s with which her friends had wrapped her waist hung heavy about her, and she moved slowly. Sweat oozed through the scented salve on her forehead. The women marked that her figure was not so fine as they had imagined. Sireli, already informed of the value of his bride's gift, brought ten whale teeth in each hand; he had reserved four others for use on the morrow. Vaulini was ashamed that his contribution was double that of hers. Had she lost by a small margin only, she would have been happy to defer the honor to her husband. Still carrying their whale teeth, the bride and groom sat upon the pile of mats, and one of Sireli's "small mothers" held a slice of pork and a slice of taro before them. She proffered it to Vaulini to bite, then fed the remainder to Sireli. Two mouthfuls of pig and two of taro were allowed the bride and groom. This is called "the eating together." When they finished, they unwound the *sulu*'s which were wrapped about them and piled them separately to await the great exchange of marriage property on the morrow. The whale teeth were held in reserve.

Then the food which remained in Toviya's house was spread on the eating-mat for the bride's family. Isacodro found the three whale teeth which Toviya had hidden in the pigs; these were his to keep. He took his place at the head of the mat and in a loud voice called relatives to eat. Only those who felt closely bound to him by ties of kin dared come. Others feared the derisive chorus with which people would greet him who presumed this familiarity on questionable grounds: "Presuming fool! What are you doing here?" Those who ate with Isacodro were almost all of Nalauvia, perhaps twenty-five in number. Their women ate afterward.

Until far into the night, Isacodro and Toviya and their wives, who were the hosts at this great wedding, apportioned among their guests the feasts which had been heaped outside. Everyone who had contributed a gift received a share. If one were overlooked, he would speak out; and this would shame the hosts. Men of "contents of household" caste, who are especially apt at this complicated task of serving large quantities of food, helped arrange the portions. Isacodro gave Ema half of the feast which he had received to distribute among her guests. Those who assisted first set aside a small portion for Isacodro and Ema. Then the guests of each were classed geographically, and they placed food portions in long rows on the village green, one row for each region. Likewise the feast which Isacodro had presented to To- viya was distributed among the guests of Toviya and Siteri. House- holds which had contributed gifts to both bride and groom received more than one portion. Thus Bici received from Ema, and his wife from Toviya. Isacodro, however, divided his feast exclusively among Nalauvia people and their guests. When the work of dividing food was complete, all gorged themselves. Even those who had brought no gifts were called to the eating-mats of their friends. Of sweet pudding there was not enough to distribute with the feast. Bundles of it were passed from hand to hand, and everyone tasted it; but only the small children were called together and fed heartily of this delicacy regardless of their liens upon the hosts of the feast.

While, in the house of Toviya, Sireli and Vaulini were sleeping to- gether for the first time, Toviya requested the young men of Nakoroka to prepare another oven to use up the uncooked food left over from previous ovens. This oven is called "making open the threshold"; it is right that it should be prepared during the wedding night. Toviya's only remaining two pigs were killed and dressed carefully. Monasa, who is skilled in butchering despite the fact that he is not of "contents of the household" caste, incised a small hole in the flank of each pig and removed the alimentary canal cunningly so that the pigs looked whole. In the throat and belly of each, a flap was loosened neatly and sewed in place again when a whale tooth had been concealed inside; in all, four teeth were so concealed. The oven called "making open the threshold" is a special honor proffered virgin brides alone; it is the custom to couch these pigs upon new mats, and flanked by neat heaps of food they are delivered at the doorway of the house which holds the marriage bed. The wedding guests rejoice, especially those of the bride's family, while her women relatives scuffle happily in search of the concealed whale teeth. These belong to her who finds them. If the bridegroom should learn that his bride has been unfaithful to her troth, he informs his kinsmen straightway; gashed wide with blows of angry knives, with limbs awry, hiding no whale teeth, the pigs are cast down in the dirt before the kinsmen of the bride so that all guests may see that the groom has been betrayed. But there was no sound of discontent from Sireli in the marriage bed. The sun was risen for an hour, and still the bridegroom slept. The young men were impatient at the oven because the food was overdone. At length Toviya ruled that the feast be served.

Bici and Namo carried the pigs resplendent on their fine mats to the threshold of Toviya's house. Commotion of rejoicing kinsmen wakened the bride and groom. Vaulini sought out Melika, who was Naicadra's wife and her "small mother," to have the long curls cut from her virgin's coiffure. The matted ropes of hair which hang from the back of the head to the shoulders as the proud sign of virginity are rare in these modern times. Melika cut the curls and spoke gently: "It is good, my child." Ratu Luke, who was watching from across the village green, whispered to Namo: "Look. So my friend Sireli had intercourse last night." But no one jested; not even a cross-cousin would remark, for instance, that the bridegroom's sleep had been uncommonly heavy, that the sun was high.

Baked food keeps for several days even in hot weather. A mouthful of yesterday's feast was enough to start this day. Men went to the taro ponds. They did not wait for the apportioning of the pig called "making open the threshold." The young men set about preparing more sweet pudding. The women of Nalauvia and Nakoroka, and some of those who had come as guests, accompanied Vaulini as she "descended into the water" to get a meal of fish for her new husband. They all brought nets and planned to catch enough to feast the multitude. All doffed what clothes they wore and hung them in bundles round their necks. The slippery boulders and the rapids of the river required full freedom of limbs. But Vaulini did not remove her pinafore; it was one which Sireli had given her. She stumbled in the water so that her dress was wet and her body showed through the wet cloth. The women saw that she was very round, that her breasts were turgid and black at the tips as she stood with hanging head in their full view. Melika cried: "Why do you stand in the water in your pinafore?" She approached Vaulini and tore her dress from her in shreds. Then all the women knew that Vaulini was long with child.

Melika shrieked and struck her. All her mothers and her sisters struck her. They started back to the village wailing the funeral cry: "My child. *Isa lei*, my child." Vaulini stood in the water for a long time. Then she loitered along the path and hid in a grove which screened her from the village.

In the village the wailing of the women resounded long before they came into view. The Nalauvia men left sweet puddings half-prepared and fled in fear to the forest. The remaining guests paused in the midst of their festivities, but they began to chat again and pretended to forget the bride's disgrace. Isacodro sat listlessly in Toviya's house while noiseless tears ran down his cheeks; it is said they made a puddle on the floor. All the Nakoroka men were angry that Isacodro had failed to watch his daughter carefully. The years of preparation were wasted because the ceremony no longer had a purpose. Despite the lavish display of food and property, ancestors would not be pleased by this honoring of a bride who was not virgin.[13] But many of the men at Nakoroka were Isacodro's cross-cousins; they suppressed their anger. They say, however, that if it had not been for the British administration and the rules of the white man's church and the sweetness of temper at Nakoroka, they would surely have killed him anyway and all the people of Nalauvia.[14] Today he is like a man who has long ago been dead. If he should raise his voice among other men, they would remind him that he is lucky to be alive, that the counsel of a man who has failed to manage his own affairs is not wanted. But he has never raised his voice. He does menial tasks in silence, and privately he takes pride in his motor skills: he is a famous builder of houses; though he is old, he can wring the juice from kava with more grace than any man. He is proud of his unique immunity to pain and disgust. He can eat raw meat. Once he deliberately cut off his little toe because a splinter had infected it. In his daughter's presence he is still uncomfortable.

After nightfall Lebu and Lui brought word that they had found Vaulini beyond the village margin and that she refused to come home because she feared her kinsmen; two young men who were wedding guests went to police her return. Ema said: "Smite her when you see her. Let her die." But the young men led her to her husband.

Ema did not cry. Silently she cooked her fish and prepared the evening meal for her guests. Bici says that she wanted to "fly away," but she gave no sign. Like Isacodro, she cannot raise her voice among

13. Pregnancy is believed to require long-continued and regular intercourse. Hence her disgrace was manifold.

14. Ema, however, would have been spared because she comes of good Nakoroka stock. Though Isacodro has claims on Votua land, these would not have been strong enough to save his life, even in combination with his cross-cousin relationship. No offense could be more serious than his.

her age-mates lest Melika remind her of the way in which she failed to watch over her daughter's betrothal.[15]

Isacodro and Ema still grieve about their disgrace. But Vaulini has borne her shame lightly. Now that many years have passed, she laughs and chatters like any other woman. People say she is a fool.

Toviya and Sireli refused to show chagrin. Sireli gave Vaulini the personal gift of mats and *sulu*'s "to dry her" after her descent into the water. Though the wedding guests had gathered their belongings and prepared to depart straightway, Toviya persuaded them to stay until morning. Hastily Ema and Siteri made the exchange of mats and *sulu*'s. But in contrast with the exchange which had occurred at the time of the Wesleyan ceremony, Siteri withheld those which were in excess of Ema's gift; she made no generous gesture.[16] Then Ema and Siteri brought forth the whale teeth which the bride and groom had held during their "eating together." This should have been the climax of the marriage exchange, because whale teeth are sacred and their value cannot be measured. Hastily Ema placed hers before Siteri in the ceremony of presentation. Before Siteri reciprocated, she counted Ema's gift and gave an equal number in return. In haste the hosts of the marriage redistributed the marriage property among their guests. Each who had contributed received an exact equivalent in return. Next morning Nakoroka was empty of its guests. As is the custom, Isacodro and Ema escorted Vaulini back home to Nalauvia.

A month later Sireli, accompanied by mothers and sisters and his grandfather Unuwale as spokesman,[17] took two whale teeth to Isacodro at Nalauvia. Despite Vaulini's dishonor, it was necessary to complete the requirements of the marriage ceremony. This gift of whale teeth is called "the women see each other"; the women who were Vaulini's cross-cousins at Nakoroka came to accept her among them and escort her to the home of her husband. Unuwale presented

15. Long ago Ema was betrothed to Naicadra, who is now Melika's husband. But Isacodro used supernatural means to gain her favor, and she married him instead. Though Naicadra is a good man, a pillar of the church, Melika has never been happy as his wife. Once a famed beauty, she is still lithe and vigorous, much younger than he. He has always suffered from various chronic ailments. One child has been born to them, the fat and virtuous Meremanini. Perhaps Melika bears a secret grudge of long standing against Ema; it was Melika who first spied Vaulini's tragedy; it is Melika who reminds Ema of her guilt. They are "small sisters."

16. The careful counting of marriage property at this time is prescribed by ceremony. It had no bearing on the discovery of Vaulini's pregnancy.

17. Unuwale was Sireli's father's elder half-brother. Unuwale's death and funeral are described below, pp. 362–67. There were, in all, eight or ten persons in the party.

the whale teeth and said: "We have come to see Vaulini. Be of good spirit. It is true that there are bad reports about her, that you have broken her. But let the marriage of our children be managed properly. *A soso ratu!*" Ema wept, partly from shame and partly because Vaulini was about to join Toviya's household at Nakoroka for the span of her husband's life.[18] Isacodro and his brothers at Nalauvia had prepared an oven. It was a small thing but suitable for this occasion. A wild pig had been roasted as garnish for the food.

Next morning Isacodro's relatives brought dishes, clothing, and household equipment for Vaulini.[19] Vaulini's friends and immediate kinsmen accompanied her back to Nakoroka. Isacodro feigned illness and stayed in Nalauvia. At Nakoroka, Toviya had made an oven. Ceremony required that this, too, be but a small thing; but Toviya had slaughtered his last domestic pig.

When three months had passed, Ema brought gifts to Nakoroka as her *sasavuta* gift. Mats which were unfinished at the time of the wedding feast are included in this gift. This was an opportunity for her to remove the disgrace of losing in the marriage exchange. If it had been possible to erase all dishonor, the entire village at Nalauvia would have joined to make a truly lavish display of wealth. But Ema brought only thirty mats. A few kinsmen of Nakoroka people came from Lekutu. Friends came from villages near by but brought no gifts. Toviya and the men of his moiety made an oven and a simple kind of pudding. Someone had contributed a domestic pig. When the food was cooked, the feast was presented to the Nalauvia people. That night the young people danced until the cock crowed. Others whose tongues were loose with kava conversed with special skill. Next day a second oven was made for the guests at large; all but natives of Nakoroka received this feast. There was another night of dancing. Even old men danced. It is said that the young people made secret trysts in the dark, and, when they again joined the dancers, no one asked where they had been. At dawn all guests, except the few kinsmen from Lekutu, who had assisted as hosts on this occasion, shook hands and departed. Then the mats which Ema had brought were divided among those who had joined in making ovens for Toviya.

Now Vaulini was heavy with child. But Sireli was a good man and

18. In all known cases of marriage "in the manner of the land" the bride and groom joined the household of the groom.

19. On occasions of this sort property obligations of both affinal and blood kinsmen are applied. The entire village at Nalauvia contributed to this gift.

felt no anger toward her. When she was confined, Sireli said he would accept the child as his own. It was a girl. They named her after Queen Victoria.

A year later Isacodro came to live at Nakoroka because of trouble with his brother.

The betrothal whale tooth (*gasau me cina*); "food of the path for bringing forth the writs" (*boqa dresui i vola*); the gift of whale teeth called "the wedded see each other" (*vei divi ni vaku mau*);[20] the ceremony by the Lekutu mission official and the feast and exchange which followed (*vaku mau*); the great marriage feast which includes "ovens of the father and mother" of both bride and groom; "the eating together" (*kana vata*);[21] the counting of the mats; "making open the threshold" (*vaka ceva ni tuba*); "cutting the curls of the virgin bride" (*tasi ni tobe*); "the descent into the water" (*laki sobu*),[22] followed by the "drying" (*vaka mamaca*) and the exchange of marriage property (*solevu ni wati*); the gift of whale teeth called "the women see each other" (*vei divi*[23] *ni alewa*); the gift of mats called *sasavuta*—all these are episodes which marriage "in the manner of the land" prescribes. The names of the episodes are distributed throughout Vanua Levu, but associated property relations vary with locality. At Nakoroka it is said that the families of bride and groom always compete with each other in giving and that the property contributed by each is theoretically equivalent to what it receives.

Yet besides the greater number of mats and *sulu*'s which Sireli's family contributed, they also had roasted twenty domestic pigs and presented twenty-three whale teeth. Vaulini's family had roasted only six pigs and given Toviya but ten whale teeth. Though Vaulini's family had supplied some wooden vessels, some coarse floor mats for the kitchen and everyday use, and some kettles, tin plates, and spoons from the Chinese store, this household equipment in no way compensated for the discrepancy in value between the bride's and the groom's marriage property. The thirty mats which Ema brought as *sasavuta*

20. Because of the peculiar meaning which *divi* may take, the translation of this ceremony is uncertain. *Divi* sometimes denotes purposive action, "to see about something." With the preposition *mai* it can mean "to bring forth." The whole phrase might mean "arranging for the wedding ceremony." I have translated it above as though it were the regular reciprocal form of *diva*, "to see."

21. This ceremony gives name to the entire occasion.

22. Also called *vei dere*, "wading together," or *vei silimi*, "bathing together."

23. See above, n. 20, on *divi*.

gift were more than outweighed by the many feasts which Sireli's family had prepared. Yet Toviya and Sireli did not feel cheated of their rightful property; like all bridegrooms at Nakoroka, Sireli was proud of having defeated his wife in giving. It is right that the bride's people should be lavishly entertained.

Ten of the whale teeth Isacodro had received were returned to those from whom he had begged the teeth he had given, but thirteen remained with him to dispose of when the occasion arose. Toviya had collected twenty-three teeth to present to Isacodro and had received only ten to distribute in return. He distributed these among his more distant kinsmen. Men at Nakoroka were so closely bound by obligations of kin that they shared Toviya's debt as though it were their own; likewise they enjoyed prestige from the wealth which was displayed at Sireli's wedding. Because Toviya's status was high as heir to the titular whale tooth for his division of Votua,[24] he was free to ask Bulisivo for support in his enterprise; Bulisivo personally supplied several whale teeth. A man of low status would not have dared to ask aid from a high chief directly. Though the debts which Toviya had incurred were remembered by his creditors, no creditor ever thought of pressing his claim. The kin group has always been interwoven with individual debt-credit relations; he who empties his coffers into the hands of a brother or cross-cousin knows that, when a need arises, he himself has many brothers and cross-cousins on whom to depend. Only conspicuous debtors lose face.

If all exchanges were like Sireli's wedding, Nakoroka would soon exhaust its supply of whale teeth. The matter is otherwise with the food distributed. After gardens have been emptied for ceremonial display, they are always replanted with zeal. Small pigs are fed carefully. For several years this zeal bears fruit, and the land flourishes as evidence that the ancestors have been pleased. But the supply of whale teeth is strictly limited. Hence those which have passed out of the community must be replaced through other channels. Ten years earlier Bulisivo's eldest daughter had married a chief of the Dama region; Nakoroka had lost gracefully in the competitive display of wealth, but its supply of whale teeth had increased. When Bulisivo's two sisters were young, rumor of their beauty had spread throughout Vanua Levu. Chiefs came from distant regions in hope of winning their favor.

---

24. It was not until the death of Unuwale in 1933 that Toviya received this title, but at the time of the wedding he was already known as potential heir. The actual title-holder, Unuwale, gave Toviya full support in this enterprise.

YOUNG WOMAN WITH VIRGIN'S
COIFFURE

Often they were betrothed with many whale teeth as gifts to guard their virginity,[25] but they always found excuse to break the marriage agreement. It is said that their father Ratu Seru became very rich. The gifts given at times of birth and funerals may also bring wealth into the village.

Despite Vaulini's disgrace, the fame of her wedding still resounds in Bua Province. Such wealth was never before assembled for a wedding feast at Nakoroka.[26] Even less elaborate marriages "in the manner of the land" warrant discussion for many years, because such marriages are rare. Virgins are few. Girls of the present generation rarely bother to dress their hair in virgin's coiffure. Thus they avoid the publicity which attends the shearing of their curls when it becomes known that they are no longer virgins. About sixteen years ago Losana and Vatili performed all the ceremonial exchanges of marriage "in the manner of the land." Losana was a virgin because she was very young; she had barely attained puberty when Vatili presented the betrothal whale tooth. Such youth is unusual. Bici says that her marriage was almost like that of an Indian in this respect. But the gift exchanges were small and not to be compared with the marriage of Vaulini. Vatili's status in his kin group was not firm enough to permit lavish accumulation of wealth; there are no chiefs or title-holders in Losana's family.

Melika had been a virgin when Naicadra betrothed her more than twenty years ago. They had fulfilled the marriage ceremonies "in the manner of the land." But they were both of Nadroro land. Their kin groups overlapped and were so closely knit that there was little motive for competitive display.

The only other Nakoroka betrothal which was consummated by marriage was that of Bulisivo. More than forty years ago his father presented ten whale teeth as betrothal gift to a noblewoman of a powerful Wainunu family. Bulisivo had not been consulted, but, like a dutiful son, he married as his father wished. Great pomp attended.

It is said that betrothals were more frequent in the old days. In recent years parents have hesitated to betroth their children because of a growing wilfulness among the younger generation. Peni's father gave a whale tooth to Nabadua to betroth his son to Nabadua's daughter Lui. A quarrel broke the engagement,[27] and hard feeling

25. When they were no longer virgins, they received another kind of gift as marriage proposal: "speaking for the woman."
26. The wedding feast of Bulisivo's oldest daughter occurred in the land of her husband.
27. See above, p. 251.

arose for a time between Nabadua and Peni's father. Ivamere's betrothal was likewise unsuccessful.[28]

Most men chose a simpler method. A gift of whale teeth to the fathers and brothers of the prospective bride states a man's intention; the gift is called "speaking for the woman." Women who receive this direct proposal are not virgins. When enough time has elapsed to purchase the marriage writs and marriage property, a small feast validates the union, and the marriage is fulfilled. If the bride and groom are of high status, this kind of marriage may lead to elaborate display of property, despite simpler ceremonial requirements. The gifts which Bulisivo's sisters received as "speech for the woman" comprised many whale teeth. Their marriage feasts would have been lavish; but these women were headstrong, as noblewomen are inclined to be, and against the will of their brother and the village they eloped with men who had given no gifts at all. Ratu Luke gave two whale teeth "to speak for the woman"; though Bulisivo and the village disapproved of his choice of a bride, his status as chief required feasting for several days. Little property was exchanged, however, because Ratu Luke's kinsmen would not support him in this wilful enterprise. Keleivi, who married in 1936, gave a single whale tooth as his "speech for the woman." He shares Raitova's household inconspicuously. He is of low birth, and he never raises his voice among men. His courage in coaxing spirits of the dead from their graves is his only claim to notoriety. His marriage feast was a boiled meal, and the village took no notice; the only persons to whom he confided his intention were the women of Raitova's household: his "small daughter" Ivamere and his "small sister" Losana.[29]

It is said that the colonial administration discourages elaborate exchanges at marriage because of the danger of dispute arising through broken marriage agreements. The betrothal whale tooth which watches over the virginity of the bride and the gift which "speaks for the woman" have brought trouble in the past. If the woman chooses to reject these gifts at the time they are proffered, they are returned to the suitor. But if she chooses to wait for a time and then finds some fault with the suitor's character, he forfeits the whale tooth. Of the long series of ceremonial gifts, that called "the wedded see each other," which just precedes the mission ceremony, is the first which meets

28. Ivamere was betrothed to Waiseya (see Chart X) until November, 1935, when she was involved in a scandal (see above, p. 295).

29. Losana is Vatili's wife, but her prenuptial ties were with Raitova's land.

with colonial approval; little time remains for increasing the productivity of gardens, fattening pigs, and seeking marriage property.

Another kind of gift exchange which culminates in a wedding feast is replacing the old-fashioned marriage "in the manner of the land." Groups of brothers or sisters have visiting relationships with the girls or boys of opposite moiety in a neighboring village. Accompanying gift exchanges increase with each visit until they attain extravagant proportions.[30] Only marriage proposals can conclude the competition honorably. To heighten village prestige, brothers aid their competing sisters; parents help their children in the entertainment of the guests. Six years ago Orisi's marriage concluded a relationship of this sort with the girls of Dreketi.

Sometime in 1933 Vaulini, who was then widowed, Lebu, and Lui had carried baskets of kava to the Chinese trader at Lekutu and purchased scarfs and new printed cloth. On their return, while they were watching a festival at an Indian village near Lekutu, a group of boys who were their cross-cousins arrived from Nalauvia. They stopped to banter. Someone suggested starting an exchange relationship. The girls gave away their newly made purchases; the boys gave them tobacco and set a day upon which they would come to Nakoroka bringing gifts. Half a year later they came laden with tobacco, printed cloth, and perfume from the Chinese trader. Namo and Jekovi, who were Lui's true brothers, made ovens and feasted the Nalauvia boys. The boys made two piles of their gifts; one they called "dead things," which canceled the gifts given by the Nakoroka girls six months before; the other they called "living things," which the Nakoroka girls would have to cancel with future gifts before any prestige would accrue to them. With each visit, "living things" must grow in quantity.[31]

In Nabadua's house the girls danced to entertain their guests. As they danced, the Nalauvia boys rolled cigarettes from tobacco and wild pineapple leaves, lit them, and gave them to the dancing girls. After a puff or two, which interrupted the dance, the girls passed their cigarettes back to their mothers and their brothers, who were singing and clapping accompaniment in the crowded house. The rhythm of the dance beat through the village. Sometimes an old woman of an-

30. This relationship is called *tau-muana*, "of a piece" (?).

31. This same classification of goods in exchange occurs during the gift exchange which accompanies the reciprocal visiting of chiefs or any intervillage feast. The same terminology applies to modern card games in which the losers always insist upon a chance to "kill" the "living" score against them.

other household who had no taboo relatives among the dancers left her mat half-plaited, wrapped a fresh *sulu* about her waist, and went to watch the dancers and clap time. Older men, however, preferred to drink evening kava with their usual friends. When three or four dance songs had been sung completely in all their verses, the girls clapped out of time as signal that it was the guests' turn to dance. When the boys hesitated, the girls cried: "Give back the dance! Give it back!" And the boys tore garlands from the hedges outside and returned to dance while the Nakoroka girls made cigarettes for them. Some older women had come from Nalauvia to accompany the dancing of their sons. Peni of Nakoroka beat the dance drum for them; they are his brothers.[32] Later the Nakoroka girls danced again. And the Nalauvia boys danced in return again and again. Toward morning the girls donned old *sulu*'s, and gave the new ones which they had been wearing to the boys as they presented cigarettes. In return, the boys gave them tobacco and all the clothing they could spare with decency.[33]

The girls returned the visit to Nalauvia, and the Nalauvia boys came to Nakoroka a second time. In September, 1935, the Nakoroka girls visited Nalauvia. With co-operation of almost the entire village at Nakoroka, their extravagance discouraged their competitors. They waited in vain for a return visit. Finally, in 1936, a Nalauvia boy proposed marriage to Lui. The formal competition was ended. But Nalauvia will exhaust its last resources to feast Nakoroka on the wedding day.

Sometimes competing villages must retire in disgrace. The daughters of Bulisivo were once involved in this kind of relationship with the young men of Duleniwai. The entire village at Nakoroka co-operated. When the Duleniwai guests arrived, they were dismayed to find colored cloth tied in streamers to the palms which line the village margin. Though a child[34] was born to one of Bulisivo's daughters, the young Duleniwai chief who was its father did not dare to propose a

32. Except for the initial exchange of gifts, this description is typical of the dancing which entertains all guests.

33. The competitive giving of personal belongings is called *vei tatau* and may accompany the dancing of any intervillage groups whose relationship is of long standing and hence competitive. The affinal ties between Nakoroka and Nalauvia are so close that sometimes even the older people dance and give away their clothes. Once Nabadua returned from a Nalauvia visit ashamed and discouraged because the *sulu* which he had given away was dirtier and more ragged than the one he had received in return. (But Nabadua's shame was a boast of a nobly generous spirit.)

34. Di Sereima, born about 1931.

marriage feast. Duleniwai was shamed. In 1936 the young chief brought a few personal gifts to the child to validate its paternity.

Once when the Nakoroka men had been building houses at the island Galoa, they cast their *sulu*'s on the beach as they were departing. As they sailed away, the Galoa girls shouted that they would soon come to Nakoroka to dance and bring gifts. When the Nakoroka men reached Lekutu, they purchased two dozen handkerchiefs from the Chinese trader and sent them to Galoa. But the Galoa girls have never come to dance. They are "weak." Except for Bici,[35] the Nakoroka men are proud of their strength in giving. Bici says that it is a stupid thing to do because you always lose your property.

These dance relationships at all times color the attitudes of those who have participated. During the housebuilding at Lekutu in February, 1936, casual dancing filled many evenings. Gift exchanges always accompanied the dancing of Nakoroka girls and Nalauvia boys even though the occasions were informal, not expressly planned as times of exchange. Lui and her sisters have been described as "belonging" to the young men of Galoa and Tavea; they are potential competitors in dance exchanges.

Young Ratu Seru and his brothers are especially lavish in their entertainment of Dreketi girls. Though the exchange relationship which culminated in Orisi's marriage is long since past, a desire for competitive display still persists. At Christmas time in 1935, Ratu Seru prepared expensive foods for the visiting Dreketi girls. The night before their departure he serenaded them; with his ukulele and tenor voice he led the procession of young people which wound across the village green in the moonlight. In European harmony they sang: "O congenial guest, your departure is sorrowful to me. What are you about, leaving tomorrow?"[36] As they approached the house where the guests were, the chorus swelled in volume. Then the young men, who were dressed in garlands and smeared with ointment, filed through the door and took places for the dance.

In the old days *tau-muana* relationship between villages was unknown. Bulisivo remembers a trading game played by the men of one

35. Bici is about thirty-five years old. He played a very mild role in the relationship with the Galoa girls. It is usual for younger people to be the major participants. The dance exchange is described by married people as a game for the young. A married man or woman should not enjoy the sexual excitement which always accompanies the dancing of young people. Yet marriage does not preclude participation in the festivities.

36. This song is known throughout Fiji by both natives and Europeans. It is played by the band in Suva.

village with the women of another, out of which he suggests that *tau-muana* may have grown. At the last occurrence of this game he was a young man. Nakoroka was playing with Tavea, with which trade has always been lively; the people of Tavea are Nakoroka's special "sea people." They decided upon an ironwood grove near Lekutu as gaming ground. The young people of Nakoroka tied bundles of sugar cane and ripe bananas in the trees at one end of the grove and built pyramids of yams and taro. They also brought sweet puddings to feast their opponents when the game was over. The people of Tavea brought sea turtles and many kinds of fish and piled them at the opposite end of the grove. While each group of young men guarded its own food, the young women of each competing village set out to steal food from the men of the other. Thus the women tussled with the men; it would have been dangerous for the men of different villages to compete so boisterously. Bulisivo was sitting in a tree guarding Nakoroka bananas when the women of Tavea approached. They grasped his foot and pulled him from his perch. He spoke to them, but they paid no heed even though they knew he was a chief. The din and the gaiety were great. Bulisivo laughs when he remembers how he could not even hear his own voice. The village whose supply of food was first exhausted lost the game. The winners gave the remainder of their food to the losers and shamed them. But all remembered the exact margin by which the winners had excelled; this was called the "living" surplus and served to stimulate a return bout. At each successive game greater quantities of wealth were displayed. But Bulisivo does not remember that a marriage was required to put an end to the competition.

FEASTS AND CEREMONIES OF BIRTH AND EARLY INFANCY

Ramo did not come to Nakoroka until November, 1935. 'Her marriage to Ratu Luke the previous April had angered the chiefly family of Votua, who were Ratu Luke's nearest relatives at Nakoroka. And she preferred to live on at Sarowaqa and take Ratu Luke into the household of her parents there.[37] Bulisivo, who is his "small father," had expected him to marry Di Kabu's daughter, who virtuously stayed at home in the evenings and plaited mats. But Ratu Luke is not dependable. The Votua chiefs blame him bitterly for marrying a commoner and scattering his chiefly blood. For six months he had been "village chief" at Sarowaqa, but he could not make the men build houses; they would not listen to him. So the Buli of Lekutu District re-

37. Ratu Luke was *vasu* at Sarowaqa, but the chiefly family had died out. No one remained through whom he could exert his claims.

moved him from his post. In disgust Ratu Luke returned to Nakoroka in October, 1935, despite the anger of the Votua chiefs. He had no house of his own, but Toviya, whose house lies between Bulisivo's and Naicadra's, offered him hospitality. A month later he brought Ramo.

Since early November, Ramo had been expecting labor pains. Everyone knew that she was carrying twins. Her pregnancy had lasted too long for the growth of a single fetus. Naicadra's wife Melika, who is skilled in these matters, had already taken Ramo to the ford in the river Votua to see whether the twins were fully formed and ready to be born; she squatted in the water for this examination. Since the time when her menstruation had first stopped, she had known she was pregnant. She knew that the forming of children takes about nine months, but she had not marked the time carefully. November was the tenth month, she thought. While she felt ill during the early months, she had lain in the house. When she felt well again and went about the village, Ratu Luke made no feast to announce that she had passed the first period of pregnancy. Had his gardens been flourishing, he might have so honored this first conception of his marriage; but the omission was not serious because everyone knew that Ramo had already borne two children out of wedlock. She visited about the village, washed clothes, plaited mats, and journeyed to the gardens. But she did not touch a cooking pot; she did not want her children blemished with birthmarks. Until Ramo's sister joined her at Nakoroka to do the chores of Toviya's household, Melika and her daughter, who were of Naicadra's household next door, prepared food and carried water for Ratu Luke and his wife; this was because their houses are close together. If Ratu Luke had observed filial obligations to Bulisivo, he might have persuaded the Nakoroka men to build a small house for Ramo so that she might have privacy during her late pregnancy and confinement; it is forbidden to prepare kava in a house where infants live. To avoid this inconvenient taboo, Toviya had to divide his time between Naicadra's household and that of his wife's people in Sarowaqa.

Ratu Luke had not slept with Ramo for a long time. A good husband always remembers that sexual intercourse during pregnancy increases the pain of delivery. Almost every man desists during the last three or four months. They would not have sexual intercourse again until nearly a year had passed and the nursing period was complete. He avoided other women, too, because he wanted his children to be well formed in Ramo's womb.

When Melika's examinations showed that confinement was drawing near, Ratu Luke and Ramo were afraid. Ancestors may snatch away the newly created soul of a child whose parents have disobeyed their elders. Ratu Luke felt guilty. Though it was he who had organized the November feast to welcome Bulisivo home from his long sojourn on the windward coast, he had not deigned to admit his guilt and beg forgiveness; though he had blamed the village for failing to honor Bulisivo's return, he had not humbled himself, and Bulisivo had not been moved to forget Ratu Luke's previous disregard for chiefly responsibilities. On December 31 twin girls were born. Ratu Luke lay in his kitchen all day. He dared not work, lest the infants suffer sympathetically; had he worked with a knife, they would have become blind. It was taboo for him to enter the house where they were being delivered. To escape his anxiety, he refused the food which his friends brought him and feigned sleep.

Melika presided at the confinement. Her daughter helped. Ramo's sister and two elderly women, Di Kabu and Iliseveci, were also there. Ramo's twins were born easily. In the old days the usual posture assumed for delivery was squatting braced against a house post. If labor was slow, the confined woman clung to a pole which was lifted high and jostled by the women attendants. Or the attendants would support the patient between them and run about the house. But Melika used the new "white man's method": Ramo lay on her side. Melika regrets that there are no young women who have courage enough to become her pupils in midwifery. The young women of today are too weak to face this ordeal.

When the infants were not eating, Di Kabu and Iliseveci held them in their laps and shaped their foreheads with the constant pressure of their hands. A bulging forehead is uncomely. When the old women slept, younger women who were their apprentices[38] held the infants. For three days the shaping continued; by that time the infant skulls had become hard and fixed. To these women Ratu Luke presented the feast which is called "the dropping of the navel cord." It was a boiled meal. Melika would have received food also, but she had helped with the cooking.[39]

38. Women teach their skills to willing pupils regardless of kin relationships, but they like to teach girls of their own families.

39. At this time a coconut should be planted. When it has sprouted and grown for a year or two, the child's navel cord, which has been preserved for the occasion, should be hidden in its crown. This tree is the child's first property. Several children at Nakoroka own such trees.

Ramo's milk was not enough for her twins. When they were three days old, Ratu Luke went to the nearest Indian village and offered to work in the rice fields there in return for the use of a milk cow. Formerly a nurse would have been chosen from among the village women; it is said that a suckling infant can stimulate the production of milk in the breast of even a childless woman.[40] But in the last two decades the European custom of feeding cow's milk has become fashionable. No one at Nakoroka knows how to milk a cow so that it will keep producing milk; rather than empty the udder regularly and let the surplus spoil (since the drinking of milk nauseates most normal adults), it is considered more economical to extract only enough to supply immediate needs. In two and one-half weeks Ratu Luke's cow had ceased to produce milk. During the next six months he made frequent excursions to the Indian village for fresh cows and spent many intervals working in the rice fields.

When Ratu Luke made the "feast of birth" (*magiti ni sucu* or *tu nu dra*), his children were ten days old. It was an oven of yams and taro which he presented to Bulisivo; if Ramo's parents had come from Sarowaqa, he would have feasted them instead. He should have made it much sooner, but he was harassed with obligations to the Indians. The food was apportioned among the chiefs of Votua, who, acting as his kinsmen, had presented a small gift of mats.

Six weeks later Ramo's parents came from Sarowaqa bringing a gallon tin of kerosene from the Chinese trader and three mats. This gift is called *cika tenetene* or *tuku mi*. It must accompany all who come from other villages to see newborn children. Ratu Luke asked Bulisivo to supply a pig for a return feast, but Bulisivo refused. Instead he offered to give taro and order the young men to prepare sweet puddings for the guests. Ratu Luke was ashamed to present such meager fare. Fortunately for him, Ramo's more distant relatives in Sarowaqa had not bothered to come. Ratu Luke kept expecting his noble mothers, who were "small sisters" of his own mother and lived as great chieftainesses in the household of the Roko of Macuata at Naduri; he had sent word to them that his children were born. He wanted them to come bringing the gift called *tuku mi*, because Nakoroka people had always respected his family connections with the great Macuata chiefs. He always imagined that they would come the next week, but they never arrived.

40. Women at Nakoroka cannot understand the stupidity of Europeans who do not know this fact.

When the children were two months old, Ratu Luke permitted
Ramo to leave the house and wander freely about the village. Now
after two months' confinement she could bathe in the river. Now for
the first time in months she could work in the kitchen. But Bulisivo
waited two weeks more before he performed the naming ceremony
which initiated the children's first contact with kava and which had
to precede their first departure from the house. He named a day.
Vatili and Monasa, who are Ramo's kinsmen at Nakoroka, helped her
parents to prepare a feast for Bulisivo, who would perform the ceremony, and for Ratu Luke and the other chiefs of Votua. No one questioned Bulisivo's right to play chief's role in this ceremony; it is an hon-
or for any child to be named by a man of such high rank. Bulisivo felt
he was being very kind to the wayward Ratu Luke; Ratu Luke was
annoyed that Bulisivo had failed to hold this ceremony two months
earlier. Monasa baked taro. Ramo's father brought a half-dozen tins
of beef, several bars of soap, and a gallon tin of kerosene from the
Chinese trader of Sarowaqa; he should have brought at least one
whale tooth for Bulisivo, but the coastal villages have come to use
trade-store goods instead. Vatili brought a small stalk of kava from his
garden.

The young men prepared kava and served it in most formal fashion.
Monasa and Vatili sat on either side of the bowl fulfilling the role of
chiefs who were presenting: they led the rhythmic clapping and the
chants of the kava ceremony. The twins lay on two fathoms of new
printed cloth spread on a new mat before Bulisivo. When he was
served, he held the cup over their heads and spoke: "Your kava,
Lanieta and Lusiana. Your kava. Be healthy. Be fertile. Do not conceive in the path." As he drank, all present clapped their hands in
syncopated rhythm until his cup was empty. Because there were not
enough commoners among Ratu Luke's close kinsmen to supply each
chief with a "messenger" for the kava ceremony (it is improper for
two chiefs to drink in succession), Vosalevu, who is Big Di Litiya's
husband, acted as "messenger" for Bulisivo because they are cross-
cousins. Ratu Luke drank as "messenger" for Big Di Litiya because
he was youngest of the chiefs and his status lowest. Naicadra drank as
a chief. When Monasa and Vatili had drunk, each chief was served
again in turn. Then the twins were removed. Their part in the ceremony was ended. Though Ratu Luke had decided long before that his
children should be named for his dead mother and her sister (one of
the noblewomen of the household of the Roko of Macuata), this was

the first ceremonial use of their names. The occasion is called "drinking with purpose" (*unu baleta*).

Informal drinking followed until the kava bowl was empty. Then the feast of taro and tinned beef was presented formally to Bulisivo and the Votua chiefs. The mat and the cloth on which the twins had lain during the ceremony should have been a gift from Ramo's parents, but Ramo's family had suffered hardships; Ratu Luke, who was anxious lest Bulisivo find flaws in the ceremony, supplied this gift which his parents-in-law were unable to provide. Ramo herself had plaited the mat. The mat and the cloth were now Bulisivo's; he rolled them up and took them to his house. If whale teeth had been presented, these too would have been Bulisivo's. Perhaps Ramo's father was ashamed that his gift had been so poor; saying that his sister's child lay ill at Sarowaqa, he begged to be excused from the ceremony as soon as the kava was finished.

Every week Ratu Luke hunted wild cattle. He kept his household supplied with wild pork. When pigs destroyed the taro and many yams of his only dry garden, he held his remaining yams in reserve because he still anticipated the visit of his "mothers" from Macuata. When he lamented that he could prepare no entertainment worthy of these noble visitors, Bulisivo offered little sympathy. Even for the food of every day, Ratu Luke was dependent upon his Votua kinsmen. He was continuously in debt to the Indians for the use of their milk cows. In spite of the fact that during the first week in May he had given four mats, twelve large yams, and twelve taro and labored in the rice fields for three days without pay, the Indians came during the night and secretly removed the cow. Although the twins could already eat small bits of yam and taro and the juice of coconut meat, they needed more milk. One of them was especially weak. At length Bulisivo consented to accompany Ratu Luke to the Indian village to hire out as laborer in payment for the rent of another cow. For four days they worked there together. Bulisivo's wife and youngest daughter accompanied them to care for Bulisivo's needs and perhaps to help him plant in the rice fields. Although Bulisivo was aged and the labor which he could perform was negligible, even among the Indians his presence lent dignity to Ratu Luke's request for a cow; not so much dignity, however, as Bulisivo imagined.

Toward the end of May, Bulisivo decided that Ratu Luke's twins were strong enough to go outdoors. Still worrying lest his "mothers" come and find him without food, Ratu Luke made the feast to com-

memorate the twins' first bath in the river. He asked Namo to supply
taro; if Namo had not belonged to commoner caste, he would have
been his "small brother." Ratu Luke made a small oven and presented
Bulisivo with baked taro and wild pig. Afterward Ramo carried the
children about the village to visit for a time in each household. Bici
says that the eldest child, who in each family is called "the old head,"[41]
is honored with a gift presentation upon its first visit to each household, that new mats are spread for it to lie upon, and that these become the child's property. Everyone knew that the twins were not
Ramo's first-born. It was said, too, that Ratu Luke had already sired
children in Macuata and on the windward coast. But the twins were
considered Ratu Luke's eldest because they were the first issue of his
first marriage. Bulisivo had performed the naming ceremony, an honor
which only the first-born receive. It was the last Sunday in May when
Ramo took the children to see Di Kabu and Big Di Litiya in their
great house. There the noblewomen remarked upon the beauty of the
children; they played with them and tried to make them laugh. Everyone enjoyed the visit. But no new mats were spread upon the floor;
they received no further honor as Ratu Luke's oldest children. The
entire village took pride in them as newborn village offspring, for the
birth of twins is rare and brings fame to the village. But no one gave
them special gifts when they went visiting.

When an oldest child is born, it is a special honor for a friend of the
parents to be *qima*. A private agreement before the time of birth establishes the relationship. The *qima* must avoid seeing the child for several
months; when he feels that he has honored the child enough, he "goes
to see" bearing gifts. In return the parents prepare a feast or present a
gift of food. During the last few decades at Nakoroka there had been
but one *qima:* Vosalevu had honored the eldest child of Samu in this
way. Ratu Luke told me that I could be *qima* for his twins. When three
months had passed, I tired of the inconveniences of this avoidance relationship and asked that a day be appointed for my presenting of gifts.
As usual, Ratu Luke was expecting the arrival of his "mothers" and
begged me to delay. When his "mothers" did not come and he saw
my impatience growing, he begged yams of Bulisivo and sent his wife
and her sisters for a mess of fish. After carefully composing a presentation speech, I went to see the twins. I presented a whale tooth and a
fathom of blue woolen cloth which had been sent to me from America.

41. If the oldest child dies, the second-born does not inherit the distinction.

As his "receiving the whale tooth" gift, Ratu Luke gave me a pandanus mat. Unfortunately I had composed no acceptance speech; but Akuila, who had received with Ratu Luke, moved quickly to my side and without embarrassment acted as my "messenger" for the rest of the ceremony. Though Akuila spoke of the mat as "our mat," his claims to part ownership in it were ceremonial only; he insisted that I keep it. But he did share the meal of boiled yams and fish which Ratu Luke presented to me later in the same evening. Next day Ratu Luke brought me a kava stalk and several baskets of uncooked yams from Bulisivo's gardens.

Still the twins were not well fed, and Ratu Luke had no more to give as rent for a cow. When the Indians came to collect, he went with them to their village hoping to do some work in payment. During this period the young men of Nakoroka were searching for means to earn tax money, and the village was empty except for women and old people; there was no one to milk the cow. When Vatili returned from an attempt to find work at the mines, Ramo complained of Ratu Luke's neglect and requested Vatili in his role as "village chief" to arraign Ratu Luke before the next meeting of the provincial officials in district court at Lekutu. Because she was still nursing her children, she could not bring food from the gardens or water from the river; women with suckling infants are considered too weak for heavy work. In Ratu Luke's absence she was completely dependent upon Melika's kitchen. When kava had loosened his tongue that night, Vatili spoke loudly against Ratu Luke: "Ratu Luke is a fool. He does no chores for his wife, and his children have no food." Vatili should not have spoken so; Ratu Luke is a chief. Though Vatili considers Ratu Luke his "small son," they are brothers-in-law (cross-cousins) through Ramo and must love each other.

During his late adolescence Ratu Luke had lived in the household of the Roko of Macuata. Some people say that the trouble started because of his attentions to a young girl who was a commoner. He ran away. Then for a time he lived with his father on the windward coast. The Roko of Bua Province offered to appoint him to high office in a district, a great honor for a man not yet thirty years old. Ratu Luke says he declined, arguing that he had no wife to manage the kind of household which an official requires. Others say that he was tired of a certain woman who has since borne his child. He returned to Nakoroka, to the land where his mother is buried, and the chiefs of Votua greeted him warmly as a prospective son-in-law. They helped him build gardens and begged him to feel at home until they found that his attention was centering on Ramo, the pretty commoner in Sarowaqa. Now when Ratu Luke heard that Vatili had threatened to arraign him, he returned sullenly to Nakoroka. The Votua chiefs, who were his nearest relatives, were willing to sit by and watch him pay for his folly. Without their support he could not hope to provide for his wife and children. He returned to Nakoroka; but, rather than carry water for his wife, he preferred to hunt wild pigs in the forest. The women of Naicadra's virtuous household continued to carry meals to Ramo and the twins.

Early in June when Vatili quarreled with his wife Losana,[42] Ratu Luke dared to speak angrily about it among the young men. Ratu Luke extolled the virtues of Losana and suggested that some scandalous act lay at the root of the family quarrel.

When a child born in his father's village has attained two or three years of age and first visits the village of his mother, his father's family must accompany him carrying gifts for the parents of the mother. This gift is called *vaka sika rara*, "pressing down the village green" (?). In return the parents of the mother make a feast which commemorates the child's return to the land where he is *vasu*, i.e., bound by maternal ties. If Bulisivo chose to honor Ratu Luke's children, he might use this occasion to organize a village-wide presentation of gifts to Sarowaqa and with a great display of wealth augment Nakoroka's prestige. But it is unlikely that his attitude toward Ratu Luke will change. When the twins visit Sarowaqa, Ratu Luke will probably present two or three mats and a basket of yams; no one but the immediate family will be interested.

If a child is born in his mother's village and the father wishes to change the child's residence to his own village, the father's family must present gifts called "the carrying forth" (*vei roqo*). Bici considers this gift a payment for the trouble caused by confinement. Ratu Luke was born in Sarowaqa, his mother's village, and his father, who was then resident at Nakoroka, "carried him forth." But such cases are rare. Among commoners confinements usually occur in the village of permanent residence. Among chiefs gift exchanges must always accompany changes of residence.

42. See above, pp. 262–63.

DRINKING KAVA TO CELEBRATE THE COMPLETION
OF A NEW HOUSE

The natives have bathed and have donned fresh clothes for the occasion

CHURCH HOLIDAY AT LEKUTU

Photograph through the courtesy of Mr. L. M. Anderson of Delanisau

Like marriage exchanges, those associated with birth and infancy range in scope from a small feast which a man prepares in order to announce publicly that he accepts the responsibilities of paternity to elaborate wealth displays which mobilize the resources of the entire village, as in the case of chiefs in good standing. Had Vaulini been a virgin when she married Sireli, elaborate exchanges between the affinal kinsmen in Nakoroka and Nalauvia would have persisted throughout their first child's infancy; occasions for gift presentation, which were inconspicuous in the case of Ratu Luke's children, would have tested the prestige of village ancestors. Tales of the extravagance of feasts would have resounded throughout Bua Province.

Usually the father is ultimately responsible for making all feasts and entertaining those who come bringing gifts. Obligations toward all guests from other villages, whether they are his wife's consanguineous relatives or his own, are equal. It is only the naming ceremony, "drinking with a purpose," in which affinal groups have distinct ceremonial function. For this rite an elder kinsman is chosen for his high rank, regardless of whether his affiliations are with mother's or father's family; he and his family receive the feast and the gifts; the family of the other parent presents.

DEATH AND FUNERALS

The villages had assembled after the Christmas holidays to build houses at Lekutu. Gaiety of the holiday time was fresh. For four nights the dance drums had been beating until dawn. Many dwelling houses had been given over to the young people, who wanted privacy to dance for their partners from other villages. Even some of the older people, who were not beating time for the dance of the young, danced for one another and gave away their clothes. It is said that Isacodro and Vatili had been very gay. On this night Nakoroka danced for Nalauvia until past midnight. Then the chiefs[43] and some of the men repaired to the house of Ratu Kitioni, who of Lekutu chiefs is kinsman to Bulisivo.[44] They retired, but they did not sink far into sleep. Vosalevu came shouting through the door and tumbled them rudely on their mats. There was a corpse next door, and the funeral wake had languished from inattention; the mourners had requested the Nakoroka people to dance.

43. Big Di Litiya, Vosalevu, and the daughters of Bulisivo. The occasion was not important enough to bring Bulisivo himself away from his land at Nakoroka.

44. The name of Ratu Kitioni's house is the same as that of Big Di Litiya at Nakoroka: "Inland Forest."

Though a commoner, the dead man had been a distant kinsman of Big Di Litiya. He had died on the island of Tavea. Early in the evening his near relatives brought home the corpse, but the wailing of this small procession passed almost unnoticed. Some paused to exclaim: "A death!" But all imagined that some other more closely related kinsman would dance at the wake and continued preparing for whatever entertainment they had already planned. In the dead man's house a lamp was hung above the corpse. A few kinsmen came bringing the "gift of death," greeted the corpse with mourning cries, and danced for a while.

But the drums of the young people, sounding from distant parts of the village, coaxed them away. Only a few tired women remained to cheer the mourners with their feeble clowning. When the Nakoroka people retired for the night in the house next door, the dead man's wife asked Vosalevu to rouse them so that the funeral wake could last throughout the night.

Reluctantly shaking sleep from nerves which four sleepless nights of dancing had already jangled, the Nakoroka people smeared their faces clumsily with scented oil and tied garlands in careless knots round their wrists and throats. Each wore a fresh *sulu* which Big Di Litiya had begged from Ratu Kitioni, whose house they shared. Somehow Di Litiya managed to present a pile of cloth and some tobacco to the dead man's family. Vatili, Samu, Big Melika, who is Naicadra's wife and Di Litiya's cross-cousin, and the daughters of Bulisivo stumbled across the threshold behind Vosalevu and arranged themselves for the dance. Vosalevu kept shouting: "The dance is good. Quick, start the song. Let our dance be strong." Di Litiya clapped her hands noisily all the while and laughed loudly for no cause except to rouse her comrades to the hilarity proper at a funeral. Vatili, Samu, and Vosalevu danced while the women sang and clapped out rhythm. It was the sitting dance of indoors. Vosalevu led the posturing until Vatili, who gained spirit with each chorus, began to swing lithely and anticipate the jerking of Vosalevu's stiffening joints. In his youth Vatili had been renowned for graceful dancing. Despite Vosalevu's sly prods with the elbow, Samu never awoke completely; he continued to make mistakes which made the women scream with laughter.

The corpse, wrapped in mats, made a long bundle in the center of the house. The dead man's wife sat before it and roused herself from quiet weeping to laugh noisily now and then and to cheer with clapping hands. An elder daughter of the dead man sat near that end of the bundle which was his head and, leaning over it, wailed mourning phrases in a piercing voice. She guarded the corpse from the dogs that came to sniff and fanned away the insects that swarmed about the lamp. But each time she wailed, the joyous clamor of the Nakoroka women welled stronger to drown her weeping. Vosalevu shouted the dance song in his hoarse voice. Big Melika leaped into the line of dancing men and with rolling eyes and awkward gestures began to mimic the dancers, lagging always just behind the beat. Laughter grew louder. People were roused from sleep in near-by houses and came to watch. Someone brought a dance drum.

Then it was the mourners' turn to dance. Di Litiya, the women, the dancing men, and the newly come spectators who crowded the thresholds all shouted at the dead man's wife and his wailing daughters: "Dance. Return the dance. Thanks for the dance." Small children, grandchildren of the dead man, leaped tumbling to the space kept clear of the crowd between the Nakoroka dancers and the corpse. The dead man's wife made way for them. She sat upon the part of the bundle which was her husband's thigh. The bundle bent a little as she pushed it to the rear to make more space. The children sang their own dance music. The dead man's wife and his wailing daughter did not watch. But the spectators shouted in appreciation to stifle every sound of mourning. "Thanks for the dance. The dance is good, unique." And all the time they laughed loudly. A fat old matron of Lekutu pushed forward from the crowd, began to swing her hips sideways, then forward and back, as she jerked her shoulders to the beat of the drum. With wrinkling nose and mouth awry, Melika joined the fat woman in this "dance of the Indians." Those who watched abandoned themselves to laughter.

The hours passed. The dance drum beat. The men's sweat glistened through their scented oil as they swayed bending. Melika rolled her eyes. The dead man's daughter wailed. His wife sat silently. And all the time there was laughter and clapping. Then they shouted: "The cock crows." Soon it was dawn, and all the people, spent with laughter, went off to their houses to sleep for an hour before the day's work began. But the smoke from some cook fires was already rising.

Within the village death is always sad. When young people die, it is a bad thing because they have had no chance to live. But the deaths of old people are even more sorrowful because their children have attained maturity and can mourn them with the full understanding of mature souls. Vosalevu was in a distant region when he heard that his mother was dying at Lekutu. To reach her bedside he traveled all night long, but he arrived too late to speak with her. People were already greeting her corpse with "gifts of death." For three days and three nights he made feasts to entertain those who had come to the funeral; guests were many because his mother was a noblewoman. Finally, he was exhausted, and he slept.

To those from other villages, however, funerals are a time for great happiness. The feasting, the assembled crowds, the deliberate joy to cheer the mourners—all these add color to funereal entertainment. Spinsters and old widows particularly will walk long distances on the muddy paths so as not to miss a funeral. When old Di Kabu's leg was infected with "Indian boils," she was too ill to accompany the village women on their expedition for swamp reeds. But when she heard that an old man had died in Sarowaqa, quickly she chose a mat as funeral gift and set off on the journey even though she knew that nightfall would overtake her on the slippery path. Only the deaths of great chiefs are somber occasions for everyone: there is no dancing then; even the wailing of mourners is forbidden; those who would weep must make conch-shell trumpets cry or beat the village drum; no one may say: "The chief is dead"; instead they say: "The sun has set." The most popular funerals are those of important commoners—a man who has held the titular whale tooth for a subdivision of the village land, who has had property to control and distribute, and who has initiated great ceremonial exchanges. To the funeral of such a man all distant kinsmen come to look upon the dead one's face and prove their kinship. At the funeral of such a man there will be dancing to cheer the survivors in his household.

Unuwale was such a man. He had fled the circumcision ceremony in his youth and so helped to lower Nakoroka's reputation. His four marriages had been stormy and childless; women laugh at a man who is uncircumcised. Yet, despite the bitterness of his tongue toward most of the people of the village, he gained status among the men, who learned to listen to his voice in council. For many years he held the whale tooth for the land division of Votua of which Toviya is now titular chief. Moreover, he had strong claims in Nadroro land and in Rokowaqa, and through a known genealogical tie which made him older brother to Nabadua, who is Tavua's title-holder, he had influence in Tavua land. With vigor he used the status which seniority permits. With the "bad soul of a commoner" he accumulated whale teeth, so that his kinsmen who would participate in wealth display had first to beg of him. Like a white man he spoke angrily to those who took his property even though they were his brothers. In his old age he had drunk kava over the heads of several Nakoroka children in the naming ceremony, a rite for which men of superior status are selected.

He died in 1933. Two weeks before his death he called upon his brothers and his children and his sisters and their children to come before him and hear his last requests. These were the "owners of the death," his brothers and sisters in moiety together with their children. Nabadua came with his children and grandchildren and Bici's family. Toviya of Votua, Melika, who is Naicadra's wife in Nadroro, and Raitova of Rokowaqa came each with his family. Close kinsmen came from Sarowaqa and Lekutu, bringing mats to hold in reserve as "gifts of death." These arrived in time. But the Tavua kinsmen from Dule-niwai who brought whale teeth, arrived too late.

Unuwale said: "I am about to die. I know that my sickness is too strong for me. Remember our land. Remember our village. Let no bad reports spring forth. Now I shall divide the land and the coconuts upon it.

"You, Nabadua, must have the nuts which the chief, your father, planted and gave to me upon his death, those large groves at Cave-of-the-Shark and The-Priest-of-the-Oyster (Nabetenidiyo).

"And Namo, son of Nabadua, yours are the coconuts at Twice-Forking, The-Swamp-Land, The-Large-Chestnut-Tree, and The-Small-Chestnut-Tree. These are scattered widely in the land of Tavua and Nadroro. But you are friendly with Naicadra of Nadroro."

To Bici he gave a large share. Bici was the child of his beloved "small sister." To Melika he gave large groves in Nadroro land. Raitova received but a few. To Radebu, daughter of Kelera, he gave but five poor trees. (Bici laughs when he remembers the poverty of Rade-bu's share.) And even to the children he assigned certain coconuts. To those who came from Sarowaqa and Lekutu, he said: "You live a long way off. When you come to this place, eat freely of the nuts, but none of the land is yours."[45]

To Toviya, who is the son of Unuwale's father by a different mother, he gave the rich groves in Votua land, but he said to Toviya: "Remember the young people in Votua: Ratu Luke and Tomasi. Remember Sakariya of Buleya. And remember the 'children of Votua':

---

45. Land is rarely given to outsiders. In the old days it was given away only to compensate the relatives of strangled widows, or "to bury the blood" of a recent war.

Peni and Narogo, who are now of Nadroro; Yani, wife of Namo, who is now of Tavua; and Samu of Rokowaqa."[46]

But Toviya did not remember Unuwale's words. He did not divide the coconuts until the angered ancestors had killed his son Sireli with a quick sickness. Then he divided them. Toviya also received the titular whale tooth for his division of Votua land, because he was the oldest man of those whose blood ties gave them rights in this land.[47] But Unuwale said: "Remember the deaf-mute Yana of Lekutu and her daughter. When they come to this village, see that they are well feasted." He spoke of all the assembled guests by name and asked them to enjoy the hospitality of the Votua people for all time.

Then Unuwale died. A mat was spread over his face, and the "owners of the death" began to weep. Then all common women of the village assembled quickly and came to wail over the corpse; they came promptly, lest as forfeit for their tardiness they need come "in the manner of the land," that is, with mat gifts as penance to avoid ancestral wrath. Unuwale died at night. The women decided among themselves who should watch near the corpse throughout the night, the next day, and the next night and weep for him and fan away the sniffing dogs. Besides two of his sisters in Tavua, they chose Little Melika, who is Toviya's daughter and Unuwale's "small daughter," and Big Melika, who is Naicadra's wife and Unuwale's "small sister." Big Melika is known for her strength in wailing. The men among the "owners of the death" wept, too, when they first greeted the corpse. Some of these made tearful grimaces and broke their voices without real sorrow, in the manner of Indians. Not all the men felt grief. For instance, there had never been great affection between Toviya and his half-brother Unuwale. And Namo said: "Now there is one less uncircumcised man to cast shame upon the name of our village." Naicadra, who is high in the church, said "Mass";[48] but, when the "owners of the death" proffered the mat which is the due of him who fills this office, he demurred, and, because his soul is good, he did not accept the gift.

Next day, while the women kept their watch, the "owners of the death" presented Bulisivo with the whale tooth called "digging-stick for the burying." Bici, who is "native of the village green" for Tavua,

46. These "children of Votua" had one parent only who belonged to Votua. Today all but Samu are considered members of other groups.

47. When Toviya dies, the title will pass to his cross-cousin, Akuila.

48. Though it is strange to me that Wesleyans should call their service "Mass," Fijian Wesleyans of my acquaintance call all short rites of prayer *masu*, which is certainly the borrowed English word.

should have made the presentation speech. But Nabadua did it because he is skilled in ceremonial speaking. Bulisivo turned the whale tooth end for end and presented it to Naicadra, who is title-holder in Nadroro. Vatili spoke for Naicadra as "native of the village green"; Big Melika is the true heir for this task in Nadroro, but she cannot speak in ceremonies because she is a woman. Bulisivo said: "Let the men of Nadroro dig the grave."[49] The men of Nadroro brought gifts of uncooked food and mats to Bulisivo and a whale tooth in return for the one which they had received. When the Nadroro men had dug the grave and bathed to wash away the dirt of it, "owners of the death" gave them a boiled meal.

Bulisivo said that it was the time for giving "gifts of death." All the village men piled uncooked food outside the house in which Unuwale's body lay. Each family in the village brought mats or *sulu*'s as its "gift of death." Those who were "owners of the death" gave several gifts. Toviya gave four mats. Bici had sent his wife to a distant Lekutu kinsman to beg bark cloth for a shroud: only the memory of the debt persists; it is unlikely that this distant kinsman will ever request a favor of Bici. Guests had been gathering from distant villages to cheer the mourners; each brought a mat or *sulu* and feasted at the expense of the "owners of the death." Melika, who is skilled at washing a corpse,[50] and the other women mourners spread the mats inside the house. Then Bulisivo ordered that the food and whale tooth which Nadroro had given him be brought to the house of Unuwale. The noblewomen accompanied him to greet the corpse; they dared not come until after Unuwale had died, for the presence of chiefs hastens death. They placed the whale tooth called "wrapping the corpse" near Unuwale's feet, and Bulisivo said: "Let the corpse be wrapped." But the corpse was unwrapped many times so that the kinsmen who came from great distances could see the face. Had he been a chief, kinsmen in the old days would have come from other islands, and the corpse would have lain unburied for many weeks.[51]

That night the guests danced until dawn to cheer the mourners. The young men and the girls of Tavua as "owners of the death" danced in return. Sometimes they poked the corpse to see how swollen from decay its belly was. The "owners of the death" killed the pig

49. Almost all the men of Nadroro were of opposite moiety from those who were the "owners of the death." Many were cross-cousins.

50. Men delegate this task to women; it is unpleasant.

51. The colonial administration has set strict limits on the time that corpses may be left unburied. Unfortunately, this rule prevents the attendance of very distant kinsmen.

which during the last months of his life Unuwale himself had been fattening for this occasion. They made the oven called *buru qaloqalo*, which they presented to those who had kept the wake. They also gave away an ax and three mats.

Next morning the "owners of the death" made the oven called "true *buru*." Before the oven was opened, young men whom the village elders had appointed as pallbearers lashed the bundled corpse with sennit ropes and lifted it high in the center of the house so that the dead man's "small children" and his sisters' children could walk stooping beneath it; thus the souls of those who had not yet attained the sturdiness of maturity were protected against the coaxing advances of the dead man's soul when it would come beseeching them to join the souls of the dead. Accompanied by all close kinsmen except the two sisters in Tavua who stayed weeping in the dead man's house, the pallbearers carried the corpse to one of the sparsely wooded slopes beyond the palm-lined margin of the village where there are many other graves. Big Melika and Little Melika walked close to the pallbearers, weeping. Only three or four of the mats which the funeral guests had brought as "gifts of death" were bound about the corpse; women kinsmen carried the rest to the burying ground, spread them about the grave and lined its walls so that no freshly dug earth could be seen. While Naicadra said a "Mass," a long mat, spread across the grave's mouth, served as a sling to lower the corpse. The occasion was solemn, but, save for the wailing of Big Melika and Little Melika, there were no signs of grief. A troop of curious children peered furtively from a grove near by and giggled among themselves. Then all the mats were folded carelessly and cast into the grave. Everyone threw a few handfuls of dirt into the grave, and the young men leaped down upon the corpse to stamp upon it and pack the mats firmly about it. Stamping continued as the grave was filled. There were sounds of the corpse bursting. When the funeral party returned from the grave, the oven called "true *buru*" was opened and distributed among the guests.

Before the guests departed, "owners of the death" gave a kava stalk to each one who had brought a gift. Those who had brought the whale tooth received mats as well as kava. When a week had passed, Toviya made the feast called "fifth night" and distributed it in the village; a month later, the feast called "tenth night." Three months later they faced the grave with stone and made the final feast for Unuwale. On this last ceremony a few kinsmen came from other villages. They were well entertained. Unuwale had been a man of importance; but, had he been of chiefly caste, the facing of his grave would have been delayed for many months, and another feast called "hundredth night" would have honored him.

As in the ceremonies of birth and marriage, the care with which funeral rites are observed depends upon the social status of the principals of the occasion. The death of an important man includes a larger group of kinsmen than that of a woman or child. Though Vilomena had held the whale tooth for a division of Nadroro, her funeral was not elaborate. Her feast of the "fifth night" coincided with that which marked the facing of her grave with stone; it consisted of a kava stalk and a boiled meal of manioc, which Vatili, who was heir to her household, distributed among those who had brought "gifts of death." Vatili had not even notified Bulisivo formally of her death; hence Bulisivo and his household paid no heed to the funeral. Vatili also neglected to inform her son Sakaru of the death; Vilomena was already buried when he arrived. Vatili, as "village chief," directed the gravedigging.

Vilomena's importance to the life of the community had been negligible. The ugliness of her face, which had been badly burned many years before, had spoiled her chances of marriage. Her two children had been born out of wedlock. Sometimes she attended meetings of the village elders, but Naicadra and Vatili were the principal spokesmen for Nadroro. Yet, as the daughter of a chief, her place in the kava ceremony was high among commoners. There had been no redistribution of land rights upon her death. She requested Vatili to hold the titular whale tooth in trust for her son Sakaru until he should reach full maturity.

Few guests came to the funeral of Sakiusa, who was Namo's son and Nabadua's grandson. His mother's people came from Lekutu, and people of other households at Nakoroka exhausted themselves with dancing to cheer the mourners. But the feasts were not elaborate. Nabadua was already impoverished, and he knew that careful observance of funeral rites for so young a child would accomplish little toward regaining ancestral favor. To notify Bulisivo of the death, Nabadua presented only a few stalks of kava.

If a spouse survives one who has died, he may ask his brothers and sisters in moiety to provide a gift of property, called *yabo*, for the kinsmen of the deceased. On January 15, 1936, the husband of one of Big Melika's "small mothers" died in Sarowaqa. This "small mother" sent a request to Melika's sisters at Nakoroka to prepare a *yabo*. From her husband Naicadra, Melika procured a whale tooth. From her "small brother" Bici she begged bark cloth which Bici had been saving as a shroud for his aged father. Melika's daughter and Ema and her daughters contributed mats. When they arrived at Sarowaqa, they heaped their *yabo* gift inside the house; had they heaped them outside, an exact equivalent in value would have been presented them in return. But this gift was a "dead *yabo*" and not a "living *yabo*."[52] Melika and her sisters received mats and kava as mere acknowledgment for the whale tooth.

The *yabo* gift occurs very rarely in this part of Vanua Levu. On the Natewa coast of eastern Vanua Levu, where there is a tradition of village exogamy and where marriages are usually patrilocal, a wife's relatives bring a similar gift to a husband's funeral. If the husband's kinsmen wish the wife to remain in their village, they return a gift of equal value; if they do not reciprocate with a gift, the wife returns to the village of her kinsmen. The transaction serves to cancel the marriage payment. At Nakoroka, however, the *yabo* gift is not considered an equaling of scores between affinal groups. Rather, it offers opportunity to honor a cross-cousin. Theoretically a "living *yabo*" could serve as an occasion for competitive display of wealth. But, within memory, a "living *yabo*" has never been given at Nakoroka.

When an old person dies, survivors in his household may honor him with "the strong throwing-away" (*qaqa dai*); the house in which they have lived may be presented to the high chief. The chief would usually give it back to the donors or permit them to continue living in it. In ancient villages households were larger; rather than test the chief's good will at the risk of removing shelter from so many persons, it was customary to build a small house as gift for the chief and as honor for the deceased. In 1930 Samu and his mother were living in the house of Unuwale. When Samu's mother, who was Unuwale's sister, died, they gave the house to Bulisivo. Unfortunately for them, Isacodro fled at this time from Nalauvia with his family and begged land and shelter at Nakoroka. Bulisivo gave Unuwale's house to Isacodro. Unuwale, who was a childless widower, joined the household of Nabadua. Though Samu was also a widower, he had two small children; the children went to live with his sister Losana in Vatili's house, and Samu joined the household of his "small brother" Raitova. Bici says that he would gladly give his house to Bulisivo when aged Kaiyava dies if it

52. See the account of a "living *yabo*" above, pp. 278–80.

were a new house. He would gladly live in his kitchen to honor his father Kaivaya. But, of course, Bulisivo would return the house to him.

Sometimes the products of a man's land supply food for a feast called *mara* to honor his death. A length of cloth tied conspicuously marks the area which is to be held in reserve for this occasion. Usually it is a stream, and the fish which live in it that are made taboo in this manner. He who trespasses will suffer some mishap. When in 1932 the father of Vilomena died, Vilomena marked the river Nadroro with the *mara* banner at the point at which it empties into the river Votua; the fish of the entire river were held in reserve. Vilomena's father was a chief and a holder of the Nadroro title. When the women of Nadroro had woven a large fishing net, a day was appointed for the feast. While the men of Nadroro made ovens, the women fished in the river Nadroro with the new net. Thenceforth the taboo was dissolved. They presented the feast and the net to Bulisivo, who apportioned the fish among the village households. Bulisivo kept the net until his "small brother" Ratu Vuki of Sarowaqa begged it of him.

The young men of Nakoroka built a platform along the path to Lekutu at the point at which Sireli felt the first pain of the illness that resulted in his death. They faced it with stone like a grave and planted shrubs upon it. Everyone who passes casts his special leaf there and thinks of Sireli. There are similar platforms along all paths, but few of them were built to commemorate a death; most of them serve to communicate knowledge of who has passed that way.

By one of several rites of humiliation and self-denial a man may honor the death of a friend who is outside the immediate kinship group. He may "eat like a pig"; his meals will be thrown on the ground outside the house; only in case of extremely wet weather may he balance a leaf upon his head and eat indoors. For a whole year Toviya "ate like a pig" for a friend in Duleniwai. At length he tired of mourning and carried a whale tooth to the "owners" of his friend's death; they presented him with several whale teeth in return for the honor which he had bestowed upon them. As an alternative to "eating like a pig," it is possible to "eat at night," or "eat like a snake": eat one day, fast the next. Toviya is the only living man at Nakoroka who has performed this rite.

Until they have presented a whale tooth or its equivalent in value to the "owners of the death," kinsmen who have not seen a corpse are forbidden village hospitality. Aside from the funeral feasts and the "gifts of death," this is the only strictly prescribed property gift which follows death.[53] Toward several villages every individual suffers the restrictions of this unfulfilled obligation. There are men of Duleniwai who for years have had to walk many miles through unbroken bush to reach the leeward coast without trespassing on Nakoroka land. The Nadroro people who for many years have resided at the village of Nasigasiga across the Macuata border were not informed of the death of Vilomena's father in time to reach Nakoroka before the corpse was interred; as a result, Nakoroka and Nasigasiga are mutually taboo. Though many residents of Nasigasiga have died in the interim, the Nasigasiga people must initiate the rebuilding of friendly relations because it was they who first neglected their obligations. A "small sister" of Vatili's, who lives at Nacula, could not come to honor Vatili's mother at the time of the feast for parents because she had no whale tooth to present as forfeit for her neglect to attend Vilomena's funeral.

On the evening of February 21, 1936, Peni and I returned to Nakoroka after a four-week sojourn in distant Macuata. Every day of our absence Peni remembered the illness of Sakiusa, who was son of Namo and of Peni's "special" sister Yani. As we traveled down the Macuata coast on our return, Peni inquired of every wayfarer as to whether news of a death had come from Nakoroka. When two days' travel still remained, he learned that Sakiusa had been buried the week before. As we passed the store of the Chinese trader at Lekutu, he bought a whale tooth, thinking of Yani, who would be chagrined at his absence from the funeral of her eldest son. As soon as he arrived at Nakoroka, he requested his father Vaula and Naicadra, his elder "small brother" in Nadroro, to present the whale tooth to Nabadua, who is title-holder for Tavua, the group to which Namo and Yani belong. Together they entered Nabadua's house. Naicadra made the speech of presentation. He spoke in a broken voice, as though he could not control his desire to weep. Old Vaula sniffled quietly. Peni sobbed for several minutes. Namo and Nabadua presented a stalk of kava in return, as their "acceptance of the whale tooth." When the formal ceremony was complete, Yani's mourning cry burst forth from behind the mosquito net where she had lain concealed: "My child, my child." Then she joined the men to greet Peni after his long journey. They smoked tobacco, joked, and asked Peni to recount his recent adventures.

53. The gift has no name. Usually it is referred to as *yaboyabo*. But this term more accurately describes the gift which "owners of the death" sometimes send to distant kinsmen to notify them of a death. It is this unnamed gift which is of frequent occurrence at Nakoroka. During my residence there it was presented on at least six different occasions.

A week later Nabadua and Namo gave Peni a large batch of sweet pudding. They should at least have baked an oven of food for him in return for his whale tooth, but Nabadua is impoverished. Namo had borrowed money from Peni to buy sugar to sweeten the pudding.

On May 12, 1936, the village at Nakoroka was crowded with guests on their way to earn tax money at the mine on the windward coast. Men of Nacula and Nalauvia filled the households of Vatili and Orisi; men of Navakasiga and the island Yaqaga stayed in Naicadra's house; and men from Bua Village were sheltered in Tavua houses, although they had no kinship ties at Nakoroka. In all there were more than fifty men. Many of the guests of Vatili and Naicadra were distant kinsmen. Many had not visited Nakoroka for several years, and during this interval two of Nadroro's people had died: Vilomena and Vilomena's father. To secure their freedom of passage through Nakoroka, the guests had brought two tins of kerosene and a dozen bars of soap and presented them formally to Vatili, Vaula, and Naicadra, who were "owners of the death."

Vatili was annoyed that so many guests had come. To feed them was a heavy chore, and Nakoroka men themselves were anxious to be off to the mine to earn tax money. Vatili knew that the chance of finding work in such a multitude of potential laborers would be slight. The gifts which the guests had brought were small repayment for the trouble of housing so many. In his capacity as "village chief" Vatili decided privately that there would be no special feast to acknowledge Nadroro's acceptance of the gifts. He considered this occasion an emergency new in history: never before had so many men traveled to the mine; they were bent on a modern errand and had not come purposely to Nakoroka to fulfil an obligation "in the manner of the land." To him, whose status as an owner in Nakoroka land is questionable, prestige of the village did not seem to be at stake.

Naicadra expected Vatili to initiate the making of an oven. Vatili and old Vaula were of Vilomena's division of Nadroro land, and the obligation was more directly theirs. Vatili was holding Vilomena's titular whale tooth in trust for her son Sakaru, and in this capacity should have accepted responsibility for the prestige of Vilomena's title. But when Naicadra saw that Vatili had provided the guests with no kava, he spoke to him and offered to assist in the preparation of an oven so that the name of Nadroro would not be shamed. Vatili refused. Naicadra spoke to Vaula, who replied that perhaps in the morning he would bring food for an oven from his gardens and that he, too, had been waiting for Vatili. But Naicadra gained small comfort from Vaula's speech, because Vaula is old and very slow. Naicadra is not strong; alone he could not make an oven for so many guests. The younger men of Nadroro were already absent in search of tax money. His kinsmen in Tavua and Votua were already busy with their own guests. He thought of asking Bulisivo for assistance. But he was ashamed because he remembered that Vatili had not informed Bulisivo of Vilomena's death; he knew that Bulisivo felt this slight because Bulisivo had not come to see Vilomena's corpse. In desperation he asked the young women of the village to come and entertain his guests with dancing.

But Melika, who is Naicadra's wife, dared to approach Bulisivo. She is Bulisivo's "small wife" and cannot speak to him directly. So she persuaded Naicadra to accompany her. Together they crawled across his threshold. She sat with hanging head and wept before the chief until he asked Naicadra what the trouble was. Naicadra said: "My gardens are a long way off, and I cannot prepare an oven." She said: "I am only a woman, and I do not understand ceremonies. But these guests will spread evil rumors about Nadroro's name."

A young chief had come with the guests. This was his first visit at Nakoroka. He was of a family who are distant kinsmen of the chiefs of Inland Forest. When a chief first passes through a new region with which kinship binds him, he must bring a gift even though the occasion is not a formal visit between chiefs. This young chief had brought a whale tooth to the house of Naicadra, where he was staying with his companions. Naicadra had already referred the whale tooth to Bulisivo with the request that the young chief be feasted in return. Bulisivo had sent Isacodro to Votua land to bring food and kava. While Melika was weeping before Bulisivo, Isacodro called forth from the center of the village green according to Bulisivo's instructions and announced the names of the men who must assist with the preparation of a feast for the young chief. Melika heard and thought that Bulisivo was already planning to assist Nadroro. She stopped crying until Bulisivo had explained the purpose of Isacodro's announcing. Then she wept again. Finally Bulisivo was persuaded. He ordered the preparation of a second oven. Later Vatili excused his neglect to honor Bulisivo's authority at the time of Vilomena's death. He said that Bulisivo had never fulfilled his duties as king of Inland Forest and that Nadroro need no longer regard him as their chief. He cited the formal visit of a Macuata chief which for thirty years Bulisivo had left unrepaid. As a result of Bulisivo's incompetence, he said, all who visit Macuata are ashamed.

The soul of one who has died may wreak vengeance upon his kins-men if they fail to observe funeral ceremonies with propriety. The soul of a chief is more dangerous than that of a commoner; an adult's is more dangerous than a child's. For many weeks after a death people avoid solitude after dark. Some six-year-olds once scampered into a house in which the men were drinking kava informally; Samu said: "Aren't you afraid to be running about after dark? There are dead souls about. Sakiusa is lurking in the path." After Vilomena's death women hastened home from fishing expeditions to reach the village before dark. When anyone went to the river at night, he carried a torch or a lantern and usually persuaded a guard of companions to ac-company him. If the wind dislodged a bucket from its hanging and sent it clattering to the ground, or if a sudden gust smote the mat hang-ings of a doorway which had been closed against the rain, someone would surely say: "Vilomena is about." And people would shiver as their own souls, uncomfortable in the presence of a dead soul, lifted the hair at the backs of their necks. Once at dusk on the Lekutu path far from the village Peni felt his soul climb high upon his neck as signal that a dead soul was near by; Peni shuddered in disgust and, as he hur-ried his steps, shouted insults over his shoulder to frighten the dead soul. He knew intuitively that it was the soul of Sakiusa, his beloved sister's child, who came seeking him. But, as time passes, souls of the dead become ridiculous. Small accidents were attributed laughingly to Vilomena and Sakiusa. The children made a game, and, pretend-ing that Vilomena was chasing them, they raced about the village green in delicious terror.

A child is in special danger when a parent dies lest this parent re-turn in loneliness to carry off the child's soul. When Bici's mother died, Bici took his present name as nickname so that his dead mother would not recognize him when she came seeking. Yet Vilomena's mentally retarded eight-year-old daughter Unaisi knew no fear. Because she was sired in the path by a wandering Solomon Islander, people were not surprised that she failed to understand what other children knew. It amused them when in her piping voice she babbled about her mother as though she had not died, but finally they made her hush because they feared the anger of Vilomena's soul.

CHAPTER XI

TROUBLE

NABADUA

AT MIDMORNING of November 2, 1935, I went to Nabadua's house. The doorways were hung with curtains of plaited coconut leaf as they are at night or when the house is empty. "Where is Nabadua?" I asked.

"Inside," someone said.

At the lower door I called, "*Duo, duo!*"

From inside, Nabadua answered. "Hello. Enter the house." I found him sitting alone in the darkened house. His hands were pressing his temples.

"I have come to ask some questions," I said.

"All right," he replied.

"I want to read a list of all the people in the village," I said. "You must tell me how you are related to each one."

"I am very sick." He spoke as though he had a bad cold.

"Where is your pain? The stomach? The head? Let me get you some aspirin."

"No," he answered. "No medicine. My head aches and my body is dead. I cannot eat."

"I shall go away," I said.

"No. Ask the questions."

As I read the list, he would clear his throat and with uncertainty say what kind of kinship bound him with each name. He would sigh: "*Isa lei!* I am dead." I read the names of his wife's brothers.

"They are just people," he said.

"No," I corrected. "That is not right. They are your cross-cousins."

"All right," he said. He was stalling; his marriage with his "sister" had been in defiance of native custom.

"Why," I asked, "did you marry a woman of your own moiety? Now your relationships with people are mixed up."

"I know nothing of moieties," he replied. "I know only that I belong to a family of chiefs;[1] that my father was a chief; that my mother's

1. The words which Nabadua used to mean "family of chiefs" (*yavusa 'uraga*) is also the name of his moiety. It is a play on words.

374

father was a 'strong' man who did what he liked, and I have named
my oldest son after him, Lisala Namosa (Namo); that all the households of Tavua—of Monasa, Bici, and Namo—look to me as chief, and
when I die they shall listen to the words of Namo, my son."

I did not know then that, the evening before, Nabadua in anger had
ordered his young wife Kelera to leave his house and never to return
and that with his infant son she was traveling the steep path to her distant kinsmen in Duleniwai. The sun was hot and dangerous for so small
a child.

Three days before, they had rested together in the shade at the edge
of the village, Nabadua, Kelera, and their infant son. Nabadua had
returned from an early morning journey to his gardens for food. Kelera
had brought a mat from the house and spread it in a quiet place as
protection from the wetness of the ground. She was nursing her son.
As the shade receded with the ascending sun, she shifted her body to
shelter him from the hot glare. He was delicate for his age. Like all
Nabadua's children, who had been pale in infancy, his body was almost white. Nabadua dried a piece of tobacco and rolled it carefully
in pandanus leaf for Kelera. Lazily he filed his machete to make it
sharp. Though they were visible from all corners of the village, the
broad expanse of close-cropped grass on every side assured them that
their words were private. The village was almost empty. The men and
the young people had gone to Lekutu to make a garden for the Buli.
The women were wandering in the forest on various errands. As usual
on sunny mornings, small children were playing tag in the deep pool
of the river Votua; steep riverbanks muffled their shouts. Older women
were plaiting mats in their houses. This is a busy time of day. Most
men would be ashamed to chat idly with their wives in the middle of
the morning and would have waited until night; what of importance
could a man say to his wife? Nabadua took his son from Kelera's arms
and held him above the mat with his curled limbs dangling, but as he
brushed the child's feet against the roughness of the mat, coaxing him
to try to stand, the child began to cry. He was much too young. With
noisy laughter Nabadua kept addressing him by name and saying:
"Now you are a strong man, chief in Tavua. You make the women
speechless." Nabadua was amused with his own humor, but the child's
large head continued to roll weakly on his infant shoulders. His cry
was feeble. Then Nabadua's seven-year-old daughter, Narieta, came
dripping from the river. Nabadua called to her impatiently, and together they started off toward the forests of Tavua to search for wild

yams and perhaps kill a wild pig. He carried his spear, and a few dogs followed. Kelera rolled the mat and returned indoors to shelter her son from the heat.

That night guests traveling to the mines were entertained at Monasa's house which neighbors Nabadua's. The dance was gay, and all the older women of the village had crowded there to clap time. Sometimes the guests would stroll outside to stretch their legs. Some, who were well known among Tavua people, called, "It is night" at Nabadua's doorway. Nabadua asked them in to join him at the kava bowl, and like an extravagant host spread a clean mat for them in the place of honor even though they were not chiefs. With vigorous interest he asked the questions which one always asks a guest. Then, reminding them that they were in Nabadua's house, he gave them tobacco, but in the sight of all reserved a specially tasty portion near the center of the leaf for Kelera, who sat at his side. Frequently he addressed her as "my friend." Soon his noisy good humor waked his infant son. With apologies for passing above the guests, Kelera retired to the upper part of the house where the child was sheltered inside a mosquito net. She lay there nursing him. Later on Nabadua and Kelera came together to watch the dance. He stood at the door while she sat just inside and clapped for a while with the women. Though he was usually uninterested in dancing, he kept exclaiming through the door upon the skill of the dancers.

As he sat alone on the morning of November 2, Nabadua was remembering these last days with Kelera. He regretted his anger. He thought, too, of how all the people of the village were waiting for disaster to fall upon his house. The night before he had overheard the elders speaking of him in council at Monasa's house. They had spoken of his evil nature, of the dire misfortune which would surely overtake him, and of his cruel treatment of Kelera. He had turned her out in the evening. The women of Isacodro's household had persuaded her to stay with them overnight so that she could journey to Duleniwai by daylight. Many times Nabadua had spoken too freely against Bulisivo and the chiefs of Votua. He wondered now whether his ancestors were truly angry. He remembered that a disease inside his eldest grandson's head was spewing forth a horrid fluid from his ear, that, as the stench grew stronger, the boy grew weaker. He worried about his own youngest son, who failed to grow sturdier each passing week as infants should. He was afraid.

He had asked Vaulini to hasten along the Duleniwai path and try to overtake Kelera, to apologize and beg her to return at least to the village if not to his house. Until Vaulini returned, he could only wait in his house and press his temples. Peni said of him: "Even though he should understand that it is the carelessness of his own words which has brought evil times upon him, he could do nothing; it is his custom to speak freely and cause trouble, and this cannot be changed."

Vaulini persuaded Kelera to come back. By late afternoon they were resting in the house of Isacodro, who is Vaulini's father. But Isacodro's house is small and crowded. Monasa, who calls Kelera "sister,"[2] offered her the use of his house: he and his wife were engaged for weeks at a time in their gardens in Sarowaqa territory, their children were away at the district school in Lekutu, and during their brief periods of residence in the village the entire family could be comfortable enough in the kitchen. During the weeks that followed, Kelera established herself in Monasa's house. Isacodro's daughters brought her meals and slept with her. Nabadua brought food from his gardens for her and often in secret he begged her to return to his house. But she would not listen. Finally, Nabadua said: "Kelera no longer lives in my house. I am too old. But that is all right. Now I am old and shall sit in the house all day. I do not need a woman. I have children and grandchildren who will bring firewood and water for me. They will prepare my meals while I sit alone in my old age. I shall braid sennit and drink kava. What good is a woman to an old man? *Isa lei*, now I am old." But he continued to take food to her. His children were busy with troubles of their own, and he did not sit in the house.

Nabetenidiyo, where Nabadua was born about 1875, was built by descendants of the ancient villages of Tavua land. It spread itself comfortably on the point of land made by the joining of the rivers Votua and Tavua; by the time it was built, the church had come to inland Bua, and there was no need for ramparts. Nabadua's father was chief there. He was of chiefly caste and held the whale tooth of chiefly authority in Tavua land. For a time Nabadua lived in his father's noble household. But, when he was very young, his father died. His mother, whose status as a commoner Nabadua refuses to remember, married a chief of Navakasiga in the far west of Bua Province. She took Nabadua with her to her new household, and it was there that he "got his soul" and began to recollect clearly. Bici remembers Nabadua as a young

2. Monasa, Nabadua, and Kelera are all "small" siblings. But Monasa felt more closely bound in kinship with Kelera than with Nabadua. Though Nabadua considers him a younger brother, Monasa prefers to think of Nabadua as Kelera's husband.

man at Nabetenidiyo in the house of the uncircumcised Kaiyava, who
is Bici's father; they slept together in a small hut and at meal time
joined the other "natives of the village green" in the large eating-house
which was shared among members of this caste. Sometimes Nabadua
slept in the eating-house with the young men. Bici says that Kaiyava
was very kind to the young Nabadua, who had no true father of his
own. But Nabadua does not recall the time that he spent in the house
of the uncircumcised Kaiyava. He remembers only that he lived in the
houses of chiefs. Living thus in noble company, he learned how ceremonies should proceed and how to speak in them.

Nabadua's mother bore no other sons. When she went to Navakasiga, she brought no other child to her new household there. After
Nabadua was ten or twelve, old enough to travel alone, he visited frequently in the village of his father. It was there that he was circumcised with Monasa, who was living in a house of the priestly caste, and
an older paternal half-brother, who now lives in Duleniwai; these are
Nabadua's age-mates, his companions at circumcision. There were
two older boys in the house of the Navakasiga chief. But with these
"brothers" Nabadua was not congenial; Vatili says that Nabadua has
never been friendly with men, only with women. When the colonial
administration recorded the names of the land of Bua Province and
classified the people patrilineally as heirs to the land, these "brothers"
made a mistake and claimed rights in land which was not truly theirs;
their ancestors were angered and consumed them with disease. Nabadua, however, knew well that his true home was Nabetenidiyo, the village where his father had been chief; he knew that his father's blood
was strong within him. He remembers telling the colonial officials that
his land was Tavua and that they wrote it in their books.[3]

Nabadua had lived with three women at Navakasiga before he sired
Namo, his eldest son. Perhaps he would not have chosen to stay with
Namo's mother if the government had not become angry and threatened to fine him. He has always been a "bad man" in his relations
with women; he has always behaved in a strong manner because his
mother's father was Lisala Namosa, whose strength and arrogance
made the village tremble and whose blood Nabadua feels within him
almost as surely as that of his father. With pride he compares his appearance with Isacodro, whom he assumes to be of the same age. Isacodro, he says, looks much younger because he has lived with one

3. According to government records, Nabadua at this time claimed to be a member of
the Sivoa division of Nadroro.

woman only. Nabadua has few teeth, and there are pouches and
wrinkles about his eyes. He is proud to have produced so many children, and this is bound to tell in a man's appearance. Seven times he
has been appointed "village chief" by the government, but each time
he has had illicit love affairs and so lost his official status; he has paid
seven fines before the provincial court for "living like a devil." Even
his brothers fear he will forget "small spouse" taboo and seduce their
wives. For many years they have mistrusted him, and there has been
no peace among them. Monasa, his companion at circumcision, drinks
kava with him, but their relationship is stiff with etiquette. Sometimes
Nabadua regrets his passions after they are spent, but more often he is
proud of their chiefly strength. Nevertheless, ancestors have been
pleased; the great number of his children prove ancestral favor. Three
women have borne him seventeen children. Nine live, eight have died.
He is proud that Namo, too, can act in a strong manner; his second
son already promises to be a scourge among the virgins of the countryside, and Nabadua and Namo rejoice.

While Namo was still an infant, Vilomena's older brother died. Her
father, who was chief in Nadroro, sent whale teeth to the Navakasiga
chief to "bring" (*sosomi*) Nabadua into Nadroro land. Vilomena's
father remembered that Nabadua was descendent on his mother's side
from Nadroro's hero, the great Lisala Namosa. Moreover, Nabadua
was of the same age as the young man who had died, and Vilomena's
father hoped to quench his grief for a lost son. Nabadua traveled there
to the old village, Yakana, in Nadroro land and lived there with that
chief. He came with Namo and the woman who is Namo's mother.

It was then that the government came to write the names of the land
and place a "village chief" as an official in each community. They sent
Nabadua to Nabetenidiyo to fill this office. It is difficult to know how
old he was at this time. Namo, who today must be thirty, since his
oldest child is nearing puberty, was still an infant. Nabadua must have
been in his early twenties, and the official position was an honor for so
young a man. Doubtless he spoke bravely among the officials and convinced them of his chiefly heritage. Doubtless he told them secret confidences of incompetence among the older men; he told them how the
land was failing and discussed reforms to right the evils of his times.
He could speak with earnest fire. And, when he set out for the village
of his birth, he felt assured that his ancestors had chosen him to be
chief and to pass their judgment among ordinary men. He returned to
Nabetenidiyo not as a visitor to the lowly household of Kaiyava the

uncircumcised but as a chief, in name at least, who would lead the
village to new prosperity. During the days of the wars Tavua population had suffered heavy losses. Old men had died and left no heirs. Before
his death Nabadua's chiefly father had already gained for himself all
titles in Tavua's depleted castes.[4] When he died, he asked Unuwale,
who was then living at Nabetenidiyo, to hold Tavua's chiefly whale
tooth in trust until Nabadua should mature. Now, with the coming of
the government, Unuwale moved to Votua and left Nabadua's leadership at Nabetenidiyo unchallenged.

But Nabadua's regency was short lived. The government decided
to combine all the scattered hamlets of Inland Forest Kingdom into
one large village; Nakoroka was built. The survivors of Tavua land
came to live in four households there. Nabadua still held the chiefly
title among them; he held the whale tooth which his father had held
before him. But at Nakoroka he had to humble himself in the presence
of the Votua chiefs, who were rightfully of chiefly caste, and especially
before the mild Bulisivo, who held the kingly title for all Inland Forest. Tavua gardens were far from this new village site. Nabadua had
to ask Bulisivo for permission to build taro ponds in Votua's fertile
land. With the fruition of each crop he presented food gifts to Bulisivo.
But Nabadua deems himself a man who does not speak much; he says
that his chiefly heritage made his temper sweet so that he could accept
the vassalage to Bulisivo with modest resignation. His only anxiety was
lest his own ancestors be not pleased with Bulisivo's rule.

Bulisivo had two sisters, Di Kabu and Di Litiya. People came from
distant kingdoms just to look upon them because rumor of their beauty
had resounded far away on the windward coast and into distant Macuata. They are of Votua land, and the she-dog named Big Vagina is
their ancestor. Di Kabu, who is the elder of the two, still wore virgin's
coiffure; it is unlikely that she was still a maiden, but no one dared
question the claims of so great a lady. Di Litiya, who was already the
widow of a Lekutu commoner, had brought great unhappiness to her
brother Bulisivo when she eloped with this person of lowly birth; Bulisivo had retired to the forest for many weeks to think upon his sorrow
in solitude. Now she was reconciled again with her brother, and her
infant son was living in his household. But except for Di Litiya's wilful marriage, both sisters had always been discreet, so that their repu-

4. Title to leadership in castes may have been of no more significance than seniority in
a household. Perhaps to justify the legend that castes were once distinct and vigorous political units, Tavua men say that the decimation of their population and the centralizing of
political authority into a single title occurred during the time of Nabadua's father.

tations were immaculate. The calves of their limbs were of a rare fulness, and their sleek thighs and hips were round with loveliness beyond compare. Nabadua saw them every day, and Namo's mother was already fading. He spoke with the noble sisters. Even his enemies admit that his conversation has always been pleasing to women. Then he was possessed with desire for them. It was a chiefly passion, and he was borne upon it. It was ancestral will. And because his mother's father was a strong man, he had courage to fulfil this will; who else at Nakoroka was better qualified by rank of birth? Now, when he thinks of the great courage of his youth, he beats himself upon the chest and says he is a man. Even today he has no words to tell of the tattooed patterns on their thighs. But Bulisivo found his sisters in Nabadua's arms, first the elder, who claimed still to be a virgin, and then the younger. The time was about 1912.

Whenever Bulisivo converses earnestly with a friend, he speaks of the trials of feeding infants. Again and again he tells of how his son, the blind Tevita, was born in 1912, of how his wife failed and died and there was no nurse to feed this weakling child. He begged cows from the Roko of Macuata, but in a few weeks the milk of each in turn was used up. Finally there were no more cows on the leeward coast, and yet the blind child cried for milk. For many years Bulisivo had been friendly with an aged British planter on the windward coast near Saolo, which is the village of Bulisivo's mother. Now he traveled there with his daughters and his ailing son; for many months they lived in the land of this old friend upon the produce of his gardens. There was a dairy herd, and the son could have milk. Bulisivo also tells of how the people of Saolo had long been pleading with him to return and live upon their land so that it would again bring forth abundant fruit. Their need was great, and he felt the blood bonds with his mother strong within him. When his son had gained strength on this friend's plantation and learned to stomach garden foods, Bulisivo departed thence and entered the village of his mother and lived there many years. At length the soil grew strong once more, and there was bounty in the land.

But Bulisivo tells of how the people of Nakoroka begged him not to leave them, of how they feared lest the wrath of ancestors descend upon them in the absence of their chiefs. Di Kabu had married hastily and joined her husband's household in Sarowaqa. Bulisivo planned to take Di Litiya with him to the windward coast that she might be a comfort to his ailing son; his daughters were young and had no skill in infant care. No member of the chiefly caste would remain. But the men of Nakoroka gathered gifts. They brought forth kava until their gardens were empty and heaped it there before him. In haste they searched among their kinsmen for whale teeth and mats. Bending in the dust, they wept and begged forgiveness for all past deeds that might have been displeasing to him. And foremost among them, clothed in rags, with ashes smeared upon his head, Nabadua lay and was their spokesman. He said: "Ai soro, ai soro." And Bulisivo was moved to weep and pity them in their fear. But in his own purpose he was firm; he departed from the village and listened sadly to the wailing voices as they faded behind him. He climbed the steep path. He made but one concession before departing; the kingly whale tooth of Inland Forest was conferred upon Di Litiya in formal ceremony. She did not journey to the windward coast with him. But the people of Nakoroka had little faith in her fitness for this title; a chief must live in his own land and remember that his blood is a sacred thing, not to be scattered. Di Litiya had married a common man of Lekutu and lived there on foreign soil as his wife; the son whom she had borne was a true chief and *vasu* to Nakoroka land, but his sacredness was not so pure as it would have been had she chosen to espouse a chief.

Years passed, and many times the village mourned Bulisivo's absence. Di Litiya sometimes failed to remember the responsibilities of her title. Though arrogant and strong as a noblewoman should be, she lacked the mild demeanor in emergency with which Bulisivo could soothe men's ruffled tempers. The whale teeth of every land group had been transferred into her keeping before Bulisivo's departure; all the land had been "emptied anew." Di Litiya delayed and did not return these teeth to the various title-holders of the land divisions. At length she married Vosalevu of Lekutu, and village anger rose high. Ancestors cursed her with sterility, and she bore no children from this second marriage. The land continued to decline.

More than the others Nabadua regretted the fate of Inland Forest's kingly title. He resented the assurance with which Vosalevu sat at his wife's side in the council of village elders and spoke his mind with ease. He knew that Vosalevu's blood had drawn no chiefliness from the father's side, and Vosalevu's mother had likewise been a chief through the mother only. Though he knew the ancient rule that makes maternal ties the stronger, he believed privately that the ancestors intended paternal ties to grow in strength and solve the needs of modern times. And when Nabadua paralleled his own status in the land with that of Vosalevu, whose ties were not of Nakoroka, he found himself secure as a true owner. He felt deep conviction in himself that Nakoroka ancestors were displeased with the regency of this wayward noblewoman and her foreign husband. He remembered Bulisivo's long residence on the windward coast. He remembered that since the death of Bulisivo's father the Votua chiefs had frequently left the land of Nakoroka deserted of a title-holder and lived about to suit their own conveniences. He knew that poverty in the land brought less sorrow to the chiefs themselves than to him, whose parents held no ties with foreign kingdoms. Sometimes, while he slept, he dreamed a certain thing. Though he is not one to speak with ancestors in his sleep, which is a priestly talent and not fitting to one who feels the tasks of chiefship strong upon him, the dream lent fuel to his disapproval of the chiefly house. He dreamed that Bulisivo and his sisters came with gifts and, drab with ashes, bowed low on the ground, saying: "Ai soro, ai soro."

When the first World War had boomed the copra market, people forgot the soil's poverty. Work for a few hours in the coconut groves bought luxuries from traders which were never known before. Nabadua's father had planted many coconuts at the village site of Nabetenidiyo. When he died, he had given them into the keeping of Unuwale, title-holder in Votua. Though other kinsmen knew Unuwale as a man of evil temper, Unuwale the uncircumcised held his "small brother" Nabadua in strong friendship. Together they shared the rich groves of Tavua land. The lavish hospitality of Nabadua's house was known even in distant villages. Even Vosalevu says that at this time Nabadua was generous to all guests alike, to kinsmen and visitors from other households and to travelers from great distances. Nabadua prospered and outshone the chiefly house itself.

He knew no shame. Like a true chief, he took whatever woman pleased his fancy. He had no regard for moiety restrictions. When the mother of Namo had borne him many children, he tired of her wizened leanness and took the young widow Kelera, whom he chose to treat as a wife though she was "sister." Men whispered evilly behind his back. But his prosperity proved ancestral sanction for his deeds; no one spoke openly against him. At this time, the young Namo also chose a wife who was his "small sister" and with his father's full approval risked the anger of her kinsmen. It pleased Nabadua that his son showed a strong spirit. It proved that blood of the father was strong in the son, that the chiefliness of Nabadua's father had passed through Nabadua to the second generation.

But a man of fresh ambition was establishing himself at Nakoroka. This was Vatili, who had recently married Losana of Unuwale's household and come to claim, through his mother, rights in Nakoroka land. Though born in the house of his mother's "small brother" at Nakoroka, Vatili had lived in his father's house at Nacula as a child. When he was barely adolescent, his father drowned before his eyes. Then his mother came to live permanently at Nakoroka. A British planter near Lekutu who had known Vatili's father took pity on the youthful son and took him to his home as houseboy. Vatili saw the comforts of a British household. He saw wealth saved instead of wantonly displayed. He saw how writing was an infallible aid to memory. Upon his own initiative, and with the encouragement of the friendly planter, he learned after a fashion to read and write in the missionary dialect. Returning to Nakoroka as a bridegroom, his relatively great knowledge of the ways of white men enabled him to grasp the mechanisms and purposes of colonial administration with greater ease than any of his contemporaries. He was well suited for the task of "village chief," and his accomplishments were put to use through long services in this office. Though all remembered that he was not truly native to Nakoroka soil[5] and chafed under his authority, his knowledge made his voice an influence among men. He knew little of observing old ceremonies to renew the land. His gardens were not bountiful. But he knew the copra market. Unlike Nabadua, he sought advancement in the church and learned its ritual, and he was not proud of coveting his neighbor's wife.

Nabadua spoke resentfully of him as a native of Nacula and indicated Nacula phonetics in his speech. Soon Vatili learned of this resentment. These two should have cherished each other as cross-cousins. But Vatili was not closely bound by the interwoven kinship bonds of Nakoroka people; he had not learned to distinguish between his agemates there as brothers and cross-cousins. Yet Nabadua was of the opposite moiety and required respect; Vatili restrained his anger, but he showed no love. He excused his negligence, saying that Nabadua had married his sister.

Then in 1926 there was a general need for money in the village. Vatili and his mother's brother whispered that Nabadua had no right

5. Though maternal ties are strong, Vatili's mother's claims upon Nakoroka land were not strong.

MOTHER OF CHILDREN PAST PUBERTY

to exclusive use of the coconut groves at Nabetenidiyo. Soon Naicadra and Toviya joined in questioning Nabadua's right to this great source of wealth. Nabetenidiyo lies at the joining of the rivers Votua and Tavua. A mile up the river Tavua from this junction the river Nadroro empties. Both these latter rivers are of equal size, and it is impossible to know by their appearance whether the river Nadroro empties into the river Tavua, or Tavua into Nadroro. When the village was built at Nabetenidiyo, Tavua people thought they were building in their own land along their own river. But Vatili was of the opinion that the government had recorded this land as Nadroro. Though Nabadua shared his luxuries generously with all the village, he was firm in his resolve to hold his source of wealth; he said that his father had planted these coconuts for Tavua people; he knew that ancestral wrath would descend upon Tavua gardens if he permitted other people of Inland Forest, whose kingly title he deemed forfeited, to share in ownership. Unuwale, whose claims to ownership in Tavua were secure, sustained Nabadua's opinion. These two stood alone. Hatred grew strong against them in the village, and there was fear of open violence. The mild Bulisivo's absence was regretted. They remembered how it was Nabadua whose deeds had driven Bulisivo from the village. Especially Sakariya, who is the last survivor of descendants of Buleya land, spoke much too freely.

Di Litiya called a council of the village elders. Vosalevu sat with her and conducted the discussion to sift all facts in the dispute and dissolve the enmity. But Nabadua would not listen to the words of Vosalevu. With fervor he defended his own case and spoke without restraint. And Sakariya, whose reputation as a trouble maker is well known, questioned Nabadua's right to speak so in the presence of Di Litiya, who held the kingly title for all Inland Forest; how could Nabadua, who was but a commoner on his mother's side, dare to speak with such assurance before a true chief to whom his land was merely vassal? Vatili, Naicadra, and Toviya sat quietly while their cause was thus espoused in angry terms; though they feared the outcome of this noisy speaking back and forth, they made no move to check their angry spokesman. Cringing in terror at the daring of his act, shuddering in his slight body with rage almost suppressed, Sakariya rose to his feet and there in the presence of chiefs punched Nabadua in the nose. Lest Nabadua strike back, Vosalevu leaped from his chiefly place at Di Litiya's side to close upon Nabadua's arms and keep him squatting. But Vosalevu tripped and fell sprawling across the space in the center of the house which held the kava bowl. He is tall and the house was small. He fell with his full weight against Nabadua, who was sitting there holding his injured nose. Startled and confused, Nabadua thrust an arm backward for support, but it crumpled beneath him as he was flattened to the floor, head bumped, neck bent uncomfortably against a house post. He thought: "It is all right if I die." He closed his eyes and lay relaxed and limp, although his arm was wrenched nearly from its socket. A tin can from some trading store lay crushed beneath him; it had served as a spittoon, but now it made a cut in his arm. Blood was drawn. Sakariya had taken flight long since and was now well on his way toward the dark forest beyond the edge of the village. There was no longer need for argument. In his own words Nabadua tells how he retired with chiefly dignity to his own household; he says his anger was well controlled.[6]

Nabadua gathered his family about him and prepared to travel to Duleniwai and join the household of his older half-brother there. But the people of Nakoroka remembered that his family was large and that his departure would seriously decrease the future population of their village. They held council and, obeying Di Litiya's bidding, gathered gifts to "bury the blood" which had flowed from Nabadua's arm. He says that all the people of the village gathered humbly before him and begged him not to leave them. He says that, as they proffered their gifts, Vatili and Vosalevu groveled in the dirt and wailed: "Ai soro, ai soro." But Vatili laughs at the suggestion that the village humbled itself before Nabadua; he says that the village begs humbly for forgiveness only before a chief. To repay him for the rough treatment, not as an apology, Nabadua received an ax and a pot of food that was merely boiled. With Unuwale, he retained exclusive rights to the coconuts at Nabetenidiyo.

For several years the fame of Nabadua's hospitality continued to resound throughout the province. But resentment grew against him in the village. Sometimes, with the gruff manner which some chiefs assume, Vosalevu possessed himself of the luxuries in Nabadua's household; through his wife he was using the authority of kingship in Inland Forest. Nabadua suffered such indignities in silence. But he consoled himself, believing that ancestors would wreak vengeance on the house

6. This episode has been reconstructed from the accounts of several informants; I have described it as I think it really happened. Vatili emphasizes Nabadua's guilt in speaking before Big Di Litiya with such authoritative manner. Vosalevu describes his own intentions as completely pacific. Nabadua is proud of his own quiet demeanor in the face of the uncontrolled anger with which the others attacked him.

of the Votua chiefs for failing in their duties toward the land: Di Litiya
had never returned the title-bearing whale teeth of the land divisions
of Inland Forest Kingdom which Bulisivo had received in ceremony
many years before. Nabadua saw that this negligence had already
made the gardens less abundant. Wild pigs gained courage and began
to uproot the crops.

It was probably during one of Vatili's terms as "village chief" that
Nabadua was embroiled in trouble with the government for his neglect to buy the writs which would have sanctioned his marriage with
the widow Kelera before the government and the church. As a right-
eous Wesleyan, Vatili disapproves of "living like a devil" and so dam-
aging the village's reputation among churchmen throughout the land.
During Vatili's terms of office, Nabadua found it especially irksome to
perform the tasks of housebuilding. As often as he found excuses to
gain honest leave from statute work, Vatili discovered some way to involve him in litigation with the government. Then Unuwale died and
left Nabadua with no staunch allies except for his young son Namo.

When about 1930 the bottom dropped from the copra market,
Nabadua was impoverished. During the last few years the business of
the Chinese traders had spread to the most remote hamlets; rice, sugar,
and other delicacies were exchanged for the valuable coconuts. Like
many other men, Nabadua had slackened in his yearly planting. The
area of his cultivated land had shrunk. And yet his reputation as a generous host persisted, and distant kinsmen came seeking entertainment
as guests in his household. Hastily he attempted to replenish the failing
resources of his gardens. But new needs assailed him. He was an "owner of Unuwale's death." Like a true chief, he made the funeral lavish.
Then in quick succession several of his children died, and many guests
came to cheer the host of this once generous household. Pigs continued
to destroy his newly planted gardens. Redoubling his attempts to hon-
or ancestors, he emptied his remaining gardens for the funeral feasts.
When the men of the village saw that his resources were exhausted,
they rejoiced secretly, Vatili and Vosalevu more than the others.

Monasa, who is Nabadua's "small brother," had profited but slightly through the copra trade. With good conscience he had kept his
gardens full and as time passed increased the number of his taro
ponds. When the moon was bright, he shunned the comfort of his
house and kept vigil in his garden to protect the crops from marauding
pigs. Nabadua speaks as though Monasa were his true vassal. He
smiles with lofty kindliness when he explains how he has always en-

couraged Monasa's work in the gardens. As title-holder of Tavua, Nabadua possessed himself of some of Monasa's garden products to augment the glory of Tavua when his own gardens had failed. But Monasa has no stomach for extravagance. He lacks a chiefly spirit. He does not look upon his own gardens as Nabadua's enterprise. Gradually he has ceased to plant in Tavua land and with the help of a younger "small brother" in Tavua has expanded those of his gardens which lie in the land of River's Mouth Kingdom, just across the river Votua, to which he has claim through his wife. Though, according to special agreement between chiefs,[7] the kingly title of Inland Forest includes River's Mouth in its authority, this land is not included under Nabadua's title. Monasa could be quietly amused at Nabadua's patronly interest in his husbandry.

As Monasa's "brother" in Tavua land, Nabadua could have begged food from him. Monasa would not have refused. But the gardens of a chief do not fail. A chief may use the products of his subjects for large feasts in which the land division as a whole participates, but Nabadua needed food for everyday use in his own house. He wandered through the forests hunting wild yams; these are meager sustenance, and his family was large.

The other Tavuan household in Nakoroka is headed by Bici, son of Big Kaiyava. Nabadua says that it was his father who arranged the marriage of the uncircumcised Kaiyava. Ordinarily such despised persons, unworthy of the name of men, cannot find wives. But Tavua population was not large. Kaiyava was the last survivor of the caste called "natives of the village green," and Nabadua's father deemed it wise to find a wife for Kaiyava that this caste might be preserved. He found a woman in Nadroro land and gathered marriage gifts to bring her to Tavua. From this marriage Bici was born. Bici's bowed legs and peculiarly twisted feet prevented him from joining in the usual games which children play. Though he could walk with ease, he could not run fast like other children. He used to stay in the house all the time. But Nabadua, using an older brother's privilege, whipped him and sent him off to the distant mission school at Nabouwalu[8] to become a scholar. But Bici has always resented Nabadua's assumption of authority. In sleep he has often dreamed of fighting with Nabadua and vanquishing him. When Nabadua chose to possess himself of Bici's

7. See above, chap. iii. The land of River's Mouth was ceded to Inland Forest to "bury the blood" of the massacre at Nabetenidiyo.

8. At this time, which was more than twenty years ago, there was no district school at Lekutu.

meager garden products, Bici sulked and whispered that he would arraign Nabadua before the provincial court. Nabadua could not humble himself before Bici, the son of a man uncircumcised, and beg for
food to feed his family; it would be fitting only for Bici to depend upon
Nabadua, as a lowly vassal depends upon his chief.

Toviya was the only one of Nabadua's "small brothers" in other
land divisions at Nakoroka who approached him in rank. Toviya held
the title to a division of Votua land. Though he had no ties with the
chiefly caste, he was respected among Nakoroka men. But the mem-
orable feud about the coconuts at Nabetenidiyo was fresh in Nabadua's
mind. Toviya had taken Vatili's side; and now in private he was enjoying Nabadua's fall from ancestral grace. Nabadua surmised Toviya's glee and could not humble himself.

Except for Vosalevu, the Votua chiefs were of the opposite moiety.
But even had Di Litiya been his own sister, Nabadua would not have
disclaimed his lifelong argument that Tavua was no vassal to a kingly
title which was negligent in its obligations to the land.

Nabadua stole. Men began to suspect him of the mysterious disappearance of their taro. Nabadua was seen behaving stealthily in the
region of Votua gardens. One day Vaula counted the taro in his ponds
at Nadroro; next day he knew that someone had taken some by stealth.
Nabadua had been seen on the path which leads to the Nadroro gardens; he had been carrying taro; he had given some hurried explana-
tion of why he should be carrying taro in Nadroro land when his own
gardens were in Votua. The council of elders met to discuss Vaula's
loss of taro. Nabadua pleaded innocence and fervently excoriated all
thieves. Vatili, Bici, and other men of the church requested the native
mission official at Lekutu to organize prayer meetings throughout the
district and ask Jehovah that death fall upon the culprit. But the mission official said Jehovah would take vengeance in his own time. Four
more of Nabadua's children died, and his guilt was known throughout
the village. Those whose belief in Wesleyan creed was not strong
thought that it was the village ancestors who were punishing the crim-
inal. Though he planted vigorously, his gardens no longer yielded in
abundance. Pigs uprooted yams before they were mature. Taro with-
ered in its ponds. And in the village after dark there was hushed
laughter whenever Nabadua's name was mentioned.

It was in November, 1935, that Nabadua said: "Now I am old.
What good is a woman to an old man?" and wished that Kelera would
return again to live in his house. He said: "Isacodro and Monasa have

brought gifts of kava to her from their gardens. If she refuses to accept, then I shall know that I am old."[9] But, before Kelera had come to a decision, other needs assailed him from all sides. Vatili had reported to the Buli that Nabadua had been truant from the village work at housebuilding, and Nabadua received a summons to provincial court. Namo's eldest son was failing slowly of his dread disease. And Namo, who lived with his wife's people at Lekutu so that his son could be under the care of the native medical practitioner, was deep in debt to the Chinese trader. Nabadua's second son, who had gone to the mine to earn money and assist his elder brother in the payment of the debt, was reported sick with a strange disease. Men at Nakoroka chuckled when they saw how the village ancestors seemed to be collaborating with the Wesleyan God to punish Nabadua for his sins.

Bici said: "Nabadua cackles like a bird, but his head is empty." Vatili said: "Nabadua is a funny man. He keeps everyone laughing." And in another mood: "Nabadua speaks but does not think beforehand of the answer to his words." Bulisivo laughed and said: "It is strange. Though his words are strong, Nabadua is the first to lie relaxed and limp when times of stress descend upon the land. When there is a hurricane, and I must command that ropes be bound about the houses lest they collapse, it is Nabadua first of all who feigns sleep and resigns himself to death. Fijians are a strange people."

While Kelera was nursing her infant son, Nabadua should have been permitted freedom from the statute work of housebuilding under official supervision. It is understood that the time of infancy is trying; men must bring food for their wives and water from the river; in those households poor in women, new fathers even carry firewood. But the Buli agreed with Vatili that Nabadua's freedom had lasted long enough. At this same time the Buli summoned Nabadua's second son, who had stayed too long at the mine, and also a younger "small brother" of Monasa. The two young men appeared before the Buli and were unable to pay the fines which he levied; Nabadua heard of their unhappy state and hastened to them lest the Buli send them to far-off Nabouwalu to work out their fines in penal servitude. Fortunately, Bici had been in my employ and accumulated funds of which Nabadua

9. Though Monasa was Nabadua's brother, he looked upon Nabadua as Kelera's husband. On this occasion he was fulfilling an affinal obligation for Nabadua as though they were cross-cousins. Isacodro was Nabadua's cross-cousin according to strict moiety principle, and they cherished each other as cross-cousins should. But because of Nabadua's marriage within moiety, Isacodro was not Kelera's brother. Nevertheless, on this occasion Isacodro and Monasa acted together as brothers supervising a sister's marital trouble.

possessed himself before departing. Nabadua was acting as Tavua chief in the best interests of Tavua men; Bici should not have begrudged Nabadua's right to put the money to this use. Nabadua met the Buli and with a grand gesture presented two five-shilling notes which bought the young men's freedom. But the Buli brought charges against Nabadua himself and sought to arrest him in the name of the colonial administration. Then, and Nabadua is especially pleased with his ingenious foresight in possessing himself of all Bici's money instead of just part of it, he drew a third note from behind his ear where he usually carries his tobacco. He tells how he proudly parted from the Buli's company, leaving him humbled and speechless with surprise.

Kelera came back to Nabadua's house, but not for long. Early in January, 1936, Namo brought his dying son home to Tavua land. Because Namo's house was undergoing repair, he brought his entire family to Nabadua's house. Namo's mother came, too, to care for the sick child. Though Kelera and Namo's mother are not enemies, they are rarely seen together in the same house. When Kelera stays with Nabadua, Namo's mother goes to the house of Namo. Now Kelera returned to the house of Monasa and lived there until after the child's death.

Toward the middle of January, a man who had distant ties with Tavua land died in Sarowaqa. Most of Nakoroka's people flocked gaily to the funeral. As title-holder for Tavua, Nabadua felt heavily obliged to contribute lavish funeral gifts. But Bulisivo remained at home, and, despite the dead man's ties with Inland Forest Kingdom, sent no gifts. Nabadua blamed Bulisivo for neglecting to seize upon this opportunity to advertise Nakoroka's wealth. In contrast with Nakoroka's reputation for abundant gardens, those of Sarowaqa are impoverished. Nabadua himself was poor; but above all else he wanted to participate in this funeral feast with the extravagance warranted by his title to chiefship in Tavua. Of his own products he could spare only a small pig. But an aged guest, native to the windward coast, was visiting Bici's household; he was returning from a funeral at the island Galoa and had a whale tooth. Nabadua begged this of him, despite Bici's private annoyance. Nabadua presented his gifts to the "owners of the death," and they lamented their poverty in food and gave him mats in return. Anxious to assert the role of Tavua as an owner in this death, Nabadua offered to bring taro from Nakoroka gardens. With a young Sarowaqa man as companion, he went directly to Bici's taro ponds without entering the village at Nakoroka. He probably told the young companion that the taro was Bici's; but he stressed his own

status as Bici's elder brother and leader in all Tavua enterprises. When
Bici discovered that one of his largest taro ponds had been emptied,
he was angry. Nabadua had not acted stealthily, yet Bici was indig-
nant that Nabadua should assume the privileges of elder brother with
such assurance; had Nabadua's own gardens been abundant and had
Bici been dependent upon him, Bici would have felt no annoyance.
But he was proud that his small gardens grew luxuriantly enough to
feed his small household; he was proud that he did not need to depend
upon Nabadua like a younger brother. He spoke angrily in his own
household, and, when he served kava in Nabadua's house, his smoth-
ered anger made him sulk.

The funeral of Namo's son was held in the middle of February. Virtuously Bici claimed that he was moved to pity for Nabadua by this
death; it was his kindliness that prevented his seeking justice from
Nabadua before the provincial court. The funeral feasts were as lavish
as the combined poverty of Namo's and Nabadua's gardens could produce. Bici, too, was an "owner of the death" and contributed foods.
To inform Bulisivo of this death, Nabadua and Namo prepared a gift
of ten stalks of kava. There was no whale tooth in Tavua. Some of the
kava was Monasa's, and Nabadua had been glad to accept a few stalks
even from the uncircumcised Kaiyava. Bulisivo was informed at night.
The kava was heaped outside his house; in the morning the women of
Votua would slice it and spread it in the sun to dry. But in the morning
there were but two stalks where ten had been the night before. A council assembled to discuss this strange disappearance. Nabadua over-
played his part; his shocked dismay was too verbose. All knew that it
was he who had stolen back his own gifts. Yet there was no evidence
against him. No one voiced suspicion in his presence. It was decided
that, since the presentation was Nabadua's, it was he who should beg
forgiveness before Bulisivo. Nabadua and Namo boiled some pots
of fish and yams (no one knew what gardens grew these yams) and,
bowing before Bulisivo, said: "Ai soro, ai soro." But Nabadua's plea
for mercy was not really humble on this occasion. He still had dreams
in which he saw Bulisivo groveling before him. Without doubt Namo
knew how the kava had disappeared; they two would have laughed
together secretly.

Nabadua had often whispered to his friends that Vatili was one who
acted stealthily. It is true that Vatili once used a small bit of tax money
to buy private luxuries; the men of the village had given him this
money because as "village chief" it was he who paid the village taxes

to the colonial administration. Individually men decided not to trust
their tax money to him in the future. But, in so doing, he had violated
no one's privacy and had put no one's status in question. He had not
jeopardized the village peace. He had merely used the money of kinsmen to serve his own convenience. Though it was true that he had
acted stealthily, his concealment was directed primarily against the
colonial administration. But his guilt had been discovered, and he was
sentenced in the provincial court to six months of labor in the Nabouwalu region under government supervision.

Now, as Nabadua's dependence upon stealing garden produce
grew, he redoubled his efforts to cast suspicion on Vatili. Despite faith
in his cleverness in covering his tracks, Nabadua began to fear lest the
already wise village begin to suspect his guilt. A nobleman of Sarowaqa, who has kinship ties with Bulisivo's house at Nakoroka, usually
plants several taro ponds in Votua land. During a visit to Sarowaqa,
Nabadua spoke too freely in accusing Vatili of stealing taro from the
gardens of the Sarowaqa chief. On March 12, 1936, this chief came to
Nakoroka angrily to investigate the charges. After ascertaining that
the products of his taro ponds were seriously diminished, he called at
the house of Bulisivo. As is becoming to a chief, he cloaked his anger
in polite restraint. Vatili was summoned to attend their discussion.
They sought Nabadua also, but as if by accident that day he was far
in the forest in search of wild yams.

This Sarowaqa chief and a "small brother" of Vatili's mother had
been cross-cousins and held each other in especially strong affection.
They called each other "friend." They had agreed between themselves
that they would share their property completely; each would regard
as his own that which belonged to the other, luxuries and products of
the land alike. Upon the death of this senior kinsman of Vatili, he had
requested the Sarowaqa chief to accept the young Vatili into his friendship with the same affection. Thus for several years Vatili had felt free
to use the gardens of the Sarowaqa chief. In the discussion before
Bulisivo, Vatili smilingly explained that, of course, he had taken a few
stalks from the chief's taro pond; sometimes, after a hard day building
houses, it had been convenient to draw upon this taro because it was
much closer to the village than his own gardens. But he could not account for the great decrease in the products of the ponds. The Sarowaqa chief was convinced that Vatili had not betrayed his trust of
friendship. It was apparent that the true culprit had been afraid to
face this inquiry: all knew that Nabadua's gardens were empty and

that his poverty drove him constantly to the forest for wild yams; not only had he himself been guilty of the theft, but he had tried to shift his guilt to another. Vatili's anger was tempered by the affection in which he held Nabadua's children: Vatili had considered Nabadua's eldest wife as sister and cherished her children. They could have brought charges against Nabadua in the provincial court, but they remembered that his young wife and infant son would suffer in his absence. Bulisivo and the Sarowaqa chief laughed in exasperation and decided to do nothing. They knew that ancestral wrath would deal punishment in good time. They waited.

When Nabadua's grandson had died, Kelera returned to her place in Nabadua's household. Namo returned to his own house with his family. His mother accompanied him. Then the eldest daughter, who was perhaps eleven years old, fell sick with a skin eruption about her waist. Naicadra dreamed that the ancestors were angry because Namo had failed to make gift payments to those men in the distant villages who had tried to cure his dead son. Hastily Namo prepared to journey through the district and fulfil these ceremonial obligations lest his daughter die. He had no property of his own; his gardens were exhausted. No longer could he turn to Nabadua for assistance; Nabadua likewise was destitute. But Naicadra had always felt kindly interest in Namo's children. Like Peni, Naicadra had accepted Namo's improperly married wife[10] as sister despite her membership in the opposite moiety; he looked upon her children as beloved sister's children. Therefore he was pleased, as a good man should be, to share the products of his gardens with Namo. He pitied Namo too, because the lot of one who is son to a man like Nabadua is difficult. With other churchmen of the village Naicadra might say: "The sins of the father are visited upon the son and unto the second and even unto the third generation."

On April 16, 1936, a group of girls returned to the village from the mine. They had traveled there to mix kava for the workmen and earn money. They brought word to Nabadua that the wife of his elder half-brother lay dying in Duleniwai. With his young wife Kelera and her two youngest children, the infant son and the seven-year-old Narieta, Nabadua set out to see the face of the dying woman. It is a bad thing to travel with an infant, but Kelera was still nursing him. As funeral gift Nabadua took a whale tooth which was rightfully the

10. Namo and his wife were of the same moiety and should have called each other sibling.

property of aged Kaiyava, father of Bici. Ten days earlier Bulisivo had
been pressed with an unfulfilled ceremonial obligation. Guests had
brought this whale tooth to Nakoroka as forfeit for their neglect to attend recent Nakoroka funerals. Except for the male pig which Bici had
been fattening against the day when old Kaiyava should die, the village had been exhausted of its supply of domestic pigs. In his role as
chief and older brother of Bici, Nabadua had volunteered to contribute this pig so that the honor of Nakoroka would not suffer. He had
given the pig as though it were a small thing. It pleased him to fulfil a
village need of which Bulisivo was incapable. But when, in return for
his contribution, Bulisivo gave him the whale tooth which the guests
had brought, Nabadua neglected to pass it on to Kaiyava. Bici failed
to hide his annoyance.

Weeks passed, and Nabadua did not return from Duleniwai. Word
came that his brother's wife had recovered. Nabadua had no reason to
loiter any longer. Tongues began to wag. His taro ponds, which gaped
in emptiness, and his gardens overgrown with weeds became common
subjects for joking. At a council of elders discussion centered upon his
poverty. They decided unanimously that he remained in his brother's
household so that his family might be fed. Yet no one proposed a plan
to assist him. All were amused. Then word came that his wife was ill.
People suspected that her illness was a ruse to explain his long absence. It was not until June that he returned. He told of how Duleniwai had been crowded during the month of May with men who were
traveling to the mine to earn tax money. Two deaths in which he was
not directly concerned had attracted funeral guests from all the villages of the windward coast. To feed the hordes of visitors, the men of
Duleniwai had baked ovens every day until their garden food was exhausted. Then they had sliced kava, dried it in the sun, and exchanged
it with the nearest Chinese trader for rice, sugar, and tea. Nabadua
told of how his brother had begged him to stay and assist with the
work of this trying time. An epidemic of "Indian boils" had broken
out in the crowded village. Both Kelera and Narieta had suffered.
But the men of Nakoroka continued to joke behind Nabadua's back.
His day was past.

Every day with Narieta and his dogs Nabadua journeyed through
the forests in search of wild yams. His kava bowl stood empty in his
once gay house. His infant son did not grow strong. Though he still
talked freely in the elders' council and concocted plans for every emergency, he saw that men no longer listened to his voice. He saw that

his poverty was amusing to them. Yet he clung to his faith in his ancestors. Though the meaning of his fate baffled him, conviction in his inner chiefliness was firm. No other man had sired so many children; though many had died, his family remained the largest in the village. Kelera was happy in his household. Perhaps he could even sire another child. Though he might be despised in the house of the Votua chiefs, one day his children and his children's children would repopulate the land. Nakoroka would become a village of descendants of Tavua land. This, he thought, was the ancestral purpose. But people said: "He cackles like a bird." They waited for his children to die.

After I had returned to America, I received a letter which Vatili wrote in July, 1936. He told me how Nabadua had gone to Tavua land in his usual search for wild yams. A wild boar charged upon him. He is not so agile as he once was. He tripped and fell from a rock escarpment, smashing several ribs. But he has convalesced and can again hunt wild yams.

Nabadua is unique at Nakoroka. He alone has forgotten that matrilineal inheritance of membership in the chiefly caste is the strictest of all regulations concerned with rank of birth. He alone has hoped that some day the community would recognize him as its chief. Naicadra is also son of a chief, yet he knows that ancestral wrath would descend upon him should he presume to expect the honors and the privileges which true members of the chiefly caste alone receive. Naicadra's status as owner of the land is firmer than Bulisivo's, yet he has never questioned Bulisivo's right to hold the kingly title of Inland Forest. He has always behaved humbly as a vassal should. He has always tried to fulfil his obligations in exchanges, but he does not flaunt his wealth. His gardens have prospered, but rather than display the surplus he has preferred to feed those who are in need. Demands are not heavy upon him because he has never tried to assert his leadership among the men of his division of Nadroro. He is not ashamed to beg of kinsmen of low caste. He is good in the eyes of the church. And his goodness is a chiefly trait as well; for this he accepts the respect of other men in silence.

Though a man may have well-established membership in a particular caste or land group, he may be called upon to perform ceremonial tasks other than those with which his hereditary ties are strong. Almost every man has served upon occasion as "native of the village green" to call announcements from the center of the village. Almost every man has drunk kava as "messenger" for a chief; though this is a ceremonial function rather than a hereditary task, it is especially fitting for those who are born to be "natives of the village green." A chief, however, never drinks as "messenger" for a commoner. Unlike Nabadua, most men know the limits within which their various caste affiliations are adjustable. Among commoners Naicadra might drink kava as a chief, but in the presence of true chiefs, he accepts his place among commoners without anger.

But a man's hereditary rank, or his precedence in kava-drinking, is independent of the relative importance of his voice in council, his wealth, or his virility. Each of these may vary separately. Each may be a means for gaining prestige, but inadequacy in one respect does not preclude participation in other social functions. Ceremonies must always be complete with all their actors, but he who fills an honorable role need not be a person of importance. When Vilomena, whose father was a chief, drank kava among commoners, she drank as a chief. In the absence of true chiefs she might even have acted as chief in the acceptance of a ceremonial gift, yet men held her words in contempt because she was a woman; her children had been conceived in the path, and even among women she was not admired. Though fat bachelor Narogo drank as "messenger" for the chiefs, and in this role might sit above the commoners in the kava ceremony, yet he was despised because he had not been circumcised until his younger brothers, smarting from his shame, had detained him forcibly at the station of the native medical practitioner. The products of his gardens were not even enough to feed himself; he was dependent upon the household of Naicadra.

The strongest voice in the council is not that of the most productive gardener or of the highest chief. Yet he who would seek influence in the council incurs criticism wherever he is vulnerable. Those of higher birth will consider him presumptuous. Those whose status as owners of the land is more secure than his will belittle him on this score. If he expresses his virility in frequent love affairs, he will be damned as a trouble-maker. If he lives peacefully with one woman, he will gain village approval, but at the same time men who are less sexually restrained will laugh at him for fearing village anger. He who would gain power by accumulating property through gift exchanges or by guarding the produce of his land is censured as a miser, one who has no regard for chiefly tradition; yet he who is poor in food and property is ridiculed as extravagant or lazy. A man who is ambitious in any respect must be prepared to face village disapproval. He must keep constant vigil lest the hostility which he evokes grow greater than his courage can withstand. He who seeks general approval in the village cannot lead his fellows; he must conduct his life as inconspicuously as possible and listen to the words of other men. But he can be proud that he is an energetic workman and that his gardens are plentiful; he is as conscious of his status in the village as are more courageous men. A suggestion that he is lazy may lead to violent resentment.

A close hereditary bond with the chiefly caste is an asset to men ambitious for wealth because it usually implies greater likelihood of inheriting title to a large area of land. Yet the exceptional Unuwale, now deceased, was of low birth. His careful cultivation of garden land and his judicious participation in exchanges caused influential men in three land divisions at Nakoroka to bequeath large tracts of land into his keeping. They knew that under his control the products of the land would increase despite ancestral approval of extravagance. Nabadua's father charged him with the responsibility for Tavua land until Nabadua should reach maturity. But Unuwale was unduly ambitious. His ambition was despised by other men as the mark of a mean spirit. He was known widely as a "bad man" with the "soul of a commoner" who refused to share his property with his kinsmen unless they begged humbly before him. If his "brothers" used his gardens for convenience, he arraigned them for theft before the provincial court. Yet he accumulated property and became a power in the village; all kinsmen who sought to initiate exchanges came first to beg his contribution; the property which was distributed at his funeral was worthy of conversation throughout the province. Perhaps it was the contempt in which the community held him because of his flight from circumcision that allowed him to risk accusation of meanness; he was already despised and had nothing to lose. It is proper for a man to take pride in abundant crops as a mark of ancestral favor; it is proper, too, to take pride in participation at exchanges. But all condemn a man who deals sharply with his kinsmen and seeks to accumulate through gift exchanges.

BICI

Of the heads of households, Bici's status is lowest in the village. His house, though not quite so small as Isacodro's, is far more dilapidated. Though he is at least thirty-five, he always sits with the young men during formal kava-drinking. Nabadua and Monasa overshadow him completely in the enterprises of Tavua people; his voice in the village council is very small. His conversation is pedantic and lacks interest for other men. Hence the additional burden of being known as one with a "commoner's soul" adds little to his ignominy. Perhaps Bici dreams that despite his failing eyesight he may accumulate wealth someday and become a power in the village. Perhaps he remembers that his father, like Unuwale, fled the circumcision knife and that this reflects similar disgrace upon the son. He alone is unashamed to show anger when kinsmen use his garden products according to the rules of blood relationship. He alone is unashamed to be a "bad man." Though he styles himself one who gives freely, he always remembers his generosity.

He is resentful of his low status. Toward kinsmen of superior status he asserts his property rights under British law and strives penuriously to gain full credit for each morsel that his meager gardens produce. Most of all, he resents the superior status of Nabadua, who is his elder brother—his mother's sister's son—and holds the chiefly title to his land. One night he dreamed that Nabadua came to him and said: "Here are the gifts which you have given to Kelera. You two have been sleeping together."

"Who told you?" Bici asked.

"Isacodro," said Nabadua.

Then Nabadua raised his knife in anger and Bici fled. But cleverly he turned upon Nabadua and struck him so that the knife fell to the ground. They fought, and Bici was strong. When he awoke, his hair was bristling with fear and he felt ready to fight. When old Kaiyava dies, Bici hopes that Naicadra will present a whale tooth to the people of Tavua and request that he join the Great River division of Nadroro.

Toward the few adults whose status is inferior to his Bici is officious. He alone is unashamed to tease Narogo about the mystical pineapple tree near Udu Point at which a man may cast a missile and gain the woman of his desire. All other men delicately refrain from topics which might embarrass fat bachelor Narogo, who has but recently been circumcised and is a laughingstock among the women. Bici alone can feel insulted by the impudence of children. Once old Kaiyava had brought a gift of food to my house; while he was loitering there to smoke tobacco in a friendly way, Vatili's noisy daughter, who is fourteen or fifteen years of age, asked him what such an old man was doing at my house. Kaiyava told Bici of the incident, and Bici went angrily to Vatili to demand that the girl be punished; though Kaiyava is despised because he is uncircumcised, yet he is old, and age requires respect. Most men, however, would not deign to feel insulted by the impudence of a young girl; they would have been maliciously amused that Vatili's daughter should display such poor manners.

Bici requires strict obedience of his wife. More sullenly than any other man, he criticizes her neglect to fulfil his slightest command. Though she complains of illness, he may insist that she go fishing so that his palate may be pleased at the evening meal.

He has a friend. Several years ago a mission teacher of low caste lived at Nakoroka. But he went mad and used to wander through the forest at night and in the rain. The men of the village spent many unhappy nights searching for him. Eventually they notified the colonial authorities, and the mad missionary was removed to the hospital for the insane at Suva. But he was discharged as cured and returned to reside with his kinsmen at Lekutu village. He plants a little and braids sennit in the house like an old man, but he cannot speak with understanding. Whenever Bici visits at Lekutu, he searches for this poor man whom he calls "friend" and gives him gifts of tobacco with patronizing kindness. Sometimes they drink kava together.

At Nakoroka it is Vaula who comes most often to Bici's household. Vaula is Bici's "small father." He came to Nakoroka at his marriage and wisely has never chosen to assert his voice in council. Though younger than Nabadua, he has grown lethargic with increasing years; in apportioning the tasks of housebuilding, he is always grouped with the old men. His gardens yield a mediocre crop. In the evening he brings kava to Bici's house, and they two drink together in silence.

When Bici's elder brothers saw that his weak legs hindered him in doing hard work, they encouraged the development of his mind. They thought his manner, which was sullen even as a child, was the mark of a precociously mature spirit. He liked to sit in the house and listen to the talking of the old men. Between them his brothers supplied the fee for his entrance into the mission school at Nabouwalu. He traveled there and lived for four or five years. A scholarship for attendance at a higher school at Suva was given to the most promising pupil below a certain age, but Bici was too old to compete. Eventually he secured a small clerical position in the government service at Nabouwalu. But there was some scandal about the disappearance of funds, and Bici was discharged. Many men would have been proud of such experiences as sign of their daring. But Bici felt that his career was ruined. He returned to Nakoroka to sit again in the house and listen to the talking of the old men. In 1935 cataracts grew rapidly in both eyes and impaired his vision. People say that blindness is the usual price men pay for drinking too much kava.

While he was still a small child, his name gained fame temporarily throughout Fiji as one beloved by the Wesleyan God. With a "small brother" of Monasa's household, he was playing near the margin of the village. They saw clusters of tender coconuts dangling above them and wanted to drink. They said: "Please Jehovah, we are hungry. We are thirsty. We haven't any yams. We haven't any taro. We would like a nut to drink." A large green nut crashed to the ground at their feet. They took it to old Kaiyava and begged him to open it. They found that it was just at the proper stage of ripeness for fine drinking. Then they went again to the coconut tree and said: "Please God, we are not quite full." And another nut fell before them. They asked for a third and received it. They asked for a fourth, but this was denied them; God thought that three large nuts should satisfy the thirst of two small children. The tale of this miracle reached the ears of Wesleyan officials. They wrote a yarn about it for the Wesleyan newspaper, which was published at Suva in the Wesleyan dialect and circulated among all churchmen in Fiji.

No other men at Nakoroka have ever gained publicity in far regions. Bici was grateful to the church and approved it highly because it did not discriminate between those of low and high birth.[11] But because of his meager education in its schools, he has had no chance for advancement as a functionary. Sullenly he has nourished an old frustration; that he was too old to win the scholarship for study in Suva. He indicates church officials in Sarowaqa and Lekutu and feels confident that, had he enjoyed their opportunities for education, he would have traveled far higher; their heads are weak and his is strong. Proudly he performs the task of holding, until the time arrives for payment, the funds which have been collected for the salary of the village missionary teacher.[12] He is resolved that his weak son, the six-year-old Kaiyava, shall have the opportunity for advancement in the church which he himself was denied. He notes the sullen manner in which his son gazes upon the play of other children; he notes the child's interest in the conversation of adults. He sees that the child resembles him; he is proud of his son's "mature soul."

But Bici's learning has gained him no prestige among the village

11. Though less ardently than Catholic missionaries, the Wesleyans extend a kindly hand to the uncircumcised.

12. For nearly a decade Nakoroka had had no mission teacher. But in February, 1936, a young native of Tavea came to inveigh against card-playing and kava-drinking on Sunday.

men. His conversation is heavy with irrelevant details. His attempts at humor are labored. His allusions to genitals or other shocking topics are always far too obvious; instead of achieving wit, he makes his talk obscene. Frequently he displays his learning and recounts Bible stories or recites the names and dates of early Pacific navigators. But his audience is unappreciative; they desert him for someone who speaks with wit. Bici knows that their lack of appreciation is founded upon ignorance. Yet he is hard put to it to conceal his resentment at their inattention.

As a young man he never joined the gay excursions to dance and woo girls of neighboring villages. When there was dancing at Nakoroka, he usually clapped and sang in the background or beat the drum with mediocre skill. His elder brothers arranged a marriage for him with a sickly woman of Duleniwai, and it was then, to the exasperation of his brothers, that he began to drink kava until his skin grew gray and scaly. Several sickly children were born of his marriage, but, except for the weak Little Kaiyava, all died soon after birth. When Kaiyava had barely passed infancy, Bici's wife eloped with a man from the windward coast. His brothers, Nabadua and Monasa, took the initiative and gathered gifts with which to request her return.

Men consider Bici lacking in virility. Yet he likes to expatiate upon his knowledge of bizarre, sexual techniques which all people know but never practice. His interest in such lore never flags. He behaves with less restraint than other men in the presence of his female cross-cousins. Often in sleep he has dreamed of committing adultery and of fleeing the summons to the provincial court. He dreams, too, of sleeping with the noblewomen of Votua.

VATILI

Unlike Bici, Vatili is too proud to whine when he feels that his status is insulted. Yet he is not ashamed to threaten with fines those who question his authority as "village chief." One day the men were cutting the grass of the village green; Isacodro saw no reason to work in line with other men who, under Vatili's direction, were proceeding in orderly fashion from one end of the village to the other. Isacodro worked much too fast and continued to move away from the orderly procession. In disgust he began to cut grass in a corner by himself. Vatili demanded his obedience; but he continued to work as he pleased. Vatili remembered, and at a later time persuaded the Buli to summon Isacodro before a session of the provincial court. He used this same weapon against Nabadua, who more freely than any other voiced his disapproval of Vatili's authority.

Except for the foolish Orisi, who once resented Bulisivo's right to censure him for entering the village noisily at night, Vatili is the only man at Nakoroka who has dared openly to question Bulisivo's authority. When Vilomena died and Vatili neglected to inform Bulisivo and present a whale tooth as "digging-stick for the grave," he was implying that Bulisivo's title held no authority in Nadroro land.[13] Though all men murmur behind Bulisivo's back, few would dare to administer a deliberate affront. Nabadua's criticisms of Bulisivo were always whispered in confidence. Like Nabadua, Vatili refuses to see his own unpopularity. Until his domestic trouble in May and June, 1936[14] he refused to admit that many of Nakoroka's men resented his strong voice.

Yet, when he is not served high among the commoners in the kava ceremony, his resentment of the slight is poorly concealed. Like Bici, he cannot help looking sullen. He knows that the village men do not enjoy his conversation. He stays at home and rarely joins a casual evening gathering at the kava bowl.

Though he has no great ambition to rise in the church, it pleases him to be known as a staunch Wesleyan. With Naicadra, Vosalevu, and Bici, he is of the inner circle which discusses the business of the church and, in the absence of a mission teacher, decides who shall tell Bible stories from the pulpit on the following Sunday.

PENI

Peni is of low birth, and his nearest kinsmen are the mild Vaula and the despised Narogo. He accepts his place in the village with humble fatalism. He does not expect much of himself because he knows that he is but a common man. Yet he is ashamed that he has no voice in speaking before men. He will never admit that he is too shy to speak in church and imagines that someday he will learn how. Namo laughs at this ambition, affectionately because they are cross-cousins. Compared with Namo, who is but a few years his senior and who speaks glibly in any company, Peni is dumb. It is only to children and adolescent boys that he can speak with courage. Among these he is inclined to be overbearing. But they do not mind because they admire his strength and the tales of his love affairs.

13. See above, p. 367.
14. See below, pp. 417–19.

Like Isacodro, he is proud of his ability to perform hard work with speed, of his gardens, which are clean of weeds, and of his many closely planted taro ponds. Though his hereditary status is very low, he takes pride in his energy. Proudly Peni, who does not dare to speak in church, tells of how once several years ago he called Sakariya to explain before the chiefs why he had called Peni lazy. A native official, high in the provincial hierarchy, had been traveling through Nakoroka. No young man could be found to carry his luggage. Peni, just returned from his gardens, met Sakariya, who greeted him with angry phrases about the laziness of Nakoroka's young men. The elders assembled in the house of Naicadra before Big Di Litiya, who was then holding the titular whale tooth for Inland Forest Kingdom. Peni asked Sakariya to cite the grounds for his charge. Peni explained that he had not known of the official's needs and that Sakariya had no just reason to think him lazy. With swelling chest, Peni tells of how he dared to stand upright in the presence of the chiefs and his elders, and how he challenged Sakariya, who is slightly built, to stand up and fight. He is proud, too, that young Ratu Seru stood by him like a brother in this emergency; Ratu Seru was waiting in the dark outside to club Sakariya when Peni should push him through the door. But Sakariya began to weep. And Peni remembered that Sakariya was his mother's "small brother" (*tubu-na*), against whom it is not proper to show violence. And Peni wept, too, and was sorry that he had stood in the presence of the chiefs and his elders. He asked Sakariya to forgive him, and Sakariya apologized tearfully.

Peni is a champion of old tradition. Though he cannot speak, he knows the ceremonies of formal presentation and acceptance. He carries the cup with grace and without error at formal kava ceremonies. He loves his garden land, and his filial respect is exemplary. He is virtuous in the eyes of the ancestors. He can sneer at other young men who, though their tongues are quicker, have deserted their families for the gay life at the mines and allowed weeds to choke their gardens.

He is proud, too, of the tales gossips tell of his secret trysts with women of the village. Among the young men he brags of stealthy adventures with young women of other villages. But he has always conducted his love affairs furtively. Though he brags that, like Ratu Seru, he too can use the strong arm (*liga qaqa*), which is a masculine privilege, and take a woman to his bed in the face of disapproval of every man in the village, other men laugh behind his back at the emptiness of his words; he has a "weak soul."

He has always been extravagantly generous. Bici and Vatili call him foolish. He heaps fine tobacco from the Chinese store upon the girls whose favor he is seeking. He is glad to share with kinsmen. Unlike Bici, he does not avidly claim the prestige to be gained from each contribution. Yet he swells in pride when he is prosperous. During the time he spent in my employ, he accumulated vast sums of money. His wages only equaled what mine workers receive, but in remote Nakoroka there was little drain upon his purse: the nearest Chinese store was half-a-day distant at Lekutu, and he earned money faster than he could bestow gifts upon young women of the opposite moiety. When the time arrived for paying taxes, several men begged humbly for his assistance. Naicadra, who is Peni's older "small brother," was among them. Had Naicadra been aggressive, like Nabadua or Vatili, he would have possessed himself of Peni's money in a strong manner. But Naicadra is a good man.

OTHER MEN OF NAKOROKA

Vaula, Raitova, Akuila, and Naicadra are all good men. (Toviya is not good because he hides personal luxuries from his kinsmen. Moreover, he is suspected of stealing the titular whale tooth for his division of Votua land; by this act he provoked the wrath of ancestors.) Good men do not speak too freely. They are generous, yet not ostentatiously extravagant. They are humble and accept the leadership of more aggressive men. When they are in need, they deign to beg of their kinsmen. Vaula and Raitova are of low caste. Both came to Nakoroka as mature men.[15] Because they are both timid men who find "it is impossible to speak," neither has ever dared to seek a strong voice in the council. They cannot even speak in church. With Isacodro, these two drink kava last of all among the older men.[16] Raitova has inherited the title to chiefship in Rokowaqa land because there is no worthier heir. But Rokowaqa functions as a part of Votua in all ceremonies; gardens are no longer planted there. His title means no more than leadership in his own household. Though Raitova's hereditary status

15. Vaula claims Nakoroka land through his mother. But he was born in Macuata and came to Nakoroka for the first time when he married a Nakoroka woman. Raitova was born at Nakoroka, but his mother took him to her kinsmen in the Sarowaqa region when his father died. He was still an infant. He lived there until his mother's death, then came to Nakoroka to claim garden land through his father. He had already married and sired two children.

16. Of younger men who sometimes join the meetings of the old men because they are householders, Bici and Namo drink late in the ceremony. Bici's place is low because of his birth, but Namo's is low because of his youth.

is quite as high as Vatili's, he has sat in silence among the other elders for many years because he has a "weak soul." Vaula has not even a household of his own, and, since his wife's death, has divided his time between the Nadroro houses of Orisi and Vatili. Hence his participation in the council would have no purpose; except perhaps for Peni, who is his son and honors his every wish, his words are the expression of one man's opinion only. He rarely sits with the elders when they convene for serious discussion. Vaula's gardens are less carelessly cleaned than Raitova's, but both prefer to work at old men's pace. They do not require abundant crops because they hold no delusions of their chiefliness. In the evenings Vaula drinks kava in Bici's house; Raitova, who does not like to drink, dozes near his own hearth, while the young people of the village use the more comfortable part of his house to play cards or to dance.

Raitova is famed for his past skill in sexual intercourse. During his wife's short life he sired six children in less time than any man in Nakoroka has required for an equivalent achievement. Once when Nabadua was citing his own large family as proof of his chiefly heritage, I suggested that Raitova seemed to be of similar chiefliness. Nabadua answered: "Yes, we are alike, Raitova and I. We have sweet tempers and we listen agreeably to the words of other men. We think only of living in peace. And these things are pleasing to our ancestors." But Raitova is a notoriously incompetent father. He loves his children and his dogs with such abandon that he cannot bear to say harsh words to them. In fits of temper his daughters and his sons are always running away from home. The entire village is amused at the stern manner which, in contrast, he assumes to keep children from whispering in church; he does not belong to the inner circle of the church but has been appointed sergeant-at-arms.

Though Naicadra proudly styles himself "dumb" in contrast with Nabadua, he can speak long in sermons at church. He leads a secluded life. Except on formal occasions, he lounges in his house in the evenings. He avoids kava except in ceremonies because it is not approved by the church. As title-holder for his division of Nadroro, he controls a large planting area of many coconuts and bananas. His own gardens are abundant, and the food of his household is rich. But he is not plagued with begging kinsmen; all know that there are many dependents in his house and that on his own initiative he sends much food to other households. Though he has never been suspected of meanness, he sometimes receives ancestral communications during sleep which work out to his material advantage. In council he has never spoken out of turn.

Akuila has sought no status at Nakoroka, either in the church or in any other field. Yet he can speak with dignity if the occasion arises. Because his wife has fertile lands in Sarowaqa, he divides his time between the two villages and seems somewhat strange in both. Unlike the other three good men, he drinks excessively of kava. Moreover, he has sinned against the ancestors, who have killed his children in reprisal; he was lacking in filial respect. But all men look forward to Toviya's death, when Akuila will receive the title to the *bota* division of Votua land and hold the title in trust for Toviya's grandson. In contrast with Toviya, he treats his kinsmen generously. He is a good worker.

None of the good men at Nakoroka has caused dispute among the village men. On only one occasion was Raitova almost provoked to violence by the troublesome Sakariya.[17] But even a good man can be angered by such a serious insult, particularly if his antagonist is of slight build like Sakariya. None has provoked the wrath of ancestors against the village. Akuila's sin was not grave enough to cause suffering beyond his immediate family.

Men who resent the circumstances in which heredity has placed them may move away from their oppressors. Monasa is a mild man, but Nabadua's overbearing manner insults him; he cannot in humility accept the status in which Nabadua would place him. Early in 1936 he built a house in River's Mouth territory near the gardens in his wife's land there; now he is beyond Nabadua's jurisdiction.

Of the four adult men of chiefly caste[18] at Nakoroka, Bulisivo and Ratu Seru alone know with certainty that birth qualified them for positions in the village which no other can covet or can test. There is no other fitting candidate for Bulisivo's kingly title in Inland Forest. When Nabadua insulted his authority many years ago, Bulisivo mildly retreated. But his flight was in itself an act of reprisal against the village because he knew that the land would suffer in his absence; Big Di Litiya was no proper king. Hence, despite his submissive temperament, he has a weapon with which to enforce his authority.

Though Bulisivo is not unaware that men find him dull in his unofficial capacity, he chooses to ignore the insult implicit in their atti-

17. When Raitova imagined Sakariya to be violating the privacy of his gardens (see below, pp. 419–20).

18. Bulisivo's blind son, Ratu Tevita, would be a fifth, but he fills no adult role.

tude. Sadly he must remember that, though men do not heed his words, it is his task to guide them in their heedlessness with his superior intellect and perspective. Actually his knowledge of some aspects of the world is greater than that of any other man at Nakoroka. It has long been customary for young chiefs to travel among their kinsmen in distant lands; Bulisivo did this in his youth, and he alone appreciates that the universe does not revolve about Inland Forest Kingdom or even about Vanua Levu.

Ratu Seru is Nakoroka's only male *vasu* of chiefly caste. Yet depriving the village of his presence would bring no marked hardship upon it; he has never taken seriously the obligations "in the manner of the land." Unlike Bulisivo, he cannot assert his authority by threatening flight, for Nakoroka has no confidence that he would exert himself to maintain its prestige. Hence, to maintain his status as a uniquely privileged individual, he must be deliberately aggressive. Perhaps childhood association with Vosalevu in his mother's house taught him the value of aggressive demeanor. Unfortunately, his youthful wandering has brought him knowledge of the decadent regions where European influence has drained all color from the old way of living. He is listless about the future and is concerned but slightly with the future of the village at Nakoroka.

Uniquely at Nakoroka, Vosalevu has courage to understand his own status in the village. Calloused to unpopularity, he knows that his authoritative role depends upon his own aggressiveness and not upon his questionable claim to chiefly caste. Unlike Ratu Seru, who is almost expatriate, Vosalevu spends most of his time in the village and must constantly maintain a forceful bearing. Yet he thrives upon the struggle which his position imposes.[19] With zest he describes frequent dreams of overcoming adversaries in physical combat. Sometimes he dreams that a stranger is sleeping with his wife, the still attractive Big Di Litiya. Unless his opponent is armed with a spear or knife, he never imagines defeat or fear. His rare nightmares are concerned with frightful supernatural beings; once a black man, who was so large that his head was invisible in the distant sky, approached him in the night calling his name in a voice which boomed awfully. There is no man at Nakoroka who does not fear Vosalevu; his anger makes even Ratu Seru cower. Ratu Luke was always wishing that he knew how to box.

19. For many years he has successfully maintained the reputation of knowing how to box with skill. But to my knowledge no one at Nakoroka has ever seen him in action. The fracas which occurred in 1934 (see below, pp. 421–22) hardly offered this opportunity.

Vatili respects every word that Vosalevu utters. Only Nabadua dares
to murmur in whispers behind his back, all the while trembling in
terror because he remembers how Vosalevu leaped upon him ten years
ago and wrenched his shoulder.

But Vosalevu uses other devices to secure his status. He claims to
have exclusive knowledge of how to make good soap from coconut oil
and caustic soda purchased at the Chinese store. It is only Vosalevu
who can eliminate the "unpleasant odor of soda" which rises to spoil
the efforts of other men. Not knowing Vosalevu's special skill, I presented Nabadua with a can of soda in January, 1936, and agreed to
make soap and share it with him if he would provide the oil. Vosalevu
saw Namo and Nabadua gathering nuts and preparing a large quantity of oil; before the day had passed, he knew their plans. With the
smiling voice which he knows how to use when he is angry, he asked
whether I had given soda to Nabadua. Then he asked: "Will the soap
be Nabadua's or will it be yours?" Ingenuously I said: "We are sharing it." And Bici, who was sitting by, congratulated me privately on
my wisdom, had I said that the soap was to be Nabadua's, Vosalevu
would surely have gone to Nabadua's house straightway and taken
possession of the soda. Though in mixing the soap I followed the directions on the can with great care, Namo sorrowfully detected the odor
of soda in the final product.

Though some commoners with chiefly souls, like Nabadua and
Namo, take great pride in the reputation of Nakoroka among other
villages, no one but Vosalevu would have traveled all the way home
across the island to bring forceful discipline to bear upon an erring
household and remove the cause of an evil rumor which had spread to
the mine where he was working.

Ratu Luke alone is in serious danger of losing his identity as a nobleman. Though no one will ever forget to address him with plural pronouns and respect his sacred person with the proper forms of etiquette,
there is nothing chiefly in the character of his household. His family
is sheltered in Toviya's house. Naicadra's wife supplies their food.
Wild pigs have outraged his chiefliness and destroyed his gardens.
Though he displays true chiefly disregard for the consequences of his
acts, his "strong soul" deserts him as soon as he must face his angered
kinsmen. Like Peni, he is shy in his relations with other men. Among
young commoners he sings and jokes with ease, but he speaks with
difficulty in a council of older men. Like Bulisivo, he takes flight without deigning to state his grievance. But his departures deprive the

community of nothing; in the past he has fled too many times. Today he is alienated from all the powerful chiefly families who might have lent authority to his whims. Like Peni, he takes pride in his strength. Only he and Peni are fleet of foot and brave enough to spear a wild cow. But the admiration which his feats can still excite in young men is poor recompense for the disgrace of poverty in a chief.

Wesleyan services, which permit men of low status like Bici to speak presumptuously from the dais in the church, amuse most chiefs. Bulisivo and Ratu Seru rarely bother to attend church meetings. The elder noblewomen are not enthusiastic Wesleyans. Yet both Vosalevu and Ratu Luke have chosen to strive for influence in the village circle of churchmen. Vosalevu likes to shout of fire and brimstone from the pulpit. From beyond the village margin, one can hear his voice swelling in Wesleyan cadences. But Ratu Luke declaims the story of the great flood with modesty; in private Bici ridicules him because he knows no other sermon.

For all men, regardless of their stock of hereditary assets, there is potential mobility of status. The ambitious seek a higher status; through virtue the meek seek approval. All, except those who choose to take flight or relax in laziness, are highly vulnerable to insult and sensitive to the regard in which the community holds them. Few among them choose to look upon themselves without illusion. Each man deliberately forgets his failures and glorifies his triumphs. Hopefully he watches among his fellows for signs to verify his self-respect. And with delicacy the community co-operates to guard each man from full knowledge of his own shortcomings: not even a child would mention incest in the presence of Nabadua; with great forbearance the village helps even the lowly Narogo to forget that it is shameful to be uncircumcised. Yet the memory of insults whispered and half-heard, the quick silences at the kava bowl when one joins a gathering unexpectedly, and the obvious flattery and hidden laughter rob every man of his trust in others' words. To dispel his uncertainty, he crouches outside the house and tunes his ear to the low sound of voices. Stealthily he must learn the truth.

CHAPTER XII

KEEPING THE PEACE: STATUS AND WEALTH

IN THE old days[1] kingdoms were always uncertain about the dependability of their allies. The whim of a chief, jealous of his prestige, could split the villages within a single kingdom into warring factions. Tense suspicion led them to betray old alliances in which they placed no trust and plot secret covenants with former enemies toward whom they felt momentary loyalty. The people of each village lived in terror of surprise attack. Hoping for protection, they vowed obeisance readily to any powerful neighbor. But before the advent of the Tongans, bent on conquest, and the Wesleyans, whose Christian zeal converted the people of Vanua Levu into two mutually hostile camps, wars were not bloody. Warring villages were usually neighbors, because, as Vatili explained, "Why should there be fighting between strangers who do not know each other and hence can feel no anger?" War was confined within the circle of acquaintances; it never overstepped boundaries within which at least the chiefs were kinsmen. Within this limited area the prescribed affection for cross-cousins and affinal relatives made it likely that villages would be warned of impending danger. Plans for the attack were slow to be fulfilled: with boasting, fierce war dances, and the numbness which kava brings, warriors had to whip themselves to a hysteria of heroism; before they ventured beyond the security of their own palisades, war priests with their supernatural talent for prediction had to assure them of success. Hence there was ample time for a dutiful cross-cousin to forewarn the intended victims. Those who feared assault could take flight in the forest until the danger passed.

There were other devices for averting disaster. The path by which the enemy would approach might be blocked with two spears crossed above a war club.[2] Perhaps one of the "messenger" caste would lie

1. See chap. iii, pp. 34–57, for historical sources of this period.
2. This ceremonial blocking of the path is called *sau rabo*. Nadroro used it before an army from Dreketi.

411

groveling there in the path and proffer tribute to the approaching warrior band; if this "messenger" were related to the warriors by the "path of marriage," his request would receive more serious consideration. Those who deemed themselves in disfavor with a formidable neighbor could formally beg his forgiveness; with ashes smeared upon their faces, they could ask forbearance for all past breaches of faith and offer gifts to strengthen their avowals of future loyalty; they would come badly clothed as a sign of their humility and in mournful voices cry: "Ai soro, ai soro."[3]

When all devices failed to prevent bloodshed, the victors lived in terror of reprisal. But, with a ceremonial presentation of gifts, this terror could be dissolved. Laden with gifts of whale teeth, food, and mats, the conquerors approached the village of their victims with humility and "buried the blood" (bulu-bulu-ni-dra) of their recent victims. Since the conquering warriors had neglected proper observance of funeral ceremonies for those whom they had slaughtered, the gifts which "buried the blood" also dissolved all obligations of funeral exchange. Sometimes rights in the land were included with this gift. Thus vengeful retaliation was checked, and feuds did not continue.

When anger kept on smoldering between villages, the chiefs from neighboring kingdoms might assemble to establish peace. With a few young men as his attendants, each chief traveled toward the troubled area. He traveled without weapons and brought gifts of whale teeth and the sacred kava. Perhaps his retainers carried a single whale tooth swinging from a pole between them and garlanded with leaves as a gift of special sacredness. For such a party of travelers there was no danger. They wore their patterned bark cloths hanging free and fastened high upon their chests, instead of bound about their loins, so that all who saw would know their mission. The chiefs presented their gifts to each disputing land division. They made their own presentation speeches because the occasion was too sacred for even one of the "messenger" caste to speak. Bulisivo of Nakoroka has attended chiefly councils to establish peace, once at Lekutu and once at Sarowaqa; all chiefs from Lekutu District were assembled.[4]

The same suspicions which disrupt alliances between villages and kingdoms lead every man to doubt the loyalty of companions in his own household. Almost every man is secretly jealous of those companions who are above him in status and is sensitive to their treatment of

3. Ai soro is the name of this procedure.
4. Such chiefly gatherings are called vei-meyau.

him. The devices which check the violence of warfare control the hostility also within the village. He who wishes to beg forgiveness can humiliate himself ceremonially (*ai soro*). When violence has actually occurred, an exchange of gifts "buries the blood."[5] Despite the regulations of kinship which outlaw violence among all but brothers, there is constant fear lest men will chafe one another's pride in casual contact; hence each man must learn to guard his words and behave with dignity on all occasions. When men work together, the tasks which each performs must be decided in advance so that work can proceed smoothly and without dispute. Among women, however, there is less need for self-restraint because women are weak and their anger cannot be dangerous. In the games which sometimes enliven times of feasting, it is the women who pit their strength against the men; it would be dangerous for men to compete and test one another's temper.[6]

When a dispute arises between men, the chief is called to hear the case and conclude the argument peacefully. This "hearing together" is a good thing, says Vosalevu, because if Bulisivo did not tell men to forget their anger, anger would persist for years; men choked with rage cannot speak or work together.

On May 18, 1936, eleven-year-old Sakaru, son of the dead Vilomena, had gone to the bush in company with some children to bring back meat which Ratu Luke had killed the day before. On their return Sakaru paused to drink at the river Nadroro and rest because his burden of meat was heavy. He was not so healthy as the other children; the lymph glands of his groins often swelled and caused pain. People said that he would die of the same disease that had killed his mother. While he rested, one of Bici's dogs who had been following the troop of children stole a piece of meat. Discovering the theft, Sakaru grasped his machete intending to strike the culprit with its flat side. But the knife slipped from his grasp. It was his first knife, and he used it clumsily. Its sharp edge struck the dog, cutting a foot, and the dog ran howling down the path to the village on three legs. That evening, when Bici returned from his gardens, he found his dog still whimpering. Angrily he learned that Sakaru was the cause and went

5. Though this procedure is known by a different name from that which "buries the blood" between villages, they are recognized as analogous.

6. In recent years soccer has become popular in the coastal villages among those who have attended school. But in former times, though men sometimes competed at dart-throwing, the only games which required rough physical contact were played against the women. Today at feast time, women may still attack a young man, smear him with mud, and throw him into the river; he submits peaceably to this rough treatment.

in search of him. When Bici found him playing cards with Ratu Luke's wife and asked who had wounded his dog, Sakaru hedged and said the dog was lazy. Angrily Bici struck him several times, and Sakaru ran home to Vatili's house, crying. The village waited in suspense to see what Vatili would do when he came home. Sakaru is Bici's "small brother," and it is all right for a man to discipline a younger brother. But Sakaru was not economically dependent upon Bici; his acquaintance with Bici's household was slight. It is more fitting that an older brother or a father with whom the bonds of kin are well established should presume to act as disciplinarian.[7] Moreover, Bici had made a child cry. He had acted in anger, and perhaps the punishment which he inflicted was far greater than Sakaru's misdeed warranted.

Vatili was Sakaru's "small father." At her death Vilomena had placed Sakaru in his charge. Vatili was guarding Sakaru's title to Vilomena's division of Nadroro. Bici was also Vatili's "small son" and subject to his discipline. But since they were of the same age, no rule of kinship prevented Bici from fighting back. Though Bici was nearly blind with cataracts and his legs had been twisted since infancy, people spoke in frightened whispers of his anger. It was sufficiently clear that Bici was impotent in physical conflict, yet anger is in itself dangerous. Vatili returned and requested a hearing before Bulisivo. Before the hearing he approached Raitova's house, in which by chance Bici was recounting his grievance. Vatili saw that Bici was inside and retreated in embarrassment; it would have been improper for them to meet before Bulisivo's words could bring assurance of mutual friendliness.

It was late at night when Vatili, Sakaru, and Bici gathered at Bulisivo's house and discussed their grievances before their chief. Vosalevu and Big Di Litiya were there also to assist in Bulisivo's judgment. Bulisivo spoke briefly in a tired voice to call the hearing to order. Had the case been more important, he would have spoken at greater length. Then Vosalevu, speaking with assurance as Bulisivo's lieutenant, asked Vatili to state his purpose in requesting a hearing. Smiling, Vatili said that he wanted to hear the whole story of the trouble between Bici and Sakaru. Vosalevu called upon Bici and Sakaru in turn. In a clear voice Sakaru recounted the events of the afternoon which had culminated in Bici's striking him. Bici, who had drunk excessively of kava during the evening, spoke humbly in the presence of

7. Cf. above, p. 281. Samu whipped his "small daughter" Ivamere. But her true father is notorious for his ridiculously soft heart. Next to her true father, Samu is the oldest man of the household. His status as Ivamere's "small father" is of long standing.

chiefs, but he felt secure in his ability to speak more glibly than eleven-year-old Sakaru. He had already explained the case to Bulisivo in private discussion over the kava bowl. He knew that Sakaru was in fresh disfavor with the chiefs: by mistake Sakaru had gone to sleep upon the mat of the young Ratu Seru who was *vasu* to the Nakoroka chiefs; upon discovering his mistake, he had failed to show a properly repentant spirit. Bici dared to contradict a detail of Sakaru's story; he had slapped Sakaru lightly instead of striking him with his fist. Bici emphasized the insolence with which Sakaru had spoken of the dog as "lazy."

Then Vosalevu spoke and, as they sat before him with drooping heads, he gave them good advice. To Bici he said: "Control your temper and remember your place." To Sakaru he said: "You are always talking as though you were big. You talk back to your elders. You speak in a manner that is not suitable to your age or position. It is true that your mother's father was a chief and that you have inherited his title in Nadroro lands. But you must remember that the blood of chiefs is very weak in you. You must remember, too, that your father is Sakariya, whose habit of big talk is well known. Though you are only a 'child of the path,' your habits strongly resemble those of your father. Remember the trouble he has caused in this village. Remember that you must change your ways if you want to live here in happiness." Sakaru looked very serious as he remembered that several years earlier his father had fled from Nakoroka in fear and anger. Vosalevu concluded with phrases of ceremonial speech. Everyone clapped quietly. Bulisivo said that the case was dismissed; with ancestral opinion his words had solved the dispute.

Two days later Bici was still explaining his blamelessness to the chiefs. Big Di Litiya agreed and said that Sakaru was indeed impudent. Bici quoted the Fijian version of the Bible, which says: "The progeny of kings are kings indeed." This proved that the blood of Sakaru's father was strong in the son.

Sakaru had been a frequent visitor in my household. Vatili's orders made him stay away thenceforth. The chiefs considered that it was unseemly for a child of commoner caste to feel at home in the house of a white man. Vatili was afraid that Vosalevu would whip Sakaru.

Disputes between women rarely trouble chiefs. When Radebu challenged Ivamere's right to wear virgin's coiffure, it was a council of old women who determined the procedure of investigation. The opinion of Bulisivo's sister Di Kabu is respected among these women, but her age and love of peace warrant this respect as surely as her chiefly blood. Until great age enfeebled Daova, who is Vatili's mother, it was she who filled this judicial role of oldest woman in the village. Only when the arguments of women involve their brothers or husbands does the case require a formal hearing before chiefs.[8]

Early in January, 1936, many young men had gathered at Nakoroka. Everyone had come home for the Christmas feasting. Eight young men who had but distant claims in Nakoroka had come from the windward coast because of Nakoroka's reputation for abundance of food. Girl kinsmen of Ivamere had come from Dreketi. For more than a week the young men had been feasting them and seeking their favors. Dispute arose among them about the cooking of the food. Young Ratu Seru had been directing the procedure; but his "small brother" Tomasi, who was the focus of discontent, seceded with a small group of followers and began to prepare a feast in another part of the village to shame the work of Ratu Seru. Rumor of the dispute reached the ears of Bulisivo and the chiefs. They discussed what plan would best remove ill-feeling and sent Vosalevu as their spokesman to address the young men. In the open, near Nabadua's kitchen, Vosalevu cleared his throat and harangued the young men who had assembled in one group. He said that it was a bad thing to dispute and that it was especially bad for them to divide into opposing factions and vie with each other in the preparation of food. He said: "As you work separately, anger will grow stronger. It is the will of Bulisivo, our chief, that you forget your anger and work together in one kitchen as you prepare the food for your guests." While Vosalevu was speaking, Nabadua, who sat alone drinking kava in his kitchen, would shout his opinion of young men's stupidity through the open door and his hearty agreement with the words of Vosalevu. Sheepishly the young men set about preparing the evening meal; they worked together in Namo's kitchen. Not even Ratu Seru would have dared to act against Bulisivo's counsel when it was voiced by the vigorous Vosalevu.

For him who is dissatisfied with a chief's decision there is no higher court of appeal.[9] In former times a commoner who was discontented in his own community might send whale teeth to a hostile village in which he had kinsmen and request that the foreign chief bring his warriors to wreak vengeance.

8. See Vilomena versus Selaima, pp. 259–60 above.

9. The colonial administration usually supports a chief's decision in his own community.

A YOUNG MAN OF GREAT MEADOW

Troubles between husband and wife rarely excite Bulisivo's notice unless the men of the village take sides and hostility threatens. Even the disruption of a marriage of long standing does not in itself warrant a hearing. The trouble between Vatili and Losana was of mild importance until Nabadua championed her cause to humor his old enmity against Vatili. There had been private disagreements in Vatili's household for many months. Twice in the past Vatili had ordered Losana to leave his house, but friendliness had always been re-established before nightfall. When Losana actually moved to Raitova's household on May 17, 1936, the village was startled; this marriage had lasted more than fifteen years. Vatili was considered a good man in family life, and Losana had never been unfaithful. Peni, who disliked Vatili's overbearing manner, and Ratu Luke, whose wife had appealed to Vatili to force her husband to accept his paternal responsibilities, pitied Losana because Vatili had no brothers who would beat him. Peni was sure that Vatili had whipped Losana many times in the past and that her sweetness of temper alone had kept her from appealing to Bulisivo for justice. Ratu Luke imagined that Vatili was planning to court the affections of Bulisivo's daughter Di Vara, who had recently quarreled with her husband in a distant village and brought her son to Nakoroka to live. But no one chose to interfere.

Vatili's lot was difficult. His house was crowded with dependents, and the everyday chores required an able woman. His own two children had reached puberty and no longer required the constant attention of their parents. But ever since the death of Samu's wife, Vatili had looked upon Samu's children as his own. Losana was Samu's true sister, and she gladly accepted the responsibility of mothering his infant daughter and his son. Vatili had grown especially fond of the small daughter who for several years had refused to go to sleep unless he held her in his arms. Then, too, Sakaru and Unaisi, children of the dead Vilomena, flourished under Losana's supervision; though Unaisi, with her scattered wits, was no child to be proud of, yet her tactless remarks were amusing, and she was always cheerful. Vatili's mother, Daova, was too old for kitchen chores. Except on her very bad days, she made leisurely excursions to the river for a bath; but she could do no work except to plait mats slowly. Moreover, a blind sister of Vatili's father had recently joined his household. When Losana moved away to live in Raitova's house, she took the small children with her. But the two old women remained with Vatili. He had to carry water for them. Old Vaula came from Orisi's household next door to help with the cooking until Naicadra's wife took pity on them all and brought meals for them.

People joked about Vatili's unfortunate plight. They pitied Vatili's mother. But Losana's status as an owner in Nakoroka land could not be questioned, and gradually she drew all the sympathy. Raitova's household, in which she had taken shelter because she shared in his land, was already crowded. Raitova's "small brother" had just brought a wife from Nalauvia who was already pregnant and unable to assist with kitchen chores. Raitova's daughters were visiting in Macuata, and the burden of the work in this household fell upon Losana's shoulders. Losana had to sleep in the lower part of the house. Some nights there was no space for her inside the mosquito net. She lived like a stranger in Raitova's household; though she did not complain, everyone knew she was discontented.

The whole village saw that two households had become disordered, but no one ventured to ask Bulisivo for an opinion. Then, in June, Nabadua returned from a long sojourn in Duleniwai, where, with his family, he had been a funeral guest. Antagonism between Nabadua and Vatili was well known. Because Nabadua had married within his moiety, people said that it was only natural that their kinship tie was confused; they should have been cross-cousins. Nabadua felt sure that Vatili was at fault; he demanded that Bulisivo hear the case and that Losana be given justice. When Vatili spoke before the chiefs, he said that only in the heat of anger had he asked Losana to go away; he had not intended that the separation be permanent; he had already requested his kinsmen in Nacula and Nalauvia to bring whale teeth for the gift called "the bringing forth"; he wanted Losana to accept this gift and return to his household. Vosalevu was absent from this hearing; he was seeking tax money at the mine, and there was no one who could present Bulisivo's opinion with firmness. Bulisivo begged for peaceful settlement, but he had no plan. Nabadua was enjoying Vatili's plight. Finally, Vatili said: "My troubles have made it impossible for me to get tax money. In the morning I shall go to Nalauvia to await the tax-collector, and when he comes I shall go to prison. When I have served my term, I shall go again to Nalauvia and live there until I die."

Early next morning Vatili left. But the men of Nakoroka held council and decided that they would distribute the burden of Vatili's tax among themselves. Rather than risk diminishing its manpower, the village humbled itself before one who felt injured. They sent a youth to Nalauvia to inform Vatili of their decision. Vatili returned, but he said that he was waiting only to see whether Losana would refuse his gift of whale teeth; if she would not come back to his household, he would go away again. She returned to him.

Despite the fear of violence which Nakoroka men allege as reason for the continuous constraint in which they live, occasions upon which men have come to blows are very rare. In 1926 Sakariya struck Nabadua. In 1934 the village rose in wrath against Vosalevu, and Sakariya clubbed him. In 1936 Bici struck Sakaru. Violence has threatened on other occasions, but only at these three times within recent memory has it broken out in the village. Now that Bulisivo has returned, men hope that the future will be safely peaceful.

Early in January, 1936, during the feast time which followed Christmas, Ratu Luke was very angry with some young men who were guests in his house.[10] Though the young guests had distant claims in Votua land, they had been reared in decadent coastal villages where old traditions are no longer honored. The naming ceremony had not yet been made for Ratu Luke's newborn children; yet these foolish young men had dared to mix kava inside the house and endanger the children's lives. When Ratu Luke heard, he hastened to his house to order the departure of his guests. Angrily he told them to leave the village. Next morning Bici, Peni, and Ratu Seru discussed his anger; speaking in awed whispers, they fitted together the details. Ratu Luke had been so angry that he almost struck his guests. Namo had encountered them as they were leaving the village; it was night, and he begged them to stay until morning. But they had left at once.

In 1931 Raitova would have struck Sakariya if Raitova's "small brother" Keleivi had not intervened. Raitova had planted taro just below Sakariya's yam garden. Next day when Sakariya pulled the weeds from among his yams and loosened the earth where it was hard packed, by accident he threw debris on Raitova's taro. He decided that the taro was planted in an unfortunate spot and that he would transplant it to a better place. But just as he had piled the stalks together in preparation for their replanting, Raitova came to see whether pigs had damaged his gardens during the night. To him it looked as though Sakariya was deliberately destroying his taro. Sakariya's troublesome nature is well known. He had already brought trouble to Raitova's household; in 1928 he had stolen the favors of Raitova's wilful eldest

10. Toviya was head of this household.

daughter so that she became pregnant. The anger of Raitova and his brothers on this occasion centered upon their foolish daughter, who fled the village and joined her mother's kinsmen in the Dreketi region. But though Sakariya is their cross-cousin whom they must love, they remember that he, too, was implicated in their daughter's disgrace.

When Raitova saw the uprooted taro, anger possessed him and he descended upon Sakariya. If Keleivi had not chanced along, Sakariya would surely have been beaten despite his cross-cousin relationship with Raitova.

At this time Nabadua was "village chief." Remembering his old grievance against Sakariya,[11] he decided that this dispute should be presented as a case at the next meeting of the provincial court, that Raitova should be compensated for the damage to his taro. Bulisivo had not yet returned from his mother's land on the windward coast. Big Di Litiya was still holding the titular whale tooth for Inland Forest Kingdom. She called a council of village elders. In her councils the men always remembered that she was a woman, and they spoke with less diffidence than under the rule of Bulisivo. Though no one else at Nakaroka was disposed to sympathize with Raitova's anger, Nabadua presented the case against Sakariya with eloquence. When the council was dismissed, Sakariya was sure that the village had turned against him. Sadly he announced his conviction that the people of Nakoroka no longer wanted him to live among them; he prepared to go to Lekutu and live there with distant kinsmen. Three times Big Di Litiya called councils and ordered Raitova to humble himself before Sakariya and ask forgiveness. On the last of these occasions the entire village knelt before Sakariya and begged him to stay among them; but he, who is the last survivor of the ancient village Buleya, departed and has never returned, except for short visits. Raitova's charges never reached the provincial court.

More than any other of Nakoroka's men, Sakariya was dangerously likely to provoke violence. Most men are relieved that he has gone away.

Banishment has been a device widely used in Fiji to discipline undesirable persons. There was a chief on the island of Cikobia who was always causing trouble among the young men. The leaders and the chiefs held a council and decided that he must live in distant lands until he should have changed his ways. For five years he has wandered

11. It was Sakariya who had struck Nabadua during the argument about Nabetenidiyo coconuts in 1926.

in the coastal villages of Macuata. Then there was a young man in Suva who fraudulently collected money on the pretext of starting a business; a high official sent him to Rotuma for ten years. Once a chief of Macuata was sent to the Lau Islands. After several years the Roko of Macuata asked him whether he was cured of his troublesome disposition; he said that he was. No matter how quarrelsome his disposition, an exile cannot cause trouble because he lives like a guest in a strange land. He has no rights, no voice with which to exert his evil will. But at Nakoroka no one has ever been banished. Long before a man's unpopularity in the community has become general, he is aware of his failing status and prepares to withdraw to the village of some distant kinsman; though an adult can rarely gain secure status as an owner of the land in a village to which he is not native, like Sakariya, he invariably chooses to seek his fortune in a new field rather than to try repairing even a slightly damaged reputation in his own community.

Vosalevu is uniquely courageous. He was born at Lekutu, and his strongest hereditary ties are with Lekutu land. Yet despite open antagonism at Nakoroka, he dared to elope during the night with Big Di Litiya; they traveled directly to Nabouwalu and bought the writs which legalized their marriage in the eyes of the colonial administration. He even dared to come to Nakoroka to live; though he was recognized as a member of the chiefly caste at Lekutu, his opportunities for administrative influence were greater at Nakoroka because his wife held the titular whale tooth for Inland Forest Kingdom. Yet when he was involved in the only outbreak of open violence which had occurred for eight years, he sought to change his residence again to Lekutu. It was in 1934 that Vosalevu quarreled with Di Merelita, the daughter of Bulisivo's sister Di Kabu, and struck her with a carrying-pole so that it broke and she cried. Alone among the men of middle age, Vosalevu knows how to play cards; he had wanted to borrow Di Merelita's playing cards to entertain a visiting native medical practitioner, but she had pretended that the cards were lost. Many people were assembled in Naicadra's large house to honor their official guest. Bici was mixing kava. The Votua chieftainesses had come to drink and pay their respects. Sakariya, too, had come from Lekutu for a short visit. When Vosalevu struck Di Merelita, Bici knew that there would be trouble; in fear, he gathered the kava utensils and retreated to a lower corner of the house. To make a noblewoman cry is forbidden. All Nakoroka men were insulted, and anger rose against Vosalevu, the outsider.

When Big Di Litiya and Di Kabu began to cry in sympathy with Di Merelita, the anger could no longer be restrained. Nabadua, who above all others resented Vosalevu's presence at Nakoroka, led the attack. Sakariya, Toviya, and Keleivi leaped upon Vosalevu and tried to strike him. But the medical practitioner was a strong man. He threw the men outside the house, one by one. Sakariya was first to find himself outside. Hastily he found a heavy timber, and, when Vosalevu came through the door, Sakariya struck him on the forehead. Then he was afraid of Vosalevu's anger, because everyone believes that Vosalevu has learned the British art of boxing. When Vosalevu regained consciousness, he vowed to kill Sakariya. But Sakariya had fled to the forest.

In anger Vosalevu gathered his personal belongings and prepared to depart from Nakoroka with his wife Big Di Litiya. Had his intentions been to go alone, the men of Nakoroka would have rejoiced. His chiefly blood connects him with a foreign kingdom; he has no bonds with ancestors at Nakoroka. But Big Di Litiya was holding the titular whale tooth for Inland Forest Kingdom. If she should depart without first transferring it in formal ceremony to Di Kabu, the only other noble at Nakoroka whose age was venerable, the crops of the gardens would wither and famine fall upon the land. Quickly Nabadua and Toviya gathered property among their kinsmen: a whale tooth, kava, and several mats. They coaxed Sakariya from the forest where he was still in hiding, and together they groveled in the dirt before Vosalevu and wailed "Ai soro, ai soro" as they proffered their gifts. Vosalevu was persuaded to stay.

He who is negligent in fulfilling ceremonial obligations or in observing proper etiquette toward those of chiefly caste violates the "rules of the land"; this is sin, and ancestors punish the offender with quick wrath. But many offenses are not sinful until they have been interdicted by chief's decree. The chief, who is less remote from village life than ancestors, must control men's relations and decide how best to keep the peace; ancestors approve his control and substantiate his judgment. It is his special office to restrain all acts which may lead to open violence. Namo has said that theft and anger, both of which are sins abhorred by ancestors, most frequently require chiefs' attention. Theft is dangerous because it may lead to anger and thence to violence; in itself it is an insult to the status of the victim.

There are methods by which guilt may be divined, but in Nakoroka disputes they are never used. Vaula knew a man of a village now defunct[12] who had learned a special technique from the spirit mentors with whom he dealt. Some forty years ago the Buli of Lekutu District called upon him to detect the culprit in cases of stealing. He would fill the palm of his hand with water and, as the names of suspected men were called, raise his arm so that the water flowed down its length; if the water dropped from his arm at the elbow, the suspected man was innocent; but if it coursed down the arm's full length and made a pool on the shoulder, guilt was proved. No such diviner is known ever to have lived at Nakoroka. A more widely known method for detecting guilt requires that all suspected persons cast the shoot of a certain plant into a pool of water; if the shoot floats, innocence is proved. But there is no faith in such innocence; this divining is a game of children. It is the council of elders, over which the chief presides, that weighs the evidence of fact and opinion until guilt is known; each elder has a voice to speak the knowledge gleaned from many nights' informal conversation. Discussion in the council is more free when all suspects are absent.[13]

At Nakoroka the word for theft (butako) describes all stealthy acts. Seduction of a virgin, adultery, and secret use of another's property all belong in this same category; all are bad because they are accomplished in a thieving manner. Theft perpetrated in a foreign village, however, is a feat of bravery rather than a crime. It is said that men may trample upon an outsider who molests their women. Among young men, he who brags of having risked such danger is a hero. Stealing a yearling or a fowl from an Indian village is a worthy deed. But within the village all such acts are bad because they may provoke anger.

Sexual offenses, however, rarely warrant chiefs' attention. At least nine marriages at Nakoroka have been disturbed by the infidelity of one of the marriage partners. Even Bulisivo's wife is not above suspicion; Toviya, who was her paramour, fled to Sarowaqa and stayed there for many months. The culprit almost always flees the scene of his guilt; the injured husband can vent his rage or his sorrow upon his wife in his own household. More probably the husband will retire in injured virtue and allow her brothers full authority to punish her. There is little danger of open violence.

12. This village was part of River's Mouth Kingdom.
13. Divining by spinning the coconut is said not to have been used to detect guilt. It is remembered only as a device to choose successors to a title.

In 1935, while Yani was still nursing her youngest son, Namo discovered that she had been meeting Samu in secret for many months. Namo himself had abstained from exciting her sexually so that his infant son should grow strong. But there was little friendliness between them. Though Namo was more than thirty years old, had sired five children, and lived in a household of his own, he liked to identify himself with the young men and took pride in his success at philandering; Yani knew that she looked much older than her husband and she resented his infidelities. But Namo was a good father and mostly kept the taboos of paternity. One morning, at an unusually early hour, he saw Yani take up a bundle of clothes and start off for the river. The village was not yet awake. Usually the sun was already well-risen when women gathered at the deep pool in the river Votua to bathe and gossip. Namo roused himself slowly and decided to follow Yani. When he reached the river, he found the bundle of clothes still unwashed, but Yani was not there. He called to her, but she did not answer. Then he began to search. He found her in a clump of cane, weeping. He asked her why she was there, but she did not answer. She only wept. That day Samu left unexpectedly to visit relatives in Nakalou. Four months passed before he returned to Nakoroka. Namo took no action, but among the young men he advertised his interest in other women. When Samu returned, Namo treated him politely. They are *tau-tubu-na*.[14] But Samu never comes to visit casually at Namo's house; he also avoids Nabadua, who is Namo's father. The village has forgiven Samu; but if he should have some trouble in the future, they will remember his adultery with Yani as a part of the sum total of his character. Had Samu chosen the "strong" method of satisfying his desires, had he considered himself a "man" worthy of chiefly privileges, he might have met Yani in the full knowledge of the village and avoided the guilt of theft. But no man, not even the rash young Ratu Seru, has ever dared openly to court favors from the nursing mother of a large family.

Except for the unique case of Nabadua, theft of property is almost unknown at Nakoroka, yet suspicion of such theft is more frequent cause for formal hearing before chiefs than is adultery. Kinship obligations create rapid fluidity in distribution and consumption of all goods. The entire community participates. Hence material wants can be sat-

14. They are of the same moiety. Though Samu is Namo's senior by only a few years, he is of an older generation. Hence they are *tau-tubu-na*, and it is unseemly for them to display anger toward each other.

isfied otherwise than by theft. Brothers, sisters, parents and children, sisters' children, and grandchildren—all have free access to a man's property. Those whose kinship bond is not strong must ask before they take, but they ask freely and without embarrassment. Only grandparents, uncles, cross-cousins, and affinals are ashamed to ask unless they have a special need. But women of these categories feel no shame. Women are "like dogs" in this respect. They restrain themselves only toward those whom they avoid because of affinal taboo. Despite such ease of distribution, the producer always retains the honor of production. The recipient must not conceal the donor's name. Even true brothers must not take by stealth lest they risk a charge of theft.

The value of property depends upon its appropriateness for ceremonial gifts or feasts. Whale teeth, kava, yams, taro, mats, and domestic pigs are all suitable for ceremonial occasions. These are "things of land"; they are relatively difficult objects for which to ask. Metal tools, cotton cloth, kerosene, and soap have high utilitarian value and are frequently included in a formal gift exchange. But it is not so difficult to ask for these. Money, tobacco, matches, sugar, salt, tea, and other luxuries which can be rapidly consumed are asked for with greatest ease. In theory every village contains an abundance of garden products and gifts suitable for ceremonial exchanges; village prestige depends upon these things. Though there is always a shortage of tobacco and of the luxuries from the Chinese store, no shame is felt for this shortage. Because demand for luxuries always exceeds the supply, and because they may be asked for practically without shame, and because no one may gracefully refuse a request, no one ever accumulates a large quantity.

He who has tobacco is always expected to distribute it freely. Yet everyone is granted slight indulgence from the rule which requires generosity so that he may hold a small amount secretly in reserve for his own use; he who deprives himself is foolish. As a rule, everyone carries a small supply of tobacco on his person; when it is ostensibly exhausted, his obligations to the community are fulfilled. When there is a shortage throughout the village, the pleasure of casual evening gatherings is seriously curtailed because each man prefers to smoke secretly in his own house. If discovered, such stealth is always ridiculed. Yet every man is guilty.

More stigma is attached to concealment of tea and sugar, because these are foods, and all men should take pride in offering choice foods to chance visitors from other households. He who conceals food may be described in slurring accents as a commoner. The man who deprives himself to entertain outsiders has, they say, a chiefly soul, but nevertheless he is a fool. There is no one at Nakoroka who does not discriminate sharply between friends and outsiders in sharing his luxuries. Thus Bici informs Vaula secretly that tea is brewing in his kitchen, and they drink together while Bici's son squats between his father's knees and sips occasionally from his cup, but usually before the tea is drunk some visitor has come and received a share. Bici often resents the visitor. Vosalevu and Big Di Litiya sip tea in the dark lest the people of Bulisivo's large household see a light and come to join them.

This secret provisioning with luxuries is extremely difficult in Nakoroka. An excursion to the Chinese store excites curiosity. Unless the shopper returns quietly after dark, crowds will gather to examine his purchases. No youngster who is sent on an errand to the store can be trusted to evade with cleverness the persistent inquiries of those who wish to know what he has purchased. Thus begging kinsmen flock to the purchaser's house to greet the child's return. Bici knows that Nabadua or the chiefs will come visiting on those rare occasions when his house is well stocked. Only young men who have not yet established households of their own distribute luxuries with a lavish hand; their generosity is most free among the girls whom they are wooing.

Within the circle of chiefs, however, luxuries are secure from the begging of commoners. All admit that the wants of chiefs require more careful satisfaction, because chiefs are of a finer essence. But when gardens are unsuccessful, which signifies that Bulisivo has failed in his duty as a chief, and the royal households continue to eat finer foods and smoke tobacco extravagantly, the more daring commoners grumble behind their backs. Frequently Bulisivo smokes cigars and discards half of each unsmoked, a most wasteful habit, because no one dares to use the discarded tobacco which his lips have touched; even the younger chiefs would suffer from contact with tobacco which has been touched by his great sacredness. The proper standard of generosity for chiefs to observe is difficult to determine because it involves contradictory principles; a chief should remember his people and distribute luxuries among them even though he himself is impoverished; yet a chief must live in a luxurious manner to advertise his chiefliness to visitors from other villages. Though commoners imagine that the chief's supply of luxuries is fabulously vast, actually tobacco and foods are exhausted as rapidly among them as among commoners. Sometimes several days pass, and no one in the royal houses smokes except by stealth.

Though no one ever accumulates a quantity of luxuries, yet all fear theft. Houses should be "inhabited" to offer hospitality to visitors, and an empty house is a disgrace to its owner; but, more than this, there is fear lest some night prowler will possess himself stealthily of some personal luxury which may be cached in the upper region of the house. "Perhaps an Indian is lurking near the village." But even kinsmen of Fijian blood are not above suspicion. No commoner would dare to explore a chief's house which had been left empty; it is improbable that a chief, even though he deigned to be curious, would dare to search the empty house of a commoner. Each house is sacred to its owner; he who goes to the upper region of another's household, even upon invitation of the owner, must clap carefully when he returns to less sacred ground.

The property which the land produces diffuses through the community along the same channels as luxuries. Taking by stealth alone is forbidden, but a man's prestige is intimately bound with his wealth in goods which have value in feasts and ceremonial exchanges, while poverty in luxuries is no disgrace. Great wealth in gardens is a symbol of ancestral favor. Chiefs and senior kinsmen hesitate to use another's garden crops lest their begging signify poverty and hence injure their status.

When property is needed to pay off a ceremonial obligation of the village as a whole, Bulisivo feels free to draw upon the private wealth of his village, as the prestige of contributing to exchanges and of supporting dependents remains with the individual producer, but the products of labor are distributed. To a man who does not value his status, however, there is complete freedom to depend upon the wealth of kinsmen, provided that he does it without stealth; to such a one, poverty involves no disgrace or physical discomfort, and he has no motive for theft.

There are signs which may be posted to show that use of certain streams or gardens or groves of coconuts is forbidden. He who trespasses against such taboo will suffer accident, but his crime will be no more serious in the eyes of ancestors than that of taking food by stealth from any garden which belongs to another. The taboo is a warning to those kinsmen[15] who have the right to take food from gardens

15. Brothers, sisters, parents, or children.

of the owner for their convenience that this special garden is reserved for a future feast. Bulisivo and the council of elders can place such taboo on many gardens and coconut groves to reserve food supplies for ceremonial occasions of village-wide importance. But the taboo is not a safeguard against theft.

Trespassing on another man's land, like trespassing in another's house, causes ancestral displeasure. A man usually searches for wild yams in the territory of his own land division. When a man invites others to take food from his garden, it is polite for them to give him a small gift in return for this permission to invade his privacy.[16] To enter another's garden stealthily is a serious insult to his ancestors and his status as a landowner. When Raitova saw that Sakariya had uprooted his taro, he was angry not because Sakariya had apparently destroyed a considerable quantity of food but rather because another had presumed to trespass in his garden. Theft is a dangerous offense because it is an insult. Likewise accusation of theft is a serious offense and immediately requires the pacificatory attention of chiefs.[17]

THE BALANCE OF WEALTH

Mats, kava, yams, pigs, and taro form the bulk of every gift display and feast. By harder work anyone can increase his production of these goods. Land, which is the source of all such wealth, is plentiful. Though many tracts of Nadroro and Votua land are spoken of as belonging to certain individuals,[18] the gardens of any one of the many persons who share claims in Nadroro or Votua, or who have vague ties of kinship with the "owner," may be found planted in the "owned" area. The title-holders of the major land divisions, and particularly he who holds the kingly title, have authority which gives them advantage in production; usually they can mobilize more assistance in planting, and their gardens occupy favored spots. But there is no opportunity for the title-holder to exploit those who share his land, because his own prestige is

16. Brothers, sisters, parents, children, grandchildren, grandparents, and sisters' children are exempt from this requirement. It applies especially to cross-cousins and those who are related by marriage.

17. See the accusation of Vatili, above, pp. 392–94.

18. See above, Maps V and VI. This ownership, which in most cases is based on verbal wills, like that of Unuwale (pp. 363–64), applies principally to wild fruits of the land. It is only since the development of the copra trade that the ownership of coconut groves, which is based upon similar claims, has come to approach the European conception of property. The luxuries which copra can buy from the Chinese trader are highly desirable and very scarce. There is one instance of open rivalry for the ownership of a rich grove of nuts (see above, pp. 384–85).

intimately interwoven with the prosperity of the whole community. Those of true chiefly blood require a higher standard of comfort because they are more delicate than commoners; but no chief at Nakoroka could live in extravagant ease in the face of actual need among his followers.[19] In former times polygamy among chiefs was the rule. Many chiefs had three or four wives. But their marriages were not a personal enterprise. The entire community enjoyed the security of military alliances so created and the opportunity to please the ancestors with displays of wealth.

The ceremonial procedure of the marriage feast and some of those which attend birth and funerals require the competitive participation of affinal groups. A group of siblings in one moiety is said to exchange with their cross-cousins in the other moiety. These sibling groups are responsible for the collection of the goods which are displayed. Actually the sibling group initiates and supervises the process of collecting. But this process follows tortuous paths of kinship of all categories so that members of both moieties are requested to supply property to both participating groups. The actual producers of the wealth are scattered through broad territory. Hence there need be but slight correlation between those in whose names the feast is held and those whose effort has produced the displayed wealth. Many persons intimately associated with the exchange contribute to both participating groups. Individuals remember those to whom they have given wealth as kinsmen with whom the obligations of kinship have been freshly validated. Because few men have courage to refuse a request, the only check upon an utterly free and undifferentiated flow of wealth throughout the circle of acquaintanceship is the timidity of those who ask: a man resorts to his affinals and cross-cousins only when the resources of close kinsmen in his own moiety have been exhausted.[20]

The feasts and exchanges associated with chiefly titles[21] are likewise dependent upon the interobligations of kin. Because goods flow most easily among siblings, groups of brothers and sisters are likely to be aligned together. But in these exchanges the territorial groups which

19. It must be borne in mind that those of chiefly blood at Nakoroka are almost all of a single family. They are a small sample from which to derive generalization.

20. Obligations between male cross-cousins usually depend upon cross-cousin marriages. Either a sister or a wife must serve as go-between. There is no flow of property between the houses of Vatili and Nabadua, who has married his sister instead of his cross-cousin: Nabadua and his youngest wife are of the same moiety, and Vatili looks upon both of them as cross-cousins; there is no one to bridge the moiety difference between them.

21. See above, pp. 208–10.

the chiefly titles represent are aligned competitively against one another.[22] However, most persons have claims on more than one land division. On different occasions they participate as members of different groups; their loyalties are not fixed.

In all exchanges which include large groups, the display of a great quantity of wealth and the fulfilment of ceremonial requirements are of far more importance than actual competition among the participating groups. By giving, every individual has a chance to strengthen his bonds of kinship. The ancestors of all have been pleased; all will profit through increased fertility in their soil. Surplus wealth has been dissipated: gardens have been emptied of food, and durable goods have been distributed over a large area. There is motive for fresh zeal in production. There is, however, a difference in the way in which the two types of exchanges are initiated. In theory any individual may challenge his affinals to an exchange, while the exchanges organized on a territorial basis depend upon the title-holder's dutiful carrying-out of his ceremonial, prescribed functions. Actually, however, the inauguration of either kind of exchange depends upon the chief's co-operation. No man would venture to initiate an exchange without the full support of the chief, who thus has virtual power of veto. Even the affinal organization of marriage feasts tends to become obscured by the land affiliations of the participating groups.[23] Nowadays large affinal exchanges are no longer necessary because most of their functions are reduplicated by those which are organized under chiefly titles. Today most occasions of birth, death, and marriage are marked only by a small family feast which serves as a public acknowledgment of a change in family organization.

Though exchanges are theoretically reciprocal, there is no careful count. In this system of giving without calculating the return, the balance of wealth depends upon the existence of surplus and the continuation throughout a large area of the desire to give. Wealth given in mar-

22. Feasts within the village, like those of Christmas and Mother's Day, which recur every year and no longer require the initiatory will of a chief, also provide opportunity for the land divisions at Nakoroka to compete with one another in display. Likewise most cooperative work is organized on this territorial basis.

23. In the feasts of Vaulini's marriage (above, pp. 331–42), classification of the participants according to their affiliation with Great Meadow and Inland Forest kingdoms brings competitive attitudes most clearly to the fore. In attempting to sort out the various mechanisms involved in the grouping of participants in exchanges, it is impossible to segregate loyalty to the land from organization centered around chiefly titles. The authority of chiefs is historically distinct and more recent than organization according to hereditary claims upon the land; in Nakoroka these two are merged.

riage feasts may return to the village through other channels during the ceremonies of birth or death, but this return of wealth is not in any way considered a repayment of past debts. The region which maintains high prestige in all exchanges must exploit its natural resources with a high degree of skill or energy; it must maintain a higher surplus of wealth. The interrelation of the desire to give and the belief in potentially unlimited surplus is illustrated by the exceptional role which whale teeth play in exchange: whale teeth cannot be produced; the supply is limited; hence the presentation of each tooth theoretically requires a return gift. It is only on such occasions as the lavish feasts which attended Vaulini's marriage that whale teeth are given with no expectancy of return. On less spectacular occasions the gift of a whale tooth is always reciprocated with kava, mats, and feast food and frequently with another whale tooth. The value of whale teeth is rated upon an extravagant standard. In impoverished regions such as the Lekutu coast, where the goods valued at feasts may be needed for everyday consumption, exchanges are seriously crippled; the desire to give has been qualified by the need to consume.[24] But even when scarcity interferes with generosity, people remain unable to refuse requests; they prefer to simulate extreme poverty and consume in secret.

The system of giving is already in the process of disruption. Private trade relations with individuals of impoverished coastal regions[25] are almost obsolete because people of the interior have found that their generosity has been exploited. It is highly probable that the natives of Nakoroka will soon learn to qualify the enthusiasm with which they prepare large feasts to shame impoverished Sarowaqa and Lekutu. The chiefly families at Nakoroka already understand that they must look to the conservation of their own resources.

24. There is, of course, no way of evaluating absolute need. But when old habits of distribution must be curtailed to meet the requirements of everyday needs, people of Lekutu District complain of a shortage. Wastefulness, which is widespread in Fiji, is not simply adaptation to the quick spoiling of food in a hot climate. Though there are few methods for preservation, starchy roots do not spoil readily, and meat which is recooked every day can be eaten indefinitely.

25. Such regions have experienced more contact with foreigners. Increased sophistication as well as actual shortage is breaking their desire to give.

CHAPTER XIII

SOCIAL COHESION AT NAKOROKA[1]

SOCIAL cohesion at Nakoroka today depends structurally upon chiefly titles. It is the authority of ancestors vested in these titles which preserves peace and directs the efforts of the population. Without a chief to initiate the work of satisfying their wants, they are helpless. Without a chief, purpose is removed from village life. It is the ceremonial functioning of the chiefly titles which binds the village population into co-operative enterprise to secure fertility. Upon this functioning of the chiefly titles, too, depends the produce of each garden. He who tries to raise a crop in his own name alone lives in fear lest wild pigs uproot his yams and floods sweep away his taro ponds. He must have rapport with the ancestors, and, along with all others who are descended from the same land, he can have this only through dependence on the chiefly title. Then together they can display greater wealth at feasts and win more ancestral favors. His village must save its face before other villages lest in a village loss of face he himself be inevitably included.

Nevertheless, all men chafe within the bonds which the chiefly organization imposes upon them. They accept in its entirety a hierarchy of theoretically hereditary titles and meticulously observe the ceremonial pageantry, heavily fraught with status distinctions, which surrounds them. Yet except for the distinction between chief and commoner, even hereditary status is subject to wide fluctuations. Every man fears lest his achievement fall short of the requirements of his hereditary category, for Nakoroka provides no objective standard of status measurement. Rank in the hierarchy depends upon subjective judgments and random proof. The most opposite virtues and acts enter into the determining of status. Virility or docility, aggressiveness or sweet temper, acquisitiveness or generosity, thrift or extravagance—all may be used to praise or to disparage. Any or all may serve equally as arguments to build the character of a friend or to destroy the reputation of an enemy. There is no socially approved method of stating one's achievement; there is no consistency in the socially respected ideal character.

1. [I have added to this chapter paragraphs based on conversations with the author.— RUTH BENEDICT.]

This structural flaw in the ethos of Nakoroka works itself out in the life and character of all men in the village. They are uncertain of themselves; they are touchy about their status. The prime qualities of the soul, they say with true discernment, are fear and shame which causes "burning of the ears, the face, and the insides." "When a man dies, then only will he cease to feel shame." And when shame overcomes the soul in Nakoroka, it does not lead to redoubled activity to rebuild a shattered reputation. It leads, except in the case of the most defiant, to passivity and flight. A man weeps, feigns sleep, flees to the forest, or takes up his residence in another village. In this alien village he is safe enough. He will receive his share of food; he will be among kinsmen. But it is defeat. There are ten adult men and one woman who have threatened flight from the village because of real or imagined loss of face.[2] Six of these have made good their threats. But except for Monasa and Sakariya, all have returned again to their true land at Nakoroka. The village at Nakoroka is still the place where every native of Nakoroka wants to live. In an alien village his status as "owner" will always be held in question. He must try to live there without asserting himself until he judges that sufficient time has passed so that his disgrace is forgotten and he dares to return quietly to his own village. The path to enhancement of status that is open to a man in Nakoroka is that of kin-organized feasts and gift exchanges which attend births and deaths.

The dissonance between theoretical hierarchy in Nakoroka and the random and confused determinants of status has a historical background. The system of chiefly titles and hereditary status is Tongan, and the prestige of Tongan invaders spread and buttressed it in this region of Fiji. Chiefly privileges are still identified with the customs of islands to the east: chiefs are said to sit "in the manner of Tonga"; their sacred backs are "Samoan." The whole complex has been accepted without complete obliteration of an earlier ethos. For each region of Nakoroka there are two sets of ancestors. The first are "owners" of the land, sometimes identified with animals; the second are chiefly immigrants who built an empire at Flight-of-the-Chiefs and then dispersed to found chiefly houses throughout the province.[3]

Tongan influence has not been so strong in all parts of Fiji as it has been at Nakoroka. Dr. Dorothy Spencer, who engaged in a year's research in the province of Tholo West, Viti Levu, tells of a region which

2. In addition, there is also Raitova's family of wilful children who take frequent refuge with Dreketi kinsmen.
3. See my *Flight of the Chiefs* (New York: J. J. Augustin, 1942).

of all Fiji has perhaps experienced least Tongan influence.[4] There chiefly titles imply little authority. There is not the hierarchal subordination that there is in Nakoroka. Dr. Spencer describes the noisy quarreling in which people at Nasanthoko are constantly engaged; there is not the careful modulation of voice and gesture that is so marked at Nakoroka. Nor is Nakoroka's constant phrase *via-via-levu*, "want want big," "acting out of place," or "acting beyond one," so common in Nasanthoko vocabulary.

In Fiji in pre-Tongan times cultural ethos undoubtedly resembled that in Tholo West and in many other islands to the west. In that epoch of the older ancestors hereditary status was rooted in ownership of land; among men whose hereditary claims upon the land were of equal certainty, leadership depended upon achievement. Kin-organized feasts and gift exchanges attended births and marriages and deaths; by these a man enhanced his status and honored the animal ancestors and secured fertility of the soil. Such kin-organized feasts and gift exchanges still exist at Nakoroka and are theoretically a way to enhance prestige by achievement. But, with the development of organization under the chiefly titles, competitive exchanges between kin groups have become redundant. They continue, but they do not mark comparative status. They are swallowed up in the ethos of chiefly titles. Village ancestors are pleased, of course, by such exchanges, but the wealth displays of the chiefly ceremonies have completely overshadowed their functions.

Thus an effective system of hereditary titles has overlain a culture in which recognized status could once depend largely upon achievement. The bases for such achievement were no longer present in the new order, and no new bases were substituted. Social ambition and obsession with status persist, but the cultural means of satisfying these have become confused and contradictory. Men are filled with shame. Self-assertion is an anomaly in a government which is organized to function independently of the persons who fill its roles, and men of Nakoroka have become poor in courage. They conjure up a loss of face and flee from their village; they arraign their fellows. Social cohesion is well provided for in the wide extension of responsible kinship bonds, in the distribution of economic goods, and in the work parties which share the labors of production. It is threatened by omissions and contradictions in methods of gaining self-respect among a people obsessed with comparative status.

4. See *Disease, Religion and Society in the Fiji Islands* ("Monographs of the American Ethnological Society," No. II [New York: J. J. Augustin, 1941]).

APPENDIX

LINGUISTIC NOTE

I have adjusted the dialect at Nakoroka to the orthography initiated widely in the South Pacific by Wesleyan missionaries. Considerable literature has already been published in this orthography, and it is widely known among Fijians themselves. Therefore, I have chosen it despite a recent trend in official circles at Suva to encourage so-called "English" phonetics. The older method is a far more efficient means of expressing Fijian sounds than any modern innovation.

	Stops	Fricatives	Nasals	Semivowels	Laterals	Trills	Sibilants
Labials	b	v	m	w	. . . . . .	. . . . . .	. . . . . .
Linguodentals	$d(t^*)$	c	n	. . . . . .	. . . . . .	. . . . . .	s^*
Palatals	q^*	k^*	g	y	l	r	. . . . . .

* Surds.

With the exception of the surd t, all stops are preceded by a nasalization which is least apparent in initial position. The degree to which they are voiced or surd depends in part upon vowel context and in part upon dialect variation within the village. Voicing has no semantic importance. At Nakoroka t is always elided and replaced with a glottal stop, which I have indicated with a prime (').[1] At Lekutu, Tavea, and Galoa, where t is spoken, it is explosive and interdental.

With fricatives, voicing is less variable. The letter c is usually voiced strongly and sounds like *th* in *then*. Almost everyone voices v, which is bilabial; k, however, is extremely variable both in voicing and in degree of aspiration. Initially, k is almost imperceptible.

Nasals are pronounced as in English. The letter g represents our *ng* in *singing* in contrast with the nasal palatal stop q, which sounds like *ng* in *finger*.

Both w and y are but slightly articulated. The speaker's mouth hardly changes position as he inserts a y or a w between two a's; clear distinction becomes apparent only in rapid speech, when *aya* becomes *ai* in sound.

Though l and r are interchangeable between dialects, they remain almost constant at Nakoroka; l is rather far forward, while r is a light apical trill.

Both p (a surd labial fricative) and j (a surd linguodental affricate: *t-s-sh*) occur in proper names. Doubtlessly j was borrowed from English; it occurs in nineteenth-century genealogies in Fijian variants of Josephine, John, and George. The letter p occurs in names which seem to have no English paronyms (as in Peni), but it is probably a surd variant of v created through contact with English phonetics.

Vowels (a, e, i, o, u) are pure and are pronounced approximately as in Italian. When vowels are not separated by consonants, each retains its full quantity; thus it requires double time to articulate *oi*, *ei*, *ou*, or *au*, although they bear superficial resemblance to English diphthongs.

1. To facilitate comparisons with other regions, I have inserted t's in most of the Fijian phrases which occur in this book.

435

Sometimes there is a tendency to palatalize before articulating *e* after the sibilant *s*. In some cases this palatalization indicates contraction. I have represented it with *y*. Variation in dialect is extreme throughout Vanua Levu. Each village has its own distinct set of phonetics. By their speech individuals can be placed geographically. The most obvious classification of dialects depends upon the use of *k* and *t*, which native informants consider a basic distinction in Vanua Levu dialects. They explain the present distribution of these primary dialect variations as a result of the immigration of maritime people who settled in eastern Vanua Levu and along the north coast; these maritime people spoke *t* and elided *k*, in contrast with the inland descendants of Flight-of-the-Chiefs and Flight-of-the-Strong, who spoke *k* and elided *t*.[2] Origin legends and methods of classifying kin agree roughly with this classification. The coincidence is particularly noticeable in Macuata: The regions which speak *t* trace descent from immigrant maritime chiefs (they claim Bau and Verata as their ancestral homes) and do not recognize moiety structure as fundamental in determining marriage prohibition. The regions which speak *k* trace descent from inland Flight-of-the-Strong, recognize affiliation with the descendants of Flight-of-the-Chiefs in inland Bua, and observe moiety regulations (see Map VII).

In the region of Savusavu Bay and western Natewa both *k* and *t* are elided. This region also has maritime tradition. Though the men of Korotasere on the eastern margin of the area claim ancestors separate from those who populated the *t*-speaking region of eastern Vanua Levu, their phonetics could easily have resulted from a fusion of *k*- and *t*-speaking dialects. In the Labasa region, which is marginal between *k*- and *t*-speaking areas, there is a tendency to elide both. Likewise the children of *k*-speaking Nakoroka who have attended the district school at *t*-speaking Lekutu elide both. But the tendency to elide both consonants when two dialects mix cannot be generalized to apply to all Vanua Levu. In regions of western Vanua Levu, which was influenced directly by the authority of Bua Kingdom, both *t* and *k* are spoken.

Within the areas of *k*- and *t*-speaking peoples there are secondary variations which can be generalized into phonetic rules. When in *t*-speaking regions the nasal linguodental stop (*d*) is voiced, *t* is an interdental surd. When *d* is surd, it tends to lose its nasalization; so that *t* may be distinguished from it, *t* becomes a surd linguodental affricate (*t-s-sh*). In *k*-speaking regions there may be a parallel relationship between *k* and *q*. Where *q* is strongly nasalized and voiced, *k* is a surd stop; where *q* is a surd stop, *k* becomes strongly fricative.

Because of the brevity of my four-week survey of Vanua Levu linguistics, I was unable to collect sufficient text material to arrive at any method of classification according to vocabulary. The vocabulary variations of which all natives are aware are concerned with differences in personal pronouns, demonstratives, and a few common words which are considered characteristic of localities. Except for the island of Tavea (and perhaps also Galoa and Yaqaga), personal pronouns seem to have parallel grammatical structure throughout Vanua Levu. At Tavea I found no true form for trial number. But there are numerous variations between parallel pronoun forms which cannot be explained by phonetic shift and which are characteristic for locality. *Akai* is the demonstrative "this," which is characteristic of Inland Forest, Great Meadow, and Flight-of-the-Strong.[3] In Nacula and Nalauvia of Great Meadow Kingdom and

2. When a consonant is elided, it is replaced with the glottal stop (').
3. See Map III, p. 32.

MAP VII

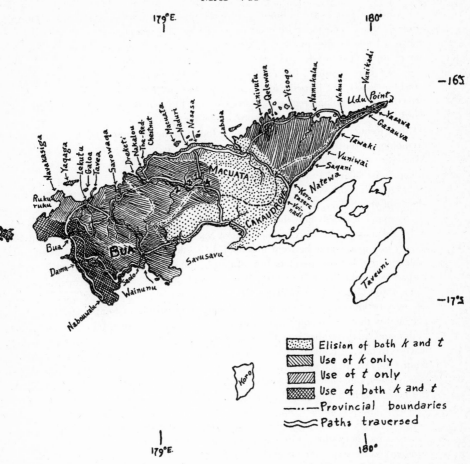

DISTRIBUTION OF THE USE OF *k* AND *t* ON VANUA LEVU

Coastal regions in which I am certain of phonetic habits are indicated by arrows. In all Macuata and Cakaudrove regions so marked, I recorded texts. Texts were recorded as well in (1) Natua, (2) Batiri, (3) Raravuka, and (4) Nacereyaga, which are villages representative of the *k*-speaking region of inland Macuata. Formerly this *k*-speaking area extended farther to the east. I have discussed phonetics with natives of villages of most of the leeward half of Bua Province; natives at Nakoroka are well acquainted with variations in these dialects. In eastern Vanua Levu the population has concentrated on the coast; from Korotasere eastward the interior is almost empty land. Hence the territorial extent of the *t*-speaking area is not commensurable with the distribution of its population. I am most doubtful of the extent of the dialect which elides both *k* and *t*, since knowledge of Cakaudrove Province west of Vuinadi depends entirely upon native hearsay. My own excursion through the Savusavu area was made at a time when I had no knowledge of the language, and results should be rechecked. The inland region of Macuata which the map represents as eliding both *k* and *t* is sparsely populated except where it has been invaded by the sugar industry. Naduri, Nasasa, and Dreketi are beyond the influence of sugar-planting, but these regions have become disturbed phonetically by a regime of progressive chiefs. In Bua Province the division line of dialects between Saolo and Nabouwalu, and between Navakasiga and Bua, is inexact.

westward and southward in Bua Province it is replaced by *qoi* or *iqoi*. The distribution of *yana*, "that," coincides with *akai; qori* coincides with *qoi*. There is similar distinction between Inland Forest and Great Meadow in the intensifying adverb which has similar meaning to English "too" in "too much": *be* is characteristic of Inland Forest; *mene*, of Great Meadow; but today both are being replaced by the Bauan *rui*. The word for "good," *re*, is used widely in inland Bua and Flight-of-the-Strong; *se'a* characterizes the *t*-speaking region of eastern Vanua Levu. *Iloiloa* is Flight-of-the-Strong's word for "morrow," which at Nakoroka is *roaroa*.[4]

Most frequent and subtle variations are found in the meanings of words of the same etymological roots. At Nakoroka *lu'u* is the verb "fall"; in the *t*-speaking region of Macuata *lutulutu* (the reduplicated phonetic paronym of Nakoroka's *lu'u*) means "deep." At Nakoroka *nobu* is the word for "deep."

Even within the village at Nakoroka there is marked difference in phonetics and choice of vocabulary. Tavua households almost neglect to nasalize *q* and so resemble Sarowaqa. The chiefly households are tinged with the dialect of Wainunu. The speech of Isacodro and of Vatili resembles that of Nacula. Bici's language is clouded with the dialect of Vuya, where he went to school. It is said that only Toviya, Nabadua, and Naicadra use the true speech of Inland Forest; but even these vary among themselves. Nabadua speaks like a Tavuan; Naicadra and Toviya bear closer resemblance to Nacula and Great Meadow. There is also variation between age levels, and a man's age may be known by the language he speaks. It is perhaps a compliment to Namo's personality that all his contemporaries and juniors have imitated him in the elision of both *k* and *t*. His mother is of the *t*-speaking region of Navakasiga, and, when Namo learned to talk, he chose to elide both consonants. Among those children who have attended the Lekutu school, Namo's early experience with the *t*-speaking dialect is duplicated. They, too, elide both consonants. But it is Namo who is known as the author of the new speech. Samu and the children of Raitova's household use many words of Macuata and are influencing preschool children at Nakoroka. Samu's five-year-old daughter speaks *t* in kinship terms, a phonetic idiosyncrasy for which the Macuatan experience of her father cannot account. Vatili says that she finds words in the forest. Among young people the vocabulary of Bau, which has the sanction of missionaries, the colonial administration, and the district school, is supplanting that of their parents.

Three kinds of pig Latin offer further examples of facility in linguistic invention. Two of these are widely known in Bua Province, but the third is a guarded secret of Nakoroka's young men; three of them learned it on an excursion to Macuata, and it is a mark of prestige among boys to understand it. As signal that the secret language is to be used, someone says: "Awa faca." The proper response is: "Kofi fa."[5]

In the face of such linguistic versatility it is difficult to understand how dialects could have become traditionally associated with specific areas. There are two complementary explanations. (1) When an individual has attained adulthood, he is highly conservative in his adoption of new speech habits; though Namo's mother has lived

---

4. Both *l* and *r* are extremely variable and in some words interchangeable, but *iloiloa* is not simply a phonetic variant of *roaroa*.

5. These words have no meaning. *Awa faca* is a variant of "Our father." The letter *f* is bilabial and borrowed; except in its context in borrowed English words, it is identical with *p*.

with Nakoroka people for thirty years, she preserves her Navakasiga dialect.[6] (2) Before the days when rising empires shuffled the population, there was far less intercourse among peoples of widely different dialects; fear of foreign lands kept them at home. Though intermarriage between neighboring communities of but slightly different dialect was doubtless frequent, it occurred after adolescence, when speech habits were already well established, and thus the linguistic mixture which such marriage might have produced was deferred until its influence became apparent among the children who issued from the marriage. Particularly within the last decade, the trend which will blur the association between dialect and locality has been accelerated, for the gold mine and the district schools affect every young native. With decreasing fear of foreign regions, desire to travel has grown strong, and greater sophistication will tend to make knowledge of all dialects universal. Inventive youngsters will receive more variant stimuli, and their speech will diverge more widely from the traditional dialects of their lands.

6. Vatili, Vaula, Big Di Litiya, and Vosalevu offer similar examples of this conservatism.

GLOSSARY OF PROPER NAMES
AND TITLES

[Names which occur in the text but once and which are fully explained in that single context, and such common terms as Vanua Levu, Viti Levu, Nakoroka, etc., are omitted. All names of residents at Nakoroka are referred to households under which they are discussed in chapter iv. A key to actual proper names is on file at the Department of Anthropology, Columbia University.]

ADI—*See* Di.

AKUILA—House III. Heir to Toviya's title in Votua land.

ALIFERETI—Commoner of Sarowaqa. Father to Ramo; father-in-law to Ratu Luke (see Chart III).

ANA—House XII. Wife of Bici.

BARI—Young man of the Savusavu region whom I brought to Nakoroka as porter.

BAU—Near Rewa off the coast of Viti Levu (see Map II). The kingdom of Bau achieved great notoriety among Europeans during the nineteenth century. Early to adopt European techniques of warfare, the fame of its empire was so great that Europeans mistook the king of Bau for the king of all Fiji. Though the British soon discovered that Bau had no authority over remoter Fiji, a permanent alliance had been established; the warriors of Bau became British police. The language of Bau has become the official language of all Fiji to both missionary and government functionaries (see chap. ii).

BICI—House XII. The scholarly "small brother" of Nabadua who approves of the European concept of private property. A diligent informant.

BIG—Means "older." Big Kaiyava, Big Melika, etc., are listed under Kaiyava, Melika, etc.

BUA—The modern village of Bua, principal village in modern Bua District, lies near the site of the old capital of Bua Kingdom, on the Bua River not far from its debouchment into Bua Bay, which indents the western coast of Bua Province (see Maps II and III). Bua Kingdom achieved great fame during the first decade of the nineteenth century as a source of sandalwood. Before the rise of Bau in the 1820's the king of Bua ranked high in the eyes of European traders as an entrepreneur in the sandalwood trade. Early contacts with Europeans during this era paved the way for missionaries who followed (see chap. ii).

BULEYA—An ancestral village of Inland Forest Kingdom (see Map III). Sakariya, the only descendant of this village who still recognizes strong hereditary bonds with its land, fled from Nakoroka about ten years ago.

BULI—Title of highest district official in the colonial administration (see p. 62).

BULISIVO—House I. He holds the kingly title in Inland Forest Kingdom.

CAKAUDROVE—A modern province which includes the coasts of Natewa and Savusavu on Vanua Levu and the island of Taveuni (see Map I).

CARE—House IV. Six-year-old son of Vaulini. Sturdy, happy, and at home in three households. A hero of the "days of the wars" had the same name (see p. 47).

441

COGEA—Modern village on the lower Wainunu River. Since the development of the gold industry at Yanawai, Cogea has become a thoroughfare through which all the men of Bua Province must pass on their way to the mine. Not far away, Captain Robby, an old and honored resident of Fiji, has maintained a tea plantation for many years (see Map I).

COLD WATER—A tributary of the river Votua. Name of the land in which Isacodro's yams were planted (see Map V).

DAMA—The old kingdom of Dama (see Map III) was a powerful adversary of Bua Kingdom during the religious wars of the middle nineteenth century. The modern village of Dama, on the Dama River, is the residence of the Buli of Dama District.

DAOVA—House VII. The aged mother of Vatili.

DARIA—East of Saolo on the Wainunu coast (see Map I). Today it is the residence of the Buli of Wainunu District.

DEGEI—Deity of the Kauvadra region of Viti Levu. He is identified with the snake. He gained great notoriety during the nineteenth century because of missionary crusades against him.

DI—Title meaning "noblewoman." It precedes the names of all women of chiefly blood. Di Kabu, Di Litiya, etc., are listed under Kabu, Di; Litiya, Di; etc.

DREKETI—Modern village on the Dreketi River in western Macuata. Also the name of the nineteenth-century kingdom of the same name (see Maps II and III).

DRITI—Modern village high on the Dama River near the ancient site of Flight-of-the-Chiefs (see Map I).

DULENIWAI—Modern village on a higher affluent of the Wainunu River. Many descendants of the Buleya and Tavua divisions of Inland Forest Kingdom live there.

EMA—House IV. Wife of Isacodro.

FLIGHT-OF-THE-CHIEFS—Ancient village site near the headwaters of the Dama River. According to legend, a group of chiefly émigrés from the Viti Levu region established a great kingdom there from which all natives of modern Bua Province trace descent.

FLIGHT-OF-THE-STRONG—A kingdom of interior Macuata which was contemporary with Flight-of-the-Chiefs. It was settled by noblewomen fugitive from Flight-of-the-Chiefs. As a political unity it may have persisted longer than Flight-of-the-Chiefs; the term "Flight-of-the-Strong" is still commonly used to distinguish inland Macuata from the region settled by maritime invaders.

GALOA—Small inhabited island off the Lekutu coast. It belonged to Great Meadow Kingdom.

GREAT MEADOW—Powerful kingdom to the west of Inland Forest (see Map III).

GREAT RIVER—A common place name on Vanua Levu. The ancient lands of Sivoa and Great River composed the Nadroro division of Inland Forest. Maki-ni-valu, chief of Great Meadow, gave another village named Great River to Bua Kingdom in return for military services; this village, Great River, is situated on a tributary of the Lekutu River. There is a third Great River on Savusavu Bay and a fourth in the Labasa region (see Map I).

INLAND FOREST—The kingdom from which the village at Nakoroka is descended. It was composed of five land divisions: Votua, Nadroro, Tavua, Buleya, and Rokowaqa (see Map III).

INOKE, RATU—Hero of Dreketi, in "days of the wars."

ISACODRO—House IV. Skilled housebuilder at Nakoroka. His arrival at Nakoroka is described on page 255. The peculiar nature of his status is explained in the account of Vaulini's marriage (pp. 329 ff.). The planting of his garden at Cold Water is described on pages 127 ff. An Isacodro of the nineteenth century occurs in a tale of the wars (pp. 43–44).

IVAMERE—House V. Daughter of Raitova. Until November, 1935, she wore virgin's coiffure.

JONE, RATU—Chief at Nabetenidiyo (see p. 49).

KABU, DI—House II. Widowed sister of Bulisivo. Though sometimes described as high chief of Rokowaqa land, her influence in the village is far less than that of her younger sister, Di Litiya.

KADAVU—Island south of Viti Levu (see Map II).

KAIYAVA—House XII. Big Kaiyava, the uncircumcised, is father of Bici. Little Kaiyava, whose soul is mature for his years, is Bici's son.

KARALAI—House V. Spry seven-year-old daughter of Raitova's oldest daughter. Her father is the philandering Sakariya.

KASI—Name of site of the gold mine at Yanawai.

KELEIVI—House V. Thirty-year-old "small brother" of Raitova.

KELEMEDI, RATU—House I. Son of Bulisivo's youngest daughter. He was perhaps ten years old in 1935.

KELERA—House IX. The youngest wife of Nabadua.

"KING FOREST"—The whale tooth which is the symbol of kingly authority in Inland Forest Kingdom.

KITIONI, RATU—Kinsman of Bulisivo. Resident at Lekutu.

KOROTASERE—Modern village on the Natewa coast (see Map I).

KUBULAU—The point of land which divides the bays of Savusavu and Wainunu. Also the kingdom and district of the same region (see Map III).

LABASA—Modern village on the Macuata coast. It is an important center of the sugar industry.

LANIETA—House III. One of Ratu Luke's twin children.

LAU—Eastern archipelago of the Fiji Islands (see Map II).

LAUTOKA—Center of the sugar industry on Viti Levu. It is situated on Viti Levu's northwest coast.

LEBU—House IV. Youngest daughter of Isacodro. Younger sister to Vaulini. The village beauty.

LEKUTU—Coastal village northwest of Nakoroka. Name of the district which includes Nakoroka (see Map I).

LEVUKA—During the early history of British expansion in Fiji, Levuka was the seat of British government. When all native uprisings had been quelled, the superior harbor at Suva, near the mouth of the Rewa River on Viti Levu, soon brought commercial development which eclipsed the importance of Levuka. Suva became the capital. Though Chinese and Indians still do business in Levuka, most of the Europeans have moved away. The city is situated on the island of Ovalau.

LISALA NAMOSA—Native of Nadroro. Hero of the "days of the wars."

LITIYA, DI—Big Di Litiya, of House II, is the younger sister of Bulisivo. During Bulisivo's lengthy sojourn on the windward coast she held title to kingship in Inland Forest. Little Di Litiya, of House I, is Bulisivo's daughter and mother of the noble child Di Sereima.

LITTLE—Means "younger." Little Kaiyava, Little Melika, etc., are listed under Kaiyava, Melika, etc.

LOSANA—House VII. Virtuous wife of Vatili. The village held her in high approval, and, when there was trouble in her household, they took her side against Vatili.

LUI—House IX. Eldest daughter of Nabadua. Once she had been betrothed to Peni. In 1936 she planned to marry a young man of Nalauvia.

LUKE, RATU—House III. Young nobleman whose wilful marriage antagonized the chiefly family at Nakoroka, his closest kinsmen.

LUSIANA—House III. One of Ratu Luke's twin children.

MAAFU—Leader of the Tongan imperialists in Fiji (see chap. ii).

MACUATA—Province of modern Vanua Levu, west of Bua on leeward coast (see Map II).

MAKI-NI-VALU—Chief of Great Meadow Kingdom in the middle nineteenth century (see pp. 37 ff.).

MASIMA, RA—A half-Tongan chief in Bua Kingdom who was first among Vanua Levu chiefs to proclaim his Christianity.

MATUA—House X. "Small brother" of Monasa. He has worked for long periods at the gold mine.

MELI, RATU—Houses I and II. Son of Bulisivo's eldest daughter. He had attended school at Suva.

MELIKA—Big Melika, of House VI, is wife of Naicadra. She is a "wise woman" famed in the village for her knowledge of obstetrics. On occasion she can be a boisterous clown. Little Melika, of House III, is the daughter of Toviya.

MERELITA, DI—House II. Industrious and marriageable daughter of Di Kabu. Peni considers her his sister.

MEREMANINI—House VI. Daughter of Naicadra and Big Melika. Fat and virtuous.

MONASA—House X. Unsociable "small brother" of Nabadua. He has affiliations with the chiefly caste and is famed for his industry as a gardener. Another Monasa, of the "days of the wars," is mentioned on page 45.

NABADUA—House IX. Holder of the Tavua title to chiefship. Polygamist and would-be chief.

NABETENIDIYO—Village in which Tavua descendants resided just before the building of the village at Nakoroka (see Map VI). Nabetenidiyo was destroyed by the army of Dreketi.

NABOUWALU—Seat of colonial administration in Bua Province (see Map I).

NACULA—Modern village inhabited by descendants of Great Meadow Kingdom. It lies but a short distance from Nalauvia, with which its name is always coupled.

NADRORO—One of the five divisions of land at Nakoroka (see Map VI).

NADURI—Seat of colonial administration in Macuata Province (see Map I).

NAICADRA—House VI. Holds the title in the Great River Division of Nadroro. His hereditary status gives him the right to hold the title to all Nadroro alternately with Vilomena of Sivoa. He is a good man and powerful in the church.

NAIRORO—A section of Tavua land near the village and well planted with taro ponds (see Map VI).

NAKALOU—A village on the Macuata coast just beyond the mouth of the Dreketi River. Many Nakalou inhabitants trace descent from Nadroro land.

NAKAWAKAWA—*See* The-Bridge.

NALAUVIA—A few miles south of Nacula on the river Lekutu. The relations of Nacula and Nalauvia with Nakoroka are strongly competitive. Marriages between the two regions have been frequent in recent years.

NAMO—House XI. Son of Nabadua and namesake of Lisala Namosa of Nadroro.

NAMOSA, RA—*See* Lisala Namosa.

NARIETA—House IX. Nabadua's eight-year-old daughter.

NAROGO—House VI. Fat bachelor and brother of Peni. Aside from an occasional ceremonial role for which no one else was available, Narogo participates but slightly in the village life. He has no social ambition.

NAROWAI—A village in the hills above Bua Bay (see Map I).

NASASA—A modern village just east of Naduri along the Macuata coast. The Buli of the district of Nasasa resides here.

NASIGASIGA—A modern village inhabited by descendants of Nadroro land. It lies just across the border in Macuata (see Map I).

NAVAKASIGA—Today Navakasiga is included in the colonial administration of Lekutu District. Formerly it was a separate district. It occupies the westernmost extension of the leeward coast.

NAVIDAMU—*See* The-Red-Chestnut.

ORISI—House VIII. Impoverished and unpopular among his age-mates, Orisi spends much of his time working in Indian rice fields.

OVALAU—Island off the northeast coast of Viti Levu. The site of the city Levuka, which was formerly the seat of colonial government of all Fiji.

OVINI—House VII. Son of Vatili. He was attaining puberty in 1935 and 1936.

PENI—House VIII. Son of Vaula. Among the young men the strongest hunter and the best gardener. A champion of propriety and of the old way of life.

RA—Title of respect similar to Ratu. It is probably an abbreviated form of Ratu.

RA MASIMA—*See* Masima, Ra.

RADEBU—House IX. Daughter of Kelera by her first marriage. She was notorious for her sexual adventures.

RAITOVA—House V. Nominal holder of the title to chiefship in Rokowaqa. The slowness with which he works is a joke throughout the village. He is also known for his incompetence as a father of a large family.

RAMO—House III. Native of Sarowaqa. Wife of Ratu Luke.

RATU—Polynesian title meaning "nobleman." It must always precede the name of a man of chiefly blood. "Sir" is perhaps its closest English equivalent. Ratu Seru, Ratu Meli, etc., are listed under Seru, Ratu; Meli, Ratu; etc.

REWA—Like Bau, the kingdom of Rewa expanded and decayed under white man's influence. Located near Bau (see Map II), its chiefs rivaled the chiefs of Bau for power and influence on Viti Levu.

RIVER'S MOUTH—Most of the descendants of River's Mouth Kingdom live in the modern village of Sarowaqa (see Map III). The status of River's Mouth in relation to Inland Forest is described in a story of the "days of the wars" (pp. 49–52).

ROCK FORTRESS—Fortress of River's Mouth Kingdom (see Map III).

ROKO—Title of highest native official of a province. For organization of colonial administration see pages 61–67.

ROKOWAQA—Ancestral village of one division of Nakoroka (see Map III). Its descendants are today considered a part of the powerful Votua group.

ROTUMA—An island lying about three hundred miles north-northwest (12°30′ S.; 177°40′ E.) of Vanua Levu.

RUKURUKU BAY—Indents the west coast of Vanua Levu between Naivaka and Naicobocobo.

SAKARIYA—The last professed descendant of Buleya land. He fled to Lekutu in disfavor about ten years ago.

SAKARU—House VII. Illegitimate son of Sakariya and Vilomena. His ready tongue leads people to predict that he will suffer from the same unpleasant traits of personality which led his father to flee from Nakoroka.

SAKIUSA—House XI. Young son of Namo. He died of an ear infection in 1936.

SAMU—House V. Widower with strong familial ties with the village of Nakalou.

SAOLO—Modern village on the Wainunu coast. The home of Bulisivo's maternal kinsmen.

SAROWAQA—A modern village northeast of Nakoroka near the mouth of the Sarowaqa River. Its inhabitants trace descent from the kingdom of River's Mouth.

SAVUSAVU BAY—Indents the Cakaudrove coast (see Maps I and III). Also the name of the region which borders the bay. More properly called "Nasavusavu."

SAYASI—House IV. Grandson of Isacodro. He attained school age in 1936.

SELAIMA—House VIII. Wife of Orisi. Her adjustment in the village was difficult because Orisi had not consulted his elder sisters about his marriage plans.

SEMI—Young man with distant claims on Nakoroka land. He is afflicted with ringworm.

SEREIMA, DI—Houses I and II. The five-year-old granddaughter of Bulisivo who has learned to expect affectionate attention from the adults of the chiefly households.

SERU, RATU—House II. *Vasu* (the right to belong to the land of one's mother) to Nakoroka and the Saolo region. Arrogant and dissatisfied with the narrow scope of village activities.

SIRELI—House III. Son of Toviya. Vaulini's bridegroom.

SITERI—House III. Wife of Toviya. Also name of Yani's sickly eldest daughter, whom Naicadra has adopted.

SIVOA—Division of Nadroro land for which Vilomena held the title of direct control (see Map VI).

SOLEVU—Region at the western end of Wainunu Bay. It is now a district. The inhabitants are descendent from a kingdom of the same name.

SOMOSOMO—A modern village on the island of Taveuni. Formerly it was a powerful vassal of Bau.

TAVEA—Island off the Lekutu coast. Its inhabitants maintain a special trade relationship with the people of Nakoroka. During the political upheavals of the nineteenth century it changed hands many times. Today it is considered a part of Great Meadow.

TAVEUNI—Island east of Vanua Levu (see Maps I and II). In early days colonies of Tongans came to Taveuni to build canoes with its timber.

TAVUA—Name of an ancient village of Inland Forest Kingdom. Today it is a land division at Nakoroka.

TEVITA, RATU—House I. The only son of Bulisivo. Blind from birth.

THE-BATH—Village of Cakaudrove to which the people of Wainunu fled when they were attacked by the combined forces of Bua and Bau (see pp. 45–48). As a small child, Vatili's mother was taken to The-Bath by her parents.

THE-BRIDGE—Modern village on the Wainunu coast near Saolo. Relation between Nacula and The-Bridge is described on page 54.

THE-RED-CHESTNUT—Modern village on the Macuata coast beyond Nakalou. Vaula has kinsmen there.

THE-SUN-IS-HIGH, RATU—Father of Ema (House IV). It was he who informed the men of Inland Forest that the Dreketi army was planning to attack Nabetenidiyo (see pp. 49–52). His affiliation with the chiefly caste is questionable.

THE-VILLAGE-IN-UNNAMED-LAND—Old village site (*Na-Koro-Tiki*) in Wainunu Kingdom. Today it is deserted except for the noble father of Ratu Luke and a few of his retainers.

TOMASI—House I. Son of Viniyana by her first marriage. He has worked for long periods in the Labasa sugar mills.

TOVIYA—House III. He has strong affiliations with the priestly caste and is skilled in all techniques for dealing with the supernatural.

TUI—I have translated this native title as "king" and have called the territory which it controlled "kingdom."

UDU—The peninsula formed by the narrowing of eastern Macuata and Cakaudrove.

UNAISI—House VII. Illegitimate daughter of Vilomena. Her mental growth is retarded.

UNUWALE—House III. Though the late Unuwale was never circumcised, he achieved high status in the community, and his funeral was a great occasion. He was "small brother" to Toviya, Nabadua, and Waiseya.

VARA, DI—House I. Youngest of Bulisivo's daughters.

VATILI—House VII. He has served many terms as "village chief." People resent his authority because they consider him an outsider. In the "days of the wars" a Wainunu warrior was also named Vatili (see p. 47).

VAULA—House VIII. Father of Peni and Narogo. He came to reside at Nakoroka upon his marriage, but in contrast with Vatili he has lived inconspicuously and without personal ambition.

VAULINI—House IV. Isacodro's wayward daughter. Her marriage "in the manner of the land" is recounted above (pp. 329–42).

VEITINIYA—House XI. Namo's youngest daughter. She was born about 1932.

VIKATORIA—Vaulini's illegitimate child adopted by Isacodro.

VILOMENA—House VII. During her life she held the title for all Nadroro land. But, despite her hereditary claims on a chiefly title, her influence in the community was not great. When she died, there was little sorrow.

VINIYANA—House I. Bulisivo's second wife. She is a commoner and of Bulisivo's own moiety. She is not well liked.

VIWA—An island kingdom near Bau (see Map II). At an early date its chiefs accepted the teachings of the missionaries.

VOSALEVU—House II. The second husband of Big Litiya. Though his affiliations with the chiefly caste were questionable, his aggressive temperament secured his place among the Votua chiefs.

VOTUA—The land division at Nakoroka which includes all the present nobles of Inland Forest Kingdom (see Map V).

WAI LEVU—*See* Great River.

WAINUNU—Wainunu Kingdom included the land drained by the Wainunu River and extended along the coast of Wainunu Bay. Present-day Wainunu District includes this same territory. The chiefly family at Nakoroka is related to that of Wainunu.

WAKESA—House VII. Daughter of Vatili. In 1936 she was attaining puberty.

YANA—A deaf-mute now resident at Lekutu. She has hereditary claims on the land at Nakoroka (see Chart IX).

YANI—House XI. The wife of Namo. She has a coconut grove in Votua land.

YAQAGA—An island off the coast of Navakasiga. It has been subject to Great Meadow Kingdom. Today it is included in the colonial administration of Lekutu District.

YASAWA—A village in the Udu region of Cakaudrove. Also an archipelago west and north of Viti Levu.

YOSALEVU—Big Litiya's first husband. *See* Vosalevu.

BIBLIOGRAPHY

BURROWS, COMMANDER W. *A Report on the Fiji Census, 1936*. Suva, 1936.

CALVERT, JAMES. *Fiji and the Fijians*, Vol. II, ed. GEORGE STRINGER ROWE. London: A. Heylin, 1858.

DEACON, A. BERNARD. *Malekula: A Vanishing People of the New Hebrides*, ed. CAMILLA H. WEDGWOOD. London: Mitchell & Hughes, 1934.

ERSKINE, JOHN ELPHINSTONE. *Journal of a Cruise among the Islands of the Western Pacific*. London: J. Murray, 1853.

GIFFORD, E. W. *Tongan Myths and Tales*. Bernice P. Bishop Museum Bulletin No. 8. Honolulu, T.H., 1924.

———. *Tongan Place Names*. Bernice P. Bishop Museum Bulletin No. 6, Honololu, T.H., 1923.

———. *Tongan Society*. Bernice P. Bishop Museum Bulletin No. 61. Honolulu, T.H., 1929.

HARRISON, TOM. *Savage Civilization*. New York: Alfred A. Knopf, 1937.

HENDERSON, GEORGE COCKBURN. *The Discoverers of the Fiji Islands*. London: J. Murray, 1933.

HOCART, ARTHUR MAURICE. "Fijian Custom of Tavua," *Journal of the Royal Anthropological Institute*, XLIII (1913), 101–8.

———. "Heralds and Envoys in Fiji," *ibid.*, pp. 109–13.

———. *Kingship*. London: H. Milford, 1927.

———. *Lau Islands, Fiji*. Bernice P. Bishop Museum Bulletin No. 62. Honolulu, T.H., 1929.

LOCKERBY, WILLIAM. *The Journal of William Lockerby*, ed. SIR EVERARD IN THURN. "Publications of the Hakluyt Society: Second Series," No. LII. London, 1925.

MARINER, WILLIAM. *Accounts of the Natives of the Tonga Islands*, ed. JOHN MARTIN. 3d ed. Edinburgh, 1827.

PRITCHARD, W. T. *Polynesian Reminiscences*. London: Chapman & Hall, 1866.

QUAIN, BUELL. *Flight of the Chiefs*. New York: J. J. Augustin, 1942.

SPENCER, DOROTHY M. *Disease, Religion and Society in the Fiji Islands*. "American Ethnological Society Monographs," No. II. New York: J. J. Augustin, 1941.

THOMSON, SIR BASIL. *The Diversions of a Prime Minister*. London: W. Blackwood & Sons, 1894.

———. *The Fijians: A Study of the Decay of Custom*. London, 1908.

WILKES, CHARLES. *United States Exploring Expedition—1840*, Vol. III. Philadelphia, 1849.

WILLIAMS, THOMAS. *Fiji and the Fijians*, Vol. I, ed. GEORGE STRINGER ROWE. London: A. Heylin, 1858.

INDEX

Abortion, 243, 316

Acculturation, 1, 7–11, 384, 431; problems of 58, 68, 70–71, 78–81, 371, 431

Adoption, 101, 262, 293–94, 379, 417

Adultery, 255, 258, 423, 424

Affinal kin: attitude toward intra-moiety marriage, 276–80, 290–94; behavior of, 53, 54, 258–61, 266–70, 272, 278–80, 290–94, 296–97, 330; brothers-in-law, 245, 290; determination of, 268–69; extended, 93, 135, 330; father-in-law, 290–93; mother-in-law, 290–93; obligations of, 134–35, 137, 269–70, 292–93, 331–32, 342, 359, 390 n., 411; sister-in-law, 258–60, 290; *vugo*, 290–93; *vuo-na*, 291, 293; *see also* Cross-cousins; Moiety

Age: determination of, 142, 158 n.; of heroes, 30; kinship behavior regarding, 269, 281–82; and marriage, 272; seniority, 112, 326, 362; status, 74, 112, 185, 247 n., 249–50, 255, 281, 290, 326–27, 354, 362, 378–79, 398, 399–400, 405 n.

Ancestor gods, determinant in choice of king, xvi

Ancestors: alienated by church, 31, 229–30; ancient temples of, 229; animal, xii, 150, 184, 241, 288, 380, 433; communion with, 30, 61, 62, 231–32, 242, 406–7; created castes, 188, 379; created land divisions, 188; etiquette toward, 234, 235; ownership of land, xiv; as protectors, 147; punishment by, 62, 230, 231, 274, 280–81, 364, 376, 378, 382, 394; rapport with, 143, 157, 161, 162–63, 429, 432, 434; role in maintenance of fertility of land, 54, 127, 140, 229–30, 329, 344, 430; songs of, 236

Anger, 385, 386 n., 399, 408, 416, 419–20, 421–22; of ancestors, 62, 230, 231, 280–81, 364, 394, 396, 422; dangers of, 414; among kin, 246, 252–57, 263, 265–66, 281, 285, 289–90, 296–97, 340, 407; unsanctioned, 363, 399

Bamboo, uses of, 86, 169, 174

Bananas, 139–40, 141, 154

Bark cloth, 82, 91, 165; as decoration, 84; manufacture of, 174–75; in priestly ritual, 230; for a shroud, 365, 368; "singing for," 40; as symbol, 205, 232, 412; as war material, 50, 51

Baskets, 86, 172–73, 218; for storage, 84

Bau Island, 16–18, 22, 174; effects of acculturation in, 16–18; empire of, 41; as model for British colonial organization,

187 n.; prestige of, increased by Europeans, 18, 26, 28

Bêche-de-mer, 17

Betrothal, 345; limited to virgins, 329

Birthmarks, cause of, 351

Bota caste, xiii, 186 n.; functions of, 186–87

Boys: activities of, 145–47, 150; circumcision of, 314–15; gardens of, 106, 112, 119, 121, 126, 138; gift exchange among, 313; and puberty, 314; sexual education of, 322; training of, 311–12

Breadfruit, 140, 154

British authorities, 44, 45, 48–49, 58; arrival of, 31; and crystallization of native political structure, 58; as district commissioners, 63, 68; influence of, on political structure, 193–94, 227–28; *see also* Colonial administration

British sovereignty, 26, 28, 48

Brothers-in-law, 245, 290

Brothers: behavior of, xvii, xviii, 248–53, 255; classificatory ("small"), 247, 391–92; kinship terms for, 248; older, xvii, 249, 281; younger, xvii

Bua, 6; civil war in, 23, 33

Buli (native district head), 62, 63, 64–67, 71, 73, 74, 75, 78, 79–80, 137, 145, 155, 157, 159, 160, 162, 177, 193–94, 211, 350–51, 390–91, 402, 423; native opinion of, 216

Buli shell, 62, 162

Burial rites, 74, 366; *see also* Death; Funeral

"Burying the blood," 52, 255, 386, 388 n., 412

Cane, use of, 86

Cannibalism, 39, 47, 55, 56, 57, 58, 149, 203

Canoe-building, 19, 21, 24–25

Carrying, 128, 142, 219; sexual differences in technique of, 219, 307; training in, 307

Caste: affiliation, and residence, 188; *bota*, xiii, 186, 186 n., chiefly, xii, 86, 106, 185, 186, 380; "contents of the household," xiii, 186; heredity in, in conflict with rights in the land, 191; and kinship, 278, 287–88, 297; kinship terms for, 244–46; loss of differentiation of, 194; "natives of the village green," xii, 53, 53 n., 186–87 (*see also* Messenger); priestly, xii, xv, 186; structure, description of, 185–90

Castes, xii, 185, 380; choice of affiliation in, open to commoners, xvi, 397; division of population into, 192; *see also* Chief; Commoner

451

Al